In memory of David Plant (1965 - 2008)

who always enjoyed a bit of

interesting transport,

and whose attitude and courage gave

inspiration to all who knew him.

JAGUAR
THE COMPLETE STORY

This edition published in 2008 by Motorbooks, an imprint of MBI Publishing Company, 400 First Avenue North, Suite 300, Minneapolis, MN 55401 USA

Originally published as Jaguar – Die komplette Chronik von 1922 bis heute © 2006 by HEEL Verlag GmbH, Königswinter

Motorbooks titles are also available at discounts in bulk quantity for industrial or sales-promotional use. For details write to Special Sales Manager at MBI Publishing Company, 400 First Avenue North, Suite 300, Minneapolis, MN 55401 USA.

To find out more about our books, visit us online at www.motorbooks.com.

ISBN-13: 978-0-7603-3447-8

German edition:
Editorial: Joachim Hack, Bad Honnef
Design: Olaf Schumacher Artwork, Königswinter
Lithography: Sabine Köse, Petra Hammermann, Collibri Königswinter

Editors for English edition: Peter Bodensteiner and Jenny Miller
Page layout for English edition: Chris Fayers

Printed in China

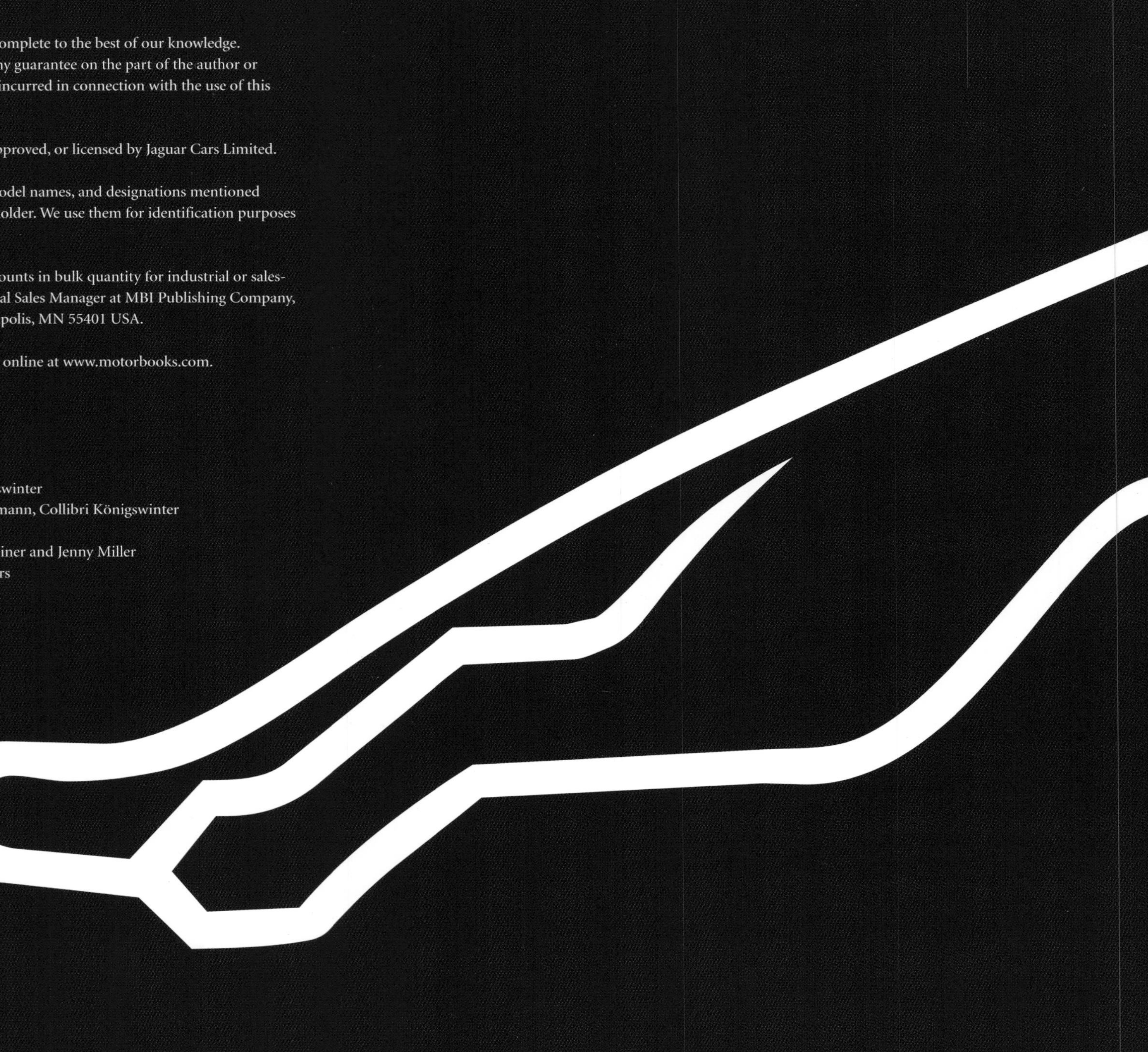

JAGUAR

THE COMPLETE STORY

motorbooks

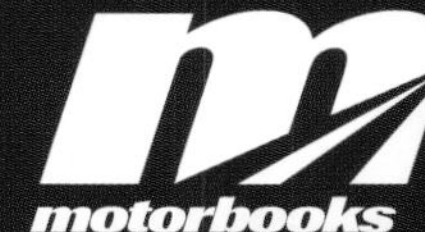

TABLE OF CONTENTS

Contents

APPENDICES

FOREWORD

To the First German Edition

In all my life I have hardly encountered any motorcar that releases emotions as does the Jaguar. Be it privately or professionally, be it in talks with friends and colleagues or with people I meet for the first time—I cannot remember ever having met someone who was not fascinated by Jaguar.

Regarding last year's increasing new car registrations, this fascination must have become stronger. In these times of more or less similar technical solutions, the character of a brand is of greatest importance when choosing a car. A car is not just a means of transport; it also reflects ambitions, dreams, and joy of life.

The character of a marque is as difficult to describe as the one of a man. Nevertheless, I would like to try it. Jaguar is elegance, sovereignty, and style. In its checkered history, Jaguar always managed to maintain this core, from the first Swallow via the legendary E-Type, right to the present XJ, XK, and S-Types. Jaguar was and still is the exceptional, beautiful, valuable. I am sure that these characteristics will remain with Jaguar in the future.

My time at Jaguar was one of the greatest but also most wonderful and thrilling experiences in my career. This is why I not only wish this book to become a great success, but I also extend my greetings to all those who share the emotional feeling for this fascinating marque.

Nicholas V. Scheele
Chairman—Jaguar Cars 1992–1999
August 2000

To the Previous German Edition

When Heiner Stertkamp asked me to pen this introduction to *Jaguar—The Complete History,* I was both honored and proud. Honored because not only has Jaguar been one of the major influences on my life, but also because the foreword for the previous edition was written by Nick—now of course, Sir Nick Scheele—with whom I had the pleasure of working for four of his seven years at Jaguar. Nick has remained a friend for whom I have great admiration.

The pride comes from being given the opportunity to capture in a few short paragraphs the essence of what, for me, makes Jaguar so special.

Daring and individual design has always been one of the strengths of Jaguar, and in these pages you will find elegant yet visually powerful cars that emphasize this. My favorite Jaguars—and every devotee will have his or her own personal view on this—are those that, from the moment you first saw them, could have been nothing else but a Jaguar.

But styling, while so vital to the Jaguar recipe, is only one ingredient in the mix. In addition, over the years Jaguars have also meant refined power, luxurious craftsmanship, and driver-oriented technology. The experience of driving a Jaguar brings these together in a way that no other car does.

And underlying all this is the strong sense of both an enduring heritage and a confident future. Just as the XK120 and later the E-Type inspired admiration and longing, so the all-new XK has those same qualities.

As I said when we revealed the new XK at the Frankfurt Motor Show in 2005, and a year later in London when we showed the new XKR, only a very few people have the privilege of launching a new Jaguar sports car. And I can promise you that whether you are a long-standing enthusiast or a newcomer to the delights of Jaguar, there is plenty more to come from the leaping cat!

Bibiana Boerio
Managing Director—Jaguar Cars Limited
September 2006

INTRODUCTION

The Jaguar motorcar is well known all over the world. Named after the large South American feline, it is individually and unmistakably composed of elegant lines inspired by the impression of a leaping cat, powerful yet, in most cases, silently powerful, with exquisite roadholding, perfect riding comfort, and exquisite, slightly old-world equipment, with nicely figured walnut dashboards and fragrant leather seats. This, at least for us foreigners, is typically British, a style that makes the Jaguar recognizable in traffic, even for those who are less interested in cars.

The Jaguar legend—it could not have been more dramatic even if it had been created by William Shakespeare—adds to this special aura: It's about gleaming chariots built with great pains, with stamina plus an element of good luck. Powerful and lithe, a Jaguar seems to have a female heart beating under the shining skin.

With the help of one of the most spirited British jockeys, Jaguars defeated seemingly invincible old heroes. History records that one of Jaguar's adversaries was a greedy giant, who one day seized it by the throat, causing it severe physical damage and—following wrong advice—poisoned it.

With good help from some dauntless friends, a courageous and industrious *deus ex machina* saved the day so that the old glory revived Jaguar, and it went from strength to strength. Meanwhile, as dark clouds rose from the western horizon, a new threat was thwarted by a transatlantic treasure, a dowry from a sudden and surprising marriage.

The real history of Jaguar is admittedly less dramatic, but is no less fascinating. The story of the Daimler marque, which reaches back to the very invention of the car more than 100 years ago, is intertwined with that of Jaguar. To tell the history of one of Britain's most famous car marques certainly is very daring for someone not a native English speaker. This book does not intend to reveal stunning news but to provide an in-depth overview with an international accent, to be a reliable source of what an enthusiast might like to know about Jaguar and the affiliated marques. I start from the very beginning and end in present times, including company history, technical evolution and data, a model guide, and racing record.

Of course, such a huge task is beyond the reach of just one person. Thankfully, I was able to benefit from the work of other Jaguar historians. Their books are listed in the appendix. I am also very thankful for the help and support of Jaguar Cars, the Jaguar Daimler Heritage Trust, Jaguar Deutschland, Jaguar Austria, Aston Martin Lagonda Limited, and the late Karen Miller of Jaguar Cars of North America, without whom this book would not have become reality. Many thanks to Paul Skilleter, Brian Long, and Prof. Wilfried M. Schön for all their helpful hints and the many photographs they contributed to this book, some of which have not been published before; to Bodo Möhrke for looking through the passages about the Panther; to Walter James for information about the early days of the Jaguar Association Germany; to Klaus-Josef Roßfeldt, Heinz Rudolf, Ulrich Echterhoff, Jürgen Dietz, Allen Hoskins, Mike Purnell, Freddie Rausch and Michael Sommer for their contributions; to Fritz-Werner Schönborn's archive, which contains so many rare documents; and to Heel-Verlag and its staff for their patience and helpfulness. Further thanks to Jochen Arden, Maria and Dr. Gerrit Balken, Friedhelm Bergmeyer, Thomas Beyer, Hans-Peter Brüggemann, Reiner König, Klaus Langenbach, Heinrich Meyer, Siegfried Ridder, Gerrit Rooswinkel, Hartwig Teismann, Angela Twelbeck, Dieter Ullrich, and Auto Welt for allowing their photographs to be included in this book. Photographs from Jaguar are marked with a "J," those from Paul Skilleter's archive (often with copyrights at Jaguar) with an "S," while "St" denotes the author's photographs.

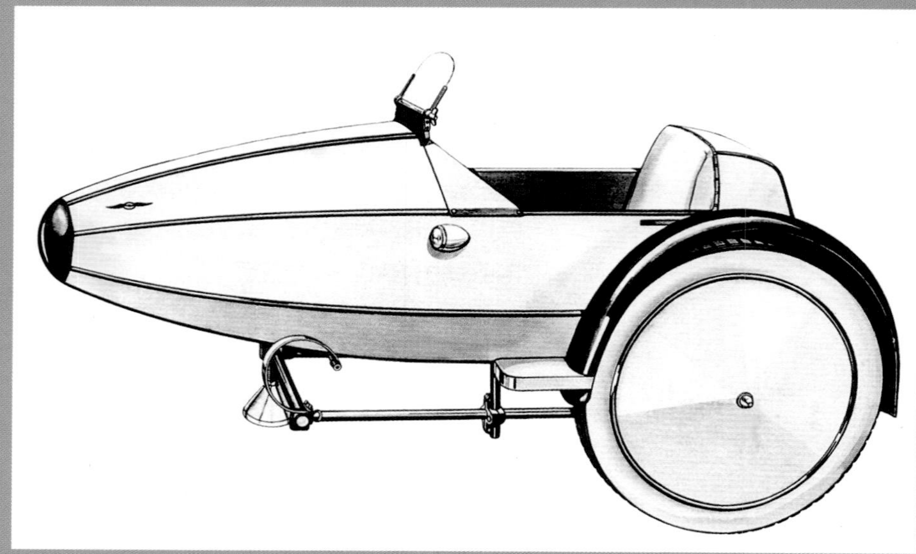

1

MOTORCYCLE SIDECARS

Triumph. The name sounds appropriately international and promising, or so salesman Siegfried Bettmann might have thought in 1886, two years after emigrating from his German hometown of Nuremberg to London. Bettmann so christened the penny farthing-style bicycle produced in Birmingham for all Europe. *Nomen est omen*, or "the name says it all"—the proverb proved to be true in this case! No wonder that the subsequent "safety" bicycles from Bettmann's own manufacture in Coventry—at the time the British metropolis of bicycle production—became an unquestionable commercial triumph!

Only a few years later, in 1894, Heinrich Hildebrand and Alois Wolfmüller of Munich started the very first volume production of motorcycles. They had run their first two-stroke engine in 1892 and a four-stroke in 1893. Encouraged by the enthusiasm of his partner, Mauritz Schulte, Bettmann occasionally imported some of these noisy machines to England, which at the time was very skeptical about the dangers posed by gasoline-engined vehicles. When the Bavarians ceased motorcycle production in 1897, Schulte not only switched over to De Dion motorcycles, but also developed his own two-wheeler machines for Triumph. In 1902, mass production of this motorcycle began at Priory Street, Coventry, where Triumph had moved just a few years before. In the following year, Bettmann had his motorcycle produced in Nuremberg as well. The single-cylinder, four-stroke engine proved to be very reliable and gained a reputation as the "trusty Triumph," highly recommended for military use—an important communications factor for the British army in World War I. Many of them were ridden by soldiers who had little or no experience, before the war, with motor vehicles of any type. These Triumph motorcycles can justifiably be regarded as the earliest forebear of today's elegant sedans and racy sports cars known affectionately as Jaguars.

The first piece of evidence comes from one of these soldiers, William Walmsley, who was born in the summer of 1892. Before the war he had worked for his father, Thomas Matley Walmsley, a coal merchant, at Stockport near Manchester. An early example of his engineering abilities was a machine that polished the brass bridles of their dray horses. The Walmsleys produced their own "jig-built" metal-clad railway coal wagons—work experience that would introduce young William to techniques and practices that would be of extreme importance to him in his future life.

When the war broke out, William, like many of his contemporaries, volunteered for duty in a prestigious cavalry regiment from his home county of Cheshire. The war over, he returned with a slightly injured leg to his happy parental home, Fairhaven, at Flowery Field, Stockport. He brought with him one of the "steel horses" of Triumph manufacture. Rather than turning to his father's coal business, William found a pastime in restoring this motorcycle. He must have done a good job, because friends engaged him to refurbish and restore their motorcycles. His father's money acted as a subsidy affording him time to pursue his interest in motorcycles—William did not have to earn his living!

Touring on a motorcycle—being equipped with just one seat for the driver—could be a lonesome pleasure. This was a problem for sociable people like Walmsley! Man's natural inclination to togetherness made more than one enthusiast put his darling into a trailer. Of course, this made conversation *en route* more or less impossible. All too often the trailer became separated from the motorcycle on rough roads, often with dramatic and injurious results.

For many, the additional seat in front of the driver—often the feature of a powered tricycle—is

Left: Despite the determined look in his eyes, this young man was not sure about his professional career—then this William Lyons established a small company that was to become Jaguar. *(S)*

Opposite: This is the beginning of Jaguar: William Walmsley's first motorcycle sidecar. *(S)*

Fairhaven, the home of young William Walmsley. In the garden he started to repair motorcycles and thereby laid the foundation of what was to become known as Jaguar. *(St)*

Typical Motorcycle sidecar from just after World War I. *(St)*

Seventy-five years later it was called Berwick: Walmsley's house at 23 King Edward Avenue, Blackpool. *(St)*

a faded memory. It was left for the passenger to take the full impact of any frontal collision and at best to protect themselves against dust, flying stones, and bad weather. All these passengers may have been thankful to the brothers Graham of Enfield, who in 1902 invented the sidecar, which, as the name implies, was safely attached—at the side—to the motorcycle frame.

Walmsley would have liked to own a sidecar, but the usual tall and bulky models, many made in wicker, did not please his eyes. So he built his own—according to his personal, discerning taste. This sidecar was of an octagonal cross-section, very low and cigar-like in shape. Its bright, unpainted aluminum panels gleamed futuristically—a rocket for the road! The seat was set low, and the passenger was able to adopt a more reclined position, reducing wind resistance. The styling was influenced by a Watsonian prototype on display at the 1919 Motorcycle Show. Walmsley's sidecar was particularly handsome, and handled well, due to its low center of gravity. Naturally, Walmsley was very proud of his design, although he later learned that Harley-Davidson had offered a similarly low sidecar some months earlier.

Such a sidecar was manufactured by hand, but in principle it was not unlike making coal wagons. He built the frame from ash and covered this with metal sheets, now of aluminum. Fred Gibson, Walmsley's brother-in-law, helped him, as did the enthusiastic Wilfried Webb, son of the owner of a nearby bicycle—and motorcycle—workshop. Webb's father had become famous by racing bicycles and had once covered over 380 miles in 24 hours, while wearing all his Victorian clothing! The manufacture of the Walmsley sidecar was a family affair, with the folding top and seats cut out, sewn, and upholstered by Walmsley's sisters. All this happened in Fairhaven's garden shed, where at least two sidecars, probably more, were assembled and mounted on chassis likely to have been made in Birmingham by A. H. Haden. Sadly this hallowed place, where the first of these historic sidecars was constructed, no longer exists.

Walmsley kept his first sidecar combination and called it *Ot-As-Ell,* following local Lancashire slang by dropping the H of "hot" and "hell." In essence this was the first pre-Jaguar, and could be seen on the road as early as 1920, displaying an Irish registration—a "red herring" to confuse the police. It was officially registered on January 28, 1921 with the number DB 1238. The second example of the low but prominent sidecar was made for Fred Gibson, and the third example was sold to a real client. Gibson took his sidecar and Webb, as his passenger, to local sidecar races. They became famous in their first year, as class winners in the East Cheshire Trial, where their sidecar outfit was the only single-cylinder combination to make an unpenalized climb of the famous Litton Slack, the steepest gradient in the event.

A letter from that first real client of Walmsley's gleaming cigar-shaped sidecar was later published in *The Autocar.* It claimed that Walmsley intended to turn his hobby into a regular business and had temporarily employed a sales agent in Manchester for the purpose. However, no other evidence exists to support this claim.

In the workshop of the nearby Bamford Arms Hotel, quite a few more Walmsley sidecars were manufactured, but by now the Gibson family was no longer involved. The sidecars were offered at 28 guineas plus 4 guineas for the hood, lamp, and the then-fashionable aluminum wheel disc that covered the spokes. (One guinea was 21 shillings, or 1 pound, 1 shilling. At the time, a good weekly wage was 4 guineas.)

Walmsley's father sold his coal merchant business, and in June 1921, the Walmsleys moved away from Fairhaven, which was taken over by one George William Swallow. The birds of the same name were synonymous with lightness and agility, as were Walmsley's sidecars, so that "Swallow" seemed a most appropriate name for Walmsley's product. Indeed Walmsley seems to have used this new identity in promotions from about this time, so it is likely that Mr. Swallow may have inspired Walmsley.

The Walmsley family found a new home on Britain's northwestern Fylde coast at 23 King Edward Avenue, Blackpool, a residential area near the town center of the well-known holiday resort. At the end of the new garden was a small brick shed, accessible via a back entry. Here William continued to build his sidecars with his wife Emily doing the sewing and trim. This is another historic landmark that no longer exists.

Some years before, and not many yards away on the other side of the street, at the corner of Holmfield Road, lived the family of William Lyons, an Irish musician and composer. One of his more noted compositions, the *Infatuation Waltz,* is said to have entertained King George V on board HMS *Medina* when traveling to

Behind the rightmost of the three garage doors is the place where William Walmsley created his first sidecars at Blackpool. *(S)*

India. William and a young Minnie Barcroft fell in love and set up home in Blackpool, where he opened a music and piano warehouse. However, he continued to play in local orchestras, and even conducted some of them. The success of the warehouse was mainly thanks to Minnie's diligence, while William remained addicted to his role as a composer. As well as daughter Carol, they had one son, born on September 4, 1901, named after his father—William. This boy, of course called Billy by his playmates, would grow into the leading man of the story that follows, although no one could have expected that at the time. Billy was an inconspicuous, average, and not-too-ambitious pupil of Arnold House, a reputable and respected school where he excelled mainly in sports. Running was his favorite discipline at the time.

Little surprise that the choice of a job or profession became difficult for the teenager. The first possibility was an apprenticeship with the famous Vickers concern. He at least mastered the entrance examination, which was described as difficult. But an alternative opportunity presented itself. Billy's father, already one of Blackpool's dignitaries, had been introduced to A. W. Hubble, chief of Crossley Motors at Gorton, coincidentally near to Walmsley's Stockport. Crossley was a well-known and respected company at the time, which had started with the manufacture of gas engines and made its breakthrough into car manufacture in 1904, with a model designed by J. S. Critchley. Billy would be trained in the technical know-how of motor vehicle manufacturing—a subject in which he had not shown

LEAVE FOR
FR.3030

any previous interest. In addition, as a Crossley trainee, he would be expected to study mechanical engineering at Manchester Technical College.

Billy Lyons found it hard to adjust to being just "another cog in the Crossley wheel" and retraced his footsteps, back to Blackpool and his father's workshop. He successfully applied his hand skills to repairing gramophones, at the same time dreaming of owning his own business. He would have liked to produce record players, incorporating his own modifications, and although he weighed the pros and cons of starting the business, it never materialized.

Young Lyons spent most of his leisure time racing motorcycles—a passion that he, to the disgust of his teachers, had discovered in his school years. As soon as the war was over, Billy, along with his close friends Arnold Breaknell and Geoffrey Nabb, were instrumental in recreating the Blackpool, Fylde, and District Motor Club and organizing the races for which the club was noted. For some time he was the club's vice captain. Billy was particularly proud of his Harley-Davidson Daytona Special—one of only three in Great Britain. The Harley was key in some of Billy's early successes against some stiff competition, particularly in hillclimbs.

At the motor club, Lyons struck up a friendship with Jack Mallalieu, the general manager of the local Sunbeam garage, owned by the Jackson brothers. Jack Mallalieu offered an apprenticeship to Billy, which he readily accepted. Soon Mallalieu went into business for himself, funded by a successful Bolton textile business owner, by the name of Brown. A Morris and Rover workshop was established at Metropole Garage, Blackpool, which Brown had acquired from a leading local bus operator, Joseph Street. This was conveniently situated only a mile away from the Lyons' home, so Billy joined Mallalieu as his odd-job man. Officially his title was junior salesman, but his duties included a wide variety of administrative work on Mallalieu's behalf, affording the opportunity for Billy to combine and expand his knowledge of both technical and commercial aspects of the business. This grounding would stand him in good stead for the future. In November 1919, the increasingly successful Billy Lyons represented Brown & Mallalieu on their stand at the Motor Show in London. The Motor Show counted as the leading car exhibition in Great Britain, and was the first following World War I. Lyons would not have dared to imagine then that one day he might fascinate the masses at this show and others worldwide with his racy dream cars!

During this time, Billy acquired his first, but hardly "racy" car. This was a pretty, but very unreliable Coventry-built Buckingham prewar cycle car, an almost forgotten marque made at the Holyhead Road workshop, which would later be the manufacturing home of the famous Alvis 12/50. However, Lyons soon replaced the Buckingham with another motorcycle.

In summer of 1921, as soon as Walmsley moved in, Billy became aware of the young new neighbor with these elegant, shining sidecars, and he purchased one. Walmsley, in turn, became interested in the motor sport club—at least the social side of it. He was more a gentleman than a gentleman driver.

In his little workshop Walmsley could only produce one sidecar per week. Takers were enough among motorcycle enthusiasts, not the least because Walmsley strategically parked his combination along Blackpool's famous "Golden Mile" promenade or in front of the Carlton Hotel. But Billy Lyons was sure that with some real advertising, many more shiny Swallows could be sold. So he proposed to Walmsley that his business should become more professional and be expanded. Walmsley did not like the idea, but his wife Emily, who was pregnant with their first child, said she would feel more secure with a more regular income for their family. After endless debates, most of them in Walmsley's family kitchen, Billy and Emily managed to persuade Walmsley of their idea. Luckily, he had already patented his sidecar design in April 1921, when still living at Stockport. They decided upon a weekly production rate of 10 sidecars, which were now officially known as the Swallow. In order to dedicate himself completely to the new task, Billy Lyons quit Brown & Mallalieu early in 1922.

In 1921, with an overdraft guaranteed by the fathers of both men, the sizeable loan of £1,000 was negotiated with William's and Deacon's Bank. A friend of Lyons' father made available the upper story of a long, narrow building at 7-9 Bloomfield Road, Blackpool. It was located above the electrical manufacturing business of a Mr. Outhwaite, and was rented as a workshop from early 1922. Billy Lyons started recruiting suitable employees who, initially, were put to work creating the

Behind these walls William Lyons lived as a young man: 24 King Edward Avenue, Blackpool. *(St)*

Opposite: In his youth, William Lyons was an enthusiastic motorcycle rider. *(S)*

Jaguar is aware of its roots and has donated a commemorative plaque to Lyons' and Walmsley's first workshop at Bloomfield Road, Blackpool. *(St)*

The upper story was where it all started: 7–9 Bloomfield Road, Blackpool. *(St)*

Right: The swallow in its artistic flight was Lyons' and Walmsley's first brand. *(Schön)*

workbenches and other equipment needed to start sidecar production. The first employee of the company (which would evolve into the prestigious Jaguar Cars Limited over the decades that followed) was Richard Binns, who started as a foreman. Two tinsmiths, Jim Greenwood and Joe Yates, were the first to work on the sidecars. Painting was the duty of Cyril Marshall, always referred to by Walmsley as "Sam." Seats and interior trim were the preserve of Arnold Hollis, who worked for the fledgling company on a part-time, as-needed basis.

Lyons occupied an office of about 50 square feet. He sat behind a desk the top of which had been covered in leather by Arnold Hollis. Lyons, as always, was as busy as the shop-floor workers. He was driven by a strong sense of duty, leading by example—at times outpacing the energy of his shop-floor workers. In later years he was known to have regretted strongly that he had involved himself in the time-consuming aspects of the business, leaving little or no time to enjoy the easier living typical of the period's industrial and commercial upper class. But once he decided to make this sidecar business a success, he remained determined and rarely allowed himself a distraction. This was a character trait that would stand him in good stead in his later business life, and it would be the underpinning of all that he and his dedicated work force achieved in making the marque a significant contributor to the history of the automobile.

The first floor location of the workshop was less than ideal for mounting the sidecars to their chassis frames, now being supplied by Montgomery in Coventry. These frames had to be hoisted upstairs and then returned to ground floor level when complete, a labor-intensive activity. Swallow continued to function despite sometimes lacking suitable equipment and sufficient manpower. As in many expanding businesses, this introduced a measure of improvisation and the need to impose flexible working practices on the work force. The shop-floor workers grudgingly accepted the seasonal aspect of employment, which was influenced by the peaks of "new-model" demand—created by introductions at major motorcycle and car shows—typically held at London's Olympia.

Lyons fully expected to become Walmsley's partner, a matter justified by the loan, guaranteed by the Lyons family. However, first Lyons had to attain full age—it was November 1922 before the contract from the solicitor was ready to be signed. In this document the operation was referred to as "Walmsley & Lyons," becoming effective, retroactively, on September 11, 1922, suggesting Lyons' 21st birthday, although this is not strictly correct.

One clause confirmed that Lyons would pay one half of the already existing overdraft of £1,000. Lyons was also committed to the payment of a license fee of £50 to Walmsley for the sidecar design, which was considered to be a Walmsley "invention." The profits were to be shared equally between both partners, and each partner was entitled to a weekly salary of £10. Shortly afterward, the operation was officially named "Swallow Sidecar Company," and this name was used in advertising just a few days after the signing of the contract.

From his 21st birthday onward, the young William Lyons no longer needed his father's signature for the banker's orders. He made a practice of collecting the workforce's weekly wages late on a Saturday morning. This was an example of the canny business side of Lyons at work—the workforce could not help but work longer than they had to in order to be present to receive their wage packets.

Advertising was another of Lyons' roles. The stylized swallow depicted on the cover of the first Swallow brochure prompted an immediate rebuff from Coventry car maker Swift, who already used a similar radiator

mascot. Lyons turned to a family acquaintance for legal advice, who confirmed that litigation was imminent, unless the brochures were destroyed. As they were of questionable quality, they were considered to be an acceptable loss. The matter was put down to experience, another part of Lyons' business learning curve.

In autumn 1922, Swallow had already contracted for a stand at the Motorcycle Show. However, Lyons was aware that one motorcycle manufacturer would not be attending and decided to take over the vacant stand, even though Swallow did not produce motorcycles. Although he would not normally have been permitted to occupy the stand, Billy Lyons' powers of persuasion won the day. Not surprisingly, a leading periodical of the day, *The Motorcycle*, contained a glowing report on the highly attractive, slim, gleaming sidecar called Swallow. Its report introduced Swallow's presence to the motorcycling fraternity throughout the U.K. One of Swallow's show sidecars was attached to an equally impressive Brough Superior Twin type SS 80—owned jointly by the Swallow partners. They had acquired this motorcycle shortly after a meeting with young George Brough, who had recently left his father's motorcycle manufacturing business to start up an independent motorcycle manufacturing company.

Lyons spread his advertising of Swallow sidecars over several newspapers, resulting in a steadily increasing demand that the small workshop and its small workforce found hard to digest. With the understanding and goodwill of the bank, a warehouse at the back of Woodfield Road—a continuation of Bloomfield Road in the direction of the sea front—was rented from a Mr. Francis. Shortly afterward, an opportunity occurred for Swallow to move to a two-story building only one block away from its Bloomfield Road premises—at the corner of John Street and Moon Avenue. Production and assembly were quickly relocated there, making the hoist redundant. These changes streamlined production and allowed the production of up to 100 sidecars weekly, a production figure that Swallow was able to maintain for many years. The management of the company's accounts and accounting function was subcontracted to O & W B Haworth (acquaintances of Mr. Lyons senior), who had provided Swallow with its first manufacturing site and their first female employee, secretary Dorothy Atkinson.

It appears that many Swallow customers were as unfamiliar with the roadholding characteristics of a motorcycle combination as they were with the name of the company. When cornering or braking, the sidecar influenced the directional stability of the motorcycle, whether fully laden or empty. Certain maneuvers and changes in direction called for conscious body movements by the rider and passenger in order to transfer weight—particularly if a pillion passenger was carried. Accidents on the maiden voyage of motorcycles with Swallow sidecars attached were not uncommon, and in consequence brought Swallow additional business. Any mishap of this nature was not covered under the vehicle guarantee—made clear in the owner's handbook under the chapter titled "Misuse."

In 1923, William Walmsley acquired a burnt-out Austro-Daimler car from Fred Gibson, who had a hand in Walmsley's first sidecars. With the help of the very young Harry Leslie Gill, who had only recently joined the company, the Austro-Daimler was to be clothed in new, strikingly attractive coachwork—which would have been the first "tailored" car from Swallow. Strange to relate, Billy Lyons was not involved in this exercise, his duties still being confined to the commercial and administrative side of the business. Another new employee, who at 17 years of age was considered quite old compared with youngsters like the 15-year-old Harry Teather, was Arthur Whittaker. Arthur was assigned the task of rectifying the mechanical state of the Austro-Daimler. Unfortunately the young man failed in his task and the car was sold off. As a Swallow salesman, Whittaker was expected to ride his motorcycle combination to visit potential and existing sources of sales throughout the country, whatever the weather, a job that he grew to dislike. Fortunately for Whittaker, his abilities as a procurement and purchasing manager soon came to light, and it was in this role at manager and director level that he was a faithful servant to Lyons for nearly 45 years.

For the 1923 Motorcycle Show some of the best-known and respected motorcycle manufacturers displayed their machines with Swallow sidecars attached. Brough Superior, Matador, and DOT (slightly optimistically translated to "Devoid Of Trouble") all displayed Swallow combinations that were sold and delivered to their new customers at the show, saving the

Arthur Whittaker, a gifted purchaser. *(S)*

A masterpiece among motorcycle sidecars: Swallow Model 4. *(J)*

cost of their transport back to Blackpool. Demand created more demand, resulting in the signing of the first dealer contracts, which were administered on the company's behalf by press agent Raymond Bailey. For some time Swallow ran a small dispatch office at Coomer Road, Fulham, West London, to be nearer to its many clients in the capital.

The amount of free publicity was increasing with the reportage of national and club competitive events, highlighting the participation of motorcycle combinations with more and more Swallow sidecars among the winners. Harry Reed, the founder of the DOT motorcycle manufacturing company, for example, was second in the 1924 Sidecar TT on the Isle of Man with his 344cc JAP engine, while Almond Tinkler on a Matador-Swallow combination with Blackburne engine took third place. At one point the Matador mechanics replaced the Swallow sidecar with a Haden, a make that had seen many previous TT wins. After one of Lyons' rare outbursts, Matador reverted to using the Swallow. Despite Lyons' own career in motorcycle racing, the Swallow Company never directly took part in racing.

Swallow prospered, and gave the partners a good and regular income. On this basis a cautious William Lyons contemplated marriage. He had fallen in love with Greta Brown, a schoolmaster's daughter. When collecting her at her parents' house he would park his motorcycle around the corner. Naturally, Mr. and Mrs. Brown were suspicious until they learned that the slope of the other road helped young Lyons to start his bike. On September 15, 1924, William Lyons married Greta. They had three children: Patricia, John, and Mary. On their honeymoon in the Scottish Highlands they bought a puppy, on impulse. Although this first canine acquisition was a very lively animal, the Lyons family would always keep dogs. At first the couple rented a flat, and then lived in a bungalow in Bispham Road. Later William Walmsley and his family moved to the same road.

In 1923, Swallow had added a new model called the Coupe Sports de Luxe, plus another model marketed as the Light Weight de Luxe. With its pentagon section—the idea came from Jim Greenwood, the tinsmith—its manufacture was much easier and less expensive than the original model, which nevertheless remained popular for some years more. Demand for the company's products increased still further, and production figures rose in an effort to satisfy the demand. Further variants were added to the range. Models 3 (a rare, more robust variant, probably with hexagonal section) and 4 brought further improvement, the latter with a long, pointed tail. Stylistically, this was a masterpiece that proved to be extremely popular, remaining in production well into the 1930s. The most popular among Swallow's early sidecars, the Model 4A had better weather protection and a full windshield, instead of the little Brooklands screen.

Walmsley seems to have had some of his best ideas by night. With this in mind he always kept a pencil and note paper on his bedside locker to record his latest ideas. One of his more ingenious ideas was a child-size or junior version of Model No. 4, in the spirit of the children's pedal cars of the time. As with a pram, a push bar protruded from the pointed back, which allowed young Bobby Walmsley to join his parents as they walked. Only a few years later the boy became independent of such good will, when his father built a pedal car for him that proudly bore the Swallow name on its hood.

Models 5 and 6 were particularly light racing models. The former returned to the original octagonal section and had a curved Perspex screen, but it was only rarely built. Model No. 6, the Light Weight Racing Sidecar, was no longer pointed at the front; instead the bottom panel was curved, ending at the upper panel just under the windshield. This also became general practice with other makes of sidecars. At Swallow, Model No. 6 was just called "Scrapper."

The most famous racing motorcycle riders used the Swallow sidecar. Sunbeam works driver George Dance, motorcycle world-record holder Bert le Vack, Tony Worters, Jack Emerson, Joe Wright, Michael Evoy, Ivan Riddoch, and Charlie Waterhouse were all devotees of the Swallow sidecar. Dougal Marchant managed to beat all of the records in his class—a total of 16—with his Chater-Lea and Swallow Scrapper combination in 1926, including the flying kilometer at 86.35 miles per hour.

Model No. 7, the Semi Sports, was similar to the previous model, but more robust for everyday use. In order to save costs, one variant had the aluminum panels replaced by fabric. Both were very popular; the army continued to use them during World War II. Model 8, the Touring Design, had more comfortable deluxe equipment and was further improved as Model 8A, the Hurlingham. This was also available with a metal roof. Model No. 9, the Sports Touring Coupe de Luxe, was distinguished by its hood sides that imitated the Vauxhall's concave hood flutes. Model 9A, designated de Luxe Touring, was another model with improved weather protection. The front of Models 10, 11, and 12 was inspired by a canoe and had polished rails around a mahogany deck. No. 12, the Sun Saloon, featured a metal roof and glass screens all around. No. 13, because of superstition, was never a production reality. No. 14 was quite light and streamlined with flush panels. Named Donington Special and Super Sports de Luxe, these models' names revealed their potential for racing. Model No. 15 was the last development under Lyons, unveiled in 1936 and produced for one year only. Its lines were taken from No. 14, but as the Ranelagh Saloon, it was luxuriously equipped and was often ordered with a metal roof.

In 1926 Emil Frey of Switzerland became Swallow's first overseas franchised dealer, and he was to become a particularly successful one. Frey, patron of motorcycle

Top: Swallow Model 2 with Perspex windshield. *(J)*

Above: Swallow Model 9 as enclosed "Saloon." *(J)*

Right: Swallow Model 9 "Roadster" attached to a wonderful Sunbeam motorcycle; the swage lines along the upper edges of the body are quite visible here. *(Rooswinkel)*

Above: Alice Fenton, Lyons' right hand since Swallow times. *(S)*

Left: In the basement of this building the first Austin-Swallows were assembled: Cocker Street and Exchange Street, Blackpool. *(S)*

"... and this is what it looked like shortly before it was torn down in 2001. *(St)*

racing on grass tracks, had started trading with motorcycle equipment in Zurich on October 1, 1924. In 1928 he won the sidecar race on the Solitude circuit near Stuttgart with an Osborne and Swallow combination powered by an Anzani two-cylinder engine—the first Swallow victory abroad. From then on until 1933 Frey ran a branch office at Stuttgart.

In 1926 Swallow moved into a larger, more modern workshop at the corner of Cocker and Exchange Streets near Blackpool's town center. Lyons' earlier employers, Jackson Brothers, had used this building shortly before; Jackson Brothers had taken it over from Joseph Street, another name mentioned previously.

Deviously, Lyons managed to use a lorry from sidecar chassis supplier Hayward to make the move to the new facility. He persuaded the Hayward driver to spend a weekend at the Blackpool seaside. By late on Sunday the total relocation was complete, with no lost production time and no extra expense incurred—typical Lyons! All the former Swallow premises had been vacated, so that the whole company and its production facilities were united under one roof, with obvious benefits.

In advertisements both the Cocker and Exchange Street addresses were given, implying an even larger organization and facility, another little Lyons ploy. Upward of 30 people now worked for Swallow. Among them was young Alice Fenton, who was originally employed at Lyons' music and piano warehouse. She would become Lyons' right hand in all matters concerning Swallow and later, those that were established under the Jaguar banner. Fenton was appointed as a Jaguar main board director in 1956, until her premature death in 1960. The scope of her company responsibilities went far beyond those of a normal secretary, including all customer relations, and she was familiar with every detail of the company's operation. In all these years there was not a single problem that Miss Fenton was not able to solve instantly—she proved to be an invaluable servant to the company and to William Lyons, and was sadly missed in the years following her demise.

In 1927, the U.K. police forces joined the very "broad church" that made up Miss Fenton's customers—many of whom, because of her good works and attention, remained faithful to Lyons and the Jaguar marque for many, many years. The honor of becoming the first Swallow-driving police department fell to Nottingham, which was equipped with glorious Brough motorcycles and beautiful Swallow sidecars.

In World War II, Swallow, under William Lyons' direction, assembled many motorcycle sidecars. *(S)*

THE FIRST CARS 2

From the mid-1920s onward, experts believed that more inexpensive cars would become available, which would seriously affect the future well-being of the motorcycle industry. This trend had already sounded the death knell of so-called cycle cars, which in essence were motorcycles with four wheels. A similar adverse forecast was directed at the sidecar industry. The advent of the Austin Seven may have influenced Lyons when he decided to expand his operations to include attractively priced sporting-style bodies for more mundane family cars.

A high degree of self-sufficiency and production cost control all linked to "good-housekeeping" had been the keynote of Swallow's sidecar manufacturing success. So it was no surprise that a paint and a trim shop for car coachwork was installed in a part of the large new building that was not occupied by sidecar manufacture. By the end of 1926, Swallow ads aimed at attracting upholsterers and painters currently employed in the Midland motor industry had appeared in Birmingham area newspapers, more than 100 miles south of Blackpool. This is how Cyril Holland, who was to become an important new employee, first learned of Swallow. Holland had been an apprentice at Lanchester, a company whose technical achievements in automobile engineering had started as early as 1893 and which was the most advanced car manufacturer in the early decades of the British motor industry. Holland had worked for several car manufacturers, honing his skills in every facet of coach building—from the first drawing to the final product—and his abilities were most impressive. Cyril Holland proved these abilities, working on a Talbot-Darracq that had crashed in a beach race at Southport, re-creating the Talbot with roadster coachwork and distinctive vee windshield.

Lyons, however, was not aiming at one-offs and restorations: His plan was to build, in volume, series of similarly specified cars, but with the style and equipment of more individual coachbuilt cars. For this reason, his company now took on a new identity—Swallow Sidecar & Coach Building Company.

In 1926, a general strike had severely damaged the British economy and small cars with low running costs were proving popular. Lyons gauged that some who had lost a fortune, but not their pride, during the depression, wanted to be seen in a smaller car that was tastefully different from the average. Similarly, Lyons sought to attract those with increasing disposable income who wished to "trade-up" and be seen in something different. A small but elegant vehicle built to high standards of quality, but that would not be much more expensive to buy and run, seemed to Lyons to be the niche to aim for. He reasoned that the answer was to transfer the principle of Walmsley's sidecar onto four wheels. He only had to find an appropriate car chassis, and that would come from the Austin Seven.

This company bore the family name of its founder, Herbert Austin. He gained his first merits with another well-known marque, having been employed as a young man at the helm of the Birmingham branch of Frederick York Wolseley's sheep-shearing machine manufacturing business. With expansion of the business in mind, Austin built for Wolseley a rather unorthodox three-wheeler similar to the French Bollée vehicle, with a small, horizontally mounted two-cylinder engine. But in May 1896, one Harry J. Lawson secured the Bollée patents for England, to a degree restricting Austin's activities. It was 1899 before Austin could create his

Swallow transformed the ubiquitous Austin Seven into the flashy Austin-Swallow. *(Schön)*

Opposite: Contemporary photograph of a very early Austin-Swallow Roadster with a hardtop and fenders forming an entity with the running boards. *(S)*

Below: Early Austins were not exactly beauties. *(St)*

The engine bay behind the imposing grille of the Austin-Swallow is not very impressive. *(S)*

second car, with a single-cylinder engine, again mounted horizontally. Series production of this car commenced in 1901, and was immediately taken over by the mighty Vickers concern. Vickers, who initially made machine guns, later shifted focus to aircraft production and owned the Rolls-Royce and Bentley marques for more than 25 years, until 1998. Successful at first, the demand for the single-cylinder Wolseley rapidly decreased from 1903 on. Obstinately, Austin decided against adapting new fashions and as a result was told to clear his desk, to be replaced in 1905 by John Davenport Siddeley. However, it was not long before the Vickers directors found reason to quarrel with Siddeley, causing him to leave the company. Siddeley—First Baron Kenilworth from 1937—created an organization that designed and built aircraft engines and aircraft that competed successfully with Vickers, and a range of quality specialist cars under the Armstrong-Siddeley marque.

Despite his dismissal by Vickers, Herbert Austin remained in the automotive industry and founded his own vehicle manufacturing business in the Birmingham suburb of Longbridge. Its great moment came when the Austin Seven was unveiled on July 21, 1922. Eighteen-year-old Austin draughtsman Stanley Edge designed the car. Edge had been inspired by the Peugeot Quadrilette. The new car's name indicated that it was taxed as a seven-horsepower car (with an annual road tax of £7) according to the British law that favored long-stroke cars against the Ford Model T with its large engine. Contrary to most cycle cars of the time, the Austin Seven was a small but fully equipped car with a water-cooled four-cylinder engine of 696cc displacement, soon enlarged to 747cc. It had simple splash lubrication, brakes on all four wheels (the pedal working the rear, the handbrake the front drums), a three-speed transmission, a separate chassis, and a small, sober body for four not-too-large persons. It was so practical and affordable, that with more than 300,000 examples to its credit, it was Britain's first seriously mass-produced car. It remained in production as the Austin Ruby until the outbreak of World War II. The German BMW (Dixi), the French Rosengart, and the American Bantam started car manufacture producing the Austin Seven under license, while Datsun in Japan chose to copy the design.

William Lyons was aware of the Austin Seven's merits, and soon after his marriage he purchased a two-year old Seven Chummy, an open four-seat tourer that he praised as being "wonderful value for money," although he did not like the austere lines of the body. It proved to be an ideal basis for his first venture in specialist car-body building.

At the time, other companies offered special coachwork for the Austin Seven, but Lyons and Walmsley were particularly impressed by the two-seater made by E. C. Gordon England at Wembley, with its fabric body. Hughes of Birmingham, who was already competing with Swallow's sidecars, also manufactured a light roadster body for the Seven. Despite its bright aluminum construction, it was not exactly beautiful, but it showed what could be done with the Austin Seven chassis. More attractive was a sketch made by Cyril Holland that, to Lyons' order, he refined and adjusted to the dimensions of the Seven chassis. This exercise determined the styling of the Swallow-bodied Austin Seven as we know it today.

Lyons purchased the chassis from local Austin dealer Stanley Parker, who was afraid that Austin might withdraw his franchise agreement. It thus took some convincing before Parker was prepared to deliver an Austin Seven minus its body. His cooperation and courage was rewarded with a sales franchise for the Austin-Swallow, which from 1928 was an exclusive franchise for the whole North of England. After many decades, Parker proudly boasted that he was the longest-serving Jaguar dealer. In January 1927, Swallow received its first chassis bearing the number CHAI 2203; it cost £114, 5 shillings. The mechanical specification remained unchanged, with only a supporting bracket for the long tail added at the rear of the chassis, and the starting handle extended. The body, with its ash frame and aluminum cladding, utilized the same construction techniques as the sidecars, negating any new manufacturing methods.

On May 20, 1927, the neat open two-seater with its helmet fenders at the front wheels, a round egg-shape tail, and its similarly rounded radiator grille, plus its vee windshield, made its debut in the magazine *The Autocar*, with which Lyons started to cooperate very closely. In these times of mostly black or dark brown, square motorcars, the rounded Swallow with its bright cream color and the fenders set off in crimson red was a sensation—to some a cultural shock. The interior was dominated by a fully equipped mahogany dashboard and comfortable seating trimmed in leather. No other "special" on the Seven chassis was equipped so lavishly. A hardtop, available via special order, turned this light touring car into a cozy coupe in cold weather.

In 1927, the first series front fenders were replaced with sweeping fixed fenders combined with running boards. In late 1927, the hardtop was more positively fixed, with two bolts at the rear and catches at the windshield frame. With its curved roof, it provided better headroom and offered a central ventilation flap. The headlining was a cord color matched to the leather trim. The windshield tapered at the base, while on the driver's side a hinged upper window was available at small extra cost. A swallow mascot was now mounted on top of the radiator shell, which bore an "Austin-Swallow" badge instead of "Austin." The rear was now higher, and legroom was greater. The alternate color scheme of pale gray with fenders and roof in bright green became available. Later, additional duo-tone finishes were made available.

By the end of 1927, the first large order for no less than 50 Austin-Swallows was placed by Percy J. Evans. The Birmingham car dealer quickly became convinced that these striking, nippy little cars could be a healthy addition to his business when offered alongside the more staid products of other manufacturers. The Austin-Swallows sold very quickly, converting Evans into yet another faithful dealer of Lyons' products.

Although Lyons was overwhelmed by his early opportunities, business jumped to an even higher level only a few weeks later. Charlie Hayes, a former colleague of Lyons' at Brown & Mallalieu and now working for Henlys, the famous car dealer in London, introduced him to his new chiefs. Henlys immediately ordered 500 Austin-Swallows for exclusive distribution in southern England with the exception of Kent, which was reserved for Martin Walter. For many decades Henlys was an important dealer for the SS and Jaguar successors of the tiny Austin-Swallow.

With this news, Walmsley declared Lyons mad. Lyons, in grabbing the Henly opportunity, seemed not to have considered the existing production capacity at Cocker Street, which was limited by the modest paint shop that only allowed a small weekly production. This was not the only production limitation to such a high-volume run.

After Walmsley's strong adverse reaction, Lyons hardly dared to confess that he had also promised Henlys an additional model, an enclosed four-seater. Despite the ensuing workload, Swallow made good on its promise and unveiled the Austin-Swallow sedan in September 1928.

The styling of this tiny four-seater sedan was again Cyril Holland's, and it had started with a sketch on a wall. Its peculiarities were the roof overhang above the windshield, as on the Alvis 12/50 sedan, resembling a peaked cap. The rear end was tastefully rounded and had a near-oval window. The "pen-nib" duo-tone scheme on the hood was inspired by the American Auburn. Most parts of the coachwork came as pressed sheets from the little company of Musgrove & Green at Birmingham. The vertically divided slide windows in the doors—remember the Renault 4—were only featured on the prototype of summer 1928. All the others had wind-down windows that had a tendency to cant in their rails. For the female passenger, a "Ladies'

A painting of an early Austin-Swallow that now belongs to the Jaguar Daimler Heritage Trust. *(J)*

The modest dashboard of an open Austin-Swallow. *(J)*

Companion Set" was provided in the glove box with all necessary paraphernalia for the re-creation of a woman's beauty en route. Similar to the two-seater's hardtop, a vent was positioned in the center of the roof, and both models now had revised radiator grilles with dumb irons in front. In that same year, Avon at Warwick introduced a very attractive special based on the Austin Seven, styled by the Jensen brothers, who in 1930 would start their own manufacture of exclusive sports cars with period American engines, a Jensen manufacturing direction that continued into the mid-1970s. Nevertheless, it was the Austin-Swallow that captured people's imagination! It could have happened otherwise, proof of which was Gordon England, whose popular Seven Roadster had once inspired Lyons. England's company did not make it through the depression that hit in 1929.

With the heavily increased production rate necessary to meet Henlys' large order, a new problem arose: Nearly all the components of the Austin Seven were made in the Midland area and had to be brought to Blackpool by train. With smaller items this was easily achievable, but the chassis from Austin caused some trouble, arriving irregularly and in large batches. At Blackpool's Talbot Road station, from time to time, a frightening number of Seven chassis stood about until they were transferred to Swallow in batches of 6. Austin obviously tried to rid themselves of as many chassis as possible, so that Lyons was forced to place orders of 50, which was a month's production of Swallow! The stationmaster certainly did not approve of this early version of the modern "just-in-time" delivery practice.

Lyons was forced to find a more practical solution and decided that transportation from the Midlands to Blackpool should be avoided altogether by relocating his manufacturing activity to the very center of British car manufacture. With his little Austin Seven, Lyons engaged in several foraging visits to Birmingham and

Coventry looking for suitable facilities. These he finally found with the help of solicitor Harry Noel Gillitt, the son-in-law of the owner of Rover, in Holbrook Lane, Foleshill, in the north of Coventry. This former bomb and shell-filling factory consisted of four blocks, two of which had not been used since World War I and which were now for sale. In order to prevent sparks, it had been equipped with wooden floors. One block was five times larger than Swallow's existing "shop" at Blackpool. Lyons persuaded the owner to lease out one block to him for three years, at an annual rent of £1,200, following which Lyons would have the option to purchase both blocks for £12,000. Despite a delay to renovate the facilities and make them suitable to Swallow's needs, the move was completed by early November 1928.

Thirty-two of the 50 Swallow employees followed Swallow—and William Lyons—to the Midlands. For months the staff had to work more than 12 hours a day. In the midst of construction work the new main electricity cable was stolen and a considerable amount of money had to be spent for a replacement, to Lyons' annoyance. Some referred to him as a "penny pincher," while others respectfully described him as "careful with money." A request for a wheelbarrow, for example, prompted his question as to what was wrong with the buckets that had been used before. After the move from Blackpool, Swallow seems no longer to have been named Sidecar & Coach Building Company. In 1929, at the latest, the designation Swallow Coachbuilding Company was in use. This may have been a limited company from then on; there was possibly a subsidiary called the Swallow Sidecar Company.

The townscape of Coventry—with the cathedral as the sole exception—was certainly not to Lyons' taste, but he also considered that Blackpool was spoiled by its mundane beach. The seemingly endless rain during the Swallow's first Coventry winter did nothing to arouse enthusiasm. Nevertheless, Lyons had to settle down in this industrious town, like it or not. He first lodged at the Queen's Hotel in Hertford Street, where he had stayed on several occasions before. Soon both Walmsley and Lyons moved to houses at St. Paul's Road, Foleshill, and then to the southern suburb of Earlsdon—Lyons preferred Eastleigh Avenue, where his family finally joined him again. Around 1930 he moved again to Woodside, Gibbet Hill Road, a particularly distinguished residential area that over the decades accommodated many notable automotive industry directors and their families.

Cyril Holland remained at Blackpool, not being prepared to pay out of his own pocket for the move to Coventry. Lyons, on the other hand, could not make an exception for any one single employee. So, he recruited Frank Etches as new head of the wood shop. Etches came from Triumph, where, under Claude Holbrook, cars had been produced since 1923. Etches claimed that he had invented a steam-bending process for wooden jigs. The wood formed using this process all returned to straight during further manufacture, whereupon Etches left sick and then disappeared altogether. Lyons grudgingly called Holland for help, who quietly solved the problem, remaining faithful to Swallow.

The production of such a wooden jig no longer took place in one single step. Instead, headed by the newly recruited Fred Gardner, the process was divided into separate tasks in the sawmill. Standardized parts accurately produced in large numbers eliminated the practice of having to adjust jigs in the body assembly shop. The assembly would not take longer than one hour now. This procedure—more typical for mass production—was at that time still quite unusual for a specialist car manufacture with its tiny series of cars. This principle sounds simple, but to turn it into reality was more than difficult. It was not easy at all to make a part exactly to the measurements of a pattern. On one occasion, the staff appeared in front of Lyons and declared the aim impossible. They would be proved

Open Austin-Swallows from 1931 (left) and 1930 (right). The younger example has a hardtop. *(Rooswinkel)*

Opposite above: In its time the Austin-Swallow sedan was a beauty in its class—this is the 1932 model. *(S)*

Opposite below: 1930 open Austin-Swallow. *(S)*

wrong, and by Christmas of 1928 the production aim of 50 cars per week was reached using the new technique. Later, however, the regular weekly rate settled down to 30 cars.

The Blackpool work force had been paid on a piecework basis since shortly before the move to Coventry. With this pay system, Lyons could calculate the production cost of his cars to the penny. A good worker earned a weekly wage of up to £5, but to achieve this figure many worked well into the night. Quantity control and payment were based upon job cards countersigned by the foreman. The workers from Blackpool as well as those from Coventry were not used to this system and would not accept it. Lyons gave them the choice to accept this system or to leave. Many preferred to go, ignoring the high unemployment rate of the day. However, at Swallow the system prevailed. With every new model, the time needed for every single work unit had to be measured with the stopwatch as a basis for payment. When timed, the workers did not work overly quickly, so that they got to appreciate the benefits of the system.

Maurice Simpson and Gordon Crosby reported in *The Autocar* on work at Swallow. They found quite a few aspects to praise, as they felt diligence, cleanliness, and rationalization all had reached astonishing levels. There was no assembly line as such. The bodies were instead put on a jig until they were mounted on the chassis. At times, parts were dealt with in a rather rough manner. Typically, when Austin introduced a new radiator in May 1929, the filler was higher than the previous filler, fouling the Swallow body. The remedy was a hefty blow to the filler, which produced the required amount of clearance with the body—such was engineering in the 1920s! The right "look" was always the highest priority. Jack Beardsley's trick of bending the leaf springs to balance out the additional weight of the sedan coachwork may have looked frightening to experts too, but it was inexpensive and effective.

In 1929 the Austin-Swallow had the honor of being tested by *The Autocar*. The magazine's judgment was that the car not only looked like a more expensive car, but also drove like one. Handling, roadholding, and directional stability, even on rough roads, seemed unexpectedly good—plus complimentary comments regarding the "fine-tuning" of the Swallow—was this a "thank-you" for letting *The Autocar* unveil the Austin-Swallow?

The poor ventilation of the sedan model was remedied when two octagonal fresh-air ducts were added to the top of the cowl in 1930. They resembled those of an ocean steamer *en miniature*. The radiator grille was once again changed, its opening now becoming broader toward the base. The floor was now made of steel sheets instead of wood. This revised Swallow was the first to be shipped to a royal address, in this case the Sultan of Perak in Malaysia—the British Empire still worked! His Royal Highness preferred the colors black and purple. The coach paint was discontinued early in 1930 in favor of synthetic cellulose (Duco from Du Pont), with the drying time becoming much shorter to allow higher production rates—at the price of much more polishing, however.

Right: Air scoops for better ventilation of the interior of the Austin-Swallow sedan; the upper part of the divided windshield on the driver's side is hinged. *(Rooswinkel)*

Far right: Dashboard of the Austin-Swallow Sedan. *(S)*

Right: Grille of the final version of the Austin-Swallow with central chromed bar. *(Rooswinkel)*

Below: Austin-Swallow sedan in its final guise—stealing the show from classic Jaguars. *(Rooswinkel)*

For 1931 the Austin-Swallow's radiator grille became lower, and a vertical center strip was added—the grille remained broader at the bottom. This center strip was chromed, as was the rest of the grille surround—gone was the time of nickel plating. The split bench seating was replaced by two separate bucket seats, and the two-seater was once again reduced in price. With regard to the numerous improvements to Austin's chassis, experts refer to this model as the "second series." It was first shown at the 1930 Motor Show.

Toward the end of 1931, safety glass was announced for the windshield. Sports-type silencers, fishtail exhausts, and chromed bumpers made by Wilmot-Breeden were added to the specification as well as a four-speed gearbox and an extended track. Prices were reduced to £165 for the sedan and £150 for the two-seater. During the 1932 model year, the Austin-Swallow went out of production after 88 sedans, between 17 and 20 two-seaters, and one "special van" were built.

Back in 1927, Swallow had introduced, as a larger brother to the tiny Austin-Swallow, a Morris with special coachwork. Oxford's famous son, William Morris, who later became the wealthy Lord Nuffield, made bicycles and motorcycles before launching his Oxford car in 1912. He astutely purchased components and equipment from first-class suppliers at particularly low rates, finally acquiring the businesses of some of his major suppliers. This is how the Morris concern was built up to become one of the major players in the British auto industry. Bill Morris (as he was first known) successfully introduced his Oxford model with its charismatic bullnose radiator, a model that took sales from the popular Model T Ford. Swallow turned its attentions to the Morris Cowley, which since 1927 featured a more conventional, flat grille. With its 1.5-liter engine it was looked on as a poor relation to the Oxford, which had developed considerably in the meantime. From autumn 1927, Swallow offered a two-seater roadster body not dissimilar that of the Austin-Swallow, but with an elegantly sloping back that included a rumble seat. To allow for a lower roofline, the steering column was lowered, the rear leaf springs were flattened, and even the clutch housing is said to have been modified. The old-fashioned artillery wheels were covered with bright wheel discs, or for an additional £10, wire wheels could be fitted. A hardtop was available for special order. The few Morris-Swallows were sold via Brown & Mallalieu, whose workshop Lyons knew well. This particular Swallow model did not last long. Cecil Kimber had Morris' support with his Oxford-based sporting M.G. and a steady supply of customers enthusiastic about the famous "octagon" marque.

In addition to the Austin-Swallow and the Morris-Swallow, Holland designed an open four-seater based on a Clyno, but despite initial plans it was not to be produced in series. The one-off was used by Walmsley as his company car, but was discarded because of the sagging of the rear section of the body. Clyno, makers of cycle cars, had with great ambitions turned to small car manufacture. But by 1927, their new, lavish works had accelerated their financial difficulties. Rumors of a new small £100 Morris made Clyno hastily reduce its prices, with dire commercial results. Of course, a series production of the Clyno-Swallow was now out of question.

In 1928 Swallow built a body for the Alvis 12/50 chassis. A young company (founded in 1919), Alvis was named after its alloy pistons. Its body form was similar

1929 London Motor Show—in the front the initial Swift-Swallow, in the background a FIAT-Swallow. *(S)*

to that of the Austin-Swallow and succeeded the "company" Clyno as Walmsley's personal transport. Incidentally, the 12/50, which was introduced in 1923, had been designed by Captain G. T. Smith Clark, who before had been employed with Coventry-Daimler. The Alvis-Swallow also remained a one-off. Alvis' chief, T. G. John, was not impressed by the car and refused to supply chassis to Swallow. Nevertheless, Swallow advertised the car for some time as if it was to be produced in series.

For the Motor Show of 1929, Swallow gained real status. For the first time it was invited to take a stand within the prestigious coachbuilders section—three new sedans were shown. The bodies, with their colorful duotone schemes, low windshields, and pointed roofs remained faithful to Swallow tradition, although the "pen-nib" treatment was discontinued. The chassis came from Standard, Swift, and FIAT.

The FIAT-Swallow had been introduced earlier in the summer of 1929 and was based on 509 A chassis, fitted with the Italian's overhead valve 1-liter engine, and too "short" gearing. Old-fashioned artillery wheels did not enhance its overall appearance. These FIAT chassis, made in Britain by Vickers, had remained unsold. Even with Swallow's colorful body treatment—a choice of nine duotone combinations was available—plus the fitting of wire wheels, which may have replaced the older wheels at extra cost, the car was hard to sell. It disappeared from the catalogs some months later when the succeeding FIAT chassis type 514 became available in England. It is said that those that remained unsold were eventually scrapped.

Swift, with whom Lyons had earlier come into conflict with his radiator mascot, had started out as a bicycle manufacturer, turning to cars in 1902. In 1929 Swift offered a light chassis powered by a 1.2-liter

Above: A Swift-Swallow during a visit at a later Jaguar plant. *(S)*

Right: The rounded rear of the Swift-Swallow is a copy of the Austin-Swallow sedan. *(S)*

The Standard Nine was quite popular in England; this is a Fulham Sedan with fabric body. *(Long)*

The Standard—in Britain a widespread car in the first half of the twentieth century. *(St)*

Right: This is what William Lyons made of the Standard: The Standard-Swallow with modified grille. *(S)*

The Wolseley, with its small, lively six-cylinder engine, was the most sporting among the Swallow cars. *(S)*

engine and running on attractive wire wheels. Lyons took on board suggestions made by Henlys when production of the Swift-Swallow came into full swing in March 1930. During the following autumn the chassis and running gear specification was improved in many different aspects. Items included attention to the fuel tank, cooling system, and the engine's combustion chamber. The radiator grille had a more modern touch with a bright vertical strip. The Swift-Swallow was praised for its spaciousness, its large doors, and its fine handling. The Swift distinguished itself by having the gear lever on the right side of the driver's seat. Again, the continuity of the model was affected by the prevailing market conditions. Financial difficulties forced Swift to cease production in April 1931, and the attractive Swift-Swallow became a thing of the past.

Another car from this era, the Standard-Swallow, marked the beginning of a very close cooperation between Lyons as a newcomer to Coventry and the established Reginald Walter Maudslay, who in 1903 had started to make cars in Coventry under the Standard banner. This name was full of glory at the time, representing an energetic, vibrant, colorful flag fluttering proudly at the head of a flagpole. Maudslay, however, had chosen this name as an expression of his idea that in his manufacture all parts should be made precisely to a common pattern so that they became interchangeable with different examples of the same model without any adjustment—standardized! Without this a spares organization, taken for granted today, would be impossible. This advanced idea—the same as that applied by Lyons and Fred Gardner in the manufacture of his wooden jigs—was more difficult to achieve then, with the still inadequate equipment of the day. In 1906, Standard became famous for introducing the first British six-cylinder car at an affordable price—the 18/20, which cost £625.

The Standard Nine introduced in 1927 was an upright, reliable, and popular vehicle with a four-cylinder engine. Its design is said to have stemmed from the French Mathis of pre-1914, another design attributed to Ettore Bugatti. The Standard-Swallow was based on the "Big Nine," which had its engine capacity increased to 1.3 liters. It was shown at the 1929 Motor Show with the typical "shoulder form" Standard radiator shell, which in company with the ultralow windshield left only a ridiculously shallow windshield aperture. Only one such example was made. Only a few months later the Standard-Swallow was offered at a slightly higher price, but with a different radiator shell. Standard obviously liked this design, as its own styling for 1931 became very similar. The drivers' side of the windshield could be opened as a whole, while previously only its upper part was hinged. This kept dust from creeping in between the two parts of the windshield. In 1930, the Standard-Swallow's hood became lower again, and bumpers were added as standard. In the 1932 model year, 40 Standard-Swallows were supplied, and in the 1933 business year (it started in August 1932) a further four.

In autumn 1930 Swallow tried again with a Morris, this time a sedan based on the small Minor chassis that had been introduced at the 1928 Motor Show. In size it was similar to the Austin Seven. The changes were less obvious than with the Austin-Swallow; the typical square Morris grille remained untouched. Again only one Morris Minor-Swallow was made, which was exhibited at Henlys. Again, it was an M.G. with a very similar Midget coupe that the public preferred.

In January 1931, Swallow introduced a rather small but attractive open sports tourer based on the chassis of the sporty Wolseley Hornet and powered by a 1.3-liter six-cylinder engine. The Wolseley marque had been taken over in 1927 from Vickers by Morris. The Hornet was in essence a Morris Minor, which in turn had inherited a Wolseley engine. As would be expected from Wolseley, the engine had an overhead camshaft inspired by the Hispano-Suiza aircraft engines it had produced under license during World War I.

Despite its lively performance, the Hornet was only available, at first, with a rather boring sedan body in typical Morris style. Specials were already available from Hill & Boll, Avon (the last model the Jensen brothers styled at Avon), and a number of other coachbuilders. Swallow waited until "naked" Hornet chassis became officially available from Wolseley. They lowered the rake of the steering column and fitted larger wheels and an open two-seater body with a sloping boat-tail. The purchase price was 20 percent higher than the standard Wolseley example. The Wolseley Hornet became the first six-cylinder with a Swallow body, later a very typical configuration that framed the destiny of the company. Sporting driver Albert George Douglas Clease—at the time nobody would have dared to question any of his opinions about cars—judged the Wolseley-Swallow wonderful. In this beautiful, sporty car he opined that the driver was "well accommodated physically and psychically."

For the 1931 Motor Show the chassis became broader and was equipped with bumpers, a second spare wheel, and the bright finished air ducts of the Austin-Swallow as standard. From late 1931 onward, a four-seater version was available, and from April 1932 a more powerful Special version with twin carburetors, increased compression ratio and thus more power, double valve springs to cope with the higher revs, and a four-speed gearbox. Of all Swallow cars, the Wolseley was the longest-surviving. In the 1932 model year 379 Wolseley-Swallows were supplied, plus 145 the following year.

The last of the Swallow cars was the larger Standard-Swallow of May 1931. It was based on the Ensign that had been introduced in 1928, with an increased capacity in 1930. Its six-cylinder engine was solidly built and reliable, but it was no longer an overhead valve engine. Thanks to its seven main bearings, it was renowned for its smooth running. Swallow tailored an enclosed four-seater body, similar in style to the previous Swallow sedans, although considerably larger. The large Standard-Swallow, however, was not a best seller. With regard to competing models of the same breed—more about these later—it would remain in production for only one year. The advertisements for this model were no longer created at Henlys but at the publicity agency Nelson, established in 1929 by the former Henlys man William Westwater Bett. He located his agency close to Trafalgar Square with its Nelson Column—hence the name. The advertisements were not very restrained, but boastful, using the motto "Swallow Exclusive Coachwork."

At the time nobody could imagine that one day the history of Swallow might be of interest to enthusiasts and historians. Everything out-of-date was thrown away. The young entrepreneurs' time was fully engaged with satisfying demand; nobody was concerned about archives. During Swallow's several moves in its early years, there was every opportunity to look through the files and throw away documents and photos that would now delight historians. For the early Swallow years, information of this nature is rather scarce.

Thanks to Alice Fenton, this changed from the model year 1932 onward. She put on record every single item produced, starting a process that documented and preserved masses of information about Jaguar. Hardly any other marque's history has been researched in such detail as Jaguar's. Precise information about every single car produced since 1931 still exists, and owners can obtain it via the Jaguar Daimler Heritage Trust. Technical and specification changes for all models still can be referred to today. Nevertheless, this is a tricky subject. Sometimes the remaining stock of old-specification parts were used up even though the change had already been announced. Model year changes sometimes did not take place in one step but extended over several months until every detail was changed to the new specification, and generally things were in more disorder at Jaguar than they became after the takeover by Ford. Even thorough research may thus result in misleading conclusions. For this reason this book will not go beyond the description of the general details of development of product and producer.

A Standard "16" Swallow—nearly 50 years after it was made. *(S)*

3 AN EXCLUSIVE CHASSIS

During the late 1920s long hoods and low roofs became a long-lasting fashion among car stylists. In its article about the 1928 Motor Show *The Autocar* wrote about this new, sporting look. A drawing—or more a cartoon—from their artist, F. Gordon Crosby, gave an illustration of a racy sports coupe with an excessively long hood and a leather-covered, very low roof with carriage top irons at the sides. However, these extreme proportions were less unrealistic than Crosby may have thought: Only a year later Auburn chief Erret Lobban Cord created a sensation with a truly low, front-wheel-driven coupe that he christened with his own name, the Cord L-29. The styling had not been created in-house, but was the art of award-winning coachbuilder William M. Murphy of Pasadena, California.

It was Reginald Chandler at Henlys who drew Lyons' attention to this car, which immediately drummed up his enthusiasm. So Swallow started to do something similar. The result was to Henlys' liking. Donald Reesby of Iliffe Press—publisher of *The Autocar*—refined and colored this drawing, thanks to Lyons' good relations with the magazine's editors. Cyril Holland created a body to these lines, which was only 48 inches high and 18 feet long. Of course, these extreme proportions would have to be adjusted to meet practical needs, particularly as no production chassis was available that would suit this body length. A second mock-up had more conventional dimensions. Helmet fenders made the hood still look longer than it really was.

The chassis of the Standard Ensign seemed to fit this body, but the low lines required a chassis frame somewhat lower than Standard's production frame. As Swallow could neither develop nor make a lower chassis, Lyons depended on help from Standard, where in 1929 John Black became Reginald Maudslay's successor as chief executive. He had come from Hillman, a son-in-law of the founder who had died in 1921, and had left in late 1928 upon the takeover by Humber and the Rootes family. Now Black had a new aim in rescuing Standard, which then was in the red. It was more than doubtful whether Black would help Lyons. Usually the small series of a coachbuilt car would not justify the effort of a separate chassis development. William Lyons would not allow any objection, because on a Standard chassis his dream could not come true. He already had some ideas how the chassis could be made lower at little cost. Because of the success of the little Standard-Swallow, Black had confidence in Lyons' young enterprise, and agreed to supply him with an extra-low Ensign chassis for 1932. The engine was repositioned seven inches to the rear. The leaf springs were mounted alongside the main chassis members, so that this could be lowered according to Lyons' design. These chassis were manufactured exclusively for Swallow—gone were the times when a Swallow had nothing technically unique to offer! This agreement cost Swallow £500 to get production under way. Swallow had to take 500 such chassis at a unit price of £130, including engine, transmission, and so on. The chassis frame was made for Standard at Mills-Fulford, who remained Standard's supplier after being taken over by Grindlays in 1935.

Lyons was not inclined to call his latest model a Standard-Swallow again. For the new chassis a new marque name had to be found. Negotiations between Swallow and Standard about whose name should have more emphasis in the new marque took a long time. In the end a compromise was found: "SS." It was part of the agreement that the interpretation of what the letters should stand for would be left open. So it was left to the public and press to determine whether this was a Standard Swallow, a Swallow Special or a Swallow Sports. They also had a "Sexy Six" or "Sissy Six" in mind—not exactly a compliment for a sports car with more masculine characteristics.

While William Lyons suffered appendicitis and endured an enforced stay in Coventry and Warwickshire Hospital, Walmsley had headaches about whether the space under the low roof of the SS would be adequate. Without consulting his business partner, Walmsley had the roof lifted several inches, so that the car became about 55 inches high. The original low and rakish lines were nevertheless used in advertisements as a teaser. As soon as Lyons had recovered, he was appalled by this change and referred to the latest body feature as a conning tower. Lyons adopted a gentleman's approach to solving the problem, first asking Cyril Holland to leave the room before he explained his reaction to Walmsley's arbitrary act, perhaps using less gentlemanly language. When his initial anger was over, even Lyons had to concede that the space under the low

Above: For its time the American Cord L-29 had an incredibly low roofline, fascinating enthusiasts on both sides of the Atlantic. *(St)*

Opposite: The second edition of the SS One was a wonderful car. *(J)*

Above: The SS One's endlessly long hood and slightly too-high cabin. *(S)*

Left: The externally fixed trunk was characteristic already for the first SS One. *(S)*

roof would have been inadequate. The Motor Show at which the SS was to be announced was soon to open, and there was not enough time for further changes. The roof, which still was about 12 inches lower than the Standard's, was already causing problems. When covering the curvatures of the roof, particularly in the corners, creases in the fabric top were inevitable. Percy Leeson, who had been poached from Midland Bodies, managed to solve the problem almost overnight—to Lyons' relief. Leeson would go on to serve Lyons as trimmer for more than forty years.

Left: The small SS Two in its original guise was well-balanced. *(J)*

Below: Few SS Twos of the early variant have survived—in this case with a somewhat overloaded front end. *(S)*

Despite this solution, the car was completed just before the Motor Show opened on October 9, 1931. The preparation was so rushed that there was no time to put the car on its correct chassis. Strictly speaking, the car's debut took place one day earlier—William Lyons had allowed the *Daily Express* to interview him and to take pictures of the new car, which was simply and unimaginatively called the SS One. Frank Hough of Henlys took the opportunity to emphasize the substantial influence of salesmen in the design. However, this statement was aimed at the coachwork and chassis changes necessitated by it. In all other respects the technical specifications were Standard's!

The new hybrid again scored well in road tests. The roadholding, which was helped by the low center of gravity found praise, as did the effective, well-tuned springing and damping. The seven-bearing engine was judged quiet and reliable, although the exhaust note seemed somewhat noisy. Long distances could be covered without much fatigue. To the experts' judgment this was an enthusiast's car at a favorable price, although not quite as fast as the body suggested. In plain terms it was more show than go.

The small SS Two, which was introduced alongside the six-cylinder car in October 1931, was similar in shape to the SS One, but considerably shorter. Strangely, its lines seemed more balanced, more harmonious. Like the older Swallow cars, it was based on an unchanged Standard chassis—the Little Nine—

which had just been introduced. This smaller car was considerably less expensive than the former Standard-Swallow based on the older (now Big) Nine, but it had the same appointments as the SS One. It was, however, notorious for its poor directional stability. The tiny car was a sight for sore eyes and scored the class win in the 1932 Ramsgate Concours d'Elégance from a Swift-Swallow. In a similar event at Bristol during the same year, the SS Two was second.

The exhausts of early SS cars, lacking real insulation, tended to raise the car's interior temperature, and the non-adjustable carburetors were problematic. Swallow and R.A.G., who made these carburetors, had not conducted cold weather tests, so carburetor performance was erratic. Attention to the carburetors was a complicated matter, which R.A.G., for good reason, carried out itself at the Swallow works. Windshields, together with the Pytchley sliding roofs, which were available from 1929, tended to leak. The fenders were again criticized for rattling, as with the Austin-Swallow, and the doors tended to sag. Technically and stylistically, the connoisseur would have desired a little more fine-tuning of both the body and certain mechanical parts. However, it has to be kept in mind that at the time other makes, perhaps with the exception of the most expensive, could not guarantee better function—car manufacturers were still light years away from today's development, test, and quality assurance techniques and procedures. Here and there, odd-job men had to rectify what had been missed; at Holbrook Lane much of this, according to the practice those days, was vested in the skills and know-how of Harry Gill, in particular.

Besides the 2-liter 16-horsepower SS One, a 2.5-liter 20-horsepower engine (the real horsepower was of course much higher than this tax rating indicated) similar to one introduced by Standard shortly before was made available. A 20-horsepower SS One was to represent the marque for the first time in a competitive automotive event, the 1,000-mile (pre-Royal Automobile Club [RAC]) rally to Torquay in March 1932. This was not in any sense a race, but contrary to the fashionable Concours d'Elégance, the cars and drivers had to show their driving abilities. The emphasis was not on sheer speed, but on driving skills. A. G. Douglas Clease, having advanced from a Swallow to become an SS enthusiast with his 16-horsepower (Chassis No. 135103), and possibly E. F. Huckvale were the drivers of note. The latter had joined Swallow soon after its move to Coventry. As company secretary and later as a Jaguar director, he had entered the cars in this event. Kathleen, Countess of Drogheda, completed the SS team, which proved not to be overly successful.

Any new marque must be prepared to work hard to gain a reputation; it was the same for the SS. Real connoisseurs with their Bentleys, Hispano-Suizas, and Invictas looked down with disgust on this *parvenu* with its too-stylish bodywork. Nevertheless, the SS became a success. Many sports drivers simply could not afford this arrogant attitude, and they were lucky that such a racy car was available at such an affordable price. Some owners of much more expensive vehicles fueled doubts about the quality of the materials used. The mantra they seeded was that SS must have cut corners. But Henlys helped stem the tide, as after 1930 they had enthusiastically, purposely, and effectively toured from town to town with their "sales circus" for Swallow and later SS.

Dealers often heard customers criticize the passenger space, which was particularly cramped in the rear—a great deal of length was taken up by the long hood. Henlys responded by adding a rumble seat in July 1932 at only an extra £10, but the open seat looked like a rather frightening place to ride.

Lyons found a more radical solution, partly because he found it difficult to come to terms with the proportions of the SS One after Walmsley's design changes. Lyons pushed forward a restyled SS One, which was put on display at the Motor Show on September 30, 1932. This car was built on a completely new, more rigid chassis with a longer wheelbase, the rear axle underslung, a lower roof, and front fenders with a sweeping form. Despite breathtaking proportions, the lines were now very harmonious and provided adequate interior space, particularly in the rear passenger space. The styling could now be described as timeless and elegant, and they contributed to the exclusive appearance. The grille bore the SS hexagon, which had already been used in advertising and which had been devised by Donald Reesby, certainly inspired by the M.G. octagon. The typewriters at Swallow were equipped with a special key just for this trademark. A. G. Douglas Clease, who has been mentioned previously, undertook a 1,000-mile journey to the Scottish Highlands in the revised SS One before it was formally launched. Contrary to his expectations, the car's floor never touched the ground, and the engine powered the car up the steepest gradients. One of the daily tours was about 330 miles, with no breakdowns! Clease once again was full of praise. The testers of *Motor Sport* were similarly impressed at the car's ability to hold high average speeds on country roads. Again, the press praised roadholding and handling. Writers emphasized that despite the long hood, the offside fender was visible from the driver's seat.

The first SS in international racing was a 20-horsepower coupe of the revised type, Chassis No. 135619. In 1933, the ambitious V. A. Prideaux Budge competed in the Monte Carlo Rally with his SS, starting from John O'Groats. But he was not lucky; on an icy bend his car slid off the road. Fifty-eighth out of 71 official finishers wasn't a glorious result, but it was a start, nonetheless.

Demand for the elegant SS was very healthy, enabling Swallow to expand quickly. This growth was all the more significant as other manufacturers stumbled from crisis to crisis or even had to cease their manufacturing activities. Swallow found itself in the lucky position of not knowing how to satisfy demand. Lyons was immensely relieved when, early in 1933, the last two blocks of the former armaments factory that Swallow occupied became available from the receiver for £12,000. These buildings had been used by Holbrook Bodies to produce fabric-covered Weymann bodies for Hillman. The access road from Holbrook Lane to Swallow's factory at that time was a thoroughfare in questionable condition; it was later tarred and called Swallow Road. It still bears this name, although for some years the site was occupied by Dunlop Rim and Wheel and Dunlop Aviation

In March 1933 an open four-seat tourer on the SS One chassis was introduced. As with many other sporting tourers of the time, the cowl was raised in front of the dashboard so that—in theory—the airflow passed above the driver's face when the windshield was folded down or only aero screens were fitted. The doors were cut out so that there was more space for the elbow, which often encouraged the sporting driver to hang his arm outside the closed door. Mechanically, the tourer was identical to the coupe. The first example of the tourer (Chassis No. 135988) went to Captain Black, most appropriately colored black, as was William Lyons' own example (Chassis No. 136386).

The open models with their folding soft tops soon gained a sporting reputation as a result of their light bodies. Consequently, the SS from now on was usually represented in rallies by the tourer. A trio in white, red, and blue (Chassis Nos. 136620, 136625, and presumably 136405) took part in the Alpine rally, which was acknowledged as a particularly hard and competitive event. In 1933 it covered a tortuous route from Merano to Nice. In addition to the privately entered coupe of Count Orssich (his success with Adler Autobahn at the Le Mans 24 Hours made him famous later), the three SS "works" cars were driven to and in the event by Charles M. Needham, who was the previous year's outright winner, honored with a Glacier Cup, and his navigator Munro; the ladies team of Margaret Allan and Mrs. Eaton; and press representative and photographer Humfrey Symons of *The Motor* with James Wright. Symons, a well-known journalist, rally driver, and aviator, later gained fame by crossing the African continent in style with a Rolls-Royce, but lost his life in the air war above Dunkirk. With Lyons' approval, a tourer tried and tested in other British rallies (Chassis No. 136416, registration KV 5523) was made available for the Alpine to the Austrian Georg Hans Koch, a well-known boat builder and skier. In 1926, Koch had already taken part in the Alpine with a Standard 18/36 and became known in the early 1930s as dealer in Vienna and sports driver for SS. His relationship with Lyons lasted all his life, and his wife

Douglas Clease on his test drive with the revised SS One in Scotland on September 30, 1932. *(S)*

Above: Tourer and sedan SS Ones with Koch (left) and Count Orssich at the finish of the 1933 Alpine Rally. *(S)*

Right: 1933 Alpine with the SS One of Count Orssich and Ingo Ernst Stahl on their way over inhospitable passes. *(S)*

The "works" team for the 1933 Alpine Rally, colored blue, white, and red. *(S)*

Above: SS One Tourer with A. G. Douglas Clease. The spare wheels in the fenders instead of at the rear and the louvered hood may identify this car as the red works car for the 1933 Alpine Rally. *(S)*

Right: The beauty of the SS One becomes evident if compared with this Avon Special, also based on a Standard. *(St)*

continued that relationship even longer. The Kochs were anglophiles enough to acquire British citizenship after World War II.

In the far-away Alps, with their never-ending ascents, the SS team was no more convincing than its competitors. Even before the start of the event, on the way to Merano, the SS had suffered overheating, which distorted the alloy heads fitted in an attempt to increase power output. Overheating occurred with the SS even at home in Britain with its moderate climate and its less demanding hills. Despite this trouble, they came in 6th (Koch), 8th (Needham), and 11th (Count Orssich), in the 3-liter class, a notable achievement against strong competition from Bugatti and other prominent sporting makes.

In 1933 the SS One achieved further success, in the hands of Douglas Clease in the Scottish Rally (with Koch's Alpine tourer); a 1-2-3 at Eastbourne; and a 1-2 at Ramsgate (both "only" Concours d'Elégance); in the Caravan Rally with Constance Carpenter and a very functional heavy Car Cruiser caravan; in the Shelsley Walsh hillclimb (E. M. Harvey, 61.4 seconds, 3rd-in-class); and in Brian Twist's class win at the Edinburgh long-distance event. In the Manx Grand Prix, an SS One tourer served as "official course car," and Douglas Clease in a 20-horsepower tourer took part in the first RAC rally (1933), although the highest acclaim that SS gained there was for the Philco radio in it.

British magazines undertook their first long-distance tests, and the SS One stood the test. In one case—*The Autocar* had borrowed Douglas Clease's twin-carburetor car (Chassis No. 136683, registration KV 5916) for in-depth tests—the only complaint was a broken fan belt, remarkable evidence of the reliability of the SS, and a tribute to its Standard heritage. The combination of a solid chassis and a reliable engine, which remained mainly untouched, was ideal for this sort of test. But this tactic also had some downsides—the clutch and brake were quite heavy, and it was only because of the mercy of the tester team that acceleration and maximum speed were mildly criticized.

In 1933 Avon, who with its Special had already been a competitor to the Austin-Swallow, unveiled its interpretation of a sporting Standard Ensign, aimed at the same market as the SS One. Styling was by C. F. Beauvais, who cleverly hid the high chassis. An increased compression ratio resulted in vivid performance. At Concours d'Elégance this model was often more successful than the much lower-slung SS, but not so in sales results. Although one of Reginald Maudslay's sons was now employed by Avon, SS became the prime address for special coachwork on Standard chassis. SS secured the market for inexpensive specialist cars, and the son played no role after Maudslay's death on December 14, 1934.

For the 1933 Motor Show, the performance of the Standard six-cylinder cars—and with them the SS One—benefited from a larger bore of 106mm. This size remained with SS and Jaguar for nearly 60 years, until 1992. At the same time a two-door sedan was introduced, virtually identical to the coupe with the exception of the carriage irons being replaced with side windows—with rear seat passengers in mind. The fenders of all SS One models were slightly revised, and the spare wheels of all but the sporting, light-weight tourers received a painted metal cover. The radiator grille now tapered off toward the bottom, and its vee-shape was more pronounced. Projecting into the wind like an arrow, the grille was quite beautiful! Avon of Warwick showed new bodies on Standard 12-, 16-, and 20-horsepower chassis. These may have been slightly lighter than the SS, but the SS was still more elegant by far.

Famous racing driver John Cobb—whose three world speed records in the Napier-Railton were still for the future—praised the SS One sedan soon after its

Left: The well-appointed interior of the SS One tourer. *(S)*

Below: 1934 SS One tourer. *(J)*

Above: The wonderful grille of the 1934 SS six-cylinder. *(Schön)*

Right: Trunk with external spare wheel of the same car. *(Schön)*

debut and was impressed by performance, roadholding, and balanced braking, although according to other sources, these tended to be erratic. In the following year, Sydney Light drove a tourer (Chassis No. 247001, registration AXB 129) in the Monte Carlo Rally as well as in the Alpine. At Monte Carlo, the tourer managed to score a win in the unlimited class for open cars in the Concours de Confort. Driving from Nice to Munich in the Alps, the SS was successful, but only as a team, winning third place in its group—its performance being affected by overheating and cylinder head distortion. In addition to Sydney Light the team consisted of Mr./Mrs. Clease and Charles Needham/Harry Gill. The latter avoided overheating by adding 25 percent benzene to their gasoline. Another team was formed of two SS Twos, driven by Prince Ernst Windisch-Graetz and Norman Black/Ruben Herveyson, who overslept the start on the fifth day. Another SS One 20-horsepower tourer was entered. At the wheel was F. W. Morgan, who managed to achieve fourth place and received—like the SS team—an edelweiss plaque. That year, Hotchkiss and Panhard were the Alpine winners.

At home on the Scottish Rally, Needham and the SS One tourer achieved a class win, and did the thousand yards of the Shelsley Walsh hillclimb in a remarkable 50.2 seconds. Equally remarkable was the lap average of 79.05 miles per hour at Brooklands achieved by T. Leather in an SS Tourer. In 1934 SS was again successful in the Concours d'Elégance, with four class wins at Eastbourne (three of them for Captain Plugge's sedan), two at Ramsgate and another four at Bexhill, with two second places. The many successes of the 20-horsepower may lead to the conclusion that this was the more popular variant, but this seems to apply to sports drivers only. The average Englishman had to think more economically, even when running a dream car like the SS One. So it was the 16-horsepower that outsold the 20-horsepower model.

The SS Two was also replaced by a completely revised model at the beginning of the 1934 model year.

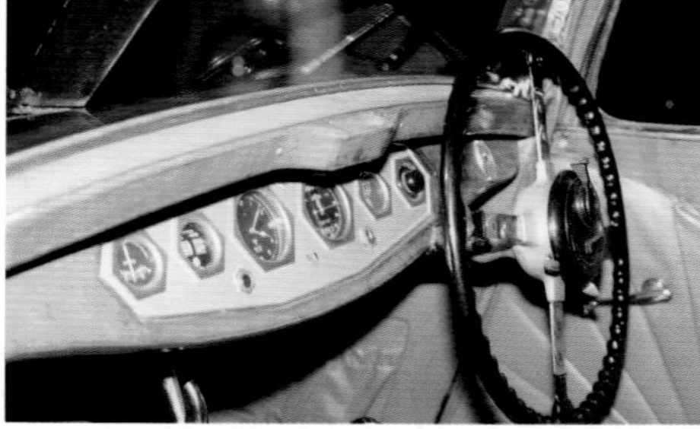

Top: Door trim of the SS One sedan with the sunbeam pattern. *(Schön)*

Above: Dashboard of the SS One sedan with hexagonal instrument surround. *(Schön)*

Right: SS One tourer also has a very attractive rear. *(Schön)*

The coupe lines with carriage hood irons and the four-window sedan were again similar in style to the SS One. When Standard revised its smaller chassis, SS grasped at the chance and used the new 10- and 12-horsepower as the basis of the revised SS Two. This made it a larger and faster car, but the opposition still was faster. In March 1934, the open four-seat tourer was introduced. Incidentally, this model was ordered for the police traffic department at Bolton in 1935, and was thus the first SS police car to see duty. For its own use, SS made two delivery vans on the SS Two chassis, but their little engines could not cope with heavy loads and they were soon scrapped.

Above: The SS One was a beautiful car; this example is still in Jaguar's possession. *(S)*

Right: A particularly carefully restored 1934 SS One tourer with the top erect. *(St)*

The tourer version of the revised SS Two of the 1934 model year is remarkably elegant. *(J)*

Opposite above: The SS tourer and its rear; later legislation made it necessary to add mirrors and rear lights. *(S)*

Opposite below: A proud owner showing his SS Two tourer. *(S)*

In mid-1934, the SS Car Club was established with William Lyons as honorary president. This club organized sporting events for SS cars, giving their owners an additional pleasure in driving and riding in their cars and adding to the marque's publicity. The foundation rally boasted more than a hundred participants, a healthy sign of the growing enthusiasm for the marque. During this period there was no factory-organized advertising program—Swallow and SS still left advertising to the dealers, but things would eventually change. Ernest William Rankin, born 1899, was engaged as public relations chief. After 1924, he had worked for the British branch of General Motors at Hendon, and after 1930 for Watney's brewery, which still uses his inspiration—the red barrel—as its trademark. Rankin established the SS magazine and liaised between Swallow, the Nelson advertising agency, and the SS Car Club. In addition, he looked after the racing and rally drivers who used an SS to add to their fame. A contest with thousands of keys was the latest publicity generating idea. The first person to open a certain garage with one of the keys was the winner of the SS One sedan in that garage.

Despite their right-hand drive, some SS cars were shipped to the United States toward the end of 1934. British-born resident Richard G. Taylor was the company's dealer. He had registered the SS trademark in the United States for himself and so made Lyons dependent on him. Taylor resided in the luxurious Waldorf Astoria Hotel in New York, where one day Alfonso, Prince of Austria, appeared before him. The prince would have been the heir to the Spanish throne—had not his father, Alfonso XIII (who gave a famous Hispano-Suiza sports car its name), been forced to abdicate in 1931. Now the prince was interested not only in the handsome car, but also in becoming an aristocrat salesman, as a replacement for his former *apanages*. The association seems to have started, but Taylor soon disappeared from the SS scene, and in 1938 the prince died in Miami. Perhaps the demise of both was no great loss to Lyons and the image of SS.

At home in England, Lyons was not satisfied with the performance of the Standard engine; the discrepancy between the appearance and performance of his cars now was nearly ridiculous. As Standard had little to offer in this respect, Swallow now had to do something about it, even if the car's reliability was at risk. Quite early, Walmsley had installed a Studebaker straight-eight engine in a "naked" SS One chassis for testing purposes. Henlys was Studebaker's main dealer for England. A Standard six-cylinder with Zoller supercharger was tried as well, probably in the same chassis, but these early exercises came to nothing.

Finally, SS spoke with the British tuning genius Harry Weslake. He was born in Exeter and was some four years older than Lyons. As a youngster he had developed the Wex carburetor just before the end of World War I, which gave many motorcycle engines additional power. In this context Weslake discovered that the gas flow was of prime importance for a good performance. He found and developed ways to improve gas flow, using tests that, even from today's high-tech vantage point, were quite accurate and effective. On this know-how his engineering office activities expanded and capitalized, after the carburetor fabrication business had been closed down. His breakthrough was certainly his work on Bentley's 6.5-liter engine, which benefited from 120- to 200-horsepower power increase. Weslake, having fallen out with M.G.'s Cecil Kimber, offered his services to Lyons. The Coventry Motor Cylinder Company, which made the light alloy cylinder heads for SS, had praised Weslake, and this made him welcome at Swallow.

At Swallow, however, only detail improvements were possible, initially. The engines were still made at Standard and powered Standard's model range as well. The typical tricks of a higher compression ratio, higher valve lift, and double carburetors had to suffice, but with these SS was able to offer livelier six-cylinder cars for the 1935 season. The RAG carburetors were still the Achilles heel. Their fuel residuals continued to affect smooth and positive acceleration, which, particularly in racing, was so important. The tiny RAG Company still skillfully "tweaked" its carburetors in the production area at Swallow themselves, but this was at their own cost—a practice that affected their operating costs, and that forced them into receivership.

The new, more powerful engines were displayed at the 1934 Motor Show. Surprisingly, the SS stand was no longer in the coachbuilders' section but could be found among the car manufacturers. For SS this was a quantum leap in status. This was thanks to support from Peter Henry, sales chief of Armstrong-Siddeley, who prevailed over Herbert Austin as President of the Society of Motor Manufacturers and Traders (SMMT), founded in 1902 with the intention of organizing the annual Motor Show, which it did for the first time in 1903 and twice in 1905. Herbert Austin's relationship with Lyons was still tense. Peter Henry may later have regretted the support given to Lyons, particularly when soon Jaguar production volumes would outstrip those of Armstrong-Siddeley, its city neighbor.

Another novelty for the 1935 model year was the Airline Sedan, which had a seemingly aerodynamic sloping back with an integrated trunk. Lyons was not very fond of the car because its roofline—again in an attempt to provide adequate space for the passengers—was much more rounded than he would have preferred. A novel feature was the missing B-post between the

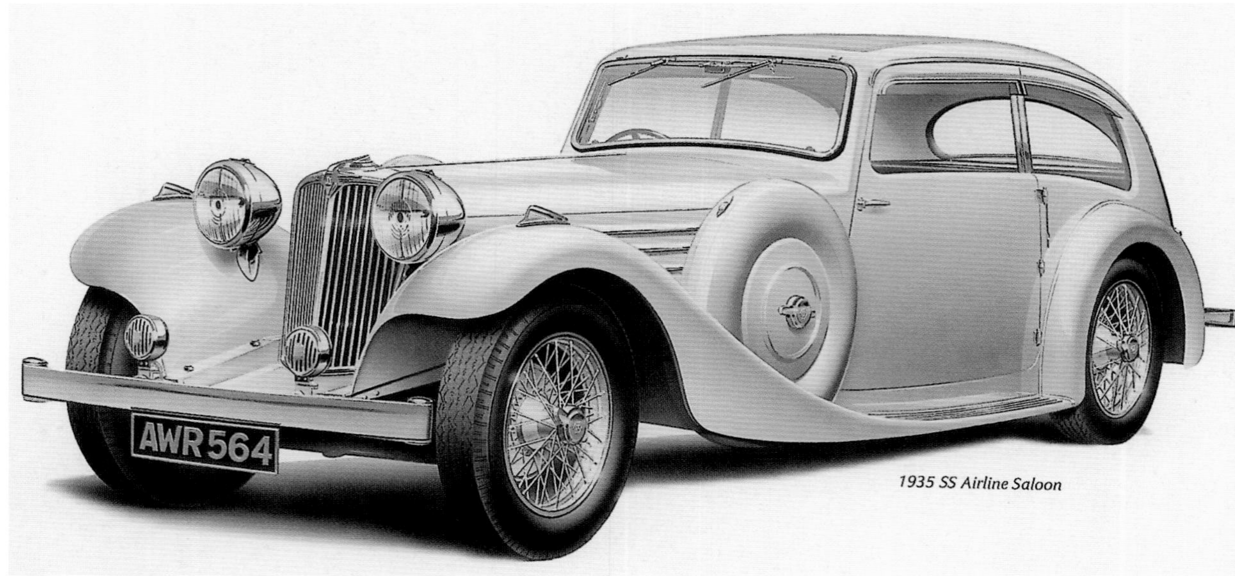

1935 SS Airline Saloon

Top: When introduced in autumn 1934, the SS One Airline was ultramodern with its aerodynamic styling. *(J)*

Above: The fine interior and well-appointed dashboard of the SS One Airline had been manufactured with great care. *(Schön)*

door and side windows—a pillarless sedan. Soon after its debut the windshield became more raked and the louvers in the hood were re-positioned horizontally, so that the car looked even faster. In this guise, the Airline is considered by many the most attractive SS, and its interior appointments matched this image. It typified SS products of the day; distinctive but never bizarre. However, its large doors were too heavy for their hinges and the wooden frame had a tendency to sag. The beautiful interior was spoiled when the car was in motion by the ingress of heat and noise to the passenger compartment. The Airline became infamous as the only Lyons' creation to be openly criticized by the man himself; as the owner of a lavender blue example (Chassis No. 248750), he certainly knew what he was talking about. Another Airline (Chassis No. 249175) was shipped to New Delhi, addressed to a certain Mr. Nehru, c/o Indian National Congress.

In rallies SS became a more familiar sight. In the Concours de Confort of the 1935 Monte Carlo Rally, an SS One tourer driven by the Hon. Brian E. Lewis again won the unlimited class for open cars, with Sydney Light's bright Airline second. The Coventry dealer Samuel H. Newsome, now also was among the SS pilots, and even one William Heynes competed, with a supercharged engine. Newsome won a First Class award at the RAC Rally at Eastbourne, together with Douglas Clease in one of the rare drophead coupes and Elsie Wisdom in an SS Two. For the record another five SSs took part in this rally (drivers were A. H. G. Hooper, V. L. Parry, G. W. Olive, R. D. Hunnam, and W. G. V. Vaughn). At Brooklands, A. Goldman in an SS Two tourer achieved an average of 60.32 miles per hour and at the Bexham Concours d'Elégance, SSs took three first places.

In March and June 1934, Walmsley created one-off, two-seater tourers on 20-horsepower chassis (Numbers 247564 and 248015) with shortened wheelbases and long, low backs. Today only one of these can be verified. A photo of one of these cars shows chromed wire wheels, proving that these can be original on an SS, contrary to many experts' belief.

The same idea resulted in the more or less secretly introduced SS 90 (or SS One 90, as it was called initially), which was completed in March 1935, just in time for the RAC rally. It had no trunk, and the model designation was reminiscent of George Brough's SS 80 and SS 100—the Rolls-Royces among motorcycles. Thus Lyons gave away his liking for the noble brand; Brough returned the compliment years later by becoming a Jaguar enthusiast. The number 90 was chosen to indicate the maximum speed this sports car was supposedly able to reach, and to be sure that the name would raise curiosity in sports driver circles.

Left: Two SS 90s at the starting line. *(St)*

Right: The SS 90 was forerunner of many classic sports cars made by William Lyons. *(St)*

Top: The SS 90 prototype had a particularly attractive, flowing back. *(S)*

Left: The SS 90 as produced in a small series had a more practical, but not as beautiful back. *(S)*

Above: The meticulously styled dashboard of the SS 90. *(S)*

One of the extremely rare SS One drophead coupes, here flagged off by no less than Sir Nick Scheele. *(J)*

The SS 90 is indeed the first outright SS sports car. With two-seater cockpit, low hood, light and effective mesh grille (like the Bentley), and again, wonderfully flowing fenders, the SS 90 is a typical example of a classic sports car. Under the hood it was similar to the SS One. The 20-horsepower engine benefited from a slightly higher compression ratio, which had been introduced before, but remained otherwise unchanged. The SS transmission and chassis also remained unchanged, apart from the shorter wheelbase. Even the chassis numbers are in SS One sequence. The famous prototype (Chassis No. 248436) has an elegant sloping back, in which the spare wheel is included. The following series of 23 SS 90s exposed the fuel tank and a nearly vertically mounted spare wheel.

This light car was ideal for hillclimbs. In May 1935 it managed the Shelsley Walsh in 54 seconds, third best time of all sports cars. The first of the little series (Chassis No. 249476, registration AVC 477), which Douglas Clease drove in the 1935 Scottish Rally, obviously was intended to become a coupe body. This did not materialize, so the car was sold off as a standard roadster, probably via Henlys.

The SS 90 prototype suffered a clutch failure in the 1935 RAC Rally with the Hon. Brian Lewis (later known as Lord Essendon) aboard. The press, which otherwise was so sympathetic to Lyons, seized upon the mishap, so it was up to Lyons to present the SS 90 in the right light. During a weekend rally of the SS Car Club with more than 100 teams—one came from as far away as Sweden—Douglas Clease's works car (Chassis No.249476) clocked the best time of day on the handling and sprint course. Other competent drivers' cars were not as well prepared, however, and the meeting ended in disharmony. The club secretary made away with the cash box, so SS had to bear all expenses. To keep this from happening again, Rankin, in addition to all his other burdens as public relations chief, from now on had to run the club.

Together with the SS 90, the SS One drophead coupe—briefly mentioned above—was unveiled. This was a well-appointed convertible with wind-down

The workforce with which Swallow started in Coventry. *(J)*

windows and a lined top filled with horsehair. It looked very similar to the old coupe, apart from its true top. The first example was on Chassis No. 249205. The drophead coupe remained in production only briefly, which now makes it a rarity, just like the SS 90. The SS One and Two, including some of the fixed-head coupes with the carriage irons, which since autumn 1934 were only made to special order, remained in production until the end of 1935. The last examples had the larger radiator grille of the succeeding model.

While SS continued to grow, the antagonism between Lyons and Walmsley became more evident. The latter immediately spent every pound gained for another pleasure, while Lyons dutifully reduced his personal demands to a minimum and reinvested much money in the company to increase its profitability. In short, a conflict between these two contrasting characters was imminent. More and more, Walmsley fled to his hobby, the model railway. He spent quite a lot of SS' manpower and material, and he felt his ownership gave him that right. Of course Lyons had a different point of view, and so a reorganization was inevitable. On October 10 or 26, 1934—the sources are inconsistent in this point—the marque SS became a company. SS Cars Limited was registered as a subsidiary of the Swallow Coachbuilding Co., with authorized capital of £10,000 in £1 shares. SS made the cars, while the sidecars continued to be Swallow's business. On November 20 or 28, 1934, Walmsley announced, to Lyons' relief, that he would withdraw from the business. The shares were split into five-shilling units and the authorized capital increased to £30,000. In January 1935, SS was quoted at the Stock Exchange with a capital of £240,000, and the refounded Swallow Sidecar Company (1935) now was its subsidiary. Lyons became chairman and managing director, which made him an autocrat. Lyons relied on the counsel of financial expert Bob Bett of the Nelson advertising agency for the floating of the shares. Other directors were purchasing chief Arthur Whittaker, solicitor Noel Gillitt, and Thomas Wells Daffern. Lyons later would add as many shares as possible to his half.

William Walmsley invested the money extracted from his half in the Airlite Trailer Company run by Clifford Dawtrey, the brother of the deputy chief engineer at Standard. In 1934 Dawtrey was still employed by Swallow, where he, among other duties, wrote the instruction manuals. His hobby was always caravanning, and so he started to build mobile campers in his spare time. As this work became ripe, Lyons sacked him. So Dawtrey made a profession of his hobby, and engaged many former colleagues for evening work. For Airlite, Walmsley developed a roof with cloth sides that could be lifted with a jack. As a towing car for his own example he chose a Bentley. The Bentley only enjoyed a short life, as the car was badly damaged in an accident caused by Walmsley, who luckily only injured his thumb. He replaced the car with a Studebaker.

Airlite did not survive for long either, so that many people who worked there returned to SS. With Walmsley's help, Dawtrey opened a new company called Coventry Steel Caravans in 1938, which made campers on ash frames. After World War II, Walmsley still gave useful advice for caravan production. He died on June 4, 1961, after suffering from pernicious anemia, shortly after having moved back to Blackpool. Whittaker and Huckvale represented Jaguar at the funeral; Lyons did not attend.

Arguably the third edition of the SS Two: The mighty Jaguar grille betrays the late manufacture of this car as 1936 model year. *(J)*

4 AN EXCLUSIVE ENGINE

Despite the power increases of the previous years, the SS still had an unfavorable reputation for being more show than go. Lyons was forced to look for much more power, and the Standard six-cylinder engine had to be revised radically. Fortunately relations with John Black were excellent, and he instantly agreed to supply SS exclusively with such engines. Lyons now assigned the boastful Weslake—whom Lyons employed as an independent contractor—with the revision of the 2.5-liter engine so that it delivered at least 95 brake horsepower (real horsepower to British standard, not to be confused with the horsepower rating for tax purposes). Weslake demanded an additional fee for each additional horsepower above the target.

Due to the complicated valve mechanisms of the day, overhead valves were restricted to high-performance engines. This did not deter Weslake, who replaced the old side valves with this configuration. Inlet and exhaust ports were placed at a more favorable angle to the combustion chamber, so gas flow became more efficient. The result was 102 horsepower from an engine that in 1931 had developed only 55 horsepower. Thanks to its solid design with seven large main bearings, no changes to the block and its internals were necessary. As a precaution—Lyons' cautiousness in technical matters was to become legendary—another expert, Dick Oats, was asked for his opinion on Weslake's ideas. He saw no snag, and for perhaps the only time, Lyons happily paid the unexpectedly high invoice.

The new, powerful engine was to drive a sedan with—a first for Swallow and SS—four doors. This was a vehicle for the discriminating owner-driver. The powerful, well-appointed sedan became the centerpiece of Lyons' professional career from that point on. It aimed at customers that preferred the Bentley, which since 1931 under Rolls-Royce had turned into a "silent sports car." Bentley offered no bodywork with its cars, so the client had to choose among the offerings of numerous coachbuilders. Park Ward's Sport Saloon was quite popular at the time, so Lyons took this as an example when creating his "silent fast sports car." The result was so similar to the original Park Ward design that it was soon nicknamed the "Bentley of Wardour Street," as this was where many London actors and artists with a bias to Lyons' latest creation were living.

Lyons had to find a proper name for his product, once again a very complicated matter. At first, he aimed at an already well-known brand name as a replacement for the less glamorous SS. He focused on Sunbeam, a brand he was involved with for a short time at Jackson Brothers. Sunbeam had started in the bicycle trade and since the beginning of the century was renowned for its quality sports cars. Before World War I Sunbeam experimented with V-12 engines, and in the most glorious 1920s it held the land speed record five times. Lasting glory was gained when in 1923 a Sunbeam was the last British car for many years to win a Grand Prix.

In 1920 Sunbeam liaised with Darracq in France—the Italian branch of which had developed into Alfa Romeo—and Talbot in London, the latter subsequently eclipsing the Sunbeam. However, even in the early 1930s the Sunbeam still was on par with Bentley or Invicta—perhaps with the exception of its maximum speed. In 1935 Sunbeam, as part of the Talbot Darracq concern, went into liquidation, due to the expenses of its racing and land speed efforts.

The name Sunbeam was particularly fitting for SS cars, as their inner door panel always had been decorated with the beams of a rising sun. In late June 1935, the receiver declared that the company would be sold to Alfred Herbert Limited, which had promised to hand on the car business to Lyons. But the Rootes brothers—they have already been mentioned briefly above—who had started as car dealers and managed to buy via Hillman and Humber a whole motor concern, were quicker than Herbert and snatched up the

Top: William Lyons' value for money as shown to the press in September 1935. The rear doors were hinged at the rear on the series production models. *(J)*

Above: One of the first OHV Standard engines made for the SS Jaguar. *(J)*

Opposite: SS Jaguar 1.5-liter—grille and headlamps were carefully styled. *(J)*

Opposite above: Engine bay of the SS Jaguar tourer. *(S)*

Opposite below: The combination of "old" tourer body and "new" Jaguar six-cylinder chassis resulted in the SS Jaguar tourer. *(S)*

company in early July. This is why the remnants of the once famous Sunbeam make now can be found at Peugeot, which does not use the name any more.

Salvation for Lyons came from a list of animal names prepared by Nelson Advertising, presumably on their own initiative. The name "jaguar" at once leaped into the eye, recalling the lithe and powerful feline from the South American jungle as well as Armstrong-Siddeley's glorious 14-cylinder aircraft engine from World War I. A more suitable name for Lyons' high-performance luxury sedan was hardly imaginable. Lyons thought so also, but was not so fond of choosing an animal name as with the Swallow. After some deliberation, Lyons decided that only the new model with the overhead valve engine should bear that name, not the whole SS company. Even on this point Lyons almost went back, but Nelson's people told a white lie, explaining to Lyons that the advertising campaign in *Daily Mail* had already been started. Thus, the Jaguar name was saved. Nobody at the time, however, seemed to have recognized that the Australian importer of Armstrong-Siddeley used the name in 1934 for its top model.

Not only did the name cause headaches to Lyons, but the technical aspects of the car were a problem as well. The chassis used by SS had become more and more distinguished from Standard's, although they were still produced there, including the engine and transmission, of course. Now that Walmsley the tinkerer had left, a proper development department became a necessity. It was obviously advisable to ask Standard to help identify some suitable engineers. Their chief engineer Edward Grinham suggested William Munger Heynes, who was born on the last day of 1903. Since 1923 he had worked for Humber, starting as an apprentice. There he helped develop the independent front suspension for the Hillman Minx. The conservative management—which included the notorious Rootes Brothers—did not dare to introduce such a development that would have seemed very bold to the traditional car buyer of the time, who still found nothing wrong with solid front axles. So Heynes' only contribution to the Minx was the four-speed gearbox. Despite the front suspension disaster, his abilities were rewarded in 1930 when Heynes became chief of the Hillman design office. In particular, he was occupied with stress calculations for the chassis frame.

By April 1935, Heynes had moved to SS. It did not matter that his brother was employed with Avon, competitors of the Swallow and the SS. Heynes' first duty at SS was to design a chassis suitable for the new engine in less than six months. He managed this with one employee and a small team of helpers. Whitley, Jaguar's modern development department, could only dream of such speed, but cars are somewhat more complex these days!

The new SS Jaguar 2.5-liter sedan was unveiled to the press at London's Mayfair Hotel on September 24, 1935, some two weeks before the opening of the Motor Show. Every attendant was asked to guess the price of the new car, and the average was more than £600. Proudly, Lyons let the cat out of the bag and announced that the Jaguar would cost no more than £385. It remained his secret as to how he got his money's worth! As a matter of fact, he did gain considerable profits.

According to Jaguar files, the show car (Chassis No. 10001) was completed on October 18, 1935. The sedan and the modified SS models were joined in the Motor Show by the SS Jaguar 2.5-liter tourer—the former tourer with the new engine and grille, which survived in the catalogs only for a few months.

Additionally, a strikingly similar, slightly smaller model was also on show, the SS Jaguar 1.5-liter sedan with the larger of the familiar four-cylinder engines. It had a shorter hood than its larger brethren but the same fine appointments.

In the shadow of the new sedans the SS 100 was unveiled, which externally was very similar to the SS 90. Only the back was changed slightly, with its inclined spare wheel—also working as a bumper—mounted on the fuel tank, which now only held 14 instead of 18 gallons. The SS 100 with the OHV engine gained a reputation for becoming less stable at higher speeds, and it did not quite reach the maximum speed of 100 miles per hour that the name suggested. It took slightly more than 11 seconds to accelerate the car from rest to 60 miles per hour. In the experts' opinion, its tire wear was excessive. But there were important advantages to report: the SS was reasonably economical, reliable, uncomplicated, and on the country roads of the time—no motorways yet—only the BMW 328 at double the price with its independent front suspension could beat the SS 100.

Racing drivers were immensely attracted to the SS 100. Among them was Paul Marx, who was assigned the third example made (Chassis No. 18003) after a long wait. He had the car shipped to the United States and used it to take part in the breathtaking races of the Colliers brothers' private club in New York, one of the first racing clubs on the east coast. Marx's letter of thanks was included in the sales brochure—Lyons thought much of advertising using the endorsements of customers.

The SS 100 was particularly successful in international road races, such as the 1936 Alpine (it had been canceled the year before), where Thomas H. Wisdom and his wife Elsie (she puzzled reporters by calling herself Bill) gained a Glacier Cup for their penalty-free run against strong competition from BMW and

Above: Strongest competition for the SS 100 came from BMW's 328 sports roadster. *(S)*

Left: There is little space left for luggage behind the driver of the SS 100. *(S)*

Right: Weather protection of the SS 100 was not perfectly watertight. *(Schön)*

Bugatti. They rode Chassis No. 18008 (registration BWK 77), the so-called "Old Number Eight" that became famous for all the modifications it later received. This SS 100 managed the Shelsley Walsh in just 51.62 seconds—much quicker than the SS 90 the year before—and came first in the class of unsupercharged cars. At Brooklands, Tommy Wisdom in the same ("rather prepared" according to press reports) car achieved an average of 104.41 miles per hour, while the unmodified car of H. Bolton managed just 87.91 miles per hour. In October 1937, Wisdom and "Old Number Eight" raised the average to 111.85 miles per hour, and his quickest lap was at 118 miles per hour. The SS 100's result in the sports car Grand Prix at the Marne was remarkable as well, with Australian F. J. McEvoy taking victory (average 69.98 miles per hour) from an Amilcar.

Just as it had the previous year on the RAC Rally, the SS had broken down, but this time the press was more discreet. The following year (1937) they had to report a 1–2 for Jack Harrop and Tommy Wisdom, who won despite the wintry conditions and strong competition from Fraser Nash, BMW, and others attracted by a new class system. The former had his car (Chassis No. 18050) modified for the Le Mans-type start so that the engine was started as soon as the handbrake was released. E. H. Jacob/Rankin and the Hon. Brian Lewis were fourth and fifth and together with Wisdom gained the team prize. In the Concours d'Elégance only a third was achieved. The 1937 Welsh Rally saw the SS 100 as winner as well (Chassis No. 18046, registration ATM 700, drivers E. H. Jacob/Rankin). Further SS 100s were driven in the event by the Wisdoms and by Lewis, together winning the team prize again.

An SS 100 at the 1936 Alpine Rally. *(S)*

In 1937 SS 100 Chassis No.18026 achieved the first outright win in a foreign competition at Vila Real in Portugal, where local hero Casimiro de Oliveira, despite an unforeseen pit stop forced by a stone chip after 150 kilometers, finished just one second ahead of Adler, BMW, and Aston Martin. The SS 100 excelled at many concours, but quick races over long distances were not its forte. Lyons therefore avoided entering the SS 100 in such events. He even reimbursed the entrance fee for the 1938 Tourist Trophy race to the team of

Below: "An engine with two spare seats" might well describe the SS 100. *(Schön)*

Right: The SS 100 is a wonderful classic sports car; fog lights have been added later on this example. *(Schön)*

Far right: The SS 100 hood covers an attractive engine with two S.U. carburetors. *(Schön)*

Cuddon-Fletcher/Dobson and its 2.5-liter SS 100, just to avoid press reports of a bad racing result.

Today the SS 100, of which only few examples were made, is rated as a classic sports racing car. With its low line and elegant fenders, it is by far the most sought-after prewar Jaguar. The no less desirable sedans are not in the limelight, although at the time the press wrote very favorably about Lyons' new model for 1936. *The Autocar* described the drive in the Jaguar as smooth and lithe (what a compliment for Heynes!), the gear change light with good synchromesh, the steering fine, the handling good, the roadholding safe even at high speeds, and the springing comfortable. The other major motoring magazine, *The Motor*, emphasized the flexible engine, the precise braking, and the good equipment provided, which even included the famous tool set in the trunk lid.

Comparable to the SS sedans and introduced at about the same time were the Triumph Dolomite and the M.G. SA (2.3-liter). The latter was introduced only two weeks after the Jaguar, but was delivered in quantity only much later, as so many last-minute changes had to be carried out. M.G. followed in 1937 with the VA (1.5-liter), and in 1939, the WA (2.6-liter). The SA was priced about the same as the Jaguar. It had less power and a less useful range of gear ratios, but it did have hydraulic brakes. The M.G. sedans were not to prevail over SS, and so they were withdrawn from the market for 1940, when the war gave an excuse.

The new Jaguar sedans even took part in the Monte Carlo Rally. A 2.5-liter sedan was second in both the Concours d'Elégance and the competition for the most handsome engine bay. The Welsh Rally in July was more of a sporting event. In the enclosed drive class, D. S. Hand was the winner with a 2.5-liter sedan in front of Jacob in a similar car. The class for smaller sedans was dominated by R. E. Sandford and his 1.5-liter in race and concours alike.

Heynes seems to have been less satisfied with the first Jaguar than were press and customers. For its second model year the chassis frame was much revised and widened for better legroom. A recess at the back of the front seats gave rear passengers a more comfortable space for their feet. A six-cylinder sedan (Chassis No. 12462, registration CDU 700) was assigned to Greta Lyons and is still owned by the works. With a similar example (registration CDU 122), Harrop achieved a still honorable 29th at the Monte Carlo Rally in January 1937.

This model year brought SS healthy profits, so a dividend of 12.5 percent of the nominal share value was distributed among the shareholders—the highest prewar dividend. Most of that went to William Lyons as main shareholder, of course. He cleverly invested £5,000 out of that sum in a manor called Wappenbury Hall, some miles to the southeast of Coventry. The park of this time-honored building—a very large front garden indeed—often served as a backdrop when Lyons had to evaluate a new design. Lyons, who had moved so often during the previous years, would remain in this house for the rest of his life—nearly 50 years! He installed a noble household with a butler and further personnel, although otherwise he was a money saver, and his wife Greta was not so comfortable with this lifestyle.

During the successful 1937 season, the SS works had the honor of being extensively described in *The Motor*. The magazine exactly described the assembly line that had only been installed the year before, and that slowly moved the cars on rails during assembly. Everywhere notes were attached with the week's production aim and warning advice. Every windshield bore a sign saying "Avoid Damage!" Every vehicle had to pass a 28-mile test drive without headlights, as these were prone to damage from stones.

The very comprehensive, well-appointed dashboard of the 1937 SS Jaguar sedan. *(S)*

Opposite above: Even the SS Jaguar 1.5-liter cast a spell over actors. *(S)*

Opposite below: This is how the SS 1.5-liter went into its second (1937) model year. *(J)*

SS 100 of Jaguar's collection. *(J)*

Top: Greta (later Lady) Lyons in the prewar years preferred a 1937 Jaguar 2.5, but not as brightly colored as this example. *(Schön)*

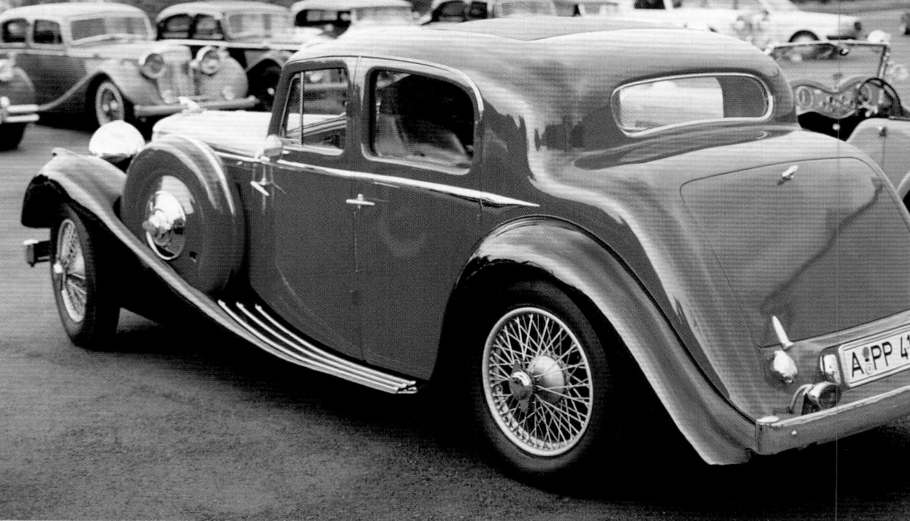

The 1937 model year remained faithful to the rear view of the SS Jaguars. *(Schön)*

The now-familiar Jaguar mascot was not yet in use. The first Jaguars lacked such decoration, although it was popular with enthusiasts of the time as a means of self-expression, such as the Spirit of Ecstasy on the Rolls-Royce, the crane of the Hispano-Suiza, or the elephant on the horseshoe grille of the Bugatti Royale. It was left to the accessory dealers to provide somewhat dreadful mascots of DESMO make for the Jaguar, which Rankin rebuked as "a cat shot off a fence." So Rankin did something about it and created a breathtaking leaping jaguar. F. Gordon Crosby, who has been mentioned above and whose racing SS painting hung in Lyons' office, reworked the sculpture to the slightly stylized shape we know today. He may have been influenced by M.G.'s tigress, because Crosby then owned an M.G. From December 1938, this mascot was available at an extra cost of 2 pounds, 2 shillings.

Much to the competitors' chagrin, SS did not intend to rest on its laurels. To the contrary, for the October 1937 Motor Show—now at Earls Court and no longer in the Olympia Hall—the sedans were revised again. The models on display were similar to the previous year's at first glance, with the exception of the spare wheel having moved from the front fender to the trunk. Nevertheless, the bodies were completely new. The stabilizing ash frame beneath the sheet metal had been replaced by pressed metal pieces. In mass production all-steel bodies were cheaper and quicker to make—forerunners going back to 1912 were the American manufacturers Hupmobile and Oakland. All-steel bodies are less susceptible to humid climates such as that found in Britain. Lyons, always fond of rationalizations, thought the all-steel construction would be suitable for his products as well—he could not know that further problems were ahead!

The steel pieces needed could neither be designed nor made at SS. Lyons thus had to rely on Pressed Steel, a company that Morris and the American all-steel

The classic face of the 1937 SS Jaguar 2.5-liter. *(Schön)*

Above: In 1937, William Lyons purchased Wappenbury Hall, the front of which was often used as a background for the evaluation of his latest styling ideas. *(St)*

Left: The 1937 SS 1.5-liter sedan was often finished in restraining black. *(J)*

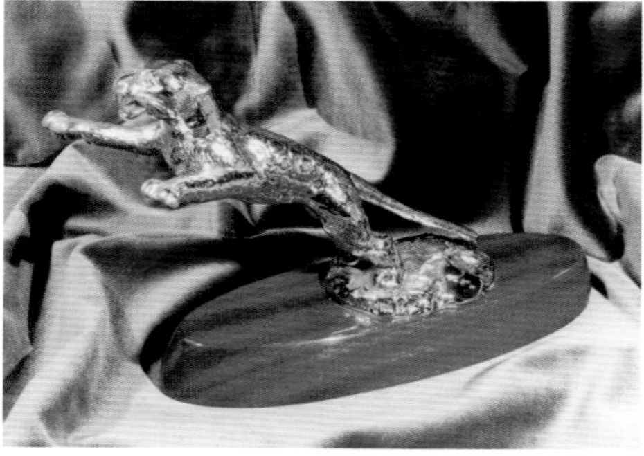

pioneer Budd founded in 1927 to provide Morris with pressed steel. The steel presses that formed the stabilizing panels were huge and impressive. Morris alone could not take as many parts as these presses could make, but other manufacturers did not dare to use Pressed Steel—they were afraid Morris might find out about their future models before they were on the market. Morris sold his entire share so that third parties like SS could be gained as customers.

But even Pressed Steel was not able to supply the relevant parts as quickly as Lyons imagined. It would take a year before delivery could start. So Lyons ordered some components from other sources like Rubery Owen, Motor Panels, and Sankey. The outer sheets had to be welded onto the supportive structure and the seams had to be leaded. The staff of 600 was increased to 1,500 for this additional work! Many employees from Briggs coachwork at Dagenham could be enticed away. When all parts were put together, however, it became obvious that most of them would not fit properly. The gaps were so big—they simply could not be bent or filled with lead! The first 25 examples had to be scrapped.

Part of the problem was solved by Harry Rogers, who had joined the company only recently. This assured him Lyons' everlasting respect. Nevertheless, all the new staff had little to do for three or four months, and no cars could be produced, as the tools for the old ash frames had already been disassembled—their space was needed for the new production. It was April 1938 before the scheduled weekly production of 100 cars was achieved, which saved SS from being ruined.

At the Motor Show of 1937, besides the new bodywork, a revised 1.5-liter engine was on display. This new engine—in fact two-thirds of the six-cylinder and thus a 1.8-liter—was derived from the equally new Standard Flying 14 and housed under a shorter and narrower hood again. Besides the sedans, new

Top: The DESMO radiator mascots were E. W. Rankin's *bête noire*. *(Schön)*

Above: SS thus decided to have its own mascots styled by Gordon Crosby—a piece of timeless elegance! *(Schön)*

Right: The SS 100 was the dream car of a whole generation; the indicators on this example have been fitted later. *(Schön))*

Left: Very early SS Jaguar drophead coupe, probably based on the 1937 sedan chassis. *(Schön)*

Below: Dashboard of the early SS Jaguar drophead coupe. *(Schön)*

Bottom: The 1937 SS Jaguar 1.5-liter sedan is a rare sight these days. *(Schön)*

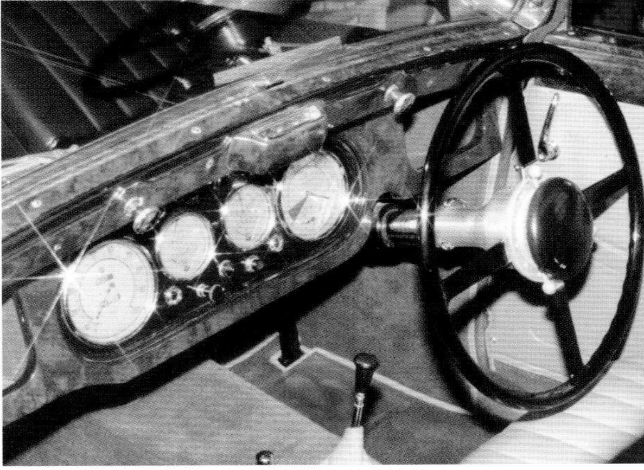

Above: The mesh grille was chosen in an attempt to save weight over the more usual bars and to improve air supply. *(Schön)*

Right: Not many cars could reach the promised 100 miles per hour—the "100" badge in front of the SS 100 grille however was well justified. *(Schön)*

dropheаd coupes were displayed. One of them bore Chassis No. 12306, which indicated a sedan of the previous model year. This may have been the result of a client urgently wanting such a drophead coupe, as this car was shipped out in December 1937. The drophead coupes revived the chromed carriage irons, their lined tops were filled with horsehair, and the folding mechanism was spring-loaded. These drophead coupes allowed a third driving position with only the part of the top over the front seats being rolled back and fixed with leather belts. The interior was as well appointed as in the sedans, with many instruments, lots of wood, and finest-quality leather. There were ash frames in doors and rear end, because with the small production numbers of these cars, using large press tools would not have been a worthwhile investment. When

William Lyons went on summer holiday in France in such a car in 1938—he indulged in the new sport of water-skiing there—he suffered a punctured tire, which forced him to empty the trunk of all luggage in order to reach the spare wheel. This experience would lead Lyons to ensure that future models had ingenious mechanisms that made the spare wheel accessible from outside.

The Motor Show of 1937 also brought a new 3.5-liter six-cylinder engine. Apart from the larger dimensions, the engine was similar to the familiar 2.5-liter unit.

Above: More than one percent of the total SS 100 production participated in the Scottish Coronation Rally. *(S)*

Left: The SS 100 is so sought-after that in England precise replicas are manufactured—with some components from more modern Jaguars. *(Schön)*

Above: Sammy Newsome at the wheel of *Old Number Eight*, which has just had its windshield and fenders removed. *(S)*

Left: The most famous of all SS 100s is *Old Number Eight*, shown here in its most developed form—bereft of its fenders. *(J)*

Below: Two examples of this SS drophead with elaborate weather protection were made for S. H. Newsome. *(S)*

This futuristically styled, aerodynamic SS 100 was made by Pycroft. *(S)*

The SS 100 now definitely reached its 100-mile per hour promised speed—an important step for the prestige of the marque. However, the new engine stressed the chassis to its very limits. The first 3.5-liter SS 100 (Chassis No. 39001) was delivered to Prince Michael of Romania—his war ministry presented it to him when he was nominated as second lieutenant in the mountain troops, and he preferred it to his previous BMW sports car.

The engine of "Old Number Eight" was swapped for a 3.5-liter and it had a successful racing debut—some weeks before the official debut—at Shelsley Walsh. Sammy Newsome ran the course in just 45.94 seconds and became class winner. At the factory, this car had been made somewhat lighter. When it was not yet fast enough for the Brooklands oval, its power output was increased further by using special fuels. During warmup it achieved a maximum of 160 horsepower for a short time. A cylinder head further refined by Harry Weslake and Dick Oats helped make this miracle possible. With a works racing car (Chassis No. 39055, registration DHP 736) Jack Harrop finally won the RAC Rally in May 1938, which further helped the reputation of the SS 100.

This reputation was built partly thanks to Harold E. Bradley. In Lyons' old hometown of Blackpool, Bradley had gained a fortune running some cinemas, and then racing and rallying became his hobby. So he entered the 1938 RAC Rally with his SS 100 (Chassis No. 39035, registration HG 6247) and finished eighth, with only five penalty points more than the winner. He seems not to have achieved an outright win in his short 1938 season, but the car was modified during the following winter with some useful hints from one Walter Hassan. In the end, its power output was not far behind that of "Old Number Eight."

In the following season one of Bradley's most entertaining races was at Phoenix Park in Dublin. Bradley achieved a record lap speed for nonsupercharged cars with an average of 94 miles per hour. At Limerick he almost won, surviving contact with a wall but suffering an engine failure just before the finish.

Above left: Freestone & Webb created this SS sedan in the knife-edge style. *(S)*

Above right: SS Jaguar drophead coupe by Maltby with very low roof. *(S)*

Below: SS 100 coupe in the United States. *(S)*

Jack Harrop scored 10th at the 1939 Monte Carlo Rally in sedan with the larger engine (Chassis No. 30797, registration DKV 101), which made it best British entrant, while the year before J. O. H. Willing managed only 42nd place, although he added a Grand Prix d'Honneur in the Concours de Confort.

Lyons proved his driving abilities in the summer of 1938 in a race with identical cars organized by the SS Car Club. Driving Chassis No. 39053, he showed no less than William Heynes and Sammy Newsome a clean pair of heels—an impressive end to a racing career that had never actually existed! Three SS 100s were delivered to Germany, and Chassis No. 39026 was displayed at the 1938 Autoausstellung (motor show) in Berlin. One of them was found years later in an all but perfect state after some military service in the ruins of Warsaw.

Despite the racing successes and the elegantly styled, well-appointed bodies, some people needed something more individual. These customers ordered still more exclusive and better-appointed special coachwork from a coachbuilder of their choice. As there now were unique chassis for SS with engines that could not be found in cars other than the SS, these transformations were considered SS specials, not Standard specials as before. The highly regarded Salmons/Tickford Company chose the chassis of the first SS Jaguar as the basis for its special coachwork, and none other than New Avon chose the SS 100 as the basis of its specials following an idea of the racing driver-*cum*-dealer Sammy Newsome. So Chassis Nos. 39109 and 39115 received special lightweight drophead coupe bodies.

Particularly noble was a sedan from Freestone & Webb for the 3.5-liter chassis in the then-fashionable razor-edge style. It took part in the Ramsgate Concours d'Elégance in July 1938. Mulliner at Birmingham, not to be confused with Arthur Mulliner in Northampton, or the even more elegant H. J. Mulliner in London, had the honor to create for John Black's wife a princely limousine, also based on the 3.5-liter Jaguar. Two conversions of sportier drophead coupes by Maltby of Folkstone, with narrow windshields and low roofs seemed perhaps a bit swanky. Nevertheless, its elongated, more rounded back gave Lyons some valuable inspiration for future models. Even in Switzerland, with support from Emil Frey, some special convertibles were fitted on Jaguar chassis—four by Worblaufen, 13 by Tuscher at Zurich, one each from Graber and Bernath, as well as four 2.5-liters and three 3.5-liters by

Marcel Fleury, the Geneva SS importer. Apart from Graber and Fleury, the Swiss coachbuilders also showed their skills on an SS 100. The Belgian *carossier* Van den Plas would do so on Chassis No. 49064 as well, but only after World War II.

Lyons reserved an exquisite novelty for the 1938 Motor Show: a two-seater SS 100 coupe with the larger six-cylinder engine (Chassis No. 39088), teardrop fenders and a roofline inspired by the raciest Bugatti sports coupes. Although offered as a normal model at £595, the coupe remained a one-off, which still is in existence.

For the 1940 model year, sedans and drophead coupes were provided with heating. The 1.5-liter was the only exception, when not ordered as Special Equipment model. In advertising this heating was described as air conditioning!

As the start of the 1940 model year collided with the outbreak of war, compression ratios in the SS engines were reduced to accommodate poorer gasoline quality. This made the engines run more quietly, and although some horsepower may have been lost, it was not stated so in the official data.

The Jaguars had given SS a reputation as a well-designed, well-built, attractive, practical, and fast

Above: Original photograph of the SS 100 coupe gives some hint to later Jaguar sports cars. *(S)*

Right: A particularly nice one-off is the SS 100 coupe that was on display in 1938. *(J)*

Roof, body and fenders combined to create one harmonic entity in the SS 100 coupe. *(J)*

touring car. Their harmonious, unspectacular power output was impressive. Even the most blasé of connoisseurs had to admit that the SS was more than just another imposter. The all-steel cars brought good profit, which now remained in the company, as Lyons had decided to take over a nearby supplier of pressed steel panels, Motor Panels. Lyons' intention was to gain independence from other suppliers of all-steel body components—a good idea considering that 20 years later most such suppliers had been taken over by manufacturers competing with Lyons. The price was very high, so that a loan had to be taken from Lloyds Bank, who generously accepted a personal guarantee by William Lyons himself. Unfortunately, Lyons had to sell off Motor Panels in 1943 because of the change of production forced by the war. Of course, car production came to a halt after war was declared, coincidently on Lyons' 38th birthday; only remaining stock was used up for some sedans in 1940. Despite all efforts, no military contracts could be obtained at first.

With the help of Howard Davies, the former motorcycle manufacturer (HRD) and Swallow salesman since 1935, the War Department awarded a large contract for the production of motorcycle trailers to SS. However, a dispute arose with Lyons about Davies' commission, and he was forced out. SS also failed to be awarded a contract for parts for the Manchester bomber, and so the business year 1940 became the only one to end with a loss for Lyons, to the tune of £22,000. In the following year, orders for diverse aircraft parts helped, and despite war damages to the factory buildings, 1941 ended with a profit of £40.000. However, heavy investments caused the debts to rise to £70.000.

Classic style was rendered in all-steel for SS' six-cylinder chassis. *(S)*

Top: The 1938 SS Jaguar 1.5-liter drophead coupe is a rarity. *(S)*

Above: Chassis and engine of the new 3.5-liter for 1938. *(S)*

The new engine of the 1.5-liter was also delivered by Standard. *(S)*

Such motorcycle trailers for war purposes were made in huge numbers at Swallow. *(S)*

The war years continued in this manner. The fuselage assembly for the Whitley bomber and the Meteor jet brought good profits, although the buildings had to be extended considerably. SS assumed this cost, of course, but after the war the company would benefit from its large premises.

With the outbreak of war, SS was confronted for the first time with military production methods. Before, most design questions had been dealt with verbally. Now drawings had to be made for every detail, so that in case of an emergency production could be taken over by another contractor. Particularly for the sidecars, such drawings did not exist. Luckily, in 1940 Tom Jones joined SS. He had the experience needed to craft such drawings.

Manufacture and repair of aircraft components were the main tasks of SS and Swallow during the war. During the war, Lyons had new fabrication buildings erected, but in November 1940 firebombs damaged six of his blocks. For a while, then, production was relocated to South Wigston. SS was spared from further serious war damage, other than to Coventry itself.

For William Lyons and his family, the war meant abandonment of the luxurious lifestyle in the countryside. Lyons even gave up cigarette smoking. The personnel had to be sent home to do their patriotic duties. As for the vehicles at the works and at Wappenbury Hall, where quite a few were stored, they were only used in case of serious need. The whole family lived in permanent fear of bomb attacks. As one of Britain's industrial centers, Coventry was a prime target for the Germans.

For wartime work, the companies' development of light all-terrain vehicles, under the codes VA and VB, was remarkable. They had unitary bodies, dispensing with a chassis frame, and independent front and rear suspensions. The hydraulically operated brakes also were an advantage over the former SS cars. However, the War Ministry lost interest in the development as soon as the cargo load of the latest parachutes increased sufficiently to support the weight of the American Jeep.

In 1942 John Silver joined SS as its first production engineer. Before, he had worked for General Motors, Lucas, and BSA. Jones, Silver, and paradoxically the war brought dramatic improvement to Lyons' previously somewhat intuitively organized production practices. So, while still at war, Lyons prepared for the time after the armistice.

The VA prototype could have resulted in an interesting addition to SS production. *(S)*

The VB all-terrain vehicle, a prototype as well, with its Ford engine, anticipated a later association by several decades. *(S)*

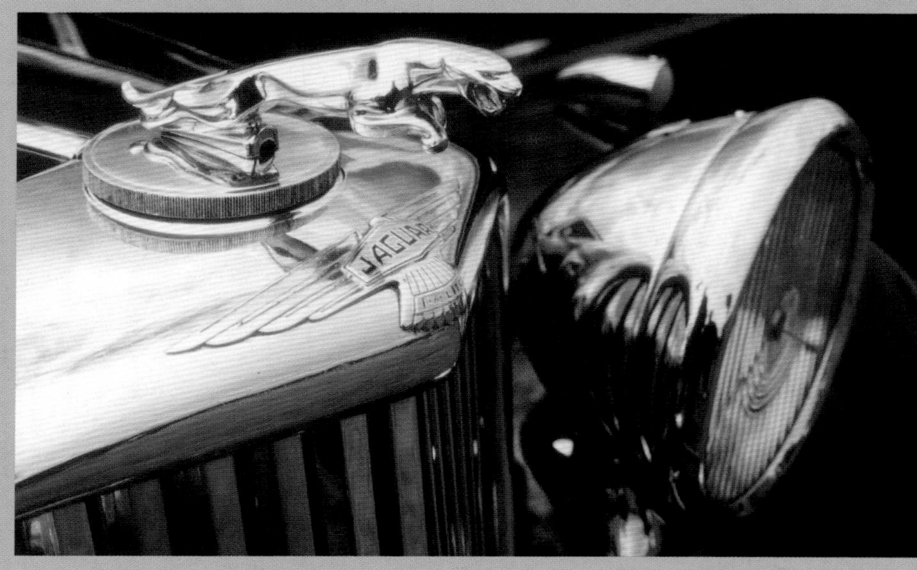

THE JAGUAR MARQUE

The years of reconstruction after the war were another difficult and exhausting period for Lyons. Change was everywhere, and the company needed to adapt to a new reality. At first he had to establish the financial basis for the return to car production. For this purpose, Lyons not only parted with Motor Panels, but he also sold off his sidecar production, thus concentrating the nucleus of his enterprise on car manufacture.

Swallow was taken over by Helliwell, and the production of the renowned sidecars was transferred to their plant at Walsall airport. But already in 1948, Swallow was sold again to Tube Investments. The new owners tried to introduce a sort of scooter in 1950, but the market was not yet ready for such a vehicle, so it was soon discontinued. In 1953 Swallow undertook a no less adventurous excursion into car production with the Swallow Doretti, which was based on the Triumph TR 2, but with a more rigid chassis of Swallow's own design. Its name is said to have come from the daughter of the U.S. importer. But this episode was already over by 1955. Wisely, the sidecar production had been continued all the time, and it was this that an old acquaintance became interested in: In October 1956, Swallow was taken under the wings of Watsonian, and sidecar production was relocated to their plant at Greet, near Birmingham. So

Above: The Triumph Renown, a small but fine car. *(Long)*

Left: With the Standard Vanguard and Triumph 1800 roadster, Sir John Black created some opposition to Jaguar's four-cylinder models. *(S)*

Opposite: The grille decor of the Jaguar 1.5-liter. *(Schön)*

Above: Export was paramount at Jaguar; this 3.5-liter was reserved for export. *(S)*

Left: The radiator mascot is well known, but the postwar product dispensed with the previous SS hexagon. *(Schön)*

Below: Another 3.5-liter drophead coupe, photographed in front of Wappenbury Hall. *(S)*

Ian Appleyard with his famous SS 100 in the 1948 Alpine Rally. *(S)*

Swallow completed its circle, ending as part of the company that once supplied the very first sidecar chassis to Walmsley.

After dropping Motor Panels and Swallow, Lyons was able to purchase the production facilities for the six-cylinder engines he used. Although the advanced Vanguard, with its 2.1-liter four-cylinder engine was still under development, John Black had decided that he would concentrate on this new model, and that the larger engines were of no further use for him. So he informed Lyons in 1942 that he could not supply six-cylinder engines after the war. Lyons' spontaneous reaction was to ask if he could purchase the production facilities. These had been mostly written off, and so they agreed to a price of only £6,000. Lyons now was sure that the OHV engines were exclusively his. In the first months and years after the war, the demand for replacement engines for SS cars was quite strong, so the investment amortized quickly.

Sir John soon found out that he had committed a grave mistake, but Lyons would never return the facilities. Black proposed to establish a joint venture for the

manufacture of these engines, but old football player Lyons, now that he had the ball, would rather keep it. Black's revenge may have come in 1944, when he took over Triumph's car production, which had been under receivership for five years. As Triumph was in SS' neighborhood, Lyons had looked into Triumph's books in 1939 to scope out a purchase, but he saw no promising future and made no offer. Soon after the war, Triumph's 1800 drophead coupe was unveiled, remarkable for its second windshield folded in front of the rumble seat. It had the same engine as the 1.5-liter Jaguar, but with this it was no real contender to Lyons' products, nor were the dinky Mayflower and Renown sedans, which seemed to be Rolls-Royces *en miniature*.

The name SS now seemed rather inappropriate with its connotation to Hitler's dreadful *Schutzstaffel*, a prime symbol for the abomination of the Nazi regime. Fortunately, the name Jaguar Cars Limited had already been registered in November 1937 as a subsidiary of SS Cars Limited, and all SS products already were called Jaguar. It was time to give the whole company the name of the South American feline—a late relief for Bob Bett, who had proposed this in 1935. In an extraordinary grand meeting in March 1945, the relevant resolution was passed. A short telephone call to Armstrong-Siddeley, who had produced a famous aircraft engine of the same name during World War I—made clear that there were no objections from that side. Many years later, the British aircraft industry would ask Jaguar for its permission to use the name for a fighting aircraft that became particularly famous during the Gulf War in 1991.

The luxury of a 1946 3.5-liter Jaguar was reserved for those who paid in U.S. dollars. *(St)*

On the rear bumper of postwar Jaguars the "SS" hexagon has been replaced with a "J" rectangle. *(Schön)*

Opposite above: Only details like the grille badge betrayed the identity of postwar Jaguar sedans. *(Schön)*

Opposite below: The face of the first post-war Jaguars was still very classical—only the indicators that have been mounted later disturb the illusion of timelessness. *(Schön)*

Upon the end of the war, capital and a good name were secured. But before returning to car production, the sourcing of material required for Jaguar production had to be clarified. During the first years after the war there were shortages everywhere in England and Europe. In particular, steel sheets were rationed. There were no allocations unless a large proportion of the products were to be exported. Before the war, SS had not pursued the export business, but nevertheless there was some demand, particularly from the British colonies. After the war, the government had to be convinced that the Jaguar would be marketable overseas.

The nitro-cellulose finish on these 1.5-liter sedans (betrayed by their chromed side lamps) required extensive polishing to ensure a gleaming appearance. *(S)*

Lyons had a brochure made for this purpose, and with this he went to Sir George Turner, the concerned secretary in the Ministry of Supply. At those times most of Britain's exports to the United States consisted of wool and whiskey, with car exports in 1946 contributing less than a half-million pounds. Nevertheless, Labor Party man Turner accepted Lyons' luxury car concept and the prospect of huge amounts of money to be gained. He allocated the necessary materials within two weeks.

In July 1945 car production could start. The new Jaguars were officially announced on September 21, but no cars left the factory before October 1945. These cars were mostly made from prewar stocks, and they were similar to the 1940 model year specifications, but the waistline moldings were thinner and the SS symbol on the rear bumper had been replaced by a large J. Acceleration suffered from the low quality of the gasoline available then, but the maximum speed was not affected.

The first postwar brochures not only showed the sedans with the three familiar engine sizes, but the drophead coupes and the SS 100 as well, production of which had not yet been resumed. The six-cylinder drophead coupes returned to production late in 1947 and were officially announced at the Geneva show in March 1948. But they were only produced for a few months, which makes them particularly rare and sought-after today. The SS 100 did not return into production after the war. Only one example (Chassis No. 49010) was registered as new, as it had been mothballed at Wappenbury Hall during the war. Its engine was replaced by the larger size, and Ian Appleyard—the son of John Ernest Appleyard, SS dealer at Leeds since 1935 and Lyons' future son-in-law—was allowed to use it for racing. In 1947 Ian Appleyard had taken part in the Alpine rally with his own SS 100 (registration EXT 207) and gained a third in class. Now, with the newer car, registered LNW 100, he was awarded an Alpine Cup for his penalty-free run. He gave away the outright win when he helped a competitor who had suffered an accident. Like most of the glorious Jaguar racers, LNW 100 survives to this day.

Immediately after the war, motor races were a rarity, and usually prewar thoroughbreds were raced. So it was not much of a surprise that the SS 100 was still successful. In 1946, for example, N. A. Bean achieved best time of the day (40 seconds) at the Bo'ness Speed Trial; Pycroft's aerodynamic SS 100 was first in the first race ever held at Goodwood; Newsome came in second at Shelsley Walsh (46.95 seconds); Parker finished second at the Bristol Hillclimb at Portisland; R. M. Dryden was a class winner at Prescott (59.7 seconds); C. Mann was second at Elstree; and J. W. Patterson was a class winner at Craigantlet (99 seconds). In 1947 Elsie Wisdom gained the Ladies' Trophy at Bouley Bay, Jersey (72 seconds, in "Old Number Eight"); Bean won again at Bo'ness Speed Trial (43.4 seconds); Pycroft and his Special finished the Ulster Trophy race in eighth place; R. M. Dryden achieved another class win at Prescott; Tom Cole took a second place at Brighton Speed Trials; and H. E. Matthews, E. I. Appleyard, and L. Parker won a First Class Award at the Eastbourne Rally. The list of successes only became shorter in 1948. Besides the Alpine success the SS 100 repeated its class win at Prescott (Dryden again, with only 53.62 seconds). Even in 1949 Ian Appleyard managed a class-win and outright second in the Tulip Rally.

Meanwhile, postwar production got under way only with many setbacks and troubles. Lyons' parsimony troubled the relationship between the managing director and his staff, from which he demanded ever-increasing performance. Inevitably this led to a first

. . . but this worker has found a helpful polishing instrument. *(S)*

walkout in the autumn of 1946. In a large convention with about 1,400 people—nearly the whole staff—Lyons managed to make peace. Allowing this convention to take place was not easy for Lyons, because it meant that he accepted the trade unions as negotiating partners for the first time. Lyons said that the weekly working time could not be reduced to 40 hours, as the competition was so strong. He argued that if the staff were not prepared to work hard, they would face hard times. Like many other industrialists, Lyons could not understand how the workforce put the whole enterprise at risk for a small short-time advantage. This view did not result from ideology, but from his serious care for his lifework, the Jaguar plant. All his life Lyons was vexed with trade unions' requirements, some of which would have ruined his company had he accepted them.

The *Jaguar Journal* was established, which for several years under Bill Rankin informed the staff about what happened at management level. The first issue reported details of the aforementioned convention. Harry Teather, one of Lyons' most faithful workers, was introduced as person of the month. He was now head of the stores and had a staff of more than 50 under him.

The economic situation was not rosy in most European countries at the time, so it was unthinkable that the Monte Carlo Rally would be revived in 1947. Rodney Walkerley and Mike Couper thought differently, so they undertook their own private "rally" to Monte Carlo in a Jaguar 3.5-liter (registration FVC 879). Despite masses of snow, they arrived safely without any breakdown or scratch in the paintwork. At the Mediterranean Sea, the reception was princely and could have suited a true Mote Carlo Rally quite well. In his first rally, Ian Appleyard scored a second place in a similar sedan at the Lancashire Automobile Club meeting in Lyons' old hometown of Blackpool.

Jaguar—like SS before the war—ran a racing service department that after September 11, 1946, was headed by the famous Frank Raymond Wilton England. He was born in August 1911 at Finchley in the north of London. Already in his youth, his father, a director at Unilever, supported his interest in racing. From 1927 until 1932, he apprenticed at Daimler's London service depot. The young man, called "Lofty" due to his build, took part in the 1932 "pre-RAC" rally to Torquay in a Daimler Double-Six with sleeve valves and Windovers body. The decisive test was to drive in top gear as slowly as possible without stopping, for which the Daimler, with its fluid flywheel (a.k.a. torque converter), was ideally suited. England, however, came in only second behind a Lanchester, which also had a fluid flywheel.

Afterward he was a racing mechanic for teams like Mike Couper and Sir Henry Birkin. England then worked for ERA, alternating with Alvis. Once, after a dispute with Alvis, the London distributor Chas Follett criticized the quality of Alvis cars in a public address. As an act of heroic revenge, England sabotaged Follett's car. During World War II England was a bomber pilot, and after the war returned to Alvis and to racing. At Jaguar he became responsible for service and spares supply, and he headed the works racing program—treating the racing drivers with more care than normal customers, of course. England was to become director in 1956, Lyons' assistant in 1961, and managing director at Jaguar in 1972. This soon ended, though, and England retired to Austria in 1975, where he died in 1995.

British customers faced very long waiting lists for a new Jaguar, and they became even longer when on Friday, January 31, 1947, Jaguar's felt store caught fire. Fortunately, the fire was extinguished after only 1½ hours. Much material for the interiors was destroyed, but only two cars were written off. The total damage was about £100,000, and production was resumed the following Monday. Delivery times had increased into years by then, and not even a driving ban for privately used vehicles in 1947 changed this. Customers who turned to Henlys found Philip Weaver there, who was engaged by Jaguar directly as its own customer representative—this happened thanks to an acquaintance with Wally Hassan from their co-operation at Bristol.

One chance for Jaguar to expand came in 1947, when Lagonda was offered for takeover. Lagonda was highly esteemed for the design of its engines, particularly the magnificent V-12 of prewar days. W. O. Bentley informed Jaguar about the not-so-favorable situation at Lagonda when he evaluated that company. So Jaguar showed no further interest, and Lagonda went to David Brown, who just had bought Aston Martin as well. Quirk of fate: much later Lagonda and

Jaguar both became affiliates of the Ford Motor Company for more than 15 years.

Who had thought that aside from Switzerland, one of the best foreign markets for Jaguar immediately after the war would be in Belgium? This was thanks to the very able importer Joska Bourgeois and the colonies that saved Belgium from severe economic damage. It may be because of this lady's influence that from 1947 on the Jaguar was available in left-hand drive form. Surprisingly, the first model so equipped was the 1.5-liter sedan. In order to avoid the import duty of £600 per vehicle, from the Brussels show in 1948 onward, the cars destined for Belgium were assembled in the former workshop of Van den Plas, which had become much smaller over the years. Jaguar production chief Ted Orr was responsible for seeing that that the assembly there went smoothly, although Bernard Hartshorn and a small team of experts represented him in Belgium. William Lyons himself drove the first car off the Belgian assembly line. But the import duty had been lifted already in 1949 and the Belgian assembly, with its emphasis on the drophead coupes, was closed down.

Another overseas market was to grow even more important. Early in 1947, Jaguar was able to start sales in the United States. The smart prewar importer Richard G. Taylor, until then, had claimed that the sales rights for the Jaguar were his. In the ensuing negotiations Jaguar was represented by an expert lawyer recommended by Studebaker, whose distributor for England was Henlys. Now that all was well on the juridical side another problem arose. Fergus Motors in New York was the first importer. Because Americans tend not to be very careful when parking, to avoid damage, overriders had to be added to the bumpers of cars that were destined for the United States. In March 1948 Fergus still was not able to supply spare parts. In the United States the Jaguar soon gained a reputation for poor quality, an only partially justified judgment that remained for a very long time. Jaguar was to blame for the windshield and doors that were not very dust-proof. However, many other problems were the result of poor maintenance.

Lyons had to do something about the situation in the United States, so in the spring of 1948 he traveled to the New World on RMS *Queen Elizabeth*. In just five weeks he established a new sales organization. Following advice from Bert Henly, he met the Austrian immigrant Max Hoffman. Hoffman was happy to take the distributorship for the eastern States and sell Jaguars in his stylish showrooms on Park Avenue in New York. In 1949, Hoffman sold 90 Jaguar sports cars based on a brochure alone.

On the West Coast Lyons signed several dealer contracts. One of his partners was the Norwegian Kjell Qvale. All dealers were expressly obliged to hold adequate stocks of spares. Only a short time later Lyons put all western activities in the hands of Chuck Hornburg, a common friend of the Earl of Warwick, who had already shown his talents as a salesman in England.

In June 1948 Lyons and Hornburg arranged a Jaguar exhibition in Hollywood. The success was similar to that seen once before in London's Wardour Street—16 cars were sold on the first day alone, among them a 3.5-liter drophead coupe to one of the greatest film stars ever, Clark Gable, who later placed a permanent order for the first example of any new Jaguar. Lyons was even invited to Gable's film studio, but his deepest impression was of the terrible tea that was served him there, confirming all the bad prejudices of the Old against the New World. During his American adventure, Lyons also took the opportunity to visit the Chrysler and Studebaker factories. Lyons traveled home on RMS *Queen Mary* with orders exceeding £1 million.

Although sales figures continued to rise steadily, complaints about the service in the United States continued. In 1952 Lyons read in the newspaper that a Dutch resident in England, Johannes Eerdmans, was going to move to the United States in order to establish a business there, following a recommendation from the British minister of labor, Sir Walter Monkton. Lyons had been impressed by Eerdmans when they were introduced to each other on a holiday trip to Salcombe in Devon. Lyons assigned Eerdmans to inspect the Jaguar sales organization in the United States. Eerdmans confirmed that by far not all was good, and so another reorganization was started.

Hoffman, who now also distributed Jaguar's strongest competitor, Mercedes-Benz, had to step away from his franchise, which went to Eerdmans. Lyons is believed to have paid more than £100,000 as compensation. Also, Hornburg was reduced to normal dealer status. Beginning in 1954, U.S. sales were put in the hands of Jaguar Cars North America Incorporated, headed by Eerdmans. From that point on, customers benefited from much better service, particularly as a result of training courses for garage staff that had already started before the reorganization. In 1954 annual sales in the United States were about 4,000, a level that continued for many years. This made Jaguar the most successful car importer in the United States, just ahead of Volkswagen. Lyons no longer had to worry about his American sales organization, and he remained closely linked with Eerdmans all his life. In 1958 Eerdmans introduced a central spares store from which the dealers were supplied quickly and in time.

Perhaps thanks to Jaguar's legendary export success, Lyons was nominated to be vice president of the Society of Motor Manufacturers and Traders (SMMT), which in his early years had denied him a stand among the car manufacturers at the Motor Show. By this time Jaguar was regarded as a full and long-standing member of the society. Even rumors that Jaguar might close down its plant and lay off 1,500 staff because of a lack of coal and steel could not damage the company's good reputation. In 1950, just when Jaguar was forced by a shortage during the Korean crisis to temporarily abandon the chrome finish on grilles and hubcaps, Lyons became president of the SMMT.

The industry's admiration for Lyons went deeper than his appointments with the SMMT. His dedication to nearly all aspects of automotive production was as impressive as his impeccable wardrobe of dark blue suits and light ties. (Although it's worth noting that before the war, his dress was not always so formal.) He directly headed sales as well as production and development. In every respect, he had the last word as the main shareholder and director of Jaguar. He had excellent control over his business and staff.

Lyons' cost-saving mentality was legendary. One day an employee drew his attention to a worn carpet in a sales room. Lyons decided that it would suffice for some time. Some weeks later, Lyons discovered a spotless carpet at the same place. He immediately dressed down his employee. When Lyons had finished, the man explained that he had just repositioned the carpet so that the worn part was hidden under a display cabinet. Lyons, puzzled at first, thought something similar might be possible at his home, and he invited the ingenious employee to look into it.

Early in 1949, the first Jaguars went out of production. The last ones were four-cylinder sedans for Jaguar managers—obviously Lyons thought the new model to

How to make a 1949 dream-car of a pre-war *belle*? (S)

be too noble for his management. Although the car's road holding and suspension still were highly acclaimed, the solid front axle was no longer up to date, at least in international comparison. The leaf springs, if they provided adequate comfort, could no longer provide adequate stability. Under braking, the springs allowed the whole axle to rotate a few degrees, and a sudden release of the brakes could make the whole car porpoise. Heynes, who admired the Citroën's front-wheel drive arrangement, had designed an independent front suspension for the Jaguar as early as 1938. It had ingenious ball joints at the outer ends of the wishbones. A 3.5-liter sedan with this arrangement was ready before the war and was tested extensively. The VB all-terrain vehicle mentioned above, which also had an independent suspension, had no influence on this or any other nonmilitary development.

After the war two further experimental cars with coil springs and elongated wishbones were tested, as proposed by Robert J. Knight. Knight joined SS in 1944, coming from aircraft engine development at Armstrong-Siddeley and Bristol after an interim stay at Standard. At Jaguar he was in charge of suspension development, with Heynes as his boss. Shorter wishbones proved to be stiffer than the half axles that were tried as well, so they were combined with torsion springs and telescopic dampers. In 1946–1947 it was decided that this was the way to go.

For the new chassis Heynes aimed at a perfect springing, as well as efficient sound deadening. For comparison purposes a Bentley Mark VI, the latest offering from Crewe, was kept at hand. This car taught Jaguar a lot about rubber's abilities to suppress suspension-borne noise and vibration.

These developments added up to a truly modern chassis, for which Lyons designed a very modern and aerodynamic body. Due to its large panels with integrated fenders, it had to be made completely at Pressed Steel. Here again, some delay occurred, so that a revision of the current body was needed in order for Jaguar

Top: Modern, smaller headlamps raised the question how to fill the emptiness on the large fenders. *(S)*

Above: Cyril Holland in his later years, at a Jaguar club meeting, of course. *(S)*

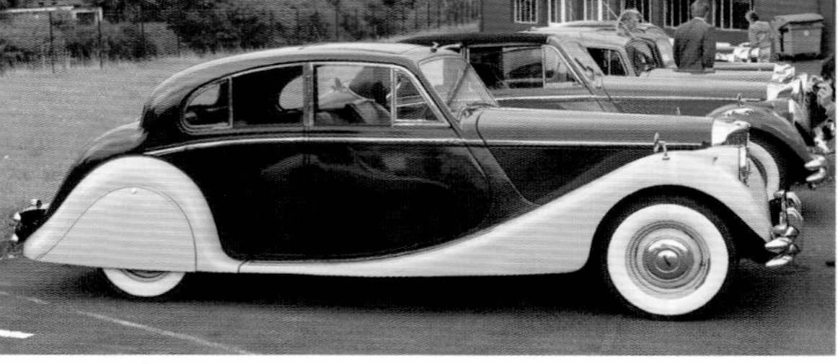

Above: With the Mark V, Jaguar completed its palette of OHV cars. *(J)*

Center: Duotone Mark Vs are particularly rare. *(Schön)*

Below: A Mark V drophead coupe in a most unusual bright red finish. *(Schön)*

to show any new model at the 1948 Motor Show, the first after the war. Although the body repeated a well-known concept, the smaller headlights that were now integrated into the front fenders, the spats over the rear wheels, and the chromed side window frames ending at the rear with a characteristic D shape gave the car a totally different look.

After the war Cyril Holland had left Jaguar. He had found the scope of his activities more and more limited over time, so styling was now up to Lyons alone. Like Holland, he did not use drawings or clay models. He would start his work in a closed workshop, together with some of his most able panel beaters, who formed metal pieces to his desires and put them on wooden jigs. He particularly trusted Fred Gardner, the sawmill chief who had been with him since 1929, and who was one of the very few employees he called by his Christian name. It was a time-consuming process to hone the perfect line, evaluate alternatives, and fit the perfect details like lamps, door handles, and body creases. Afterward the mock-ups were set up outdoors and finally in the park of Wappenbury Hall to evaluate the effects of light. Lyons' eye was so critical that the people around him may have become desperate more than once! Only when the design was faultless and Lady Greta and the rest of the family liked it, drawings were made as a preparation for production. At the time this

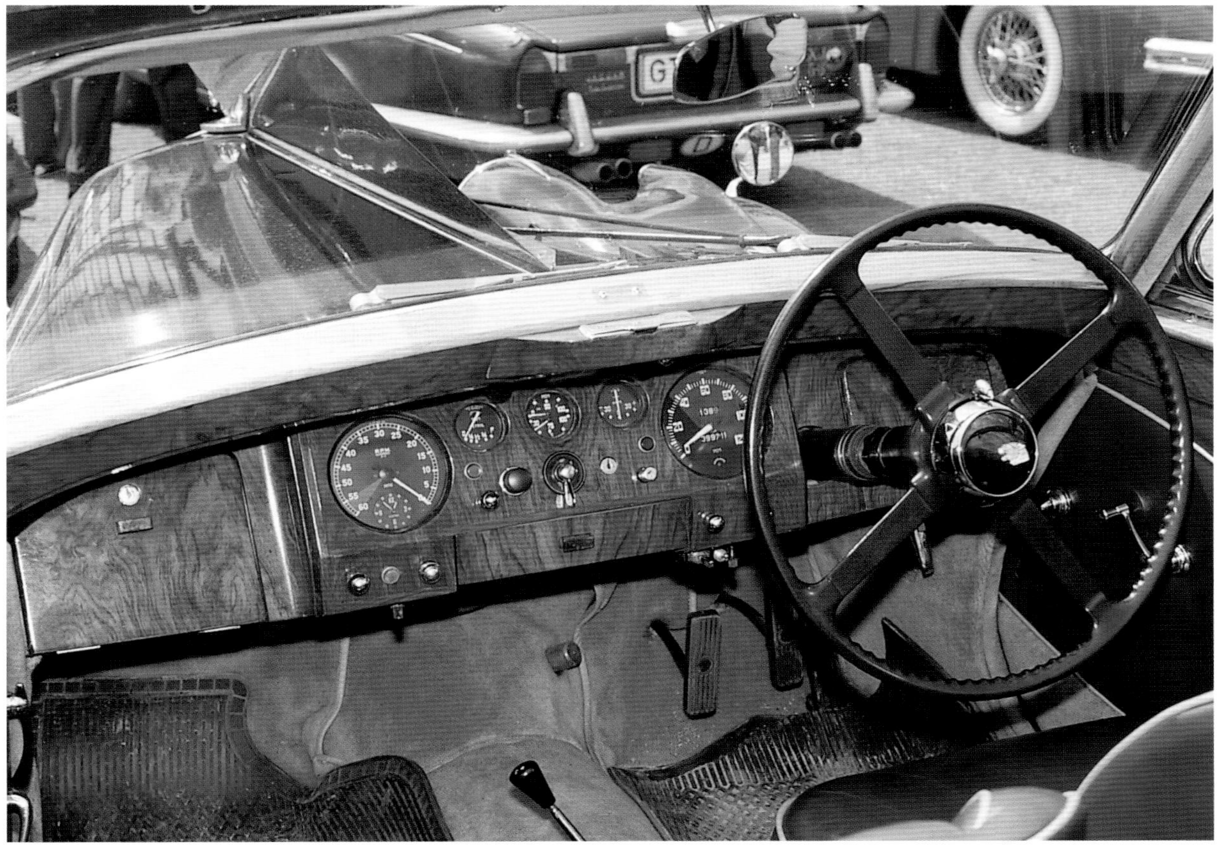

Above: Loyalty is to give one's Mark V a Lalique radiator mascot and drive it for more than a half century, as a British enthusiast managed to do. *(Schön)*

Left: The dashboard of the Mark V shows progress in detail. *(Schön)*

Above: This very early 3.5-liter drophead coupe shows the pointed front edge quarter light. *(S)*

Left: This Mark V 3.5-liter drophead coupe was once owned by Nelson Rockefeller. *(St)*

The Mark V finished third overall in the 1953 Monte Carlo Rally. *(S)*

trial-and-error was typical for technical development as well, and may be one of the secrets of the pragmatic progress during that period.

Allegedly in reference to the fifth variation of SS/Jaguar, but certainly influenced just as much by Bentley's nomenclature, the new sedan got the fanciless name Mark V. After the SS One of 1931, its successor of 1932, the SS Jaguar of 1935, and the all-steel cars of 1937, this was indeed Lyons' fifth six-cylinder car. The predecessors immediately were called "Mark IV" by the trade, but this was an unofficial designation. The four-cylinder version was no more, as this engine would not have provided adequate performance for the heavy new body. The four-cylinder engine had been the last component made for Jaguar at Standard.

Just before the official press debut on September 30, 1948, Lyons withdrew the drophead version of the Mark V and had the waistline strip positioned slightly lower. Only after this revision—one that might have escaped the eye of the uninitiated—did Lyons find the styling perfect. Both sedan and drophead coupe versions of the car were then displayed beginning October 27, 1948, at the Motor Show. Testers took note of the comfortable drive offered by the Mark V, particularly on long journeys. But they also experienced some brake fading, as the wheels had become smaller according to the latest fashion, and no wire wheels were available but only steel wheels with hubcaps. For the first time the police ordered large quantities of vehicles from Jaguar, as this latest model soon gained a reputation for extraordinary reliability. The police in particular, but many "normal" clients as well, benefited from the operator training that was offered at the Jaguar works from 1949 onward.

The Mark V combined its civil virtues with a good deal of sportiness, as was proved in many events. However, the Mark V did not finish the grueling Carrera Panamericana in 1950, driven by Jay C. Chamberlain and Jorgen Thayssen. The team of Cecil Vard/"Bill"Young was more successful in January 1951 on the Monte Carlo Rally, where they finished third in a 3.5-liter (Irish registration ZE 7445), while Douglas Sharp/Wally Waring/W.H. Wadham (registration JAA 915) finished ninth in the sporting event and second in

Cecil Vard under way in wintry Monte Carlo 1953. *(S)*

the Concours de Confort. In 1953 Vard and navigator Arthur Jolley finished fifth in the same car and event. No wonder that in 1954 another Mark V competed at Monte Carlo with J. A. D. Lucas and L. H. Handley. In the same year, R. W. Blackhurst did the RAC Rally in a Mark V. Caravan manufacturer Sam Alper and companions Martin Lumby and Graham Hoare towed one of Alper's Sprite caravans with a Mark V around the Mediterranean Sea—10,000 miles in 40 days—and the only damage suffered was to the exhaust.

Smaller variants of the Mark V, equipped with a 2-liter four-cylinder engine or a six-cylinder scaled down to 1.9-liters, were also tried, but were not developed beyond prototype status, nor were they sold.

THE XK ENGINE 6

Lyons' desire for more power had existed for some time. In the first years after World War II he aimed at producing a 100-mile-per-hour luxury sedan. To achieve this, an engine far more powerful than the then-renowned 3.5-liter was needed. The latter allowed a maximum speed of only 90 miles per hour. Harry Weslake could provide Lyons with the engine design know-how he needed. But it was an assiduous young man whose genius was of greatest importance to the new engine: Walter Hassan. Born in 1905, he was the 14th person to be hired by W. O. Bentley for his car manufacture at Cricklewood in north London. From 1931 onward, when Bentley went under Rolls-Royce's umbrella, Hassan remained with Bentley's ex-chairman Woolf Barnato. At Brooklands he looked after Barnato's 8-liter racing car as well as after Bill Pacey's car. After a short stay in 1936–1937 with racing car manufacturer ERA, he joined Thomson & Taylor, who prepared racing cars at Brooklands as well. Thomson & Taylor also imported the Italian Alfa Romeo sports car, famous for its impressive double overhead camshafts. There Hassan worked, among other things, on John Cobb's world speed record car.

In 1938, with the help of the gifted SS racing driver Tommy Wisdom, Hassan joined SS. There he was in charge of racing preparations as well, culminating in the fabulous 160 horsepower 3.5-liter engine for "Old Number Eight." But again, Hassan did not stay very long. In 1940 he went to Bristol, were he worked with Charles Newcombe and Phil Weaver. In 1943 Hassan returned to SS because he was interested in the development of the VA and VB all-terrain vehicles. He stayed at Lyons' company for seven years—astonishingly long for Hassan. During that time the famous XK engine entered production, and Hassan also had a hand in the hiring of Lofty England, Charles Newcombe, and Phil Weaver. He then joined Coventry Climax, where he developed the featherweight ("FW") pump engine, a masterpiece of engineering from which so many successful racing engines were derived. Later, when Coventry Climax was taken over by Jaguar, Hassan returned to his former team. He died in July 1996 a contented man, having enjoyed a long and inspiring life.

Besides Walter Hassan and Harry Weslake, chief engineer William Heynes and Claude Baily contributed significantly to the development of the new engine. Baily, who once had designed the Morris Eight engine after the pattern of the Ford Eight, had the duty to work out most of the details.

When developing the new engine it was clear that the existing 3.5-liter engine would be used as a starting point. It was essential that the engine would produce power reliably and consistently, as with the high-performance engine of "Old Number Eight," but on normal gasoline.

Two engine sizes were envisioned from the very start, either a four and a V-8 or a six and a V-12. Heynes proposed an engine of the type he had described in a paper for the Institute of Automotive Engineers—a four with two overhead camshafts and hemispherical combustion chambers, intended for a motorcycle. According to Wesley, this was still the best compromise among the needs of good gas flow, efficient cooling, and low production cost, although from a technical point of view the second camshaft could have been dispensed with. It was due to the reputation that Alfa Romeo had gained with a twin-cam engine that the second camshaft nevertheless became a feature of the new engine. The Riley Nine of 1926 had shown that overhead-cam engines could be produced in some quantity. However, Lyons insisted on using the complicated dual overhead cam mechanism that had first been seen combined with hemispherical combustion chambers on the Peugeot racing car of 1912 designed by Ernest Henri. Lyons expected that the outward appearance of the engine should suggest accuracy and technical competence.

Experiments with hemispherical combustion chambers started in 1943. Baily designed some variations of cylinder head and block, called XA, XB, and so on. The first experimental engine that became reality was called XF. This was a dual overhead camshaft (DOHC) four with 66.5mm bore and 98mm stroke, resulting in 1,360cc. Its crankshaft was too weak for high-rpm operation. This experiment was followed by XG, with the block of a Standard four-cylinder, but a very complicated head with pushrods *à la* the BMW 328. This complicated valve mechanism turned out to be rather noisy. Next was the XJ with a 98mm stroke (just like XF) but an 80.5mm bore, resulting in 1,996cc. This engine reverted to DOHC. Harry Weslake tested

From the top: Claude Baily, technical draftsman with an enormous talent. *(S)*

Wally Hassan, the horsepower magician. *(S)*

Harry Mundy, one of the most important fathers of the XK engine. *(S)*

Above: Goldie Gardner's MG EX 135 with a Jaguar four-cylinder engine is shown here during its record runs near Jabbeke in Belgium. *(S)*

Below: The XK four-cylinder engine in its final development stage. *(S)*

many variants of valve mechanism and port design on this engine. For the first time the ports fed the chambers tangentially, and a venturi effect was introduced. Both improved mixture swirl, which helped prevent self-ignition. By building lots of patterns and metering the gas flow, Weslake found the optimum design.

A variant of the XJ engine equipped with special pistons for a compression ratio of 12:1 and capable of 146 horsepower at 6,000 rpm was lent to Major A. T. G. "Goldie" Gardner, who put it in his aerodynamic MG experimental car, the EX 135. This car had started its life in 1933 as a K3 Magnette but was now hidden under a very low-slung, cigar-shaped body. In August 1948 on a straight motorway near Jabbeke in Belgium he achieved an average speed of 176.72 miles per hour on a flying kilometer. Even the average for the flying five kilometers was above 170 miles per hour. For use in the Mark V and an XK 100 sports car, the four-cylinder engine's power was reduced to 95 horsepower or, as stated in brochures, 105 horsepower at 5,000 rpm. Neither car saw series production, because production cost was only marginally less than the six-cylinder variants, the demand for which alone exceeded Jaguar's production capacity. There was, however, one XK 100 prototype (Chassis No. 470001), but it was soon scrapped. At least five of these four-cylinder engines exist today, one at the Jaguar works. Rumor had it that about 50 such engines were discovered at Jaguar in the 1980s, but there was no truth behind this idea.

A single Duplex chain driving the camshafts via sprockets directly from the crankshaft produced a whine that could not be suppressed. The only convenient solution was to use two duplex chains with intermediate sprockets. The lower one was tensioned hydraulically with neoprene-covered dampers. The upper one was tensioned by an eccentric sprocket situated between the camshafts. In an address to the Institution of Mechanical Engineers, Heynes described the difficulties experienced with the complicated valve mechanism, particularly that oil would be sucked along the valve stems into the combustion chambers.

Following the XJ four was an XJ six-cylinder experimental engine (83mm bore, 98mm stroke, 3,200cc). As predicted by Weslake, this engine did not deliver convenient torque at low revs. A longer stroke of 106mm was the answer, as increasing the bore seemed more difficult. So the capacity rose to 3,442cc, and the engine got its famous name, XK. It proved its reliability in a 24-hour endurance test, where it was held at 5,000 rpm and then every two hours revs were increased for five minutes to 5,250, 5,500, or 6,000 rpm. The XK was a wonderful piece of engineering that had cost more than £100,000 for tooling in 1947 alone. It was to become the classic power supply for Jaguar, and was fitted in everything from the compact everyday sedan to the most successful racing car.

The XK engine also had success on the seas, although this is not often mentioned. In 1947, Norman Buckley had reached an average 65 miles per hour for one hour with his speedboat *Miss Windermere*, powered by a 4-liter Lycoming engine. In October 1949, Buckley received one of the first XK engines. With a Lucas magneto, direct seawater cooling, and an additional oil cooler, he made the XK engine seaworthy and put it into *Miss Windermere*, which he towed to its destinations with a Mark V sedan. During the following years the power output was increased continuously. In 1952 a C-type head was employed, and in 1954 three Weber carburetors were added. Again and again Buckley and *Miss Windermere* set world records in its

This early XK 120 prototype was photographed early in 1948. *(S)*

Right: Fascia and rear are nearly perfect, but not yet the windshield. *(S)*

Below: After some few changes the XK 120 is nearly there—this is the version shown at the 1948 London Motor Show. *(S)*

Left: According to Jaguar legend, Lyons had been inspired by this BMW 328 that was equipped with an aerodynamic body for the 1940 Mille Miglia. *(Auto Welt)*

Top: Very early XK 120s ready for export to the United States. *(S)*

Above: William Lyons admittedly liked curves, the XK 120 face being proof. *(Schön)*

800 kilogram class. For some time Buckley was challenged by Christoph von Mayenburg in a similar boat. Von Mayenburg set a class record in 1954 with an average of 76.5 miles per hour for one hour. Buckley did even better in 1956 with *Miss Windermere II*, reaching 79.6 miles per hour. In 1957 Buckley set a top speed of 113.5 miles per hour, and two years later even exceeded 120 miles per hour. In 1960, with a new engine, Buckley's hourly average exceeded 80 miles per hour.

Back in 1948 the launch of a new high-speed sedan with ultramodern coachwork did not become a reality. Lyons didn't believe it advisable to unveil the new engine paired with a warmed-up sedan of traditional lines. Lyons thought a breathtaking sports car would be a better fit for the unveiling of the new XK engine, a proposition for which he was already prepared. Lyons may have been inspired by a BMW 328 sports racing car with special aerodynamic coachwork for the Mille Miglia that was handed around in the British auto industry. Lyons also took inspiration from the slim but high grille of the Alfa Romeo.

In February 1948 a prototype was ready at the works, but with many imperfect details and a four-cylinder engine under the long, slim hood. With a little more attention to detail, the XK 120 evolved. The number was chosen to indicate the top speed—as on the prewar sports car. This breathtaking roadster was presented to special guests at the Grosvenor Hotel in London on October 22, 1948, and five days later to the public at Earls Court. It still had the 3.2-liter engine under the hood, which was kept deliberately closed. At first the car was also called "Super Sports," recalling the prewar SS make. The front bumpers had yet to be relocated somewhat higher, and the windshield sides were not yet curved. In this guise the car (Chassis No. 660001) received its registration HKV 455.

Ronald M. V. Sutton joined Jaguar in 1948 as test driver. He was called "Soapy" because some shaving foam often remained behind his ears. Sutton had gained a reputation as a fast driver before the war driving a Lea-Francis, and he was chosen to prove that the XK 120 was capable of the promised speed. In the early morning of December 10, 1948, a test drive near Coventry ended with a not very satisfying 102-mile-per-hour maximum. During the winter the engineers worked to improve this performance, and in April 1949 the 120-mile-per-hour target was reached.

Chassis 660001 later became an experimental fixed head coupe at Jaguar's experimental department. Years later this chassis was turned into an XK 140 experimental car. The car then seemed to have gone missing, until in 1998 it was rediscovered. Seams visible on this very first chassis show clearly that it was derived from a Mark V that had been shortened and made somewhat narrower. This parentage made the XK 120 a very docile animal, quite a difference from the uncompromising springing and rough manners usually associated with sports cars at the time. Even the pedals and gearlever could be operated with surprising ease.

William Heynes did not agree with Lyons' idea that this wonderful sports car should also be offered as an XK 100 with the four-cylinder engine derivative that was tried during experimental stage. So Heynes did what he could to obstruct production of this engine. Not a single XK 100 was sold, possibly because it was offered at the same price as the much more charismatic six-cylinder engine.

In recognition of the XK 120's breathtaking styling, Lyons was named Royal Designer for Industry by the Royal Society of Arts. This was the first time that a car stylist was so honored. The public response was also quite positive—rather than produce a small series of only about 200 examples, Jaguar started full series production.

On May 30, 1949, Sutton officially tested the maximum speed on the Jabbeke motorway which had been so beneficial for Goldie Gardner's record trials. With a

Above: Wally Hassan, Ron Sutton, William Heynes, and XK 120. *(S)*

Left: Leslie Johnson and his XK 120 earned some cups at Palm Beach in January 1950. *(S)*

Below: The car that proved to be the fastest in the world at Jabbeke. *(J)*

Above: William Lyons, Tazio Nuvolari, and the XK 120 specially repainted red. *(J)*

Below: Silverstone 1949: A great victory for the brand-new XK 120. *(S)*

standard XK 120 (Chassis No. 670002, registration HKV 500), minus the windshield but with undershields, Sutton recorded 132.6 miles per hour, and in completely standard guise reached 126.5 miles per hour. The Royal Belgian Automobile Club, using Gardner's distance markings on the motorway, operated the stopwatches. As a proof of the engine's flexibility, Sutton cruised past the press and officials after the high-speed runs at 20 miles per hour in direct gear, which prompted further acclaim for the new fastest nonsupercharged production car in the world. Soon after this record, Sutton left Jaguar, heading for Alvis.

A downright historical success was achieved by the XK 120 in August 1949 in its first production car race, which was organized by the *Daily Express* at Silverstone—Britain's new motor sport Mecca after Brooklands was damaged during the war. As usual, Lyons was very skeptical whether Jaguar should dare to take part in that race. In order to make sure that the car was likely to win, he insisted that during testing before the race the car should run faster than the previous record for at least three hours without breakdown. Hassan and England achieved this, and even Lyons himself did a stint. Lyons noticed just after starting that he had forgotten his glasses. Rankin, Lyons' co-driver, had to announce every braking point. Astonishingly they arrived safely at the finish. In the race itself, Chassis No. 670002 (or HKV 500, the Jabbeke car which had been changed to right-hand drive) was driven by Leslie Johnson. Johnson won the race with an average speed of 82.8 miles per hour, followed by Peter Walker in a similar car, while the third XK 120 driven by Prince Bira (Bongse Bhanutej Bhanubandh of Siam) did not finish because his tubeless tires were erroneously fitted with tubes. His car, by the way, was the exhibition car from the 1948 Motor Show.

In January 1950, the XK 120 started its first overseas race at Palm Beach. Bill Spear's car broke down, but Leslie Johnson finished second in class and fourth overall. Alfonso Gomez Mena scored the first outright

overseas win for an XK-engined car on February 24, 1950, at a production car race in Cuba. In April 1950 Leslie Johnson took part in the Italian Mille Miglia with Chassis No. 660040, but after 14 hours racing only came home fifth. The similar cars of Biondetti, Haines, and Wisdom broke down, the latter only 30 miles from the finish! Generally Jaguars were not very successful racing on Italian soil.

Around this time the true series production of the XK 120 started, after 240 examples had been made in the traditional coachwork manner, with aluminum sheets over ash frames. Fifty-seven of them were right-hand drive and 183 were left-hand drive. Dispatch from the factory did not start before the second half of 1949. Of these first examples, RHD cars went to Australia and New Zealand; 18 RHD and 21 LHD cars to Europe; 7 RHD and 4 LHD to Asia and Africa; 4 RHD and 136 LHD to North America; and 19 LHD to South America. Six RHD and 2 LHD remained in Great Britain; the destination of one LHD car is unknown. One of the cars delivered to America went to Briggs Cunningham—it was the first in a series of most illustrious Jaguars to make their way into his hands.

The series production cars had all-steel bodies (just like Chassis No. 660172, which was built as a precursor), with doors and hoods made of aluminum and that were slightly heavier than the former ones. The rarity of the aluminum XK 120 has elevated it to a higher position (and value) among enthusiasts.

With the steel body exports to the United States, the success of the XK 120 was extended beyond anything Lyons had dared to hope even in his most optimistic moments. Racing was the best advertising even in the New World, where the brilliant California racing driver Phil Hill took his XK 120 to success at the highest levels of U.S. road racing. Sherwood Johnston and others scored further remarkable wins for the car.

In a speed and endurance test, Leslie Johnson and Stirling Moss drove an XK 120 (Chassis No. 660040, registration JWK 651) for 24 hours at the Montlhéry high-speed circuit west of Paris at a record average speed of 107 miles per hour. The fastest round was at an average 126.20 miles per hour, and one year later this was improved to 134.43 miles per hour.

The Tourist Trophy race of September 1950 at Dundrod in Ulster deserves particular attention. An XK 120 (Chassis No. 660057, owned by Tommy Wisdom) was the outright winner. Although this was the first win for Jaguar in a long-distance race, in this case the driver was more remarkable than the car: It was the first major race for Stirling Moss, which he won at an average speed of 75.15 miles per hour, with Peter Whitehead in another XK 120 placing second. Together with Leslie Johnson, the third driver in the race in an XK 120, Jaguar was awarded the team prize. Moss, now Sir Stirling, internationally renowned for his later wins for Mercedes-Benz, was able to adjust to so many different types of cars that he deserves to be called one of the best racing drivers of all time.

Famous names were attracted by the Jaguar name then as they are now, and so it was no surprise to find the legendary among those who tried the XK 120. With HKV 500, a car already mentioned, Moss took part in practice for the 1950 *Daily Express* production car race at Silverstone, but ill health kept him from racing. Victory nevertheless again went to Jaguar, thanks to Peter Walker (the Shelsley Walsh winner, in Chassis No. 660042, registration JWK 977), ahead of Anthony P. R. Rolt in a similar car. Major Tony Rolt, born in 1919, became famous during the war by escaping seven times from German captivity. At Castle Colditz, he built a glider that, because of the Allied victory, did not see completion. The car with the next chassis, No. 66043 (registration JWK 977), was lent to Clemente Biondetti for the Targa Florio, which was run in Sicily. He suffered a broken con-rod, which led to an improvement for the engines in series production.

Even Ian Appleyard abandoned his faithful SS 100. In July 1950 he participated again in the Alpine with his new wife Pat, who also happened to be William Lyons' daughter. With his famous XK 120 "NUB 120" (Chassis No. 660044), he achieved a class win and another Alpine Cup. In the subsequent years and at other rallies, he succeeded with the car in a most impressive manner.

F. le Gallais constructed his L.G.S. special around an XK engine and took it to the Bouley Bay hillclimb beginning in 1950, when he finished third in class. In 1952 he was second behind frequent winner Lord Louth in an XK 120. From 1953 onward they competed in different classes. Thus they could both achieve class wins on the same day, his Lordship until 1955 and le Gallais until 1957.

Ron Sutton, generally known as "Soapy." *(J)*

Above: Pat and Ian Appleyard, the couple with the golden Alpine Cup. *(S)*

Above right: Stirling Moss in an XK 120 in 1951. *(S)*

Below: NUB 120, winner of the Alpine Rally, is one of the most famous XK 120s. *(J)*

The racing year 1951 was quite a good one for the XK 120; the most notable triumphs were:

• Appleyard's wins in the Tulip Rally (from Rudi Habisreutinger from Switzerland in another XK 120), the RAC Rally (in which the Ladies' Prize went to Miss M. Newton in an XK 120 and seventh place in the sporting event to Lyons' son John in his XK 120, registration no. KRW 923), the Morecambe, the London Rally (sole penalty-free entrant, thanks to navigator Gordon Wilkins) and the Alpine (class win over 3-liters, another Alpine Cup for penalty-free run and the Soler team prize with Habisreutinger in an XK 120 second and Grant-Norton/Loades eighth in another XK 120)

• Johnny Claes/Jacques Ickx' win of the Liège-Rome-Liège Rally in HKV 500 (the first ever to finish penalty-free; second were Herzet/Baudion in another XK 120)

• Hache/Crespin's class win in the first Tour de France Automobile (a mix of rallies, circuit races, and hillclimbs at different places in France; second were Simone/Schlee and third Descollas/Gignoux, all in XK 120s)

• F. P. Grounds/J. B. Hay's class win in the National Rally, the concours of which was won by Dame Snow in an XK 120 with leopard fur as seat cover

• W. B. Black's class win at the Boreham Meeting, the sports class of which was dominated by Parkes with an M.G. Magnette special called Jaguette, with XK engine and SS gearbox

1953 XK120.

• Peignaux, Taylor, and Bray's 1-2-3 finish in the Rallye Soleil

• Moss, J. C. P. Davidson, and J. Duncan Hamilton's 1-2-3 finish in the famous production car race at Silverstone (Moss with an average of 84.5 miles per hour)

• L. Wood's win in the Scottish Rally (in the same car he also achieved a third place at Castle Combe)

• W. F. Mead's win in the Edinburgh Rally

• Johnny Claes' win in the One Hour Race at Spa (average 81.22 miles per hour)

• R. L. Sangan and A. Owen's 1-2 finish in the Bouley Bay hillclimb

• Scherrer's victory of the Bremgartenpreis at Bern

• John Fitch's win in the Six Hour Race at Sebring

• Sherwood Johnston's win in the Grand Prix sports car race at Watkins Glen

• D. Parkinson's win in the Reno Road Race, and a second place in Palm Springs

• Second and third places for B. R. Hawes and F. M. Ferguson in the Grand Prix of Malaya at Johore

• Second and third places for Wilken and Craig in the Goodwood Easter Monday Race

At Montlhéry the already well-known JWK 651 covered 131.81 miles in the "flying" hour. The races in Italy were less satisfying, with an eighth place in the Giro d'Italia for Clemente Biondetti in a special consisting of a sort of Maserati birdcage chassis, a Ferrari body, and his duly repaired XK engine, which nevertheless did not stand up to the Mille Miglia. For all the successes during 1951, Jaguar was awarded the Dewar Trophy by the RAC.

One of the most amazing photographs of a Jaguar in motor sport: Ian Appleyard's XK 120 in front of the unique panorama of the Alps. *(S)*

The following rally year again brought many victories and top placings:

• In July 1952, Appleyard did the third consecutive penalty-free run in the Alpine in the same car, for which he received the first-ever golden Glacier Cup. When in the 1980s another dealership of the Appleyard group was opened, this cup was handed over by Ian—who died on July 2, 1998—to the then-Jaguar chief Sir John Egan, and it has been kept since then at Jaguar. Second in the Alpine was Maurice Gatsonides with another XK 120

• In the RAC Rally XK 120s finished second (J. C. Broadhead) and third (Appleyard) in class, and won the Ladies' cup (Miss Mary Newton). In the same race, Leslie Johnson was disqualified for having removed the spats from the rear wheels

• The Morecambe Rally brought a sixth place for John Lyons and the Ladies' cup for his sister, Pat Appleyard

• The Rallye du Soleil ended with a 1-2 finish for D. O. M. Taylor/Mrs. Taylor and Rudi Habisreutinger/W. Horning, as did the Tulip Rally with Habisreutinger/Horning and F. P. Grounds/Mrs. Grounds

• G. P. Denham-Cooke won the Scottish Rally

• F. S. Mort won the Bo'ness Speed Trials, with S. Black as the winning lady

• Habisreutinger/Horning also were class winners at the British National Rally

• Laroche/Radix were class-winners in the Rally Liège-Rome-Liège

• The three-day Highland Rally ended with an overall victory for the XK 120 of G. P. Denham-Cooke. In the Sports car handicap race M. W. Head came second

• J. Neilson in his XK 120 won the Rest-and-be-Thankful hillclimb

• Berthomier won his class in the Tour de France

• Simone's XK 120 was class winner in the Coupe du Salon at Montlhéry with a speed of 81.85 miles per hour

• Ian Stewart won the sports car race at Turnberry from P. J. Kenneth while he was only second in the Formula Libre Race, with Scott-Douglas behind him.

• E. W. Holt (70.24 miles per hour) and J. B. Swift finished 1-2 in the Easter Monday sports car race

• In the 12-Hour Race at Sebring the XK 120 driven by C. Schott/M. Carroll finished second behind a Frazer-Nash

• In the Grand Prix de France sports car race at Reims, Scott-Douglas finished third

• On the Isle of Man, Sir James Scott-Douglas of the newly established team won with the XK 120 with an average speed of 65.22 miles per hour

• The Bridgehampton handicap race in the United States ended with a 1-2-3 for M. B. Carroll, J. Koster, and W. H. Saunders, the unlimited class race with a 2-3 (W. Hansgen and P. Timmins) and the modified sports car race with a third place (J. Fitch)

In the 1953 Alpine, Appleyard was again penalty-free, but now he drove a new XK 120 (Chassis No. 661071, registration RUB 120) and won from Fraikin/Gendebien, who also received an Alpine Cup, in another XK 120. Appleyard also won the Morecambe (the last battle for NUB 120), RAC, and Hastings Rallies. In the Rally Lisbon he finished second and Appleyard could see he had a chance of winning the newly established European Rally championship. For the Viking rally, to which only four-seaters were admitted, RUB 120 was quickly converted into a drophead coupe with two tiny seats in the rear, but Appleyard did not dare to take part in the race with that car. Appleyard thought that he still had gained enough points, but as only the four most successful results were counted, he finished a close second. Appleyard thought this was unfair and withdrew from rallying, apart from some inconsequential starts.

Stirling Moss winning the 1950 Tourist Trophy with an XK 120. *(Schönborn archive)*

An early XK 120 open two-seater, heavily modified for historic racing. *(Ridder)*

An early steel roadster, recognizable by its window frame following the body curve more precisely, and its separate sidelight housings. *(S)*

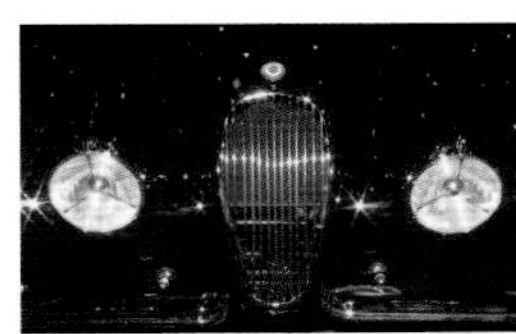

The XK 120 grille, a masterpiece of elegance. *(Schön)*

Far left: The interior of a well-restored XK 120. *(Schön)*

Left above: The Jaguar XK 120 with aero screens as supplied with early Special Equipment models. *(Schön)*

Left below: An XK 120 was modified for record drives in 1953—Guy Broad has built this faithful replica. (St)

Above: XK 120 fixed head coupe with the then-fashionable painted wire wheels. *(Schön)*

Left: The roof fits neatly into the curved lines of the XK 120. *(Schön)*

Top: The fine interior of the XK 120 fixed head coupe. *(Schön)*

Above: XK 120 open two seater and fixed head coupe for comparison. *(Schön)*

In 1953:

• Gendebien/Fraikin finished second in the grueling Liège-Rome-Liège

• The Bennett couple won the Rally Evian-Mont Blanc

• The Hally couple won the National Rally

• W. Dewess finished second in the Great American Mountain Rally

• The Highland (J. M. Cringean) and Scottish Rallies (J. H. Cunningham) brought further victories

• In the Easter Monday Races at Goodwood two XK 120s took second-place finishes (E. Protheroe and M. W. Head)

• In the Snetterton Sports car race J. Farrow finished second behind le Gallais and his L.G.S.

• Balaracco's XK 120 won the Grand Prix sports car race at Bern

• Sherwood Johnston became sports car champion that year in the United States

In the following years the XK 120 racing successes thinned out, not least due to more modern challengers from Jaguar's own stables. For 1954:

• A third place in the Scottish Rally

• A class win in the National Rally (both E. Haddon/ C. Vivian)

The dashboard of the XK 120 fixed head coupe—here in its later guise—is magnificent. *(J)*

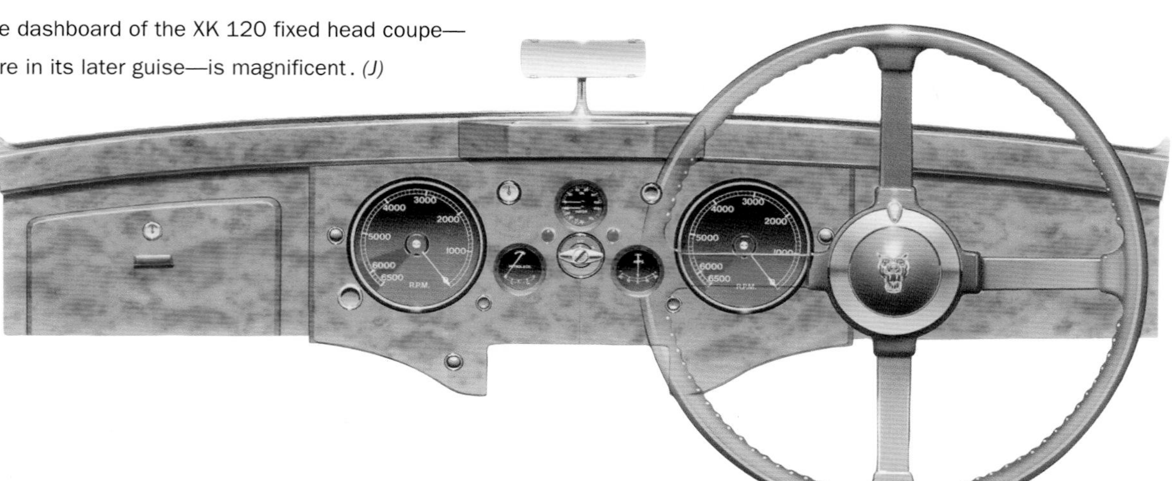

Above: In recent years the XK 120 fixed head coupe has become much sought-after. *(Schön)*

Right: Contemporary photograph of the dashboard in the nearly finished prototype of the XK 120—the telescopic steering column is clearly visible. *(S)*

• M. Salmons' class win in the Bo'ness Speed Trials in June and his overall win there in September

• E. Protheroe's win in the sports car handicap "A" race at Goodwood

• Bob Berry's third place in the Snetterton International sports car race and his second in the Curragh handicap race

• J. Sears' third place in the Snetterton five-rounds sports car race

• R. Perrin, G. Constantine, and W. Smith's 1-2-3 at Watkins Glen

In 1955: Scheid finished fifth at Spa in an XK 120, Meunier third in the Grand Prix des Frontières at Chimay, and M. D. Heather won at the Munster handicap race at Cork in Ireland

In 1957: Peter Sargent managed to win the production car race in the Autosport series at Goodwood.

In 1958: R. A. Gibson became class winner in the sports car race at Snetterton.

The rear of the XK 120 fixed head coupe with twin exhaust; the complicated profile of the bumpers is in evidence. *(S)*

Top: The record run of the XK 120 fixed head coupe at Montlhéry was much exploited for advertising. *(S)*

Above: LWK 707, the XK 120 of Montlhéry, with Stirling Moss, Jack Fairman, and Nick Scheele. *(J)*

Above: XK 120 fixed head coupe at the 1952 Alpine Rally with René Cotton at the wheel. *(S)*

Below: LWK 707 again, in a very detailed airbrush painting. *(J)*

In 1959: E. Protheroe won the Autosport championship race, R. Taylor won the Sedan and GT race at Snetterton, and Protheroe became class winner in the three-hour night race at the same circuit.

The normal XK 120 that Dewis, with considerable aerodynamic aid, had accelerated to a breathtaking 172 miles per hour by then already had a sister. At the Geneva show in 1951, Jaguar showed a fixed head coupe with a rounded roof, nearly half-moon rear side windows, and no pillar between its glass and the door—following the example of the Airline. At the occasion of this show German tester Hans Uwe Wieselmann from the magazine *Das Auto* had the opportunity to drive an XK 120 open two-seater for the first time in his life. "A dream of sports car drivers has become reality—the engine is not temperamental at all—and all this with normal gasoline from the pump," he exclaimed. In the same year a more powerful S.E. version (Special Equipment, a designation already used just before the war) with 180 horsepower was earmarked with a chassis

XK 120 drophead coupe for America with the whitewall tires still protected. *(S)*

Left: The XK 120 drophead coupe, with its speed and style, filled the gap left by the demise of the Mark V drophead coupes. *(S)*

Below: Ian Appleyard with his XK 120 drophead coupe at the 1954 Alpine Rally. *(S)*

number prefix S and equipped with additional small aero screens to replace the roadster's windshield in racing (only available until summer 1953), wire wheels, twin exhaust, and stiffer torsion bars.

The coupe with the rounded roof was of course aerodynamically more efficient than the open two-seater, and therefore was the right choice for the high-speed trials at Montlhéry in August 1952. The bronze-colored car (Chassis No. 669002, registration LWK 707) with Johnson, Hadley, Moss, and Fairman as drivers, ran seven days and nights and covered 10,000 miles at an average speed of 100.31 miles per hour. The average for 10,000 kilometer was 107.30 miles per hour. Speed records for 72, 96, 120, 144, and 168 hours were set as well. The car did 17,000 miles during the week. With the aerodynamic fixed roof, the fixed head coupe was a good racing car despite its additional weight. It won the National Rally (Moss/J. A. Cooper).

In 1953 Reg and Joan Mansbridge finished third in the Alpine behind the aforementioned Jaguar open

Above: Early prototypes of the twin cam sedan were made soon after the war, but as the Mark VII it debuted in 1950. *(S)*

Below: The chassis of the Mark VII, then state-of-the-art. *(S)*

Above: The rear of the Mark VII with its tiny lights. *(S)*

Above left: Following precise orders from the boss, steel sheets were formed and painted black before being assembled to a prototype, which Lyons would study endlessly in the sunlight. *(S)*

Left: A nearly finished Mark VII prototype. *(S)*

two-seaters. In the Australian 24 Hour Race on New Year's Day 1954, "Geordie" Anderson was the winner, after a carburetor breakdown was repaired with parts from a visitor's car. In May 1954 G. Tyrer finished second in the enclosed car race at Ibsley.

The third variant of XK body was unveiled in April 1953. It was a luxuriously appointed convertible with the wooden dashboard of the coupe, a fully lined top, and wind-down side windows—the car was also a late replacement for the Mark V drophead coupe. The side windows did not allow the curved windshield frame, so the open two-seater's beautiful chromed frame was replaced by a stiffer one made from steel metal that was integrated into the body.

From April 1954 onward, a competition cylinder head ("C") was offered for the XK 120. This provided 210 horsepower but did not markedly improve the car's performance.

Long before that time Mark V production—in itself only the result of unhappy coincidence—ended. In 1950 Pressed Steel started production of the body for the "twin cam saloon"—as Lyons' dream of a high-speed express was called during its development. The modern lines and integrated fenders of this body required it to be made of unusually large sheet sections.

Top: Lots of wood created a lavish atmosphere in the Mark VII. *(Schön)*

Above: "Grace, Space, Pace" were the advantages pointed out in Mark VII advertising. *(J)*

Top: The Mark VII was breathtaking in 1950. *(Schön)*

Above: Like the XK 120, the Mark VII had wonderfully sculptured rear haunches. *(Schön)*

Right: An advertising photograph of the Mark VII. *(S)*

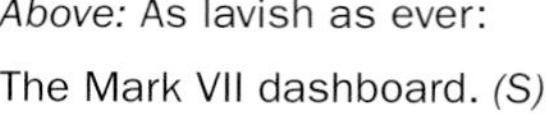

Above: As lavish as ever: The Mark VII dashboard. *(S)*

Right: A huge trunk was hidden under the nice rounded skin of the Mark VII's rear. *(S)*

Top: Mark VII with works lightweight body at the 1954 Monte Carlo Rally on the Col des Lecques. *(S)*

Above: Mark VII in the 1953 Monte Carlo Rally at a special test on the Col de Braus. *(S)*

Above: The tiny taillights of the Mark VII were deemed quite normal at the time. *(Schön)*

Left: Mark VII armada at the 1955 Monte Carlo Rally. *(S)*

Adams, Bigger, Johnston, and the Mark VII M were the overall winners in the 1956 Monte Carlo Rally. *(S)*

In deference to the Bentley Mark VI, Lyons called the successor of the Mark V the Mark VII. However, in the files, two cars with Chassis Nos. 620004 and 623053 from Mark V sequence are called Mark VI, and they had XK engines under their elongated hoods. Two convertible prototypes were made using the Mark VII body structure, but they lacked the stiffness required for series production. These were not shown to the public, but were secretly scrapped.

The new Mark VII was unveiled two years late at Earls Court on October 22, 1950. The Jaguar staff was offered the opportunity to travel to London in a chartered train to witness this moment of vital importance to the future of the company.

The engine in the new car was identical to the one in the XK 120, and it allowed the car to travel at up to 100 miles per hour, as Lyons had requested. Otherwise the chassis was much the same as under the Mark V. There was no traditional mascot, as the radiator filler cap had been relocated under the hood. Instead, a growling jaguar head with two wings was put above the grille—a strange combination of Swallow and Jaguar symbols. With the advertising slogan "Grace . . . Space . . . Pace . . ." the car became a success all over the world, particularly in the United States. Jaguar allegedly was not aware that M.G. had used a similar motto for its 1936 SA, VA, and WA sedans.

Several test reports of the Mark VII were published in British magazines. The magazines usually drove the demonstrator (Chassis No. 710006) with registration LWK 343. This was one of the few cars available, because a strike delayed the start of series production for six weeks. In production form, the car delighted testers with its power, comfort, noise suppression, spaciousness, and general refinement. Similarly powerful and roomy cars were available from the United States, but these sedans were a disappointment to enthusiasts with their poor roadholding and damping. The Mark VII also deserved some minor criticism with regard to its drum brakes, which were barely adequate for the car's superior performance, and the steering, which felt a bit light for European tastes. The prominent, bullet-shaped steering wheel boss was not well loved either. The quality of the car was highly praised; at the time the quality of the materials used was most important to consumers, panel fit being of minor relevance.

The demand for the Mark VII once again exceeded Jaguar's expectations by far, and could hardly be met using the existing production facilities at Foleshill, although the floor space had been increased from 40,000 to over 600,000 square feet back at the start of Swallow production there. When journalist Gordon Wilkins paid a visit to Swallow Road in 1951, he saw modestly appointed offices and only adequately equipped rest rooms, revealing Lyons' money-saving philosophy. Wilkins also mentioned the surprisingly small staff, noting their enthusiasm and efficient organization.

Jaguar had applied to the highest government agencies for assistance in undertaking further expansion at the present site, but this was denied. Once again Lyons had to build a completely new plant. For war production, the government had built a plant in 1939 for Coventry-Daimler, only two miles away at Browns

Lane, Allesley. Daimler could afford to dispense with the plant. Lyons managed to buy the more than 1,000,000 square feet, but the government usually did not sell its property, preferring to engage in lease contracts. So Lyons had to sign a long-period lease agreement before he could buy the plant. At least the presence of plenty of land around the plant would allow further expansion. At the same time Jaguar took over the manufacture of the Meteor tank engine, which Daimler had been building there alongside buses. Fortunately for Lyons, this contract was worth as much as Jaguar's whole car production.

Moving started when the Mark VII went into series production late in 1951 and continued step-by-step without interrupting car production—a masterpiece of organization by John Siver. The paint shop, which was started at Browns Lane in November 1952, was the last part of the production to make the move. Instead of cellulose, synthetic resin varnish was used to paint the cars. This eliminated the arduous and time-consuming polishing process. At the same time Jaguar began using a special drying facility for the wooden interior pieces, which reduced the process of veneering from 12 hours to 10 minutes—obviously Jaguar still used every opportunity to improve efficiency!

An important addition to the technical specification of the Mark VII was the Borg-Warner automatic gearbox, which was introduced as an optional extra at the 1953 New York Auto Show. American customers were accustomed to this sort of transmission, so Jaguar had to follow the trend. Additionally, a supply shortage of manual gearboxes could be elegantly circumvented this way. British customers, however, were not able to specify the automatic. In 1954 the car rental company Victor Britain became the first British client allowed to order automatic Jaguars. The Board of Trade commanded that these cars could only be rented by customers paying in foreign currency—the relations of government and trade have come a long way since then!

In 1952, the Thonning couple drove a luxurious and heavy Mark VII all the way from Indian Calcutta to London—and they managed to arrive there safely. Apart from an oil pan protection and a 24-gallon fuel tank (with a tendency to leak), the car was completely standard. The production car race at Silverstone was kindly divided into sports car and sedan classes, so the Mark VII could show its sporting potential. It was Stirling Moss' privilege to win the race at an average speed of 75.22 miles per hour in LWK 343, the well-known press demonstrator. Bertie Bradnack finished fourth in another Mark VII. The car was better suited to rallies. René Cotton/L. Didier finished the Monte Carlo Rally in fourth with Jean Herteaux/Crespin sixth, while W. H. Wadham/Waring won the concours. Another eight Mark VIIs took part in this rally, among them Ian Appleyard (registration PNW 7), Raymond Baxter/Gordon Wilkins (registration LWK 343), Bob Berry/Allan Currie (OKV 76), Bradnack, and Mansbridge. In the Lisbon rally of 1952, Sosa finished second in the unlimited class, and Appleyard also came in second with PNW 7 in the Tulip Rally.

In April 1953 Jaguar test driver Norman Dewis tried the Mark VII on the motorway near Jabbeke in Belgium and managed 121.7 miles per hour. That year many Mark VIIs again participated in the Monte Carlo Rally. The Appleyards very nearly missed victory, and together with Cecil Vard and Don Benett, they added the team prize to their second place. In the Tulip Rally, Appleyard scored a class win and fifth overall, but he did not finish the Norwegian Rally. Major J. E. Osborne/F. Lt. D. Brown finished the National Rally with military precision as class winners. At Silverstone, Moss was victorious again in the same car as the year before, as the car had been improved and the opposition was not particularly strong. In 1954 the row of winning Mark VIIs at Silverstone changed as Appleyard (registration SUM 7) won from Rolt (LHP 5) and Moss in the proven LWK 343, which suffered a jammed starter. In the Monte Carlo Rally, Ronald Adams/Desmond Titterington achieved sixth place, and Charles Lambton won the concours. Cecil Vard had advanced to a Mark VII but together with Arthur Jolley and Frank Bigger he only captured eighth place. Even this year a Mark V could be found in the rally, driven by J. A. D. Lucas/L. H. Handley. Another one could be seen in the RAC Rally (driver R. W. Blackhurst), where J. Ashworth finished second in class with the newer model. The Mark VII achieved class wins in the Tulip Rally (J. P. Boardman/J. A. Duckworth), in the Alpine (E. Haddon/C. Vivian) and in the Scottish Rally (J. M. C. Shand). Third place there went to E. R. Parsons/Mrs. J. G. M. Vann, who also won the National Rally.

7
FAME AT LE MANS

One of the most famous motor races in the world is the 24 Hours of Le Mans. With a very fast, long straight, and some narrow bends it presents man and machine with a difficult challenge. In England the race became famous in its early years with Bentley's victories in the 1920s. As the Jaguar in the early years after the war still was not as highly regarded as other, more traditional makes, the company believed a win at this very special place in the northwest of France would be very desirable. In 1950 Jaguar went to Le Mans to find out if it had a chance to win this grueling race. From a technical point of view Jaguar's effort did not seem too ambitious, but at the time most racing cars were a far cry from today's standards of technical perfection. Jaguar entered three rather standard XK 120s against racing cars with more or less prewar technology. The result was encouraging: Peter Clark/Nick Haines (the latter was an Australian and Royal Air Force pilot in the war who had been seventh overall in an Aston Martin DB 2 at Le Mans the year before; their XK 120 was Chassis No. 660041, which later acquired registration MGJ 79) finished 12th, just behind the American Briggs Cunningham in a Cadillac Special. Peter Whitehead/John Marshall (Chassis No. 660042, registration JWK 977) was 14th. The third car (Chassis No. 660040, JWK 651), driven by Leslie Johnson/Herbert H. Hadley, was running in good position toward the end of the race but suffered a clutch failure. Lofty England, who was in charge of Jaguar's Le Mans adventure, thought Johnson should be blamed for this damage because he tried to relieve the brakes by shifting down through the gears while decelerating.

In total this was an unexpectedly good result. England and Heynes were convinced that with much the same mechanics, a lighter chassis, and a more aerodynamic body, the XK could become a Le Mans winner. It was September or December 1950—both dates are quoted in historical sources—before Jaguar decided to establish a racing department and take part in the next 24-hour race. Rumor has it that the Belgian importer Madame Bourgeois believed that private entrants, which she felt were often ill-prepared, were a detriment to Jaguar's reputation. It is said that she convinced Lyons that a works racing department was a necessity. Phil Weaver became head of this department while Lofty England would organize and look after the teams participating in the races.

In order to improve the car's aerodynamic efficiency, Malcolm Sayer was employed in September 1950. He had been born in Cromer, Norfolk in 1916, and studied aerodynamics at Loughborough College. He finished with unparalleled marks and then entered the automotive division of the college in 1933. In 1938 he was awarded a degree as an automotive engineer. From then on he worked with the aircraft manufacturer Bristol. In his spare time he developed the body for the unhappy Gordano car. In 1948 he moved to Iraq, attracted by the largely fictional engineering faculty there. From a German professor he learned mathematic means to calculate the behavior of a body in the air stream. This gave him an incredible advantage over the rest of the automotive industry, which was why Jaguar was interested in Sayer. His good relationships within the aero industry gained Jaguar access to wind tunnels prototype testing.

The mechanics under the aerodynamic skin of the Le Mans racer were the responsibility of Bob Knight and the more practically inclined Tom Jones. The process, from the first sketch to the finished car, took seven months. Heynes used broomsticks to build the first model of the tubular frame under the body, which, according to Lyons' requirements, had to resemble the XK 120. His idea to integrate sheet metal to further

Above: A Jaguar pit stop during the company's first appearance at the 24 Hours of Le Mans in 1950. *(S)*

Below: Phil Weaver, the man behind Jaguar's racing. *(S)*

Left: This is one of the XK 120s that did so well in the 1950 Le Mans 24 Hours. *(Schön)*

Opposite: Lofty England at work, suitably dressed in double-breasted suit. *(S)*

Above: The XK 120s prepared for the 1951 Le Mans race were not started—this is a replica owned by a German collector. *(St)*

Right: Another XK 120 for the 1951 Le Mans race with shorter hood and doors. *(S)*

Below: The trunk lid was omitted for reasons of stability. *(S)*

strengthen this structure was remarkably advanced. The suspension generally remained unchanged versus the road car, but side movement of the rear axle was better controlled, and the steering gear was of the rack and pinion type. The engine also was very close to the standard type, but a special competition cylinder head provided some useful additional power. The name of the sports prototype signified the close relation to the XK 120 as well: it was called XK 120 C ("competition"), or more unofficially "C-Type." As a precaution against possible delay in the manufacture of the prototypes, Lyons had three XK 120s prepared with special lightweight aluminum bodies. Body LT 1 was finished in green and LT 3 in white on Chassis No. 660741. Both went to Hornburg in California but suffered overheating and braking problems when raced. LT 2, on Chassis No. 660748 and registered JSV 482, was modified by Bob Berry to be a serious contender. These LT bodies are easy recognizable by the shortened hood (ending above the grille) and doors that do not hide the sills. A German collector owns a replica of the LT cars. Heynes did not bother too much with these cars, correctly believing that the XK 120 C would be ready in time for Le Mans.

During the relatively short prerace testing at Le Mans a young American student named Bob Berry hung around with the team, his only apparent qualification being his knowledge of the French language. With his father's Mark V he had gained some racing experience, but Berry turned out to be a dyed-in-the-wool Jaguar enthusiast with a knack for public relations. In 1964 he would become Rankin's successor as public relations chief. Rankin himself, by the way, was not to enjoy his twilight years, as he died after a long illness on February 18, 1966.

For the 1951 race at Le Mans, the XK 120s were finished in a very dark shade of that famous racing green that, in 1903, Napier had chosen for the Gordon Bennett Race in Ireland, and which since then has been deemed the only appropriate color for a British racing

car. The cars were entered privately by the drivers, so that any defeat or other calamity would not rest at Jaguar's feet.

Immediately after the start the cars showed that this cautiousness was unnecessary. During the first 50 laps all three XK 120 Cs were leading, but then the race became more exciting: Clemente Biondetti, who shared XKC 001 with Johnson, stopped at the pits with a lack of oil pressure, the reason for which remained unclear at first. Shortly after midnight Moss (in XKC 002, shared with Jack Fairman) broke down with a broken con-rod caused by the same symptom. It became apparent that a broken oil pipe in the sump was the cause. The steel tubes were too brittle, and all subsequent racing engines were provided with copper pipes. Peter Whitehead and Peter Walker thus had to defend their lead with minimum stress to their engine. As soon as England thought the lead was sufficient he signaled "slow" to the passing XK 120 C. Lyons thought this was the wrong tactic and made England signal "faster," which he only did as long as Lyons watched him, thus creating some confusion for the drivers. During the next pit stop England secretly advised the driver to ignore the "faster" signal, and with this artifice the car safely reached the finish as winner. The privately entered XK 120 of Bob Lawrie/Ivan Waller finished 11th with an average 82.52 miles per hour, while the winners averaged 93.49 miles per hour.

With this win Jaguar proved that its cars were fast and reliable—as the Bentleys of their period had been. At once Jaguar was regarded as a true enthusiast's car. William Lyons was satisfied; his make had reached the worldwide fame he had sought for so long. As a further proof, Jaguar managed a 1-2-4 at the Tourist Trophy Race at Dundrod in Ireland (Moss in XKC 002, Walker in XKC 003, and Johnson/Rolt in XKC 001, the latter setting a lap record). Jaguar also won the team trophy.

At the motorway straight near Jabbeke, an XK 120 C driven by Norman Dewis reached the maximum speed of 148 miles per hour, while a slightly prepared XK 120 did 142 miles per hour and a Mark VII reached 121 miles per hour.

While Jaguar was preparing the XK 120 C for its second race at Le Mans, David Murray founded Ecurie Ecosse in Edinburgh. This melodious name means nothing more than "Scottish racing team." He started with four XK 120s and one XK 120 C, all of which were elegantly finished in a metallic blue to match the Scottish flag. The illustrious driver team consisted of Ian Stewart, Sir James Scott-Douglas, and J. Duncan Hamilton. It gained a reputation even at Jaguar, who first offered them their racing cars before selling them elsewhere.

Preparations for the Le Mans race included testing of disc brakes, which had previously been used by aircraft, in cooperation with Dunlop. This was the first major challenge for test driver Norman Dewis, who had taken on Soapy Sutton's job at Jaguar earlier in 1952. On Easter Monday 1952, Stirling Moss drove XKC 003 with this new braking system in the Goodwood race and finished fourth. A lot of common technical development projects between Dunlop and Jaguar companies were to follow, to the benefit of both.

Above left: Stirling Moss broke the lap record in 1951 at Le Mans with the brand new XK 120 C. *(S)*

Above: An XK 120 C is handed over by William Heynes to Tommy Wisdom, famous racing driver from prewar days. *(S)*

Below: The XK 120 C and its powerful, reliable XK engine were as good as unbeatable at long-distance races. *(J)*

From top: An XK 120 C in the flag-blue finish of Ecurie Ecosse. *(Schön)*

An XK 120 C in front of the racing transporter of Ecurie Ecosse that thankfully has survived. *(Schön)*

Hardly any other car brought as much fame and honor to Jaguar as did the XK 120 C. *(Schön)*

Above: A roaring Jaguar racing car even suits the ambience of an old castle. *(J)*

Left: Stirling Moss and his XK 120 C in the 1951 Tourist Trophy. *(Schönborn archive)*

Among these projects was the Maxaret antilock brake, which had been tested extensively in the Mark VII as early as 1952.

The Le Mans race did not bring the desired triumph to Jaguar. The reason was the brand new Mercedes-Benz 300 SL, with which the Germans wanted to continue their prewar successes. Stirling Moss had reported from the Mille Miglia how quick the 300 SL had been, and that he had not managed to hold the same pace with his XKC 003 despite its disc brakes. Together with Dewis he had been in third position, but a relatively minor failure in the steering gear forced retirement—once again Jaguar was not successful in

Italy. Hastily, Sayer improved aerodynamics for Le Mans, modifying the front and rear ends of XKC 001, 002, and 011 with a "droop" snout. The drivers were Rolt/Hamilton, Whitehead/Stewart, and Moss/Walker. The low hood line required the header tanks on top of the radiators to be placed elsewhere. Tests showed that this and the rather thin piping reduced cooling efficiency. On two cars some measures were taken to improve cooling just before the race, but in the race the Jaguars soon suffered overheating and retired.

As compensation, Moss won at Reims with XKC 005 (wearing the original body) with an average 98.18 miles per hour. Also, Mercedes-Benz and Ferrari were not among the entrants, which made it an easy victory for Jaguar. This was the first-ever victory for a car with disc brakes.

At Silverstone, Moss drove the XK 120 C and won the sports car race with an average 84.02 miles per hour. In a "Race of Champions" of six identical XK 120s he also won against foreign icons German Paul Pietsch, Siamese Prince Bira, Swiss de Graffenried, Belgian Johnny Claes, and Australian F. A. O. Gaze. The XK 120 C still was not always sufficiently reliable and retired in the British Empire Trophy Race and under Moss at Monaco. However:

• Moss and Walker won the nine-hour race at Goodwood

• Moss alone won the 24-hour sports car race at Boreham and the sports car race at Turnberry (from Hamilton and Ian Stewart, both also in XK 120 Cs)

• At Shelsley Walsh, Prescott Walker won with 41.14- and 47.53-second times

• In the Wakefield Trophy Race at Curragh, Ian Stewart was the winner (and Scott-Douglas in an XK 120 was third), as well as in the Jersey sports car race

• The first successes of the XK 120 C in the United States were Phil Hill's victories in the 4-liter class in the Elkhart Lake Race and John Fitch's victory in the Seneca Cup race at Watkins Glen

• Ian Stewart also was the winner in the sports car class at Castle Combe and Charterhall, where Moss was second in his XK 120 C

Duncan Hamilton purchased XKC 004 and Tommy Wisdom XKC 005, which has been mentioned above already. With this pastel green car (registration MDU 212) he finished sixth in the 1952 sports car Grand Prix

The practical cockpit of an XK 120 C. *(Schön)*

Above: Norman Dewis, Jaguar test driver since 1952, greatly influenced the further development of the XK 120 C. *(J)*

Left: The XK 120 with its unlucky "droop snoot" for the 1952 Le Mans race. *(S)*

of Monaco. Dr. Giuseppe Farina, the most famous Ferrari works driver of the period, was also interested in the car and attempted to purchase one. Jaguar was aware, of course, that he acted as front man for the curious Ferrari engineers, but the company nevertheless sold XKC 032 to him.

In April 1953 Norman Dewis competed at Jabbeke in XKC 012 and achieved a maximum speed of 148 miles per hour. This was to some degree thanks to three Weber carburetors tried before by John Heath in his HWM racing car and then ardently recommended to Harry Weslake. Jaguar showed its thankfulness by awarding HWM full Jaguar dealer status.

In 1953 the XK 120 C again took part in the Le Mans race. One of the cars entered (XKC 047) was destroyed in a road accident. So XKC 012 was quickly transferred to Le Mans where it was transformed to the specification and chassis number of the damaged car, including the rubber bag fuel tank. With Roger Laurent/de Tornaco as drivers, the car finished in ninth place. Tony Rolt/Duncan Hamilton drove the winning XKC 051 (Registration 774 RW, average speed 105.85 miles per hour), while Stirling Moss/Peter Walker finished second in XKC 053, and Peter Whitehead/Ian Stewart took fourth in XKC 052. For the first time ever the race had been won with an average of more than 100 miles per hour.

Also in 1953:

- Whitehead/Stewart won at Reims with an average speed of 105.45 miles per hour in the now 12-hour race
- At Sebring, S. Johnston/R. Wilder finished third
- Moss/Rolt again retired in the Mille Miglia
- Scott-Douglas/G. Gale of Ecurie Ecosse came in second behind Hawthorn/Farina's Ferrari in the Spa 24-hour race
- I. Stewart/B. Dickson finished third in the Goodwood nine hours, while Moss/Walker and Rolt/Hamilton retired
- In the first 1,000-kilometer race on the Nürburgring, Ian Stewart/Roy Salvadori finished second while Jimmy Stewart/J. Lawrence were sixth and Roger Laurent/Olivier Gendebien in XKC 047 retired
- Ian Stewart won the seven-hour race at Ibsley with Jimmy Stewart third
- At Charterhall Ninian Sanderson finished second, followed by Jimmy Stewart
- In the West Essex Sports Car Race in May, the XK 120 C finished second and third with the same drivers as at Charterhall, while in the June race Ian Stewart won from J. Lawrence and O'Moore, the latter in a HWM-Jaguar
- Ian Stewart, J. Lawrence, and Scott-Douglas won the team prize in the Leinster Trophy race
- Ian and Jimmy Stewart finished second and third in the Charterhall international race
- J. Kelly finished second in the Wakefield Trophy Race at Curragh
- Peter Walker and le Gallais, with his special, won the sports car and racing car classes in the Prescott hillclimb
- Simone finished second in class at the Montlhéry Coupe du Salon, while A. Hug in an XK 120 won his class there
- Toward the end of the season the Dundrod Race had a thrilling finish when the leading XK 120 C of Moss and Walker retired just before flag. Without hesitation, Moss pushed the car past the line and finished fourth. This was sufficient to capture second place for Jaguar in the newly established FIA European Championship

In 1954:

- Jimmy Stewart finished second in the Castle Combe Sports Car Race
- Jimmy Stewart won the Easter Monday race at Goodwood from Tony Rolt
- Jimmy Stewart also won both the Ibsley Sports Car and Formula Libre races (both from Sanderson)
- At Goodwood Jimmy Stewart won the Johnson Challenge Trophy, followed by Sanderson and G. Dunham. In the sports car handicap race run there the same day, M. W. Head finished third and "Dick" Protheroe won in an XK 120
- Walker finished the International Sports Car Race at Silverstone third in the sports car class
- In the Wakefield Trophy Race at Curragh, Hamilton finished second and Kelly third
- At Zandvoort Sanderson/Laurent were second behind a Cooper-Bristol
- E. Erickson finished second in the National Capitol Races held in Washington, D.C.
- In Buenos Aires Jimmy Stewart retired while F. C. Cranwell and Scott-Douglas/Sanderson captured third and fourth places

Above left: William Lyons' famous "Brontosaurus." *(S)*

Top: The last XK 120 C was the prototype for a new generation of racing cars. *(S)*

Above: Phil Weaver, Peter Sargent, Stirling Moss, and Frank Rainbow. *(S)*

Below left: The same car in side elevation. *(S)*

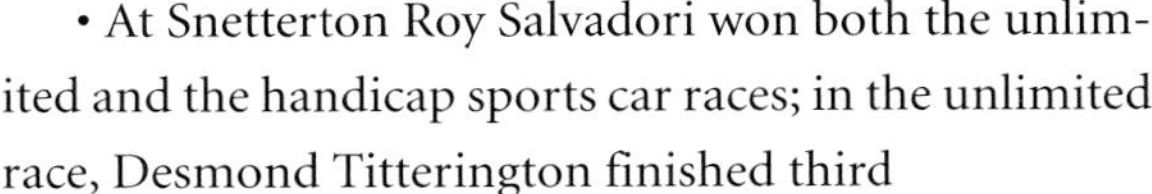

• At Snetterton Roy Salvadori won both the unlimited and the handicap sports car races; in the unlimited race, Desmond Titterington finished third

• At Oulton Park Titterington won from Sanderson

• In the Empire Trophy Race, also run at Oulton Park, Hamilton was fourth

• Salvadori and Titterington finished first and fourth in the September race at Goodwood

• Hamilton won at Aintree, where Jimmy Stewart finished third

• J. Kelly won at Wicklow

• M. W. Head finished second in the international sports car race at Snetterton

• At Charterhall, Salvadori and Sanderson achieved a 1–2 win

• At Watkins Glen, M. R. J. Wyllie won from Walt Hansgen in a special with a Jaguar engine

• The year ended with a third for D. Margulies at Brands Hatch on Boxing Day (The following year, W. A. Scott-Brown was to achieve the same result in a similar car.)

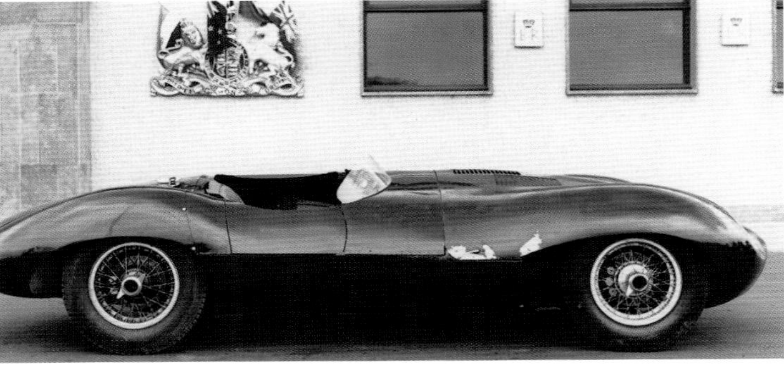

In 1955: Margulies' victory in the Sardinian Trophy Race was remarkable, as was his seventh place in the Nürburgring race. Even in 1957 the XK 120 C still achieved wins—the two class wins of J. Bekaert and P. M. Salmon in the Welsh National Spring Meeting.

For Goldie Gardner—he has been mentioned above for the world record he achieved using Jaguar's four-cylinder engine—a rather bulky but obviously very aerodynamic one-off was made. It was based on the XK 120 C. Lyons was involved in the styling, but the car was not a beauty. It was soon known as the "Brontosaurus," and Norman Dewis tested it extensively in late 1953. Thereafter it was not used any more, apart from some inspired test drives by the chairman in his plant. Later it was scrapped.

A version of the XK 120 C was to have a future, however. These changes led to a completely new design. Its unit body, with a tubular frame under the large hood and along the propshaft, resembled the latest Alfa Romeo sports racing car called "Disco Volante," and indeed, it looked a bit like a flying saucer. At the time it was thought that this would be a particularly aerodynamic shape, although its drag coefficient of exactly 0.5 was disappointing. This car became known as the D-Type, D being the next letter in the alphabet, and not denoting the car's disc brakes, with which late C-Types had already been equipped.

Top: Preparing D-Types for the race at Le Mans. *(S)*

Above: C is followed by D—this is the 1954 D-Type. *(Schön)*

Above right: The first genuine D-Type, still unpainted, during test driving at Le Mans under the eyes of Lofty England. Still nobody had recognized that the registration number on the car was not identical to that on its papers. *(S)*

With better weather protection and a lower point of gravity than the XK 120 C, the prototype underwent tests at Le Mans in 1953. At Jabbeke, Norman Dewis achieved nearly 180 miles per hour with this prototype (only slightly faster than the aerodynamically optimized XK 120), despite its engine not running properly at full throttle. Soon this car achieved a lap record at MIRA, a proving ground established in 1946 by SMMT and the British government at Lindley near Coventry. In the works the prototype was called the "light alloy car" because most of its parts were from aluminum. Rather late in its prototype stage the car was allocated Chassis No. XKC 201. For most people it was (and is) XKC 054, as if the XK 120 C numbering had been continued.

The D-Type had low profile radial tires of the better-wearing Stabilia type that Dunlop had developed especially for Jaguar. Just like the disc brake, these tires were developed under Joe Wright of Dunlop. They were mounted on light alloy steel wheels that incorporated holes for better brake cooling. Dry sump lubrication ensured better oil supply under racing conditions and allowed the engine to be mounted lower in the frame. This allowed a lower body profile and thus helped aerodynamics. Injection systems developed by Lucas and by S.U. were tested, but the fuel pumps suffered from the heat of the returning fuel. The injection system was first used in a race by XKD 601 at Sebring on March 24, 1956.

In the spring of 1954, the brand new D-Type (with the misleading Chassis No. XKC 401) managed to break the Le Mans lap record previously held by Ascari's 4.5-liter Ferrari by no less than five seconds. In the June race, however, Tony Rolt/Duncan Hamilton (chassis XKC 402, registration OKV 1) unluckily finished second, only 105 seconds behind the Trintignant/Gonzales Ferrari. The Jaguar was hindered by debris in the fuel. Roger Laurent/Jacques Swaters were fourth, driving the famous C-Type XKC 047 that had been ninth the year before. Two further D-Types retired. These were Moss/Walker in XKC 403 (registration OKV 2), and Whitehead/Wharton in XKC 404 (OKV 3). At Reims a satisfying 1-2-4 finish followed for the D-Type (Peter Whitehead/Ken Wharton, Rolt/Hamilton, and Laurent/Swaters)—most impressive for a brand new racing car! In the Tourist Trophy Race, however, all three D-Types retired (Rolt/Hamilton,

Whitehead/Wharton, and Moss/Walker, the latter with a 2.5-liter XK engine). William Lyons incurred further mishap when, during loading at the Belfast port, a heavy container fell onto his private Mark VII. Nevertheless, Jaguar finished second in the British Sports Car Championship.

In the following year (1955) the D-Type got larger inlet and exhaust valves for Le Mans. Later, these would be made even larger, up to 2 2/32 and 1 11/16 inches. In order to provide sufficient space above the relatively compact combustion chambers of the long-stroke engine, the exhaust valves had to be inclined further, to 40 degrees from the cylinder axis.

The magnesium alloy that had been used for the front tubular frame since the C/D prototype was replaced with steel for ease of repair. In this case a particularly stiff material was procured from Reynolds (531), which was also used for motorcycle frames. This was the first time that the D-Types were not shipped to Le Mans, but instead crossed the Channel by airplane. XKD 505, with an aerodynamic "long nose" (registration 774 RW) and drivers Ivor Bueb and Mike Hawthorn won the race with an average speed of 107 miles per hour. Hawthorn had just replaced Stirling Moss at Jaguar after having driven a Briggs Cunningham D-Type at an average of 79 miles per hour in the Sebring 12 Hours to achieve a much-publicized win over Ferrari. At Le Mans, Claes and Swaters (Equipe Francorchamps) were third in XKD 503, but Rolt/Hamilton (XKD 506, registration 032 RW), Beauman/Dewis (XKD 508, registration 194 WK),

In 1955 Mike Hawthorn and Ivor Bueb managed the first victory at Le Mans for the D-Type. *(S)*

and Spear/Walters (XKD 507) retired. Tony Rolt's racing career was nearing its end, and in the following year he worked as an engineer for Ferguson, who in the 1960s created the four-wheel drive and antilock brakes of the Jensen Interceptor.

The 1955 Le Mans race was controversial for the epic accident that occurred in front of the pits. During the battle against Fangio and his Mercedes-Benz 300 SLR, which was equipped with a spectacular air brake that operated by the trunk lid opening backward, Hawthorn decelerated for a pit stop after overtaking a slower Austin-Healey. The Austin-Healey consequently veered to the left, and Pierre Levegh, who was approaching very quickly in another Mercedes-Benz, could not avoid the Healey. His car launched into the crowd and exploded, causing more than 80 deaths. Mercedes-Benz withdrew its cars from the race later in the evening. Hawthorn needed some persuasion from England to continue the race. Despite some early accusations, he was not responsible for the gruesome accident.

For Lyons the race also brought a personal tragedy. His 25-year-old son, John, who just had joined his father's company and occasionally raced his XK 120, was involved in a head-on collision on the road en route to Le Mans. The cause of this accident remained unclear; despite his Continental experience, he may have been in a hurry when he tried to pass oncoming traffic on the left side, which had fatal consequences in France, where cars drive on the right side of the road. It was Lofty England's duty to inform Lyons of his son's death. John would not have wanted the Jaguars to be withdrawn from the race, and so they were not. Having lost his only son, Lyons now was without an heir for his company—a stroke of fate he had in common with other famous car manufacturers like Ettore Bugatti and Enzo Ferrari, whose sons Jean and Alfredino also died rather young.

Jaguar only entered the D-Type in one more event in 1955, the Tourist Trophy at Dundrod. For this race XKD 505 got an independent rear suspension, but this car did not start.

Also in 1955:

• Hamilton won the sports car class in the Coupe de Paris race at Montlhéry

Preparing for the 1956 Le Mans race. *(S)*

• Hamilton finished third in the Easter Monday race at Goodwood

• In the Whitsun sports car race at Goodwood, Hamilton won from Berry while Protheroe's XK 120 C finished third

• In the Johnson Challenge Trophy races at Goodwood, Hamilton won again while Protheroe's XK 120 C finished third

• M. W. Head won the Helsinki sports car race from Lincoln

• Titterington won the Ulster Trophy Race from W. T. Smith in—like Lincoln in Helsinki—an XK 120 C

• Hamilton also was third in the Grand Prix of Portugal at Oporto

• At Snetterton, Titterington was third in the 24-hour Formula Libre race and won the sports car race from Sanderson and W. T. Smith (the latter in an XK 120 C)

• Sanderson and Titterington achieved a 1-2 finish at the Aintree sports car race

• Hamilton and Head won at Silverstone race followed by J. Barber in an XK 120 C

• In the Silverstone Sports Car Race, Rolt was third, followed by Hawthorn, Hamilton and Titterington

• At Aintree, Hawthorn was fifth behind the Aston Martins, followed by Sanderson

• Titterington won the Charterhall Meeting

• In the Goodwood Nine-Hour Race Titterington/Sanderson were second

• Briggs Cunningham intensified his Jaguar racing efforts in the United States, where Sherwood Johnston won the Watkins Glen and Hagerstown races, while Cunningham himself finished second at Elkhart Lake behind Phil Hill's Ferrari

• Sherwood Johnston, at the Bahamas' Governor's Trophy Race, and Hamilton, at the Dakar Grand Prix, captured third places

The following year the Le Mans race was delayed about two months. Following the tragedy of the previous year the pit area was rebuilt with an eye toward improved safety. Therefore, Reims came first, a race that by now had established itself as a "little Le Mans." D-Types finished 1-2-3-4 (Hamilton/Bueb, Hawthorn/Frère, Titterington/Fairman, and Ron Flockhart/Ninian Sanderson, the latter two teams from Ecurie Ecosse). During the race Duncan Hamilton, driving the winning car, had ignored England's "slow" signs and set a new lap record instead. At the end of the race England sacked him for his disobedience.

For the 1956 Le Mans race, full-width windshields were obligatory and gasoline consumption was restricted by limiting the fuel tank capacity to 130 liters and prohibiting refueling before the 35th lap. The nearly standard XK 140 of Peter Bolton and Bob Walshaw was wrongly disqualified for breaking this rule in the 21st hour of the race while lying in 12th position, an unbelievable placing for a mere road car in this toughest of races. The D-Types entered had "long" noses and one had fuel injection. Flockhart/Sanderson (XKD 501, registration MWS 301) won with an average speed of 105 miles per hour (a little less than the winners in the year before), while Jacques Swaters/Freddy Rousselle of Equipe Nationale Belge (XKD 573, registration 164 WK) finished fourth. Hawthorn/Bueb (XKD 605, registration 393 RW) were sixth, but Fairman/Wharton (XKD 602, registration 351 RW) and Frère/Titterington (XKD 603, registration 774 RW) retired after accidents. XKD 606 suffered an accident while being driven by Desmond Titterington in practice and thus did not start the race.

Despite Malcolm Sayer's sketches of a Grand Prix racing car, Jaguar announced its withdrawal from international racing on October 13, 1956—a step deeply regretted by many racing enthusiasts. The reason given was that a new racing car would have to be designed in order to keep ahead in the next racing

In 1956 long and short nose D-Types were at the start at Le Mans. *(S)*

Ron Flockhart and Ninian Sanderson won the Le Mans race in 1956. *(S)*

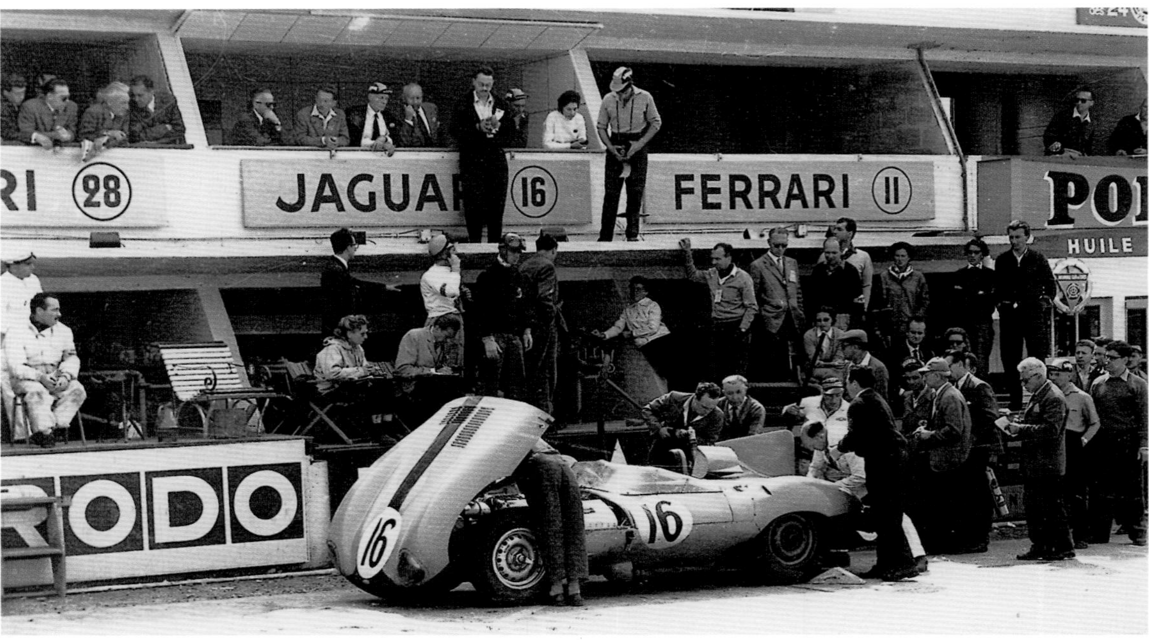

D-Type of Equipe Nationale Belge driven by Frère/Rousselle in the 1957 Le Mans 24 Hours. *(S)*

season, and that this could not be done with Jaguar's resources without neglecting the passenger car operation. The three works D-Types were sold to Ecurie Ecosse. Jaguar expressly said that no decision had been made whether to return to racing in 1958, but in the end, the break lasted about 20 years. Phil Weaver and his competition shop, which now was renamed the prototype shop, still took on interesting projects, like a fiberglass body for XKD 544—a challenge, as this was essentially a monocoque design. Engineering chief William Heynes also regretted the withdrawal from racing as this had helped him hire a qualified and dedicated team. During a lecture in 1976, Bob Berry lamented that the pleasure he took in looking after a team of racing drivers was long since lost.

In retrospect Jaguar rightly had already extracted the maximum possible publicity out of their racing efforts while devoting a minimum of technical development. (Meaning that as many standard production parts as possible were used on the racing cars.) The gain in prestige Jaguar experienced during the early 1950s could never have been achieved with advertisements alone.

Even during the period of factory support, drivers and private teams usually—with the exceptions of Le Mans and, since 1951, Reims—raced on their own dime. Thus, the public happily recognized that this withdrawal did not mean the absence of Jaguars from racetracks. To the contrary. At Sebring in the United States, the D-Type now started for the first time with an enlarged 3.8-liter engine with 270 horsepower (Hawthorn/Bueb, third behind two Maseratis). Also in 1957 Ecurie Ecosse won the 24 Hours of Le Mans, a brilliant 1-2-3-4 sweep for Jaguar with Flockhart/Bueb (XKD 606, registration 376 SG, 3.8-liter, average 114 miles per hour), Sanderson/Lawrence (XKD 603, registration 341 SG), Los Amigos Lucas/Jean-Marie Brussin ("Mary," XKD 513, registration 6478 AT 69) and Frère/Rousselle (Equipe Nationale Belge, XKD 573, registration NKV 479). Last of the successful D-Types in this race were sixth-place finishers J. M. Hamilton/Masten Gregory with XKD 601 (registration 2 CPG, 3.8-liter). On the salt flats of Bonneville, the D-Type did its highest ever officially confirmed speed, 185 miles per hour. In the Buenos Aires 1,000-kilometer race, Sanderson/Mieres (Ecurie Ecosse) finished fourth behind Ferrari and Maserati, but Flockhart retired in the Mille Miglia once again. The same day (May 12) at Spa, H. Taylor and Rousselle finished third and fourth behind two brand new Aston Martin DBR 1s. At Monza, however, Fairman (3.8-liter), Lawrence, and Sanderson were fourth, fifth, and sixth. At the Nürburgring, Flockhart/Bueb only achieved seventh. In the Goodwood Trophy Race, Taylor was third behind Archie Scott-Brown in a Lister-Jaguar and Jack Brabham in a Tojeiro-Jaguar. J. Bekaert/Mould won the Snetterton 12-hour race, and Walt Hansgen became U.S. sports car champion in a D-Type.

The D-Type's track record continued into 1958. For the Le Mans race the engine capacity had to be reduced to 3 liters, and all cars entered retired (Hamilton/Bueb

Among the specials with Jaguar engines, the Lister was the most famous. *(Schön)*

XKD 513 at Le Mans. *(S)*

The functional styling of the D-Type is aesthetically pleasing as well. *(Schön)*

Right: This elegant badge explains the identity of a rare racing car. *(Schön)*

Right above: Ecurie Ecosse D-Type with seat cushions covered in tartan. *(Schön)*

Below: The eye-catching engine of the D-Type, in this case perfectly restored. *(Schön)*

Right below: The Tojeiro's interior is more functional than comfortable. *(Schön)*

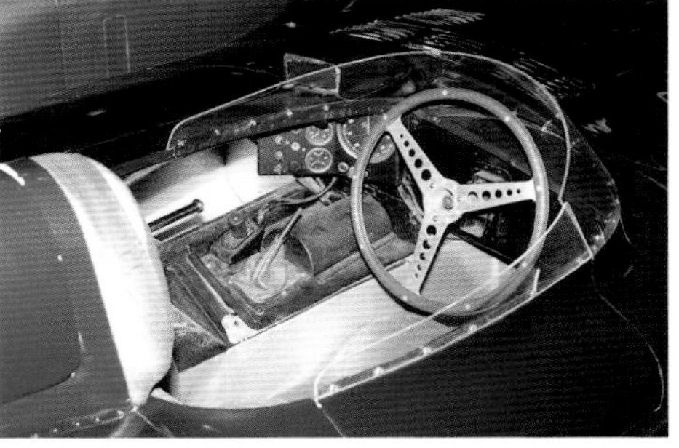

The interior of the D-Type is totally different from its predecessor. *(Schön)*

From top: This is the crest under which the D-Type achieved many racing successes. *(Schön)*

The Tojeiro was remarkably elegant; it also had an XK engine under its hood. *(Schön)*

This is the famous, aerodynamically efficient long nose of the later works racing D-Types. *(Schön)*

A D-Type works racing car with the long nose and the rear fin to provide directional stability at high speeds. *(J)*

The D-Type is only rarely seen in the Italian racing color. *(Schön)*

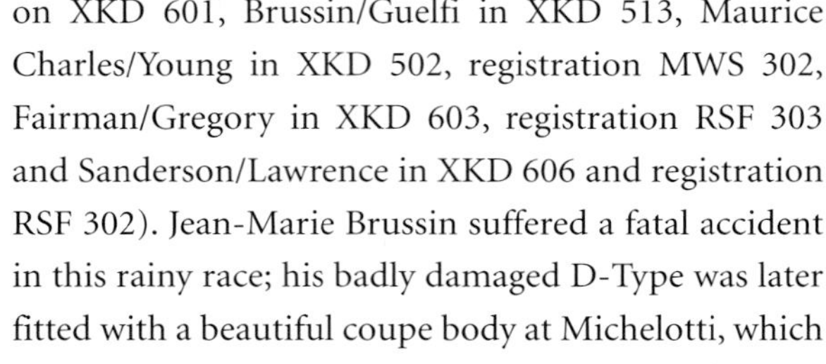

on XKD 601, Brussin/Guelfi in XKD 513, Maurice Charles/Young in XKD 502, registration MWS 302, Fairman/Gregory in XKD 603, registration RSF 303 and Sanderson/Lawrence in XKD 606 and registration RSF 302). Jean-Marie Brussin suffered a fatal accident in this rainy race; his badly damaged D-Type was later fitted with a beautiful coupe body at Michelotti, which survives to this day, but on an E-Type chassis. Gregory/Flockhart, Bueb/Sanderson, and Fairman/ Lawrence started 3-liter D-Types at the Nürburgring, but again, only 7th place was reached by the latter team. At Monza, Bueb came home 9th place with his 3.4-liter D-Type, while Fairman and Gregory finished 11th and 12th. Moss won the sports car Grand Prix race at Silverstone

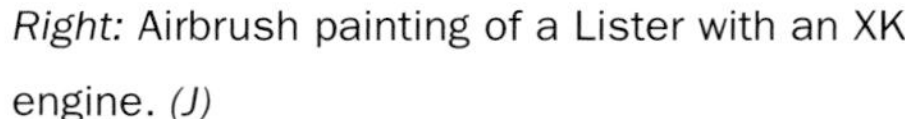

Right: Airbrush painting of a Lister with an XK engine. *(J)*

With small bumpers and a real glass windshield, the XK-SS was a ferocious sports car. *(Schön)*

in a Lister-Jaguar 3.8-liter. Bueb followed in fourth in a Tojeiro-Jaguar and Innes Ireland in a D-Type finished 9th. Hamilton took 3rd in the Sussex Trophy Race at Goodwood, as did B. Krause with a 3.8-liter D-Type at Riverside and W. Pitt in the Melbourne Veteran TT. Walt Hansgen again won the U.S. sports car championship, this time in a Lister-Jaguar.

XKD 603 again took part in the 1959 Le Mans race (drivers Innes Ireland/Masten Gregory) but again retired. However, the participation of one car in four editions of this demanding endurance race is most remarkable. In 1960 XKD 606 (registration RSF 301) with Flockhart/Halford was the last D-Type to race at Le Mans, and it also retired. The XK engine had gained a legendary reputation in the C- and D-Types and was the engine of choice for many sports prototype manufacturers. Some such artifacts have been mentioned in the lists of honor above. In 1956, a two-year-old Cooper with an XK 120 C engine started at Le Mans but soon retired. Later, Brian Lister adorned his sports cars with Jaguar engines and started them at Le Mans (1958 with Rousselle/Dubois and 1959 with Bueb/Halford and Hansgen/Blond). In 1959, the Tojeiro sports car also took part with Flockhart/Lawrence driving. The car was made by John Tojeiro, who had designed the A.C. chassis.

Some decades later a D-Type became the first Jaguar to be sold for more than £1 million. This happened at an auction at Monte Carlo on May 3, 1989, during a time when classic car prices exploded.

Above: The taillights of the XK-SS were shared with the XK 140. *(Schön)*

Left: The sporting lines of the XK-SS remained rare, as the car was only manufactured for a month. *(J)*

Below left: In this XK-SS, the XK engine and Weber carburetors combine to create a powerful machine. *(Schön)*

The cockpit of an XK-SS. *(Schön)*

By the end of 1956 Jaguar had no further use for the D-Type production facilities. Bob Blake, a gifted coachbuilder from America who had made nearly all the bodies for Briggs Cunningham's cars, remembered that Cunningham once had a D-Type mildly modified for road use and then tried unsuccessfully to get it homologated by the Sports Car Club of America (SCCA) as a production sports car. Blake used this inspiration to modify the D-Type into a super sports car for road use by adding a roof. Duncan Hamilton had a similar idea and had his D-Type modified this way to make it saleable. Whether Blake or Hamilton prompted Jaguar to produce something similar is an open question, but on January 21, 1957, the XK-SS was introduced. Sixteen were built during the following weeks. The car's somewhat awkward windshield was taken from a Ford Consul, a bread-and-butter car. The car not only was faster than the Mercedes-Benz 300 SL, but at $6,900 it was also less expensive! As a tailor-made, long-distance high-performance car, the D-Type already offered much more comfort than the usual racing car of the period. With even more wind protection from the new windshield, the XK-SS was a pleasure to drive in normal traffic.

Jaguar's offering for the normal sports car buyer of the mid-1950s, the XK 140, was unveiled at the Earls Court Motor Show on October 15, 1954. It was offered in the same three body variants as its not very different predecessor, the XK 120, of which the remaining stock was sold late in 1954 at a considerable discount. The engine in the XK 140 was enhanced to 190 horsepower or, with the help of the C-type cylinder head, 210 horsepower. The latter was designated by the "S" chassis number prefix instead of the "A," and was available only as XK 140 S.E. or—for some inexplicable reason—XK 140 M in the United States. The engine was moved 3 inches forward in the chassis, which made a larger interior possible, particularly in the footwells, and the steering was changed to rack and pinion. Solid bumpers at both ends of the car were a requirement

Despite its luggage rack the XK-SS did not offer much space for touring. *(S)*

Right: D-Type plus some comfort is the XK-SS. *(J)*

The unforgettable face of a racing car for the street. *(S)*

Above: 1954 Jaguar XK 140 open two-seater. *(Schönborn archive)*

Far left: Jaguar XK 140 fixed head coupe, at the time a much sought-after touring car, now a bit forgotten. *(S)*

Left: XK 140 fixed head and drophead coupes had two occasional seats in the rear. *(S)*

Opposite above: 1954 Jaguar XK 140 drophead coupe. *(Schönborn archive)*

Opposite below: 1954 Jaguar XK 140 fixed head coupe. *(Schönborn archive)*

American Raymond Loewy had his own idea of a Jaguar sports car in 1955. *(S)*

Left: Italian Michelotti had ideas that led to a completely different style. *(S)*

Below: Among the three body styles of the XK 140, the drophead coupe is particularly sought after. *(J)*

from the U.S. clientele to counter the less careful drivers of typical American sedans. The car's other chrome ornamentation—its grille—may also be attributed to American taste. Cast in one piece together with its seven bars, the grille was not universally acclaimed. Both coupes now had two tiny seats in the rear.

The sporting career of the XK 140 was, of course, overshadowed by the D-Type. But Ian Appleyard relied on one with the registration VUB 140 during his rare returns to rallying, such as the RAC Rally of 1956 where he finished second overall. Baillie and Jopp started in 1957 at Reims, when only production cars were admitted, but they were not very successful; even the little Alfa Romeo Giulietta proved to be quicker.

To explain why there was no XK 130, *Jaguar World*, a magazine created by Paul Skilleter in 1988, created the following legend: In his usual cautiousness, Skilleter said, Lyons had ordered another lightweight XK 120 for Le Mans and called the car XK 130. During assembly a tie-pin had dropped into one of the cylinders. As this had remained undiscovered, it caused severe damage when the engine was run. The engine was saved by

boring that cylinder out to 87mm and using a piston of the American Tucker (a very advanced sedan with rear-mounted engine of the late 1940s, which was loved by the press, but not accepted by the market). A credulous reader contacted Lofty England himself for further detail. He was told that the larger cylinder was then used only as a supercharger for the other five—now this reader realized that he had been April fooled!

A more serious request was that of Colonel Rixon Bucknall, who asked for an XK 140 chassis without body in the mid-1950s. He had a coachbuilt two-seater touring body made for it, in which every part that could be of use for his epic continental tours—down to an umbrella—had its place, and each of those items had provisions to be safely fixed so that they could not rattle. This truly unique vehicle with its modified SS grille still exists in an enthusiast's collection.

At the Motor Show in 1954, the XK 140 was accompanied by a revision of the Mark VII with the 190-horsepower engine of the XK 140, distinguished with the suffix "M" to its name all over the world. A dark red or "claret" (a color used for royal vehicles

Above: The wonderful curves of the XK 140, in this case combined with a non-original radiator mascot. *(Twelbeck)*

Below: An impressive XK 140 fixed head coupe with some of its open siblings. *(Schön)*

Above left: Most attractive even in real life is the XK 140, particularly with such a registration number. *(Schön)*

Above right: Still more lavish than in its predecessors are the interiors of the XK 140 fixed head and drophead coupes. *(Schön)*

Above: Mark VII with elegant 1954 styling from Ghia-Aigle. *(S)*

Right: The fog lamps make the difference: 1954 Mark VII M. *(Schön)*

The late Queen Elizabeth, the Queen Mother, had a Jaguar Mark VII M to which the Mark VIII insignia were later added. *(Schön)*

during Victorian times) example of the Mark VII M was prepared for the then Queen Mother Elizabeth, after a similar order for a Mark V had not materialized. The car (Chassis No. 727554) had an automatic transmission, because Her Royal Highness wished to drive the car herself occasionally. It also had the traditional royal lion mascot and an additional horn-push on the dashboard. The car was later modified to incorporate the Mark IX appearance and brakes. Popular Queen Mum loved the car and used it often; in 1974 it was returned to Jaguar, where it is still proudly kept.

The Mark VII M again played a prominent role in rallies, such as SUM 7 of Pat and Ian Appleyard, PWK 700 of Ronald Adams/A. T. MacMillen, and PWK 701 of Cecil Vard. These three took part in the Monte Carlo Rally of 1955, where they gained the Faroux Team Prize. Adams was the best of the team, only finishing eighth, while Appleyard lost a core plug and thus only placed 83rd. L. S. Stross/K. F. Pointing won the large production car class of the RAC Rally and the team prize in the Liège-Rome-Liège Rally. J. P. Boardman/J. W. Whitworth scored a class win in the Tulip Rally. The Mark VII also dominated the production car race at Silverstone, which Hawthorn won with good old LWK 343 from Jimmy Stewart (PWK 700) and Desmond Titterington (PWK 701). Appleyard again had bad luck and retired in a cloud of steam.

In 1956 Jaguar finally won the Monte Carlo Rally with drivers Ronnie Adams/Frank Bigger/Derek Johnston in the works-prepared PWK 700. Reg and Joan Mansbridge/P. Stramson (OVC 69) and Cecil Vard/Arthur Jolley/Jimmy Millard (LWK 343) finished much further down the field; the latter was involved in an accident but helped to score third among the teams. Winning Le Mans and Monte Carlo in the same year had never before been achieved by one make, and it's possible that reaching this summit may have contributed to Jaguar's decision to withdraw from racing while at the top. In this remarkable 1956 season Jaguar even achieved some success in the Mille Miglia, with Guyot's production sedan class win in a Mark VII. Bueb won at Silverstone with an average of 80.01 miles per hour, with Frère third, and Hamilton (in a 2.4-liter) in fourth position. Toward the end of the season R. W. Russell scored a class win in the National Rally.

Above: Jaguar's mightiest engine was this 9-liter V-8. *(S)*

Left: The hubcaps and the rear bumpers extended toward the spats are the telltales of the Mark VII M. *(S)*

8

UNITARY CONSTRUCTION

Many auto manufacturers had switched to unitary construction around this time. This style of car design dispensed with the heavy, bulky chassis frame and thus made new styling ideas possible, which Lyons liked. In order not to put his whole company at risk, it seemed advisable to try out the new unitary construction with a type of car to be added to the existing Jaguar range, rather than by replacing an existing model. Engineering calculations for structures as complex as a car body were still not very developed, so a smaller sedan than the typical Jaguar seemed to be the right choice. This car would aim at the sort of clientele that had been ignored by Jaguar since the demise of the 1.5-liter. In particular the XK four-cylinder—the development of which already had been completed—seemed to be the right engine for such a car. At Pressed Steel this project was called the "Utah."

As the new car aimed at the sporting driver with a family, Lyons took his inspirations from the XK sports car. Adding two doors and seats to this beautiful vehicle showed what the new car would look like in principle. The engineering details were left to Pressed Steel. Like many contemporaries, they were somewhat overcautious, and so the elegance of the initial idea fell victim to large roof pillars. To keep costs down, the door window frames were not chromed but instead were integral parts of the door skin, which did not help looks either. The suspension had to be reworked completely, as there was no chassis frame to which it could attach. For the front suspension a subframe was employed, and the torsion bars were replaced by coil springs, which could be mounted in the subframe. The engineers were not sure that the body would be stiff enough to bear the loads of the torsion bars. The live axle at the rear was mounted at the rear ends of leaf springs, the center and front of which were fixed to the floor of the body.

Unitary bodies have an unfortunate tendency to amplify like a drum any noise and vibration transferred via suspension and engine. William Heynes found a way to prevent this by insulating the suspension twice with rubber mountings. In the rear this caused some problems, and a perfect solution could only be found after a lot of experimental work. Jaguar eventually scrapped the original idea to put a four-cylinder in the car and instead remained faithful to the six-cylinder. However, they did reduce its capacity to less than 2.5 liters by shortening the stroke, as had happened occasionally for motor racing. The production of the four-cylinder would have cost only a little less per unit, but would have made stock-keeping much more expensive.

Jaguar did not spend much time testing the new 2.4-liter, as it was modestly named. It seems that only two prototypes were tested. Anyhow, Norman Dewis regretted that he had not had the opportunity for further testing and optimizing the car.

With the introduction of the 2.4-liter (now commonly called the Mark I), Jaguar's staff increased to nearly 4,000. The body-in-the-white came complete from Pressed Steel's Oxford plant at a price of £375. Whittaker, when negotiating the price, had surprised his opponent with the absurd idea that the price had to be 10 percent below the large sedans because the new body was 10 percent lower.

Top: An early 2.4-liter with its grille in the style of the XK 140. *(S)*

Above: Early prototype of the 2.4-liter with an XK 120 grille and Mark VII radiator mascot. *(S)*

Opposite: Grille and mascot of the Mark II. *(Schön)*

Top left: The trunk of the 2.4-liter. This retouched photograph shows no vertical bars along the number plate. *(S)*

Top right: The rear of the 2.4-liter also resembles Jaguar's sports cars. *(S)*

Above: Idealized drawing of a compact Jaguar—advertising the 2.4-liter in 1955. *(J)*

Assembly of the new sedan took place on a new line that had previously been used by Standard-Triumph. It moved 30 cars at the same time and would serve Jaguar for nearly 40 years! Its advantage over the previous trolley was its variable speed. At the end of the line, the completely assembled body was lowered onto the suspension.

The British press was delighted by both the concept and realization of the 2.4-liter. The noise suppression achieved after a lot of trying and testing was rated as good, and the hanging pedals were welcome. The gearbox was no longer up-to-date with its long throw, weak synchronization, and noisy lower gears. The testers recommended a higher tire pressure for improved roadholding. They also remarked that the car leaned spectacularly in fast bends, but this was harmless and passengers hardly noticed it. John Bolster of *Autosport* rated the 2.4-liter as the best car his magazine had ever tested. Although it was nearly as fast as the Mark VII, there was of course a demand for even better performance. From 1956 onward, Jaguar offered tuning kits to increase power output to up to 150 horsepower. In racing the 2.4-liter was not as successful as the Mark VII, although it was nearly as fast and competed in a lower class.

With the New Year's Honors List young Queen Elizabeth II honored Lyons for his export achievement and created him a Knight Bachelor, so that he now became *Sir* William. Lyons was somewhat afraid of official duties connected with this title, as he did not like giving public speeches. At last his patriotic attitude prevailed and he accepted the title; thereupon the royal family visited Jaguar in March 1956. The Duke of Edinburgh was most interested in the design office, and Prince Charles was given a 1:10 scale D-Type model. In the same year a 2.4-liter—full size, this one—was delivered to Prince George of Denmark.

In October 1956, the successor to the large sedan was unveiled, the Mark VIII. A curved chrome molding, duotone finish, and a recess in the rear wheel spats made the car look less bulky than its predecessor. The one-piece windshield returned, now slightly curved. The chrome frame around the grille became thicker, and a more traditional leaper replaced the growler-cum-wings mascot. As this now was mounted on the hood instead of the radiator cap, the leaper could be made slimmer at its base—thus the rear legs were now stretched, which gave a much better representation of a leaping jaguar.

In the 1957 Mobilgas Rally two such Mark VIIIs toured 10,500 miles round Australia. Mrs. Geordie Anderson/Bill Pitt/Jim Abercombie finished seventh behind six Volkswagens—who had the benefit of dealerships everywhere—while Dunning/Cash won the class for automatics. The Mark VIII was the first Jaguar that indicated the presence of this transmission with chromed letters on the trunk lid.

Everyday life was much less glamorous; still war damages had to be repaired. The Suez crisis resulted in additional gasoline rationing, and Jaguar was forced in November and December 1956 to a four-day workweek. On February 12, 1957, the tire store in the northern part of the plant caught fire and destroyed large parts of the assembly and testing area. The damage was estimated at £3.5 million. Although Bob Berry and others drove as many cars as possible out of the burning buildings before the fire brigade stopped this dangerous situation, 270 cars were lost. This included in particular the four D-Types that had remained with Jaguar, a client's car of the same type, and the body patterns for the model. Production of XK-SS, which had started only a month before, could never be resumed. The press was invited to witness the scrapping of the cars, which was done in order to prevent any damaged parts from being sold as original spares. As a combined effort of staff, suppliers, and other companies, it was possible to resume production within two weeks, partially in tents. After six weeks, normal production figures were reached again. Dunlop, for example, allowed Jaguar to use its former

Foleshill works for running in their engines. Before, the test beds had been attached to generators so that electrical energy was produced when the engines were run for two hours each.

In spite of this setback, Jaguar introduced a new model only two weeks after the fire. Sir William was forced to do so, as the public had already learned of his plan to put the 3.4-liter engine of his larger cars into the unitary body of the smaller Mark I sedan. The result, which Americans particularly had longed for, was unveiled on February 26, 1957. Briggs Cunningham, whose workshop in New York's Queens was by then integrated into Jaguar's dealer network, had already hired the nearby Alfred Momo Corporation to transplant the 3.4 into the 2.4's hull. Jaguar's 3.4-liter distinguished itself from its smaller sibling by the larger grille with slimmer chromed bars and recesses in the rear wheel spats. Customers who wished further ease of driving were offered an automatic transmission, available for the 2.4-liter as well from autumn 1957. When testing the 3.4-liter for *The Motor*, Christopher Jennings found the brakes inadequate in relation to the performance of the engine, which was soon countered by the availability of disc brakes. Further criticism concerned details of more interest for non-racing drivers: The ventilation was poor as long as the windows were closed, and more than four steering wheel turns from lock to lock seemed inconvenient.

The 3.4-liter was quite successful in racing and rallying, similar to the older Mark VII. In particular, fame was gained at the Tour de France Automobile, which from 1957 had a touring car class that suited the 3.4-liter ideally. That year, however, the 3.4-liter was not lucky, and none of the three cars made it to the finish (drivers were Hermano da Silva Ramos/Monnoyeur, Jopp/Baillie, and Consten/Renel). The sedan race at

Above: Even African governments had a demand for representative sedans and sometimes preferred unusual color combinations, as on these red and white examples. *(S)*

Left: The Mark VIII is adorned with a wonderful mascot. *(St)*

Right: The heavily chromed grille made the Mark VIII's face look different. *(S)*

Top: The interior of the 3.4-liter was not less well-equipped than its larger brothers. *(S)*

Above: The 3.4-liter anticipated the XK 150 grille. *(S)*

Above right: What remained after the ferocious fire at Browns Lane in 1957. *(S)*

As a journalist Paul Frère made the 3.4-liter known in many countries; here he is posing in the Alpine XK 120 "NUB 120," which he never drove at the time. *(St)*

Silverstone brought a 1-2-3 sweep for Hawthorn, Hamilton, and Bueb, while Scott-Brown retired and Flockhart in a 2.4-liter Coombs-prepared car finished fifth. The winner's car, by the way, was a 2.4-liter (Chassis No. 900007) upgraded to 3.4 liters.

In the 1958 Monte Carlo Rally—the previous year the rally had been canceled because of the Suez crisis—30 Jaguars were entered, but the best of them was Carris/Beziers who only finished 24th. In the RAC Rally, Brinkman in a 3.4-liter won his class. Ian Appleyard's last rally, the Tulip Rally, was not a success; his 3.4 retired after damage to the exhaust. Baillie/Jopp scored a third in the touring class in the Tour de France, while Sopwith/Goldthorpe suffered an accident, as did brothers Graham and Peter Whitehead, and Peter tragically lost his life. The March and July races at Snetterton were won by Sopwith, and Sir Gawaine Baillie won the sedan car race at Aintree from Flockhart, while the third 3.4-liter (Sopwith) retired with brake failure. P. Blond, in a 2.4-liter, scored a class win. Hawthorn also won the May sedan race at Silverstone (average 84.22 miles per hour) ahead of Sopwith and Flockhart, and in July Walt Hansgen also won there. Sopwith and Baillie scored a 1-2 finish at Brands Hatch, where later Baillie and Sears were also victorious. At Goodwood in May, Baillie finished second, and the Whitsun race ended with a 1-2-3 sweep by Hamilton, Sopwith, and Baillie, as did the Crystal Palace Race (Sopwith, Baillie, D. J. Uren). Sopwith also won the October races at Brands Hatch and Snetterton.

In 1959, Hermano da Silva Ramos/Jean Estager Noumours were overall winners in the Tour de France, and they earned the yellow ribbon. The 3.4-liter's racing career reached its climax with the Faroux Team Prize in the Monte Carlo Rally (George "Bobby" Parkes/Geoffrey Howarth/Arthur Senior in 8th position; Philip Walton/Michael Martin in 9th; Eric Brinkman/John Cuff in 37th; and Vernon Cooper/Geoff Baker in 56th). The spring races at Goodwood, Aintree, and Silverstone resulted in 1-2-3 finishes with drivers Bueb, Salvadori, and Baillie. Donald Morley again won the Tulip Rally, this time with navigator Barry Hercock, but Eric Brinkman/Frank Ward had to retire after an accident. Parkes/Senior just missed an Alpine Cup because they were a little bit too fast at the Stelvio. In the aforementioned RAC Rally with lots of snow, Bobby Parkes finished 5th in class. Plant/Heinemann won the Sestrière rally, and Walt Hansgen won the two-hour race at Sebring ahead of Phil Forno (also of the Cunningham team) in 3rd.

Late in 1957, the first test of a Jaguar was published in German's leading car magazine *Das Auto, Motor und Sport*. The piece was written by Paul Frère, who finished fourth at Le Mans that year (and later was to win the race with a Ferrari). Frère tested the 2.4-liter and 3.4-liter sedans. Despite winter conditions during the test, Frère reached 198 kilometers per hour (123 miles per hour). He praised the handling and the roadholding and asserted, "There is no true touring car that could beat the 3.4 liter on long distances and mixed roads. With all its power, the 3.4 liter is a true touring car with ample room for four or five persons and large doors. The springing is good, although the sports driver might appreciate more damping at the front. Driving comfort, particularly on the front seats, is excellent." To William Heynes' honor Frère added, "Sound damping is particularly good, and irritating drumming of the body is avoided altogether. With the eyes closed a passenger can hardly guess if the car is driven on medium tarmac or on pavé. Jaguar cars have always had excellently executed first-class equipment, and the 2.4 and 3.4 liter do live up to this tradition." There was only one minor criticism: "The fact that Jaguar Chief Sir William Lyons is a nonsmoker is revealed by the fact that the door key, if attached to the ignition key, dangles in the open ashtray." Frère resumed, "Finally it can be said that the 3.4 liter Jaguar represents among motor cars the iron fist in silken glove, and there are few touring cars as pleasing to the hottest sports car enthusiast as the latest Jaguar."

Jaguar's base of enthusiastic customers formed the Jaguar Drivers' Club (JDC), a rather late successor to the SS Car Club that had not survived the war. JDC enjoyed no direct link to Jaguar itself. From this group two other clubs, the now-defunct Jaguar Car Club and the Jaguar Enthusiasts' Club, evolved.

For the enthusiast, Jaguar had another ace in the sleeve, the successor to the XK 140, only two years old. The XK 150 as unveiled on May 22, 1957, had cautiously revised lines; Lyons had styled a completely new sports car but rejected it because of the high tooling cost. The fender was higher to give the XK styling more like that of a modern car with fully integrated fenders, an impression to which the broader hood added. The previous tooling for the fenders and hood could be used with minimal changes, which saved Sir William a lot of money. Despite the reluctant changes to the exterior, the interior offered much more comfort and space. The wheels hid the most important technical advance, as the disc brake that had been tried and tested in racing was now available for the first time on a road Jaguar. Officially only available in the S.E. models, it seems as if very few examples of the XK 150 left the factory with the old drum brakes. The engine of the S.E. was equipped with the torquey "B" head and still provided 210 miles per hour. Other than the coupes, the open two-seater was available only from early 1958 onward. At the same time a more powerful three-carburetor variant with a straight-port head of Claude Baily's design that produced a nominal 250 horsepower became available. This was the famous XK 150 S—it nearly had been designated CS according to Baily's proposal—which is a much sought-after rarity these days. The 150 was not often seen on racetracks: Brothers Peter and Graham Whitehead retired in one in the Tour de France, and in the Rest-and-be-Thankful hillclimb A. McCracken was fastest in the large sports car class with an XK 150 S (65.47 seconds). Eric Haddon/ Charles Vivian in a similar car won the 4-liter GT class in the Tulip Rally. In May and June 1960, Don Parker won at Snetterton and Oulton Park.

In mid-1958, Paul Frère tested the XK 150 fixed head coupe, again for *Das Auto, Motor und Sport*. Now the Belgian registration of the car was made visible, and this car also failed to break the 125-mile-per-hour barrier. "For British standards it seems like a little revolution that the dashboard is no longer covered with walnut veneer." Despite the importance of wooden appointments, Frère found a positive result: "Although there now are sports cars running even faster than the XK 150, there is hardly one that combines the

For the XK 140's successor Sir William Lyons had many ideas. *(S)*

This coupe seems to be more closely related to the 2.4-liter—another idea for an XK 140 successor? *(S)*

Even a convertible was taken into consideration; again the 15-inch wheels betray the close relationship with the smaller sedans. *(S)*

Below: Compared with the XK 140, the ultralow lines of the prototype become evident. *(S)*

performance that should do even for the most demanding driver with such a civilized behavior. Its price is still quite moderate. However, the question remains open what Jaguar could offer in the sports car class if instead of this sophisticated but 10 years old design, the experience gained in motor sport would be properly exploited." This was a question that would only be answered years later.

For the 1958 Motor Show, the Mark IX with disc brakes replaced the Mark VIII (the so-called Mark VIII b being the military version of the Mark IX without power steering and overdrive, but with manual gear change). It was supplied with an overbored, 3.8-liter variant of the XK engine with 220 horsepower. This became necessary despite earlier doubts whether the XK engine could accommodate an increase in capacity. Because American customers demanded more torque in order to regain dominance over the domestic sedans, dealer Alfred Momo in New York had experimented and shown that overboring of the XK engine was possible. The 3.8-liter engine could now also be ordered for the XK 150 as an option.

In the XK 150 S, the 3.8-liter engine with the straight port head was rated at 265 horsepower. This variant was distinguished with a chassis number prefix "T" but erroneously the first examples still bore the prefix "S" on the chassis. During development, the 3.8-liter block was prone to distortion due to the lack of cooling water between the cylinders. This was cured by slots between the upper endings of the bores. Before its official introduction, the XK 150 3.8 S scored a third place at Sebring for Mike Hawthorn/Ivor Bueb. A similar car (Chassis No. T 825146; due to a reading error it was called ISOS) was modified with a fastback body style by Eric Richardson so that he could travel with his family from England's south to weekend stays in the north. The owner's correspondence with the works shows that the 160-mile-per-hour speedo was not sufficient to cope with the car's improved performance! This car is still in existence.

One would think that these wonderful Jaguars sold like hot cakes, which generally was the case. But it was difficult to reach some customers in foreign countries because of import restrictions. In order to avoid such

As a fixed head coupe, the XK 150 may well have been the most practical of all XK variants—in this drawing the grille badge stems from the XK 140 for some reason. *(J)*

Above: For some time the drophead coupe was the only open variant of the XK 150. *(J)*

Below: The XK 150 fixed head coupe was well balanced and had an air of modernity. *(J)*

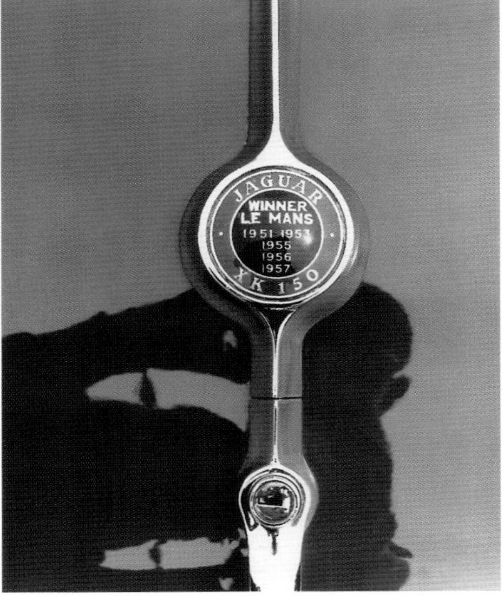

Top: Proudly, all Le Mans victories were listed on the back of each XK 150. *(S)*

Above: A brighter grin in the face of the XK 150. *(Schön)*

Below: Rear view of the XK 150 fixed head coupe, still with XK 140 taillights. *(S)*

Still in the style of the British Empire: The dashboard of the Mark IX. *(J)*

From top: Hidden behind this grille is a 3.8-liter XK engine—the 1958 Jaguar Mark IX. *(Schön)*

Discretion for military purposes: The partition for Jaguar's Mark VIII b. *(J)*

Later Mark IXs had larger taillights with separate lenses for the indicators. *(Schön)*

obstacles, Jaguar, on the initiative of importer Mario Padilla, decided to assemble cars in Mexico, where 152 2.4-liters and 62 3.4-liters were made. All the parts had been shipped from Coventry. Soon the assembly workshop, which was operated in cooperation with Mercedes-Benz, was nationalized. In November another assembly line, which was to remain operative much longer, started production in South Africa. Cars had been assembled in Ireland since 1949.

In Germany, the Jaguar was more or less nonexistent during the first postwar years. The Neumann Company in Berlin had been the importer in 1938, when they displayed an SS 100 at the Berlin show, but nothing further was heard of them. After the war, car magazines occasionally reported on Jaguar's legendary racing successes and on some exquisite special coachwork from Ghia, Pinin Farina, and the like. The German economic situation in general, the fact that only customers paying in foreign currencies were allowed to buy foreign cars like the Jaguar, and high import duties made sure that the Jaguar was not a common sight in German traffic. Until the late 1950s Jaguar did not manage to sell more than a few dozen cars per year in Germany; prices in deutsche marks were quoted from 1953 onward. For southern Germany, the dealer was Emil Frey in Zurich across the Swiss border, in connection with Wilhelm Speck at Freiburg. Apart from occasional activities from Overseas Motor Sales GmbH in Frankfurt, northern Germany was served exclusively by Fendler & Lüdemann in Hamburg, who imported their first Jaguar in 1954. Overseas Motor Sales had been founded by an officer of the British Rhine Army named Mayhill. At first he supplied only his colleagues, and not only with Jaguars. His business was located at a Frankfurt showroom.

A similar Jaguar source appeared in Düsseldorf, where many British soldiers were stationed. A small workshop called Birkelbach, which previously had specialized in two-stroke engines, gained a reputation. Jaguars came there for repair quite frequently. Because of trade restrictions, customers had to bring in spare parts themselves or have them handmade at Birkelbach. The business grew, and in 1949 was reorganized as Birkelbach & Unkrüer, who later sold new Jaguars that were shipped in along the Rhine river.

It was, however, due to the enthusiasm of young Peter Lindner that Jaguar started to sell better in later years. Legend has it that a garage was situated in the basement of his parents' home, and when he inherited the house after the premature death of his parents, he decided that he would become the Jaguar importer for Germany. Jaguar was skeptical but allowed him to import cars, at least for 1958. Lindner took his new venture, which included other British makes as well, very seriously. He started by taking over the Overseas Motor Sales showroom in Frankfurt. Sales figures rose steadily, and Lindner gained official importer status by 1961.

At this point, *Das Auto, Motor und Sport* introduced Jaguar to its readers with a long article by Dieter Korp, a German. It was titled "The Great Loners," and that was a precise description of Jaguar in Germany because, despite the competitive prices, only 420 Jaguars were registered in Germany by then, kept alive by just 13 garages. It was claimed that new Jaguars were delivered to Germany by airplane, but it seems more likely that Lindner simply drove the cars from the Düsseldorf port to Frankfurt. Customers were most interested in the 3.4-liter sedan. The maintenance usually carried out by Jaguar drivers was described in detail: The usual interval for greasing was an astonishing 1,200 miles, and the shock absorbers had to be replaced every 6,000 miles, which was deemed to be quite good, considering the weight and performance of the cars.

Back in England, Jaguar had the opportunity in 1959 to buy the Browns Lane Plant after GEC had left their block. Since 1951 Jaguar had used the plant on a lease basis.

A further boost to Jaguar's sales figures came from a revamped version of the compact unit-body sedan: the Mark II. It had its debut at Earls Court on October 2, 1959. It distinguished itself from the previous model with much larger windows and slim, fully chromed door window frames, an increased rear track, and the optional availability of the 3.8-liter engine with the "B" head, as in the Mark IX. The new rear axle required the rear spats to be revised so that the wheels would not scrub. Pressed Steel use a jack to push the spats outward

A particularly nice 1958 XK 150 open two-seater 3.4-liter S. *(Schön)*

Another XK 150 open two-seater. *(J)*

Right: Still more practical than the fixed head coupe was the fastback special called ISOS. *(Schön)*

Below: One of the most abundant Jaguar sedans was the Mark IX. *(J)*

Right: Scandinavia appreciated the Mark II—this is the garage of Danish importer Erik Sommer. *(J)*

to make them fit—and that was the pattern for Pressed Steel, no drawings at all!

For its introduction in the United States at the 1960 New York Auto Show, a white Mark II with white leather had all of its chrome parts covered in genuine gold. The importer presented the car alongside a lady with a golden gown wearing a golden tiara that once was Napoleon's gift to his beloved Josèphine. The tiara contained more than a thousand diamonds! Unfortunately the car was changed to normal specification after the exhibition. Thirty-eight years later, however, Paula and Bob Alexander from Boston turned their Mark II into an exact replica of the show car.

The 3.8-liter Mark II, with its further improved performance—only bettered by the finest sports cars—was tested frequently by various publications. Its interior was well appointed and adequately roomy, and the engine ran smoothly even in thickest traffic. The larger windows and lighter interior were much praised. In the United States, the Mark II contributed to Jaguar's reputation as a classy import car. The car's standard radial tires helped roadholding. Reader surveys revealed quality problems, however—malfunctioning instruments, oil drops under the car, bleaching paint. Jaguar changed many a detail to counter the criticism.

The revised compact sedan is remembered as the Jaguar Mark II. *(Schön)*

Some of the problems could be traced back to the policies of purchasing director Arthur Whittaker, which were in line with those of the parsimonious Sir William. The Smiths rev counter, for example, was available in Rolls-Royce quality at one pound extra per unit, but Jaguar purchased the cheaper unit.

A single Mark II 3.8-liter was transformed by Jones Brothers (Coach Builders) Limited into a station wagon, according to drawings of the Nockolds brothers. This one-off (Chassis No. 207515) was called County. Jaguar used it as service car, and it survives to this day. Rumor has it that a second example may have been made. Duncan Hamilton and Mike Hawthorn indeed had the same idea, but based on the preceding car. The project was abandoned after the latter's fatal car accident. He had on loan from Jaguar a 3.4-liter (Chassis No. S970806, registration VDU 881). Just having ended his racing career on January 22, 1959, he was accelerating quickly on the Guildford bypass in third gear when he was caught by crosswind. He lost control and hit a tree; the incident cost Hawthorn his life.

The 2.4-liter XK engine of the 1959 Jaguar Mark II. *(Schönborn archive)*

In racing, the 3.8 was a touring car to be taken seriously. (The smaller-engined cars were rarely raced, and around 1960 there were hardly any serious contenders.) In particular, the Coombs-prepared Mark IIs enjoyed success, particularly the one with "BUY 1" on the number plate. The Equipe Endeavour founded by Tommy Sopwith and named after his father's yacht added further wins. On Easter Monday, 1960, at Goodwood, Salvadori and Sears were beaten by Moss' Aston Martin DB 4. In April at Snetterton, Baillie was more successful with an average 81.98 miles per hour. J. P. Boardman/J. W. Whitworth scored a class win among the prepared touring cars, and Parkes/Howarth won the standard touring sedan class. At Silverstone, Lotus boss Colin Chapman in a Mark II won his class from Sears and Baillie. In the production car race at the same venue, the 1-2-3 winners were Salvadori, Moss, and Hill. Jack Sears, W. A. Powell, and W. Aston scored another 1-2-3 sweep at Brands Hatch. In the 1960 Alpine, José Behra/René Richard won the touring class with Bobby Parkes/Geoff Howarth third; both earned Alpine Cups. The Tour de France, with its many races testing diverse qualities, became an ideal background for Bernard Consten/Jacques Renel to excel. In 1960 they won for the first time, with Jopp/Baillie second and Behra/Monneret fourth. Baillie and D. Taylor managed a 1-2 placing in the October race at Goodwood, and W. Aston won at Snetterton. Jack Sears/William Cave won the touring class in the RAC Rally, and Sears together with Equipe Endeavour

Top: 1959 Jaguar Mark II—a contemporary photograph. *(Schönborn archive)*

Above: The dash of the 1959 Jaguar Mark II. *(Schönborn archive)*

Top: The cultivated rear compartment of the 1959 Jaguar Mark II. *(Schönborn archive)*

Above: The rear of the most desired touring car of its time. *(S)*

Below: Looking and driving wonderfully: Jaguar Mark II. *(J)*

Jacques Renel (far left), Bernard Consten (far right) and a Mark II on the 1960 Tour de France. *(S)*

became British touring champion. In the United States, Hansgen and Pabst scored 1-2 sweeps at Elkhart Lake and Riverside. The season ended with Baillie winning the Brands Hatch Boxing Day race with an average speed of 64.21 miles per hour.

Starting out 1961, the Monte Carlo Rally was disappointing for Jaguar, with Eric Brinkman and Philip Walton finishing in 104th and 130th positions, although Walton won the bonus prize at Mount Angel. Peter Sargent won the spring race at Snetterton, still in an old 3.4-liter. The Easter Monday race at Goodwood ended with a win for Mike Parkes (average 76.3 miles per hour). Baillie/Jopp won the Alpine with comparatively little serious competition. In the Tour de France they were second behind Consten/Renel; Consten also won the Coupe du Salon at Montlhéry with the car of C. de Guezac. John Casewell/H. Davenport/A. Austin finished the RAC Rally in a disappointing 49th position. But Bobby Parkes/Geoff Howarth won the Circuit of Ireland Rally, where John Cuff, in a modified 3.4-liter, scored another class win. At Silverstone, Hill won from Parkes. Here the advantage of the immensely powerful American V-8 engines showed as Dan Gurney's Chevrolet Impala was in the lead until it retired with tire damage. Parkes, Salvadori, and Sears scored a podium sweep in the touring car race at Brands Hatch. At the Lowood race in Australia, the name of Bob Jane appeared for the first time, but his Mark II, boosted to more than 300 horsepower, retired. Later, particularly in the 1963 and 1964 seasons, he was practically invincible, managing 38 consecutive wins.

In 1962 the American contenders became more serious, but Jaguar still enjoyed success:

- At Brands Hatch Salvadori, Baillie, and Dodd scored second to fourth places only
- Graham Hill won the Scott-Brown Memorial at Snetterton (86.87 miles per hour), the Sussex Trophy race at Goodwood (average 86.59 miles per hour), the International Trophy Meeting at Silverstone, and the race at Aintree. Peter Sargent won in the Snetterton March and April races at Snetterton and P. Woodroffe won at Goodwood.
- Hill scored a second at Mallory Park on the same day
- Mike Parkes/James Blumer won the six-hour race at Brands Hatch, while Salmon/Sutcliffe retired
- Salvadori won at Crystal Palace, with Sears second and Baillie fourth
- The Aston Martin Owners' Club race at Silverstone was won by W. Powell (in a Jaguar Mark II, of course)
- The Grand Prix touring car race at Aintree was another win for Sears, and at Brands Hatch, Parkes, Sears, and Salvadori enjoyed a 1-2-3 podium sweep
- In the Alpine, Parkes/George Humble/Roy Dixon retired with piston failure
- Consten/Renel won the Tour de France again, this year from Rosinski/Charon, Richard/de Montaigu, and André Chollet, while Sears/Lego and Baillie/Jopp suffered accidents
- Kraft won the Geneva Rally
- Rodriguez Larreta ("Larry")/Jack F. Greeve won the Buenos Aires 500-kilometer race from three Alfa Romeos and Reyes/Salerno in another Mark II
- Ian Fraser-Jones/Chris Griffith scored a class win in the nine-hour race at South Africa's Kyalami circuit

In 1963 Consten, against even stronger opposition, managed a fourth consecutive win in the Tour de France, which now covered more than 3,600 miles, including 12 hours of high-speed racing and seven hill sprints.

Above: The Alpine was a challenge to the Mark II, here in 1961. *(S)*

Left: The Tour de France at speed with a Mark II. *(S)*

In early 1960, Dieter Korp tested the Mark II 3.8-liter for the German magazine *Das Auto, Motor und Sport.* His first impression was: "This car has such a British air that it invites one to have tea in it." How many authors have repeated these words, not knowing it is a compliment! Korp continued, "True in the best sense of the word are the large instruments for speed and rpm. In this regard, the British are leading because they are behind their time." The author was enthralled by the car's styling and the looks of the engine bay in particular. The only fly in the ointment was the not very up-to-date Moss gearbox. All this acclaim contributed to rising sales figures in Germany, reaching nearly 500 in 1962, mostly Mark IIs.

9 ENGLAND'S OLDEST CAR MARQUE

Since the end of the nineteenth century, Daimler cars have been made at Coventry. No other British car manufacturer has such a long tradition. The name is, of course, derived from German gunsmith Gottlieb Daimler, who was born on March 17, 1834, at Schorndorf in Württemberg as a baker's son. As graduate of the Stuttgart Royal Industrial School he visited France and England, particularly Birmingham and Coventry, with the Whitworth Company, which had gained worldwide fame for its precision machines and its invention of a thread standard. After several other jobs he started at engineer Eugen Langen's Gasmotorenfabrik (gas engine manufacture) Deutz in 1872. There Nikolaus Otto, once a coffee and tea merchant, was would soon invent the four-stroke engine, for which he received a patent in 1877.

This four-stroke engine was superior to the most advanced gas engine of the time—which Etienne Lenoir from Luxemburg had invented in 1860—because it compressed the mixture of air and fuel. Lenoir's engine ignited uncompressed gas in the cylinder, which then expanded abruptly. The principle of moving a piston using pressure produced this way had been patented by Brit Robert Street in 1794. A piston moved by steam had been invented by Christian Huygens as early as 1673! The energy produced by the explosion in Lenoir's engine was disappointingly small, while the sudden ignition of compressed gasoline and air produced much more power: Increasing an engine's compression ratio still is a most convenient means of increasing power in modern gasoline engines. Another detriment of Lenoir's engine was the complicated starting procedure, even requiring quick-heating the boiler.

Otto's engine turned over at less than 200 rpm. The coal gas in the cylinder did not ignite itself in the process of being compressed—it was ignited by a pilot light located outside the cylinder. The flame was introduced to the combustion chamber by opening a slot between the two at just the right moment. Because there was no usable range of rpm and the power-to-weight ratio for the 2-horsepower engine was quite poor, it could only be employed as a stationary engine. Another obstacle was that no fluid fuels could be used for this engine because the reservoir of fuel necessary for a longer trip required far too much space.

Despite these disadvantages, the invention of the Otto cycle engine was a milestone. Nevertheless, Daimler had permanent disputes with Otto, so they parted in 1881. With the money gained working with Otto and Langen, Daimler created his own workshop in the garden of his mansion at Cannstatt. There he continued his research with Karl Maybach, who first met Daimler at the machine workshop of the Bruderhaus at Reutlingen. They tried to find a more elegant and quicker way of igniting the gas and they found it by using an 1808 invention from Sir George Cayley: a tube heated by a flame burning outside the cylinder.

Daimler and Maybach built a single-cylinder engine that did 750 rpm and produced 1.1 horsepower. The exhaust side valve was operated via a camshaft, while the overhead inlet valve operated automatically by being sucked into the cylinder during the intake stroke. A similar engine of 264cc, which produced 0.5 horsepower, was fearlessly mounted in a sort of bicycle frame to create the "Petroleum-Reitwagen." In August 1885, three months before the first test run, Daimler was granted his first patent. As his ideas were based on inventions made by Nikolaus Otto, further dispute between them was inevitable. But Otto lost his patent on January 30, 1886. It was proven that French Beau de Rochas already had the four-stroke patent in 1862, so Otto had no patent right.

In the summer of 1886, without having heard of Karl Benz, who just had completed a three-wheeled, self-propelled vehicle at Mannheim, Daimler ordered a solid used coach with a wooden chassis. He mounted his engine in this coach, in this case a 1.5-horsepower single-cylinder to which rudimentary water cooling was added later. The primary drive from the engine to the two-speed transmission was via leather belts, while a chain transmitted power to the solid rear axle. In 1889 the "Stahlradwagen" (a wagon with steel wheels) followed. It was designed by Karl Maybach, and had little similarity to a coach. The second example of this had each front wheel mounted in a fork-like a bicycle, and the wheels could be turned sideward via a central lever. For this vehicle Maybach invented the spray carburetor to replace of the evaporation unit used before. The engine had its two cylinders positioned in a very narrow angle and it produced 3.5 horsepower at 700 rpm. Four speeds were now available via sprockets.

Opposite: Daimler mascot. *(J)*

Daimler's total car production in the first years was limited to these three vehicles. The creation of these cars was intended to show the advantages of the new type of engine; Daimler was not interested in horseless carriages per se. His engine was also mounted in boats, railways, and even balloons—and it was used as a stationary engine, of course.

In the United Kingdom, the Daimler history starts with Frederick Richard Simms, who was born into a renowned family of Warwickshire smiths on August 12, 1863, in Hamburg. There his grandfather provided equipment to a fleet that fished near the Newfoundland shores. Simms was as familiar with technical drawing as he was with patent laws. In his young years he had already developed a sort of tram that was widely recognized.

In 1890 Simms exhibited his achievement at an engine show at Bremen in Germany, where another tram was on display. This one was said to have been used successfully since 1887 in normal traffic in Swabia. Simms was fascinated by its light, compact, and powerful engine—Daimler's four-stroke with hot-tube ignition.

Simms introduced himself to Daimler, soon gained his confidence, and became director in the newly established Daimler Motorengesellschaft, where he remained until 1892. A loyal friendship developed between Daimler and Simms. On February 18, 1891, Simms paid for the exclusive license to sell the Daimler engine in the Commonwealth, which extended all over the world in those Victorian times. For the exploitation of the license Simms, together with his partner Alfred Hendricks, founded an engineering office at the Billiter Building in London in July 1891. It was from this location that the Daimler car company would later emerge.

The first Daimler engine arrived in Great Britain on May 16, 1891. Simms intended to run a chocolate and cocoa machine with it at the Earls Court Exhibition, but the fearful organizers would not allow this. They also prohibited the allegedly illegal display of a car and the operation of a boat with a Daimler engine on the Serpentine River (actually a 28-acre lake) in Hyde Park. The reason for the reluctance was the widespread fear of explosion hazard caused by the fuel used by these machines. Simms proclaimed that he used oil that was less volatile than the fuel usually used. He called this "petrol," a name that remains in use today. This fuel was a residue from petroleum production that could be cheaply purchased from Carless, Capel and Leonard, after they had it distilled twice and deodorized. Of course, this petrol was volatile as well, and so it also could cause an explosion. The Brits remained skeptical, although they certainly did not know this fact and could not disprove what Simms said. In the end permission for the demonstration of the boat on the river Thames was granted.

In England the Daimler engine was used for many purposes, but not in cars. This was due to the influence of the large railway companies: After Richard Trevethick built his first high-pressure steam engine in 1801, some frightening steam-powered monsters were operated as stagecoaches on Britain's highways. The landlords who owned the highways claimed high tolls from these monstrosities, which was good luck for the railways, which soon became the less costly alternative. The railway barons were well represented in Parliament, so that from 1861 (with the creation of a 12-ton weight limit for road vehicles) until 1878, any competition from highway transit was restricted more and more by laws. At last the speed of these vehicles was limited to 4 miles per hour, and until 1878 a person had to walk in front of the machine waving a red flag. In towns only 2 miles per hour was allowed, which made pedestrians quicker than these machines. So the railway had a speed advantage that was guaranteed by law!

This completely unfair law was also applicable to motor vehicles with Daimler engines, which at the time were called light locomobiles. There was thus no sense in using a car. No wonder the car arrived so late in technically advanced Great Britain!

Meanwhile, Simms learned that Hendricks had falsified the company's accounts. So, early in 1893 Hendricks had to leave the company after having paid back the missing money. On May 26, 1893, Simms reorganized the company with £6,000 raised with the help of family and friends. Daimler Motor Syndicate Limited was the first British company to bear the Daimler name. In the first year this company suffered a loss of £577 in trading with modern Daimler engines. The address was at Arch No. 71 by Putney Bridge Railway Station—located under a railway bridge arch—but it moved to the Billiter Building in 1894.

Because of the aforementioned laws, Simms had no interest in cars. Other, more idealistic personalities were not as bothered by the restrictions. So it was John Henry Knight who became the first Brit to create an automobile. In 1895 he completed a steel three-wheeler that was driven by a four-stroke engine. A second front wheel was added in the following year, which made the car accidentally resemble Daimler's Stahlradwagen. Afterward, Knight was fined heavily for violating the patents; he built no more motor vehicles!

On July 3, 1895, the first automobile with a Daimler engine finally was brought to Great Britain. It was a 3.5-horsepower Panhard & Levassor of French origin, built under Daimler's license. Only two days later the Hon. Evelyn Ellis took it on an illegal (but not fined) test drive to his home in Berkshire, about 55 miles. With this drive, Ellis, one of the directors of the Daimler Motor Syndicate, prompted no fewer than 80 orders for similar cars. With his many test drives Ellis tried to provoke the authorities to charge him with a violation so that he could bring the matter to the House of Lords. The mayor of Royal Tunbridge Wells supported Ellis' initiative against the absurd speed limitation and organized the first car exhibition in Great Britain, which was opened on October 15, 1895. It consisted of Ellis' Panhard & Levassor, the mayor's Peugeot, a Daimler fire brigade car, and—the only exhibit with no Daimler engine—a tiny De Dion.

On June 7, 1895, Simms received approval from his board to form the Daimler Motor Company Limited for the production of engines according to Daimler's patents. The authorized capital was £40,000, and Ellis was to be one of the directors of the new company. But before it was founded, fate was to befall this company.

Harry John Lawson, the 43-year-old son of a puritan preacher, was an adventurer of the worst reputation, whose obscure transactions (haphazardly) helped the motorcycle industry to its feet. Lawson made himself a very rich man, to the detriment of many innocent associates, who thought to have their assets invested in a safe company but were left with nothing.

This Harry Lawson, accompanied by two gentlemen of not dissimilar character, purchased the Daimler patents at £35,000 from the Daimler Motor Syndicate Limited. This doubled the price Simms had paid Daimler for the license. So Simms transferred the license to the British Motor Syndicate Limited, which Lawson had founded in July 1895 for exactly this purpose. The immense profit was immediately distributed among the shareholders of the Daimler Motor Syndicate Limited. They expressed their thankfulness with a silver cup dedicated to Frederick Simms. With his new company Lawson collected quite a few patents relative to the automobile and the fast-running four-stroke engine. His idea was to create a monopoly in car production and trade for Great Britain. Thanks to its Daimler engine, Lawson collected a fee for every Panhard & Levassor sold in Great Britain!

On January 14, 1896, Lawson founded the Daimler Motor Company Limited, again residing in the Billiter Building. The shares at a total nominal amount of £100,000 were oversubscribed by £10,000, despite all the reservations against Lawson. Forty thousand pounds was immediately transferred to the British Motor Syndicate (one-third going to Lawson himself) for the Daimler license. This company was Lawson's first that aimed at car production, and so this company is regarded as the origin of the present Daimler. At the time this foundation was not deemed to be worth celebrating, as the press saw no technical expertise represented on the board apart from Gottlieb Daimler, who was constantly absent.

Henry Sturmey is another interesting person among Daimler's directors. This schoolmaster and

1895 Knight, the first automobile designed in Great Britain. *(St)*

Harry Lawson on his Daimler-engined Panhard in the Emancipation Run, during which Otto Mayer from Cannstatt drove the car; he is seen here behind the front wheels. *(Long)*

bicycle enthusiast presented the first issue of *The Autocar* magazine on November 2, 1895, long before any car was on sale in Great Britain. The magazine was a seemingly independent advertising instrument for Daimler cars—no mean contribution to the success of Daimler in its early years. Sturmey was most concerned of the lack of technical knowledge at the Daimler board, and so the employment of James S. Critchley was to his merit. Critchley seemed to have a talent in designing technical apparatus. This was worth an annual salary of £400, at least initially.

His Royal Highness, the Prince of Wales, later to be King Edward VII, had taken notice of the activities in Billiter Building and was inclined to learn more about the production of automobiles that was planned there. So Ellis chauffeured His Royal Highness through the galleries of the Imperial Institute in his Panhard & Levassor. His Royal Highness was most impressed—the importance of this test drive for the cause of motoring in England simply cannot be overestimated. His words were, "I shall make the motorcar a necessity for every English gentleman." His mother, the declining Queen Victoria, however, adhered to coach and railway.

Daimler Motor Company took its first steps in preparation for the production of horseless carriages. For this purpose the directors undertook a business trip to companies in more advanced foreign countries that cooperated with Daimler, such as Panhard & Levassor in Paris, Peugeot near Belfort, and the Daimler works at Cannstatt. The directors learned that as a first step for car manufacture, a suitable factory site had to be found. Upon their return to England the search began, ending in April 1896 when the factory of Coventry Cotton Spinning & Weaving, which had not been used for three years, was discovered. Coventry, unusual for a British city, is situated far from the sea. Despite a network of canals this made it difficult for Coventry to develop trade and production, as ships were the usual means of cargo transport. So early on, Coventry specialized in weaving ribbons and manufacturing clocks, both light products of considerable value that could reasonably be transported on land. Weaving suffered a crisis in the 1870s, while clock manufacture trained workers in the skills needed for bicycle production, which thereupon expanded quickly. Thus it was quite natural that this industry, which had already attracted Gottlieb Daimler, concentrated in the Midlands. Now the bicycle industry suffered a depression, and Daimler could benefit from the technical experience of the underemployed workforce. Additionally, Lawson and Sturmey had excellent contacts at the place of their earlier success.

The Wool Mill, the factory's new name, was large enough to house the Great Horseless Carriage Company that Lawson just had founded with an authorized capital of £750,000. This company bought the licenses from the British Motor Syndicate for the incredible sum of £500,000. In addition, Daimler provided engines at a 10 percent discount for the MMC cars the Great Horseless Carriage Company produced. It is obvious who benefited most in all these transactions. As no engines were delivered, the company started selling French Bollée cars, which were called Coventry-Bollée or later Coventry Motette. Other adventurous motor enterprises were called Beeston, Bersey, Pennington, Kane, and Motor Sociable.

From May 9 until August 8, 1896, another motor show was held at Imperial Institute, organized by Lawson. As car production in England had not yet really started, this was an import show. Daimler exhibited several Peugeots with engines according to

Daimler's design, among them light "Victorias" with 4-horsepower engines of the new Phoenix type, but also Daimler's Petroleum-Reitwagen of 1886.

The publicity gained with this exhibition, the propaganda of *The Autocar*, and the support of the Prince of Wales helped bring an end to the unreasonable restrictions to motor traffic on roads. The speed limit would be raised to 12 miles per hour on November 14, 1896. The issue of *The Autocar* on the day the new policy was announced was printed in red, and Lawson tried to organize a motorcar run from London to Brighton for October 24, but it was not allowed to take place before November 14th. Lawson took part in the run with a Cannstatt-Daimler landau, which he called *Present Times*, and which, embarrassingly, failed to complete the distance on its own power. As no British Daimlers yet existed, some vehicles with Daimler engines were entered. The victory, however, went to the brothers Bollée and their two cars, the most convincing of the approximately 10 vehicles that reached the finish without help. This first motoring contest in Great Britain is said to have attracted more than a half-million spectators. Its impact was so immense that, despite the usually unpleasant November weather, the race is still repeated every year with period cars participating.

Meanwhile, the Daimler Motor Company was purchasing the machines for its factory. As there was no production yet, complete chassis were brought in from Panhard & Levassor to begin sales. The first English Daimler car had its engine mounted longitudinally at the front below a hood, following the configuration of the Panhard & Levassor after 1891 and the latest Phoenix from Cannstatt. It had two pairs of seats, all facing the front. This was a remarkably modern layout, one that had already been introduced with the Bollée steam car, *L'Obéissante* ("the obedient one") of 1873. The Phoenix also contributed the engine, a 4-horsepower straight two-cylinder with Maybach's spray carburetor and a radiator at the rear. The transmission was a modern, fully enclosed four-speed gearbox with a chain drive to the rear axle instead of the formerly popular belt, which had a tendency to slip. The change between forward and reverse drive took place in the differential, so that all four gears were available for driving backward. Such a car was intended to enter the Paris–Marseilles race but hold-ups in getting production under way prohibited this. The hesitant mailing of patent blueprints from Cannstatt was another obstacle; the Brits often had to find their own way. Usually the British Daimler designers found answers and inspiration from the French Panhard & Levassor.

The first Daimler of British production had its maiden voyage on March 2, 1897. A photograph published of a "very first" Daimler does not show this car but a mock-up, as closer inspection reveals several nonfunctioning mechanical components, despite the determined faces of the car's occupants. On the first drive, Ellis managed to climb the famous Malvern Hill near his home in July 1897. Despite special hill gears, the car barely managed the 20-percent gradient. The rudimentary water-cooling was a particular problem, as the car did not have a closed circuit but allowed the water to evaporate to release heat, so that fresh water had to be added quite frequently. In this car and others of the period, the driver would vary speed not by changing the engine rpm, but by selecting the appropriate gear. The car had no accelerator; the driver was equipped only with a lever with which to control the engine speed limiter at the exhaust valve. So, in these early days driving was done at full throttle all the time, although at three-figure rpm!

Although Ellis' hillclimb was only just successful, one Charles S. Rolls took notice, thanks to the publicity it caused. He ordered Chassis No. 6 made by Daimler in Coventry. The car was delivered in August 1897, but in reality it was a Panhard & Levassor chassis that—replacing the British Daimler—had won the Paris–Marseilles race. Only years later Rolls, with his partner Henry Royce, set out to build his own cars.

Daimler only offered one chassis type but with varying bodies, all of which had picturesque names and all of which were sold for about £300. The first "true" customer who was not related with the works that produced the car (and thus the first buyer of a British car) was Major General Montgomery of Winchester. He was supplied with his car in August 1897, just like Rolls. It is thus evident that car manufacture in the Wool Mill was under way that summer.

Henry Sturmey had to yield to Rolls and the major general before he got his hands on a vehicle for his remarkable drive from John O'Groats in Scotland to Land's End in Cornwall. This journey was delayed until

The 1897 Daimler two-cylinder was the first car made in series in Great Britain. *(J)*

With this two-cylinder Coventry-Daimler, Henry Sturmey drove from John O'Groats in the north of Scotland to Land's End in Cornwall. *(Long)*

October 2, 1897, but the car managed to finish the trip under its own power by October 19. At the end of the journey the car had 929 miles on the odometer over 93.5 hours of operation. The same car was demonstrated to the Prince of Wales late in 1897, together with an example owned by Northampton coachbuilder Arthur Mulliner. On a hunting event shortly before this, the prince had seen the Duke of York driving around in a car. His Royal Highness had to wait until June 1898 before he was actually driven in a car on a public road, accompanied by the Countess of Warwick, Lady Randolph Churchill, and the Duke of Marlborough. Despite a damaged silencer, the engine proved its abilities, although at a steep gradient the car had help from servants hidden in the roadside ditch. Later, deteriorating weather made the party swap for a coach with a protective roof.

This is how car production got going at Daimler. Cautiously, Daimler adhered to the French and German designs. In 1897, after some chassis were made with two coupled two-cylinder engines, Daimler moved to an 8-horsepower four-cylinder engine, which had been in use in Germany for some months. These were the first four-cylinder cars in the world. In 1898 an experimental shop was established to improve the somewhat questionable reliability of the early cars. Technical improvements such as the use of diesel oil or alcohol as fuel were investigated in close cooperation with the Germans, but they did not see production.

Above: This early two-cylinder Daimler is owned by Jaguar. *(J)*

Right: The 1898 two-cylinder Daimler, in a contemporary photograph. *(Long)*

In 1898 the first Daimler omnibus was made, a 16-seater that was purchased for £750 by the London Steam Omnibus Company—their first nonsteam vehicle. At the time the loads that would be experienced by the clutch and other components when used for public transit, with its many stops and starts and with a heavy load of passengers, were simply underestimated. It would be 1905 before London got its first fleet of motorbuses. Bus production at Daimler did develop into a helpful second product line alongside car production. Through increased rpm, the two-cylinder engine now produced 5.5 horsepower.

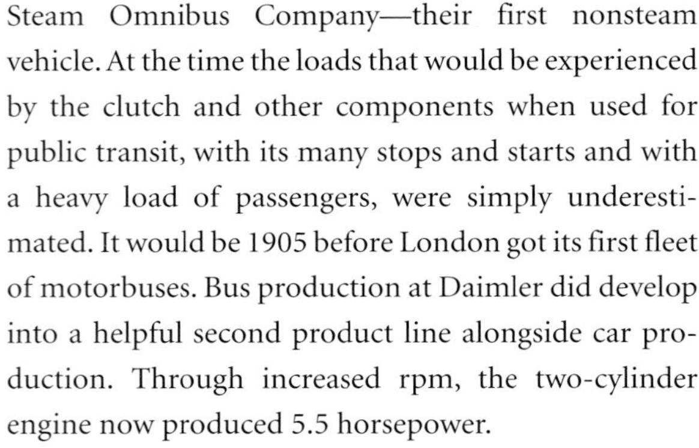

Daimler and the Great Horseless Carriage Company had many disputes caused by the all-but-rosy economical situation faced by both. The latter was renamed Motor Manufacturing Company (MMC) in 1898 and started its own car production, often using Daimler chassis but replacing the chassis identification plate with their own. This contributed to further disputes with Daimler. However, MMC supplied bodies to Daimler, who had no body shop of its own. This is why Daimlers often were bodied by the aforementioned Arthur Mulliner.

Meanwhile, the Daimler board was also occupied with internal quarrels. Had the directors not also been shareholders with an interest in the survival of the company, its collapse would have been imminent. Good news came in 1898—a profit of £9,381 had been gained, which helped reduce the disputes, and the era of new chairman Edward Jenkinson indeed started in a friendlier atmosphere.

However, the era was one of cost cutting. The London administration was closed down altogether. Staff at Coventry was reduced by two-thirds, and the rest often had Mondays off. Accounting was reformed so that management was granted a minimum of survey. In retrospect it is a miracle that the company survived at all.

Stocks of two-cylinder engines that once before had been supplied from Germany were used up in a Critchley Light Car, a vehicle of particularly simple design with belt drive and (at first) no rear springing at all. It had only one brake, and a strange, vertically mounted steering wheel column. This stopgap filled the Daimler catalogs for several years.

Unfortunately Daimler was also the pioneer with regard to fatal car accidents in Britain. On February 25, 1899, the driver of a Daimler wagonette belonging to the factory lost control on a slope during on a test drive. The vehicle broke its artillery wheels and scattered its passengers around. Driver Edwin Sewell and one passenger were killed. Daimler had to face claims for damage, and the large artillery wheels were deemed a flawed design. Henry Sturmey interfered in the subsequent public discussion with an article in *The Autocar* where he claimed that Daimler was not liable. However, his reasoning was indefensible, and in the end he was forced out as a Daimler director.

In 1899 the (not yet royal) Automobile Club of Great Britain and Ireland (ACGB&I), founded by Simms in 1897, held its first motor show in Richmond, after the first hillclimb competition ever held for cars in Britain. Daimler earned many acknowledgements and plaques. The power output of the four-cylinder had been increased to 12 horsepower. Aboard just such a 12-horsepower, Lord Montagu of Beaulieu set off for a reliability run from Paris to Ostend, thus becoming the first Brit to participate in a race abroad. Daimler started to use a closed-circuit cooling system with a tube winding in front of the hood that would cool the water flowing through it. In the newly designed gearbox, the gear teeth were permanently meshed, and gear changes were achieved using claws. The first pneumatics replaced solid rubber tires sporadically, and they suffered many punctures from horseshoe nails and glass splinters. In place of the steering lever, the steering wheel became more popular. The year 1899 ended with a profit for Daimler of £4,430.

In 1900, Daimler claimed the honor of supplying the first car to the royal household—a 6-horsepower two-cylinder, which was on loan. In the 1,000-mile run Daimlers won many medals in this event, which Alfred Harmsworth, later Lord Northcliffe, the editor of the *Daily Mail*, started. The race began at Hyde Park corner on April 23, and went via Bristol, Manchester, Edinburgh, Leeds, Nottingham, and back to London. Only one MMC car and not a single Daimler finished this ambitious race, however. This first long-distance race in Great Britain laid bare the shortcomings of the early designs, particularly the disadvantage of the hot-tube ignition in comparison with new electric ignitions under development. Karl Benz, who like Daimler was experimenting with fast-running explosion engines, had tried ignition systems that created sparks and were fed by a battery, as had Lenoir before. The technical apparatus of the time, however, did not allow such a system to work at the rpm that the Daimler engine ran. Coventry-Daimler soon made use of a Bosch license for the low-tension ignition with magneto and breaker contact that far-sighted Frederick Simms had purchased in 1897.

Daimler's Critchley Light Car was of very simple design, propelled by an early variant of the Daimler two-cylinder engine. *(Long)*

In 1900 Gottlieb Daimler died, his early death possibly being caused by his excessive labor and strains caused by permanent arguments with his colleagues at the board of Daimler Motorengesellschaft. With him a strong link between the German and British Daimler companies was lost.

Daimler produced more than 150 cars in 1900. In the same year all directors resigned, which brought Harry Lawson back to the scene. He wanted to buy the shares held by the directors, and at quite good prices. This was not to happen, however, and Lawson sued Daimler with several patent claims.

The 20-horsepower four-cylinder unveiled to the public in February 1901 was Daimler's first model that did not completely rely on hot-tube ignition. It had a device for decompressing three of the four cylinders in order to facilitate handle starting, a large radiator, and two pumps for the cooling water.

In a 500-mile reliability run in 1901, Daimler tried a driveshaft drive, but the differential could not bear the load and was damaged. Daimler had no option but to revert to the traditional chain drive. This lesson

made Daimler one of the last car manufacturers to change definitively to a driveshaft.

A historically significant event for Daimler was the first use of a car for a funeral in Great Britain—of a Daimler employee, by the way. Today the Daimler Hearse still is an indispensable part of a traditional British funeral.

In summer 1901 Edward Jenkinson had just resumed his post as chairman after an enforced interruption—the financial situation of the company made a merger with Motor Manufacturing Company a worthwhile proposition, but MMC soon discontinued negotiations. Despite several further attempts, this merger never took place. In November 1901, the company's losses amounted to £20,000.

Daimler presented the climax of its development, the most elegant 22-horsepower designed by Sydney Straker. Its engine was remarkable in that its engine block and cylinder head were a single part. This made decarbonizing—the gasoline quality of the day required this operation to be carried out quite frequently—rather complicated. Thanks to cooling water

Above: This 12-horsepower Wagonette had been delivered by Daimler to the Royal Mews. At the wheel is Mr. Letzer, His Majesty's chauffeur. *(Long)*

Right: The first Daimler supplied to the Royal Mews was this Daimler 6-horsepower Mail Phaeton. *(J)*

circulating above the combustion chambers, these engines were very well cooled indeed with inlet and exhaust valves of immense diameters. Front and rear wheels were the same size, which allowed slightly lower bodies. The rear wheel brake was operated by pedal, as was the one at the gearbox. For the first time an accelerator lever was included.

Oliver Stanton's famous Chat Noir (black cat), with its 30-horsepower engine, was based on this formidable chassis. Black with golden instruments and coachlines, it was a treat for the eyes. King Edward had some features of this car added to his as well. Although the company held orders for 84 cars at a value of £62,000 by the end of 1901, Daimler had no cash. Had Evelyn Ellis not spent £13,000 out of his private money to keep the company afloat, Daimler would have been bankrupt.

Daimler made it into 1902 and gained a profit of £1,200 while producing 120 cars. In the 1,000-mile reliability run of September 1 to 6, 1902, a Daimler 12-horsepower finished third, and two MMC 10-horsepowers were sixth and eighth. In the following year many cars of both makes could finish the 1,000-mile run. But in April 1903, when the paint shop and seven cars were destroyed by fire, the company again faced bankruptcy.

Stress tests showed that the valves supplied from outside were of varying quality. So Daimler had to install its own valve manufacturing facilities, which involved further cost.

The legal situation for motorists improved in Great Britain again in the beginning of 1904. The new Motor Car Act allowed speeds of 20 miles per hour. This was instigated by John Scott, Lord Montagu of Beaulieu and his magazine *The Car Illustrated*, which addressed elegant society. However, speeding was punished severely, so motorists did not appreciate the law, as police had already learned how to ambush speeders. In the end the seemingly liberal law was a threat to manufacturers of powerful, fast vehicles. Drivers of cars had to be at least 17 years old and hold a license that carried an annual fee in addition to the vehicle tax of more than £2. Each vehicle had to have a number plate.

In 1904 the lighter four-cylinder 16/20 and 18/22 were introduced. Daimler's flagship was the similarly designed 28/36-horsepower. With 5.7-liter capacity, this was Daimler's largest engine to date. The horsepower

Daimler 22-horsepower *Le Chat Noir* with Oliver Stanton at the wheel. *(Long)*

figures described the power available at 750 and 1,000 rpm, respectively. These cars showed the genius of the American engineer Percy Martin, who had invested a lot of his private money in Daimler, where he became factory manager in 1900. Martin came up with a radiator that had a fluted header tank and better cooling efficiency. This fluting was to become a typical attribute of every subsequent Daimler. The new dashboard, with the sides curved backward, contained glove boxes at both sides. This was Martin's idea, as was the subframe for engine and gearbox. The longitudinal chassis members now were made of steel instead of wood, which allowed a longer wheelbase. The crankshaft mountings being fixed to the engine block made removal of the oil sump easier. The navigator also had an easier life, thanks to an improved lubrication system; he no longer had to look after the proper oil supply to all bearings. New silencers made the car less noisy, an advance for passengers as well as for passersby. In 1904 a new two-cylinder was offered, closely related to the 1897 engine but of more orthodox design than the Critchley.

Daimler hoods now were hinged at the rear, opening in the "alligator" manner that would become popular many years later. In order to make parts further down in the engine bay accessible, the side panels were removable as well—a rather complicated arrangement that left no obstacles for the mechanic.

On October 19, 1904, a Daimler had the honor of being the first car ever used by the king in an official ceremony. Step by step, the car replaced horses even in their most dignified duties.

Below: Another 22-horsepower, now of 1903, with a very spacious phaeton body called Mayfair. *(Long)*

Bottom: The first Daimler with the crinkled grille surround came out in 1903, here an 18/22 HP. *(St)*

10

DAIMLER'S NEW START

On December 8, 1904, Daimler, with its permanent lack of money, had to be reorganized again as the Daimler Motor Company (1904) Limited. The newly issued shares brought in fresh money, so the new company could take over the assets of the old one. With the new line of cars designed by Percy Martin and a sound financial footing, Daimler's future seemed to be safe.

The Motor Manufacturing Company was not so lucky. It was closed down without having a successor. With it, Lawson left the motor industry as well. In 1904 he had received a one-year labor camp sentence. In 1925 he died with assets worth no more than £99. Daimler rented the MMC workshops, installing its own coachbuilding shop there.

The year 1905 marked the appearance of first the four-cylinder Daimler with driveshaft, instead of chain drive, and a differential as used by the technologically advanced Lanchester. Due to Daimler's bad experience of earlier years, it was another three years before the last chain-driven Daimler was built. The 28/36-horsepower was developed into the 30/40-horsepower with 7.25 liters of capacity in its four cylinders. Now only roller bearings were used in the transmission. The magneto fed a battery, which supplied the new, modern lights with electrical energy. With a still larger four-cylinder of 10.6-liter capacity (35/45-horsepower) this series of design reached its climax. Even the most spectacular multicylinder Daimlers of later years would make do with a smaller capacity! Daimler's majestic, versatile bodies of the period were styled by Frenchman Maurice Charles.

In these years the large, cumbersome Daimlers actually were quite suitable racing cars—hardly imaginable today. At that time, only the largest cars had powerful engines, and light sporting cars were created simply by reducing body and equipment to the minimum. Philip Dawson with a 35-horsepower took part in the first of three Herkomer runs (August 10–17, 1905) and gained a silver plaque of honor. Grigg finished 11th in the second (June 5–13, 1906), where Lord Montagu of Beaulieu won a golden plaque; Robert Stotesbury, William Rendie, and William Herdman won silver plaques, and Edward Manville's wife Maud won a special prize. Barwick finished second in the Graphic Challenge Trophy race on September 26, 1906, completing the 4-plus-mile distance in five minutes and three seconds.

Daimlers also were quite successful in the Shelsley Walsh hillclimbs that were held from 1905 onward. Many long-distance races included Daimlers; even in the Prince Henry runs in Germany, Daimlers were entered regularly. Daimlers were not that successful on circuits, apart from exceptions like winning the Daimler memorial plaque at Brooklands on July 6, 1907, when the oval with its rough brick paving was opened.

With this background the company prospered, and in 1906 profits amounted to £185,785. A bonus system was begun for staff, as was a scheme of studies for employees who wanted to graduate as engineers. The prices of Daimler cars were reduced by up to £200. This increased demand; in 1906 about 500 Daimler cars were sold, more than any other make. In the same year, Sir Edward Jenkinson retired. Edward Manville was his successor as chairman, and Percy Martin became managing director.

The top-line Daimler was the new 45-horsepower, another elegant four-cylinder car. The engine was Daimler's first mono-bloc four-cylinder (bore and stroke were 150mm, as with the 35/45-horsepower). The crankshaft ran in roller bearings. For the first time the chassis was completely made of steel, with tubular crossmembers. The engine had fully automatic lubrication, with pressure provided by exhaust gases fed into the oil tank. There was still no camshaft cover over the engine, which must have turned out about 80 horsepower. By the end of 1906, the 30-horsepower was introduced. It was derived from the 45-horsepower, but it had a camshaft cover and was mounted lower in the chassis, allowing the radiator to become less prominent. The wooden artillery wheels were finally replaced by Rudge wire wheels.

In 1906 a sales organization for Italy, the Società Anonomina Officine de Luca Daimler, was established. It assembled cars and later built more individualized cars, but did not exist many years.

In 1907 a court confirmed that the Daimler name was owned by Daimler Motor Company. The British Motor Traction Company—formerly Lawson's Great Horseless Carriage Company—had founded a Daimler Wagon Company Limited in 1901, and the court now forbade this name—despite the existence of the French

Above: Daimler logo.

Opposite: The first high-performance Daimler from Coventry: 1905 45-horsepower. *(J)*

1904 Daimler 28-horsepower, still with chain drive. *(Long)*

Above: A Daimler 38-horsepower with landaulet body made by Windovers, made in 1906 for the Viscount Hirchinbrooke, Earl of Sandwich. *(Long)*

Lanchester's 5-horsepower Stanhope was the first four-wheel vehicle with an internal combustion engine wholly designed in Great Britain. *(Long)*

Milnes-Daimler selling cars in England, and the original Cannstatt-Daimler, which now called its products Mercedes. The British Daimler cars were only improved in detail during 1907, with a lower floor and leaf springs elongated to up to four feet for more compliant suspension.

The success of the Daimler in the early twentieth century is due in no small part to the know-how of the ingenious Dr. Frederick Lanchester. Born as the son of an architect on October 23, 1868, in London, he studied engineering at the Normal School of Science and School of Mines and also at the Finsbury Technical School in the evening. In 1884 he became works director at T. B. Barker, who produced gas engines based on Lenoir's patent. Just like Gottlieb Daimler, he was looking for increased rpm, but another of his aims was developing flying machines. With his younger brothers Frank (born July 20, 1870) and George (December 11, 1874), Lanchester managed to develop his own internal combustion gas engine and mount it in a boat. At home they were called the unholy trinity as their hobby often made them miss the divine service, which of course did not go unnoticed. The boat was christened in the autumn of 1894.

Lanchester 8-horsepower at Richmond in June 1899, where it gained a gold medal. *(Long)*

Of course, Lanchester did know of Daimler's and Benz' inventions in Germany, but to his high standards, the German engines were "bone shakers." The Lanchester brothers aimed at a more scientifically satisfying concept, and it certainly is no exaggeration to call Lanchester's car the first with a four-stroke engine of genuinely British design.

This vehicle was unusual in more than one respect. Its chassis, made of 2-inch tubes, was the first deliberately designed to resist distortion under normal stresses. The spokes did not point to the center of the hub but were attached tangentially, which resulted in increased stiffness. The wheels were one-offs manufactured at Dunlop—the first specifically made for a car. The body was mounted upon the chassis with two three-quarter-elliptic leaf springs at the rear and a transverse half-elliptic leaf spring at the front. In the middle of the rear axle, the first differential in automotive history was mounted. It was chain driven. In front of it was the epicyclic three-speed gearbox with sun and planet toothed wheels and brake bands regulating the power flow. The gear change was controlled via pedals and not, as usual for the period, with a lever. The gearbox was very advanced in being completely enclosed and thus protected from road dirt. The fastest gear was a direct-drive gear, as with no car before. A bit less futuristic were the two brake blocks at the rear wheels. The engine was mounted horizontally in the center of the chassis and below the floor of the body. It was an air-cooled single-cylinder of 1,689cc displacement, with the first-ever oil ring around the piston, and an oil filter. Engine speed was regulated with a knee-operated lever. The inlet valve was operated via a camshaft, unlike the Daimler with its "automatic" inlet. In the fuel tank many cotton threads soaked the fuel, which increased the surface for evaporation many times over, thus helping to produce a sufficiently rich air/fuel mixture. The engine had two counter-rotating crankshafts, which made it run much more smoothly. This made 1,000 rpm running speeds possible, at which it produced about 5-horsepower. The high-tension electric ignition first specified proved to be unreliable, so Lanchester invented his own low-tension system with very special spark plugs.

In late February 1896 the Lanchester brothers undertook their first test drives in the dark of the night. The engine only accelerated the car to 15 miles per hour, and it was not able to climb even small ascents. Next time around, the car got a 3,459cc two-cylinder engine that would achieve 1,250 rpm with a power output of 10 horsepower. In order to make sure that the engine was perfectly counterbalanced, each piston had three con-rods and permanently meshed, toothed wheels at both crankshafts. A cone-shaped clutch was added to the gearbox. Braking could be accomplished by choosing reverse. The chain at the diff was replaced with a worm drive. Steering gear was remarkable by being of the rack and pinion type, ahead of the rest of automotive manufacture by about half a century. In this guise the vehicle did nearly 20 miles per hour and overcame steeper gradients.

A similar engine was mounted in a second vehicle that was made at the same time. The axles were attached to the ends of cantilever-type leaf springs (another "first" in a car). Lanchester made the roller bearings in his own workshop, at a tolerance of 0.00002 inch—a nearly unbelievable achievement with the technical equipment of the time!

A leather-covered, hinged board in front of the seats was to become a typical Lanchester earmark. This two-seater was called the Gold Medal Phaeton; it had been honored with such a medal by the Automobile Club of Great Britain and Ireland (ACGB&I) for its careful design in 1899 in a comparison with 17 other cars at Richmond, in which the Daimler excelled as well. The Lanchester, with its light weight and good springing, did 30 miles per hour, much faster than the police would allow.

In 1898 a third Lanchester car was completed, a Mail Phaeton with two benches positioned face-to-face. By November 30, 1899, the Lanchester brothers had borrowed enough money to establish the Lanchester Engine Company Limited in an equal partnership with the brothers Whitfield.

The money was spent for the workshop, which was situated at Armourer Mills Factory in Birmingham (formerly occupied by BSA), plus the necessary equipment. Fred Lanchester paid special attention to ensure that standardized parts were manufactured precisely, with tolerances as fine as possible. Many people at the time thought this unnecessary, but some years later Standard and others followed the same aim. A failure in the 1,000-mile run of the ACGB&I did not help the board trust its General Manager Fred Lanchester, however.

After careful preparation—which was to become the basis of the marque's reputation for unsurpassed quality—production in quantity started in summer 1901. The air-cooled 4-liter two-cylinder 10-horsepower engine made 16-brake horsepower at 1,250 rpm. It had an unusual cylinder head, with one valve in the combustion chamber and another one above, which allowed either the air-fuel mixture in from the inlet port, or exhaust gases out to the exhaust pipe. The incoming gases helped keep the valve seat rather cool, giving an advantage in longevity over other air-cooled engines of the era. A gravity-fed oil supply, from the oil tank mounted above the engine, made an early form of automatic lubrication possible. The transmission allowed preselection of gears—40 years before the automatic transmission was invented!

The body was quite similar to the 8-horsepower, with no hood at the front. The fenders were the first to

A 1903 Lanchester 12-horsepower, already with water cooling. *(J)*

Above: The larger Lanchester 20- and 28-horsepower were regarded as aristocrats of the road. *(St)*

Below: 1910 Lanchester 28-horsepower with extended ground clearance for use in the colonies. *(Long)*

be made from aluminum, and the tonneau model was the first-ever car with a hardtop. The chassis consisted of two longitudinal steel members with a robust aluminum sheet in between. Suspension was improved with radius arms both above and below the leaf springs. Spring deflection was exceptionally long. Soon the Lanchester gained a reputation for its unrivaled suspension, assisted by the unusually long wheelbase of more than 90 inches.

Not much different from the 10-horsepower was the 16-horsepower. Its roller bearings were made in-house and allowed up to 1,750 rpm, resulting in a power output of 23 horsepower. This model, of which about 20 examples were made, was intended for sporting events. On July 2, 1903, the 16-horsepower took part in the Gordon Bennett Cup contest, which was named after its sponsor, who was editor of *New York Herald*. Such contests took place every year from 1900 until 1905. In the knockout the Lanchester made it to the semifinal.

From 1903 the cooling fan would be replaced by conventional water cooling, which improved performance; these models were called the 12- and 18-horsepower. Of the latter only six examples were made—a true rarity, even at its time. Additionally, Lanchester's latest invention could be specified, the disc brake. Dirt and humidity caused trouble with the not yet very advanced copper brake pads, and none survived. The 10-horsepower could be converted at Lanchester to water cooling, and was then called the 10/12-horsepower. All these models were produced until early 1906.

The elaborate and costly design of the cars hardly left any profits for the Lanchester Engine Company to reduce credits. Financial problems were the inevitable consequence, and after a not very successful floating of shares, Lanchester went under receivership in late March 1904. In order to provide the necessary capital, the company was restructured as Lanchester Motor Company on December 19, 1904. Hamilton Barnsley became managing director, and Fred Lanchester was just technical consultant with a much lower income than he had had before as partner. The change left him with less to do, however, and allowed him to spend time doing other things, so Lanchester could live with the new situation.

Fred Lanchester's reduced influence at Lanchester was highlighted by the fact that from 1905 onward, the engines were mounted vertically instead of horizontally. The first of these vehicles was the 20-horsepower, introduced early in 1905 and designed in most part by Fred Lanchester. It was very advanced with its five white metal main bearings, an oil pump, and lightweight alloy pistons. The gearbox was operated by a single lever, and top speed was 50 miles per hour. Throttle was regulated by a lever (for adjusting idle) and a sliding valve, which soon were replaced with an accelerator pedal and butterfly valve. At the same time a Bosch high-tension ignition and magneto were employed. In November 1906 the bodies got extremely wide doors. In 1908 a battery and coil ignition was introduced. The forward-pointing steering lever was often replaced with a steering wheel, as enclosed bodies became more fashionable.

Lanchester unveiled its first six-cylinder car at the Olympia Motor Show in November 1906. The inevitably long crankshafts of such engines are prone to oscillations, causing unnecessary noise and damage. Lanchester carefully harmonized the dimensions of his 28-horsepower engine to avoid this. The engine was similar to a 20-horsepower but with two additional cylinders; power output was 42 horsepower at 2,200 rpm. Production lasted until 1912, while the 20-horsepower was discontinued in 1911.

In 1910 Fred Lanchester agreed to a further reduction of his hours for the Lanchester Company, thus winning time for other jobs. One of these was his consultancy to Daimler. There, Lanchester added to the expertise on hand, which included Charles Yale Knight, who had a similar influence. He came from America (as had Percy Martin), in this case northern Wisconsin. There he studied the adversities of agriculture and wrote newspaper articles about the subject. Through this work he came to Washington, where he first encountered the automobile. His first impression was spoiled by the noise produced by this machine, and so it became Knight's mission to find quieter-running engines.

Quite rightly, Knight thought that most of the noise was caused by the valve mechanism, particularly the camshaft. He studied technical literature, hoping that he could find more silent valves. Through this he learned of L. B. Kilbourne, who had more experience in engine design. Together in 1903 they invented a valve mechanism that not only was much more complicated but also noisier than the usual arrangement. Nevertheless, they applied for a patent.

Then, still in 1903, Knight had the idea of inserting vertically moving sleeves into the cylinders. These had slits that at the appropriate moment would open inlet and exhaust passages at the sides of the combustion chambers. After some trial and error a mechanism was found that moved the sleeve in the intended way, but this again was too complicated to assure silent running.

With a second sleeve between cylinder and piston, the mechanism could be simplified in a satisfactory manner. In October 1904 an engine was made using this system and mounted in a Panhard & Levassor chassis.

Early in 1906 Edward Manville, now Daimler chairman, met a friend of Knight who told him of the revolutionary sleeve engine. Manville asked for drawings, and soon the Wool Mill was very curious about this mechanism. A demonstration of a test engine by Knight himself confirmed Daimler's highest expectations, and soon Daimler had secured the license rights for the United Kingdom. This gave Daimler a rough diamond to polish, which became Fred Lanchester's duty.

The public was more skeptical about this invention. The pistons now were much smaller than the cylinder bore because the sleeves required space between the two. Also, it was doubtful whether the sleeves could be lubricated sufficiently.

As a reassurance, Daimler 22- and 38-horsepower four-cylinder engines were changed to sleeves and tested by the RAC. (The former ACGB&I now had the support of the King and thus become "royal.") This test consisted of a 133-hour run on a test bed, after which the engines were mounted in two chassis, driven to Brooklands for 1,920 miles of racing, and then returned to the test bed for another five hours, during which power output was measured. After this triathlon-like exercise, both engines were dismantled. No wear could be measured, and so all reservations against the new design were removed. As a consequence, participation in further reliability runs and racing became superfluous.

Ironically, it was now the Daimler Motorengesellschaft of Cannstatt that applied for a license for the sliding sleeves. Although this license was granted, in Germany only Benz (long before being merged with Mercedes) built a noteworthy number of engines employing the Knight principle. In other countries luxury makes such as Panhard & Levassor and Voisin in France employed the sleeve valves. Another to do so was the fine but later hapless Minerva from Belgium—the problem of starting these engines in winter with cold, thick oil around the sleeves became an impediment.

Although others used rotating sleeves, which were deemed superior to those in the Daimler design that moved up and down, Daimler retained Knight's idea and used it for all its engines for the 1909 model year. (The six-cylinder engine also introduced in November 1908 only got the sleeve valves in 1909.) The very first British six-cylinder engine had been made six years earlier by Napier, the keenest competitor to Daimler's expensive chassis before the advent of Rolls-Royce. The Daimler six-cylinder, with its bore of 124mm and stroke of 130mm, had a capacity of 9.4 liters and was called the 57-horsepower. All these engines had a vibration damper coupled with the crankshaft, which was noticeable to passengers who said that the engine ran particularly smoothly and without the least vibration. This vibration damper was again Fred Lanchester's invention, although some sources say that Henry Royce had been some months ahead of Lanchester in this case. Daimler's spray carburetor with several jets was no longer fed by gravity but by pressure in the fuel tank caused by exhaust gas. As an antithesis to the 57-horsepower, Daimler in late 1909 introduced its cheapest model in years, the 15-horsepower.

Further technical masterpieces were the hybrid buses called KPL, after the first letters of the patent

Top: One of the first cars with sleeve valves was this 1910 Daimler 15-horsepower. *(Long)*

Above: At that time, advertising was picturesque. *(J)*

Above: The revolutionary KPL bus. The early variant of the Daimler logo may be of particular interest. *(Long)*

Right: A Daimler 57-horsepower limousine for the King who particularly liked to use this car. *(Long)*

Below: Daimler chassis, with their powerful engines, seemed ideal for buses. *(St)*

holders Knight, Pieper, and Lanchester. These were equipped with an oversized dynamo that could operate as an electric motor to aid the four-stroke engine if a gradient demanded particularly high power output. The idea was inspired by Ferdinand Porsche's Lohner, which had electric motors as hubs that were provided with electrical energy by a four-stroke engine. The KPL buses were offered from 1910 but only 12 examples were sold, although they already had a unit body of steel and aluminum—many years before Lancia's famous Lambda.

Back in 1692 no firearms were produced in Britain, but in that year Sir Richard Newdegate arranged for five gunsmiths from Birmingham to be awarded a governmental order for no less than 200 muskets per month. This order created a tradition of smiths out of which the Birmingham Small Arms Company (BSA) was created in 1861. Under the BSA name, this company is well known to classic motorcycle enthusiasts.

Around 1880, in an era of persistent peace, BSA saw the demand for weapons decrease and decided to diversify. So BSA turned to the booming bicycle business, discarded Lawson's safety bicycle as rubbish and soon concentrated on the production of subcontracted parts for the bicycle industry. In 1908 BSA started the production of complete bicycles, followed a year later by motorcycles. Starting in 1907, BSA even made its own cars, but they were not very successful and are hardly remembered. So BSA kept an eye out for a car manufacturer to swallow and soon concentrated on Daimler, whose sales and profits had well risen over the past years, the latter now having reached six-figure amounts.

So the Daimler Motor Company was recreated once again in a merger with BSA as Daimler Company Limited in 1910. It cost BSA more than £600,000 to become the sole shareholder. Manville as chairman and Martin as managing director continued their work, but the board was joined by the extraordinarily shrewd BSA manager F. Dudley Docker, instigator of the takeover, and some of his BSA colleagues. Daimler cars benefited from the new parent in that they added BSA wire wheels, adding a filigree aspect to the looks of the formerly staid luxury cars. The BSA range of cars was broadened by a new 2-liter car of Daimler design, the BSA 14-horsepower four-cylinder tourer with a three-speed gearbox. In 1911 Daimler's radiator design was improved by slanted tubes instead of vertical ones, which were less prone to leaks even after long usage.

In 1912 Daimler started to move from the Wool Mill to nearby Radford. This site had already been purchased in 1908 and remained in use for Daimler engine production until 1997. Also in 1912, Daimler introduced a revised 20-horsepower engine with detachable cylinder heads, which made decoking the combustion chambers a far easier job. Switches and instruments that previously had been scattered all over the dashboard now were concentrated on an aluminum dashboard to which the steering column was fixed as well. In 1913 the spray carburetor was improved with seven instead of only three jets, which resulted in quicker reaction to the accelerator. In 1914 the 20-horsepower drew attention with its new gearbox that was linked directly to the differential, and with its cantilever leaf springs at the rear. An electric starter now was standard equipment, and after World War I more complete electric equipment became standard at Daimler.

World War I caused many a change for Daimler. The company offered many completely different products, more in line with the BSA tradition, including flying apparatus, steam tractors, an early form of tank, and early aero engines. After that war the situation for car manufacturers was similar to the one after World War II. Development had been stopped for years, and the factories were badly damaged and worn from war and war production, and raw materials were scarce. Nevertheless, the Society of Motor Traders & Manufacturers scheduled its 13th Motor Show at London's famous Olympia Hall in 1919 (its first since 1913). Of course, Daimler had to show its colors!

The first step, however, was to restart production of the 1914 models, 30- and 45-horsepower, the latter being particularly lavish with silver-plated fittings. The extravagance of a new model was beyond reach, apart from a shorter wheelbase 30-horsepower called the Light Thirty for the established owner-driver. Under the hood little development was achieved, apart from the semiautomatic lubrication of the main bearings. The honeycomb radiator was remarkable, as was its height now being on level with the hood. Fred Lanchester had developed a prototype with hydraulic, independent suspension on all four wheels (35 years before the hydropneumatic was introduced), a hydraulic clutch, and a single-spoke steering wheel with levers and instruments concentrated in front of the driver. This prototype was kept a secret and did not go into production, as it was deemed too advanced for the typical Daimler customer.

Another small revolution did take place: Instead of selling the cars directly from Daimler to customers, a dealer network was established. This was not an easy or quick task; the low number of Daimlers sold made it difficult to attract competent dealers, except in London. Daimler had a long-standing sales office there with personnel qualified to maintain Daimler cars and to look after customers. An acquaintance of Frederick Simms, Ernest M. C. Instone, had joined that office in 1897 as company secretary. Together with Undecimus Stratton, Daimler's London manager since 1903, he continued the business for himself under the name of Stratton & Instone. The abbreviated telegraph address of Stratstone later became the name of the whole company, which still supplies Britain's finest society with Jaguars and Daimlers. Later, 10 such dealerships were established all over Britain.

The organization of dealerships shows that even Daimler cars did not sell automatically. Quite a few people who would borrow a dress coat for a prom would not allow themselves the horrendous cost of maintaining a Daimler. The obvious solution was a car rental business, and for this purpose Daimler Hire Ltd. was founded in 1920, continuing what the manufacturer in fact had already started in 1897.

In 1923 Daimler Hire even was awarded the Royal warrant, although all cars supplied were returned to the works. In the interwar years this was a good business, but

Above: A 1912 Daimler 30-horsepower convertible. The carefully handcrafted body was made at Arthur Mulliner in Northampton. *(Long)*

Right: In 1911 the latest Daimlers—in this case a 12-horsepower—still looked much like the 1905 models. *(J)*

A very large coupe on the 1911 chassis TA 23. *(J)*

1913 Daimler 30-horsepower. *(J)*

Top: 1923 Daimler 16-horsepower doctor's coupe with Shaw body. *(Long)*

Above: 1922 Daimler 20-horsepower chassis TT4. *(Long)*

later the interest in Daimler rental diminished. Daimler Hire was ultimately integrated into Hertz, an American car rental company closely associated with Ford.

Daimler Hire also offered customers travel by air with Daimler Airways, which was established in 1922. In these pioneering days it was difficult to convince long-distance travelers that airplanes were a safe means of transport. With government money and financial support from BSA, Daimler Airways thus was more focused on cargo transportation.

Despite being founded quite early, Daimler Airways was not without a predecessor. It continued the business of Airco (or Aircraft Manufacturing Company), which BSA had taken over in 1920. In 1922 Daimler employed the first "cabin boys" in aviation while Swissair created their female counterparts more than a dozen years later. Despite its slogan, "Daimler–Hire by Land, Sea and Air," Daimler Airways was not overly successful. In 1924 it was merged with three other British airlines to become the state-owned Imperial Airways that existed until 1940.

Returning to the cars, it is worth pointing out how the long six-cylinder engines and formal bodies led to the classic Daimler proportions. The hoods of these cars were much lower than most other makes, only a few inches higher than the fenders. At the time, however, it was the impressively high radiator grille that inspired the enthusiast. These low, horizontal hoods caused a problem; the bottom edge of the windshield needed to be set high in order to avoid ugly proportions caused by the high roofs necessary to accommodate the large hats that passengers of the day wore. A bulkhead considerably higher than the hood was a usual sight on a Daimler of that period.

Other makes had turned to the torpedo look, an idea fostered by Théo Masui who, despite his exotic name, lived in London. The torpedo look made the hood and body look like one purposeful, elegant unit, with no steps visible in the side elevation. Daimler only followed in 1921, offering low and high hoods to provide the right proportions for both enclosed and open bodies.

Daimler, after purchasing MMC's workshops, usually supplied its own coachwork, which was quite unusual in this market segment. A true snob of the "roaring twenties" would not accept the idea that he might meet a car similar to his in traffic. So Daimler also delivered "naked" chassis, but unlike most makes Daimler added a steel frame to support the coachwork. This ensured that the body was properly fixed to the chassis and that there was a solid foundation for the artwork of the coachbuilder.

Despite any ingenuity, demand for the most expensive cars was inconsistent, and even Daimler had to reduce prices. The Light Thirty chassis was now £900 instead of £1,125.

In July 1921 came a 20-horsepower similar to the prewar car of the same name—it was in fact a 30-horsepower minus two cylinders. Daimler's last four-cylinder car, it was offered only for a short time. At the 1922 Motor Show, Daimler had no technical innovation to present, and even the latest BSA models were Daimlers in miniature. So the interest of the public was diverted to the first automotive radio, made by pioneer Marconi and mounted under the front seats. It was operable on several frequencies and had a rather awkward antenna mounted on the roof. The silent engine made audible all the shortcomings of early broadcasting, plus it was not shielded from radio interference caused by other vehicles. With these shortcomings, demand was very low, and the radio soon disappeared from brochures.

In November 1922 a truly new Daimler was unveiled, finally. A six-cylinder with sleeve valves, the 12-horsepower had just 1,542cc of displacement, and thus was smaller and more manageable to drive than the typical Daimler. This was Daimler's first monobloc six, its first car equipped with a single-plate dry clutch instead of the leather conus, and had its first centrally mounted (instead of outside) gearshift lever. Shifting gates were not visible any longer. The carburetor included an autovac system, while the cooling system relied on gravity. The splash lubrication with which the oil was moved directly to the places where it was most needed was quite advanced. The whole car cost just £550. An even less expensive BSA 14-horsepower with quarter-elliptic springs and disc wheels—a successor to the 1923 four-cylinder (BSA chassis, 1,444cc)—was available. At the same time, new 16- and 21-horsepower Daimlers (2.2-liters or 3-liters) were announced. Thanks to the new models, Daimler offered 56 types of cars in 1923—a far cry from many competitors who offered just one type.

In the autumn of 1923, the 35-horsepower was introduced, the first Daimler with four-wheel brakes. In early times it was thought that a car could not be steered as long as the front wheels were used for braking—despite typically low speeds of the day, the risk of locking wheels was thought too high. The 35-horsepower had a chassis of particularly light design and half-elliptic springing. The sleeves in the engine were made from aluminum instead of steel, which had replaced the cast iron used initially. Consequently, the sleeves were now thinner, so that within the same bore larger pistons could be employed. This resulted in an increased capacity of 5.8 liters instead of 5 liters (in the case of the 30-horsepower, or 8.5 liters instead of 7.5 liters for the 45-horsepower). The same trick transformed the only one-year-old 12-, 16- and 21-horsepower models into 16-, 20-, and 25-horsepower models. The new 16-horsepower was again available as a still less expensive BSA—another early example of what one day would be called badge engineering. The older 21-horsepower remained in production until 1925. The narrow but high radiator became typical for the Daimler for decades. In 1924, some 57-horsepower models were made, allegedly, exclusively for the royal household. These models were on chassis of the latest specification, but with engine dimensions from the prewar 57-horsepower.

In 1925 the semiautomatic lubrication was replaced with a forced lubrication, but little else was changed. However, most models were given new designations in that the effective brake horsepower was added with a hyphen to the HP figure, i.e., 16-55, 20-70, 25-85, and 35-120. The flagship, which was soon to disappear, remained the Forty-Five.

Top: This 1924 Daimler 35-horsepower already had four-wheel brakes and lighter steel sleeves. This elegant phaeton body was made at Hoopers. *(Long)*

Above: Forgotten times: The luxury of the 1920s. *(Long)*

Left: The six-cylinder Daimler 25-85 was a masterpiece. *(J)*

11

DOUBLE-SIX AND DOCKER

After 57-horsepower production was discontinued for the second time, a gap was left open at the top of Daimler's model range, despite the negative effect on the prestige of the marque. At that time Lawrence Pomeroy of Vauxhall fame—he had designed the 1912 Prince Henry sports car—joined Daimler and filled this gap by siamesing two 25-85-horsepower engines at a 60-degree angle to a common crankshaft. The result, introduced in 1926, was called simply but accurately the Double-Six. The chassis was remarkable for its Dewandre vacuum-assisted braking system, which soon was used for other large Daimler models as well. The Double-Six was a heavy car of immense power and flexibility. According to *The Autocar* the engine could drive the car at speeds from 2 to 102 miles per hour in top gear without any fuss. Daimler was now well ahead of Rolls-Royce—it would be nine more years before Derby introduced its first V-12 car, and then there were problems with it. Daimler's was the first series-production V-12 made outside the United States. It developed about 150 horsepower at 3,000 rpm. This may sound quite impressive, but the largest six-cylinders of the day were much lighter and less expensive, yet they achieved nearly the same power output.

In the summer of 1927 a smaller Double-Six was added with a 3.7-liter engine, which in effect was twice a 16-55. This was called Double-Six 30, while the larger car became the Double-Six 50. As there were 74 types of cars in Daimler's 1927 brochure, it was not easy to distinguish these. The Double-Sixes now featured a vertical bar in the center of the radiator to help them stand out. Soon this bar was to become part of every Daimler grille, and it still features in every modern Daimler's face. Joseph Mackle from Stratton-Instone proved that even the smaller Double-Six could be a good sports car if it was built as a light two-seater. His very special example was made to his detailed specification at otherwise rather mediocre Hoyal Body Corporation. This *Magic Carpet*, with its aerodynamic boat tail body, was finished in a mayonnaise color with copper-colored instruments and leather seats. The car reached 90 miles per hour—a very high speed for a luxury car of that period.

In 1927 Daimler started to employ friction dampers and balloon tires. Daimler management held negotiations aiming at taking over Sunbeam—as would SS some years later.

Left: Simple elegance: 1927 Daimler Double-Six 50 on chassis P; the limousine cost £2,800. *(Long)*

Opposite: Daimler stand at the 1927 London Motor Show with a Double-Six on the left. *(Long)*

In 1929 the light alloy pistons were changed in order to improve lubrication of the sleeves and reduce oil consumption—still, a Daimler could be recognized by the blue smoke emitting from the rear. One year later, the 25-horsepower was the first Daimler with a light alloy engine block.

The next technical improvement was a very significant one. It had to do with the clutch. The leather-covered conus had been a Daimler earmark for many years. Lawrence Pomeroy had looked beyond car engineering and found a German invention in shipbuilding: the fluid flywheel invented by Professor Hermann Föttinger for Vulcan shipyard. Basically this

Modestly, England's royalty had not chromed their Daimler grilles; this is a 1929 Double-Six 50. *(J)*

Right: The raciest Double-Six of all time was this 50-horsepower low-chassis roadster for C. B. Wilson. *(Long)*

Far right: 1932 Double-Six 40/50 on normal chassis but with a particularly low sedan body made by Martin Walter for one Mr. Webber. *(Long)*

consisted of two turbine wheels face-to-face in a common oil bath. If one turbine was moved the other one would also be moved, with surprisingly little loss of energy. Engaging this clutch never would result in a jerk, which happened so often in everyday use of traditional gearbox transmissions. The first idea had been to employ the fluid flywheel just to assist the normal clutch on Daimler buses. But quickly it became obvious that the fluid flywheel could replace the traditional clutch altogether.

Thinking about transmissions, Fred Lanchester and Percy Martin remembered the preselector gearbox that Armstrong-Siddeley produced and had used since 1928 and that was so similar to Lanchester's early epicyclic boxes. Combined with the fluid flywheel, this transmission was very nearly a full automatic—one decade before the Americans had their breakthrough in this regard. At last even the least talented chauffeur could parade his master at the lowest speed without the risk of stalling, an art that is hardly in use these days—with the exception of the funeral trade, which besides royalty, encompassed Daimler's most faithful customers. Pragmatic Lawrence Pomeroy and cautious Fred Lanchester could not agree on the right date to unveil this novelty, which resulted in Lanchester retiring on October 31, 1929!

Another royal Double-Six (Queen Mary), which however had a six-cylinder engine, from 1946. *(J)*

Despite this quarrel, the new transmission was soon part of every new Daimler. Although Daimler had large and flexible engines, the fluid flywheel made driving considerably easier—a significant advantage over their competitors. Nigglers objected that the clutch housing could not be held oil-tight, that the energy lost in the oil bath was excessive and that these cars could not be push-started. As with the sleeve valves, Daimler ignored these critics and obstinately maintained its course.

In autumn 1930, when Daimler, for reasons of space, had to interrupt supply of its own bodies, the larger Double-Six was replaced with the new 30/40 and 40/50 types, with light alloy engine blocks. The smaller unit was similar to twinned 20-70s, which resulted in 5.3-liter capacity. The larger engine was bored out to 6.5 liters and thus was only marginally smaller than its predecessor. With the fluid flywheel these cars were much superior to the earlier, much-admired Double-Six. The two magnetos were replaced with a battery as source of energy, with one coil for each cylinder bank. These large vehicles remained in production for only two years. Reid Railton at Thomson & Taylor, who prepared racing cars at the Brooklands circuit, carried out some significant modifications of this type. These were two particularly low chassis, one an elegant convertible coupe and the other an impressive roadster with what seems to have been the longest hood of that period. These were impressive cars that rivaled the proportions of the fantastic Cord L-29 and Duesenberg of the era.

In 1931, two years after Fred Lanchester had left Daimler, BSA decided to take over the Lanchester Car

Company, the control of which Fred had lost more than 25 years ago. As Napier had left this market and Rolls-Royce was about to take over Bentley, this step reduced the number of competitors to just one.

Since the days of the 20- and 28-horsepower, Lanchester had made big steps forward, thanks to the engineering genius of George Lanchester. In 1911 Lanchester introduced the 38-horsepower. It had C-section chassis rails, and the rear leaf springs were mounted on the outside, still in cantilever style and with rubber bushes. In a time when windshields were no longer hinged, the leather wind protection was replaced with more conventional bulkheads, but still without an engine in front of them. The 38-horsepower was the first Lanchester with a vibration damper—a Lanchester invention—added to the lighter crankshaft, with which the 5-liter six-cylinder could top 60 miles per hour. Removing two cylinders resulted in the new 25-horsepower that was unveiled at the Motor Show in November 1911. It had an electric starter which, after a surprisingly long period, became available on the 38-horsepower as well.

The last Lanchester in which Fred had a hand was the Sporting Forty, which was introduced just before the outbreak of war in 1914. This was the first Lanchester with the engine in front of the passenger compartment—customers preferred a stylish appearance to a practical layout! The side valves were operated directly by the camshaft, in classic style. The combustion chamber was thus not a very effective shape. The front axle was made from pressed steel sheets instead of a tube, and worm-and-nut steering was attached to it. The bodies—nearly all of which Lanchester made in-house—were styled by George Lanchester, who used mock-ups carved from cheddar cheese. These were certainly the most nutritious in the industry! With about a 6-liter capacity, a top speed of 70 miles per hour was within reach.

During the war, Lanchester made armored cars based on the 38-horsepower chassis, which proved themselves even under the worst and coldest conditions of the Russian winter. When the end of the war was near, George Lanchester improved the Forty with still larger chassis rails. The spring leaves were now made in-house, with polished surfaces that improved their qualities quite considerably. For cost reasons the four radius arms had to be given up, so the suspension was inferior to the earlier cars. Conventional half-elliptic springs were now employed at the front. The mono-bloc engine was improved with a cross-flow head and a bevel shaft driving the overhead camshaft and valves. For the first time on a Lanchester, the wool thread evaporative fuel system was dismissed in favor of Smiths' four-jet spray carburetor, provided with fuel by autovac.

The extraordinary silence and comfort of this car prompted test drivers to believe that it was propelled by an elastic band when this first-class car was unveiled at the November 1919 Motor Show. In 1922 the car followed the fashion of higher radiators, and in 1924 a four-wheel brake system and further improvements were carried out (such as the reinvention of the vibration damper) that made the engine run even smoother. A side effect was that the engine became more powerful as well, now achieving a top speed of nearly 90 miles per hour—much faster than Rolls-Royce's New Phantom that was deemed to be so sporting. One example of this Forty belonged to the Duke of York, and young Princess and later Queen Elizabeth II had her first public appearance in that car.

The Lanchester marque now seemed to have a more sporting image. Tony Hann had lapped Brooklands in

Top: The flashiest Daimlers between the wars were the low-chassis types by Thomson & Taylor. *(J)*

Above: The only surviving low-chassis Daimler Double-Six has a drophead coupe body by Corsica. *(Long)*

Top: Lanchester 40-horsepower drophead coupe; the largest Lanchesters remained in production for a while after Daimler's takeover. *(Long)*

Above: Lanchester 40-horsepower straight eight-cylinder with landaulet body. *(Long)*

1911 already and was on par with the likes of Lea-Francis, Bugatti, and Aston Martin as late as 1924. A Forty prototype with racing body set long-distance world records (five hours' average of more than 75 miles per hour and others) in the 8-liter class G with Selvyn Francis Edge at the wheel—the famous racing driver who previously had been so closely associated with Napier. Lionel Rapson had acquired a similar car in order to test the tires of his production. Some racing at Brooklands—with successes even against Woolf Barnato and his legendary Bentley—gained Lanchester further records in 1924, like a 400-mile average of 98 miles per hour. Unfortunately these achievements were never exploited in advertising so that they remained almost secret.

Acceleration took place in other areas. Because the coach enamel the company had been using needed such a long time to dry, Lanchester changed over to the less perfect finish of quicker-drying cellulose paint, which had just been introduced by American Du Pont. Progress in tire design resulted in 1926 in the use of the much more comfortable balloon tires that, despite much lower pressures, ensured good roadholding even at higher speeds. In 1928 a last batch of Forties was produced, and some of them became armored bodies. This batch was equipped with the Dewandre brake servo. However, the 40-horsepower remained available beyond 1929 through special order.

In autumn 1923 a smaller 21-horsepower was added to the Lanchester range of models. It had a 3-liter capacity, produced 60 horsepower at 3,400 rpm, and could go about 60 miles per hour. It was much praised by the press, and the lower price made it affordable for more customers. The 21-horsepower was bored out in 1925 to a little over 3.3-liter capacity. The name remained unchanged although it now was a 23-horsepower, according to the taxation. The year 1927 was a disappointment, as the company failed to gain a profit for the first time since the war. Thus, the 21-horsepower was modernized only by an improved front suspension with Luvax dampers.

In September 1928 a 30-horsepower was unveiled, which was a 21-horsepower with two more cylinders, i.e., a straight eight. Power and performance were on par with the older 40-horsepower. In 1929 an improved exhaust manifold, thermostatically controlled slats in front of the radiator, and Lucas P 100 headlights made the 30-horsepower still more attractive. The 30-horsepower was the only true Lanchester to be supplied with coachwork from outside sources like Hooper or Windover.

The depression of 1929 made it difficult for Lanchester to find enough customers for its expensive cars. The situation was aggravated by a lack of capital when Frank Lanchester took control of the commercial side of the business in 1930. By the end of the year the bank insisted on being refunded within two weeks. Although only £28,000 had to be repaid—much less than the worth of material in store—this was not possible. Rolls-Royce and Napier would well have liked to help Lanchester, but the time left was too short for them—as it was for some customers who tried to help. So the mighty BSA took over the debts on December 28, 1930. Persistent rumors said that BSA had influenced the common bank to kill off Lanchester. Hamilton Barnsley, then Lanchester chairman, was so horrified that he suffered a heart attack. BSA immediately took over control and closed down production in Birmingham on February 2, 1931. Some last classic Lanchesters were assembled from stock until 1932. The price achieved for the premises alone was much higher than what BSA had to pay altogether for the takeover—it still raises one's hackles!

Under BSA, Lanchester was now aimed at the customers just below Daimler level, while BSA was restricted to even smaller cars, often with only three wheels. Under new leadership, Lanchester thus started with a 15/18-horsepower model, a 2.5-liter six-cylinder with a fluid flywheel. In order to produce this model at the Daimler factory that was already bursting at the seams, the body shop was closed down temporarily. Contrary to Daimler's practice, the engine's valves were operated conventionally as on the previous Lanchesters. This model is unforgettable in that it won the "prototype" of the RAC rally that was held in 1932 in Torquay. The small sibling of this car was a 10-horsepower introduced in 1932 that was very similar in design to the 15/18-horsepower.

Daimler also suffered from the depression and no less than His Majesty King George V ordered five new cars to attempt to improve morale.

In autumn 1932 despite—or perhaps as a consequence of—the financially tight situation, a new model was introduced that according to format and technical design might well have become a Lanchester: the 15-horsepower. It was a rather small but well-appointed car with a six-cylinder measuring 1.8 liters and a fluid flywheel, but its poppet valves revealed its Lanchester heritage. This set a trend at Daimler, where in 1933 the larger models also moved to poppet valves. These valves had been greatly improved since 1909 and had become much more silent, while allowing less oily and odorous exhaust gases than slide-valve engines. The small Daimler was particularly modern in that the accelerator pedal was on the right, not between brake and clutch pedals. The 15-horsepower was the first Daimler with mechanical fuel pumps.

The 15-horsepower was exactly right for the times. Many formerly affluent people had lost some of their wealth in the stock market crash and thus could no longer afford a large car and chauffeur. The 15-horsepower offered a similar level of comfort and quality, including the easy-to-handle gear change, and combined this with much lower cost. It was not only *The Autocar* who found that this was a particularly attractive package. The hydraulic brakes came in for particular praise, but it would still be a long way until they were established in all Daimler models.

Soon after the introduction of the 15-horsepower, in March 1933 the long-time chairman Edward Manville (since March 1923 Sir Edward) died. Fortunately, he witnessed Daimler's slight economical improvement after 1929. After an interim period under Sir Alexander Roger, meritorious engineer Percy Martin chaired the company from early 1934 until 1936, when Sir Geoffrey Burton took over.

In the meantime, the 15-horsepower showed its potential and became a 2-liter through an increased stroke in 1934. This was the first Daimler with the "D" motif on the hubs. In 1937 the car developed into the "new" 15, although it now was taxed at nearly 17 horsepower as a consequence of the engine being bored out to 2.2 liters. The car was quite advanced with its independent front suspension. In the following year, the capacity was increased again to 2.5 liters, which remained typical for the small Daimler models even after World War II. Some coachbuilders offered particularly attractive convertible bodies. One of them was Salmons, who called its designs "Tickford," which later became the name of the whole company. Salmons had

Above left: Lanchester 15/18-horsepower and its owner Colonel Loughborough, winner of the 1932 Rally to Torquay. *(Long)*

Top: The famous 1934 Daimler 15-horsepower, the first model with the D motif on the hubcaps. *(Long)*

Above: Daimler also made some BSA cars like this 1934 10-horsepower; the similarity is significant. *(Long)*

A rather small 1931 Daimler 16-horsepower. *(J)*

Above: Queen Mary's 1935 Double-Six was one of only nine with poppet valves. *(Long)*

Below left: The Straight Eight was the most advanced Daimler before World War II. *(J)*

Below right: 1935 Daimler Light Straight Eight with sport sedan body by Arthur Mulliner. *(Long)*

been established in 1925 at Newport Pagnell and specialized in open cars with a crank for folding the convertible top.

The Lanchester range was substantially revised for 1934. A Light Six was added with an overhead valve six-cylinder engine of 1,378cc capacity. A similar model was available as a BSA Light Six, as a late successor to their former four- and six-cylinder cars, which had gone out of production in 1926. The smaller BSA was replaced with a variant of the Lanchester 10 with 1,185cc engine (1,298 from 1936 onward). Both had mechanical brakes instead of the more advanced hydraulic Lanchester brakes.

After these new models were introduced, the company needed to turn its attention to its largest models. In comparison to these modern cars, the Double-Six seemed like a dinosaur. Again Daimler made use of what it had gained with the Lanchester takeover; its Straight Eight engines were a promising concept. Lawrence Pomeroy developed from them an exceptionally silent (even for the most fastidious Daimler customers) 3.7-liter OHV engine, which was unveiled in 1934. This engine owed some of its smoothness to rubber mounts between engine and chassis. In the meantime, the coil ignition had become reliable enough for Daimler to dispense with the second one. The lever that had to be pushed forward to operate the handbrake at the gearbox now was a thing of the past. The brake pedal now operated the brakes at all four wheels, as did the handbrake with a more conventional lever. The spray carburetor that had been made in-house now was replaced with two Stromberg downdraft carburetors and a mechanical fuel pump. This Straight Eight was cataloged as Chassis V 26.

In 1935 the Straight Eight was enlarged to 4 liters (Chassis type V), and it replaced the last Double-Sixes, which still had sleeve valves. It was joined by a 3.4-liter Light Straight Eight (Chassis type E). In 1936 the 6.5-liter—similar to the much older 57-horsepower—was revived for a short while. Provided with poppet valves, nine of them were made specifically for the coronation of King Edward VIII. But in May 1937 Edward abdicated to follow the voice of love, so it became the coronation of George VI. Aside from the Double-Sixes, the coronation involved 150 Straight Eights and presumably more than 800 other Daimlers. Certainly there has never been another opportunity to see this many Daimlers in one place.

In 1935 the medium range of models was replaced with a new 20 and Light 20, the latter with a smaller engine and shorter wheelbase, ideal for the gentleman owner-driver. At Lanchester, the 18-horsepower was revised and received a slightly smaller engine. A Lanchester 14 was added, which was a slightly enlarged variant of the Light Six.

In 1936 the engine of the Lanchester 10 was enlarged and now was an 11. The 18 was replaced with a new model, although it was only one year old. The new 18 was a close relative of the Daimler Light 20, an affront to Lanchester enthusiasts of old times.

In 1937 the Lanchester 14, now called Roadrider, was joined by a sibling called de Luxe, with the body and suspension of Daimler's New 15, combined with a smaller engine of course. The Light Six was deleted from the catalogs.

In 1937 Daimler moved out of the traditional Wool Mill and concentrated all production at its newer Radford plant. Adjacent to the new plant, a so-called shadow factory was under construction for war production. The foresighted government had installed a scheme of such shadow factories as a precaution against damages caused to other factories by air raids.

In 1938 the 3.4-liter was enlarged to a 4-liter of which particularly the pillarless sedan made by Van den Plas gained popularity among enthusiasts. (A particularly nice example could be seen many years later in the film *Remains of the Day.*) The Lanchester Roadrider became even more similar to the Daimler 15 this year.

A variant for cost-conscious customers was the ELS 24, also unveiled during 1938. It combined the Straight Eight chassis with a 3.3-liter six-cylinder engine from the 24; it carried very large bodies at little running cost.

In April 1939 Daimler used the base of the 15 to introduce the Dolphin sporting tourer and an elegant Ritz sedan. The Dolphin was the first Daimler in years to play a role in the RAC Rally. In the same year the ES 24 was introduced as a variant of the 24, with a luxurious six-window body. The grille was curved backward for the first time on a Daimler; this remained typical until well after the war. However, soon the production of fine cars was discontinued in favor of aero engines and the like. For this purpose, Daimler built a second shadow factory two miles away in Browns Lane at Allesley, which was not yet completed when war broke out. As already mentioned, this factory became Jaguar's home some years after the war.

The Dolphin was based on Daimler's small chassis. This example took part in the 1939 Monte Carlo Rally and then received this four-seater body. *(Long)*

During the November 1940 air raids, both factories were severely damaged, and in April 1941 Daimler again suffered from the Blitz. Production was relocated to other factories, but Managing Director George Hally managed to resume the former production volume within just two months. To the regret of historians, the Daimler archives were lost in the fires caused by the bombs.

Car production was not interrupted altogether. Representative cars were manufactured sporadically, but the armored vehicle was the order of the day. The Scout, developed under the name Dingo, was available in late 1939. This evolved into the even more practical Mark I Armored Car, which, with its conning tower, was similar to a true tank with wheels instead of tracks. The engine was a four-liter six-cylinder with 100 horsepower.

Besides producing further war material, in 1940 Daimler managed to take over Hooper & Company, which had made the coachwork for nearly all Daimler

Below left to right: Straight Eight 4.5-liter touring limousine by Gurney Nutting, made for Lady Roger, Daimler's then "first lady." *(Long)*

The light color of this Ritz makes it resemble Jaguar's 3.5-liter sedan. *(Long)*

The Ritz was the finest among the small Daimlers. *(St)*

This Daimler DE 36 limousine by Hooper already has the later rear style. *(Long)*

Above: An early DB 18 cabriolet by Tickford. *(Long)*

Below: An eight-cylinder DE 36 as made for the Royal Tour to South Africa. *(J)*

cars supplied to the Royal Mews. In 1938 Hooper had taken over an even older coachbuilder, Barker (founded in 1710; Hooper was only established in 1807), and took over two factories at Acton and Chelsea that were suitable for war production. Many Daimler bodies were made under the Barker name after the war.

Daimler's parent company and its then almighty Dudley Docker provided the company with a new chairman: Sir Bernard Docker, Dudley's son. Just before his death, Dudley put him at some key posts within BSA, and in 1946 Sir Bernard became Daimler's chief. The Docker era is remembered as one of the darkest in Daimler's history. Admittedly, Sir Bernard had to make do with products and production methods that only rarely in the company's history had generated big profits.

During the war, Daimler's financial situation had not been too bad at all. Nevertheless there were rumors that Daimler would stop all car production after the war, but this was not the case. Instead Daimler regarded

Above: Daimler DE 36 sport sedan by Freestone & Webb for the 1949 Motor Show; a similar car was exported to Jamaica. *(Long)*

Right: An open DE 36 on the Australian Tour of young Queen Elizabeth II. *(Long)*

it as a matter of honor to reinstall all prewar machinery and resume peacetime production. The DB 18 was available already in February 1946. This was the prewar 2.5-liter with higher compression (7:1), raising power to a lofty 70 horsepower. The standardized steel body was made at Mulliners, in Birmingham, but special coachwork was available as well. The Tickford convertible was offered again, and there was a similar variant from Barker, which was less expensive.

Soon larger models were also available. As a flagship, Daimler introduced another Straight Eight, called the DE 36, with a 5.5-liter capacity. The engine was similar to the prewar unit, but with both bore and stroke extended by 5mm. Its sister, called the DE 27, was inspired by the earlier ELS 24 and used the larger car's chassis, shortened by 8 inches. The engine was taken from the Armored Car, and with a compression ratio of 6.3:1 it developed 110 horsepower. For better noise and vibration suppression the engine and transmission were rubber-mounted.

Chassis design of the DE models was virtually identical. The DE 36 engine, with its 150 horsepower, ensured a top speed of 80 miles per hour. The demand for such an expensive vehicle was minimal, and so no standard body was offered. The customers ordered their coachwork from distinguished companies like Hooper, who alone made 114 bodies for the DE 36. Others came from Freestone & Webb, Windovers, and so on. Customers were even more distinguished, with some royalty among them. According to the latest fashion, the doors now were curved outward at the bottom so the running boards were hidden.

For the rich and famous, Daimler thus had the right cars. The company also had to take care of more normal customers, and this was, as before the war, Lanchester's duty. Its LD 10 had already been developed just before the war as a replacement for the 11-horsepower, and it would have been introduced for the 1940 model year had war not intervened. So the introduction was delayed by six years. Its 1.3-liter four-cylinder engine developed 40 horsepower, and even this small car had the fluid flywheel. Its not overly attractive all-steel body was made by Briggs at Dagenham. It was a fine car, but at £661, no real threat to Morris and Wolseley.

In 1947 King George VI visited South Africa, and this meant some additional business for Daimler. For this royal tour, five DE 36s were ordered, plus some DB 18s. For use in Britain two more DE 36s and a DE 27 were ordered as well. On February 2, 1948, Princess Elizabeth (now the Queen) took delivery of her personal DE 27 with a Hooper limousine body. Despite its appropriate registration HRH 1 (Her Royal Highness),

Top: The Special Sports was a relatively small but fine car. *(J)*

Above: The wonderful Daimler Special Sports had considerably more power than the standard DB 18. *(Long)*

Left: The small Lanchester LD 10 was ready for production just before the war, but was introduced only after. *(Long)*

The Green Goddess of the 1948 Motor Show was a most lavishly equipped luxury sports car. *(Long)*

Right: The Empress also used the approved DB 18 chassis. *(Long)*

she did not really like the car and disrespectfully called it the funeral car.

In autumn 1948 the first Motor Show after the war was held. With the DB 18 Special Sports, Daimler again offered an attractive, sporty car. Its more powerful engine was somewhat similar to the pre-war Dolphin. It assured adequate performance with, in most cases, open coachwork from Barker and in some rare instances, Hooper.

The most inspiring car of the show, Jaguar's XK 120 left aside, was Hooper's Green Goddess. This was a five-seat convertible based on a DE 36 chassis. It was unusual in having three seats in the front row. The front fenders extended along the Green Goddess' sides to the rear bumper, while the rear ones were invisible. Instead, the rear wheels were completely hidden behind large, detachable spats. The headlamps were integrated into the front fenders with Perspex aerodynamic covers and chrome frames that imitated the grille. At about £7,000 this was presumably the most expensive car exhibited, but one of the largest and most lavish as well. Even the top was operated electrically. The car was so attractive that eight examples were sold, despite the horrendous price.

The large Daimler cars drew the attention of twice-divorced Norah Collins upon Sir Bernard. The public suggested that she might as well have been interested in Sir Bernard's yacht *Shemara*—the biggest private yacht under the British flag apart from the royal yacht *Britannia*. They married on February 3, 1949. Normally, the chairman's marriage would have no impact on the company, but in this case it was to have dire consequences. It started, hardly noticeably, with a very Special Sports given to her, which incorporated the Green Goddess' headlights.

The engine of the normal Special Sports was an inspiration for the Consort, which was introduced in the autumn of 1949 with partially hydraulic brakes, larger wheels, and a silent hypoid diff. The body of this car closely resembled its DB 18 predecessor and was made at Mulliners in Birmingham. At first the Consort was reserved for export. It was distinguished by its curved grille and integrated headlights in the style of the larger models. The DB 18 and its deriva-

Lanchester LD 14 at the 1953 Monte Carlo Rally. *(Long)*

tives would disappear from the catalogs during the next years.

The real sensation was created again at Hooper, where a Straight Eight chassis underwent some special treatment for the 1949 Motor Show. This time a Sedanca de Ville was to emerge, a limousine with an open chauffeur compartment in true knife-edge style.

For the 1950 Motor Show another Sedanca was created, but with a shorter compartment for the passengers. Its flowing lines were inspired by the Green Goddess and the Special Sports. The front fenders extended to the rear bumper, where they met the curved waistline, which was emphasized by the color combination of black and cream—a fashion at the time.

With a similar sedan style and a completely enclosed body, Hooper made the Empress, the name of which was soon generally used for the body style. It was based on the Consort chassis, but with the more powerful engine of the Special Sports. Another 1950 novelty was the Lanchester 14 or Leda, which replaced the LD 10. With four cylinders, 2 liters of capacity and 60 horsepower it was underpowered for its size, and technically it resembled the prewar 14-horsepower.

In 1951 the DE 27 was replaced by the Regency, which was slightly larger than the Consort and Empress, and made it harder to sell these models. The engine was a Lanchester 14 with another two cylinders that produced 90 horsepower. The chassis was an extended variant of the Consort, while the body

Top: Hooper Sedanca on DE 36 chassis for the 1950 Motor Show. *(Long)*

Above: Surprisingly clear styling for the face of the *Golden Car*. *(Long)*

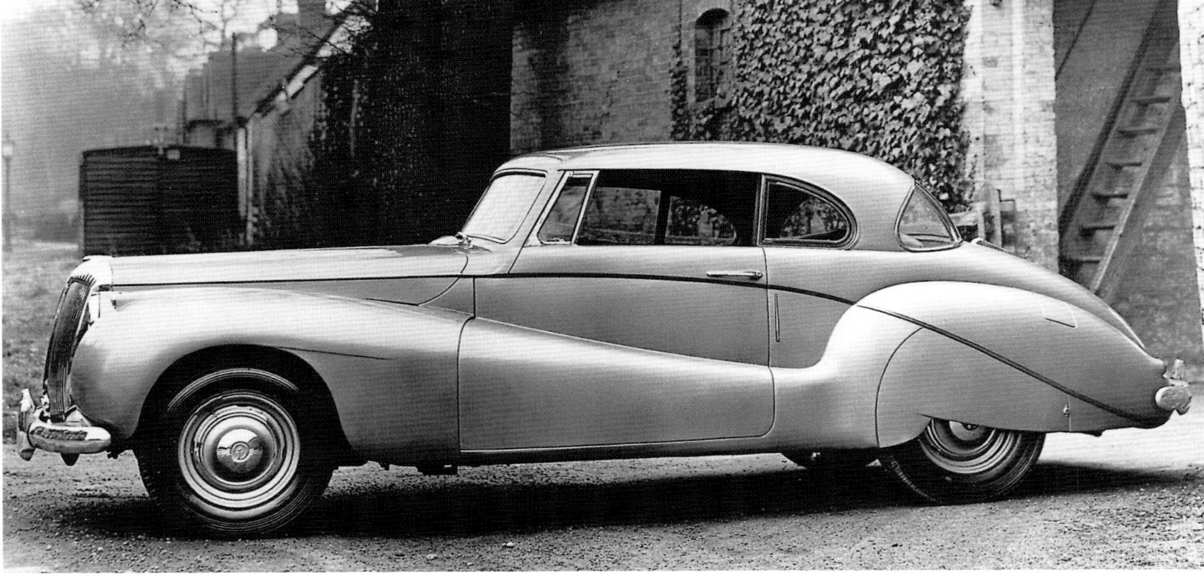

The Daimler Regency fixed head coupe seemed more aggressive than other Daimler models. *(Long)*

Above: Blue Clover was Hooper's idea for the 1952 Motor Show. *(Long)*

Right: The Conquest, successor to the Consort with its nearly flat sides. *(Long)*

resembled the Lanchester. Two benches offered sufficient although not generous space for six. At £2,334 this car was considerably more expensive than the Jaguar Mark VII, which offered nearly twice as much power. All persuasiveness was required from the dealers to sell this car, but fortunately there was still a considerable loyalty to the Daimler marque among the mostly noble customers!

Hooper's Sedanca de Ville was shown again in a revised edition at the 1951 Motor show, but the sensation was the *Golden Car*, a creation of Lady Docker who, contrary to most ladies of the time, took a serious interest in what her husband did professionally. She had decided to strongly support his work. The Daimler name, she reasoned, needed to be brought back into the minds of the masses, instead of being victimized by its own tradition. Her good intentions resulted in some overdone cars, like this golden calf—sorry, car.

The *Golden Car* was a limousine on the DE 36 chassis with all normally chromed parts gold plated; even the seats were covered with golden cloth. It had seven thousand small golden stars on the shining black finish, a manifestation of the lady's very individual taste. There was a cocktail cabinet in the passenger compartment with golden picnic crockery and any other imaginable amenity. A set of suitcases made of black crocodile leather fitted the trunk exactly. The windows and partitions worked electrically—the side windows even had double glass in order to keep heat, frost, and noise outside. A separate heating fan for the rear window was installed.

This very extraordinary vehicle cost over £7,000, and the normal Brit, still living in postwar austerity, was just overwhelmed. In retrospect these too-lavish show cars did not really suit the traditional, conservative style Daimler customers were used to. Nevertheless, with this sort of car, the Daimler and Hooper names were to be the talk of quite a few more Motor Shows.

In 1952 BSA took over Triumph Motorcycles to reinforce its own motorcycle activities. Part of the deal was the Ariel name. At the same time the Special Sports was replaced by the Regency Convertible. With an increased compression ratio of 7.5:1, the engine produced 100 horsepower. The price tag was quite lofty at £2,661. The beautiful Empress II remained unchanged externally but now was based on a Regency chassis. The Motor Show sensation of 1952 was *Blue Clover*, a very large coupe covered with many blue-gray cloverleaves. It was based on the DE 36 chassis that went out of production in 1953.

A new model for the normal customer was the Conquest, which successfully replaced the Consort. Basically this was a Regency with the bore reduced to create a 2.5-liter capacity and 75 horsepower, resulting in a top speed of 80 miles per hour. It was more than a 100 pounds lighter than the Consort. From the Lanchester Leda (the former 14) to the Daimler Regency, all models were now technically very similar, which certainly helped reduce production cost.

At the 1953 Motor Show, Daimler introduced the Conquest Roadster with a remarkably low look for the high chassis—a very sporting car for a manufacturer of luxury cars. The dashboard was covered in vinyl instead of wood and included a rev counter. It seemed as if Daimler's standard range of models imitated the flamboyant show cars more and more. It was unclear, however, whether this new direction, an abrupt deviation from tradition, would be accepted by customers. Fortunately, the twin S.U. carburetor, higher-compression, 100-horsepower roadster was well received by the press and public.

Another new car at that Motor Show was the Lanchester Dauphin, a shortened two-door Empress based on the Leda chassis equipped with a 2.4-liter six-cylinder engine with 92 horsepower (thanks to twin carburetors). This very exquisite-looking small car was so expensive that only two would be made.

Lady Docker was now a director at Hooper with her husband's help; her 1953 show car was the *Silver Flash*, based on the now largest Daimler chassis, the Regency. Hooper manufactured a particularly low and light coupe body. It was remarkable for its oval grille, which was quite different from the traditional pattern. The roof of this very large and thus all but sporting coupe included a glass section with a shade to protect the noble species inside from excessive sun.

A major event for Daimler in 1953 was the young Queen Elizabeth's tour to Australia and New Zealand, for which Daimler had to provide some cars. This tour had been planned long before and was postponed because of King George's ill health. So, the Straight Eights that had been ordered years before only now came into service.

In 1954 BSA took over Carbodies, a company that had been established in 1926 by Bobby Jones, a former employee of Daimler who had gained experience in coachbuilding at famous companies like Charlesworth and Hollick & Pratt. After the war, Carbodies was renowned for its FX taxi, a successor of which is still in production at the renamed company.

The Lanchester Dauphin was a limousine in miniature. *(Long)*

Silver Flash was certainly the most radical of Daimler's show cars. *(Long)*

The Conquest roadster was much lower than the sedans. *(Long)*

12

DYNAMIC DAIMLER

In 1954 the Daimler Conquest got a more powerful sibling, using the engine of the Roadster. It was called the Conquest Century (for its 100 horsepower) and it reached 90 miles per hour. Although externally unchanged, the rear legroom was increased by 4 inches, as the rear bench had been moved further back. Priced at £1,736 it offered better value for the money than previous Daimler models. An example with power further increased to 116 horsepower took part in high-profile touring-car races and was second only to Jaguar's famous Mark VII. A Conquest Convertible similar to the Special Sports had already been added to the range during the previous autumn.

At the 1954 Motor Show a Conquest Coupe and the Regency Mark II were introduced. The latter had an engine increased to 3.5 liters to make 107 horsepower; later the compression ratio was raised to reach 114 horsepower. The body was 5 inches longer and more than 2 inches lower, while the wheelbase remained unchanged. The interior boasted picnic tables hinged at the back of the front seats. The Empress evolved into IIA, also benefiting from the Regency's improvements. A variant with 130 horsepower was called the Regency Sportsman, easily distinguishable by its three-piece panoramic rear window.

But this was not all: There was also a variant of the six-cylinder engine enlarged to 4.5 liters, producing only 127 horsepower—nevertheless the DF 400 was a worthy successor to the more flamboyant Straight Eights. On special order, this engine also went into the Regency Sportsman and also propelled the new Limousine Regina, which with its 130-inch wheelbase and 60-inch track was substantially larger than its brethren. Regina was the first Daimler with Burman recirculating ball steering and enlarged brake drums.

Daimler's 1954 Motor Show sensation was a slightly shortened Regina, very similar to the 1951 *Golden Car*. The smallest car in the range, the Lanchester Leda, was replaced with the Sprite, which had a modern unitary body, using the Conquest's suspension and the 2-liter four-cylinder with 60 horsepower. Although the car was much lighter, it still seemed underpowered. Part of the problem was the Hobbs automatic transmission, which replaced the fluid flywheel. Its double clutch and hydraulically operated three-speed epicyclical gearbox changed gears without interrupting power transmission. Although this gear change was not too jerky, the Sprite was not very successful, with only three examples made!

At the 1955 Motor Show a new Regency variant was introduced, the One-O-Four, to trumpet its top speed of 104 miles per hour. To achieve this, the power of the 3.5-liter had been pushed to 137 horsepower. The brakes of the One-O-Four were servo-assisted. The price of £2,670 mirrored the very full equipment of the car. Additionally, there was a Lady's Model with appointments for the requirements of elegant female customers. The Regency Sportsman was renamed Four-Light Saloon, and the Empress became No. III. At the same time the 4.5-liter was boosted to 167 horsepower, a very useful improvement given the large bodies that these chassis usually had to carry. The Regina was renamed DK 400. A special variant from Hooper with eight seats was not very popular, and only seven of them were made.

The *Golden Zebra*, Lady Docker's showpiece for 1955, also was based on the DK 400. This was a sort of coupe variant of the *Green Goddess* with a different face, finished in white with zebra-covered seats. This one-off, priced at £15,000 was the last of Daimler's Motor Show specials. Despite all this change, no model in the range rose to become terribly popular. The

The Regina, with 4.5-liter engine, was Daimler's 1955 flagship. *(Long)*

On the Regina chassis Hooper created the *Stardust* show car. *(Long)*

The Conquest drophead coupe was intended for the sporting owner-driver. *(J)*

Opposite: The 100-horsepower Conquest Century was used in touring car races. *(J)*

Above: 1957 DK 400 in typical Hooper style. *(Long)*

Below: With its rear fins, the plastic-bodied SP 250 was a quite unusual Daimler. *(Long)*

Above: 1958 Daimler Majestic with conservative style. *(Long)*

Right: The Hooper Continental at the 1956 Motor Show was much less exalted than preceding show cars. *(Long)*

Below: The 1959 SP 250 certainly had a more sporting appeal than any other Daimler. *(Long)*

limousine market had become Rolls-Royce's (who now held the royal warrant), and the more sporting segment went to Jaguar. Daimler could neither rival any of them nor find its own niche in the market.

Daimler's decline certainly had a variety of causes, in addition to the strong competition. The loss of the royal warrant was the unexpected result of the extravagant lifestyle of Sir Bernard and Lady Docker. Neither royalty nor the average Brit still suffering from postwar rationing could sympathize with them. At first they had been adored, but people began to wonder about their many expensive overseas travels, as the normal Englishman was not allowed more than £25 to take with him when traveling abroad. Eyebrows were raised over many court cases that Sir Bernard was involved in, particular in the south of France. The Dockers should not have spent more than £8,000 (Daimler money, of course) for their exquisite wardrobe at the 1954 Paris Show, and they should not have spent £2,000 to ship the *Golden Zebra* and another special car, the *Stardust*, to the Monaco marriage of Prince Rainier and actress Grace Kelly, and so on.

May 30, 1956, was the end of the line for Sir Bernard, who stayed in Monaco, as he was sacked that day. This was quite a scandal. The Dockers bought two Rolls-Royces and never had anything to do with the automobile industry again. Many former clients who had become friends of the Dockers now were lost for Daimler, and in the aftermath Daimler seemed to fall into oblivion.

This was the background for the start of the Jack Sangster and Edward Turner era. Both had come from Triumph Motorcycles, which for financial reasons had been separated from car production in 1936, with the motorcycles finally being swallowed by BSA, Daimler's parent company. Because the Phase II variant of the Lanchester Sprite had not raised any interest at various shows—the once famous Lanchester name disappeared altogether in 1956. Today the name is hardly remembered—a fate that the ingenious Fred Lanchester and his brothers certainly have not deserved!

The next thing to be dismissed was the fluid flywheel, which was replaced with a much more modern Borg-Warner automatic, which had a hydraulically operated gear change and a torque converter that admitted less slip. A torque converter consists of flywheels in an oil bath with a nonrotating guide wheel between them. Buick first used one in its famous Dynaflow Automatic in 1948, the first fully automatic transmission. The first model benefiting from this change was the One-O-Four, Hooper's *Continental* coupe variant being a much-admired stopgap at the 1956 Motor Show. It was greatly influenced by the Bentley with the same name. The *Continental* remained a one-off, as the aftermath of the Suez crisis did not seem like a good time to introduce such an expensive and impractical car. The Conquest models went automatic only in 1957.

In July 1958 the Majestic was introduced as a further development of the One-O-Four. The completely new body closely resembled the predecessor, but had flatter, more modern sides. The engine had been thoroughly improved with a power output of 147 horsepower. Disc brakes were standard equipment. The automatic chassis lubrication that had been so prone to defects had been discarded altogether.

A much more thrilling car was the Dart, unveiled in the United States on April 4, 1959. As Dodge intervened, having rights to that name, the car had to be renamed after its chassis designation SP 250. The fiberglass body looked slightly awkward, as it was much lower even than the Conquest roadster. Its engine was a highly remarkable 2.5-liter V-8 with hemispherical combustion chambers—a brainchild of Edward Turner, who was more accustomed to the dimensions of motorcycle engines—with 140 horsepower and respectable performance. Turner (1901–1973), as an engineer at Ariel, had in 1935 awakened the interest of his chief, Jack Sangster, in the takeover of Triumph Motorcycles. In 1942 Turner moved to BSA, which took over Triumph Motorcycles and Ariel in 1951. Jack Sangster had instigated the coup against Docker, became his successor, and became Turner's chief again. Turner, in the meantime, had become Daimler's managing director.

SP 250 production started in September 1959. For the 1959 Motor Show Hooper prepared an SP 250 with coupe body, a higher front end, and tail fins even at the roof. The very unusual design did not go down particularly well, and so it was left to the Ogle styling studio to show a much more pleasing coupe in 1962 with completely individual styling. However, only very few of these SX 250s were made. The styling was then exploited

Above: The style of the SP 250 was somewhat awkward. *(J)*

Below: The SP 250 interior after being revised by Jaguar. *(Long)*

Majestic Major was externally similar to the Majestic but had a powerful V-8 engine. *(Long)*

DR 450 Limousine. *(Long)*

Below: The large V-8 was particularly suitable for formal bodies like this DR 450 landaulette. *(J)*

with great success by Reliant, particularly in the form of the Scimitar with its sports estate back.

SP 250 and Majestic shared the Daimler stand at the 1959 Motor Show with the slightly dated DK 400. This was soon to be replaced with a mighty 220-horsepower 4.5-liter V-8, which was very similar in design to the smaller V-8. Rumor has it that in reality the power was much higher than the published figure, as the torque was beyond the scale of Daimler's dynamometer. This combination was called the Majestic Major (Chassis name DQ 450) and was soon joined by an extended-version DR 450 with an additional two folding seats. These cars went into production during 1960–1961. From a technical point of view these were the last true Daimlers.

At this point it may be helpful to give an overview of the milestones in Daimler's history:

- August 12, 1863: Birth of Frederick Simms
- February 18, 1891: Simms purchases the Daimler license for the Commonwealth
- May 26, 1983: Simms establishes the Daimler Motor Syndicate Limited
- July 3, 1895: The first car with a Daimler engine arrives in Britain
- July 1895: Harry Lawson establishes the British Motor Syndicate Limited to hold licenses
- November 2, 1895: First issue of Henry Sturmey's *The Autocar*

- 1896: Lawson establishes the Great Horseless Carriage Company as a successor to the Syndicate for the production of MMC cars (renamed Motor Manufacturing Company in 1898, wound up in 1905)
- January 14, 1896: Lawson establishes the Daimler Motor Company Limited for car manufacture
- February 14, 1896: HRH Prince Edward's first drive in a car
- April 1896: Lawson purchases the Wool Mill at Coventry as home for Daimler and MMC car manufacture
- November 14, 1896: More liberal speed limits for motor vehicles introduced
- March 2, 1897: Maiden drive of the first Daimler made in Britain
- 1900: First Coventry-Daimler supplied to the Royal Mews
- December 8, 1904: Restructuring as Daimler Motor Company Limited (1904)
- 1908: Daimler purchases the Radford factory
- September 1910: Daimler is taken over by BSA, which was established in 1861
- 1926: Daimler introduces the first European V-12 engine made in series
- 1931: BSA takes over the Lanchester Motor Company Limited that was established on December 13, 1899, and had made cars since 1901
- 1936: Erection of the No. 1 Shadow Factory at Radford
- 1939: Erection of the No. 2 Shadow Factory at Browns Lane, Allesley
- 1940: Daimler purchases coachbuilders Hooper, which was established in 1807 and took over coachbuilders Barker (established 1710) in 1838
- 1952: BSA takes over Triumph Motorcycles
- 1954: BSA takes over Carbodies
- May 30, 1956: Dismissal of Sir Bernard Docker

As Daimler's model range was very complicated it is not easy to keep track of all the many variants, particularly because for years before 1903 only scarce technical data are available. Due to the German air raids the Daimler archive was lost. All models of a period seem to be closely related to each other, so it is not difficult to find substructures in the process of constant improvement and variation. For the earliest years differentiation has taken place with regard to engine capacity only.

Earliest Coventry-Daimlers

Name	Cyl.	cc	Ignition	Carb.	Drive	Chassis & wheelbase	Years
4 and 5.5 HP	2	1527	Hot tube	Spray	Chain		1897–99
8 to 24 HP	4	3054	Hot tube*	Spray	Chain	C, D, F, G and TA	1898–1901
6 and 8 HP	2	1551	Hot tube, 8 HP*	Spray	Chain		1901
8 HP: driveshaft						A and B	1900, 8 HP –1901
9 HP2		1804	Hot tube	Spray	Chain	TA, 78″ or 90″	1900–02
7 HP2		1773	Hot tube	Spray	Chain		1904
Critchley Light Car	2	1100	Hot tube	Spray	Belt		1899, Kimberley –1901

* With additional magneto

Pre– World War I Lanchesters

Name	Cyl.	cc	bhp	Ignition	Carb.	Drive	Wheelbase	Track	Years
10 HP	2*	4029	15	Magneto	Wool	Driveshaft	93″, later 94″	58″	1901–03
16 HP	2*	4420	23	Magneto	Wool	Driveshaft	93″, later 94″	58″	1903–06
12 HP	2	4029	18	Magneto	Wool	Driveshaft	93″, later 94″	58″	1903–06
18 HP	2	4830	30	Magneto	Wool	Driveshaft	93″, later 94″	58″	1903–06
20 HP	4	2470	28	Magneto	Wool	Driveshaft	113″	58″	1905–11
28 HP	6	3710	42	Magneto	Wool	Driveshaft	137″	58″	1907–12
38 HP	6	4942	48	Magneto	Wool	Driveshaft	138⅝″ or 127″	58″	1911–15
25 HP	4	3295	32	Magneto	Wool	Driveshaft	127″ or 115″	58″	1912–15

* Air-cooled

Early Metal Dashboard Daimlers

Name	Cyl.	cc	Chassis	Wheelbase	Track	Years
12 HP*	4**	2324	TA			1902–03
14 HP	4**	3402	TB			1903
22 HP	4**	4503	TA	78″ or 90″		1902
22 HP	4**	4503	TD and TE			1903
16/20	4**	3309	TC			1904
16/20	4**	3309	TA, TB and TC***			1905
16 HP	4**	3309	CA			1906
17 HP	4**	3309	TD			1907
18/22	4**	3827	TA***	96½″ or 118½″		1904
28/36	4**	5703	TA***	114″		1904
28/36	4**	5703	TB***	132″		1904
28/36	4**	5703	TC***	96″		1904–05
28/36	4**	5703	TD***	102″		1904–05
28/36	4**	5703	TE***	120″		1904–05
28/36	4**	5703	TG***	132″		1904–05
28/36	4**	5703	CA***	132″		1905
28/36	4**	5703	TH***	102″		1906
28/36	4**	5703	TJ	120″		1906
28/36	4**	5703	TK and CB	132″		1906
30/40	4**	7247	TD***	102″		1905
30/40	4**	7247	TH***	102″		1906
30/40	4**	7247	TJ***	120″		1906
30/40	4**	7247	TK***	132″		1906
35 HP	4**	8462	TD***	102″		1905
35 HP	4**	8462	TH***	102″		1906
35 HP	4**	8462	TJ***	120″		1906
35/45	4**	10,604	TA*** and TH***			1906
45 HP	4**	10,604	TL***	114″		1907
45 HP	4**	10,604	TM***	126″		1907
45 HP	4**	10,604	TP***	108″		1907
28 HP	4**	6787	TL***	114″		1907
28 HP	4**	6787	TM***	126″		1907
28 HP	4**	6787	TO***	138″		1907
28 HP	4**	6787	TP***	108″		1907
36 HP	4**	6787	TL***	114″		1908
36 HP	4**	6787	TM***	126″		1908
36 HP	4**	6787	TO***	138″		1908
36 HP	4**	6787	TP***	108″		1908
30 HP	4**	7965	TL***	114″		1907
30 HP	4**	7965	TM***	126″		1907
30 HP	4**	7965	TO***	138″		1907
30 HP	4**	7965	TP***	108″		1907
42 HP	4**	7965	TB***	126″		1908
42 HP	4**	7965	TC***	126″		1908
35 HP	4**	9237	TL***	114″		1907
35 HP	4**	9237	TM***	126″		1907
35 HP	4**	9237	TO***	138″		1907
35 HP	4**	9237	TP***	108″		1907
48 HP	4**	9237	TB***	126″		1908
48 HP	4**	9237	TC***	126″		1908–09
30 HP	4**	4942	TA			1908

Name	Cyl.	cc	Chassis	Wheelbase	Track	Years
38 HP	4**	6281	TA			1908
38 HP	4	6281	TB	114″		1909
38 HP	4	6281	TC	126″		1909
38 HP	4	6281	TD and TE	126″		1910
38 HP	4	6281	TG and TH	126″		1911
38 HP	4	6281	TJ and TK	126″		1911
38 HP	4	6281	TL and TM	131½″		1912
38 HP	4	6281	TO and TP	131½″		1912
38 HP	4	6281	TR and TS	132″		1913
58 HP	4**	10,431	TB***	126″		1908
58 HP	4**	10,431	TC***	126″		1908
58 HP	4**	10,431	TD***	126″		1908
22 HP	4	3764	TB	114″		1909
22 HP	4	3764	TC	126″		1909
22 HP	4	3764	TD and TE	126″		1910
33 HP	6	5646	TB	114″		1909
33 HP	6	5646	TC	124½″		1910
33 HP	6	5646	TD	138″		1910
57 HP	6**	9421	TC	138″		1909
57 HP	6	9421	TD and TE	126″		1910
57 HP	6	9421	TG	138″		1911
15 HP	4	2614	TA and TB	114″		1910
15 HP	4	2614	TC and TD	116″		1911
15 HP	4	2614	TE and TG	123½″		1912
15 HP	4	2614	TH and TJ	123½″		1913
12 HP	4	1705	TA	106½″		1911
BSA 14	4	2015				1911–14
20 HP	4	3308	TA	123½″		1911
20 HP	4	3308	TB and TC	123½″		1912
20 HP	4	3308	TD and TE	123½″		1913
20 HP	4	3308	TG and TH	123½″		1913
20 HP	4	3308	TJ and TK	131″		1914
20 HP	4	3308	TL and TM	131″		1914
20 HP	4	3308	TO and TP	131″		1915
25 HP	4	4208	TA and TB	126″		1911
25 HP	4	4208	TC and TD	131½″		1912
25 HP	4	4208	TE and TG	131½″		1912
23 HP	6	3921	TA and TB	124½″		1911–12
38 HP	6	6312	TA and TB	138″		1911
38 HP	6	6312	TC and TD	141½″		1912
30 HP	6	4960	TB and TC	138½″		1912
30 HP	6	4960	TD and TE	138½″		1913
30 HP	6	4960	TG and TH	141½″		1914
30 HP	6	4960	TJ and TK	141½″		1915
30 HP	6	4960	TL and TM	141½″	56½″	1919–22
30 HP	6	4960	TS	141½″	56½″	1922
30 HP	6	4960	TS	135¾″	59″	1923
30 HP	6	4960	A	142″	57″	1924–25
Light 30	6	4960	TO and TP	128¼″	56½″	1919–22
Light 30	6	4960	TO	128¼″	57″	1923
26 HP	4	4576	TA and TB	132″		1913
39 HP Special	6	6864	TA and TB	143″		1913
45 HP Special	6	7410	TB and TC	146″		1914
45 HP Special	6	7410	TD and TE	146″		1915
45 HP Special	6	7410	TG and TH	146″	141½″	1919–22
45 HP Special	6	7410	TJ	146″	141½″	1922
45 HP Special	6	7410	TJ	146″	142″	1923
45 HP Special	6	7410	A	146″	142″	1924
30 HP	4	4942	TB and TC	132″		1914
30 HP	4	4942	CC and CD	132″		1914
30 HP	4	4942	TD and TE	135″		1915
20 HP	4	3308	TT-4	132″	57¼″	1922

* Ignition by hot tube and magneto, front and rear wheels with different diameter, last Daimler with old-style radiator

** Poppet valves

*** Chain drive, some 16/20 with driveshaft already

World War I and Later Genuine Lanchesters

Name	Cyl.	cc	bhp	Ignition	Carb.	Drive	Wheelbase	Track	Years
Sporting 40	6	5560		Magneto	Wool	driveshaft	145″ or 152″	58″	1915
40 HP	6	6178	96	Magneto	Spray	driveshaft	141″ or 150″	58″	1919–29
21 HP	6	2932	60	Magneto	Spray	driveshaft	129″ or 133″	54″	1924–25
21 HP	6	3340	65	Magneto	Spray	driveshaft	129″ or 133″	56″	1926–32
30 HP	8	4437	98	Magneto	Spray	driveshaft	142½″	56″	1929–32

Daimler Chassis Introduced in the Twenties

Name	Cyl.	cc	bhp	Chassis	Wheelbase	Track	Years
12 HP	6	1542		TB	117″	50″	1923
BSA 14	4	1446			Like BSA 10		1923
16 HP	6	2167		TB	129″	52″	1923
21 HP	6	3022		TC	133″	52″	1923
21 HP	6	3022		TB	135¾″	57″	1923
21 HP	6	3022		A	136″	57″	1924–25
BSA 14	6	1594			117″	50″	1924–26
16 HP	6**	1872		D1	117″	50″	1924
16-55	6**	1872		L	117″	52″	1925–29
20 HP	6**	2648		C	129″	52″	1924–25
20 HP	6**	2648		S	133″	54″	1924–28
20 HP	6**	2648		T and V	139″	54″	1924–28
20-70	6**	2648		M	131″	52″	1927–28
20-70	6**	2648		Q	121″	52″	1927–30
20-70	6**	2648		V	135½″	56½″	1928–30
20-70	6**	2648		M	131″	56½″	1929–30
20-70	6	2648		M and Q	131″	57″	1931
20-70	6	2648		M and LQ	133″	57″	1932
20-70	6	2648		M and LQ	130″	57″	1933
25 HP	6**	3568	70	S	136″	54″	1924–28
25 HP	6**	3568	70	O and T	142″	54″	1924–27
25 HP	6**	3568	70	A	142″	57″	1925
25 HP	6**	3568	70	C	143″	52″	1925
25-85	6**	3568	70	O, R and V	145″	60″	1925–30
25-85	6**	3568	70	N and P	152″	60″	1925–28
25-85	6**	3568	70	M	141″	56½″	1929
25-85	6**	3568	70	V	145″	56½″	1929
25-85	6	3568	70	M***	133″	57″	1930–34
25-85	6	3568	70	V3	135½″	56½″	1930
25-85	6	3568	70	V4***	142″	57″	1930–34
35 HP	6**	5764		C	102⅝″	52″	1924–25
35 HP	6**	5764		S	102⅝″	54″	1924–28
35-120	6**	5764		T and V	148″	54″	1924–28
35-120	6**	5764		O and R	148″	60″	1924–32
35-120	6**	5764		N and P	156″	60″	1924–32
45 HP	6**	8458		R	154″	60″	1924–25
45 HP	6**	8458		M and N	162″	60″	1924–26
50*	12**	7136	150	W	155½″	57″	1927–30
50*	12**	7136	150	O	155½″	60″	1927–30
50*	12**	7136	150	P	163″	60″	1927–30
30*	12**	3744	100	Q	121″	52″	1928
30*	12**	3744	100	M	141″	52″	1928
30*	12**	3744	100	V	142″	54″	1928
30*	12**	3744	100	O	145″	60″	1928
30*	12	3744	100	M	141″	56½″	1930
30*	12	3744	100	V	145½″	56½″	1930
30*	12	3744	100	M	141″	57″	1931–32
30*	12	3744	100	V	145½″	57″	1931–32
30/40*	12	5296	125	***	138″	60″	1931–35
30/40*	12	5296	125	***	147½″	60″	1931–35
30/40*	12	5296	125	***	157″	60″	1931–35
30/40*	12	5296	125	***	133″	57″	1933
30/40*	12	5296	125	***	142″	57″	1933
40/50*	12	6511	155	***	138″	60″	1931–35
40/50*	12	6511	155	***	147½″	60″	1931–35
40/50*	12	6511	155	***	157″	60″	1931–35

* Double-Six

** Magneto in addition to coil (until ca. 1929)

*** Fluid Flywheel

Daimler Chassis with Poppet Valves and Fluid Flywheel

Name	Cyl.	cc	bhp	Chassis	Wheelbase	Track	Years
20	6	2687		LQ2	124″	56″	1934
20	6	2687		LQ3	127″	56″	1933–35
15/18*	6	2504					1932–34
18*	6	2390					1934–36
Straight 8	8	3746	75	V26	142⅛″	57½″	1935
Light 20	6	2565	62	E20	114″	56″	1936–39
18*	6	2565	62		114″	56″	1936–39
Light Straight 8	8	3421	85	E 3 1/2	123″	57″	1936–37
Light Straight 8	8	3421	85	E 3 1/2	123½″	57″	1938
Straight 8	8	4624	105	V	142″	57″	1936–39
Straight 8	8	4624	105	F	151″	57″	1937–39
Double-Six	12	6511	140		157″	60″	1937
20	6	3317	75	LQ3	114″	56″	1936–37
24	6	3317	75	EL24	114″	57″	1938–39

Name	Cyl.	cc	bhp	Chassis	Wheelbase	Track	Years
24	6	3317	75	ES24	114″	57″	1938–39
24	6	3317	75	ELS24	142″	57″	1939
Straight 8	8	3960	95	E 4	123½″	57″	1939
Straight 8	8	4095	110	DE27	138″½	60/63″	1946–51
Ambulance	8	4095	110	DC27	138½″	60/63″	1950–54
Straight 8	8	4095	110	DH27	148″	60/63″	1952
Straight 8	8	5460	150	DE36	147″	60/63″	1946–53

* Lanchester

Smaller Daimler Chassis

Name	Cyl.	cc	bhp	Chassis	Wheelbase	Track	Years
BSA 10	4	1185					1933–35
BSA 10	4	1398			99″		1936
10*	4	1203					1933–34
10*	4	1203					1935
10*	4	1444					1936
11*	4	1444			102⅝″	48″	1937–38
LD 10*	4	1287	40		99″		1946–51
Light 6*	6	1378			99″		1934–35
BSA Light 6	6	1378			99″		1935
Light 6*	6	1378			109½″	50⅝″	1936
BSA Light 6	6	1378			109½″	50⅝″	1936
14*	6	1527	40	LA-1			1936–38
15	6	1805	42		109½″	50⅝″	1933–34
15	6	2003	46		109½″	50⅝″	1935–36
Road rider*	6	2003	46		110″	52″	1938–39
15	6	2166		DB17	109½″	52″	1937
New 15	6	2166		DB17**	114″	52″	1938
15 2-½ liter	6	2522	64	DB18**	114″	52″	1939
Ritz	6	2522	90	DB18**	114″	52″	1939
Dolphin	6	2522	90	DB18**	114″	52″	1939
DB 18	6	2522	70	DB18**	114″	52″	1946–50
Special Sports	6	2522	85	DB18**	114″	52″	1949–52
Empress	6	2522	85	DB18**	114″	52″	1949–52
Consort	6	2522	70	DB18**	114″	52″	1950–52
14*/Leda*	4	1968	60	LJ200/201**	104″	52″	1951–54
Dauphin*	6	2433	92	LJ252/253*	104″	52″	1954
Conquest	6	2433	75	DJ250/251**	104″	52″	1953–57

Name	Cyl.	cc	bhp	Chassis	Wheelbase	Track	Years
Conquest Convertible**	6	2433	75	DJ252/253**	104″	52″	1954–56
Conquest Century (open models)**	6	2433	100	DJ254/255**	104″	52″	1954–57
Conquest Century**	6	2433	100	DJ256/257**	104″	52″	1955–57
Conquest Century***	6	2433	100	DJ260/261**	104″	52″	1958
Sprite*	4	1622	60	LM150/151**	100″	52″	1955
Sprite Phase 2*	4	1622	60	LM150/151**	100″	52″	1956

* Lanchester

** Independent front suspension, RHD/LHD

*** Automatic, not Fluid Flywheel

Daimler Regency etc.

Name	Cyl.	cc	bhp	Chassis	Wheelbase	Track	Years
Regency	6	2952	90	DF300/301	124″	56″	1951–53
Empress II	6	2952	100	DF302/303	124″	56″	1952–53
Continental	6	2952	100	DF302/303	124″	56″	1952–53
Regency Mark II	6	3468	107	DF304/305	124″	56/57″	1955
Empress IIA	6	3468	107	DF304/305	124″	56/57″	1955
Empress IIA	6	3468	114	DF306/307	124″	56/57″	1955–56
Regency Sportsman	6	3468	130	DF308/309	124″	56/57″	1955–57
Regency Sportsman	6	4617	127	DF400/401	124″	57,5/57″	1955
Regina	6	4617	127	DF400/401	124″	57,5/57″	1955
DK 400	6	4617	127	DK400	130″	60/63″	1954–56
Four-Light Saloon	6	3468	137	DF310/311	130″	60/63″	1956
One-O-Four	6	3468	137	DF310/311	130″	60/63″	1956
Empress III	6	3468	137	DF310/311	130″	60/63″	1956
Four-Light Saloon	6	3468	137	DF314/315*	130″	60/63″	1957–58
One-O-Four	6	3468	137	DF314/315*	130″	60/63″	1957–58
Empress III	6	3468	137	DF314/315*	130″	60/63″	1957–58
Regina	6	4617	167	DF402/403	124″	57″	1956
DK 400	6	4617	167	DK400	130″	60/63″	1957–1959

* Automatic instead of Fluid Flywheel

The merger of Jaguar and Daimler is symbolized by the Daimler 2.5-liter V-8 with its Jaguar body. *(Teismann)*

I am overdue in explaining why I have devoted so much space to Daimler in a Jaguar book: Well, in the late 1950s BSA had lost interest in its once noble and distinguished car manufacture. Jaguar, on the other hand, urgently needed space for further expansion that was not possible at Browns Lane. Daimler's nearby Radford plant with the 1936 shadow factory No. 1 constituted 56 acres of land in all. So Jaguar, by taking over Daimler, could expand without moving to a less developed part of the country. Daimler's financial situation had been suffering because of strong competition from Jaguar's less expensive but technically superior products. A similar situation had faced Armstrong-Siddeley, which stopped car manufacture for just this reason to concentrate on aircraft.

Negotiations between BSA and Sir William Lyons took place in a relaxed but secretive atmosphere. At a rather late stage it was discovered that some £10,000 of pension accruals had been overlooked. Jack Sangster and Sir William flipped a coin and Lyons won, so no extra charge was added. Jaguar announced the takeover of Daimler and Lanchester (not including Barker, Hooper, and Carbodies) on May 26, 1960, which cost £3.4 million. Jaguar's directors learned of the deal from the newspapers! The price was adjusted according to the value of Daimler's production facilities alone, without any goodwill connected with the Daimler marque. The takeover pushed Jaguar's workforce over 8,000. Jaguar relocated its engine assembly to Radford, where bus production continued until the early 1970s.

Daimler's new V-8s were very interesting engines, which were tested extensively at Jaguar. The large V-8 was used exclusively in the Daimler Majestic Major and DR 450, which already had been introduced but production of which had not fully started. Daimler had already thought about using the smaller V-8 in a compact, but luxuriously equipped sedan. A unit body would have been too expensive to be developed and produced for Daimler alone, so Daimler investigated whether a Vauxhall Cresta body shell might do the job. The results were not very encouraging. With the new parent company, the obvious solution was to use Jaguar's Mark II body shell. Fortunately, the wide V-8 fit the engine bay well. With an adjustable backrest and "Daimlerized" grille, the combination was introduced as Daimler 2.5-liter V-8 at the 1962 Motor Show.

Above: Daimler 2.5-liter V-8, barely distinguishable from Jaguar's Mark II. *(Long)*

Right: Revitalizing Daimler took place with some Jaguar genes in the 1962 2.5-liter V-8. *(J)*

Its oval grille was more than slightly reminiscent of the *Silver Flash* show car. John Bolster was delighted by the sporty touring car's sweet high-revving engine, regretting only that for a long time it was available only with an automatic transmission.

Soon after the Daimler takeover—the Royal Mews had just dispensed with their last Daimler—Norman Dewis turned his attention to the SP 250 and found its chassis unacceptably weak. This was cured with B-specification changes beginning in 1962. Sir William put some effort in making the car look less ugly, but in the end his own sports cars seemed to be of greater importance for him, and the production of the SP 250 ended in 1964. The large Daimler Majestic Major and DR 450—the last true Daimlers—remained in production for another four years.

Meanwhile, Sir William seemed to have gained interest in takeovers. In October 1961, after long negotiations with the receiver, he bought bus manufacturer Guy at Wolverhampton for £800,000. The company had been established in 1914 and produced commercial vehicles and buses. Just after World War I a few cars had been made there, among them Britain's first V-8 engine. With Daimler, Lyons had entered the manufacture of heavy vehicles, and as Daimler only produced buses, Guy seemed to be a good complement to the model range. At the time about one-third of the buses used in public transit were made either by Guy or Daimler. It took Lyons only one year to bring the company its first profits.

On March 7, 1963, Jaguar purchased Coventry Climax, the famous manufacturer of fire pump engines, by exchanging shares. The company had been called Coventry-Simplex until 1917. Between the wars, its simple engines for mundane car makes like Swift, Triumph, Clyno, and others were in high demand. During World War II, engines that had been left over after Swift's collapse in 1931 were transformed to fire pump engines. An evolution of this engine developed by Wally Hassan and Harry Mundy turned out to be invincible on the race track—it powered the Formula One champions in 1959, 1960, 1963, and 1965. Rumor was that Lyons took over Coventry Climax mainly because he wanted to secure the services of Wally Hassan for the design of his V-12 engine. Today Coventry Climax is no longer associated with Jaguar, specializing instead in forklift trucks.

In 1964 Jaguar very nearly had the opportunity to take over Lotus, which was very successful in racing. Colin Chapman faced problems with his company because of difficulties with its fiberglass bodies. The details of the merger were agreed upon while Lyons was on a business trip to South Africa. When he returned, Chapman had changed his mind—to the relief of Lofty England, who predicted a lot of disturbance arriving with Lotus. Sir William generously accepted Chapman's withdrawal. Another version of this story says that Lyons and Chapman had already shaken hands over the merger.

In 1965 Jaguar swallowed Henry Meadows, which made truck engines at Wolverhampton and had produced engines for smaller cars before the war. In this case, Lyons really was interested in the plant adjacent to Guy, as he planned to extend Guy production. Cooperation with Cummins Diesel in the United States was scheduled, but their engines would not fit in the Daimler or Guy chassis. The whole project came to nothing and was soon discontinued.

Also in 1965, negotiations about a merger of the small Jaguar group and the large utility vehicle producer Leyland took place. Leyland had already taken over Standard/Triumph in 1961. Although Leyland chief Donald Stokes and Sir John Black offered Lyons the responsibility to head all car production in the group, Lyons decided against the merger.

Wally Hassan, in his older years, as blithe as ever. *(S)*

13 INDEPENDENT REAR SUSPENSION

Left: William Heynes fine-tuning an XK engine. *(S)*

Opposite: E-Type headlights. *(Schön)*

Back in 1960, when Jaguar took over the conservative Daimler Motor Company with its mostly old-fashioned range of cars, it also gained access to Daimler's V-8 engines. These made the SP 250, Majestic Major, and DR 450 much more modern than they appeared.

The SP 250, with its small engine, was not powerful enough to equal the XK 150's performance, but its engine was far superior to the small XK unit used in the 2.4-liter Mark II. The Major, with its extremely powerful engine and excellent suspension could play a cat-and-mouse game with Jaguar's Mark IX on the road, had their drivers wanted to.

Jaguar's XK series had been in production for 12 years and the big sedan range for 10 years, while the compact sedan now was nearly 5 years old. Behind the scenes William Heynes—he had been awarded the James Clayton Prize of the Institution of Mechanical Engineers in March 1959—was busy with new developments. After the disc brake coup, he intended to introduce fuel injection and antilock brakes to series production, but this was still a long way ahead, in no small part because of the hesitation of suppliers. When refining the Daimler range was added to Heynes' duties, things started to become a bit too complex.

In order to add some organization to the project work, soon after the Daimler takeover each project received its own number, together with an XJ (for "experimental Jaguar") or XDM (for "experimental Daimler Motors") prefix. These replaced former more complicated file numbers that had started with ZX or later, ZX/XJ or ZX/XDM.

For obvious reasons Jaguar was always very reluctant to let the public know what these codes stood for. However, many of these secrets could be disclosed; they are explained in an appendix to this book.

Officially Jaguar had stopped all racing activities, but the development of further sports cars had been continued secretly. A memo of June 10, 1958, discusses a "G-Type" that was intended to beat Aston Martin and Lister at Le Mans. It was probably intended to be powered by a V-12 engine positioned

This was the first E-Type prototype; it was scrapped and only some photographs taken by Margaret Jennings remain. *(S)*

Top: A Malcolm Sayer mock-up with aerodynamically less effective headlights. *(S)*

Above: An early prototype showing the style of the coming E-Type, despite its lack of chrome. *(S)*

Above right: One of the first E-Types at Browns Lane headquarters. *(S)*

Below: A very early E-Type with a hood that could be opened by turning a T-handle. *(S)*

between the driver and rear suspension. Only 13 years later did the public learn of this project—under the designation XJ 13.

Jaguar's other sports car project was the further development of the D-Type, which consequently evolved into the E-Type. Sir William, who now was often respectfully called "The Old Man," eagerly followed the early development of this racing-cum-sports car.

The project had started following new regulations for the 1956 Le Mans race, which prohibited prototypes of more than 2.5-liter capacity. It was Phil Weaver's idea to turn one of the enclosed prototypes into a roadworthy car for normal customers—and this was to become the famous E-Type.

Based on the D-Type, a light racing car with a 2.5-liter short-stroke XK engine was developed. The

engine was equipped with two 2-inch S.U. carburetors. The body also closely resembled the D-Type. Having gained confidence in unitary construction, Jaguar engineers dared to dispense with the reinforcing subframe extension along the driveshaft.

The new car made its first secret test run on May 15, 1957. It was a very pure design, with no headlamps or door handles to spoil its looks. Its aluminum body made it a very light vehicle. This prototype was soon scrapped but later became famous thanks to the photographic documentation of ex-SS rally driver Margaret Allan (who in the meantime had married Christopher Jennings, publisher of *The Motor*). This was remembered when, in 1990, two large body parts of the car were found in a scrap yard. The light green car with Chassis No. XK 101 never had a real name, and the body number E1A seems to be preferred as a designation for the whole car, although it still was a very close relative to the D-Type.

A mockup for Malcolm Sayer's detail styling, created on a wooden stand, was elongated at Lyons' request in early February 1958. The metal sheets from this mockup were then pop-riveted and equipped with the chassis and systems necessary to make the whole thing drivable. This pop-rivet special of February 1958 had no long life. Lyons "played" only a little with it, but otherwise left it for Sayer to define the final looks of the E-Type.

In the meantime the engineers thought about the rear suspension of E1A, which began as a live axle. This

Above: The E2A at Browns Lane just before handing-over to Briggs Cunningham. *(S)*

Left: The rear of E2A still recalls the D-Type. *(S)*

The E2A looks like a rocket, but was the prototype of a sports car. *(J)*

E-Type, dream car of a whole generation. *(J)*

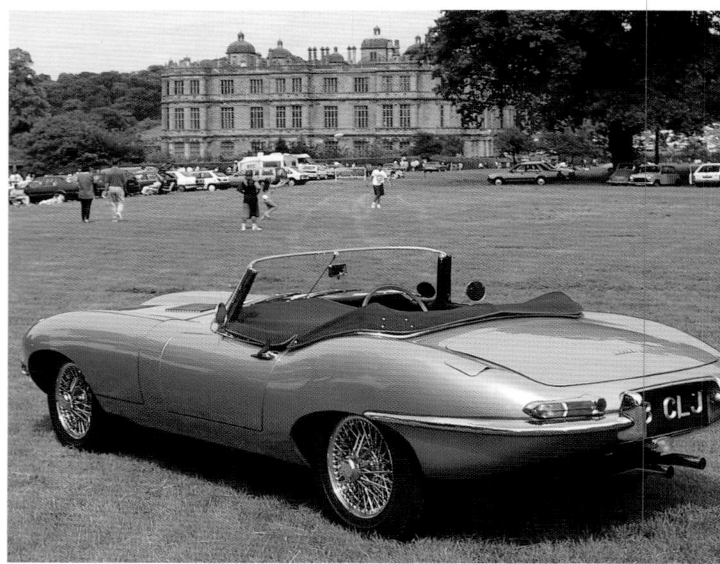

Right: The low rear end was thought to be aerodynamically advantageous. *(Schön)*

Below right: Dashboard of a very early E-Type. *(S)*

Middle: This conversion shows how the ambience of the E-Type can change. *(Schön)*

Bottom: Original flat floor on the right, but fitted later with a deeper floor on the left. *(König)*

Below: Normally the dashboard of the E-Type was dominated by vinyl and metal, but instead of an airplane cockpit it can also have the charm of a cabinet. *(Schön)*

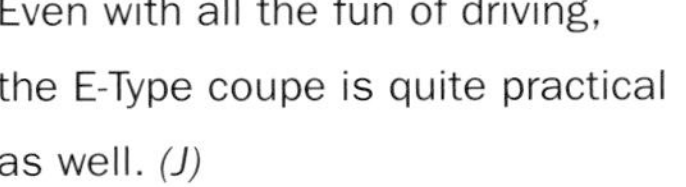
Even with all the fun of driving, the E-Type coupe is quite practical as well. *(J)*

Right from top: Three carburetors were most impressive in the 1960s. *(Schön)*

This engine bay during restoration gives clear views of the various components. *(Schön)*

The wonderful engine of the E-Type. *(Schön)*

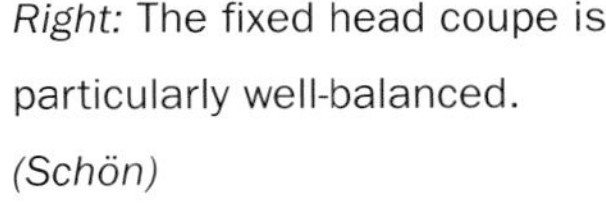
Right: The fixed head coupe is particularly well-balanced. *(Schön)*

Far right: The back of the E-Type fixed head coupe in its original guise. *(St)*

was no longer up-to-date, as its differential was unsprung weight, which was detrimental for handling. Robert Knight also was thinking about independent rear suspension in a subframe. His choice was neither a swing-axle, used for decades by Mercedes-Benz, nor semi-trailing arms, which were becoming increasingly popular. A de Dion axle also was not acceptable to him. Lyons managed to bet against Knight that he would not be able to build an independent rear suspension with a new design within four weeks.

Knight won the bet, and his solution was basically what was to be used in the E-Type when it was unveiled in 1961. It was a very complex design, with a lower transverse link below the half shaft, which worked as a second transverse link. A radius arm mounted at the body floor, together with two coil springs on each side and dampers in their centers, completed the suspension. All this was connected with rubber bushings to a subframe, and the subframe itself, through four Metalastik blocks, mounted to the body. In order to reduce unsprung weight, the disc brakes were mounted inboard at the differential. Georges Roesch of Talbot came up with the idea of using the half shafts as transverse links in the 1930s. So this suspension was nothing completely new, but it had respectable ancestry.

On December 4, 1959, Norman Dewis tested the first prototype. It still suffered from vibration generated by the transmission at low speeds. In the course of testing, a racing prototype evolved that was kept secret by Jaguar until it started in the 1960 Le Mans race. Its styling was very similar to the pop-rivet special, with the addition of a D-Type-style fin behind the driver and scoops over the rear wheels to channel cool air to the brakes. For test driving, the car inherited the VKV 752 registration from E1A. American Briggs Cunningham, eager to win the race, had become famous with his own prototypes and now persuaded Jaguar to let him race this prototype. Alas, Dan Gurney and Walt Hansgen broke down with the car. Its XK engine had been reduced to 3 liters in accordance with the regulations and it suffered from a not-sufficiently-tested injection system, which resulted in a holed piston. Jaguar's press department, with telltale eloquence, denied that this was a precursor to future Jaguar sports cars. After the race the car went back to Jaguar, where a 3.8-liter engine was installed. Then it was shipped to the United States, where Cunningham entered it in several races. Hansgen achieved an honorable third place at Elkhart Lake behind strong Ferrari and Maserati opposition. The car then returned again to Jaguar, where it was used over several years for testing Dunlop's Maxaret antilock system, the development of which had started more than 10 years before.

Contrary to all denials, a street version of the racer was finally introduced, with the most powerful of the engines that had been available for the XK 150. As this engine was much taller than the 3-liter unit, a bulge had to be added to the hood. Sayer gave the bulge a striking shape as if its only purpose were to give the car an even longer, sleeker appearance.

The public saw the new sports car for the first time on the eve of the Geneva Show on March 15, 1961, where just 10 years before the XK 120 fixed head coupe had been unveiled. This new E-Type was breathtaking in every sense of the word. Completed just in the nick of time, the coupe (Chassis No. 885002, registration 9600 HP) had to be driven nonstop to Geneva by Bob Berry. It is said that it arrived there only 20 minutes before the presentation for the world press started.

It was worth the trepidation: The style of the car, in the hands of Malcolm Sayer, revealed a strong emphasis on aerodynamics, and it was met immediately with fascination. The coupe's back, with its tailgate incorporating a large rear window (similar to the Aston Martin) was the idea of Bob Blake. When it was presented to the Jaguar board for confirmation, the reaction was restrained until Harry Rogers—although not a board member—championed the style. He immediately won the support of Sir William, and both were confirmed by the public reaction.

The car with the outrageously long hood was a unique sensation. Innumerable drives were undertaken at the testing area of the show. Thanks to the excellent performance, roadholding, and refinement, demand immediately outstripped Jaguar's production capacity, which admittedly was very low during the first months after the show. In best Jaguar tradition, the price was about half that of any competition. Production cost of the E-Type was £514—£2 less than for the most powerful XK 150! Production got under way rather slowly, and it was July 1961 before the first batch of 50 E-Types was ready for shipment to dealers. Of these, German and

Swiss importers Fendler & Lüdemann, Lindner, and Frey each received one example. The styling has retained its allure; in 1996 the New York Museum of Modern Art even purchased an E-Type for its permanent exhibition.

German journalist Fritz B. Busch wrote a tribute to the E-Type that added to the fame of the car in Germany. It was called "For Men who smoke pipes—Pure Whiskey or the Flounder." With his unmistakable sense for the irreverent he cited the chapter on tire pressure from the operator's manual: "For normal driving speeds up to 130 miles per hour . . . " though today we hardly feel the goose pimples this figure caused at the time. Busch's quips are unforgettable: "At first I walk round the car. This takes some time, as it is a long way. The car measures exactly 175⅜ inches, and not an inch less. Half the inchery is spent for the hood. It is a hood with two jump seats. Italian *La Lollo* could sit beside the car in a bikini—I would not notice her. The hood must have been tailored skin-tight—now I fear that I ever get it closed again. Before my very eyes 265 impatient SAE horses paw in the oil sump, and torque of 260 lb-ft literally bares its teeth. And people instinctively hide behind the straw bales, which strengthens my self-confidence. The car is pop-riveted to my back. It behaves as firmly as I sit in the car . . . the car acts as if it were my legs. This is not a ride on a lumpy cannonball; it is as if I were a thread uncoiled off a spinning wheel. I would like to be an endless thread. Like a big cat it darts forth and growls from 90 to 120 miles per hour, what a joy! Regarding its possibilities its driver should have a shooting instead of a driving license.

"What a car!"

A true test was published in *Das Auto, Motor und Sport* late in 1962. The title page displayed unbelievable performance figures along a photo of the nearly aeronautical cockpit of the car: "256 km/h, 0-100 km/h in 7.2 sec" (160 miles per hour, acceleration from standstill to 62 miles per hour in 7.2 seconds). This must have been the result of an error in measuring, as *The Autocar* had difficulties in achieving 150 miles per hour, the top speed promised by Jaguar, while testing the particularly powerful Geneva test car on a European motorway. The German figures were taken from a coupe registered in Britain with racing tires that Belgian Paul Frère tested for the Italian magazine *Quattroruote*, a truly international effort. The deficiency Frère revealed was the otherwise excellent disc brake system, which was prone to fading. The brake fluid tended to boil after the end of the fading test, making the brakes temporarily inoperable. Paul Frère was impressed, however: "With its conception and performance the Jaguar E is certainly the most brilliant production sports car of our time. At the same price no other car can offer nearly the same performance figures."

Early E-Types were met with criticism because of the cramped interior, uncomfortable seats, and old-fashioned gearbox with no synchromesh on first gear. So, there were plenty of opportunities for improvement. After some months, the impractical hood latches with an exterior lock were replaced with levers in the interior. Following legislation, cars destined for Germany had a steering wheel lock from March 1962 onward. From June 1962, wells in the floors offered much more space for the legs. A subsequent change to the sheet metal behind the seats allowed them to be pushed further backward, so that now even large drivers found adequate space in the E-Type.

From the very beginning of production the E-Type went racing, with some remarkable victories. *(S)*

Briggs Cunningham's racing car in white and blue livery as is typical for American racing cars. *(J)*

Right from top: The Low Drag Coupe awaiting its next racing start. *(Schön)*

Peter Lindner's Low Drag Coupe has become quite famous. *(Schön)*

In its Lightweight guise, the E-Type had a second racing career. *(Schön)*

The E-Type grew into a symbol of 1960s Britain, not least because of its racing success. Its first win was achieved in its first race, on April 15, 1961. At Oulton Park, gifted Graham Hill scored a win in the totally standard roadster (Chassis No. 850005, registration ECD 400) of Equipe Endeavour with an average 83.22 miles per hour. The second E-Type in the race was a John Coombs car (Chassis No.850006, registration BUY 1; this car was later transformed into a semi-lightweight, registration 4 WPD). With Roy Salvadori as driver it finished third behind an Aston Martin, despite suffering from brake fade. Four weeks later the E-Type's international career began at the Spa sports car race in Belgium. Mike Parkes was beaten by Mairesse in a Ferrari, but second place still was a very good result. In May 1962 an E-Type was seen at the Nürburgring 1,000-kilometer race. Werner/Olsen finished second in the large prototype class, again behind a Ferrari (Mairesse/Parkes).

While Jaguar mostly refrained from modifying E-Types for racing, the Peter Sargent/Peter Lumsden team with Chassis No. 850009 (registration 898 BYR, another example of the first E-Type batch) received a heavily retouched fastback made of aluminum. It also had additional air scoops in the alloy hood feeding the improved brakes. With this car they entered the 24 Hours of Le Mans, where Briggs Cunningham was also at the start, with an allegedly works-prepared E-Type coupe. A wrongly mounted seal blocked Lumsden's lower gears for the last hour of the race when he was in fourth position, so that the Cunningham/Salvadori entry had a chance to overtake. They could not catch up the three leading Ferraris, but they finished the race at an average 107.87 miles per hour. A further E-Type in the race, driven by Charles/Coundley, broke down quite early in the race.

The E-Type definitely had the potential to become invincible with the usual racing improvements. The car

Above: E-Type, entered at Le Mans by Briggs Cunningham. *(Schön)*

Left: A battery of Weber carburetors—a must-have for high-performance engines like that of the lightweight E-Type. *(Schön)*

had to become lighter, more powerful, and more aerodynamic, and as a consequence it would need wider tires. With this aim, Malcolm Sayer modified Chassis No. 860004, reduced the aerodynamic profile of the greenhouse, and added a true fastback. With some mechanical improvement, the car went on its first test drive in July 1962.

Again it was racer John Coombs who was most interested in a mighty Jaguar racer. Although he was a Jaguar dealer, at the time he saw no alternative but to replace his works-prepared E-Type, for the upcoming season, as Ferrari and Maserati had improved their cars considerably. First choice for 1963 was Ferrari's latest 250 GTO, which seemed to be invincible. But as soon as Coombs' new Ferrari was delivered from Italy, Jaguar had an opportunity to study it in detail and test it. It was compared with Coombs' 1961 and 1962 E-Type hardtop roadster as well as with the new fastback coupe. The data that was acquired was most helpful for Jaguar's specialists, who provided Coombs with the first E-Type Lightweight for the 1963 season.

The body was made completely new in aluminum, the sheets being pressed on the normal tools at Abbey Panels. Welding the aluminum sheets turned out to be difficult, so pop-rivets were used instead. Only the front subframe was made of steel. The XK engine received a wide-angle D-Type head with inlet valves increased to 2 inches in diameter, an alloy block, dry sump lubrication, and fuel injection. A ZF differential in alloy housing improved the rear suspension. The car gave up its old chassis number and now became 850658.

In March 1963 Roy Salvadori tested the improved Coombs car, 4 WPD, as well as the fastback coupe. The former was faster, and so it was chosen as the pattern for a small series of special E-Types that carried the next 11 chassis numbers in series. As a distinguishing feature a prefix "S" was added to the chassis numbers, and a similar suffix was added to the engine numbers.

Peter Lindner's greatest race was the 1964 Le Mans 24 Hours. *(S)*

Left: Peter Lindner's cockpit. *(Schön)*

Below left: Peter Lindner's luggage trunk. *(Schön)*

Below: In June 1962 Briggs Cunningham and Roy Salvadori took part in the Le Mans race with this E-Type. *(S)*

Some of these engines had even larger inlet valves of 2³⁄₃₂ inches in diameter. The next six numbers were not used, as initially a series of 18 specials was planned.

Another Lightweight, with thin steel sheets, was made for Dick Protheroe (Chassis No. EC 1001). These Lightweights were not made for works entries but were sold to private racing teams. For homologation purposes (Group J) the aluminum body was declared as standard, and the steel ones as specials. The fastback coupe was later sold off to Protheroe, who gave the car its registration number CUT 7 and often drove it in British races. The first Lightweight, the car that had been prepared for Coombs, also was an active racer, usually driven by Hill. Hill won at Goodwood (Easter Monday race, from Salvadori and Salmon, and the Sussex Trophy race with Salmon finishing third), Mallory Park (with Salvadori finishing third), and Silverstone (with an average of 101.02 miles per hour from Salvadori and Protheroe). Further successes of the 1963 season were Jackie Stewart's victory at Oulton (Chassis No. 850216, registration FSN 1, a heavily but invisibly prepared demonstrator from his father's dealership), which was the breakthrough in international racing for Jimmy Stewart's younger brother. Scragg won the Prescott hillclimbs in May and September, as well as Shelsley Walsh (56.43, 55.86, and 39.93 seconds); Ken Baker/H. Walkup won at Mallory Park in April and August, T. Yokohama won at Suzuka, and J. Dean won the Boxing Day race at Brands Hatch. Roger Mac and

J. Dean managed a 1-2 placing at Aintree, and Hansgen finished the 500-mile race at Bridgehampton in third.

In 1964 Scragg repeated his hillclimb wins, A. J. Lambert won the Silverstone GT races (average 82.73 and 82.87 miles per hour), and Sutcliffe won at Montlhéry. Jimmy Stewart was second in the Ilford Trophy race at Brands Hatch, as was Mac at Snetterton, while Sutcliffe was third at Limburg and at Brighton Speed trials. Pat Coundley won the Ladies' Trophy with a D-Type. This list could be extended much further—Philip Porter filled no less than 50 pages of his definitive E-Type book with E-Type racing successes. However, the E-Type was not as unrivalled in motor sport as were the C- and D-Types in their time, often being a close second to Ferrari's mighty 250 GTO.

In 1965 Scragg remained successful in hill climbing. W. R. Pearce won at Brands Hatch, J. Oliver/C. Craft finished third in the 1,000-mile race at the same venue, and R. Ward won the GT race at Snetterton. Lutz Hillesheim scored third in class in the Norisring race near Nuremberg, and in the Street Marathon at the Nürburgring, Ernst Brem and Erhard von Käuel finished fifth and sixth. In smaller races the E-Type was successful over several further years. For example, Faber's second in the 1967 Wittlicher Bergpreis and Barret's third in the Eberbach hillclimb.

One of the Lightweights (Chassis No.850663) was for the two Peters, Sargent and Lumsden, and Chassis No. 850662 was delivered to Peter Lindner, Jaguar importer to Germany. He provided the only major contribution from Germany to Jaguar's racing legend. In the late 1950s Lindner raced for promotional purposes, driving a Jaguar 3.4-liter or an Aston Martin DB 4 GT, which he also imported. When he was introduced to hobby racing driver and ready-mix concrete entrepreneur Peter Nöcker, this effort was transformed into a serious one.

Nöcker had preferred the Mercedes-Benz 300 SL until Lindner offered him his Jaguar 3.4-liter, the engine of which came from Hawthorn's crashed car and was considerably prepared—racing engines from Jaguar's experimental shop are identifiable by the "EE" prefix to the engine number. In 1961 Lindner/Nöcker won the Nürburgring 6 hours with a 3.4-liter Mark II. In further GT and touring car races, particularly the Nürburgring 12-hour race, Lindner was just as successful, and he became touring car champion that year.

In 1962 the two German Peters formed a team of three works-prepared, dark-green Mark IIs with beige leather. These cars were made in parallel with four cars for the French racing enthusiasts Consten, Dutoit, Lego, and Rosinski. Lindner and Nöcker scored numerous wins again. The Nürburgring 6 hours ended with a 1-2-3 finish for Lindner/Nöcker, Schadrak/Baumgartner and Kreft, while Peter Lindner/Hans-Joachim Walter (the latter was German rally champion) won the Nürburgring 12-hour race: together with the Jaguars at third and fifth positions, he also won the team prize.

In 1963 the Nürburgring 6 hours was the first race in the new European Touring Car Championship. Lindner/Nöcker were very keen on winning this historic race, and they did, while Böhringer/Glemser finished second with their Mercedes-Benz 300 SE. The 12-hour race became even more thrilling. Early in the race, Lindner lost 37 minutes for the repair of a Panhard rod. Instead of giving up, Lindner pushed the accelerator as even he had never done before, cut corners more than even he was used to and after this tour de force won the race only two seconds ahead of a FIAT-Abarth 2300 driven by Paul Frère, who had also gained some fame by racing Jaguars. At Zolder Lindner suffered an accident. Nöcker and John Sparrow were second and third. Lindner now had hardly a chance to win the championship, so in a heroic act of self-discipline he gave the priority in the team to Nöcker, who consequently won the Hannover airfield race, the Timmelsjoch hillclimb, and the final race in Budapest (with Lindner and Schadrack at third and ninth position). This is how Nöcker became the first European Touring Car champion.

According to Nöcker, Lindner could not drive faster when he knew the circuit better—he usually was as fast in the first lap as he was in the last, even on circuits he didn't know. His tense posture and his inaccurate way of changing gears seemed to be the reason for the quite frequent damage to his cars. All in all, Peter Lindner was not the genius at the wheel he was held for later, but nevertheless he was a determined, fast, and untiring driver.

Other drivers like Hans-Joachim Walter and later Roger Schweickert—he had a Jaguar dealership that still exists at Pforzheim—with their less spectacular

Peter Lindner, Jaguar importer and racing driver. *(S)*

driving styles could not match Lindner's popularity. Schweickert purchased Lindner's famous Mark II with the personalized registration WI-PL 1 and still owns it. Friedrich Bryzmann's Mark II was another one that won many races in 1965, such as the touring car race held in conjunction with the German Grand Prix, the Wittlicher, and the Bielbronner Bergpreis, as well as the Eberbach hillclimb. Theo Kirchhoff won the 1965 Hansapokal (where Martin Räth finished second in class with his E-Type); Ditzler was fourth in class at the Ste. Ursanne-Les Rangiers touring car race, and Dutoit/Meert third in the Marathon de la Route.

In 1966 Schweickert won the Heilbronn and Eberbach hillclimbs, the Krähbergrennen, and was second in the Teutoburger Wald. Bryzmann won the AVUS race in Berlin and the Taubensuhl hillclimb. He was second in the 100-mile race at Hockenheim and at the Mainz-Finthen airfield race. In 1967 Schweickert won the Heilbronn and the Schwäbische Alb Bergpreis, the Ratisbona, Eberbach, and Stadtsteinach hillclimbs; he finished second in the Hockenheim touring car race; and third in the Schauinsland race. Hillesheim/ Schiewer scored a class win in the Nürburgring touring car race, as did Kleiber at the Hockenheim 100-mile race. In 1969 Schweickert was still victorious at the Eberbach and Wasgau hillclimbs, while at Eberbach he was followed by Mark IIs driven by Lampert and Burkhardt. In 1970 Milosaljevic was third in the Krähbergrennen, Schweickert won the Kaufbeuren airfield race, and Sauer was third in the Eberbach hillclimb.

Back to Lindner, who started with his Lightweight E-Type in the 1963 Nürburgring 1,000 kilometers. A Ferrari started ahead of Lindner, who sounded the horn, causing the startled Ferrari pilot to a sidestep, so that Lindner could overtake. Lindner arrived first at the *Südkurve* and was still in the lead after the first lap. Later in the race he had to retire, as did Lumsden/Sargent in their Lightweight E-Type. Later it was claimed that the furious start mentioned above was Sargent/Lumsden's but this must be an error: The report in *Auto Motor und Sport* (the name having recently been changed) mentions the silver color of the car—typical for Lindner's, while Lumsden/ Sargent's always was dark-colored.

In 1963, three Lightweights started at Le Mans. It was Briggs Cunningham's fleet, all with ZF five-speed gearboxes. Of these only Cunningham/Bob Grossman made it to the finish—after a brake failure at the end of the Mulsanne straight and a nearly two-hour repair of the badly damaged hood. They still finished ninth! Lumsden/Sargent started in a Lister, but they retired.

In 1964 Lindner's E-Type had been aerodynamically improved with a most attractive "low drag" coupe body. Sargent/Lumsden had their car modified in a similar way, using the know-how of engineer Samir Klat. Lindner's car still had a reputation of being a difficult handling machine. The engines of both cars had been modified independent of each other, but both achieved 350 horsepower, which certainly made them the most powerful 3.8-liter XK engines ever. Nevertheless, these cars were not very lucky. In the Nürburgring 1,000 kilometers and Le Mans 24 Hours both cars retired—for a long period these were the last Jaguars to start at Le Mans. In the 1,000-kilometer race, Protheroe was not lucky either, but in the Nürburgring 12 Hours he won the GT class, and Nöcker won with the E-Type at the Norisring.

All in all, the Lightweight E-Type was not a dominant car, but it made GT racing a bit more thrilling. Some complained that the works had not sufficiently supported the teams and prepared the cars so that some opportunity for follow-on sales was lost. No wonder that Bob Berry, who was obsessed with racing, called it a half-hearted affair.

In October 1964 in the Montlhéry 1,000 kilometers, Lindner had a serious accident in the rain. He was flung out of the car and sadly died shortly afterward in the hospital. The completely damaged Lightweight was kept at the circuit for a long time, but in the late 1980s this historically important car was restored at Lynx in England. Nearly all the body panels had to be replaced. Rumor has it that the Lindner family held Jaguar responsible for the accident, but Jaguar supported Lindner's widow in continuing the Jaguar dealership.

With additional publicity gained in racing, the Mark II and the E-Type were the first Jaguars to gain some popularity in Germany. In 1962 alone, Jaguar sales in Germany rose by 50 percent, in France even more, and in all of Europe by 40 percent.

The large Mark IX sedan was virtually unknown in Germany. If one was offered for sale as a used car, it was necessary to explain in the advertisement that it was similar to a Rolls-Royce (to German eyes). It was thus hardly noticed in Germany when this noble and old-fashioned car was replaced with an ultramodern, low sedan with the engine and suspension of the E-Type, called the Mark X. Originally, it was intended that this would be the direct replacement to the Mark VIII, but Lyons found it difficult to find the right styling. This resulted in considerable delay. Some joker called the project "Mark Time" instead of "Mark Nine." This car retained the wheelbase of its predecessor but was slightly longer and 8 inches lower. It was of unitary construction, and thus benefited from the experience gained with the smaller sedans. Finally in the spring of 1961 the first "Zenith" cars were ready for testing (this was the code for the car when it was under development). Norman Dewis decided that the good, low-traffic roads in the southwest of France would be ideal for testing. One of the two prototypes had an accident (Chassis No. 300050, registration 5437 RW), while the other one (Chassis No. 300051, registration 5438 RW) did 40,000 miles—this was Jaguar's first extensive testing program on public roads.

Four million pounds had been invested to make production of the Mark X possible. At its launch on October 10, 1961, the Mark X was much better tested than the 2.4-liter six years before. But this was not of much benefit. U.S. importer Eerdmans just called it a lemon because of its many problems with cooling. The intense 1962–1963 winter, the first winter with many salted roads, caused severe wear to the Metalastik bushes. This did not help the car gain popularity. At home and in Europe the more sporting Mark II was serious competition, while the Mark X simply was too large, and particularly too wide. The U.S. market was slightly disappointed with the performance of the car. Nevertheless the Mark X started with good sales at least, and helped to make sure that the staff had work during the winter of 1961–1962.

The Mark X was praised in the international press, which emphasized that the car was so easy to handle that its size was soon forgotten. However, the comfortable springing made the car dive under braking and roll excessively in fast corners—both emphasized by the flat and wide, little-contoured seats. For this reason alone it was advisable to wear the safety belts. Entering the car over the large sills was somewhat awkward. In the United States the styling was not universally acclaimed; one magazine saw similarities with the 1948 Hudson. However, the Mark X was to define the looks of Jaguar sedans for about a half-century!

In 1962, Reinhard Seiffert tested the bulbous Mark X for *Das Auto, Motor und Sport*. He started with the innovative rear suspension: "This unit is so beautiful that one is tempted to put it into a glass cabinet in the living room. With regard to its good springing, the Mark X's roadholding abilities command respect."

Its lavish, well-equipped interior prompted dismissive remarks about the domestic competitors from Untertürkheim. The conclusion was: "We would say that the Mark X belongs in the first row among its competitors; it should be seriously taken into consideration. The Mark X is of particularly impressive appearance, and its technical abilities make it one of the top prod-

Above: It took William Lyons much effort to find the right style for a new large sedan. *(S)*

Below: Mark X was the first Jaguar sedan to experience extensive testing, here at MIRA. *(S)*

ucts of the European motor industry. It is not undemanding, needing an owner with good financial backing, interest, and knowledge in motoring."

Nevertheless, Jaguar development sought ways to improve the car. With its large engine bay, the car was an ideal test bed for different types of engines. An obvious idea was to implant Daimler's mighty 4.5-liter V-8. This allegedly reduced acceleration figures to 60 miles per hour from 11 to 6 seconds, increased top speed to 130 miles per hour, and yet the gasoline consumption was lower than with the XK unit. A Mark X 4.5-liter was not to be, due more to the lack of mass production facilities for the V-8 than regard for the iconic status of the XK engine. (William Heynes, head of engineering for Jaguar, reportedly lost his composure over the undisputable superiority of the alien engine.) Jaguar already had a V-12 under development, which came from the racing department, and Claude Baily had already proposed in 1958 that this engine could be used in the sedans as well. Different variants of this engine were tested in Chassis Nos. 1D 50002, 50003, and 50004 reaching a top speed of 150 miles per hour. A V-12 with a cast-iron block was tested in a Mark X as well, but it was nose-heavy and difficult to drive with brakes that were not up to the task of stopping the heavier car.

Above: A grand car with a grand luggage trunk: 1961 Mark X. *(Schön)*

Right: A new grand style shown here in front of Wappenbury Hall. *(J)*

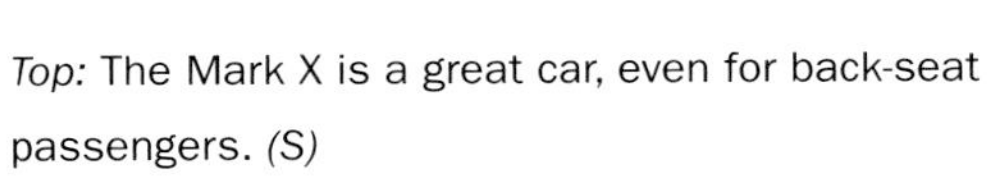
Top: The Mark X is a great car, even for back-seat passengers. *(S)*
Above: Picnic table with its own mirror for Mark X. *(S)*

Above: To have a cup of tea in a Jaguar—a dream comes true in the rare Mark X with a partition. *(S)*

Above: Sir William Lyons and a row of early Mark Xs in front of Browns Lane headquarters. *(S)*

Left: The spacious interior of the large Mark X. *(S)*

UNIQUE FEATURES OF THE JAGUAR MARK TEN

- Luxury-equipped, spacious, five-seat sedan
- Independent suspension and four-wheel disc brakes
- Six-cylinder Jaguar XK engine with double overhead cams
- Completely new, high-performance heating and ventilation systems
- Completely new body style in the best Jaguar tradition
- Steel monocoque construction offers maximum strength and security
- Choice of manual transmission, with or without overdrive, or automatic transmission

1961 Mark X. *(Schönborn archive)*

Left: The wonderful independent rear suspension of the Mark X is too nice to be hidden beneath a car. *(Schönborn archive)*

Below: Today the Mark X is still impressive. *(Schönborn archive)*

14

A HUGE CONCERN

While the Jaguar workshop had developed into a group of companies, Sir William was concerned about his smaller sedan. In retrospect it seems hardly believable, but he thought that the demand for this perfect sports sedan might soon fall. So he decided that it was the right time for a revision of these cars. Thoughts immediately went to the rear suspension, as the Mark II was the last Jaguar with a live axle. So Chassis No.208829 was equipped with the independent suspension of the later models and—to compensate for the space taken by this unit—a longer back end that was similar to the Mark X, as were the eyebrows over the headlamps and the indicators. In order to hide its origins, the car got a new chassis number, 1B 50029, which seemingly made it a normal example of what would be called the 3.8 S on its introduction alongside the similar 3.4 S in Paris on September 30, 1963. Both cars were soon known colloquially as "S-Types." The 3.4 S was not exported to the United States. All over the world, most customers preferred the Borg-Warner DG automatic to the old-fashioned Moss gearbox, with or without overdrive. As the new cars were not as well received as expected, and because the Mark II remained as popular as before, the "predecessor" remained in the range side-by-side with the S-Type.

Auto motor und sport issued Paul Frère's test of the 3.4 S early in 1964. He particularly liked the servo-assisted steering, and this was Frère's first watertight Jaguar. "The loss in sporting character has been won twice in refinement and roadholding. The S-Type has grown into an excellent car." Reinhard Seiffert confirmed this result in his 1966 test of a 3.8 S with Peter Lindner's car, registration F-PL 1. But there were also

Above left: The luxurious interior of the 1963 Jaguar 3.8 S. *(Schönborn archive)*

Above: The 1963 Jaguar 3.8 S is a typically British car. *(Schönborn archive)*

Opposite: In 1964 the engine was enlarged for the Mark X 4.2-liter—the side molding was added later. *(J)*

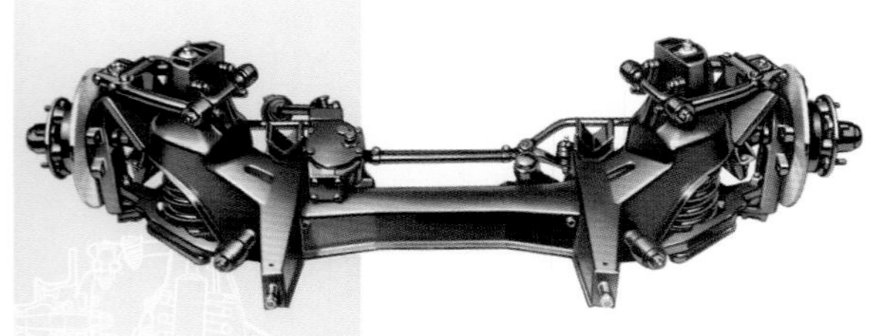

Above: The 3.4 S was a Mark II with independent rear suspension. *(J)*

Right above: Front suspension of 3.4 and 3.8 S. *(Schönborn archive)*

Right below: Still more elegant than the Mark II was the interior of the 3.8 S. *(S)*

Below: Peter Lindner's collection of Mark II, 3.8 S, and E-Type 2+2. *(Schönborn archive)*

some oddities that caught the attention of the down-to-earth engineer. He wondered about the complicated, vacuum-assisted regulating mechanism for the all-but-efficient heating system. Seiffert found reason to praise the new, full-synchromesh gearbox, but he detected an unwanted tendency for the rear suspension to steer the car. Even the price of the lower-range 3.4 S was judged unfavorable compared with the Mercedes-Benz, even though the Jaguar was equipped with a much more lavish and fully equipped interior.

Jaguar's "new" paint facility was taken over for as little as £350,000 as a used item from Mulliners coach building plant in Birmingham. Mulliners in turn had taken over this facility from Standard in 1958. In August 1964 it went into service at Browns Lane. Jaguar's workers only applied the top coat after the traditional test drive of the car. This saved the previous touching-up of stone chips.

Shortly afterward Jaguar announced its latest and largest engine, the 4.2. In the United States, which took about half of all Jaguars produced, the horsepower race under the motto of "keeping up with the Joneses" was still in progress. Jaguar customers were thus demanding improved torque for a quicker start off the traffic

lights. Alfred Momo and Briggs Cunningham urged another boring-out of the XK engine. This, however, was not easy to achieve, as the space between the cylinders was too little for adequate cooling to remain. The new engine was introduced with the Mark X for the 1965 model year. Performance had improved slightly, and the acceleration at low revs improved, in particular. The new Varamatic steering servo gained much acclaim, as did the brakes. From autumn 1965 the car was—similar to the Mark VIII B for military service—available as a limousine with a partition. One of them (Chassis No. 1D 51762) became Sir William's official car. Still, the cars were not too reliable. A collector from Westphalia once purchased the former 1964 Motor Show exhibit car, but it broke down repeatedly, and repair was always very expensive. So he sold the car, warning the purchaser of the proven unreliability. But, to the seller's annoyance, the car then worked perfectly for many years.

On October 9, 1964, the new engine became available in the E-Type as well. Jaguar's experimental test bed had been a coupe that in the works files was called "Series 2," although it had none of the later changes that were described in brochures as "Series 2." Originally the press had been informed that the 3.8 would continue as an alternative to the 4.2-liter E-Type, but further 3.8 E-Types were made. Test reports said that the 4.2 lost out on performance to the 3.8, but this impression may be due to the particularly powerful early 3.8 test car. At last, the Moss gearbox was replaced by a full synchromesh unit developed at Jaguar—as it had on the Mark X, where this was judged as a major improvement.

One week before the 1966 Geneva Show the E-Type 2+2 was unveiled. Due to a major strike at Jaguar in the autumn of 1965, its debut had to be postponed. Extending the wheelbase and raising the roof made room for two small additional seats but also diminished the perfect balance of the coupe lines. Meanwhile, in England the E-Type had become so popular that in 1966 it was even displayed on a Royal Mail stamp.

On October 13, 1966, Jaguar displayed an S-Type with the face of the Mark X and a 4.2-liter XK engine having only two S.U. carburetors. This new model was called the Jaguar 420 or Daimler Sovereign (named after the coin). The latter was the first Daimler that was a Jaguar in every technical detail. It was distinguished from the 420 only by its level of equipment, the fluted grille, and number plate plinth, and its badges.

The 420 was a bit of an interim solution, instigated by Sir William after he saw little interest in the 3.8 S at the 1965 Motor Show. Pressed Steel Fisher—

Left above: Timeless and elegant—the face of the Mark X 4.2. *(Schönborn archive)*

Left below: Luxury in the Mark X 4.2. *(Schönborn archive)*

Below: The 1964 Mark X 4.2 was almost too large. *(Schönborn archive)*

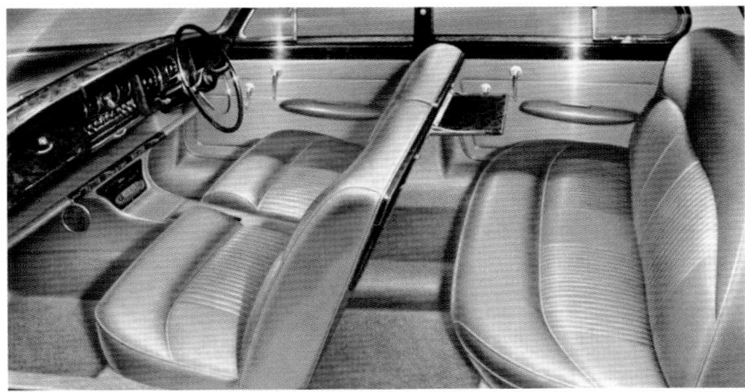

Above: 1964 E-Type 4.2 fixed head coupe—the swinging sixties. *(Schönborn archive)*

Below: Thicker cushions and vinyl covered center console in the E-Type 4.2. *(S)*

Right above: The E-Type had the 4.2-liter engine from 1964 onward. *(Schön)*

Below: An early E-Type 4.2 open two-seater with hardtop. *(S)*

Above: The fixed head coupe also benefited from the larger engine. *(Schön)*

Right: E-Type 2+2 in a crash test—for the safety of its passengers. *(S)*

Below: 1966 E-Type 2+2, a sports car for the whole family. *(Schönborn archive)*

Light blue seems to have been particularly popular for the Jaguar 420. *(J)*

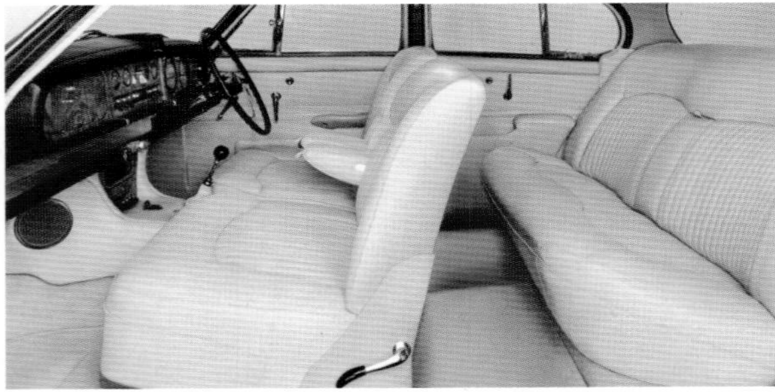

Above: The modernized interior of the 420. *(Schönborn archive)*

Below: Only two Jaguars are said to have found their way to East Germany: This 420 for actor Manfred Krug was one of them. *(JAGMAG archive)*

1966 Jaguar 420 grille. *(Schön)*

Daimler Sovereign, the first of its make that was a Jaguar mechanically. *(Long)*

Test reports praised the 1966 Jaguar 420. *(J)*

A Mark II with a long back: 1966 Jaguar 420. *(Schönborn archive)*

The Jaguar 420 is a Jaguar 3.8 S with the face of the Mark X—the latter was re-named 420 G. *(J)*

The first Daimler Sovereign, introduced in 1966. *(Schönborn archive)*

Above: The picnic tables for 420 G were carried over from the Mark X. *(Schönborn archive)*

Right: The interior of the 420 G was still lavish. *(Schönborn archive)*

Left: In 1966 the Mark X was renamed 420 G, distinguished by side moldings that made it look even longer. *(J)*

Below: The 420 was the last Jaguar for many years with a radiator mascot. *(Schön)*

the new name was a result of the merger of the British branch of the American Fisher Body Corporation (Fisher & Ludlow) with Pressed Steel under the auspices of BMC—under the threat of losing this contract in favor of Abbey Panels, only just managed to adhere to Sir William's tight time schedule for the supply of 420 bodies.

The British press was impressed by the improved flexibility of the engine, while the Varamatic steering suddenly came in for criticism of a lack of feel, prompting drivers to turn the steering wheel more than necessary. According to contemporary tests the automatic had hardly any effect on performance or fuel consumption.

Early in 1967, Reinhard Seiffert tested the 420 for *Auto Motor und Sport.* The "Gentleman from Coventry," as Seiffert called it, again impressed with its refinement. With a manual gearbox, it achieved a maximum speed over 200 kilometers per hour (125 miles per hour). The car's tendency to oversteer and its unimpressive directional stability came in for criticism.

The new name of the Mark X—420 G—caused some confusion. The name probably was instigated by the U.S. public relations people. The meaning of the "G" was unclear; perhaps it stood for "grand." The only *raison d'être* was the need to distinguish the car from the "simple" 420. The name change gave designers the opportunity to add a bright vertical bar in the center of the former Mark X's grille, and a chrome strip over the swage line at the sides of the car. The latter had already been seen on some early Mark X prototypes. There were some 420 G limousines, such as Sir William's

official car (Chassis No. G1D 55943). In the 1980s, Classic Cars of Coventry transformed some Mark Xs and 420 Gs into striking convertibles. As the roof did not contribute to the stiffness of the car, this was an easy task.

In the following year Mark II models also were given three-figure names according to their engine size. However, the level of equipment—which, had been reduced during the previous model year in combination with lower prices—remained unchanged. Enthusiasts were appalled to see real leather replaced by ambla and the picnic tables discarded altogether. For 1968 the level of equipment of the 3.4 and 3.8 S also was reduced, and the Mark II 3.8 disappeared from the brochures, although a dozen 340 3.8s were made to special order. The 240 still gained acclaim for its road-holding, its new synchromesh gearbox, and the still (for its class) remarkable level of equipment. Fuel economy, however, was not much better than with the

Above left: The 240 continued the tradition of the previous year's low-spec Mark II. *(J)*

Above top: Face and engine of the Daimler 250 V-8. *(Schön)*

Above: The slightly modernized interior of the Daimler 250 V-8. *(Schönborn archive)*

Below left: Jaguar 340, still a competitive touring car. *(S)*
Below center: The Daimler 2.5-liter V-8 was renamed 250 V-8 in 1967. *(J)*
Below right: The Daimler 250 V-8 was more lavishly equipped than its siblings, Jaguar 240 and 340. *(S)*

Above: 1967 E-Type Series 1½" fixed head coupe. *(Schön)*

Below: The E-Type Series 1½ open two-seater was only made for one year. *(Balken archive)*

larger engines. The relatively high cowl was old-fashioned by now, and the heating was downright useless. The price of the 240 was only little higher than in 1955, thanks to the reduced equipment, but the pound had depreciated by half in that time.

Nuccio Bertone presented his ultralow, very modern Pirana sports car at the 1968 Motor Show—a car that was covered heavily in the British press. Jaguar was not much impressed with the effort. At the same venue Jaguar unveiled its interpretation of a "Series 2" E-Type on October 18, 1968. There was not much visual change. Preheating of the intake air, the adjustable seat back, new safety belts, and more flush-fitting switches as well as protruding headlamps without Perspex covers already had been introduced the year before, following U.S. legislation. Thanks to the protruding headlights, the shade caused by the protruding hood almost disappeared, and the light provided better matched the speed potential of the car. This interim model is unofficially known as "Series 1½" although the transition from Series 1 to Series 2 could more appropriately be regarded as a metamorphosis. With the official Series 2, the headlights protruded even further, degrading looks and aerodynamics alike. The larger oval grille was beneficial for cooling. Indicators and rear lights were enlarged for safety reasons and were moved below the bumpers, where the new square rear number plate was situated as well. The bright cam covers were replaced with fluted black ones, the tops of the flutes being bright. Fortunately the customers were delighted with these cars, despite decreased performance for U.S. customers because of emissions controls.

Jaguar, which had developed into a large company itself, merged with large British Motor Corporation (BMC, with Austin, Morris, and other car makes, also was the parent of Pressed Steel Fisher) on July 12, 1966. In the years past many coachbuilders had joined with competing car manufacturers, and thus were no longer open to orders from Jaguar. Therefore, the new alliance with Pressed Steel Fisher seemed to be a worthwhile strategy. Furthermore, the death of Sir William's only son meant there was no heir to his empire, and his autocratic style kept him from developing young, talented management at Jaguar. The new parent seemed to guarantee Jaguar's survival past the Lyons era. The public was quite surprised by the merger of these two dissimilar partners, which was called British Motor Holdings (BMH). The Jaguar group had been guaranteed the utmost freedom and independence. Nevertheless, the classic Jaguar period of the XK, Mark II and E-Type was nearing its end.

Until 1965 Jaguars were imported to Germany by Fendler & Lüdemann in Hamburg and by Lindner, who had succeeded R M Overseas, in Frankfurt. The former had sold only a few Jaguars and thus were dropped in 1966. At that time Germany had about 60 Jaguar dealers, mainly thanks to Peter Lindner's efforts.

In England an even larger merger was announced on January 19, 1968, affecting BMH and the large Leyland commercial vehicle group. This merger became effective on May 14, 1968. Rumor had it that Sir William had not been informed of the already ongoing negotiations with Leyland when he merged with BMH. Again, there seemed to be considerable advantages for Jaguar: the financially sound foundation, common development, production and quality enhancement. As the financial year had to be adjusted to Leyland's, the 1968–1969 business year was 14 months long, ending with the month of September.

The E-Type Series 2 was the first to suffer from emissions legislation in the United States. *(Schönborn archive)*

Right from top: Larger grille and headlights betray the Series 2 E-Type. *(Schön)*

Jaguar E-Type Series 2 2+2 was suitable for sporting enthusiasts with children. *(Schönborn archive)*

A 1968 E-Type Series 2 fixed head coupe with some compromises for American legislation. *(Schönborn archive)*

Below left: The E-Type Series 2 2+2 had a more raked windshield. *(S)*

Below right: The E-Type Series 2 family. *(S)*

Much press attention surrounded Bertone's Pirana, which was based on an E-Type Jaguar. *(S)*

A 3.8 S for North America without fog lamps, which were dispensed with for the rest of the world as well during its last season. *(St)*

This new British Leyland Motor Corporation (BLMC) comprised a nearly unbelievable number of former independent motor manufacturers:

Jaguar Group (merged in 1966 with BMC, forming BMH)

- **Jaguar** (established in 1922 as Swallow, in 1934 as SS, car manufacturer since 1927)
- **Coventry Climax** (engines, established in 1904 as Coventry-Simplex, joined Jaguar in 1963)
- **Daimler** (established in 1896, car manufacturer since 1897, joined Jaguar in 1960)
- **Guy** (commercial vehicles, established in 1914, car manufacturer from 1919 until 1924, joined Jaguar in 1961)
- **Lanchester** (established in 1899, car manufacturer since 1901, joined Daimler in 1931)
- **Meadows** (engines, established in 1920, Frisky car manufacturer from 1957 until 1964, joined Jaguar in 1965)
- **Star** (established as Sharrah & Lisle in 1883, car manufacture from 1897 until 1932, joined Guy in 1928)

Austin Group

- **Austin** (established 1905, car manufacturer since 1906)
- **Vanden Plas** (coachbuilding, established as Théo Masui Limited in 1912, joined Austin in 1946)
- **Morris Group** (merged with Austin in 1952, forming BMC)
- **Morris** (established as WRM Motors in 1912, car manufacturer since 1913)
- **Austin-Healey** (car make of BMC from 1953 until 1972)
- **Autovia** (car make of Riley from 1937 until 1938)
- **Bollée** (car manufacturer from 1895 until 1933, joined Morris in 1924)
- **Fisher & Ludlow** (coachbuilding, joined BMC in 1953)
- **Hollick & Pratt** (coachbuilding, joined Morris in 1924)
- **Hotchkiss-England** (car manufacturer to French license, joined Morris in 1923)
- **Metropolitan** (car make of BMC and Nash from 1954 until 1962)
- **M.G.** (established as Morris Garages in 1910, car manufacture since 1925)
- **Pressed Steel** (body panels, established by Morris in 1926, soon sold, joined BMC in 1965)
- **Rhode** (established as Mead & Deakin, car manufacturer since 1921, joined Morris in 1929)
- **Riley** (car manufacturer from 1898, joined Morris in 1937)
- **Stellite** (car make of Wolseley from 1913 until 1919)
- **S.U.** (Skinner Union carburetors, established in 1905, joined Morris in 1926)
- **Wolseley** (established 1887, car manufacturer since 1896, joined Morris in 1927)
- **Wrigley** (gearboxes, joined Morris in 1922)

Standard Group (joined Leyland in 1961)

- **Standard** (established in 1903, car manufacturer from 1903 until 1960)
- **Alford & Alder** (steering gear, joined Standard in 1960)
- **Auto Body Dies** (body panels, joined Standard in 1960)
- **Bean** (established 1901, car manufacturer from 1919 until 1929, joined Standard in 1950)
- **Dawson** (established ca. 1918, car manufacturer until 1921, joined Triumph in 1921)
- **Hall Engineering** (coachbuilding, joined Standard in 1960)
- **Mulliner** (coachbuilding in Birmingham, joined Standard in 1958)
- **Triumph** (established 1889, car manufacturer since 1923, joined Standard in 1944)

Leyland Group (merged with BMH in 1968, forming BLMC)

- **Leyland** (established as Lancashire Steam Motor Company, car manufacturer from 1920 until 1921)
- **Albion** (established 1899, car manufacturer from 1900 until 1904, joined Leyland in 1951)

Jaguar Dealers and Service in Germany

VS	(J)	547	Andernach	Autohaus Fred Altenhofen	Koblenzer Straße 71	(02631)	4 44 47
V	(JD)	89	Augsburg	Ludwig Krehle	Am Leonhardsberg 17	(0821)	3 64 26
S	(JD)	89	Augsburg	Ludwig Krehle	Zugspitzstraße 181	(0821)	37 94 00
VS	(JD)	757	Baden-Baden	Georg Erhardt, Automobile	Lichtentaler Straße 83	(07221)	40 34
S	(J)	534	Bad Honnef	Peter Reuffel	Hauptstraße 45	(02224)	24 06
S	(J)	6587	Baumholder	Autoreparatur & Handels GmbH	Kuseler Straße 26	(06783)	3 68
V	(JD)	1	Berlin	Herbert Schultze	Kurfürstendamm 152	(0311)	8 87 92 45
S	(JD)	1	Berlin	Herbert Schultze	Wilhelmsaue 100	(0311)	87 24 98
VS	(J)	48	Bielefeld	Auto-Handels-Gesellschaft	Hermannstraße 53—55	(0521)	6 70 51
V	(J)	552	Bitburg	Carl Metzger KG	Mötscher Straße 49	(06561)	34 62
V	(J)	53	Bonn	Armin Siefener	Bornheimer Straße 88	(02221)	3 53 61
S	(J)	53	Bonn	Gebr. Siefener	Dransdorfer Weg 27—31	(02221)	3 53 61
S	(J)	53	Bonn	Ernst Mahlberg	Hubertusstraße 2	(02221)	3 66 56
VS	(J)	28	Bremen	Autohaus W. Weiß	Waller Ring 123—125	(0421)	38 38 45
S	(J)	31	Celle	G. Sperling	Harburger Straße 75/77	(05141)	20 41
V	(J)	46	Dortmund	Autohaus Mulfinger KG	Brüderweg 6—8	(0231)	52 51 82
S	(J)	46	Dortmund	Autohaus Mulfinger KG	Glückaufsegenstraße 86—94	(0231)	4 33 41
S	(J)	516	Düren	Wolfgang Mannsfeld	Arnoldsweiler Weg 92	(02421)	7 15 72
V	(JD)	4	Düsseldorf	Birkelbach & Unkrüer	Corneliusstraße 20	(0211)	68 47 25
S	(JD)	4	Düsseldorf	Birkelbach & Unkrüer	Rethelstraße 139	(0211)	68 47 25
V	(JD)	4	Düsseldorf	Auto-Supermarkt (Auto-Becker)	Karl-Rudolf-Straße 167	(0211)	34 30 34
S	(JD)	4	Düsseldorf	Auto-Supermarkt (Auto-Becker)	Suitbertusstraße 150	(0211)	34 30 34
V	(J)	41	Duisburg/Hamborn	Autohaus Scharmach OHG	Kaiser-Wilhelm-Straße 249	(02131)	5 42 11
S	(J)	41	Duisburg/Hamborn	Autohaus Scharmach OHG	Hagedornstraße 37	(02131)	5 42 11
S	(J)	41	Duisburg	Auto Loeffeck	Heckenstraße 66	(02131)	33 55 51
S	(J)	43	Essen-West	Heinrich Schmitz	Haskenstraße 3	(02141)	6 51 23
VS	(J)	239	Flensburg	F. Becker	Hafendamm 13	(0461)	2 72 00
VS	(JD)	6	Ffm.-Rödelheim	Peter Lindner GmbH	Westerbachstraße 59	(0611)	78 00 76
V	(JD)	6	Frankfurt	Peter Lindner GmbH	Niddastraße 42—44	(0611)	23 61 67
VS	(J)	78	Freiburg i.. Br.	Franz Speck	Habsburgesrtraße 99—101	(0761)	4 51 17
V	(J)	851	Fürth	Franz Schmid	Waldstraße 57	(0911)	77 77 60
S	(J)	851	Fürth	Petes Garage	Oststraße 110	(0911)	77 04 63
VS	(J)	81	Garm.-Partenkirchen	Autohaus Maier & Jörg	Burgstraße 12	(08821)	37 76
VS	(J)	466	Gelsenkirchen	Fa. Damke	Dieselstraße 16	(02322)	7 30 91
VS	(JD)	63	Gießen	Autohaus H. Mohr	Grünberger Straße 86—87	(0641)	7 30 72
V	(J)	2	Hamburg	Vidal & Sohn	Angerstraße 22	(0411)	2 00 66 32
S	(J)	2	Hamburg	Vidal & Sohn	Pappelallee 22	(0411)	25 70 21
VS	(JD)	2	Hamburg/Altona	J. A. Woodhouse & Co.	Allee 333	(0411)	43 20 88
V	(J)	645	Hanau	Hanau-Motors, Inh. Roy Sirett	Bundesstraße 8/40	(06181)	2 24 41
VS	(J)	3	Hannover	Gerhard Koch	Am Listholze 70	(0511)	69 11 50
VS	(J)	69	Heidelberg	Raichle & Kuhn GmbH & Co. K. G.	Bergheimer Straße 159	(06221)	2 03 30
VS	(J)	71	Heilbronn	Autohaus Heermann GmbH	Wilhelmstraße 23 u. 26	(07131)	8 65 56
VS	(J)	867	Hof/Saale	J. Semmelrath KG	Wunsiedler Straße 8	(09281)	39 60
V	(J)	675	Kaiserslautern-Einsiedlerhof	Paulin & Kelly	Kaiserstraße 6	(0631)	5 06 77
VS	(J)	75	Karlsruhe	Hertenstein Automobile GmbH & Co.	Zeppelinstraße 10	(0721)	59 10 41
VS	(J)	54	Koblenz	Autohaus Fred Altenhofen	Hohenzollernstraße 127	(0261)	3 44 78
V	(J)	5	Köln	Kirschbaum Automobile	Aachener Straße 90	(0221)	51 43 42
S	(J)	5	Köln	Kirschbaum Automobile	Schmalbeinstraße 7	(0221)	52 28 69
S	(J)	5	Köln-Ehrenfeld	Lutz Hillesheim	Simrockstraße 63—65	(0221)	52 94 63
V	(J)	415	Krefeld	Motor Fahrz. Handel H. Drehmann	Ostwall 224	(02151)	2 88 59
S	(J)	415	Krefeld	Motor Fahrz. Handel H. Drehmann	Neustraße 12	(02151)	2 88 59
VS	(J)	68	Mannheim	Raichle & Kuhn GmbH & Co. K. G.	R 7—31 Friedrichsring	(0621)	2 45 02
VS	(J)	405	Mönchengladbach Rheindahlen	Kremer & Diemer	Shopping Centre Rheindalen	(02161)	50 26
V	(J)	8	München	Auto König	Gabelsbergerstraße 54	(0811)	52 26 80
S	(J)	8	München	Auto König	Neußer Straße 21	(0811)	36 48 61
VS	(JD)	8	München	Plank & Co.	Ottobrunner Straße 35	(0811)	40 49 22
S	(J)	8	München	Hugo Oppel	Amalienstraße 38	(0811)	22 01 78
S	(J)	8	München	Kaspar Pichler	Schleißheimer Straße 141	(0811)	37 28 86
VS	(J)	235	Neumünster	H. Kocheim	Schützenstraße 45—51	(04321)	30 54
VS	(J)	85	Nürnberg	Siegfried Panzer	Johannisstraße 96	(0911)	3 32 55
VS	(J)	2901	Oldenburg/Metjendorf	Franz Heinje		(0441)	8 33 39
VS	(J)	45	Osnabrück	A. H. G. Beinecke	Neulandstraße 4	(0541)	5 24 42
VS	(J)	798	Ravensburg	Autohaus Wald KG	Gartenstraße 11	(0751)	25 64
VS	(J)	84	Regensburg	Autohaus Heddram	Bischof-Wittmann-Straße 12	(0941)	3 08 12
V	(J)	741	Reutlingen	Auto Specht	Lederstraße 93	(07121)	59 79
S	(J)	7411	Reutlingen-Ohmenhausen	Auto Specht	Bühlweg 2	(07121)	59 79
VS	(J)	7702	Singen/Gottmadingen	Autohandels K. G. Klopfer	Hilzinger Straße 15	(07731)	30 69
VS	(J)	7	Stuttgart-Botnang	Auto-Verkaufs GmbH	Franz-Schubert-Straße 2/3	(0711)	65 52 33
V	(J)	55	Trier	Carl Metzger K. G.	Neustraße 83	(0651)	7 28 30
VS	(J)	773	Villingen	Autohaus Saftschek	Schwenninger Straße 1 a	(07721)	30 06
V	(JD)	62	Wiesbaden	Peter Lindner GmbH	Taunusstraße 52	(06121)	2 03 00
S	(JD)	62	Wiesbaden	Peter Lindner GmbH	Kranzplatz/Spiegelgasse	(06121)	37 17 85
S	(J)	56	Wuppertal	W. D. Kniese Automobile	Stuttbergstraße 56—58	(02121)	45 00 20
V	(J)	87	Würzburg	H. Hartmann Automobile	Sanderstraße 31	(0931)	5 46 46
S	(J)	87	Würzburg	Auto Körber KG	Sanderstraße 31	(0931)	5 46 46

V=Verkauf S=Service J=Jaguar D=Daimler Stand: März 1967

A listing of German Jaguar dealers in 1967 suggests the marque's rapidly growing popularity. *(J)*

- **Alvis** (established 1919, car manufacturer since 1920, joined Rover in 1965)
- **Associated Equipment Corporation** (**AEC**) (bus manufacturer, joined Leyland in 1961)
- **Crossley** (established 1869, car manufacturer from 1904 until 1937, joined AEC)
- **Land Rover** (car make of Rover since 1948)
- **Maudslay** (mechanics for ships, established ca. 1800, joined AEC in 1948)
- **Rover** (established as Starley 1877, car manufacturer since 1904, joined Leyland in 1967)
- **Thornycroft** (established 1896, car manufacturer since 1903, joined Leyland)

For the sake of completeness: BLMC itself created further makes; for example, Mini was created in 1969 and Princess in 1975. Furthermore, BLMC acquired a stake in Innocenti in 1972 but this was handed on to de Tomaso in 1976.

In 1968, however, Jaguar was combined with Rover and Triumph to form the Special Cars Division. Again, Jaguar seems to have been guaranteed the utmost independence by Sir Donald Gresham Stokes, deputy chairman and managing director of the successful Leyland concern. In the following years Sir William Lyons was to experience more and more limitations to his formerly unlimited power over the Jaguar works. On the other hand, he was able to axe some competing development projects that could have been a danger for Jaguar; these were the very large Rover and a 4-liter Austin-Healey, called ADO 24 (an abbreviation for Austin Drawing Office) and later ADO 30. In 1966 it had been investigated whether the XK engine would fit, but Lyons rejected this. Lyons had advocated the merger of the British automobile industry in order to gain an advantage in international competition, but now he was very sad about the limitations that were imposed upon his company. In the ensuing chagrin it was not easy for his wife, Lady Greta, to save him from self-pity.

In the new corporation, Jaguar was not the most exclusive marque, nor was Daimler. This honor went to Vanden Plas, with a history going back to 1870, if not earlier. At that time a Belgian, William Guillaume van den Plas, inherited his uncle's smithy. In keeping with family tradition, he manufactured wheels for all sorts of vehicles. Soon he started to make complete axles for coaches. In 1884 he moved from Brussels to Antwerp, and added complete coaches to his range of products. This was a huge step, as now filigree work was added to the hard work on iron parts; coaches had to be equipped with all the amenities that would please the eye. This he must have done quite well, as his coaches soon were deemed to be *très chic* in noble circles.

William was proud to have three sons—one for each of the major disciplines in coach making. Antoine

Carosserie Van den Plas—one of the finest coachbuilders at the turn of the century. *(St)*

Majestic cars like this Belgian FN were chosen to carry the noble bodies of Guillaume Van den Plas. *(St)*

was educated as a smith; Henri studied the most renowned designs of the competition in Berlin and Paris; and Guillaume, the youngest, was sent to London, where he studied the plush way of life and the appointments of the finest coaches reflecting this style.

In 1898 as the family business was reestablished as Carosserie Van den Plas, which was soon to become very famous. Henri headed a staff of more than 100. A branch office was established in Brussels. The new company was very prosperous, and it managed to have its own stand at the 1900 world exposition. The carriage displayed by Van den Plas was awarded a Grand Prix; no other Belgian carriage builder had been or would ever be so honored.

In those days cars were little more than horseless carriages; their bodies were similar to coaches. So Guillaume thought he also might provide the *haute volée* with bodies for their latest hobby. To these he applied the same standards of quality as to the coaches, and he fabricated them for quality chassis like De Dion-Bouton or domestic Germain, Métallurgique, and so on.

So Van den Plas expanded. Even exacting clients from countries like Great Britain or France, who had access to the best quality manufacturers in their own countries, were attracted by Van den Plas carriages and cars, at least until World War I put an end to this. Belgium in particular suffered from this war. In the 1920s Russian designer Alexis de Sakhnoffski added a new, elegant style to Van den Plas, but still few customers could afford Van den Plas luxury. Métallurgique and Minerva (which already had swallowed Imperia, Excelsior, and Nagant, and whose chassis so often had been bodied by Van den Plas) suffered financial trouble and merged, but just before World War II both makes were extinguished. By the way, in 1935 one Mr. Van den Plas applied for a job in SS' styling department, but he was not employed there.

The story of Oscar Cüpper has a great deal to do with why the Van den Plas name survived beyond its Belgian incarnation. Although he was of German parentage, he had his business in London, importing Métallurgique cars to Great Britain. As a racing driver Cüpper had gained a plaque in the second Prince Henry trials in Germany (June 10–17, 1909; these trials replaced the former Herkomer trials). Among the cars sold in London were some with Van den Plas bodies. These were so admired, even in patriotic Britain, that Cüpper could afford showrooms at the most exclusive location at Regent's Park. In exhibitions the Van den Plas bodies always earned admiration and medals.

About 1908 Cüpper joined forces with Warwick Wright, who not only imported fine Belgian Minerva cars but also ran a coachbuilding workshop behind his showroom at St. Marylebone. As partners they concentrated on Métallurgique, which held the sole right on the exclusive Van den Plas name in Britain.

Théo Masui represented Germain, the third Belgian maker of prestige cars, in London. He had started dealing with cars and making bodies in 1901. Germain also frequently had their bodies made by Van den Plas. Théo Masui's styling genius was more than equivalent to Van den Plas. He invented the so-called torpedo style, with no breaks or steps in the side elevation of the body. Masui had this style evolved as early as 1908, and with licenses he made good money.

Together with Cüpper and Wright, Masui opened a new coachbuilding workshop on June 17, 1912. Its name was changed to Vanden Plas England on March 13, 1913. This simplified spelling remained a distinguishing feature between British and Belgians, the former being taken over by the Aircraft Manufacturing Company (of later de Havilland aircraft fame) at the beginning of World War I in 1914. Similar to Daimler, which despite the original license soon started to produce individual designs, London Vanden Plas bodies soon had their own style, independent of the Belgian ones. Crossley and Buick were the chassis most often noted in the order books. The first order for a Rolls-Royce chassis was noted in 1919, and July 1920 saw the first Daimler order.

Despite many good orders, Vanden Plas went bankrupt in 1923. Edwin Fox, then managing director at Vanden Plas, managed to purchase the name rights from the receiver. Under the old name, he opened a new coachbuilding company and was able to fulfill some of the orders of prebankruptcy days. He found a suitable workshop in the north of London at Kingsbury. There the Aviation Company—mentioned earlier under its Airco name as a predecessor to Daimler Airways—had just given up building aircraft. Before that the workshop housed the production of the infamous Kingsbury cycle car, one of the many lost cases of the early days of motoring.

Vanden Plas' success was mainly based on light touring car bodies, many of which were made for Bentley chassis from nearby Cricklewood. Later, flexible sedans were built using Weymann patents; their ash frames were covered with fabric instead of metal. Despite their flexibility these bodies ran more quietly than the usual designs. At the time, the combination of Bentley and Vanden Plas was quite successful in racing as well. Starting from the second 24 Hours at Le Mans in 1924, Bentley managed five wins, to which the sufficiently durable yet lightweight bodies contributed.

Vanden Plas was upset by Rolls-Royce taking over Bentley in 1931, as this was the end of a great era. Newly employed designer John Birkin switched to the latest Alvis Speed 20, a chassis just as sporting as the Bentley, and created elegant and popular sports bodies, again with an emphasis on light weight. After World War II, the one-off body was no longer a requirement for a gentleman, and even Rolls-Royces were offered with "standard steel" bodies. So, there was no longer much for Vanden Plas to do. Hardly more than two dozen bodies were made in the traditional way before this activity was stopped early in 1947. Vanden Plas also provided the paint finish on Humber bodies, but the traditional coachbuilding business stopped on both sides of the Channel at nearly the same time.

The survival of Vanden Plas was Herbert Austin's achievement. He had the intention to offer a car similar to a Rolls-Royce, but at the moderate price typical for his own products. Edwin Fox, his know-how, and his underutilized workforce were exactly what Austin needed for this purpose. So Austin bought the whole Vanden Plas works, which by the end of 1946 was no more than a cog in the large Austin wheel.

The new, large Austin was announced before Christmas, and in March 1947 the Austin A 120 Princess debuted at the Geneva show. The 120-horsepower indicated by the name was produced by a completely new 3.5-liter overhead valve engine with a compression ratio of only 6.8:1, dictated by the poor gasoline quality of the time. The chassis was similar to the equally new Austin Sheerline. The heavy body made the car more ponderous than the less spacious Jaguar of the same capacity, and priced at £1,917 (including purchase tax) it was considerably more expensive, but still much cheaper than a similar Rolls-Royce. However,

Top: An Alvis Speed 25 with elegant, sporty sedan body by Vanden Plas. *(Long)*

Above: A collector's car was the Daimler Straight Eight 4-liter pillarless sedan by Vanden Plas—this was the 1938 show car. *(Long)*

Right: Daimler Straight Eight pillarless sedan with Vanden Plas body, accompanied by a later successor. *(J)*

Top: An Austin Princess IV from the late 1950s, elegantly combining modern and traditional styles. *(König)*

Above: This was the smallest Vanden Plas—an upgraded Austin 1100. *(St)*

Right: The Vanden Plas 1500 was small and unusual . . . *(Stertkamp archive)*

Above: . . . but its interior was most lavishly equipped. *(Stertkamp archive)*

this model gained little popularity. On the continent, the Princess remained generally unknown, rated as a Rolls-Royce without the famous Emily mascot.

After only 32 examples of the Austin Princess were built, the engine was enlarged to 4 liters and 135 horsepower, which helped the car's performance. From late 1948 a limousine-style partition could be specified—still indispensable in some particularly fine circles. In 1950, after 760 chassis were produced, the rear side window was changed and the car was renamed Princess II. Late in 1952 a longer-wheelbase, six-window limousine with two occasional seats was added. The first two were delivered to the Royal Mews, which mourned the king's death and expected the coronation of a queen. One of these cars, while carrying Princess Anne and her husband Mark Phillips, was ambushed in 1974. Royalty escaped the gunfire unscathed, but the chauffeur, some guards, and the car itself did not. It was of course an honor for Vanden Plas to restore the car.

In the meantime the standard model had evolved into the Princess III, with a more attractive radiator with slim chromed surround in 1953. The front fenders ended further up in the front doors, aping the style of the longer model. These soon took over the more beautiful grille of the sedan. A total of 350 examples of the third series were made, including naked chassis. Although the Sheerline had been out of production for two years in 1956, the short Princess still had not reached the end of its lifetime. A further facelift with the fender line just below the waistline was introduced as the Princess IV. The side elevation now seemed to be almost flat—a style not convenient with the longer model. The Princess IV was the last Princess with the standard chassis, and it remained in production until May 1959; 200 examples were made. The longer Princess had a much longer life, being produced until March 1968, resulting in a total of 7,462 chassis. From August 1957, both long and short versions of the car were called Princess without the Austin name. Beginning in May 1960, the Vanden Plas make was added.

In 1955 another member of the van den Plas family presented himself at Jaguar and was employed in the body drawing office—although one wonders what this office had to do under Lyons, who conceived body designs without drawings. Jean-Paul van den Plas gained some fame for adding a rather academic description of the Jaguar style to Jaguar's Apprentices' magazine.

Vanden Plas at Kingsbury was not overly busy, so the idea was born to apply the Vanden Plas treatment to a more economic range of cars. In the autumn of 1957 a special series of 500 Austin 3-liter sedans was converted into Princesses with a fine interior. Even an estate car was transformed this way. From the autumn of 1959 a series production of the 3-liter's successor, with the flashy Pininfarina body, was made in true series production as a Princess 3-liter or Vanden Plas Princess 3-liter. After 4,719 3-liter Princesses were built, and a further 7,984 Mark Is were built with wheelbases extended by 2 inches, the game continued with the Vanden Plas Princess 4-liter R. Featuring external changes and a Rolls-Royce engine, 6,555 examples of these were made, from 1964 to 1968, among them one estate car for young Queen Elizabeth.

According to a similar pattern, the particularly fine Austin 1100 (16,007 examples built from 1963 until 1967, including two estate cars), 1300 (27,734 examples built from 1967 until 1974, including the Mark II with shorter tailfins starting in 1968) and, finally, Allegro (as Vanden Plas 1500 from September 1974 onward) were made until 1979, but these belonged to a class much below the ones to which this book is dedicated.

The most important dates of Vanden Plas' history are:

- 1870: Guillaume van den Plas inherits a smithy at Brussels
- 1884: Relocation to Antwerp; first complete carriage built

1992 Daimler DS 420, still "olde world" when production was ended. *(J)*

Top: The DS 420 landaulette is a rarity, as Vanden Plas only made two of them in the mid-1970s. *(J)*

Above: A bench for diplomats and senators: the 1980 Daimler DS 420. *(J)*

Below: Daimler's DS 420 was subjected to a process of continuing improvement—this is the 1984 model. *(J)*

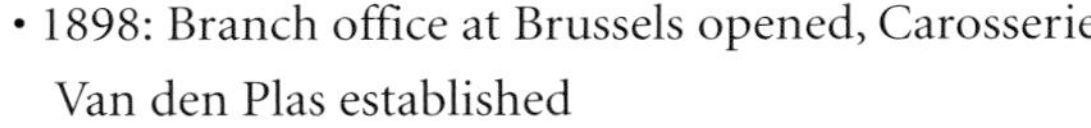

- 1898: Branch office at Brussels opened, Carosserie Van den Plas established
- Ca. 1900: First Van den Plas body made for a car
- Ca. 1905: First car with Van den Plas coachwork exported to Great Britain
- 1907: Cüpper and Wright establish their first common coachbuilding company in London
- 1908: Théo Masui invents the torpedo body style
- June 17, 1912: Cüpper, Wright, and Masui merge
- March 13, 1913: Company renamed Vanden Plas England Limited
- 1914: Aircraft Manufacturing Company (de Havilland) takes over Vanden Plas
- 1923: Re-establishment of Vanden Plas by Edwin Fox
- August 23, 1923: Vanden Plas moves to Kingsbury, North London
- June 1946: Austin takes over Vanden Plas
- December 18, 1946: Debut of the Austin Princess Saloon

Right: The Daimler DS 420 remained dignified in the worst of traffic. *(J)*

Below: The noble rear compartment of a DS 420, in West of England cloth. *(J)*

Above: Even the chauffeur could indulge in pure luxury, with some ingredients well known from the Jaguar Mark X. *(J)*

Right: Daimler DS 420, a car with royal style. *(J)*

Above left: The Daimler DS 420 entered the 1980s in slightly modernized guise. *(J)*

Above: The chromed side molding betrays this Daimler DS 420 as a 1968 model. *(Long)*

Despite its life of more than 21 years, the Austin Princess escaped major revision. When Austin and Jaguar merged in 1966 to create BMH, Austin engineers were busy with a facelift, but progress was rather slow.

Sir William Lyons thought the large Daimler limousine could use replacement as well, with a unit-body construction. So the first new car from the newly established BLMC was the Daimler DS 420, introduced on June 11, 1968. Its lines were breathtaking, although the style was in best Hooper tradition. This eight-seater limousine was more than 6 feet wide and 18 feet long, the longest unitary body of its time. The body was made at Motor Panels in Coventry, based on a platform of the Mark X provided by Pressed Steel Fisher, which was elongated by 21 inches. Austin management was sufficiently convinced by the style and execution of this car to allow the Princess to be succeeded by the DS 420 as well.

To offset the lack of work at Vanden Plas at Kingsbury, where the Princess had been made, the paint and interior work for the DS 420 would be carried out at Vanden Plas. This brought Vanden Plas closer to Jaguar.

The engine of the DS 420 was the XK unit as used in the Daimler Sovereign. The wonderful Daimler V-8 was not to survive, as rationalization and uniformity of spares spoke against it.

The 420 was a long runner in every sense of the word, as it continued in production for many years, although the yearly production figure usually was in the 200s. A shorter variant without the occasional seats could have stimulated demand, but this close-coupled sedan, with the rear wheel arches just behind the rear doors, remained a prototype. Although not many people know about it, a V-12 was tested under the dignified hood of the DS 420. A wonderful car was the result, but because only very limited demand would exist for such a vehicle, the cost involved with such a change could not be justified. In 1978 Jaguar supplied one DS 420 to Eastern Germany, while only one other example came to West Germany officially (for Jaguar Deutschland's very important guests). Some further DS 420s were privately imported to Germany as used cars.

In 1992 only, after a few minor revisions, this majestic vehicle ended production. It was the last car that was available as a Daimler only, and the last with the now legendary XK engine. Many hearses have been created on the DS 420 platform. This type of car gained maximum exposure when in September 1997 a DS 420 was chosen to transport Princess Diana to her last resting-place at her family's home. Even more remarkable are two Landaulettes that were made around 1974. Some further DS 420s were transformed similarly until 1995, but Jaguar and Daimler were not involved in these. The 1984 office car, equipped with advanced office equipment, was extensively described even in Germany's *Auto Motor und Sport*, and from 1985 onward two seats could be ordered instead of the bench in the front compartment. Even after 1992 some quasi-new DS 420 were offered by Beacham, complete with a Jaguar X 300 engine. Beacham had a fine reputation of restoring classic Jaguars to as-new standard, but its workshop was very far away in New Zealand.

15
THE CAR OF THE YEAR

Like the large limousine, a slightly smaller sedan was produced from 1968 until 1992, the XJ series. Its development started much earlier, in 1961, when the E-Type had its American debut, April 1–9 at the International Automobile Show at the New York Coliseum. Sir William was there of course, and he learned firsthand of the criticism about the limited interior space of the sports car. He phoned home and requested that a coupe with two occasional seats in the back be built. This prototype was completed under the XJ 4 designation in 1961.

In the following years Sir William had many new prototypes built, with ever-new proportions. Lyons wanted the car to be longer, Heynes primarily wanted it wider. Most of these prototypes were made by Bob Blake, Geoff Joyce, and George Mason. They would cut E-Type bodies in half and then rejoin the halves to the desired dimensions. At one stage, Mason added telescopic tubes to a blue prototype in order to facilitate easy dimensional changes.

The side elevation caused particular problems. At one stage three prototypes with different sides were built at once. Putting the result of this test into production would have cost £2 million. Sir William thought this was too much, and so it was all scrapped.

On November 15, 1963, William Heynes wrote a memo that tried to bring some order to the search for a four-seater E-Type. In this memo he described a prototype of October 1961 that was 7 inches longer than the E-Type, but with the roof at the original height it didn't offer enough interior space. The next prototype had the roof lifted by 3 inches and the sills lowered by 1 inch. This, however, made the sides look a bit clumsy. So a third layout had a less lofty roof, the sills were raised a little, and the hood sloped toward the front. This car was a mechanically complete prototype; remarkably it had an automatic instead of the manual gearbox.

Next was a wider prototype, with the Mark X's track of 58 inches. One variant of the face resembled the E-Type, while another had twin headlamps. It appears that there was some argument about the advantages and disadvantages of these versions. A compromise made in Weaver's shop became the solution, and the panels of this—with the exception of the roof—were disclosed to Pressed Steel. This prototype was then shortened by 4 inches; it had strong appeal, but not a typical Jaguar style. Heynes thought the prototype's narrow track might be useful for European markets, for which a narrower track would be advisable, but this would result in an unfavorable compact classification in the United States.

As a consequence, Heynes thought it advisable to follow two different paths: One model for the United States with a wide track, V-12 engine, and a face similar to the E-Type (over a decade later this winding path would lead to the XJ-S), and another one for Europe, 4 inches narrower and with a square face and a six-cylinder or V-12 engine. The latter would be a suitable replacement for the Mark II. This path would lead to one of the most famous sedans in Jaguar's history, the XJ 6. At this stage, however, its back was still rounded like the E-Type's. Later it was cut back some 12 inches, resulting in the look with which it would be introduced to the public some years later.

In 1965 or 1966 the sedan that still bore the XJ 4 code was developed into the now-familiar style. On June 21, 1966, this style was tested in a wind tunnel. The advantage of the older, more rounded shape became obvious. Sir William would have liked to launch the car immediately, but again it was Pressed Steel Fisher who needed a further two years to fully develop and prepare for the production of the new sedan. Alongside the engine of the 420, two smaller six-cylinder derivatives of 2.6- and 3-liter capacity had been envisaged; soon that plan was revised in favor of only one alternative engine, with a 2.8-liter. A 5.3-liter V-12 was planned, but this was delayed and could only be introduced in 1972. A 3.5-liter V-8 was derived from the V-12. For production reasons its banks of cylinders were set at an

Above left: Early XJ 4 mockup with a face that later evolved into the XJ-S.

Right from above: XJ 4, a late mockup nearly identical with the production XJ 6. *(S)*

XJ 4 as six-window sedan with a rear end to become familiar with production XJ 6. *(S)*

XJ 4 as two-door coupe. *(S)*

Opposite: Grille badge of the Series 1 XJ 12. *(J)*

Above: Rear end of the early XJ 6 with reflectors along the indicators and straight tailpipes. *(S)*

Right: Jaguar XJ 6, the best car in the world, in its later livery with matte black instrument bezels. *(J)*

angle of 60 degrees, and with this the engine would certainly produce more noise and vibration than a 90-degree V-8. A balance shaft could not be incorporated, again for reasons of production, and the hope that suitable engine mounts might cure the problem also turned out to be ill-founded.

Developing the XJ 6 cost about £6 million. It was the work of about a dozen engineers, headed by William Heynes, who retired in 1969. Among them Bob Knight's meticulous efforts to suppress noise and vibration deserve particular mention.

The XJ 6 designation was of course influenced by the project code, its similarity to the XK designation, with its fame particularly in the United States, and the number of cylinders. It was unveiled to the press at the Royal Lancaster Hotel in London on September 26, 1968, on the eve of the Paris Show. Due to the 4.2 engine's height, a highly attractive bulge had to be added to the hood. Production of an XJ 6 with this 4.2 engine initially cost £788 (compared to £727 for the Mark II 3.8-liter), but its list price was about three times as much, the difference covering overhead, development, and cost of transport and distribution. In England, demand was much higher than the production rate; delivery times stretched out to two years. On the secondary car market, a premium of up to £1,000 was paid for a new car that could be

Above: On England's new motorways, police needed to have fast XJ 6s. *(S)*

Right: The XJ 6 was again a very elegant car. *(J)*

One of the last engine bays exuding an air of functional beauty: Jaguar XJ 6. *(J)*

supplied immediately. In May 1970 customers from Switzerland flew over to Berkeley Square, the BLMC headquarters, bringing signs that expressed that after 14 months of waiting they now wanted their XJ 6s. Lord Stokes invited them for lunch, secretly delighted by the Jaguar's popularity. The delays were at least partly caused by strikes at Pressed Steel Fisher over piecework rates.

In the United States, where until 1970 the car was simply called the XJ, the sedan was introduced with the Series 2 E-Type in the ballroom of the New York Hilton Hotel. However, the supply of cars to the United States did not start before late 1969 for the 1970 model year. Only when emissions tests had been finished and production reached full scale did the regular supply to the United States start.

Despite its not-exactly new engine, the XJ 6 was fifth in the European Car of the Year contest, but won the similar election organized by the *Car* magazine. According to Alec Issigonis, the genius behind the Mini, the XJ 6 was the best of all cars in production.

Although technically conservative, the XJ 6 broke new ground in roadholding, safety, and what later was to be called NVH (noise, vibration, and harshness). For Jaguar the XJ 6 was a departure similar to what occurred with the introduction of the Mark VII; practically all older sedan models were to be replaced by the XJ 6. Remarkably, the name Jaguar appeared nowhere on the outside of the car nor in the interior. This didn't cause too much confusion, as the XJ was substantially similar to the appearance of a Mark X "with the air let out," according to the not inappropriate words of one joker. The relation of body and glasshouse was now much better proportioned, and the wheel arches were well filled with fat tires.

In June 1969, *Autocar* tested the 4.2-liter with Borg-Warner automatic, which was the most popular variant right from the start. Springing and noise suppression were most impressive(it was hardly believable that such a result could be achieved with steel springs). In both respects the testers could not remember ever having experienced anything better, including the Rolls-Royce

Above: The Daimler Sovereign variant of the XJ 6 Series 1 was not officially available in Europe. *(J)*

Right: Willy Ehling's Jaguar taxi in Munich. *(JAGMAG archive)*

Silver Shadow and the (air-sprung) Mercedes-Benz 600. Handling was superior even to the E-Type and was unique in the sedan class. Only a sharp edge in the road surface could cause some—well-suppressed—audible noise. Despite only two instead of three carburetors, the engine's performance was only marginally inferior to the Mark X's. *Motor* also found this car nearer to perfection than anything else, including the most expensive. In an endurance test that soon followed, no serious flaw was revealed.

The American magazine *Car & Driver* found some irritating details, like the oil cap that for more than 15 years had been very difficult to open—due to the camshaft cover expanding under the heat of the engine. This was only one of quite a few details that nobody at Coventry seemed to worry about.

On October 9, 1969, a new Daimler Sovereign was introduced. In effect this was an XJ 6 with a fluted grille (and vertical bars only) and trunk plinth, plus different badges. This Sovereign won the Styling Gold Medal at the Motor Shows of 1969 and 1970. Officially, this model was not offered in Europe.

Also in October 1969, the first German test of the XJ 6 was published in *Auto Motor und Sport*. The car was a left-hand drive model but with British registration. Although the article mentioned new engines that might be introduced in the near future, the exceptional refinement of the long-stroke engine was highly praised, partially a result of the well thought-out noise suppression at the bulkhead. "The main impression when driving the XJ 6 is effortlessness and good handling for a car weighing in about 38 cwt and not being exactly small," the article said. "Besides, the excellent springing and low noise level make the XJ 6 a very comfortable car in the top range." The brakes were faulted for some slight judder. "Summing up its character, the XJ 6 is a far cry from a car for the masses, much further than a German car could ever be. So the XJ 6 ranks among the relatively small group of European top-class automobiles, while it never hides its typically British character."

In mid-1970, the same magazine brought together a comparison of 2.8-liter cars, including the BMW 2800, FIAT 130, Mercedes-Benz 280 SE, Opel Diplomat, and the 2.8-liter XJ 6 with a 1969 British registration. All cars had automatic transmissions. In this group the Jaguar was the most expensive (in deutsche mark terms), which could be explained both by the lavish standard of equipment and the customs duties for the import from Britain, which was not part of the European Economic Community. In this comparison the Jaguar seemed to be slightly cramped; the ends of the car were not clearly visible from the driver's seat. Its heating was good, but not its ventilation. Acceleration to 60 miles per hour with the automatic took about 16 seconds—this is why Jaguar avoided press testing of similar cars in Britain. The engine was silent and flexible but not very dynamic. Alas, in the practicality of handles and levers, it was last. In suspension it was way ahead of its competition and among the best in roadholding, where the Mercedes-Benz with its swing axle was last. The test revealed the very different characters of the cars, but all in all advantages and disadvantages leveled out so that the difference in total points was minimal.

A survey in the United States in which 107 Jaguar drivers took part revealed that 25 found their car excellent, 42 good, and only 2 found it appalling. Compared with other makes, this was a remarkably good result, although the American press tended to stress the unreliability of Jaguar cars. Obviously these complaints were caused by poor maintenance—not the only example of a prestige brand ruined by poorly informed reporters.

For Queen Elizabeth's visit to Mauritius, the Taylor-Smith Limited wharf created a 2.8-liter XJ 6 de Luxe convertible sedan. German Willy Ehling gained less publicity with his no less unusual Jaguar taxi in Munich.

At many earlier points, Jaguar had severally thought about using a V-12 engine for racing, being impressed

Above: The XJ 13 V-12 racing car was kept secret for many years. *(Schön)*

Left: This is how the car was reconstructed . . . *(S)*

. . . after an act of self-destruction. *(S)*

by Ferrari's success. Tom Jones had a V-12 in mind as early as 1951, and a mid-engined configuration was George Buck's idea in 1957. The team of Heynes, Hassan, and Harry Mundy were pivotal in the eventual development and implementation of the V-12, however. Before the war, Mundy had worked for Alvis, ERA, and Morris; during the war for the Royal Air Force; after the war for BRM, and from 1950 until 1955 for Coventry Climax. Besides his work on the V-12 engine, Jaguar owed him for the five-speed gearbox that never went into production but was the basis of Rover's gearbox in the 1970s. It was he who first suggested that a completely new six-cylinder unit would have to be designed—three years after his retirement in 1980 this happened as the legendary XK engine was replaced.

For racing, the engineers could agree on four overhead camshafts and 5-liter capacity as the 3-liter limit was no longer applicable for sports prototypes at Le Mans. The result was two very free-revving, short-stroke XK engines being siamesed to a common crankshaft. The engine was installed centrally in a racing car evolved by Malcolm Sayer. After about two years, the car was ready early in 1966, but first tests were not performed until March 1967. At the MIRA proving ground at Lindley, David Hobbs and Norman Dewis reached a record lap of more than 160 miles per hour, and this was valid until in 1998 a McLaren F1 was even quicker. Nevertheless, the car was no longer up-to-date with regard to tire size and power-to-weight ratio. As a further limitation of engine capacity was announced by Le Mans officials (but not set in force) Jaguar stopped development of the prototype. For some years the public knew nothing about this racing prototype. On January 20, 1971, the car suffered a blown tire at high speed just after some filming at MIRA. The car turned over several times and was severely damaged. Fortunately, test driver Norman Dewis was unhurt. Jaguar repaired the car, and it is still with Jaguar.

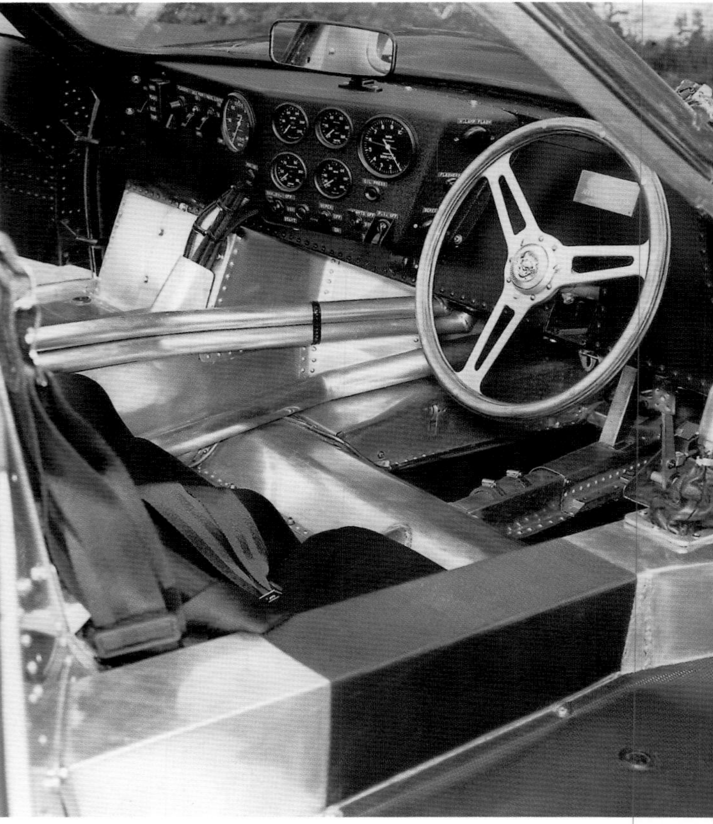

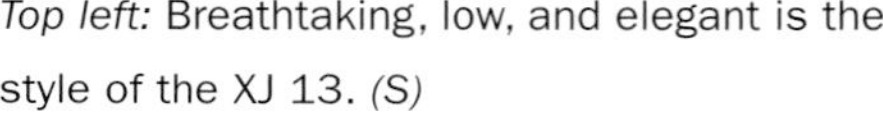

Top left: Breathtaking, low, and elegant is the style of the XJ 13. *(S)*

Top right: The XJ 13 interior. *(S)*

Above left: Four camshafts identify this engine as the unit for XJ 13. *(Schön)*

Above right: The wonderfully curved rear end of the XJ 13. *(S)*

Following its extensive repair it could be regarded as more of a replica than an original. In the meantime some true-to-detail replicas of this attractive thoroughbred have been created by others.

For series production, the V-12 had to be changed in several respects. The most important modification was boring out of the cylinders from 87 to 90mm for better low-speed torque, and the dismissal of one of the camshafts at the top of each bank. The engines were assembled at Radford, which formerly had been used for the Daimler buses, and Jaguar invested £3,000,000 for tooling. Three large Archale machines were bought for the 57 steps of work on the engine block castings; they cost about £850,000, while the tooling for work on the cylinder heads, including a Huller 42-step transfer machine, cost £700,000. The assembly of the V-12 was highly mechanized on a line with 52 stations. At each station, the engine was moved into the ideal position for the relevant work. A run in a test bed was obligatory before the engines were transported to Browns Lane.

With some considerable delay, the engine was introduced on March 29, 1971, at Palm Springs in the United States. It was not presented in the sedan but in the E-Type. Once again the sports car was the first step toward the everyday use of a newly designed engine. The engine's Achilles heel was the heat it generated. Even in the well-ventilated engine bay of the E-Type, this caused some problems with the amplifier, which already was seriously strained by the electrical load necessary to provide sparks to all 12 cylinders. This, and the valve seats' initial tendency to go loose, did no good for the reputation of the new, complicated engine. The E-Type Series 3 was similar to the previous Series 2, with its safety features, but the roadster now was based on the longer two-plus-two wheelbase, while the two-seater coupe was discontinued altogether. A very controversial item was the grille that now filled the oval mouth of the E-Type. The 4.2-liter XK engine was offered as an alternative in the first Series 3 brochures, but none were made apart from five experimental cars that were already completed in 1969. One of these chassis, but with the engine replaced by a V-12, became Production Car champion in a racing series organized by *Autocar*, with Peter Taylor as the driver.

The press was impressed by the V-12 engine under the long hood and the wider track, which improved roadholding and looks of the car. However, some old-time charm was lost along with the silky-smooth engine and the roomy interior with its comfortable seats. All in all, performance was not better with the complicated V-12 than it had been with the six. The E-Type Series 3 had a rather short and not very happy life. Soon after its introduction, the public was no longer interested in the E-Type. The last coupe was completed in September 1973, and a year later roadster production was over as well. This was kept secret for some months as otherwise the large stocks of cars could have become even more difficult to sell. Early in 1975 a final series of 50 black roadsters was announced. They bore a commemorative brass plaque signed by Sir William, who had already retired. The E-Type, once an idol of a whole generation, now caused Jaguar the hitherto unknown problem of large inventory meeting little demand.

In Germany the introduction of the Series 3 E-Type in April 1971 coincided with the introduction of Rover Deutschland as sole Jaguar importer to Germany, while mundane Austins and Morrises remained the business of Brüggemann in Düsseldorf. However, Rover Deutschland was closed down by the end of 1971, and Brüggemann took over Jaguar imports as well. This

Above: Drawings of the very last E-Type. *(J)*

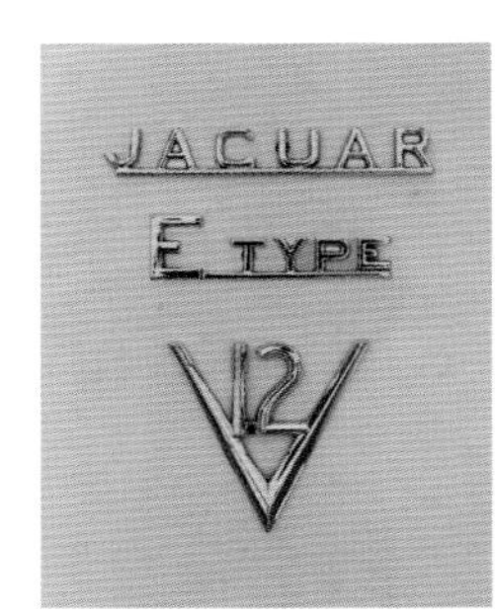

Left: The insignia of a legend. *(S)*

A V-12 E-Type in racing trim prepared by Bob Tullius' American Group 44. *(S)*

The Guyson was the very fashionable reconstruction of an accident-damaged E-Type. *(S)*

Above: An E-Type V-12 2+2 at Bath. *(S)*

Below: Some few Series 3 E-Types were made with six cylinders, but these all were prototypes. *(J)*

In its time the E-Type V-12 was not easy to sell. *(J)*

Interior of a 1971 E-Type V-12 2+2. *(Schönborn archive)*

company was taken over by Leyland in 1975–1976 in two steps. After relocating at Neuss, the company much later acquired the name Rover Deutschland in an ironic twist of fate.

The Austrian importer was the Salzburg BLMC branch (British Leyland Austria). Its ownership and name changed subsequently to E Janko GmbH and then to IGV (Industriegütervertriebsgesellschaft mbH).

Much more important for Jaguar's future was when Sir William retired and Lofty England became chairman and chief executive on March 3, 1972. Seventy years old, Lyons remained honorary president of Jaguar. Even after retirement Lyons was often a guest at Jaguar, where the younger members of the staff called him "Swilly" behind his back. He had an office there, and a consultancy agreement secured him influence on Jaguar's styling. Now his motto was that without excellent mechanics a car was no good.

Much has been written about the reasons for Lyons' commercial success with only one year of losses in nearly fifty years. Even in seemingly hopeless situations, Lyons was lucky in the end, thanks in part to his determination. To single out one reason for this achievement would be impossible, as otherwise there would be many more profitable car manufacturers.

Certainly Lyons was the right man at the right place at the right time. His lack of education for the "top job" was balanced by diligence, patience, and knowledge of human nature. He felt that a seemingly luxurious product only slightly more expensive than its standard counterpart would always remain in demand. Consequently this was what all his products represented, and what he found in Walmsley's sidecars. It was to Lyons' credit that he transferred the idea to the automobile and that he managed to keep his products ahead of the ever-increasing demands of the market, so that in the end they could be called the best in the world. While most other specialist car manufacturers believed that simply a sporty ambiance and performance were sufficient, Lyons always incorporated a touch of luxury. Driver and passengers simply had to feel good in Lyons' cars, all of which had an aura of Britishness; a combination of sport and comfort that particularly appealed to the Americans. This was part of Lyons' "value for money" ideology.

Lyons was aware that the look of his cars was of utmost importance. This was the reason Sir William was so involved in styling, particularly postwar after the loss of Cyril Holland. His only preparation for this job was his critical eye and his infinite patience when it came to decision-making. He was clever enough to integrate the family and some reliable personnel into the process of finding the right style. He constantly invited people to judge his designs—and contrary to man, he took these opinions seriously!

Lyons was lucky in that other manufacturers who offered elegantly styled quality cars demanded much higher prices than Jaguar or—like the early, less powerful SS with its promising long hood—had technical disadvantages. Moving from his specialist bodies to mass production techniques, Jaguar had become invincible, as other older-established makes were not in a position to underprice the Jaguar. Sooner or later they left the market segment just below the absolute top.

Cautiousness was Lyons' characteristic behavior in business. Starting from minor work on aluminum sheets his company evolved step by step into full coachbuilding, soon with enclosed bodies and four doors, improved engines and suspension, and ending with the complete design of cars. Two of these steps were

Top: Sir William Lyons and the work of his life: SS, Jaguar, and Wappenbury Hall. *(S)*

Above: Lyons indulged in five decades of leadership in his enterprises. *(J)*

The more traditional grille made the 1972 Jaguar XJ 12 a particularly handsome car. *(S)*

particularly big. One was the relocation to Coventry, and the second was the introduction of all-steel bodies. Naturally both of these caused considerable trouble, and so Lyons may have learned a lesson quite early: any abrupt change was to be avoided. For the introduction of the unitary body Lyons even created a completely new line of models, so that in case of a failure the reputation of the existing models would not be affected.

Vehicle development was in the hands of a remarkably small, determined team that derived its motivation not from high salaries or elegant offices, but from the honor of having contributed to several Le Mans wins and other important racing successes. Lyons spent as little money as possible for production facilities. One example is the track used to anchor the assembly line of the unitary sedans, which Lyons bought used. His cautious policy of small steps also helped save money. This cost-consciousness, supported by Whittaker's purchasing, made it possible for Jaguar cars to be so much less expensive than the competition.

Some employees complained that Lyons always kept a distance, but it must be recognized that this was his way of treating people fairly and equally. He tried not to favor anyone. This is why he called all his staff by their surnames—with the notable exception of Fred Gardner. He kept his private contact with his directors at a minimum, and Jaguar people were not very often guests at Wappenbury Hall, so that nobody had reason to feel aggrieved. Rivalry among staff members under Lyons' autocratic regime was thus the exception and not the rule. This helped shop morale, but Lyons' demanding nature could deflate it just as easily. However, because everyone was treated more or less equally in this regard as well, even this seemed to be all right, and people achieved much more than they would have in a company with lax management.

Despite his immense duties, Lyons kept his sense of humor and always managed to see the funny side of things. He also found time to enjoy the benefits of his affluence. At Wappenbury Hall he enjoyed the life of a provincial lord, and if work allowed he took holidays in Devon, where he had transformed a former little cafe at the seaside at Salcombe into a nice holiday home. While formal at work, he was relaxed and casual in his spare time.

In two regards Lyons did not achieve his aim: He did not manage to create a successor for himself after his son's tragic death, and he did not manage to purchase or build a body plant that was required for modern, unitary, all-steel designs. The solution for both was integrating Jaguar into BLMC, where Lyons' influence was subsequently restricted. The bad consequences of this step—this may suffice here to prepare the reader for what is to come—have led to occasional criticism of Sir William, ignoring his legacy of success directing Jaguar.

Shortly upon Sir William's retirement, trouble was imminent at Jaguar. BLMC planned to abandon Lyons' piecework pay system—once introduced against severe opposition from the workforce—in favor of a time-oriented system. Already by July 1972, this grew into an outright strike lasting 10 weeks, much longer than any previous strike at Browns Lane. Nevertheless the new system, with its many supervisors, was installed. It contributed significantly to the loss in productivity typical for most BLMC plants during the 1970s.

On September 7, 1973, Lord Stokes introduced Geoffrey Robinson as managing director. Born in 1939, Robinson was a very young member of the Labour Party; later he would represent Jaguar's area in the House of Commons. In the previous 18 months he was—and remained for some further time—managing director at Innocenti, the Italian branch and Jaguar importer that BLMC had taken over with Robinson's help in 1972. The Lambretta scooter and, from 1961 onward, some BMC cars had been produced there under license. As the separate Jaguar company had been dissolved on October 1, 1972, it now was just an organizational unit within the larger company.

At the side of young and dynamic Robinson, England had no more than a representative role, which did not satisfy him. He retired early in 1974, and Robinson had free hands. As Robinson came from BMC, some were concerned that Jaguar might be forced into common development efforts with other BLMC makes, leading perhaps to the sharing of technical components. Robinson, however, was convinced that Jaguar's technical independence was vital. His decision-making took place in a cooperative way, and he used this approach to reconcile with the unions. With an investment of £60 million, he planned to double Jaguar's output in an attempt to make the waiting lists shorter, but BLMC would not grant the money. Even so, he found some bottlenecks to eliminate so that production could be increased moderately. Robinson did not care much about quality; at the time of his appointment Jaguar's quota of warranty claims was still far below that of other BLMC makes. This advantage would vanish under Robinson, and for many years afterward Jaguar would have to atone for these wrongs.

A much more delightful part of the Jaguar history is the transplant of the V-12 engine into the XJ body shell—the place for which it had been developed. Nevertheless it was very difficult to fit all the accessories along with this mighty engine. Many solutions were tried with wooden dummies until one was found that was reasonable, even from the point of view of a mechanic. People joked that when all parts were mounted in the engine bay, a cup of tea could be emptied over the engine without a drop reaching the ground. This engine bay was much less ventilated than the E-Type's; heat was thus the worst problem. Heat shields at the exhaust and a ventilated battery compartment were necessary. One of the prototypes (Chassis No. 1L 2927, a former six-cylinder car, registration RHP 133 H) that was used for the test-fitting was given as a present to the Silverstone race circuit, where it served many years as a fire safety vehicle—a no-cost advertisement for Jaguar! Another prototype from 1969 is said to exist at Jaguar (probably Chassis No. 1L 4449, which was made for Lyons). As far as is known, Harry Mundy's exciting test car, with its engine enlarged to 6.4 liters and equipped with a Jaguar five-speed gearbox (Chassis No. 2R 3757, registration HRW 75 N) is no longer in existence.

Top: XJ 12 for the United States with its special lights. *(J)*

Above: XJ 12 engine bay filled with complicated mechanical items. *(J)*

After the problems of heat and space had been solved more or less, the XJ 12 and its Daimler twin, called the Double-Six, were unveiled on July 27, 1972, as the only V-12 four-door sedans of their time. This glorious event was covered extensively by the press, although it coincided with the aforementioned strike. For some time only three XJ 12s were available outside the factory. The Double-Six designation had been Lofty England's idea, recalling Daimler's prewar V-12s—England had finished second in the 1932 Torquay Rally with one. In the United States the XJ 12 in its original guise was not available, a consequence of the many time-consuming safety and emission tests required.

On September 26, 1972, the Daimler Double-Six Vanden Plas was unveiled to the public; the press already had seen the car in July. It was distinguished from its XJ siblings by a wheelbase that was 4 inches longer, with similarly longer rear doors. This was a quick reaction to similarly extended Mercedes-Benz 300 models. The Vanden Plas was about 200 pounds

Top: The most expensive wood and leather were unique to the Daimler Double-Six Vanden Plas. *(J)*

Above: Even in his later years Lofty England was very interested in things Jaguar. *(S)*

Above right: The Daimler Double-Six Vanden Plas was still much more luxurious than an XJ 12. *(Brüggemann)*

Below: Unforgettable advertising in Germany for the E-Type V-12. *(Stertkamp archive)*

heavier than the normal Double-Six, and acceleration to 60 miles per hour took a second longer. Interior and paint (three layers over the primer applied by Pressed Steel Fisher) were accomplished at Vanden Plas' Kingsbury workshop, where the same work was carried out for the DS 420 limousine.

The longer wheelbase car was very well received, and for the Motor Show in October 1972, the similarly extended XJ 6 L, XJ 12 L, and Daimler Sovereign LWB were introduced. At that time, the 2.8-liter XJ 6 had been dropped from most markets; from March 1972 it was available only in Belgium, France, Greece, Italy, and Portugal. Long-wheelbase cars—the Vanden Plas included—were normally not exported, so left-hand drive examples of these cars are true rarities.

In May 1973 *Motor* published a comparison of Double-Six Vanden Plas and Rolls-Royce Silver Shadow. The latter had a slight advantage with regard to quality and ride, while the Vanden Plas excelled in performance, roadholding, and steering. It was the much better car from the driver's point of view, but also offered better rear springing and the more spacious interior. The Rolls-Royce was generally the more silent car, but noise from the suspension was better suppressed in the Vanden Plas. Gasoline consumption was similar on both cars, but the Rolls-Royce was twice the price of the Vanden Plas.

Strangely, German magazine *Auto Motor und Sport* did not test the E-Type V-12 or the XJ 12, possibly attributable to the importer's inability to provide test cars. Brüggemann did, however, come up with a wonderful advertising slogan: "In his life a man should have built a house, planted a tree, beget a son, and driven a 12-cylinder car!"

It is quite surprising to learn that Jaguar experimented in 1972 with an all-wheel drive XJ 6 with antilock brakes. The engine and transmission were borrowed from the Jensen FF, the FF standing for Ferguson Four. The Ferguson company at the time was headed by Tony Rolt, who earlier had contributed to Jaguar's racing legend. The antilock brakes were not yet perfect, lacking a sufficiently quick electronic management. The seemingly old-fashioned style of the Jaguar makes one forget about the marque's technical advances!

An enthusiast who tailored a truly old-fashioned style for his Jaguar was Robert Jankel, whose wealth derived from a clothing factory. In 1971 he created exclusive coachwork—a very nice classic-style aluminum body—for an old Rolls-Royce. He planned to create an SS 100 replica using mechanical components from more modern Jaguars. Jankel had his first prototype on the road for testing in September 1971, making the roads unsafe around Walton-on-Thames, where his Panther West Winds was located. With its 3.8-liter engine and the live axle, the car's Mark II parentage was obvious. Many other technical components, right through to the instruments, were taken from Jaguar's spares bin. The breathtaking Panther J 72 was unveiled in October 1972 at the Motor Show. Even old Sir William Lyons paid respect to Jankel's achievement. The J 72 cost £4,380, and acceleration to

60 miles per hour took just six seconds—quicker than any Porsche of the time.

About 25 examples of the Panther J 72 with the 3.8-liter engine were made, nearly half of them with the doors hinged at the rear. In the summer of 1973—Panther just had relocated to Byfleet in Surrey—*Auto Motor und Sport* reported about the first J 72 in German, equipped with the 4.2-liter engine of the XJ 6. The large air cleaner in the engine bay required a similarly large bulge at the offside hood. This dark green rarity must have made an impression, as in Germany the demand for the J 72 was relatively high, although with a 54,300-deutsche mark price tag, it was very expensive. The customers came from illustrious circles—Arabian royalty like King Fahd of Saudi Arabia and King Hussein of Jordan among them—but also some idols from show business like Elizabeth Taylor and Sammy Davis Jr.

It was an obvious idea to put Jaguar's new V-12 into the J 72, and indeed this became reality at the 1973 Frankfurt show. Bulges on both sides of the elongated hood were telltale features, as was a stylishly enclosed auxiliary radiator near the number plate. For the less experienced car spotters, a V-12 badge was added to the grille. The price of this masterpiece was £9,500, and only 12 examples were made. The last was made on August 17, 1976, and despite considerable further demand, production of the J 72 V-12 was not continued. Seven of them—one being a left-hand drive car with an automatic—are still known to exist.

The 4.2 continued until 1978, and 177 cars were made. Late in 1976 a second series was introduced. These had an independent front suspension (no further chromed front axles!), and Jaguar's latest changes to many other items were adopted. Remarkably the rear wheels still had drum brakes! The headlights were moved slightly further apart, requiring a little recess in the front fenders. The radiator enclosure of the V-12 now became part of the six-cylinder variant. About 150 examples of the second series were made until 1980. Further cars were made under Korean management, raising the production total of the J 72 to 368—the replica thus was more successful than the original!

Robert Jankel would not have been himself had he not gone to further extremes. In 1974 he already had completed a large limousine, the de Ville, that was somewhat reminiscent of the Bugatti Royale. This car seemed much longer than the measured 204 inches would suggest. It had a majestic aura, to which the large chromed horseshoe grille contributed. The first examples were adorned with a real amethyst on top of this grille and—of course—a Jaguar V-12 engine behind it. It was unveiled in October 1974 at the Earls Court Motor Show—with a price tag of £17,500. The happy few who could—and would—afford this were King Feisal, Elton John, Johnny Halliday, and Rock Hudson. A few de Villes were equipped with Jaguar six-cylinder engines.

Any Jaguar enthusiast will immediately appreciate the de Ville convertible. The doors, which for the sedan had been borrowed from the Austin 1800, in this case stemmed from Jaguar's XJ coupe, as did the side windows. As the 142-inch wheelbase remained unchanged, the convertible was mechanically similar to the sedan. The Sultan of Brunei particularly loved his convertible-door de Ville, so he had an externally similar example with a fixed roof made for him. Production figures were 47 sedans, 11 convertibles, and 1 coupe. The last sedan was extended 36 inches by Panther and had six doors.

The J 72 and de Ville, with their immaculate aluminum bodies made by underemployed tinsmiths of the nearby aircraft industry, can justifiably be regarded as the climax in Jankel's *oeuvre*. Other projects were perhaps driven more by creative urge than genius, such as the Six, with its four front wheels, or the excessively angular Lazer. The Lima, however, was a nice, popular roadster, but it had no mechanical relationship with

Top: In its second year, the capacity of the Panther J 72 engine was increased to 4.2 liters. *(Möhrke)*

Above: The one-off Panther de Ville coupe. *(Möhrke)*

The doors of this royal Panther de Ville were in fact sourced from Austin's parts bin. *(Möhrke)*

Top: The new Jaguar XJ 12 L Series 2 with the bumpers set higher. *(J)*

Above: The functional dashboard of the Series 2 XJ. *(J)*

Above right: The well-proportioned face of a 1973 Series 2 XJ 6. *(J)*

Right: Rear view of a Daimler Series 2, varying only in detail from earlier variants. *(S)*

Jaguar. Perhaps it was this creative urge that led Jankel to bankruptcy on December 18, 1979. A Korean group of investors took over the ailing company, developed the Lima into the Kallista, and produced this until 1993.

Back to the true Jaguars, for which the Frankfurt show that opened on September 13, 1973, was of utmost importance. There, the XJ was reintroduced as "Series 2." Higher front bumpers demanded by American legislation and the consequent changes to the grilles made these cars easily distinguishable from the earlier models. Many felt the look was a definitive improvement to the proportions of the Jaguar face. The revisions to the dashboard were similarly drastic, with the imposing row of easily interchangeable switches above the center console being replaced by steering column levers for flashers and wipers. The headlight switch was also positioned behind the steering wheel. The switches were illuminated by a bulb in the center console, via fiber-optic cables. This most advanced arrangement was called "Opticell."

At the same Frankfurt show, Jaguar unveiled the coupe variants of the XJ 6, XJ 12, Sovereign, and Double-Six. With its pillarless style, this body imitated the many hardtop variants of American road cruisers, wherein the roof seemed to levitate above a wide opening, particularly when the windows were wound

down. The pillarless construction had fascinated Lyons before, but this was the first time that the rear windows could be opened as well. The 1935 Airline was such an exercise, as were the XK fixed head coupes (including a low prototype for the XK 150 that resembled the Mark II). In 1969 a first prototype of the XJ coupe was completed—of course based on the first-series XJ 6. This regency red car was sold off to a scrap yard, which was intended to become its graveyard. For some time the car remained hidden, but in Australia it was finally restored to its former glory.

It was a difficult task to make the side windows water tight and avoid wind noise, and Jaguar failed to achieve this goal. The door windows tended to push outward, so that a gap occurred between the side windows. The start of full production was delayed until about April 1975, following endless trials intended to remove this imperfection.

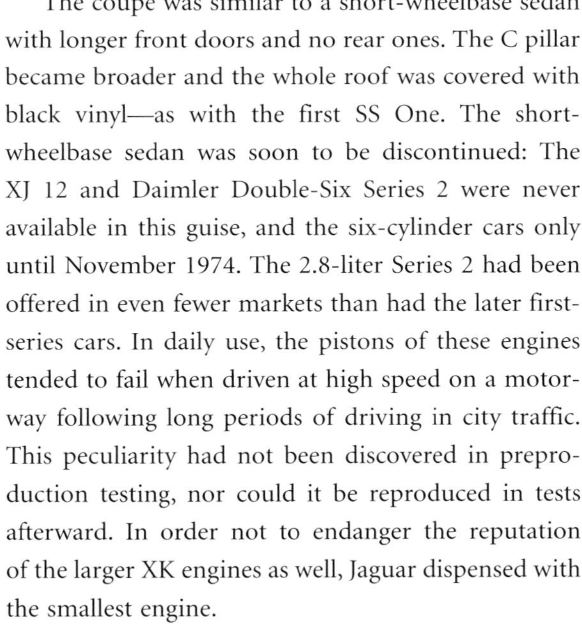

The coupe was similar to a short-wheelbase sedan with longer front doors and no rear ones. The C pillar became broader and the whole roof was covered with black vinyl—as with the first SS One. The short-wheelbase sedan was soon to be discontinued: The XJ 12 and Daimler Double-Six Series 2 were never available in this guise, and the six-cylinder cars only until November 1974. The 2.8-liter Series 2 had been offered in even fewer markets than had the later first-series cars. In daily use, the pistons of these engines tended to fail when driven at high speed on a motorway following long periods of driving in city traffic. This peculiarity had not been discovered in preproduction testing, nor could it be reproduced in tests afterward. In order not to endanger the reputation of the larger XK engines as well, Jaguar dispensed with the smallest engine.

The energy crisis after the 1973 Yom Kippur War in the Middle East did not encourage demand for large cars, particularly those as thirsty as the XJ 12. Thanks to the older XK engine, sales remained relatively steady. Testers were impressed with the new heating, air conditioning, and ergonomics, but still complained about the occasionally jerky gear change with Borg-Warner's slightly outdated automatic and the high gasoline consumption of the V-12.

The 1973 Frankfurt show also included a Jaguar with ultramodern looks, presented by H. R. Owen Limited, who called their futuristic coupe the "Sedanca." A sedanca actually is a coachbuilt car with an open compartment for the chauffeur. They were made by companies like Gurney Nutting who, like Harold Radford and Freestone & Webb, by this time were under the wings of H. R. Owen. This Sedanca had a fastback coupe body with the rear door completely made of glass and integrated black bumpers designed by Chris Humberstone. Below the shell, the mechanical components of a standard first-series XJ were used. As a granturismo, the Sedanca anticipated the XJ-S, which also had crash-resistant bumpers. Its exquisite interior comprised amenities like silver hair and cloth brushes, a Dictaphone, and a silver notebook that opened when an equally silver pencil was slid out of it. Instead of walnut, the dash was leather covered. The aluminum body had been made at Williams & Pritchley, together with reinforcing tubes in the doors and glasshouse. Panther was to assemble the cars. The prices were adjusted at £8,500 for the 4.2 and £9,500 for the 5.3 variant, but only three were made, all with the six-cylinder engine. Unfortunately this interesting project became a victim of the oil crisis, enhanced by the later difficult relationship between Jaguar and Owen.

Above left: V.I.P. in Germany created this impressive XJ convertible. *(Langenbach)*

Top: The XJ 12 coupe was very similar to the sedan. *(J)*

Above: Interior of the one-off Daimler Vanden Plas coupe. *(Brüggemann)*

Below: XJ coupe transformed into a convertible by Avon. *(J)*

CRITICAL TIMES 16

Above: The Broadspeed XJ 12 C at Silverstone. *(Schönborn archive)*

Left: Daimler 4.2 Vanden Plas. *(J)*

British Leyland Motor Corporation (BLMC) saw its first losses in 1974, and they were not small. Suddenly BLMC needed interim credit from the Labour government under Premier Harold Wilson. Tony Benn, minister for Industry, granted the credit under the reasonable condition that the large company analyze its (perhaps too) extensive production sites with the aim of improving profitability. Sir Donald Ryder was assigned this analysis. The result was submitted on March 26, 1975, and a shorter version was presented to the public four weeks later. This Ryder report recommended that the companies within BLMC be closer integrated under one single make, which would reduce the variety of vehicle types. This would save cost and avoid competition between BLMC products. All this sounded good on paper, but it was to end in catastrophe for Jaguar with the loss of the independence that once had been granted to Sir William Lyons. Leyland people now had access to Jaguar's purchasing department and learned that little Jaguar generally had achieved lower purchase prices than BLMC—a late compliment for Arthur Whittaker, who had retired in 1968.

Lyons immediately recognized that this loss of independence would mean the loss of Jaguar's own development, purchasing, production, and marketing—the latter being perfectly attuned to the fine character of the products. Geoffrey Robinson also could not find any good in Ryder's proposals; he called "the whole thing mad," and he gave up his job in early May 1975. The staff was not happy to lose him, and they even went on strike to try to keep him. Robinson found a new stage in political life, and nearly a quarter-century later he became paymaster general in the latest New Labour government. In a scandal involving preferential, secret loans to highly placed Labour politicians, he had to resign from his office, endangering the whole government with this affair. Robinson's successor at Jaguar—or the remains of it—was Tony Thompson of Morris, who hardly left any mark at Browns Lane. After that, everyday business in what now was called "Leyland Large Car Plant No. 2" was with Peter Craig until he died in 1977.

At the time of Geoffrey Robinson's withdrawal, the Jaguar range was affected by the energy crisis: In spring 1975 a 3.4-liter variant of the XK engine was re-introduced in the XJ sedan to fill the gap that the 2.8 had left. These cars were offered as the XJ 3.4 and Daimler Sovereign 3.4, while the larger-engined six-cylinder cars now were called XJ 4.2. In the United States the familiar XJ 6 designation remained in use, as the 3.4 was not offered there. The 3.4 combined lower gasoline consumption with other cost savings. Thus it was able to be priced competitively in its class and was highly appreciated in the U.K. *Autocar* characterized the manual XJ 3.4 in a test as, "An intelligent compromise of economy and performance." The engine's smoothness even bettered the 4.2, at the cost of low-range torque.

Motor confirmed the result, but still found the steering too light, judged the ventilation as just adequate, and wished that it offered more adjustment. The familiar 4.2 was now available as a Vanden Plas, while the V-12 became more economical with electronic fuel injection and the new name XJ 5.3 L (again, not used in the U.S.). For completion's sake, a single Vanden Plas coupe needs to be mentioned; it was equipped with a Vanden Plas-style interior and finish at Kingsbury and built upon a left-hand drive XJ 12 coupe. Jaguar decided against series production of such a variant, and the one-off now lives at Bremen, Germany.

At that time Jaguar was not yet tarnished by the bad reputation of BLMC, as evidenced by the fact that a

Jaguar XJ 6 coupe finished in typical period Carriage Brown. *(St)*

Opposite: The Daimler 4.2 Vanden Plas was introduced on April 30, 1975. *(S)*

prototype XJ 12 C was chosen as John Steed's transport in the cult series *The Avengers*—at the time a must-see, even abroad! After the most serious problems with its side windows seemed to have been solved, production of the coupe started around April 1975. In November 1975 *Autocar* stated that, thanks to the injection system, fuel consumption of the V-12 now was much more acceptable, but they still complained about wind noise.

In October 1975 *Auto Motor und Sport* finally published another test of a Jaguar, this time an XJ 4.2 C Automatic. Klaus Westrup's summary about the "mellow character" read: "Stylistically clean coupe version of the XJ sedan with average visibility conditions (relatively small windshield) and sufficiently large trunk, very completely appointed, good seats, practical levers, etc. Extremely silent six-cylinder engine with sufficient power and good low-range torque. Average performance for the price and engine capacity, adequate gasoline consumption, excellent riding comfort."

In November 1977 the production of the coupes was finished, but they had been too expensive for the United States. This helped save one assembly line. The Daimler Sovereign 3.4 was not offered any more either. Of the full dozen XJ types once offered, only seven remained in production, namely the XJ 3.4, and the two larger engines in Jaguar, Daimler, and Vanden Plas guise.

Autocar tested the XJ 5.3 in September 1978 and was once again delighted with the suspension. The lack of an interval setting for the windshield wiper was noted; the magazine found the dance of the wipers before finding their parking position amusing. The central locking mechanism worked somewhat loudly; unfortunately the trunk was not included in the system. The otherwise perfect new GM automatic came in for criticism due to the unnecessary detent between the "D" and "2" positions; this was designed to better prohibit an unwanted change from "D" to "N." The XJ 6 for America had electronic fuel injection from May 1978 onward, a "first" for a production XK engine but more than 20 years after its use in Jaguar's racing department. Testers and customers alike were delighted by the additional performance and reduced fuel consumption.

Avon Coachworks (or more precisely New Avon, since its reconstruction only shortly after its abortive start in the 1920s) had by now been taken over by Graham Hudson, and offered a convertible variant of the XJ coupe from 1979 onward. Jaguar ordered some of these conversions for preproduction cars used by its management. Similar convertibles were made at Lynx, which had been established in 1971 and had gained a reputation for its carefully executed C- and D-Type replicas.

The premature end of XJ coupe production certainly also had to do with its nearly total failure in racing. The idea of racing XJ coupes was the brainchild of an outsider named Ralph Broad. In 1971 he approached Jaguar with the not very surprising statement that the V-12 engine could turn out 500 horsepower. Jaguar's point of view was racing would only be supported if they had a reasonable chance of winning, which they thought was not the case with Broad. In 1973 Jaguar repeated its point by revealing the several-year-old XJ 13, with its 500 horsepower V-12, to the public at Silverstone, accompanied by the statement that Jaguar had no intention of returning to racing. At this point Broad contacted England but failed again. In 1974 he did no better when trying to convince Geoffrey Robinson of his ideas.

After Lord Stokes withdrew from active business, former Ford man Derek Whittaker was responsible for Leyland Cars under Alex Park. It was Whittaker who announced in March 1976 that Leyland would participate in the European Touring Car Championship with an XJ 12 C prepared by Broad. Broad had run Triumph Dolomites quite successfully in the British championship, and thus had gained some trust. According to Broad, the XJ-S was not eligible for this series as its interior was narrower than Annex J Group 2 would require.

After Robinson's resignation there was nobody at Browns Lane who should have been asked officially. At the time Jaguar's marketing and public relations functions had been completely Leylandized, and Leyland believed in Broad's success. The changes to the XJ 12 C were so extensive that the result was a completely new technical specification. They were carried out at Broadspeed at Southam near Coventry. Work started in September 1975. The engine was bored out by 0.6mm, giving a 5,416cc capacity. Higher piston crowns resulted in a compression ratio of 12:1, and with know-how from Cosworth Engineering, the promised 500 horsepower was achieved. Baffles were added to the oil

Above left: In the United States late XJ Series 2 models had further reinforced bumpers. *(S)*

Top: Sir Donald Stokes, BLMC chief in the company's dark days. *(S)*

Above: Derek Bell, David Hobbs, Andy Rouse, and Steve Thompson had the difficult task of bringing the Broadspeed XJ-C to finish its races. *(S)*

sump in order to prevent centrifugal forces from allowing the oil to flow away from the pump. (The wet sump had to be retained in order to comply with Group 2.) A mechanical Lucas fuel injection system was chosen together with particularly long inlet ports to effect a mild kind of supercharging created by optimizing the pressure waves caused by columns of air rushing into the intake valves. At least three of these engines were destroyed in test beds before the first car was ready for a test drive.

Although hardly any customer could purchase a manual XJ 12 C, the racing model had an allegedly standard close-ratio five-speeder from the XJ-S, with hydraulically operated single-plate dry clutch. A strong spring was used to avoid clutch slippage under fast acceleration. Behind the excessively wide wheels and the disfiguring changes to the bodywork necessitated by them, Lockheed four-piston disc brakes were hidden.

Endless technical problems delayed the appearance of the car. The team did not dare to start before the Tourist Trophy race at Silverstone in September 1976. Derek Bell/David Hobbs were first in the practice with special tires mounted, but in the race the car retired with damaged suspension.

During the winter the coupe was further enhanced with 19-inch wheels and a large plastic spoiler at the trunk lid. But the streak of bad luck continued throughout the 1977 season with the driving teams of Derek Bell/Andy Rouse and Tim Schenken/John Fitzpatrick. The cars failed to finish at Monza and at Salzburgring. In the latter race, Lofty England (who enjoyed retirement in Austria) was in attendance; after the race he invited Broad to his home at Altmünster for some days of recreation. At this stage a break was necessary until stronger half shafts could be found. At Brünn, Schenken/Fitzpatrick saw the finish at last, although because of a burst tire they were only 16th. On July 10 Derek Bell/Andy Rouse finished second at the Nürburgring behind Nilsson/Quester's Alpina-BMW. At Zandvoort and Silverstone, Jaguar finally had a dry sump engine available (these had been allowed since the Nürburgring race as BMW also had incurred serious lubrication problems during cornering). Nevertheless, both cars retired again, although Rouse

Top: The XJ-S of 1975 was the E-Type's successor. *(J)*

Above: In particular, the rear aspect of the car was unusual for Jaguar. *(Schönborn archive)*

Above right: Not everyone liked the style of the XJ-S. *(Schönborn archive)*

Below: A convertible version was not planned for the XJ-S. *(J)*

lasted until eight laps from the finish and was awarded fourth place. The final race at Zolder ended with the typical catastrophes for Broadspeed. Although the coupe had the lead at one stage in every race it took part in, Leyland was wise enough to end the Broadspeed effort. Ralph Broad himself lost his daughter in a traffic accident in 1977, and this caused him to quit racing anyway—so Jaguar's shortest and least successful racing program came to an end.

The V-12 had a more successful racing career on the sea: In 1977 Tony Fahey achieved with a 5.7-liter class world record of 128.375 miles per hour with *Vladivar V*. *Vladivar V* was Norman Buckley's *Miss Windermere V* of 1964, but with the Maserati engine replaced by a Jaguar V-12. This had been slightly bored out and improved at Forward Engineering under Phil Weaver's eyes. Harry Mundy could hardly believe that this only slightly modified unit turned out more than 500 horsepower.

As mentioned above, the XJ coupe was a sideline that in Heynes' eyes could have been a serious challenge to the American Ford Thunderbird, an extremely popular car in the early 1960s. This sideline gained some impetus in 1968 under the XJ 4 GT and XJ 27 codes. A distinguishing feature of the new development line was its so-called "flying buttresses"—extended C-posts *à la* Ferrari 246 GT, a car Sayer had been much impressed by. Sayer had finished the styling of the project car before his premature death in 1970. He was convinced that the extension of the rear pillars to the rear of the car would perfectly guide the passing airstream to the typical rear vortex. For this reason they already had been added to some of his later race car designs.

At one stage a mid-engine configuration was considered. It was rejected, however, because of its disadvantages in crash situations, cabin dimensions, noise suppression, Jaguar's lack of experience in the design of mid-engined cars, and the unique stock of spare parts such a configuration would demand. Thus the floorpan for the new coupe was taken from the XJ 12, shortened and with lower sills, which saved a lot of development time. The project was heavily influenced by the latest safety requirements in America.

The first prototype was finished in 1969. This was soon followed by a proposal from the styling department under Doug Thorpe and by another one from Lyons and Sayer, which was preferred of course. On the basis of his consultancy agreement, Lyons still had a hand in styling details This design, with its only mildly curved skin, was much different from previous Jaguar style. The large headlamps with their thick chrome rings were very individual items; they included special reflectors made by French CIBIÉ. The "flying buttresses" made the car look heavy; Thorpe in particular hated them. The most notable styling change after Sayer's death was the addition of the black front spoiler, which improved both front-end stability and cooling. The manufacture of the new coupe, particularly its body shell and assembly, required an investment of £6.5 million. The weekly production figure was intended to grow from an initial 60 to 150 cars.

For quite a long while it seemed as if "XK-F" would be the name of Jaguar's new *granturismo*, following the name of its predecessor in the United States. The alternative name "Le Mans" was already used by Pontiac. Bob Berry finally proposed "XJ-S," the last letter standing for "Special." A rather late BLMC management decision set the car's price quite high, so that the XJ-S became Jaguar's flagship, reaching Ferrari territory for the first time. The XJ-S was thus aimed at dynamic, young managers who would more easily be granted a GT than a sports car like the E-Type.

Although the press had written about it extensively since June 1975, the XJ-S was officially unveiled at the Frankfurt show on September 19. The public, who had looked forward to a racy successor to the E-Type, was somewhat disappointed by the air of the car, particularly its somewhat ponderous side elevation. For the first time in its history, Jaguar had to face overcapacities with a new model—not exactly a comfortable situation. With its heavy weight and thirsty V-12 engine, this wonderful grand tourer did not fit the mood of the time, which was dominated by rising oil prices. Even sales of the sedans were affected by this energy-mindedness. To defend the XJ-S it has to be pointed out that despite its less sensational styling—if its charismatic predecessor is the yardstick—its handling and performance simply had been underappreciated.

Bob Tullius (right), Brian Fuerstenau (center), and their racing E-Type. *(Schönborn archive)*

Autocar, in its first XJ-S test, aptly pointed out the advantages of the car as a comfortable long-distance tourer, not as a true sports car. The silent engine, audible only at high revs, was regarded as ideal for this type of car. Riding comfort was rated excellent, similar to the sedan's. The bland interior, with no wood veneer but barrel-type minor instruments, could hardly drum up enthusiasm. The XJ-S was still somewhat quicker and easier to maneuver than the standard XJ 12. A slight high-speed roll on minor undulations—well-known from the sedan—was deemed to be disconcerting in this car with its more sporting character. The V-12's flexibility was demonstrated by starting the car in its direct gear without using the clutch and then

accelerating to 140 miles per hour, a process that took only 70 seconds.

Motor thought that this all might have been achieved with less weight, fuss, and fuel consumption, naming the much less comfortable and reputedly less reliable Lotus Elite as the only evidence. Unforgettably, John Bolster of *Autosport* felt inclined to compare the manual XJ-S (only 352 examples were made of this) to

Top: Bob Tullius (left), founder and chief of the Group 44 racing stable. *(S)*

Center: With the XJ-S Bob Tullius became Trans-Am champion in 1977. *(S)*

Above: Graham Whitehead—America's Mr. Jaguar. *(S)*

the hitherto most flexible car of all times, the Rolls-Royce Silver Ghost, and the XJ-S won, despite having a maximum speed twice as high as the Ghost's! The starter was criticized for its noise—even the half-century-old Bullnose-Morris had had a more silent one.

U.S. magazine *Car & Driver* described the XJ-S as a dark, mysterious product of a plagued British motor industry, fantastically overqualified for the driving conditions of our times.

Early in 1977 *Auto Motor und Sport's* Götz Leyrer tested the XJ-S. He talked about quality deficiencies for the first time. The not very delicate bumpers and headlights also came in for criticism, as did the dark interior with its small instruments. However, the tester was delighted with the silky-sweet injected engine and its power. Fuel consumption was less of a delight, as was the very high price, even if compared to Jaguar's second V-12. "No doubt: The strongest competition for the new Jaguar comes from the same stable," he wrote.

Although the XJ-S really did not look like a racing car, American Bob Tullius chose one as a successor to his E-Type with which his Group 44 team—that he had established in 1965—had become 1974 B-Production champion for northeastern U.S. and 1975 National SCCA champion.

In August 1976 he had his first race with the XJ-S, sponsored by Quaker State and British Leyland. Jaguar themselves had investigated the racing potential of the XJ-S, but expense soon rose sky-high and the project had been given up. Only some aerodynamic tests with rear spoilers had been carried out, and Group 44 was allowed to exploit the test results. Group 44 reduced the weight of the XJ-S by around 700 pounds, while the engine developed 476 horsepower at 7,600 rpm. The Group 44 XJ-S could hit 60 miles per hour within five seconds, and 100 miles per hour in 10.3 seconds. In the engine, only the pistons (Arias), camshafts (Crane), and camshaft bolts were nonstandard parts. Contrary to Broadspeed, Tullius had dry-sump lubrication available from the start.

Its first race was at Mosport Park in Canada. By 1977 Tullius already had become Trans-Am Category 1 champion with the further lightened XJ-S. Out of 10 races, he won 5. In the following year Tullius even won seven consecutive races. Toward the end of the season, Tullius entered a similar car with driver Brian Fuerstenau, which helped Jaguar secure the constructors' championship.

In 1979 and 1980 Tullius ran the less exquisite Triumph TR 8. Then Tullius gained financial support again from the BL importers, represented by Graham Whitehead and Mike Dale. They also introduced Tullius to Jaguar management. Shortly thereafter a silhouette XJ-S with a tube frame and nearly 500 horsepower materialized for the Trans-Am championship. Only the outward appearance and the engine block had been retained from the standard XJ-S. This new car won three races in 1981 and made Tullius second in the championship. This particular engine had gained Tullius 29 victories between 1977 and 1982!

A close relative of this silhouette XJ-S was the racing prototype dubbed XJR-5, with Kevlar bodywork on a supporting aluminum structure. Its V-12—basically still the 1976 unit—had been enlarged (bore 90mm, stroke 70mm) to 6 liters, and was fed by six Weber carburetors, resulting in 600 horsepower, or miraculously, 650 for the 1985 season. This made the car, with its unique, aerodynamically efficient lines and Goodyear racing tires, capable of about 200 miles per hour.

For the design work, Tullius relied on genius designer Lee Dykstra, who had been recommended by a friend named Al Holbert. Dykstra had a reputation as the only U.S. designer to be on par with European racing car designers. The project very nearly had to be stopped, but as a last minute rescue, Jaguar sponsored Group 44, so the XJR-5 could be developed further. The engine took part in the Daytona 24 hours in the Silhouette XJ-S before the XJR-5 debuted at Elkhart Lake (Road America) on August 22, 1982. The car was not overly successful in the United States—six wins in 57 races. In 1983 Bob Tullius/Bill Adam won at Road Atlanta, Lime Rock and Mosport Park, while the Pocono win was Tullius/Doc Bundy's. Second place at Laguna Seca and thirds in Charlotte and—again—Elkhart Lake made Tullius second in the International Motor Sports Association (IMSA) championship, just behind a veritably invincible Porsche.

Nineteen eighty-four brought only one win (at Miami, Drivers Brian Redman/Doc Bundy); seconds at the same Miami race (Bob Tullius/Bob Bedard) and at Charlotte, Portland, Sears Point, Pocono and in the Daytona 3 Hours; while the XJR-5 was third in the Daytona 24 Hours, at Elkhart Lake, Charlotte, Watkins Glen, and Sears Point. Nineteen eighty-five added another single win (Elkhart Lake, drivers Brian Redman/Hurley Haywood from Tullius/Chip Robinson); further seconds at Laguna Seca, Charlotte, Lime Rock, and Portland, and thirds at Riverside, Laguna Seca, Mid Ohio, and in the second Watkins Glen race; whereas in the first race there and at Miami, Sebring, Charlotte, and Portland, the XJR-5 finished fourth.

Despite its not overly encouraging racing career, two XJR-5s started in the 1984 Le Mans 24 Hours with drivers Claude Ballot-Lena/John Watson/Tony Adamowicz and Bob Tullius/Brian Redman/Doc Bundy, but both cars retired with relatively minor failures (gearbox and wheels). In the following year the XJR-5 of Bob Tullius/Chip Robinson/Claude Ballot-Lena saw the Le Mans checkered flag (in 13th position) as the first Jaguar finisher in 20 years—while its twin, with Brian Redman/Doc Bundy/Hurley Haywood, retired again.

By late 1987 Tullius' racing prototype had evolved into the XJR-7, weighing in at roughly 1,800 pounds, with much improved cooling and even stronger aerodynamic ground effects. Only the 650-horsepower engine and the rear suspension had remained substantially unaltered. It debuted in 1985 at the Daytona 24 Hours, where it remarkably finished with a fourth place. In 28 races, the XJR-7 scored 3 wins. Before it had sufficiently matured into a championship contender, Jaguar had transferred its support for transatlantic racing to Tom Walkinshaw. Chief engineer Randle even hoped that XJR production might be transferred to Jaguar itself. However, Tullius and genius Lanky Foushee (not Lee Dykstra!) designed and built a new racing prototype for the 1988 and 1989 seasons. Thus ended Tullius' racing for Jaguar.

Top: Jaguar historian Bernard Viart takes a look at the V-12 engine of the XJR-5. *(S)*

Above left: Bob Tullius' XJR-5. *(S)*

Above right: This XJ-S held the speed record for crossing the North American subcontinent. *(S)*

The American company Hess & Eisenhardt transformed early XJ-S into remarkable roadsters. *(S)*

The second American who added considerably to the XJ-S' accomplishments was David Heinz from Florida. In 1979 he and his friend Dave Yarborough from South Carolina and a black XJ-S took part in the Cannonball Run across the United States. This unofficial and illegal race aimed at crossing the continent (that year starting from Darien, Connecticut, and finishing in Los Angeles) as quickly as possible. This race was organized every year since 1971 by Brock Yates, and in the first year he and Dan Gurney in a Ferrari Daytona had been winners. Over more than 3,000 miles the Jaguar averaged 87 miles per hour, or 32 hours and 51 minutes. A Mercedes-Benz 450 SEL 6.9 was second with only 8 minutes difference.

Two years earlier, in 1977, a one-off XJ-S was created for the 25th coronation jubilee of Queen Elizabeth II. Under the eye of Count Albrecht Goertz, who once had designed the BMW 507 roadster and the successful Datsun 240 Z coupe, the car was finished in gold with a leaping Jaguar over the windshield. A more elegant approach with wonderfully flowing lines was Pininfarina's "Spyder" of the 1978 Motor Show, part of his series of banana-shaped aerodynamic cars. This car was to have strong influence on later open Jaguars. The restorers at Lynx offered an XJ-S roadster variant from 1979 to 1982 (and in a few cases even years later) as a sort of substitute to the convertible XJ coupe, long before Jaguar had an open model on offer again. The diligently carried-out transformation was quite expensive, costing £6,000 initially.

Demand declined every year from 1976, and in 1980—when no more XJ-Ss were supplied with manual gear change—yearly production was just above 1,000. XJ-S production was interrupted during September and October 1980, just after the V-12 with a compression ratio of 10:1 was introduced for the H.E. variant. This revised engine increased performance and reduced fuel consumption. Thinking about the future of the XJ-S, a prototype with a floorpan extended by 4 inches was made. It had longer doors and side windows, while the c-posts were cut back. This idea did not go down particularly well, so it was not investigated further and the single prototype was soon scrapped.

During the years following the Ryder report, BLMC did not really progress, continuing with its weak management and its staff striking for almost any reason. Soon the products could no longer hide this neglect. Critical remarks about their reliability and build quality became louder and louder. This and the lack of a really practical, modern car in the model range resulted in further reduced production and sales figures—it was as if Leyland had forgotten how to build cars!

Jaguar suffered from the same symptoms as Austin, Morris, Triumph, etc. Jaguar's reputation for quality soon reached an all-time low, particularly in the United States. In 1978 a U.S. magazine asked Jaguar customers how content they were with their cars. Two-thirds of the 178 participants had cars made from 1972 until 1974. Cooling was a problem with half of all V-12 cars, engines with a quarter, and electrics with a fifth, while one-third of the six-cylinder owners had experienced problems in these areas. Power steering, instruments, exhaust, tires, the automatic transmission and water-tightness of the body also were criticized more often than with other makes. So the fine Jaguar became third from last of all makes the magazine had ever investigated in this manner! This report did not enhance Jaguar sales.

Contemporary comments tended to see the problem connected to the frequent strikes of the day. Management found no way to counter this erosion of its power. In these dark days, hardly any British companies could overcome such problems. It seems that at least part of the reason for this misery lies outside BLMC, being caused by more general social and political circumstances. However, Jaguar aficionados clearly placed the blame at the feet of BLMC.

The most constant stalwart to resist Jaguar's integration into the unlucky conglomerate after Geoffrey Robinson's departure was Bob Knight, with his development department. Indeed he managed to avoid any Leyland influence. If negotiations seemed to go wrong, he filibustered with endless speeches until his counterparts gave up. His masterpiece in this battle against Leyland was his narrow design of the engine bay for the XJ successor. This made it unsuitable for Rover's V-8 engine, which quite a few Leyland managers imagined in there.

Knight even managed to report directly to Derek Whittaker, chief of BLMC Automobiles. In this case good luck was with Knight: Early in 1975 Sir Donald Ryder ordered a Jaguar XJ 6 to fill in for his burned-out Rolls-Royce. Knight made sure that he was supplied with a preproduction injected XJ 12 instead. After Ryder's first trip with the car he immediately called Knight to praise this wonderful car. This gave the chief of the BLMC-governing National Enterprise Board some confidence in Jaguar's abilities and he thus gave Jaguar some free rein.

At the time, Jaguar development—unlike other BLMC makes—was at the very forefront of technical advance. In 1976 a five-speed manual gearbox had been developed, eagerly awaited by press and public alike, as was a quick-action antilock brake system. For unclear reasons Leyland management prevented their introduction, giving an advance to the German competition, which was soon to offer similar developments, overtaking Jaguar. Jaguar, with its seemingly old-fashioned wood-and-leather interiors, was particularly dependent on showing its technical competence with innovations like these.

In August 1977 Lord Ryder, now member of the House of Lords, finally gave up his chair at the National Enterprise Board. Solutions contrary to the Ryder plan now got a chance. The winds of change affected the BLMC board as well: Michael Edwardes arrived from the Chloride group in November 1977, and he made efforts to distinguish the traditional makes. In 1978 he shortened the BLMC name to BL (British Leyland). In the same year, Jaguar became a separate entity again, with Bob Knight as managing director. He reported to American William Pratt Thompson, who was head of the equally new Jaguar Rover Triumph Division.

Edwardes wanted John Leopold Egan as the new Jaguar chief. Egan was born on November 7, 1939, the son of a Rootes dealer in Lancashire. He went to school at Coventry, where he had gained respect for Jaguar. At Shell he had learned some engineering and at GM'S AC-Delco, organizational skills. Since 1971 he had successfully reorganized the UNIPART spares organization. He had also worked for Massey-Ferguson (which in its early years used Standard engines and now was in Canadian hands). Egan's political and economical views were conservative. In his view the trade unions had caused severe damage to Britain's economy with stubborn opposition against essential modernization efforts. In March 1979 Egan decided against Edwardes' offer because, in his judgment, the Jaguar Rover Triumph conglomerate could not survive.

Later that same year the useless Jaguar Rover Triumph Division was wound up again, just after Percy Plant had become official Jaguar chief. Edwardes (now Sir Michael) reduced the size of his management staff through retirements, with an American psychologist separating the wheat from the chaff. Soon Edwardes reached the limits of his possibilities at Leyland and had to apply to the new Conservative government under Margaret Thatcher for a £1 billion credit. He cleverly combined this request with complaints about the increasingly strong pound, which made Leyland export more difficult. The "Iron Lady" granted the credit, but soon became aware that she had started to fill a money sink. The lady felt duped and became angry with Edwardes, which did nothing to help Leyland.

In these dark days for Jaguar, Wally James, a Brit with Maltese pass, moved to Munich in Germany, where no Jaguar clubs were active at the time. Without hesitation he gathered some fellow enthusiasts and founded the Jaguar Association Germany (JAG) in 1979, still the most influential classic Jaguar club in Germany. Some meetings like Suebian Mark II days, rallies in the Lower-Saxonian Stemwede area, or the yearly meeting at Thuringian Ranis were occasions to meet interesting Jaguar owners, and where tips for restoration were spread and monthly regional meetings were organized. Intended to extend all over Germany, the JAG now has about 1,700 members and regional sections in all parts of Germany.

Robert J. Knight—would Jaguar still exist today if not for him? *(S)*

17

JOHN EGAN ARRIVES

In 1980, a not very successful year for Jaguar, the company's staff felt alienated when rumors surfaced that Jaguar production might be relocated to Solihull or given up altogether. So on April 9, 1980, a strike started. BL chief Sir Michael Edwardes appealed for the workers to return to work in order not to lose their jobs, but without success. He guaranteed that Jaguar would continue to exist if it were to prove its potential for survival. It was exactly this guarantee that made John Egan finally join Jaguar's management. On April 17, 1980, he chaired his first board meeting. After long discussions on April 26 and 27 he managed to bring the strike to an end, although the staff had to accept considerable wage cuts. Egan had explained that he regarded Jaguar as his personal affair—and he must have been convincing.

Even without the strike the list of problems at Jaguar was frighteningly long: bad reputation of the marque, bad workshop morale, poor productivity, supply problems, high rates of warranty claims, worn tools, adversity between management and staff. So there were quite a lot of things to do before Jaguar could return to its previous strength. Egan was keen to hear Sir William Lyons' advice. He quickly learned that Jaguar's design was beyond (nearly) all criticism, but quality was not, which he initially did not believe. Bob Berry informed John Egan of the real situation at a major dealers' meeting in June 1980. A survey of April 1977 made in the course of preparations for the imminent XJ sedan was helpful in proving the point that quality had to be the top issue. The old 1960s motto "Poor quality cannot be tolerated" seemed to have fallen into oblivion.

Manufacture in what still were Leyland plants had to become much more careful. About 150 problem areas had been identified with the help of dealers. Jaguar aimed at equaling Mercedes-Benz quality, which was a high standard.

Interestingly, more than two-thirds of the problems were traced to outside suppliers. Some suppliers had such superficial quality control that about half of their deliveries had to be rejected at Jaguar; many saw no reason to change anything even after being criticized by Jaguar. Now these suppliers were summoned and requested to fulfill their contracts properly. As previous criticism had changed nothing resistance was expected, but Egan was surprised to find most suppliers supportive. His statement was, "Improve your product, or you are going to lose your contract." The threat that consequential damage might be charged to the suppliers was just as convincing. In the end this was hardly necessary and only a few contracts had to be canceled. The quality of supply improved dramatically—and generally without any extra cost to the supplier. Management tips and technical advice led to further quality improvement.

The next logical step was to eliminate quality flaws from the in-house production process. Again Egan chose a practical approach and sent his management to visit German and Japanese car factories and see how they managed to achieve better quality. One valuable model that was discovered was Japanese quality circles, in which relatively small groups of employees of all ranks discussed quality matters on an *ad-hoc* basis. Generally shop-floor employees had the most convenient solution on hand—so many good ideas finally had a chance to be realized. Quality circles made clear to each employee his own responsibility for the quality of the product, even if all the recommendations emerging from the circle needed approval of the management. On the other hand the effectiveness of the quality circles should not be over-emphasized. Not each exchange of ideas was helpful, and a bonus system for inventions also had some benefit.

Egan also fought to decrease the influence of the shop stewards, who were still regarded as the natural foremen rather than the ones that management had installed. Egan strengthened the position of the real foremen and sent them for psychological training in order to improve their contact with subordinates. Instead of just choosing older employees for the job—which generally was the previous custom—foremen were now selected by their personal and functional abilities. More competent foremen and more autonomy for the workers were the keys to breaking the dominance of the trade unions. The quality circles helped as well, as shop stewards could hardly fight against what the workforce itself had proposed.

Like Lyons, Egan often took a car from normal production home in the evening for testing. So he saw first-hand how his measures worked and really improved the product step by step. Further important information was gained from customer surveys that dealers had to carry out 1, 9, and 18 months after

Top: The large leaping cat for Jaguar dealers. *(Bergmeyer)*

Above: John Egan came on board to save Jaguar. *(J)*

Opposite: The 1984 XJ-S TWR had some great victories. *(J)*

the delivery of a new car. The results were so valuable that soon buyers of other makes were included in the survey. As a signal that some considerable success had been achieved, the initial inspection at 3,000 miles was deleted. This early inspection had seemed outdated in the 1960s already. The regular inspection interval was extended from 6,000/12,000 to 7,500/15,000 miles. In mid-1981 the warranty period was extended in the United States to two years or 36,000 miles—so most of the risk warned about in tests now was covered by the warranty!

Better quality was one issue, cost reduction another—and Jaguar needed both! Particularly in assembly, Jaguar had to reduce personnel. Partially because of the dramatic sales decrease in the late 1970s, productivity of the 10,500 employees was just 1.3 cars per employee per year. Layoffs were inevitable in order to reduce wage expenses. When sales figures rose, new personnel could be recruited again. Egan managed to simplify production procedures and thus the productivity per employee and year increased to 3.4 cars by the end of 1983. Soon staffing levels reached new heights. Staff instruction was improved so that mistakes would be avoided, and work progressed even more quickly.

Roger Putnam, Jaguar marketing and sales chief under John Egan. *(S)*

Parts and supply storage was completely reorganized. Step-by-step "just-in-time" supply schemes were employed, but this required new organizational skills, otherwise just-too-late delivery would occur.

This progress impressed Leyland management, and the promise that Jaguar might be given back its production facilities came true. In 1983 Jaguar bought back the Browns Lane plant for £3.5 million, Radford later for about £1 million, and finally Castle Bromwich from Pressed Steel Fisher for £7 million. Lyons, still most interested in Jaguar's fate, must have been particularly satisfied about the purchase of the fully tooled-up body plant, as he never had managed to have one for Jaguar. The plants also caused some burden in that Leyland had not kept them in good repair, so it was up to Jaguar to modernize tooling, seal the roofs, and so on.

Egan was keen on having a family atmosphere among personnel, to create a feeling of togetherness. So he promoted organized company-facilitated sports activities and family events, such as open days for staff and their families. Briefings informed all personnel about important visitors to Jaguar, the latest racing successes, and quality achievements. Video films—produced to the highest standards—followed by discussion sessions also reinforced employees' identification with Jaguar and a feeling of pride. However, even in 1986 there remained complaints that parts of the staff were not sufficiently encouraged to express their opinions. Indeed, there were still differences in status within the workforce.

Another difficult task was to separate Jaguar's figures out of Leyland's centralized accounting system—since 1975, there had not been separate figures for Jaguar. For 1980 a not-too-accurate balance sheet for Jaguar was established by John Edwards and others, who had tried to filter the Jaguar figures out of the general BL balance sheets.

John Egan's thinking even went beyond his newly acquired plants. He also had to think about how to strengthen the dealer network. Many of them were hardly qualified to provide Jaguar maintenance and could not assure adequate service. Under BL it had become commonplace to use a Jaguar franchise as a lure to bring insubordinate BL dealers into line. So the Jaguar dealer network, particularly in the United States (which still took about half of Jaguar's production), was not very competent. By setting new standards that dealers had to fulfill if they wanted to keep their Jaguar franchise, the quality of the dealer network became better and better.

With sales improving after 1981, Jaguar also regained control over its marketing, just as Edwardes had promised. In July 1982 Roger Putnam—coming from Lotus—took control of Jaguar's marketing. Coming from Vauxhall, chief stylist Geoff Lawson (born in 1945) joined Jaguar in 1984. He walked through the 1984 Motor Show at Birmingham NEC at the side of Sir William Lyons, carefully listening to his great predecessor's comments. This was a rich source when in future years he had to maintain Jaguar's individuality in styling.

Meanwhile JRT Inc., the U.S. distributor for Jaguar and a number of other Leyland makes, no longer had M.G.s and Triumphs to sell in the United States, plus the pound was getting stronger and stronger in relation to the dollar. This prompted Leyland to stop deliveries to the United States—a strategic mistake that in the long term did great harm to the British motor industry as a whole. Egan himself traveled to the United States to obtain firsthand information about the dealer network. They lacked motivation as sales figures still were so small but warranty claims were so frequent. Also the dates given by Jaguar for the delivery of new cars were unreliable. Safety and emission tests often were delayed by the simple fact that the cars that were to be tested simply did not arrive in time in the United States—one of the reasons why in the United States a new model often was introduced later than in the rest of the world.

In 1984 the number of Jaguar dealers in the U.S. was once again reduced considerably. The U.S. legal system requires that the dealer must consent to the loss of a franchise, which cost Jaguar $5,000 per car sold during the twelve months. Two years later only 150 Jaguar dealers were registered in the U.S. With considerably fewer dealers, sales figures per dealer rose even more quickly than the sales figures as a whole. This made investments in garages worthwhile, and optimism was back.

Egan's measures—if regarded in hindsight—look logical and consequent. However, at the outset it was not easy to find a way to improve Jaguar's desperate situation. Diagnosis of Jaguar's disease was not easy, and it was even more difficult to cure it. Jaguar was a patient under intensive care, and Egan as the surgeon could not risk a game of trial and error, as his patient's life was at risk. Leyland often made Egan's work even harder. However, Jaguar soon prevailed, and in 1983 the company broke all previous production records.

New models played a fairly minor role in the recovery of Jaguar—a compliment to the well-designed XJ and XJ-S models. Bob Knight and Harry Mundy had retired in 1980, and Jim Randle and Trevor Crisp followed as director of product development and chief engineer. The most significant technical advance concerned the V-12 engine, and this had been initiated by Harry Mundy. It all started with a visitor from Switzerland, Michael May. He had become famous for his turbocharger kits for Ford engines. He explained to Mundy his latest ideas with regard to the shapes of combustion chambers and demonstrated his ideas with a modified Volkswagen Passat engine. His invention was a tangential channel between the valves and a combustion chamber concentrated around the exhaust valve. This shape caused a swirl of the fuel and air mixture inside the combustion chamber, thus allowing a higher compression ratio, which made the engine run more economically without the danger of self-ignition. Mundy was intrigued, and so some Jaguar V-12s were transformed according to May's ideas for testing purposes. The results were very promising, so Jaguar immediately purchased an exclusive license for the "Fireball" combustion chamber—the similarity to Buick's straight eight engines of the 1940s was certainly accidental, as these had nothing in common with May's advanced technology. Production of these highly efficient (hence the H.E. designation) engines required a £500,000 investment at Radford, where these engines were made.

Together with the modernized engine, the XJ-S benefited from some visual refreshment beginning July 15, 1981. Wood panels on the dashboard and lighter colors for the interior helped the car's looks. New chrome embellishment for the bumpers also gave the car a more elegant appeal. For markets other than North America these bumpers were reduced in size. Only now demand for the sports car began to rise, and some commented that the XJ-S just must have been too far ahead of its time!

In October 1981 *Motor* recognized that the fuel consumption of the XJ-S H.E. was a remarkable 21 percent lower than with the earlier model, now equaling the carbureted XK engine. Early in 1982 Wolfgang König tested the "silent mover" XJ-S H.E. for *Auto Motor und Sport*. "Besides its now acceptable petrol consumption, the V-12 deserves acclaim for many other qualities. Its excellent riding comfort would grace any top-class sedan. The refined manners of the XJ-S are now equaled by a homelike interior. Another positive trait is the visibly improved quality of the XJ-S."

Based on the XJ-S H.E. Lynx introduced its Eventer, with its sporting estate back, at the Jaguar Open Day on September 20, 1982. Contrary to the still controversial coupe the Eventer was a much more beautiful car, unusual for a station wagon, particularly as Lynx is said to have cut corners and borrowed some glass panels from the French Citroën Ami 8. Having been developed in just five months, during which five different stylings were tried, the Eventer makes a strong case for

Top: Jaguar administration was freshened up externally as well under John Egan. *(St)*

Above: The entrance was relocated to the former back side of the Browns Lane plant in order to avoid too much traffic at Browns Lane. *(Schön)*

Top: The H.E. engine, a (relatively) economic V-12. *(J)*

Above: The 1981 XJ-S H.E. was the first new model under John Egan. *(Schön)*

Below: With Tom Walkinshaw, Jaguar regained confidence in racing. *(S)*

quick and effective development. Initially the modification cost £6,950, and the quality of the work executed was more than equivalent to Jaguar's own standards. Total production was nearly 70 examples, including some XJR-S models. Even the XJ-S' 1991 rear end styling revisions allowed transformation into an Eventer. After the production of the XJ-S had come to an end, some more Eventers were created, finally costing £21,500.

Lynx also created a turbocharged six-cylinder XJ-S with 450 horsepower. This car might have been inspired by the successful career of the XJ-S in the European Touring Championship. In 1982 FIA had created a new Group A with a more liberal definition of touring car. The racing cars were intended to look like the standard cars, while the maximum permitted wheel size depended on the engine capacity.

Tom Walkinshaw, born in 1948, was a racing driver from his youth, starting with a Mini. When he was 20, he got his own racing car, a Lotus Formula Ford. During the 1970s he marched through Formula Three and Formula Two, and from 1976 he drove for BMW, assisting in developing and driving their touring coupes, thereby witnessing the racing debacle of the XJ-C. In 1976 he established TWR (Tom Walkinshaw Racing), trading tuning parts for makes like Mazda, BMW, and Rover. Tom Walkinshaw recognized that the XJ-S, with its transverse control arm suspension, could easily be transformed for the new group A. He asked Randle and Egan to help him with his new racing project. Walkinshaw made clear that he would not repeat Broadspeed's mistake of changing the car's entire specification. He intended to stay as close as possible to the standard design, which would grant a better chance of winning than the XJ-C had. Of course, Jaguar was skeptical, but it allowed Walkinshaw a free hand, promising support if he showed his ability to win.

So TWR modified a black XJ-S H.E. on its own, sponsored by Japanese consumer electronics manufacturer Akai and French oil brand Motul. After initial tests with Weber carburetors it was decided that fuel injection would be more suitable to racing. For reasons of reliability, the power output was limited to 400 horsepower. Due to homologation rules, the XJ-S had to weigh in at more than 3,000 pounds—even more than the Broadspeed coupe. As the wheel arches were not allowed to be modified externally, the wide wheels needed more space toward the diff. The necessary changes to the platform were declared during homologation by Walkinshaw as winter equipment for the Third World, whereupon TWR was nicknamed Third World Racing. At the rear the trailing arms were eliminated and the lower transverse arms grew into wishbones. The brakes were located behind the wheels, not inboard near the diff. With this not yet totally reliable racing car, Walkinshaw, driving himself, won at Brünn, in Austria, at the Nürburgring, at Silverstone, and at Zolder. He finished third in the driver's championship, while his team partner Chuck Nicholson (his true name being Charles Nickerson) was fourth. The second XJ-S TWR, with drivers Pierre Dieudonné/Jeff Allam, was second in Austria, at Silverstone, and at Zolder.

Thanks to this initial success, TWR received financial support from Jaguar and finished its racing cars in an elegant combination of white and green. In the first race, at Monza, a loose hood required an extra pit stop, and Walkinshaw ended the race second, only three and a half seconds behind a BMW. After winning Donnington (John Fitzpatrick/Martin Brundle, Walkinshaw/ Nicholson were fifth), Pergusa, Brünn (each Walkinshaw/Nicholson), Österreichring at Zeltweg (Walkinshaw/Brundle, followed by Pierre Dieudonné/ Enzo Calderari), and Salzburgring (again Walkinshaw/ Nicholson), and finishing third at Vallelunga (Nicholson/Dieudonné/Walkinshaw) and

Mugello (Walkinshaw/Fitzpatrick), Walkinshaw lost the Drivers Championship by a very small margin to Dieter Quester of BMW.

In 1984 the TWR cars arrived in British racing-green livery with a white strip along the sides; the engines now turned out 460 horsepower. The team now had three cars and won at Monza and Mugello (Walkinshaw/Heyer), in the challenging Spa 24 Hours (Walkinshaw/Heyer/Percy), and at Donnington (Percy/Nicholson). The team scored 1-2 finishes at the Österreichring (Walkinshaw/Heyer, and Percy/ Nicholson) and Salzburg (Percy/Nicholson and Calderari/ Sears), and 1-2-3 sweeps at Enna Pergusa (Brundle/ Calderari, Walkinshaw/Heyer, and Percy/Nicholson), and Brünn (Walkinshaw/Heyer, Percy/Nicholson, and Calderari/Sears). Additionally, Calderari/Sears were second at Silverstone, and Walkinshaw/Heyer third at Valleglunga and Zolder. On the Nürburgring, for the last time on the grueling *Nordschleife*, Heyer/ Walkinshaw only finished fifth. So Walkinshaw finally was touring champion, followed by his teammate Hans Heyer, while Jaguar became constructors' champion. For Egan the goals of racing in Group A were now achieved, and Jaguar retired from this class.

The XJ-S TWR continued racing, however. At Macao, Walkinshaw and Heyer managed a 1-2 win in November 1984. In October 1985, TWR dared to start at the breathtaking Bathurst 1,000 Miles in Australia, the circuit having a summit at a very fast section which renders cars airborne and demands a lot of courage from the drivers. This most thrilling race "down under" was won by Armin Hahne/John Goss, Hahne being the first non-Aussie to win this race. Walkinshaw/Percy added a third place to this triumph. This was the 20th and last win for an XJ-S in Group A racing, but in 1987 Hahne/Percy finished second at Pukehoke in New Zealand.

The more standard XJ-S got a sibling on October 12, 1983—the new Cabriolet XJ-SC: an open top Jaguar at last! Similar to the Triumph Stag of 1970, the roof rails would not fold away, and behind the driver and passenger an anti-roll bar was added to the construction. Thus, strengthening of the underside was not necessary, saving cost and time. Over the driver and passenger were two removable plastic roof panels. These could be stowed in a large, quality case that could be attached with straps to the spare wheel. When driven open with the rear portion of the roof erect, some bad wind noise occurred, as is common with wide-open sunroofs. Unfortunately it was not easy to make the roof panels watertight. The rear part of the roof with the Perspex rear window could be folded down in a Landau fashion. As the flying buttresses had been cut off, the car looked particularly sleek. The cabriolet had no rear seats, as the room available was rather cramped. The seat cushions were replaced with a large lockable box. Development of the XJ-SC had started in 1980, continuing the former convertible development

In 1984 TWR was officially supported by Jaguar. *(J)*

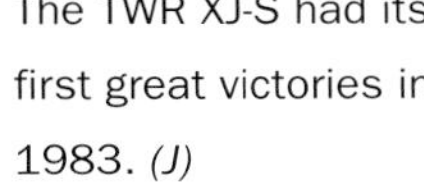

The TWR XJ-S had its first great victories in 1983. *(J)*

TWR XJ-S at Silverstone in 1982. *(S)*

Top: Stylish package for the XJ-SC's roof panels. *(S)*

Above: A six-cylinder XJ-S at last: the 3.6 of 1983. *(J)*

Above right: The first open Jaguar in many years was the XJ-SC 3.6 in 1983. *(Schön)*

project XJ 28. Assembly of the XJ-SC was a complicated matter in which Aston Martin's subsidiary Tickford was involved. It is said that Tickford designed the folding top mechanism. No wonder that only few cars could be made—long waiting lists were the inevitable consequence. Burberry had an XJ-SC (VIN 116005) made with the trunk cover and parts of the interior covered in their typical cloth pattern of checkered beige, red, and black—a felicitous advertisement for the typically British style of both marques.

The SC had a completely new engine (AJ or Advanced Jaguar 6). It was designed as a replacement for the renowned XK engine, which with regard to weight and efficiency was no longer up-to-date. Development started with a V-12 minus one bank and a capacity of 2.6 liters, intended for the XJ Coupe of the mid-1970s. This was not sufficiently powerful, so the stroke was extended to 90mm and 3.4 liters. This would have necessitated an engine block higher than could be produced on the existing tools. Another experiment was the 3.8-liter XK engine with an alloy block and 24-valve cylinder head. Production of this could have been made possible at little cost, but this engine did not seem to be advanced enough, although tests with prototypes showed promising results. As tooling for the XK engine was already well-worn it seemed advisable to address some other shortcomings of the XK engine at the same time (weight, the block not extending below the crankshaft axis, position of the bolts, and so on.)

Initially it was planned to create a diesel version of the new engine. This is why the basic dimensions (91mm bore and 92mm stroke) were so similar to a five-cylinder Mercedes-Benz diesel engine that had been purchased for evaluation. In the case of the Jaguar six-cylinder, the capacity was 3.6 liters. The AJ 6 had the same cylinder axis as the XK unit, so that at least some basic tooling could be used again, thus avoiding expensive new equipment. In February 1979 it was decided that the new engine would be unveiled in the XJ-S, not the forthcoming XJ 40. The previous XK and V-12 engines also had been first introduced in smaller-series sports cars (XK 120 and E-Type Series 3) rather than the sedan (Mark VII and XJ 12). During development tests showed that the AJ 6 would not run as smoothly as the XK. A more careful balancing of the crankshaft was necessary.

Despite delivering performance not much inferior to the V-12, the new AJ 6 was particularly economical to run, but in everyday use disadvantages like a lack of flexibility (the most noticeable merit of the XK) and smoothness became obvious. Enthusiasts were thus very reluctant to accept the new design. The gear lever, with its four planes, was also criticized, although the lack of an automatic version was not—it was delivered only from February 1987 onward. All in all the 3.6—which was of course available in the XJ-S coupe as well—had a much more sporting character than the large V-12.

Early in 1984 the XJ-S 3.6 took revenge for a not very favorable comparison against Mercedes-Benz in *Auto Motor und Sport* of 1977. Its interior was a great advance, while Mercedes-Benz now had a much-improved 500 SEC. The XJ-SC 3.6 also compared favorably according to the German magazine, which acclaimed the new engine's looks, sound, and performance, despite some jerk at part-throttle, which still had to be remedied by new programming of the throttle cut-off. "The legend grows—a true and suitable slogan," wrote tester Klaus Westrup. When testing the XJ-S 3.6 in 1984, Wolfgang König discovered the lack of low-range torque, a problem that Jaguar engineers were working overtime to remedy. "The taste is right, but some more maturity would benefit," König said.

The new engine again helped raise interest in the XJ-S, so that Jaguar thought about further variants. In 1984 another prototype convertible, without the flying buttresses, but unlike the 1980 effort, on the normal wheelbase, was completed. With Daimler crinkles on its grille and trunk plinth, this would have been a Double-Six S, but the project was not continued.

Instead, the XJ-SC with a V-12 engine was unveiled on July 17, 1985. The assembly of both Cabriolets was relocated to Jaguar alone. Soon *Auto Motor und Sport* had a test car available, and Wolfgang König resumed, "Now it shows that only the V-12 makes open motoring a true therapy. With the V-12, performance was effortless. If power is needed, it is just there, most discreetly and nearly inaudible." In the course of a general renaming this model lost its H.E. abbreviation and now got the even more complicated but clearer name XJ-SC V-12. As such, *Auto Motor und Sport* soon compared it with the Mercedes-Benz SL, Porsche Carrera, and the less popular Ferrari Mondial—at the appropriate Côte d'Azur location. The coupe also did quite

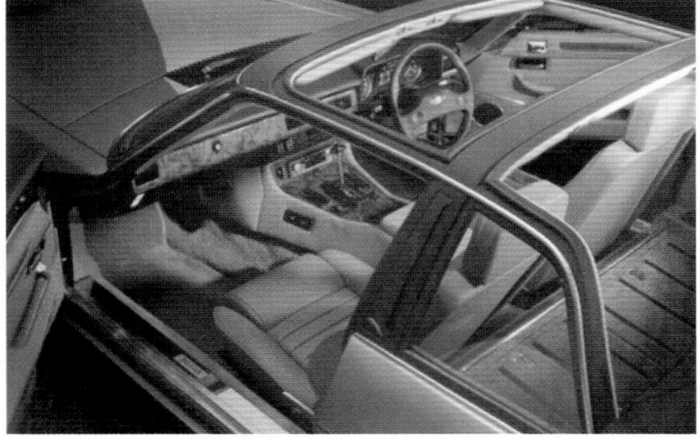

well in a comparison with the equivalents of the same competitors. Götz Leyrer repeated his inevitable lyrics about the merits of the Mercedes-Benz, but even he had to admit: "Finest exclusivity and refinement are offered by the Jaguar."

In 1985, Jochen Arden brought out his XJ-S full convertible, which he called "Roadster." Arden had started a Jaguar dealership in 1981 at Kleve, also offering appearance and engine modifications for different Jaguar models—in Germany he had no competition in this field! In 1988, Arden introduced a twin-turbocharger upgrade for the six-cylinder (330 horsepower was the result) and rear seats for the XJ-SC of best Jaguar quality. In September Arden unveiled his highly elegant interpretation of an XJ-S coupe *sans* flying buttresses, aerodynamic improvements, (suitable for the standard coupe as well) and a 320 horsepower V-12 with an optional five-speed manual gearbox. British dealer Guy Salmon found other ways to improve the XJ-S. He had an H.E. coupe (VIN SAJJN-LAW3BC115439) extended behind the front seats by 10 inches, clad in duotone silver and blue leather, finished in similar shades, and registered "JAG 2."

Only from April 1986 onward, the XJ-SC was available in the United States as a V-12 only. From October 29,

Above left: The XJ-SC V-12 was a very luxurious car. *(J)*

Above: The XJ-SC's top allowed some interesting variations. *(J)*

Left: Open drive with style—the Jaguar XJ-SC V-12. *(J)*

Above: Jochen Arden always found ways to improve Jaguars. *(Arden)*

Below: Cutting off the flying buttresses made the XJ-S much more attractive. *(Arden)*

1986, until early 1988, Leonia, where Jaguar's U.S. distributor was now located, offered a full convertible with an electrically folding top. This was made at Hess & Eisenhardt at Cincinnati, Ohio, established 1876. This car had two fuel tanks—the upper emptied into the lower one, although the pipe joining them had a tendency to leak. The modification was truly hand-made, and thus the car was rather expensive at £47,000.

XJ-SC production ended in September 1987 for the 3.6 and February 1988 for the V-12. The XJ-S 3.6 coupe had stiffer spring and damper settings for the 1988 model year, which was more to the taste of sporting drivers, while the V-12 remained the elegant GT.

In May 1985, a team of 12 within Jaguar had been advised by Egan to design a full convertible to replace the XJ-SC. This team decided to subcontract the design of the top mechanism and the prototype building to Karmann in Osnabrück. Thanks to this Westphalian aid the XJ-S V-12 convertible indeed debuted at the Geneva show in March 1988. The floor pan was ingeniously strengthened, although this could not eliminate the flexing that is so typical for convertibles. Developing sound- and vibration-damping engine and gearbox mounts caused considerable headaches. Thirty combinations were finally tested in the desert near Phoenix, Arizona. The first prototype ran in March 1987, but final prototype tests stretched out to November at MIRA.

The top of the XJ-S convertible was special in that it could be opened electrically in 12 seconds; only two clamps at the windshield frame had to be opened manually. The top was fully lined with light cloth; the rear window was glass and could be heated. Unfortunately, the rear side window could not be wound down completely, so the looks of the open car were a bit untidy. A hand crank was among the tools supplied with the car, just in case the electrics would not work. Although the convertible seemed to be very similar to the coupe, about one-third of the body panels differed. The bodies were again made at Castle Bromwich, where electronically steered trolleys transported them from station to station—a system that cost Jaguar £3.6 million. The very rigid top frame, which had to be made to very exacting standards, was the only body part made at Browns Lane, and it was mounted to the car there as well.

The XJ-S Convertible was tested by Klaus Westrup for *Auto Motor und Sport.* "With this XJ-S convertible, Jaguar has created a new superlative: It is the only V-12 convertible in series production. It is a car for estates, the owners of which have no reason to complain about bad agricultural results." Modern times took their toll, in this case in the form of the catalytic converters: "In combination with the lethargic three-speed automatic, the car is not more than well powered," Westrup wrote. But in the end the question was: "What is it that was better in former times?"

On August 22, 1988, a sporty XJ-S debuted as XJR-S, the first product of Jaguar Sport Limited, a 50/50 joint venture of Jaguar established on May 9 with Tom Walkinshaw, who was as successful as a businessman as he was at the steering wheel of his racers. Jaguar Sport Limited was situated at Kidlington, where Walkinshaw also prepared his racing cars. Distribution of the XJR-S was at first limited to select dealers, but was later opened to all. The first 100 XJR-Ss were called Celebration, after another win in the Le Mans 24 Hours; these were finished in dark metallic gray with beige leather piped gray. The doorsills carried numbered plates. The sporting XJR-S differed from its normal siblings by spoilers, sills, large wheels with unusually wide Pirelli P 600 tires, and stiffer suspension. The typical Jaguar ride comfort was generally maintained, however. The body parts had been offered separately by TWR since 1984, a business that Walkinshaw gave up when establishing Jaguar Sport.

On June 16, 1989 the XJ-S Collection Rouge was introduced to the United States. This was a standard XJ-S V-12 coupe finished bright red with golden coachlines, diamond polished lattice alloys, and an interior in breathtaking magnolia leather with bright red piping—even the steering wheel and gear lever were magnolia. The wood panels on the dash and doors were veneered elm.

A new XJR-S was ready in August 1989, and a 6.0 badge indicated the new engine size. *Autocar & Motor* (the magazines just had merged) detected only slightly improved performance with the complicated engine with its elaborate cylinder head. The springing was stiffened again. In Europe the car was only available from May 1990.

Auto Motor und Sport was impressed by the performance of the 6.0: "The Jaguar gains speed in a

Above left: The XJR-S from Jaguar Sport was a very powerful grand tourer. *(J)*

Above: XJ-S convertible interior in typical Jaguar tradition. *(S)*

Below: Only the 1988 convertible was a truly open Jaguar. *(J)*

unique and unrepeatable way, with well-subdued sound and gentle jerks indicating the change of gears, which in the worst case only happens twice when accelerating." The power must have been a bit too much in one or another corner for Klaus Westrup: "A dinosaur—in the long term an endangered species."

On September 18, 1990, the XJ-S V-12 Le Mans Special Edition was unveiled at the Motor Show at the Birmingham NEC. Only 280 examples were made, with quad headlamps, forged 16-inch alloy wheels, particularly smooth Autolux leather, selected burled walnut veneers, a four-spoke steering wheel, and thick Wilton carpets. Again the model number was engraved on the kick plates. At the same time, a special Classic Collection model was introduced to the United States.

The XJ-S was chosen by many as a foundation for their tuning efforts. Most advanced among these seems to have been Lawrence Pearce with WP Automotive, established around 1985. After 1987 he called his products Lister, with Brian's permission. The latter-day Mark 3 Lister of 1989 had 6-liter capacity and 465 horsepower. With a Getrag five-speeder, the racer accelerated to 60 miles per hour in just five seconds! The coupe cost £55,000, the convertible a lofty £73,000. In April 1989 the Lister Le Mans arrived, with a hood extended further forward, an accordingly elongated front end, and a 7-liter engine (bore 94, stroke 84mm) with 496 horsepower at 6,200 rpm. This monster had 10-inch-wide wheels at the front and 13-inch at the rear, with 245 and 335 tires. Acceleration time to 60 miles per hour was reduced to under five seconds. From mid-1990 the Le Mans was available as a convertible at £165,000. From 1993 the Mark 3 and Le Mans were offered with twin turbos and 540 horsepower. The Mark 3 alterations cost £65,000. Despite these prices, about 150 Mark 3s and 35 Le Mans are said to have been sold.

18 A SECOND SERIES 3

Contrary to Jaguar's plans, its range of models was still mainly derived from Sir William Lyons' legacy, the XJ sedan. The inability of Jaguar and Leyland to decide on the styling of a completely new Jaguar sedan gave the older model a longer life. In order to counter an anticipated sales decrease, the existing car had to be given a fresh look—as with the Mark VIII and 3.8-liter S. In 1974 under Robinson, another modernization of the existing sedan had been investigated. In 1976 it was decided that this was the way to go, with the help of no less than master stylist Sergio "Pinin" Farina. As briefed, he left the lower body more or less untouched—cost had to be saved—but his firm formed a completely new glasshouse with larger windows, now all curved, and more headroom for the rear passengers—at the cost of the feline rounded roofline. The new bumpers with large rubber elements were practical but not very nice, while the enlarged rear lights now extended toward the trunk lid, giving a marvelous impression, considering the limited possibilities. So the Jaguar XJ became the only car in which the brilliance of both the Italian and the British design geniuses of their period were combined in a sculpture of downright objective beauty. Under this fascinating hull the car offered practical modernizations: improved front seats with adjustable lumbar supports and an injection system for the 4.2-liter, saving fuel and reducing emissions alike. With its 205 DIN horsepower (for all countries with less severe emission laws) this variant may well have been the most powerful variant of the XK engine apart from racing specials. The former, higher figures were to SAE standard, which ignored the power lost through exhaust and auxiliaries and had been somewhat rounded up, as had been customary in the old days. Tooling-up for XJ Series 3 production cost Jaguar about £7 million.

In this form the XJ had its third introduction at Torquay on March 28, 1979. Jaguar models now had the number of cylinders and engine capacity as part of their names. For the first time the XJ 6 3.4 was officially imported to Europe, as were the Daimler and Vanden Plas variants, the latter as the Double-Six, however. In the United States the XJ 12, with its still considerable thirst, was not a politically correct car, so only the 4.2 was offered there.

Above: An early XJ 12 with amber badges. *(J)*

Right: The chromed flush-fitting door handles were exquisitely styled. *(J)*

Below right: XJ Series 3s were the first Jaguars with headlamp washers. *(J)*

Opposite: Pininfarina made the XJ style much clearer with the 1979 Series 3, this car being a 3.4. *(J)*

Above: The noble Vanden Plas Series 3 was the first to be officially exported to Europe. *(J)*

Right: The Daimler Vanden Plas 4.2 Series 2 is a rarity outside Britain. *(St)*

While the Series 2 was always in ready supply, the Series 3 4.2 initially was in high demand and production could not keep up. Supply was hampered by the paint shop that, after a delayed start, only had a limited output. This new paint shop had cost Leyland £15.5 million; it was the most advanced in England, covering more than 50,000 square feet over two floors at Castle Bromwich north of Birmingham, where the XJ-S and (since 1978) XJ bodies were made. Castle Bromwich was another shadow factory erected in 1938 for Morris. After World War II it had been taken over by Fischer & Ludlow which, after its merger with Pressed Steel, was involved in the supply of bodies for Jaguar.

Until 1979 the painting had taken place at Browns Lane so that the final coat would be applied after the test drive, thus avoiding damage during the transport from Castle Bromwich to Browns Lane and the test drive. Now the paint had to be applied before delivery to Browns Lane and eventual blemishes had to be rectified by hand. This was only one of the disadvantages staff was more aware of than management: The thermoplastic acrylic paint gave a mirror-like surface superior to any other paint, but this required efforts from everyone involved that a layman could not imagine. The metal below the paint had to be just as mirror-like, as this perfect paint would make the slightest unevenness visible, particularly in lead-loaded joints, of which the Jaguar bodies had so many. The lead was prone to melt during the heating process that allowed the paint to produce this mirror-like surface. For this reason it seemed advisable to choose paint with a low melting point. If it was too low, however, sun or engine heat could make the color melt, causing cracks and creases—to the despair of thousands of Jaguar customers. This became a huge challenge for Jaguar, and it was 1981 before the whole range of colors was available in acceptable quality.

A further change in production concerned Vanden Plas in Kingsbury, where the noblest XJ variants and the Daimler limousine had received paint and interior. In the course of a certainly sensible rationalization, this plant was closed down, and the painting transferred to the new shop at Castle Bromwich. This resulted in the loss of individual color schemes for the Vanden Plas variants. (Until mid-1980, some Vanden Plas were still painted with traditional schemes.) The interior was

now assembled at Browns Lane, the leather colors now being unified for all Jaguar, Daimler, and Vanden Plas models as well. The high level of trim was maintained with the Vanden Plas, and this is why a considerable part of the nearly 300 Vanden Plas employees at Kingsbury also moved to Coventry.

After all these changes it took some time until magazines could be provided with test vehicles. *Motor* published its report on an automatic 4.2 in September 1979, noticing moderate fuel consumption and good performance. In their opinion the automatic preferred the upper gears a bit too much. *Car* compared a similar car with the new Mercedes-Benz V-8, which was livelier and more economical, while the Jaguar offered more luxury and refinement.

The American magazine *Road & Track* tested an XJ Series 3 in September 1980 and surprisingly disapproved of the new seats with lumbar supports, reported more wind noise than before, and reminded readers of Jaguar's bad reputation for quality.

Since 1980 Wolfgang König was the expert at *Auto Motor und Sport* for Jaguar and other British makes, and his reports always were a pleasure to read. He started with a test of the latest XJ 6 and XJ 12 sedans. He recalled the German importer's (now called Leyland GmbH) latest advertising campaign showing the XJ in a sort of jungle. König praised the newly sharpened claws which were so helpful in the fight for new customers. "Through today the Jaguar has kept its attractive appearance. One of the most impressive aspects of living with a Jaguar is the engine bay, which is completely filled with obviously complicated mechanics. Speedy traveling is its domain rather than hectic rushing, and in this the Jaguar excels with its extraordinary refinement. Only true enthusiasts will attain happiness with it."

Avon Ladbroke, who already had transformed XJ coupes into convertibles, took Series 3 sedans—and sometimes older XJ variants—and made somewhat bizarre estate cars, using—like Lynx with the Eventer—the parts bin of a French manufacturer, in this case the hatchback of the Renault 5. When introduced at the 1980 Birmingham Motor Show, the car won a gold medal for its design although its proportions were somewhat reminiscent of a hearse. This transformation was only offered for a few years.

At the same time Jaguar introduced a more practical XJ variant, reducing the level of equipment. With a simpler radio and manual aerial, the 3.4-liter could be offered at £12,750—less than typical business cars like the Ford Granada Ghia or the Rover 3500. Jaguar also looked at giving the XJ VM diesel engines, but these experiments did not end up in the range of models. Independently, Austrian Steyr tested its somewhat unorthodox diesel engine in a Series 3 XJ because the car's perfect noise suppression helped hide the clatter of this self-igniting engine. This project also stopped before it left prototype stage.

While the higher compression V-12 was secretly used in the XJ 12 in 1980, the H.E. engine was officially announced for the sedans in June 1981. When *Auto Motor und Sport* compared the H.E. with its BMW and Mercedes-Benz competitors in mid-1982, the Daimler Double-Six Vanden Plas was chosen deliberately, as its full equipment made it about one-third more expensive than the others. The testers made a disadvantage of the armrests' convenient position close to the seats: "Driver and front passenger are downright walled in between door and transmission tunnel." But he added, "The Daimler has all that is convenient for driving comfort." "In a hurry happiness will not be attained with the Daimler." The engine was praised: "The engine teaches what smoothness can mean for a piston engine." It was emphasized, of course, that the smoothness of this free-revving short-stroke engine was due to the automatic preferring the upper gears.

Only weeks later the 1983 range of models for Europe was changed: The Daimler Sovereign was renamed Jaguar Sovereign, the Daimler Double-Six became the Jaguar Sovereign H.E. (replacing the XJ 12 5.3 as well), and the Vanden Plas became the Jaguar Vanden Plas H.E. Only the basic XJ 6 3.4 and XJ 6 4.2 retained their names. Obviously too many customers were puzzled by the Daimler name having no connection with the Stuttgart manufacturer. A true improvement was the new center console with wooden panels instead of metal, but otherwise radical change was avoided.

For the 1983 model year the Daimler Vanden Plas 4.2 was made available in the United States, albeit under the Jaguar Vanden Plas designation. The similar V-12 variant was introduced in parallel in Canada.

Around this time supply of the five-speed manual gearbox started in quantity (for the six-cylinder engines) at last. This was developed from Jaguar's own five-speeder project of the early 1970s with smaller diameter shafts (saving weight), now somewhat readapted by Jaguar and made even more silent. The first test of a five-speed Jaguar was published in *Autocar*. It was claimed that the lack of a torque converter made vibrations from the long crankshaft perceptible as well as distortion of the rear subframe. The position of the clutch pedal in the narrow footwell was not ideal, but fuel consumption was low. With the XJ 6's gigantic torque at low revs, the testers were tempted to a drive in top gear from John O'Groats to Land's End—as had been done in a Sheffield-Simplex in 1911, and the long-stroke engine calmly acquiesced to this torture. Meanwhile, Wolfgang König reported in *Auto Motor und Sport*: "Never before has it been as attractive as now. It did not remain unnoticed at Jaguar that the XJ 6 is not just a piece of art, but an object of utility in the first line.

Top: Not the most elegant station wagon, this XJ variation was carried out by Avon. *(St))*

Above: Nevertheless, even Daimler was not safe from the operation. *(St))*

The gear change is light and exact. Finally it cures the filling-up trauma many Jaguar drivers suffer from. If engineers talk of a torque engine these days, this classic engine exemplifies what they talk about. Experts expect a successor with a completely new engine for the spring of 1984. It remains to be seen if this will have similar genes of a delightful classic."

Some weeks later Klaus Westrup confirmed the positive impression the five-speed gearbox made in conjunction with the less powerful 3.4-liter engine. "Nice to have such cars around!" Some further weeks later the manual 4.2 was compared to the Mercedes-Benz 280 SE: "The Jaguar confirms what is promised in its name, and takes a very short run before jumping." However, the Mercedes-Benz handled better and was more economical and solid. All in all the merits of these two very different characters balanced out.

From September 1983, Harrods offered a particularly fine variant of the XJ 6 4.2, finished dark green with light beige leather. The doors were covered in cloth with Harrods emblems arranged in a pattern. The all-but-frugal equipment comprised TV, video, and audio units, a golden mantel clock and a refrigerated bar. The price of £35,000 was £20,000 above the normal price. The car was made by Panther chief Robert Jankel, hence the Panther badge at the trunk lid, and no second example was ever made. Soon after that, RS Panels of Nuneaton took the idea even further and extended a few XJ Series 3s by 32 inches and increased their height by 4 inches, the result of which was a quite attractive chauffeur limousine.

At the same time the range for Great Britain was changed according to the previous year's European changes. The two Vanden Plas models were now named Daimler 4.2 and Daimler Double-Six.

At this time Otl Aicher published a book *kritik am auto* which indulged in plain *Bauhaus* style. It was all about car styling, and the Jaguar was one of the subjects. The author accepted the Mark II with its dead straight door cut-outs. "Jaguar elevated above fashion,

Above: For the 1983 model year, a new center console with wood veneers was introduced. *(J)*

Right: Maggie Thatcher preferred Daimler cars—here a 1987 Double-Six. *(J)*

creating the style of unadornedness," despite all its chromed grilles, carefully designed badges, chrome, and wood! Of its sporting contemporary the author found less favorable words: "The E-Type was a soft, wavy, long cigar with much space for the engine, empty space for a seemingly aerodynamic nose but a trunk sufficient for a weekend trip only." Not knowing about the car's real history and Malcolm Sayer's talent, it was presumed: "and its line was not developed in a wind tunnel." No wonder that even the XJ sedan, with its nearly undoubted beauty, would not stand the academic test—the XJ-S came off even worse: "The functional car changed to a representative gesture." This statement may be right, but it also describes what some cars are intended for, and the Jaguar has the honor to belong among these.

John Egan's quality drive had prompted a 50,000-mile endurance test of an XJ 6 4.2 in *Auto Motor und Sport*."Why not a spleen?" was the title. It became obvious that more than most other cars, the Jaguar's reliability depended on the quality of inspection and maintenance. It also showed that the five-speed gearbox was barely strong enough for the mighty torque of the 4.2-liter engine. The Jaguar stood the test without breaking down, and this was quite an achievement, considering the bad reputation of the marque then. The lavish equipment made minor faults inevitable, but these were not rated too highly.

The most important change for 1986 was the replacement of the H.E. designation with the clearer V-12. At the same time the standard Jaguar models received wood door panels similar to the Sovereign.

The Sovereign 4.2 now had new alloy wheels with holes in two circles, reminiscent of peppermills. Fog lights, two electrically adjustable door mirrors, electric seat height adjustment, trip computer, rear headrests, safety belts and reading lamps, thick Vanden Plas-style rugs and automatic air conditioning were new Sovereign features. The Sovereign V-12 also had headlamp washers and wipers and a better radio. Both Daimlers were separated from the Jaguars by a sunroof, old-style Kent alloys, individual rear seats instead of a bench, and whitewood inlays in the wooden door panels.

When in late 1985 the top model XJ for Europe was, after only three years, again renamed Daimler Double-Six, the Vanden Plas name disappeared from all but the North American markets. This had been agreed upon with what now was Austin Rover. *Auto Motor und Sport* tested it early in 1986 as a "grille specialty" as it was Daimler's 90th anniversary. Wolfgang König explained about Daimler that "outside the British Isles ignorance still prevails." This was quite true, as was proven once again when German magazine *Der Spiegel* illustrated a report about Rolls-Royce with a photo of a DS 420, in this case the example that had been delivered to Her Majesty Queen Elizabeth the Queen Mother in 1974! Coming back to the test it was "assured that in this case only the very finest ingredients have been chosen, while the equivalent Jaguar makes do—by now quite believably—with the finest." The Daimler also did well in comparison with the flagship of Mercedes.

All the more, Arthur Wolstenholme was delighted with the qualities of the XJ chassis. Beginning in 1981 as Ronart Cars Limited he tried again what Robert Jankel had done, although in a different manner. His classic roadster had no particular 1930s sports car as an archetype. However, it took some years before his car was fully developed. The result was unveiled at the Birmingham Motor Show in October 1986 under the name Ronart W 152. With its separate fenders, its light, rounded body, and visible exhaust pipes, it exuded a classic appeal. The body was mainly from fiberglass. In its home country the W 152 was a success, but internationally it was not as well known as the Panther J 72 had been.

Production of the XJ 6 ended in Europe with the 1986 model year and a special series of 100 cars finished in dark green with beige leather. In North America it soldiered on another season until May 1, 1987, with VIN 477823 as the last car delivered to a customer (in Los Angeles) and 477824, a Sovereign finished metallic red for the Jaguar-Daimler Heritage Trust (JDHT) museum. Production of the XJ 12 continued in small numbers on what had been the pilot assembly track for the succeeding six-cylinder sedan. In Germany for the first time a V-12 sedan could be rented from one of the large companies (Avis). Arden also had assorted parts for enhancing the classic sedan, including more wood for the interior. The most impressive items were a front center console seemingly carved from a solid block of wood, and a rear console filled with electronics.

Sovereign 4.2 and Sovereign H.E. had been Daimlers before. *(St)*

Top: In the late 1980s a Jaguar was available for rent in Germany for the first time. *(JAGMAG archive)*

Above: The XJS steering wheel did not perfectly suit the 1991 Jaguar V-12 sedan. *(J)*

The XJ Series 3 carefully improved by Arden. *(Arden)*

From August 1, 1990, (and in Germany one year earlier), the renowned Series 3 was modernized with antilock brakes and a three-way catalytic converter. On September 22, 1990, Ital Design unveiled its Kensington study, a much-admired sedan based on the Sovereign V-12. The latter still remained in production, even if some felt it was out of date by then. However, there were quite a few experts who still preferred the Series 3 to its successor for a long journey, even when its production ceased with VIN 487641 (a black Daimler Double-Six with doeskin leather for the JDHT) on November 30, 1992, more than six years after the successor had been introduced.

The conservative British government under "Iron Lady" Margaret Thatcher would have liked to privatize British Leyland, but this was not possible as long as no profits could be expected. The solution was a partial privatization. From the end of 1981 this concentrated around Jaguar, as its XJ and XJ-S became more and more popular, bringing the company back to profit. Sir Michael Edwardes did not like the idea of privatizing Jaguar. But he did not prolong his five-year contract and left Leyland in 1982. Egan, however, saw the opportunity to secure Jaguar's individuality and separate it from the rest of Leyland. Egan was a Thatcherist indeed; he saw conservative ideas as the only way to salvage British industry. In 1983, privatization became the center of Thatcher's economic politics, making Jaguar a darling of the conservative government.

On January 1, 1984, a newly established Jaguar Deutschland GmbH at Schwalbach (but then moving to elegant new premises in nearby Kronberg in 1985) became responsible for Jaguar imports to Germany. This was a joint venture of Jaguar and Swiss importer Emil Frey. Its first managing director was Otto Prinz zu Sayn-Wittgenstein, followed after March 1, 1987, by Lars-Roger Schmidt, who came from Porsche. The spokesman was Peter Schack who was well known in classic car circles. Similar to the German arrangement, a Jaguar Austria GmbH was established at Salzburg.

In May 1984, Minister of Industry Norman Tebbitt officially made way for Jaguar's privatization. Until then he had tried unsuccessfully to convince his colleagues that 25 percent of the shares should remain with the government. A management buyout was vetoed by Austin Rover (previously Leyland Cars).

Egan and his colleagues had arranged financing of the £50 million that Jaguar had been estimated to be worth in the beginning—but this dream was not to come true for John Egan. In order to make possible Jaguar's survival after separation from Austin Rover, some further changes were necessary. One of them concerned the spare parts organization UNIPART, the BL spares organization, with which a special contract had to be concluded to secure future Jaguar spares availability. This happened in July 1984. The contract survived the privatization of UNIPART, which only took place many years later. Another contract with Austin Rover was about the supply of body panels, which were not made at Castle Bromwich. At the same time the Jaguar Daimler Heritage Trust was founded as Jaguar's archive and museum. All classic cars in Jaguar's possession were transferred to the JDHT. However, it still took many years before a museum could be opened to the public. Still today, Jaguar owners can order a certificate from the JDHT confirming their car's specification and other data of their car's history.

As announced per June 14, a total of 180 million 25-pence shares of Jaguar plc, the holding parent of Jaguar Cars Ltd., became available on August 3, 1984, at the Stock Exchange. The sale could have resulted in foreign companies gaining power over Jaguar. General Motors, Ford, and BMW showed interest, but such a solution was politically unadvisable. Only a so-called golden share remained with the government for six years, prohibiting an unfriendly take-over of more than 15 percent of the shares. The shares were over-subscribed eightfold at the Stock Exchange, a great success, not only for Margaret Thatcher. Only Jaguar workers were reluctant. Only 20 percent of them acquired shares of their employer, which totaled to no more than one percent of all shares. Many of them later regretted their reluctance, as the value of the Jaguar shares rose steadily!

During 1984, Jaguar's improved quality allowed the company to reduce its number of quality testers from 700 to 350. Customers appreciated the improved quality of their Jaguars. The Consumer Satisfaction Index in the J. D. Power Report of 1985 saw Jaguar in fifth place among all manufacturers. This yearly study was based on interviews with buyers of new cars. Sir William Lyons thus was satisfied seeing the mistake of 1968 corrected and Jaguar back on the road to success! It was a great consolation to him to see his company recover after the bitter 1970s. On February 8, 1985, he died peacefully at Wappenbury Hall. His always beloved wife Greta only survived him by 14 months. Of his two daughters, Patricia had long since been married again.

In June 1986, John Egan, the first guiding light among Lyons' successors, was named a Knight Commander of the British Empire for his achievements in the course of Jaguar's privatization, at the opportunity of the Queen's 60th birthday. As Sir John he had the opportunity to unveil the successor to Sir William's heritage, the XJ sedan on October 8, 1986, at the Paris show.

Already back in 1972 Jaguar had been contemplating a possible new range of sedans that could be introduced in 1977. At that time it was intended to stick to the mechanics of the existing cars, but with a new six-cylinder engine derived from the V-12 and, perhaps, the V-12 itself. Retired Sir William was cautious not to interfere too much and participated only occasionally in the styling of the front and rear ends, which were reminiscent of the then also still-born XJ-S. Such a works prototype was rejected by Sir Donald Stokes on October 26, 1973, being too similar to previous Jaguar sedans. At this occasion Stokes had been presented the first 1:1 clay model ever of a future Jaguar; it followed an idea of Cyril Crouch. Ironically, this car was quite similar to the final point of development 13 years later.

Geoffrey Robinson, then Jaguar's managing director, made use of his Italian connections and ordered models from the three leading designers: Pininfarina, Bertone, and Ital Design. Pininfarina just had exhibited a six-window XJ 12 with very modern lines. The masters presented their ideas in the summer of 1974. Ital Design showed both a conventional and a more futuristic design. These four 1:1 models were studied in company with Jaguar's own ideas and competitors, at Browns Lane. The question of styling grew into a political one when BLMC tended to prefer a modern shape without any typical Jaguar cues, while Knight and his crew preferred more classical lines. As a consequence, it was all stopped—with the exception of the conservative study from Ital design, which became reality as the

From top: Jaguar Deutschland had nice premises at Kronberg am Taunus. *(J)*

Otto Prinz Sayn zu Wittgenstein, chief of Jaguar Deutschland. *(JAGMAG archive)*

Lars-Roger Schmidt, his successor. *(J)*

Top: These were designs from which the BLMC board had to choose in 1974. *(S)*

Above: The rear view of the same car—not very British. *(S)*

Top: An Italian proposal for the XJ 40. *(S)*

Above: The XJ 40 as imagined by Bertone in 1974. *(S)*

Below: Pininfarina's idea of a Jaguar V-12 sedan. *(S)*

Maserati Quattroporte. From 1976, when Ital Design and Bertone showed revised models, BLMC people started to call the project LC 40 (LC standing for Leyland Cars), to the chagrin of the Jaguar development people under Bob Knight. They obstinately continued to call the new car XJ 40 and to propagandize the traditional Jaguar styling.

Among these development people was Jim Randle, who until 1965 had worked for Rover, where he had been part of the team that had developed the then ultramodern Rover 2000. It was Randle who, in 1978–1979, made Jaguar stylist George Thompson delve into the current Jaguar models and then sketch the new car. This sketch was more or less what was to be unveiled as a successor to Lyons' design in 1986. When the design was presented to the Leyland board in May 1980, it was by no means sure that the money for further development would be granted. But now the right decision was taken, and in February 1981, £77.93 million was granted for development and tooling up. In the end the project was to cost more than £200 million, including £50 million for development alone by the remarkably small development team of only about 300 people. The BMW 7 series, which was developed at the same time and was targeted at the same market, cost a multiple of that sum.

Now the detailed specifications had to be determined. Development aimed at reducing complexity in order to make production cheaper and improve quality. Another aim was better reliability with a reduction of warranty claims by 50 percent—compared to the XJ Series 3—and a lifetime for the engine of 150,000 miles without major revision. The latest toy for development engineers was computer-aided design (CAD), which made changes to drawings much easier and could be linked to preparation for production. Randle was well aware of the advances, but also cautioned that human intelligence cannot be fully replaced by computer know-how.

The first XJ 40 prototype ran in July 1981. The rising sales figures for Series 3 gave additional time for development and testing. From 1983 to 1986 around 400 prototypes were made on a special pilot assembly line and then tested over 5.5 million miles. This pilot line in particular is said to have helped considerably to avoid teething problems. Test drives were undertaken in all parts of the world in order to verify the effects of different climatic conditions. Prototypes were exposed to

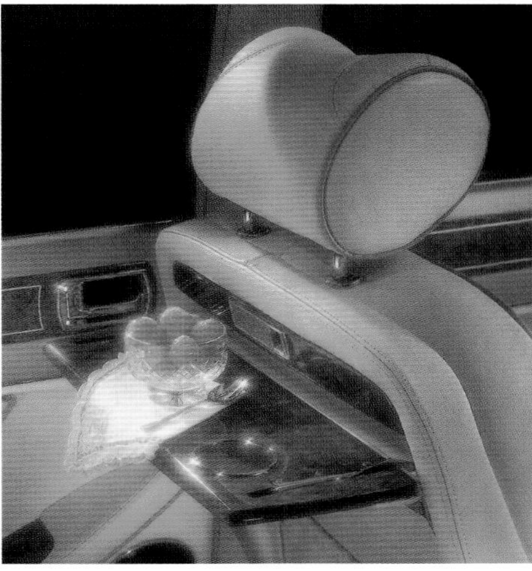

The wonderfully executed picnic tables of the Daimler were much applauded. *(J)*

desert heat and arctic freeze, put to the acid test in humid and dusty climates, rushed at high speed along German autobahns, and ruthlessly shoed through the worst potholes of Manhattan. When all weak spots seemed to have been discovered and rectified, series production quietly started in July 1986. So the longest gestation period for a new Jaguar model came to an end.

The new XJ 6 debuted during the Paris show on October 8, 1986, with 2.9- and 3.6-liter engines of the AJ 6 series, which had been introduced before in the XJ-S 3.6. They were combined with manual gearboxes of German Getrag manufacture or automatics from ZF (Zahnradfabrik Friedrichshafen). Both were also available as better-equipped Sovereign models and the 3.6 as a Daimler as well. The car had been introduced to the press earlier at Scottish Dunkeld. More than 400 reporters took the opportunity to be spoiled by Jaguar. While England was delighted with the new design and Europe was relieved that no more radical change had taken place, the design did not really appeal to the otherwise less traditionally minded Americans, who bemoaned the loss of the Series 3.

When XJ 40 production started, some minor assembly problems arose. Despite all engineering

Above: The perhaps too advanced dashboard of the XJ 40. *(J)*

Below: The XJ 6 2.9 was the least expensive XJ 40. *(J)*

Top: The dawn of a new era with the XJ 40 in its three levels of equipment. *(J)*

Above: The rear end of the Daimler 3.6 was rather staid. *(J)*

efforts the Series 3, which stayed in small-scale V-12 production, became the most reliable model with the lowest rate of warranty claims. Creation of the highly innovative electrics of XJ 40 was a most challenging task for the engineers, and the electrics were to become the Achilles heel of the model. With all sorts of setbacks, it would be 1988 before full production was reached.

During the early 1980s it was feared the XJ 6 could be too expensive and thirsty for a modern society that was no longer interested in luxury cars. An economy version had seriously been considered, but it turned out that the lack of a V-12 variant was the loudest criticism when the car was unveiled; Jaguar's German competitors were preparing such variants. Jaguar had to redesign the deliberately narrow engine bay of the XJ 40 to fit the V-12. This was another reprieve for Series 3 V-12.

Thanks to some refinement of the front suspension and to the new design of the rear, ride comfort and roadholding were excellent—*Motor* even found it superior to the Mercedes-Benz. In international comparison the fuel consumption was slightly excessive. The very modern dash with its digital readouts—the pride of Jaguar's engineers—was not accepted by the mostly conservative customers. This had showed at customer clinics during 1980 and 1981 but Jaguar had been determined to build a very modern car! The indicator stalk was criticized in particular for turning off by pushing it a second time in the same direction, not the opposite one as with all other cars.

The first test of XJ 40 in *Auto Motor und Sport* was a "good show." Nevertheless Wolfgang König stated: "Regrettably she goes, the classic Jaguar, the Mona Lisa of sedans." With relief he pointed out that in general nothing had changed to the worse, but had become somewhat more modern, up-to-date. Even fuel consumption had been reduced. With regard to the already well-known engine, the test said: "Smoothness . . . could be improved all over the rev range." "For Jaguar drivers the new automatic is a big step forward." The revised rear suspension was appreciated: "The advance becomes evident particularly on twisty country roads." "It certainly is the improved handling that adds a new dimension to Jaguar driving." The comparison with BMW 735i and Mercedes-Benz 420 SE showed that the Jaguar now was much more similar to them, with some minor exceptions like "functionality." The new model had a more efficient air, while the older was more charming. "If style is more important than function, then the Double-Six offers the optimum."

In 1988 Arden added two IHI turbochargers to the XJ 40, which lifted the maximum speed above 155 miles per hour. The car was called AJ (Arden Jaguar, not Advanced Jaguar as in the six-cylinder engine's designation) 5 Biturbo. In 1991 Arden moved from Kleve to Krefeld. A center console completely made of wood soon was added to the Arden range of parts for the XJ 40—a Belgian masterpiece of craftsmanship.

At RJ Design Limited, established by the well-known Robert Jankel, a two-door coupe "le Marquis" version of the XJ 40 could be ordered; the transformation cost was £20,000.

At the Birmingham Motor Show in October 1988, the XJR 3.6, with stiffer suspension, spoilers, and color-coded accessories was introduced by Jaguar Sport. Like the similarly modified XJR-S, this model was not for export.

In September 1989 the stroke of the 3.6 engine was extended by 10mm to attain a capacity of 4 liters. Finally the AJ 6 engine had the low-range torque that was associated with a Jaguar six. Engine management was improved and extended; a catalytic converter causing less exhaust backpressure was standard. The increased capacity returned the power that before had been swallowed by the catalyst. The dashboard had much more wood and dispensed with the higher-tech look; instead it had more round dials. Götz Leyrer was satisfied in his *Auto Motor und Sport* test report under the title "Silent Night" (reminding the expert of Daimler's old motto "Silent Knight"). The changes to the dashboard, fuel consumption, and power were welcomed. "The flaws of the Jaguar have been thoroughly cured," he said. An endurance test showed progress compared to the predecessor, but the list of failures—while limited to minor items—was still quite long. Leyrer wrote that, " . . . in direct comparison with the BMW, the British have created a convincing luxury car." The comparison with the 12-cylinder brother

Above: With the 4-liter engine, Jaguar reverted to round instruments. *(J)*

Right: The restrained lines of the Daimler 4.0. *(J)*

Above: The 1989 4-liter six-cylinder was an engineering masterpiece. *(J)*

Left: An interesting estate conversion of the XJ 40 was made at Whitley. *(J)*

Above: The 3.2-liter was a sufficiently fast vehicle for cost-conscious drivers. *(J)*

Right: As the Daimler Double-Six the long wheelbase Majestic was the Jaguar flagship. *(J)*

from the same stable ended in a tie, despite the latter's power having suffered considerably from emissions controls: "The V-12 still offers greater refinement, particularly if driven slowly. Its fans still have good reasons to love it . . . More Jaguar for the money is just not possible." In 1991 a similar comparison in *Jaguar World* (previously *Jaguar Quarterly*) ended surprisingly positive for the older car, with its more spacious interior but less precise roadholding. Its refinement—particularly with regard to the sound of the engine—was still unsurpassed. The newer car was not deemed to be more reliable than the old one. The older one's greatest disadvantage was the three-speed automatic.

On June 16, 1989, the Vanden Plas Majestic debuted in North America, a further enhanced version of the Vanden Plas (the U.S. variant of the Daimler 4.0-liter). At the same time Jaguar experimented with an estate version of a Sovereign 4.0 with very well-appointed interior. The prototype was much used by Jaguar management, but it was never added to the range of models because the elegant, sporting image of Jaguar might have suffered.

In October 1989 a new XJR was unveiled, with more power from the new 4-liter engine. After some styling changes in July 1990, the car was also available in Europe. In October 1990 the smaller engine was increased to 3.2 liters. This was now also available to European customers, although only with basic equipment. It nevertheless gained a good following. The 3.2

was tested by Thomas Fischer of *Auto Motor und Sport*, who discovered nothing surprising, as the relative lack of low-end torque could have been foreseen. Again, comments about Jaguar build quality were repeated.

Two years later a version of the XJ 40, extended by 5 inches, was introduced under the Majestic name that had already been introduced in the United States. It was available with all engine sizes. The warranty had been extended to three years or 60,000 miles. Shortly afterward a study by the British government about the consequences of traffic accidents showed that the XJ 40 was the safest car among all types offered on the British market—a slap in the face of other makes who boasted of safety in their advertisements.

After seemingly endless production, the good old XJ 12 finally came to its end late in 1992, although it had its resurgence as a 6.0-liter in an XJ 40 at the

Left: The 3.2 S helped bolster dwindling sales of XJ 40. *(J)*

Below: Only some detail betrays the 6-liter XJ 81. *(J)*

Amsterdam Auto RAI on February 3, 1993. A month later its sibling, the Daimler Double-Six, was introduced at the Geneva show. Both were available in short wheelbase or Majestic form. The 6-liter engine differed from the TWR engine of the XJR-S in that it had a less complicated cylinder head that required much less time for assembly, and thus saved a lot of money. Such an engine found its way into a Spitfire pursuit plane replica. For this unusual application the engine was equipped with four oil pumps, assuring good lubrication even when flying upside down. With 350 horsepower at 5,000 rpm, the engine was as powerful as it was reliable—an essential attribute in flying.

In mid-1993 the 3.2 was introduced in a sporting but less expensive variant called 3.2 S with rosewood on the dashboard, and for the 1994 model year a similar 4.0 S followed suit. In March 1994 a particularly fine variant with color-coded chrome parts and contrasting piping was introduced as the 3.2 Gold, again with a very favorable price in order to stimulate demand just before the model change.

19

YET ANOTHER NEW MASTER

Tom Walkinshaw, unforgettable already for his racing successes with the XJ-S, could easily convince Sir John Egan—being keen on publicity generated by racing successes—that a sports prototype with the Jaguar V-12 could be a potential winner in the Group C world sports car championship. Instead of borrowing the XJR-5 of Group 44, Walkinshaw soon decided that a completely new car would be designed with the help of Tony Southgate. The V-12 of the resulting XJR-6 had a capacity of 6,222cc (92mm bore and 78mm stroke) and again 65 horsepower. The under-floor aerodynamics of the carbon fiber body, with its channels on both sides of the narrow oil sump, produced considerably more downforce than the archrival Porsche with its boxer engine. The first test drives were carried out in June and July 1985. The XJR-6 had its first race on August 11, 1985 at Mosport in Canada, finishing a promising third (drivers were Brundle/Thackwell/Schlesser). Thanks to a contact with Gallaher (the manufacturer of Silk Cut cigarettes) provided by marketing director Neil Johnson via sponsoring expert Guy Edwards, TWR entered the scene in mauve Silk Cut colors in 1986. The engine was now bored out to 94mm, giving 6,496cc and 690 horsepower. On May 5, 1986 Derek Warwick/Eddie Cheever managed the first Jaguar win in the world sports car championship since 1957 at Le Mans in the Silverstone 1,000 kilometers. At the 1986 Le Mans race, the XJR-6s with their longer, more aerodynamic backs (distinguished by the LM suffix, which was retained for the successors) retired, however. All in all, Jaguar barely missed the constructors' championship that season.

By 1987 the XJR-6 had matured into the XJR-8 with more than 60 changes and a further enlarged engine (84mm stroke, 6,995cc, 720 horsepower). The team achieved no less than eight wins in just ten races. Raul Boesel won the drivers' and TWR-Jaguar the constructors' championship, although at Le Mans only Cheever/Boesel/Lammers made it to the finish, arriving fifth, while Lammers/Watson/Percy and Brundle/Nielsen/Hahne retired. Win Percy had an accident at over 200 miles per hour on the Mulsanne straight when suddenly his car became airborne, but fortunately he was not seriously hurt.

In 1988 TWR-Jaguar created an IMSA team at Valparaiso, Indiana, with team chief Tony Dowe, chief engineer Ian Reed, and sponsor Castrol. Guy Edwards had struck this deal on the very day of the crash at the New York Stock Exchange. The car had been further developed into the XJR-9, with 6-liter capacity and a 120-liter fuel tank for the United States, and 7-liter, 750 horsepower and a 100-liter tank for Europe. On June 11 and 12, 1988, victory finally came at Le Mans with drivers Jan Lammers/Johnny Dumfries/Andy Wallace averaging about 136 miles per hour, which is approximately one-third quicker than the D-Types in the 1950s. Kevin Kogan/Derek Daly/Larry Perkins arrived fourth, Pryce Cobb/Davy Jones/Danny Sullivan 16th, while Martin Brundle/John Nielsen and Raul Boesel/Henri Pescarolo/John Watson retired. The rest of the 1988 season also was quite successful for the XJR-9. At Brands Hatch, TWR-Jaguar was by exception forced to run a four-valve version of the V-12 that, with its additional power only just balanced its disadvantages in fuel consumption and weight.

XJR-9s also started at Le Mans in 1989 but could not repeat the previous year's win. Jan Lammers/Patrick Tambay/Andrew Gilbert-Scott finished fourth and brothers Alain and Michel Ferté/Eliseo Salazar were eighth, while Nielsen/Wallace/Cobb and Jones/Daly retired. At Tampa in the United States, Cobb achieved the last win of the long-serving XJR-9.

XJR-10 and -11 debuted, both with new V-6 engines of 3 liters and 650 horsepower (U.S.), or 3.5 liters and 750 horsepower (Europe), four valves, Bosch injection, Zytec engine management, and two Garrett turbochargers. They were well suited to the shorter sprints. The 1989 season was not quite satisfactory due to the neglected V-12 and the somewhat unreliable new engines. The only win for XJR-11—with a Bosch Motronic engine management system it was more reliable than before—was Martin Brundle/Alain Ferté's at Silverstone on May 20, 1990, from Jan Lammers/Andy Wallace. The championship in 1990 had become more of a challenge because of the newly participating Sauber-Mercedes. The V-12 XJR-12 was more successful. After a 1-2 sweep of Jones/Lammers/Wallace and Brundle/Nielsen/Cobb in the 1989 Daytona 24 Hours, the XJR-12 achieved another 1-2 sweep at Le Mans on June 16 and 17, 1990, (drivers Pryce Cobb/John Nielsen/Martin Brundle and Jan Lammers/Andy Wallace/Franz Konrad) where now a chicane on the famous

Top: Johnny Dumfries. *(J)*

Above: Eddie Cheever. *(S)*

Opposite: X 300 headlights. *(J)*

At last, the XJR-9 managed to win at Le Mans. *(J)*

Above, from left: Martin Brundle, Derek Warwick, Jan Lammers, Patrick Tambay, and Andy Wallace. *(all J)*

Right: The XJR-8 was equipped with 720 horsepower for the sports car championship. *(J)*

Mulsanne Straight reduced speed somewhat. The two other TWR-Jaguar teams (Davy Jones/Michel Ferté/Eliseo Salazar and Martin Brundle/Alain Ferté/Eliseo Salazar) retired.

In 1991 the XJR-12 returned to Le Mans with 7.4 liters, more than 750 horsepower, and weighing in at exactly 1 ton, as required by the regulations. Behind the winning Mazda Wankel racer a most impressive result was achieved for Jaguar, with Davy Jones/Raul Boesel/Michel Ferté second, Theo Fabi/Bob Wollek/Kenny Acheson third and Derek Warwick/John Nielsen/Andy Wallace in fourth position. The privately entered car of David Leslie/Mauro Martini/Jeff Krosnoff retired.

Under strictest secrecy Walkinshaw's U.S. branch, with significant involvement from Ross Brawn (an exceptionally gifted racing car designer of later Formula One fame), developed the XJR-10/11 into the XJR-16 and XJR-17 for 1991. While the latter never won a major race, the former collected two wins.

In the European sports car championship, with the capacity now being limited to 3.5 liters and turbochargers being prohibited, the new Brawn-designed XJR-14, with a 3.5-liter V-8 (Ford-Cosworth type HB) with more than 650 horsepower, space-saving torsion bar suspension at the front wheels and light weight, which allowed the placement of ballast to improve handling and lift total weight to the required 750 kilograms (1,657 pounds), won the constructors' championship, with Theo Fabi winning the drivers' championship.

Back in 1988, on May 23 the new development center at Whitley in the south of Coventry was officially opened. Armstrong-Whitworth (later Siddeley) had made airplanes there after World War I. The premises were sold to Rootes in 1969, later taken over by Chrysler and in 1978 by Peugeot, which used them for vehicle development. When Jaguar announced that its engineering would be relocated there it was estimated that £37 million would have to be spent at the site, but in the end it was £50 million, with which 850 engineer positions were created.

With this background it fit perfectly that in 1988 Jaguar had a technical masterpiece to unveil, the XJ 220, which it revealed at the Birmingham Motor Show. This high-speed sports car (in true Jaguar tradition the name suggested the maximum speed) was derived from the XJR-9 by a group of engineers around Jim Randle, who since December 1984 had met in their spare time—mainly on Saturdays, for which they were called the Saturday Club. The V-12 with 48 valves and 6.2-liter capacity turned out 550 horsepower. Like Porsche's 959, the car had all-wheel drive. The light alloy tube frame was taken from the racing car; the body was completely different and made of aluminum instead of carbon fiber. Keith Helfet had styled the nearly 17-foot-long vehicle with visible influence from Pininfarina's 1978 XJ-S Spyder study, with its even but curved skin and the longish-oval mouth. It was intended to remain a one-off, but the prototype provoked considerable demand. So in 1990 a series of 350 XJ 220s was announced, but with a different conception: The V-6 engine from the XJR-11 was not that powerful, so rear-wheel drive was sufficient and the body could be somewhat shortened. As a result of the saved weight, performance was not affected. By mid-1992 the XJ 220 was in full production at Wykham Mill, Bloxham, where Jaguar Sport had moved the year before. The bodies were supplied from Abbey Panels. In the same year the car had its first major victory at Silverstone with driver Win Percy. Production ended in 1994 with a smaller number of cars built than anticipated. Because of the changing economic climate and a declining interest in super sportscars, many clients had withdrawn their orders, which had cost them a

Derek Warwick, Theo Fabi, and Martin Brundle, 1991 at Monza. *(S)*

From left:
Derek Daly,
Pryce Cobb,
Davy Jones,
and John Nielsen. *(all J)*

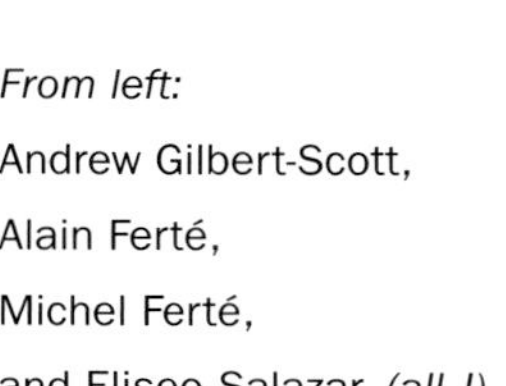

From left:
Andrew Gilbert-Scott,
Alain Ferté,
Michel Ferté,
and Eliseo Salazar. *(all J)*

Above: The V-6 engine of the XJR-11. *(J)*

Right: Nearly 250 miles per hour on the famous Mulsanne straight: XJR-9. *(J)*

Above: With the XJR-10, TWR continued to develop its concept. *(J)*

Top right: June 12, 1988, at 136 miles per hour—on the way to victory. *(S)*

Above right: XJR-14 made do with half of 12 cylinders. *(J)*

Below: In 1991 Jaguar unfortunately could not win at Le Mans again. *(S)*

Right: The compact yet powerful engine of the XJ 220. *(J)*

Right: Drawing of the planned development center at Whitley. *(J)*

Below: The Whitley development center in reality. *(J)*

penalty of £50,000 each. Even years later some cars still were unsold.

Auto Motor und Sport tested the "Cat of Prey" in mid-1994 and discovered a lack of trunk capacity, visibility, and refinement, but an excess of performance, joy of driving, turning circle, and publicity. "No, this Jaguar is not a sports car for everyday use," Götz Leyrer reported, asking: "Where is a territory for animals as wild as this?"

Well, Tom Walkinshaw had an answer and initiated an XJ 220 racing series for which he created some XJ 220 Cs with plastic body parts and suspension parts from Kevlar. The victory of this model in the GT class at Le Mans in 1993 was much-publicized (drivers were David Brabham/John Nielsen/David Coulthard). The organizers, Auto Club de L'Ouest, deprived Jaguar of the win due to an alleged minor infringement of regulations for fueling, but it never asked for the trophy back. Soon it became obvious that the allegation was unjustified, but it may well be that Tom Walkinshaw's not very calm reaction upon disqualification had made the officials stick to it. The second XJ 220 C in that race (Win Percy/Armin Hahne) suffered a blown cylinder head gasket after only 24 minutes of racing. In 1995 two privately entered XJ 220 Cs were at the start at Le Mans (Olindo Iacobelli/Bernard Thurner/Win Percy and Tiff Needell/Richard Piper/James Weaver), but both retired.

Below left: The 1988 prototype of the XJ 220 was long, stylish, powerful, and quick. *(S)*

Below right: The rear aspect of the V-12 prototype. *(S)*

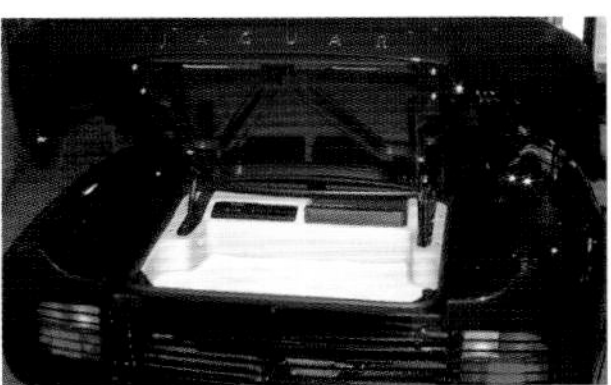

Top: The aerodynamic face of the XJ 220, the fastest production car in the world. *(Schön)*

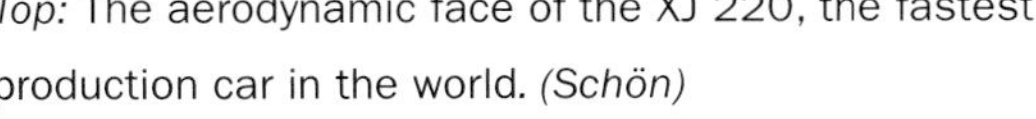

Above left: The long and low lines of XJ 220. *(Schön)*

Above right: The rear was styled with less imagination. *(Schön)*

Right: A V-6 propelled the XJ 220. *(Schön)*

Top: A luggage trunk for short travels in the XJ 220. *(Schön)*

Above: The comfortable interior of the XJ 220. *(Schön)*

As an even more sporting model Tom Walkinshaw started—initially without Jaguar Sport being involved—developing the XJR-9 into project R9R, which later became XJR-15, with a V-12 engine with "more than" 450 horsepower, of which 50 were made. The impressive styling was by Peter Stevens. It was not very lucky that both super sports cars were in production and offered at the same time. For XJR-15 Walkinshaw organized a small racing series in conjunction with the Monaco, Silverstone, and Spa Formula One races. In the last race, Armin Hahne won and the prize money of £1 million went to the owners of his car, brothers Wolfgang and Uwe Eickwinkel.

Despite the beautiful new XJ 6, the exchange rate between the pound and the dollar, which had helped Jaguar for many years, became less favorable for Jaguar from 1987 onward. At first losses from overseas sales could be compensated by hedging strategies and additional sales efforts in Europe. However, Jaguar was forced to save production cost in order to avoid losses. In 1988 the productivity rate, despite still prevalent tension between workforce and management, had risen to 4.6 cars per person per year. Nevertheless, profits melted and Egan explained this with the fact that many high-technology components were no longer available from the British market and had to be paid in foreign currencies—this caused additional currency risks, but eliminated others.

Sales figures—particularly of the new XJ 6—did not increase as much as expected, due in part to reliability—again particularly of the XJ 40—which was not yet fully satisfying if compared with the competition. The stock exchange crash of 1987 had cast a cloud over luxury markets. In the United States—the most important market for Jaguar—Toyota in the late 1980s stole some market share with its luxury brand, Lexus. With its near-perfect 4-liter V-8 and four-speed automatic it was particularly appealing for rational, businesslike customers—this competition did not help Jaguar sales.

Soon Jaguar's capitalization became rather thin; even urgent investments had to be postponed. A few opined that these problems still were the result of Sir William Lyons' autocratic style that had not encouraged young management and spent little money for production. As he had retired no less than 15 years earlier, these problems certainly should not be attributed to Sir William. Anyway, he had managed to make a profit for 50 years and left behind a range of models that after many years still guaranteed good sales. He certainly would have found a solution—as he always had—but of course we do not know what it would have been.

Egan and the British government saw the solution in fresh capital. In 1989 it appeared likely that, after the expiration of the government's protective "golden shares," 29.9 percent of Jaguar shares would be taken over by General Motors, which supplied the automatic for V-12 cars and air conditioning units. Egan and his colleagues prepared for this future. But on September 19, 1989, Ford announced purchase of an equity stake just below the 15 percent limit. Ford, the second-largest car manufacturer in the United States, already had a luxury marque in Lincoln. But Lincoln was no longer as brilliant as it had been in the 1940s, and Ford was in dire need of a real luxury marque. Ford management at far-away Dearborn believed that the luxury markets would expand in the near future. Ford proclaimed that cooperation would also benefit Jaguar, as Jaguar engineers now had access to a broad, highly advanced array of technologies like airbags, the development cost of

Below right: Born to race: the XJ 220 C. *(J)*

Below: This XJ 220 C raced at Le Mans. *(Schön)*

In its core, the XJR-15 was a racing car. *(S)*

Jaguar Sport was a joint venture of Jaguar and Tom Walkinshaw. *(Schön)*

which Jaguar could save. Additionally, the production know-how of Ford could help Jaguar to improve and rationalize Jaguar's plants.

Without warning Browns Lane, Industry Secretary of State Nicholas Ridley announced the early expiration of the "golden share" on October 31, 1989, after Ford had informed the Jaguar board of its not very welcomed interest in taking over all Jaguar shares. Ford and Jaguar management negotiated on November 1 through the early morning of November 2, fixing some guarantees with regard to the autonomy of Jaguar and lifting the price per share slightly. The takeover bid presumably cost Ford more than £1.5 billion for a Jaguar valued at an estimated £300 million. General Motors made no similar offer, quite rightfully stating that Ford's bid was rather high. Instead, General Motors took over a share in Swedish Saab Automobiles, which Ford had been interested in before it turned to Jaguar. Egan recommended Ford's bid to the shareholders, and it was only a matter of weeks before Ford reigned supreme over Jaguar.

On March 27, 1990 John Egan—not very surprisingly—announced his resignation as of the middle of the year. *De facto* he left his office immediately, his successor being William Hayden of Ford Europe (born 1929, since 1950 with Ford) who moved in on April 2. As Ford in its haste had missed out on any opportunity to learn much about the state of production facilities at Jaguar, Dearborn was horrified at what they now came to see. Hayden stated that one car manufacturer's production facilities were worse than Jaguar's, and that was the one at Gorky in Russia! This statement made many

Below left: The dashboard underlines the racing character of the XJR-15. *(Schön)*

Below center: The XJR-15 delivered by Jaguar Sport was even more of a racing car than the XJ 220 C. *(Schön)*

Below right: Armin Hahne and the brothers Eickwinkel were winners of the XJR-15 series of races. *(S)*

Bill Hayden represented Ford at Jaguar. *(J)*

customers in the United States cancel their Jaguar orders—in this case Hayden, renowned for a sharp tongue as well as for his strictness toward the workforce, had been too sarcastic. An employee showed—internally—a different kind of humor when announcing to his coworkers that due to reasons of economy the light at the end of the tunnel had been switched off.

Jim Randle resigned as well. After Ford canceled some of his pet projects he made use of a new early retirement scheme and promised that he would never work in the automobile industry again. Despite this commitment it was he who helped to bring new life to Lea-Francis cars when they unveiled a new retro sports car at the 1998 Motor Show.

Ford's first aim was to find a clear structure for the XJ and XJ-S replacement projects, and it soon adopted a new system of project codes (see appendix). Dearborn had a critical eye on what was going on in Jaguar development, because it was essential to economize with the restricted financial means. The adoption of larger mechanical components, like a 4-liter V-8 engine that had recently been put into production in the United States, was something that Ford would not expect from Jaguar with its discerning customers.

In 1991, Bob Dover became new Jaguar chief engineer. Only five years later he became chairman of Aston Martin, also part of the Ford group, but he continued his functions in Jaguar and Land Rover management before he retired in 2003.

Although aficionados were not very enthusiastic when Ford took over Jaguar, it has to be thanked for its financial input. Ford helped Jaguar survive a period of high losses—in some months from 1992 until 1994 Jaguar lost more than a £1 million per day—and investment in new production facilities. Without this helping hand Jaguar might not have survived into the 1990s. Upon the takeover Jaguar reduced the number of employees from 12,000 to 8,000 in 1992 and to 6,000 in 1997 through an early retirement scheme, but also by outsourcing. This improved the productivity factor, although not necessary productivity itself. The trim shop was one example, as was accounting, which now was carried out at Ford.

In September 1990, Special Vehicle Operations (SVO) was created from the crew responsible for the DS 420—or what had survived from the Vanden Plas spirit of Kingsbury. The enhancements offered from 1992 under the Insignia name (special colors for leather and wood, special hubcaps, and more extensive use of leather) were carried out at SVO, but for only two years.

Of course the Ford takeover raised some concern among dyed-in-the-wool Jaguarists who were keen on keeping out American influence. Contrary to British Leyland, however, Ford soon recognized that a mass producer should not prescribe a specialist manufacturer's development and marketing. This helped avoid paralyzing discussions, as both sides quickly learned that cooperation would be more beneficial than confrontation.

In May 1991 Jaguar took over Emil Frey's 65 percent stake in Jaguar Deutschland, which Peter Schack had left shortly before. The new chief at Kronberg was Hartmut Kieven beginning on September 1, 1991; he had been a Ford employee since 1964.

As of April 1, 1992—the year in which Jaguar leaped from 25th to 10th position in the much-recognized Customer Satisfaction index—Jaguar in Coventry also had a new chief, 48-year-old Nicholas ("Nick") Scheele. He arrived from Ford's Mexican production operations, where he had served for four years and had been Hayden's deputy since 1992.

During the factory holidays in July 1993, Hayden's criticism resulted in the replacement of the two 40-year-old assembly line tracks by a completely new line with only one track. All parts approached the line from the sides, freeing up much space. The installation of the new track took just three weeks!

In order to avoid currency risks in purchasing, some foreign suppliers like Nippondenso and Hella were convinced that production in England would be viable. Late in 1994 it was announced that the production of pressed steel sheets would take place at Ford's own pressing plant at Halewood, which had excess capacity. As recently as February 10, 1988—in pre-Ford days—Jaguar and GKN Sankey had formed Venture Pressings (like Jaguar Sport, a 50-50 joint venture) in order to become independent of Austin Rover's supply from their Swindon works. For this purpose a new plant was installed at Hedley Castle, Telford, which cost £35 million, but in the end the operation only fabricated the steel sheets for the first model revised under

Ford control: The XJS. Otherwise, Ford's interests were supreme and Venture Pressings was given up.

The revised XJS was unveiled on May 1, 1991, at the Barcelona show. It had the 4.0 or V-12 engine, and the styling of the side windows and rear had changed. The body had been completely revised—although this was hardly visible—and now consisted of fewer but larger panels and parts which—as before—were joined at Castle Bromwich, where £4 million had been spent for computer-controlled welding. Although completely designed during the Egan era, it reached production under Ford. The new look, including the color-coded plastic bumpers which—allegedly for cost reasons—were only introduced in 1993, had already been designed by Geoff Lawson's department in 1985, and were intended to be introduced in 1988!

The XJS was tested by *Auto Motor und Sport's* Klaus Westrup, who commented, "The same procedure as every year," as the character of the coupe had not been affected by the latest improvement—"still a very attractive car."

On September 11, 1991, a revised and even more powerful XJR-S 6.0, with body revisions as per the XJS, was added to the range of models for the Frankfurt show. Suspension was rated better than Jaguar's sports setting, offering a more comfortable low-speed ride without sacrificing to the handling. It was thus available as an option for other models for £1,157. After isolated criticism about the previous XJR-S' build quality, the new XJR-Ss were quality checked in the same way as normal Jaguars. A special series of 50 XJR-S

Above: This view shows the styling changes for the XJS. *(J)*

Below: The XJS convertible still was an impressive car. *(J)*

coupes and—exclusively for America—50 convertibles was made.

On May 11, 1992, the 4.0 convertible was introduced, with automatic transmission only. In Australia the importer had the dramatic idea to unveil the convertible on a pool—seemingly swimming. The XJS was the first Jaguar to receive an airbag in the steering wheel, while it still was absent from the sedans—severely hampering sales, in Germany at least.

Wolfgang König described the 4.0 convertible in *Auto Motor und Sport* as "of the best sort." Silence and torsional stiffness of the open body were impressive, as were engine torque and the harmonious automatic.

May 1993 brought further change to the XJS in that the already mentioned color-coded plastic bumpers were introduced. At the same time the V-12 was replaced by the sedan's 6.0, so the XJR-S disappeared. The convertible now suggested four seats, with seat cushions added as Arden had offered for quite a few years. Before, SVO had modified some U.S.-bound convertibles in the same way. This had raised considerable demand, and thus Motor Panels was contracted to develop the changes to the body structure that were required to offer at least a little bit of space for the rear passengers. In the course of this operation the hydraulic pump for the convertible top was relocated above the battery.

In the early summer of 1994, the 4.0 engine was revised for the XJS. The engine was now called AJ 16, with more power and smoothness. On May 10, 1995, Jaguar introduced convertible Celebration models in Britain, in recognition of 60 years behind the name "Jaguar." They cost £38,950 or £48,950. However, the days of the XJS were soon over—the last one was completed on April 8, 1996.

The platform of the XJS survived in the Aston Martin DB7 that was unveiled at the Geneva show in 1994. It appeared alongside a Lagonda Vignale sedan with bold styling that some experts believed to be a foreshadowing of future Jaguars.

Aston Martin is one of the most legendary British car marques. Lionel Martin, the founder, was only interested in racing cars. In 1913 he already had tuned an Isotta-Fraschini with a 1.4-liter Coventry-Simplex engine—the predecessor of Coventry Climax—and gained much success at the Aston Clinton hillclimb. A production of further examples was hampered by the war and its

Above: With some months' delay, the XJR-S was modernized as well. *(J)*

Right: The XJR-S 6.0 alongside a Jaguar fighter. *(S)*

Below: The luxurious interior of an XJR-S. *(S)*

Left: The last revision is recognized by the color-coded bumpers. *(J)*

Below: XJS convertible for 1994. *(S)*

Above: The XJS 4.0 convertible was much welcomed. *(J)*

Right: In May 1993 the XJS V-12 adopted the six-liter engine from the XJ 81. *(J)*

The close relationship between Jaguar and Aston Martin was manifested at Jaguar's headquarters in the 1990s. *(St)*

1999 Aston Martin DB7 Vantage coupe. *(Aston Martin)*

1999 Aston Martin DB 7 Vantage Volante. *(Aston Martin)*

aftermath, beginning only in 1922 under the Aston Martin name, reflecting the early racing success.

As Martin put sports above economics, he frequently ran out of money. Nevertheless the most renowned racing drivers ordered their cars from Aston Martin, giving the marque an excellent reputation. When Count Zborowski—the man with Chitty-Chitty-Bang-Bang—died, the essential patron was lost. Only in 1929 was small-series production of Aston Martin racing and sports cars resumed at Feltham in Surrey, under the direction of August Cesare Bertelli, the affluent brother of the even more famous racing driver Enrico Bertelli. However, financing remained a problem. With good luck it was possible to keep the high-class production running.

In 1947 the company was bought for £20,000 by gearbox manufacturer David Brown, who had been informed of the opportunity by a newspaper advertisement. In the same year, Brown also bought Lagonda (which cost £52,500, the premises not included), and in 1955 coachbuilding company Tickford (previously Salmons) at Newport Pagnell, where Aston Martin production was relocated.

Much fame was gained with the DB sports car series with a Lagonda engine that originally had been designed by W. O. Bentley. The most famous example of this series is a DB 5 that played a major role in the 1964 James Bond thriller *Goldfinger* with some special equipment like changing number plates, smoke grenades, machine guns hidden behind the rear lights, an ejection seat, and so on. Although the marque was sold off in 1973 and a 75 percent stake taken over by Ford in 1987, the old series of names was revived when the relatively less costly DB 7 was added to the range of handmade V-8 sports cars.

The DB 7 was based on a Jaguar design with the code name XJ 41, simplified by Tom Walkinshaw as Project XX, with rear-wheel drive and the XJS floorpan and then sold to Aston Martin, as Jaguar was not interested in purchasing the project back. With a 3.2-liter AJ 6 engine and an Eaton supercharger, it was a Jaguar through and through. It was produced at Bloxham after XJ 220 production had been finished there. Officially, Aston Martin Lagonda denied any similarity between the DB 7 and Jaguar's sports cars. It was admitted, however, that the engine block was derived from Jaguar. It was stated proudly that Bridgestone had developed a new ultralow profile tire especially for the DB 7. Ian Callum's styling for the DB 7 was very successful, winning numerous awards. It was also elected as "one of the most beautiful automobiles in the world" by a board of Italian artists. Callum, born in 1954 at Dumfries in Scotland, had studied at Coventry, Aberdeen, and Glasgow before he joined Ford in 1979, where he spent many years at the Ghia design studios at Turin before moving on to TWR in 1991.

The convertible variant called DB 7 Volante was just as attractive. It debuted on January 6, 1996, at the Detroit show. As the price was still much higher than that of a comparable Jaguar, these beautiful cars, particularly the Volante, remained rarities, although unlike Aston Martin's other much more expensive cars these were mass-produced.

Early in 1995 *Auto Motor und Sport* tested the Aston Martin DB 7: "The Aston Martin has a lot of style," was Klaus Westrup's opinion. He enjoyed the functional if slightly cramped interior, the admirable ride comfort, and the torquey engine. A DB 7 with a V-12 engine as a one-off at TWR remained a dream for the time being. As "Project Vantage," another one-off with a quasi-double Ford V-6 engine was presented to the public at the Detroit show in January 1998. With its macho body and modern-cool interior—all the wood was replaced by Kevlar and aluminum—the car was a sensation. The aluminum body (partly "sandwiched") with aluminum extrusion profiles, and with a tube frame at the front and supporting plastic elements, was of a very advanced design. The 255/40 (front) and 285/40 ZR 19 (rear) tires on large 9½-inch wheels were very impressive. The V-12 dream became reality only at the Geneva show in March 1999, obviously a descendant of the Project Vantage.

According to Aston Martin tradition the new variant was called DB7 Vantage, combining the impressive hull of the DB 7 with a hot V-12 developed in Detroit with "only" 420 horsepower instead of the 450 of the Project Vantage. Technically the engine was derived from the 3-liter Ford V-6, with each bank elongated by three units. It had already been used for a Ford Indigo prototype of 1996 and then had been optimized at Cosworth. The front suspension had been redesigned during the 2½-year gestation period. Tires

Above: 1997 Aston Martin Volante of 1997, destined for the United States. *(Aston Martin)*

Left: Jaguar project XJ 41. *(S)*

Above: 1994 Aston Martin DB 7 coupe. *(Aston Martin)*

Left: Aston Martin DB 7 Volante interior. *(Aston Martin)*

The 1994 Jaguar XJR with its supercharged engine—a great step forward. *(J)*

were 245/40 and 265/35 ZR 18 on 8- and 9-inch wheels. The six-speed manual gearbox was made at Tremec (formerly Borg-Warner); alternatively a five-speed automatic was offered. The interior was only slightly redesigned, and at the price of nearly two supercharged Jaguar coupes the Aston Martin remained a very exclusive car.

Testers were as impressed by its roadholding as they were with the engine, which made a nearly 190-mile-per-hour top speed possible. In October 2002 a variant called GT was added to the range. It had even larger tires and 435 horsepower. Two months later an even more exclusive variant of the DB 7 was unveiled: The Zagato was limited to 99 examples. This car was named after the Italian coachbuilder that had created a very light sports coupe body for the Aston Martin DB 4. In the case of the DB 7 the changes were limited to a larger grille and two bulges on the roof extending along the rear window. Power output now was 440 horsepower. In convertible guise the Zagato was shown in February 2003 as AR 1 ("American Roadster 1"), but by the end of 2003 the DB 7 era was over. Its successor, the DB 9, was related to the larger Vanquish, which had less in common with any Jaguar than the DB 7 family.

Back at Jaguar it had become evident that the angular XJ 40 had lost its following in the early 1990s. On September 28, 1994, a thoroughly redesigned successor with a more classical four-headlight face was introduced—stylistically an extraordinarily successful conversion. This X 300 had the AJ 16 engine as introduced shortly before in the XJS, a supercharged variant (XJR), a similarly modernized 3.2-liter, and the unchanged V-12. With a precision-built body, door gaps were reduced by 25 percent, and the rear door panel extended below the front door to make this gap nearly invisible. *Auto Motor und Sport* would have wished for some more functionality like more recent designs, but for the suspension Klaus Westrup had nothing but praise.

In a mid-1995 comparison in *Auto Motor und Sport* the 3.2 Jaguar had no chance against Audi, BMW, and Mercedes-Benz, but despite the tester's Teutonic attitude (showing particularly with regard to ergonomics, roadholding, and even riding comfort) the Jaguar kept up surprisingly well with the competition.

The XJR, with its fine manners being spoiled only by the sound of the supercharger, also did not find the praise in the German press that it had deserved. So few enthusiasts were informed of the diverse merits of this sports sedan with the mesh grille that recalled glorious Bentley Blower days. One such XJR became a fire tender to Andy Green's Thrust SSC when it became the first land vehicle to break the sound barrier on a dried-out American lake in October 1997—a reminder of the XJ 12 fire tender that once was presented by Lofty England to the Silverstone circuit.

In October 1995 the long-wheelbase X 300 was unveiled, becoming the standard size for the Daimlers. Short-wheelbase Daimlers were delivered only on special request. Contrary to the exquisite Majestic, these cars could be assembled on the same track as the short models, which made them much less expensive to produce. The 100th anniversary of Daimler was celebrated with a limited version of 200 Double-Sixes, called Century. The typical Daimler "D" was stitched into the headrests. In the 1997 model year the Sovereign 4.0 also was normally supplied on the longer wheelbase (in the United States, the traditional XJ 6 L designation was revived for this model) but the shorter variant remained available on special request.

Special Vehicle Operations manufactured an even longer X 300 as a one-off, with front and rear doors being elongated. The duotone metallic gray made the car look even longer.

On May 17, 1996, at the Daimler Centenary Gala, Jaguar unveiled a shortened variant of the Daimler Double-Six with a convertible top called the Corsica, and thus recalling a London coachbuilder that had manufactured the body of one of the fabulous low-chassis Double-Sixes of prewar years. This was the first car from Browns Lane with a metal cover for the folded top, this cover being of course integrated in the electrified opening mechanism. Wherever this car was on show it was acclaimed. Nevertheless its fate was no better than that of a 1993 XJ 40 Coupe prototype, as both remained prototypes.

Daimler Double-Six Century limited edition, Jaguar's 1996 flagship. *(J)*

Daimler Double-Six as derived from the X 300, still with a very luxurious interior. *(J)*

Interior of the X 300 Sovereign. *(J)*

20 EIGHT CYLINDERS

When Ford took over Jaguar, a more sporting sibling to the XJ-S was under development. Its gestation took an even more complicated route than that of the XJ 40. In order to obtain a green light for that one, it had to be accompanied by a sports car based on the same platform. This bore the code XJ 41 for the coupe and XJ 42 for the convertible. The XJ 40 platform was shortened behind the front seats, and the front suspension was moved somewhat further forward. In 1985 a new department, "New Vehicle Concepts," was established with a team of very young engineers. They adopted the project and, with the help of the latest computer technology, development was continued mainly on monitors. In 1989 Karmann made two prototypes that are still with Jaguar. Instead of a planned weight just over 3,000 pounds, the car finally weighed in at nearly 3,700. The car was a beauty, with excellent roadholding and ride comfort. But its disadvantages were a cramped interior, inadequate visibility through the narrow windows, and a minimal trunk. The sales department rated the car as uncompetitive with regard to the high price necessitated by its complex twin-turbo engine and all-wheel-drive system. The separation of design and development had lengthened information channels and thus news about feasibility came late. Communication between development and production also was limited. Marketing chief Roger Putnam advised Ford immediately upon takeover that this sports car project was not viable. Ford soon stopped the project, which by that time had wasted £15 million (with the exception of some developments that were beneficial for the Aston Martin DB 7).

In late 1991 development started on a completely new baseline, now leading directly to a new sports car. For £99 million a new front and rear end for the present XJS had to be developed. However, the number of unchanged parts became smaller and smaller, until

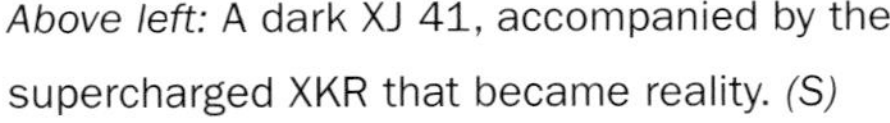

Above left: A dark XJ 41, accompanied by the supercharged XKR that became reality. *(S)*

Above: Early clay model for the XK 8. *(J)*

Left: The rear aspect of the XK 8 was intended to be dominated by curved lines. *(J)*

Opposite: XKR badge. *(J)*

these were limited to the central section of the floorpan. For reason of spares storage, it would have been better if the X 300 platform could have been used, but its rather high sills were not suitable to a low sports car. The XJS floorpan might have been suitable for the sedan, but this also would have required a lot of changes. By the end of 1991 it had been decided to make four different 1:1 styling mock-ups with various styling changes. Ford's Ghia design studio was involved, albeit only as consultant. The last design out of this group was called "clay M," which was accompanied by a completely new design called "clay A." This was the first one boasting a single oval radiator opening in a slightly shortened front overhang and a seemingly inclined bumper under the rear (reminiscent of the XJ 220). In a customer clinic at the Birmingham NEC, where both clays were displayed together with competing sports cars, clay A was preferred. All cars had dark tinted glass, were finished silver, and all badges had been removed so that the approximately 300 customers could concentrate on the general styling. For the interior, six designs were evaluated. Again it was the last design that was chosen, this decision being taken in June 1992. With regard to rationalization during product development, many lessons were taken from Ford's own Mustang "SN 95" development.

Early in 1993 Jaguar's losses made Ford seriously think about dropping X 100 development to replace it with another XJS face-lift. This project was called NPX, but soon it was put aside. Jaguar asked for state subsidies in order to continue development of X 100 and the new eight-cylinder engine, AJ 26. The vehicles were intended to be produced at Castle Bromwich and Browns Lane, while the engines were to be produced at Ford's plant at Bridgend in Wales, which had been opened in 1980. This would have reduced Radford's duties to suspensions as soon as the old-type engines went out of production. With this concept, Ford turned to the British and Welsh governments, but without success. The Portuguese government was more generous, but on the whole this would have been more expensive than unsubsidized production in Britain. This, together with problems with the Nikasil coating of the cylinders, caused a more than six months delay in X 100 development. By November 7, the Chancellor of the Exchequer was prepared to subsidize X 100 with £9.4 million, and only then did Ford management allow the project to continue. Further styling clinics in an underground parking garage in Los Angeles were unusually positive and showed the best result Ford ever had achieved in such clinics. In the course of this clinic, the need of a height adjustment for the seats became obvious.

The transformation of the clay models into real sheet metal, and the production of pressing tools for them, was carried out with state-of-the-art computer technology. All measures of the body and interior parts were taken from two precisely defined base points, and these provided the data for feeding the computers for press tool manufacture. This resulted in a perfect fit on the assembly line, so that even minor adjustments during assembly were no longer necessary.

Early in 1994 a particularly sporting X 100 C (an analogy to the XJ 220 C) was taken into consideration. This lightweight variant would have served as a basis for racing versions and as a showpiece for the 1995 Detroit show. For weight reasons the floorpan was sandwiched like in the XJ 220, but unfortunately this project was soon dropped.

From a technical point of view, the brand new engine was the most interesting aspect of the X 100—as with the XK 120, the E-Type V-12 and the XJ-S 3.6. Jaguar started the development of this V-8 after evaluating the impressive performance of the near-perfect Lexus engine and transmission—in other words, before the Ford takeover. Jaguar recalled the old 3.5-liter, which had been unsuccessfully derived from the V-12. Two balance shafts were added to this design and then tried in an XJS. Well, the results were such that a completely new design seemed advisable—for the very first time in Jaguar's long history! The project name was AJ 26, the figure allegedly deriving from the sum of possible cylinder configurations (6, 8, and 12), although it is possible that the figure just continues the line of AJ 6 and 16. The six-cylinder had a hydrocarbon emission problem that could not be solved, and it had become rather heavy. The V-12, despite its complicated design, was not much superior to the simple V-8. Even boxer engines and a 10-cylinder configuration had been considered, despite problems in balancing. The development of the engine was headed by David Szczupak under development chief Trevor Crisp, who

Above: Wonderful 1998 XKR dashboard. *(J)*

Left: XK 8 represented the latest state-of-the-art. *(J)*

reported to old Ford man Jim Padilla, who was production chief as well.

After the Ford takeover it allegedly took more than a year before the new masters showed interest in Jaguar's engine development. The Americans proposed that their new "Modular" 4.6-liter V-8 with 300 horsepower could be used, but Jaguar engineers and particularly Clive Ennos, who represented Ford among them, managed to convince the chiefs that only an engine developed at Jaguar would be publicly acceptable. Jaguar wanted a sort of quantum leap. The original bore of 83 and stroke of 92mm were replaced by square dimensions, as these resulted in a stiffer crankshaft. The result was a 4-liter V-8 with plastic intake runners, four camshafts, and 32 valves. Weighing in at only about 200 kilograms (442 pounds) its power output was nearly 300 horsepower. This engine even emitted an exhaust note similar to previous Jaguars. As planned, production of the new engine was located at Ford's plant near Swansea.

The first true X 100 prototype undertook its first test drives late in 1994 at places like Timmins (Canada), Phoenix (Arizona), Nardo (Italy), Detroit (Michigan), New York, minor roads around Coventry, and many other places placing a particular strain on automobiles. The cars were compared with the competition frequently in order to make sure that the Jaguar was superior in most respects. Jackie Stewart, long associated with Ford, whose engines had made him Formula One champion three times, tested the X 100 extensively in April 1995 and gave valuable advice on suspension settings. The first production car was completed on June 4, 1996. Even at this stage, thousands of quality improvements were incorporated; statistically, each part had been changed three times before production began. The result was impressive indeed: Manufacture took 30 percent less time than with the XJS. A weekly production of 250 was scheduled.

As XK 8—a designation chosen for its similarity with the old American XK-E designation—the X 100 debuted on March 8, 1996, at the Geneva show. Like the E-Type 35 years before, the new car was hidden under a transport crate, which was lifted with much press sensation. The convertible had a similar unveiling in New York on April 4. Only after October 2 were normal customers allowed to lift the hood and admire the brand new V-8 that left behind any previous Jaguar engine. In England the introduction was supported by a hot-air balloon with the lines of the XK 8. The car's father, Clive Ennos, retired in April 1997 when his masterpiece was completed.

The test in German *Auto Motor und Sport* was again Wolfgang König's privilege. He was delighted with the new transmission and the important fact that two golf bags would fit the trunk. "The XK 8 reacts quickly and sensibly to the steering, likes winding roads and gives the impression it were somewhat smaller and lighter." The money spent for suspension design was not wasted! Some weeks later Klaus Westrup declared an open XK 8 "seventh heaven" and placed it ahead in a comparison with a Mercedes-Benz SL 500 by two percentage points—a result that had been unthinkable before! The greatest disadvantage was the boot cover that, despite the car's electrically folding top, had to be mounted manually.

A comparison with the Aston Martin DB 7 was interesting, as it relied on the older XJS platform. British tests emphasized the new car's better directional stability despite wider tires, the much-improved riding comfort, and the electronic traction control. As the Aston Martin had been rated as the best handling sports car worldwide, and the XJS had inherited the superb riding of its earlier variants, the progress achieved with the revised suspension perhaps could have been expected. The choice to use the XJR rear suspension helped unification between sedans and sports

The XK 8 convertible was particularly sought-after. *(J)*

cars. The XK 8, however, was more spacious than the DB 7, had a more economical engine, and was much less expensive. No wonder that in its first month, October 1996, the best sales figures of the XJS were bettered by the XK 8, and it even beat its arch-rival Mercedes-Benz SL in the United States. This the XJS had never achieved! The XK 8 also was wonderfully reliable. Although some of the many technical gizmos forced an extra visit to the garage, the overall reliability of the convertible as tested by *Auto Motor und Sport* was even better than the Mercedes-Benz SL.

The V-8 presented in the sports car was of course also destined to propel the sedans, where it replaced both the 6- and 12-cylinder engines. So the model designation XJ 12 disappeared for the 1997 model year while on April 17, 1997, upon the end of production of the Daimler Double-Six, a last Jaguar XJ 12 was made, again for the JDHT museum. The last V-12 engine had been built on February 17, and its number, 161996, reveals the tremendous success of this engine during the quarter-century in which it was in production. The V-12 engine with the highest production figure was not Jaguar's but that made by Lincoln (another Ford subsidiary) for its Zephyr during the 1930s and 1940s.

Meanwhile, Jaguar engineers under the X 308 code were busy shoehorning the new V-8 into the sedan. Smaller styling revisions had already been sanctioned in February 1995, but the mechanics took some more time—barely camouflaged prototypes were on the roads beginning in February 1997. Jaguar announced the XJ 8 sedan at the Frankfurt show on September 11, 1997, two days after a press presentation for the Executive, Sovereign, and Daimler V-8 (Vanden Plas for the United States). The 3.2 Classic and Executive models were replaced with a V-8 of similar capacity. This engine was very closely related to the larger V-8, but it dispensed with the variable valve timing. So the tradition of straight six-cylinder engines, which had been carried on since 1931, was over. Following a rather late decision, not only the XJR but also the XJ 12 was equipped with a variant of the V-8, in this case a supercharged 4.0-liter with more than 370 horsepower. The impressive torque of the new XJR and Daimler Super V-8 forbade the use of the ZF five-speed automatic, so Jaguar switched to a similar gearbox from Mercedes-Benz.

Top: The X 308 was hardly distinguishable from its predecessor. *(J)*

Above: The 1996 XK 8 exuded power and competence. *(J)*

Styling improvements included the bumper chrome, which was reduced to bumper-like segments at each corner; new headlight technology, and a still more rounded grille between the headlights; a very successful redesign of the interior (which in the beginning was intended to remain much more superficial); and the first-time use of side airbags in a Jaguar. Further refinements to the suspension following the XK 8 made the sedans much more attractive and proved that Jaguar still had faith in its already 11-year-old design. The use of high-strength steel sheets and improved welding techniques helped make the structure even

Above: 1997 Jaguar XJ 8 Sovereign LWB. *(J)*

Below: The 1997 Jaguar XJ 8 had a dashboard inspired by the sports car. *(J)*

more rigid without adding weight, and also reduced the noise level in the interior.

Thus equipped, the car delighted Wolfgang König of *Auto Motor und Sport* with its powerful, willingly revving engine, and its suspension, while the interior was deemed to be somewhat narrow on the standard-wheelbase cars. On the other hand, some electronic gimmicks, which the German competitors had introduced recently, were missed. The dismissal of the switch panels behind the steering wheel was welcomed, although that happened in favor of somewhat overfunctional steering column levers. The radio and telephone switches on the steering wheel were appreciated, while the switches at the central console were irritating (the majority of them belonged to radio and telephone). Compared with the German basic upper-class models, the 3.2 lacked a bit of torque and interior space. Good marks in acceleration, fuel economy, and suspension made up most of the lost points, so that styling and image were reason enough to make the Jaguar a worthwhile alternative. The comparison of the XJR with an AMG-modified Mercedes-Benz ended similarly. The truly exceptional performance of the heavy Jaguar was admired, less so the sound of the supercharger. In a more detailed comparison of the Sovereign 4.0-liter against Audi, BMW, Cadillac, and Lexus, the Jaguar was best in acceleration and most fuel efficient. Riding comfort and roadholding were also acclaimed. Interestingly, the Jaguar was considered the car that would suffer the least depreciation! The car's limited interior space cost enough points that the German competitors passed by.

Wolfgang König's report "Changing of the Guard" in *Auto Motor und Sport* was plaintive about the replacement of the silky, silent Daimler Double-Six by the Super V-8, particularly as others like Volkswagen dared to develop engines like theirs! The V-12's negatives were forgotten in favor of unalloyed praise: "The charm of its presentation is timeless. If it's not about what it does but how it does it, the V-12 prevails." Even the "once seemingly hovering Jaguar suspension" now was glorified while the Super V-8 transmission had a much more modern and functional character with its—sad to say—unmistakable supercharger sound. Performance of the V-8 was superior to the predecessor, equaling the best competitors. The further refined interior was another advance. It was also much less expensive and lighter. "The Double-Six would not have a bit of a chance."

A further changing of the guard took place at Jaguar Deutschland, where Jeffrey L. Scott (formerly at Lexus) became chief in January 1998—just after Jaguar, for the first time under Ford management, had shown a quarterly profit. At first he remained marketing director, but in late 1998 handed these duties to Stefan Schulte, who came from Porsche. Scott's intention was to increase the number of dealerships from 70 to 150. Shortly afterward, on March 3, 1998, Jaguar presented a dream that had become reality: At the Geneva Show Browns Lane displayed a combination of the supercharged V-8 of the XJR with the marvelous XK 8 body, thus creating the XKR, a somewhat logical designation. The mouth now fortunately lost the chrome bar and was filled with a racy mesh grille. This masterpiece, with its charismatic louvers in the hood and minimal spoiler at the rear, was again tested for *Auto Motor und Sport* by Wolfgang König. Performance was rated top-class despite the non-availability of a manual gear change (quite unusual for a sports car), and the interior was rated "first class." The supercharger noise was found embarrassing on long drives—not every Jaguar enthusiast would share this view. The fuel consumption of 17 miles per gallon, a lot if compared with standard cars, seemed to be justified by the performance offered. The prices were rated "nearly irresistible"—and many customers agreed. However, compared with the Porsche Carrera, Mercedes-Benz SL 500, and Chevrolet Corvette, the XKR was not first, which may be partially attributed to the testers' lack of familiarity with the foreign product. It was deemed much superior to the attractive, new Maserati 3200 GT, which, with regard to horsepower and price, was a close match to the Jaguar. Even with the automatic and the supercharger, consumption was only marginally higher than the Porsche's higher-octane fuel needs, which made the XKR a somewhat economical proposition.

Meanwhile at Browns Lane, some construction work had been carried out. The result was a gleaming, white cube with large windows that, in September 1998, was occupied by Jaguar's public relations department and the JDHT. The basement was a large hall for the permanent display of changing selections of JDHT

Above: Jeffrey Scott's first time as chief of Jaguar Deutschland lasted only two years (1998–2000) but he returned to that post in December 2004. *(J)*

Left: Stefan Schulte, sales manager at Jaguar Deutschland. *(J)*

automobiles. Upstairs, the new archive with racks (a donation of the Jaguar Enthusiasts' Club) and cabinets for files, papers, and photographs was also available to the public. The Americans were so impressed by this museum that until 2001 they planned to build something similar at their Mahwah, New Jersey site, with a $1.5 million donation from Ford. This, however, was not to materialize.

Well, Jaguar knew of other unrealized dreams: Special Vehicle Operations, renowned for its exquisite work, took an XKR and shortened it by 14 inches so that it became a close-coupled two-seater like the earlier planned XK 100 C. This was a brainchild of SVO chief Gary Albrighton, while the styling was—as with XJ 220—Keith Helfet's. He had started with an asymmetric prototype that had a coke-bottle line more akin to the E-Type at the right side. Even the D-Type's rear fin was almost revived for the car but it was soon discarded as aerodynamically inefficient. The aluminum panels were formed—as were those for the XK 120 in the 1950s—by the Abbey Panels Company, with its

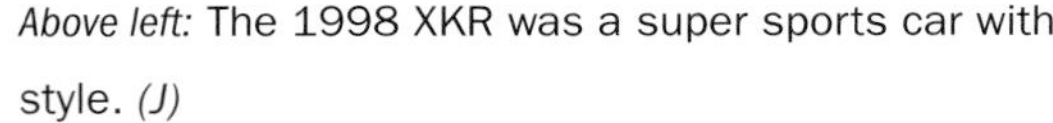

Above left: The 1998 XKR was a super sports car with style. *(J)*

Above center: First studies at the new JDHT archives. *(J)*

Above right: The JDHT museum and archive was opened in 1998. *(J)*

Below left: A spoiler was to become one of the distinguishing features of the XKR. *(J)*

The slightly modified XKR engine produced 450 horsepower in the XK 180. *(St)*

Above: The 1998 XK 180 was not for sale. *(J)*

Below: The clean dashboard of the XK 180. *(J)*

The curved windshield is a styling gimmick reminiscent of the D-Type. *(St)*

The revised XKR sports coupe for 2001. *(J)*

experience in light alloy, but now renamed Loades, after its owners.

Dramatic elements were included, like the classical oval headlights, the very low double-bubble windshield reminiscent of the D-Type, which carried through right to the rear ends of the doors. These gave a racy appearance to the car that was unveiled as the XK 180 at the Paris show on September 29, 1998. It had no top, but viewers did not notice. Its finish changed from blue to gold to green as one walked around the car. This was somewhat reminiscent of Ecurie Ecosse's flag blue, but it was discarded for regular models as too gaudy, so the XK 180 became the only Jaguar in "Teal Gold." The aluminum dashboard, with its instruments and levers arranged in neat rows, was dissimilar to the XKR's. No less than Paolo Pininfarina suggested that the XK 180 had been the most beautiful car at the Paris show. Thanks to a higher-revving supercharger and further modifications selected at Whitley (an intercooler, a larger exhaust without catalyst but with motorcycle-type silencers) the engine produced 450 horsepower.

In terms of performance, no comparison had to be feared. The engine bay, with its many polished aluminum parts instead of standard plastic, was particularly beautiful. The limited-slip differential (2.88:1) was inherited from the previous XJS. The 20-inch tires were very wide (255mm at the front and 285 at the rear) and low (35 and 30 series). It was astonishing how quickly the development had been carried out, although no computers had been used. Previously,

Special Vehicle Operations had kept a low profile and limited its activities to bodywork enhancements. SVO undertook its first step into mechanical improvement with this car. The sequential gear change, with buttons in the steering wheel, reflected the latest fashion with super sports cars, although these operated a standard automatic. Classic Jaguar enthusiasts may have complained about the lack of wood in the interior, which was replaced with brushed aluminum. The technology of the backlights is remarkable in that it used two dozen light-emitting diodes. Unfortunately this prototype was not to be added to the range of Jaguar models.

Meanwhile, customers acknowledged the constant efforts in improving Jaguar's standards of service. In 1998 Jaguar scored fourth in the U.K. and fifth in the U.S. in the J. D. Power Customer Satisfaction Index. For 1999 all models were revised to meet the latest German D3 emissions standard with even smoother running engines and detail improvements to suspension steering and brakes. ZF Servotronic II now became standard for all models, and supercharged models were equipped with larger brakes. A sensor system automatically switched the lights on at dusk.

In breakdown statistics Jaguar had climbed to the top bracket, practically lying level with German competition. In 1999 Jaguar scored first in the Customer Satisfaction Index and was also among the best non-Japanese makes in British breakdown statistics. So the invention of "Royal Service" in 2000 was not too much of an adventure. This included all maintenance, inspection, and repair costs for three years or 60,000 miles and was covered in the basic price. On the technical side, the latest enhancement was adaptive cruise control (ACC) for the XKR, with a 77 GHz sensor from Delphi Automotive Systems. It kept the correct distance to the car in front, but Jaguar felt reason to point out that the driver still was responsible for driving correctly. Under the R performance designation the sports cars were equipped with 8.5-inch-wide, five-spoke BBS wheels that revealed large four-caliper Brembo brakes behind them, and a handling package that made the whole car 10mm lower. The Brembo brakes were also available for the XJ, where a special spare wheel was required in order to clear the large calipers. R performance options were carried out by Special Vehicle Operations.

The magic year 2000 was started by Jaguar with a special saluting gun on January 11 at the North American Motor Show in Detroit, where another two-seater not dissimilar to the XK 180 was unveiled: The still more compact, very racy and desirable F-Type. The styling of this F-Type recalled of the E-Type as well as the taste of Geoff Lawson, who sadly had died the year before. Nevertheless, it was the work of Keith Helfet, who now under Ian Callum was responsible for Jaguar styling. Chassis dimensions could be chosen more freely than with the XK 180. The interior again showed no wood but brushed aluminum, which was not available on standard Jaguar products. Although not developed into a running car, the F-Type had an improved variant of the 3-liter V-6 from the latest small Jaguar under the hood.

Jaguar was very noncommittal with regard to possible series production of the F-Type. Nevertheless it was an open secret that Jaguar chief Wolfgang Reitzle and his boss at Ford, Jacques Nasser, thought this might be a worthwhile addition to the Jaguar range. Many customers shared this enthusiasm and ordered F-Types from their dealers without ever having seen one. In the end, however, financial reasoning prevailed and in mid-2002 Jaguar decided against production of the F-Type. It was too dissimilar to other Jaguar models, so that its assembly could not be intertwined into the existing assembly line. This was a serious setback for Jaguar prestige in the eyes of younger customers, whom Jaguar allegedly was so keen on. It is said that at Zuffenhausen some bottles of champagne had been opened upon this news, but prematurely, as the Porsche equivalent of the F-Type, the Boxster, experienced falling sales figures in the following years.

For the Silverstone Formula One race on April 23, 2000, Jaguar introduced, for reasons to be explained elsewhere, a limited series of 50 silver XKR coupes and convertibles with 20-inch BBS wheels called Detroit (9 inches wide at the front, 10 at the rear), black leather with red stitching, dark-gray birds-eye maple veneer, integrated navigation and telephone system, and special Silverstone badges on the hood and the locker lid. The price remained unchanged, however!

Slightly revised variants of the XK 8 and XKR were unveiled by Jaguar on August 28 (in Britain only on August 30). Hardly recognizable changes to the front

Left: Dashboard of the 2000 F-Type concept car—functional and very "Jaguar" in design. *(J)*

Below: The F-Type concept car incorporates every ingredient of a true Jaguar sports car. *(J)*

Above: Unfortunately the F-Type was not sanctioned for production. *(J)*

Right: Front and rear of the F-Type concept car are very similar in design. *(J)*

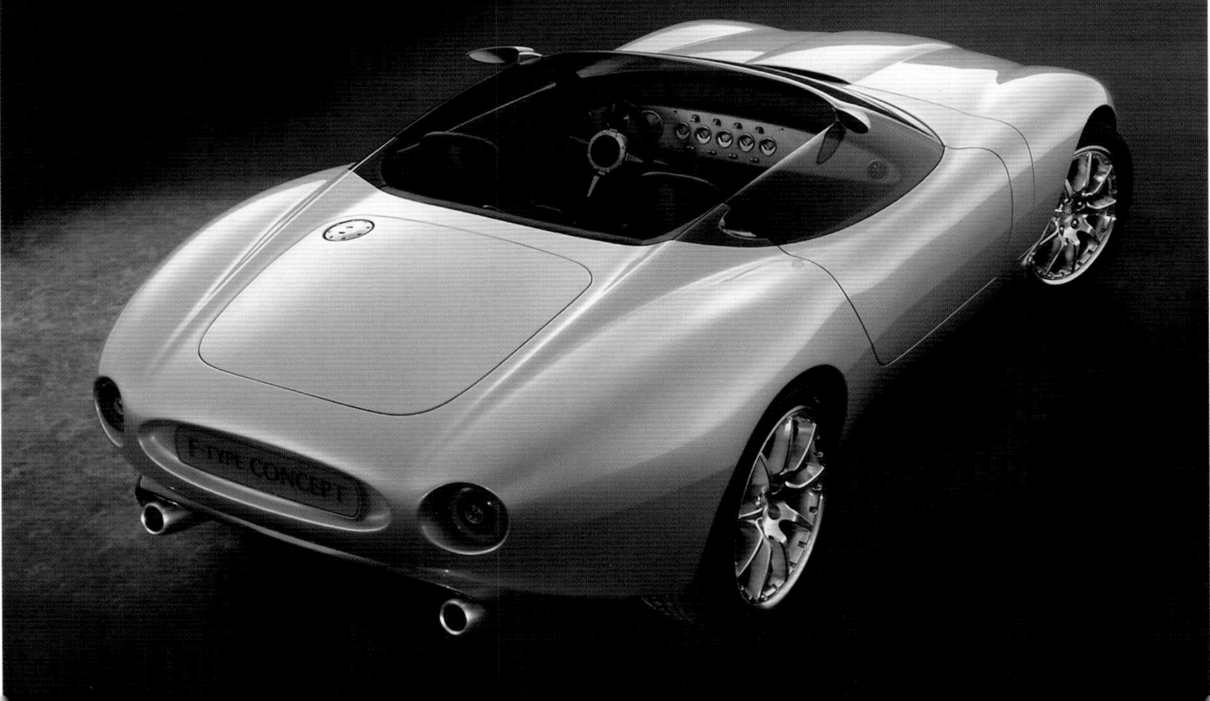

Above: ARTS helped tailor airbag deployments to the passengers in the XK sports car. *(J)*

Right: Slightly revised interior for the 2001 sports car. *(J)*

and rear included nearly flush-fitting fog lamps, with radar sensors for the adaptive cruise control hidden behind them; a chromed trunk plinth with a button for opening the lid (previously this had to be done with the remote control); a changed chrome bar in the mouth of the XK 8; rear lights with clear glass lenses; new seats with integrated side airbags; and headrests separated from the backrest. Mechanically, everything remained with the tried and tested. This was supplemented by new adaptive airbags called Adaptive Restraint Technology System (ARTS)—a first for the whole industry. Among all brands (for any products, not just automotive ones) Jaguar now scored in 18th place for recognition, for reasons much more complex than just this revised model.

In Germany an XKR Silverstone was unveiled in conjunction with the 2001 model year, limited to 200 coupes and convertibles of the new model year. In Germany these were considerably more expensive than the standard models.

At the same time Jaguar, or, to be more precise, its Special Vehicle Operations, thought about making the XKR even sportier. The result was a masterpiece of British tradition: The XKR-R, hardly recognizable by its slightly lower grille and wider 20-inch wheels, was shown late in June 2001, in a very dark shade of green metallic. With only minor modification, power output could be increased to around 400 horsepower, and the gear change—other than with the standard model—was carried out manually with a six-speed model T56. Suspension was carried over from the R-Performance model, but with even sportier settings. In an early development version, the ride of this car must have been very harsh, as according to factory publications the last six months of development were more or less devoted to regaining some ride comfort without spoiling the wonderfully precise handling. With only 2.2 turns from lock to lock, the steering was remarkably direct. The interior, again with a very dark green leather with red stitching, displayed the efforts in weight reduction, with particularly light Recaro front seats and the deletion of the rear bench. Of the two XKR-Rs, one was equipped with carbon panels instead of wood.

Jaguar's attention to detail showed in the sedans for the 2001 model year as well. All models of the XJ range were equipped with cruise control, rear parking distance control, a CD player for six CDs, and a rain sensor for the wipers. For the first time a Motorola dual-band telephone set (900 and 1,800 MHz) was installed in the automobile, with a voice-controlled choice of 20 telephone numbers, in addition to steering wheel switches. This telephone set was available for the XK as well. The XJ 8 3.2 Executive (with much chrome like the Sovereign, traditional piped leather seats, touring suspension, and carpets in contrasting colors) and the revived 3.2 Sport (no chrome, gray birds-eye maple veneer, sports seats, dark carpets) replaced the basic XJ 8 3.2. The Sovereign and XJR were enhanced with heated front seats, and the noble Daimlers came with the Motorola telephone standard. It was such an XJ 8 that was celebrated in July 2001 as the 1,500,000th automobile made by SS/Jaguar.

A further limited model of the XJR and XKR, called the 100, was introduced to celebrate the 110th birthday of founder Sir William Lyons. Finished in black, the equally black leather was stitched red, and some R-Performance extras were provided, as were a new steering wheel, gear lever, and nine-spoke Montreal alloys made by BBS. The series production was 500 each (in case of the XKR 100, coupe and convertible models together). The XKRs were also enhanced with Recaro seats, some aluminum accessories on the instruments and central console, and perforated aluminum pedals. A more sporting feel was delivered through reduced servo assistance in the steering and stiffer shock absorbers. In the context of the birthday celebrations, Jaguar Managing Director Jonathan Browning opened a jaguar enclosure at Chester Zoo, which Jaguar had strongly supported financially.

Another year later, on July 17, 2002, the last example of the second-generation XJ was completed, a dark-blue Daimler V-8 for the works museum. In August 2002 the engines for XK and XKR were bored out by 200cc to provide enhanced low-speed torque, but only slightly higher power output. Another mechanical highlight was the ultramodern ZF six-speed automatic. The interior was adorned with aluminum rings around main instruments, door handles, and transmission lever, as well as with aluminum pedals. On special request an automatically dimming interior mirror was available in connection with a compass.

The new rectangular chrome badges looked pleasant and facilitated washing—the edges of the former XK badge having disappeared. The XKR returned to a color-coded trunk plinth while the XK 8 continued with a chromed item. Headlights, although externally unchanged, were of the Xenon type for the XK 8 at special order only . . . while they became standard for the XKR. The Xenon light automatically switched on and off as required and had an automatic level adjustment. Nearly inevitable was the redesign of the wheels, now ranging in size from 17 inches to 20. The Brembo brakes now were standard on the XKR, while brake assist, which provided additional braking power in case of panic braking, became standard for all XK models.

Coinciding with the introduction of the improved XKR was its promotionally effective role in the latest James Bond thriller, *Die Another Day*, although it was only the adversary's transport—Her Majesty's agent suitably drove an Aston Martin. The bile-green XKR showed with its headlights that it did not belong to the latest generation. In the summer of 2003, 200 examples of a limited Portfolio model for the United States were based on the XKR convertible with the enlarged engine, and were finished either Jupiter red or Coronado blue. Special 20-inch five-spoke wheels and parts of the leather on the special Recaro seats that were dyed according to the paint finish were the distinguishing features of this model, which was about $7,000 more expensive than the normal XKR.

On April 1, 2004, Jaguar introduced further redesigned front and rear ends as well as new sills for the XK line. The mouth was set somewhat lower, thus imitating the SVO XKR-R, while the sills now had a straight crease instead of the bulge. Both overriders disappeared behind the XKR's mesh grille, as had been proposed by several suppliers of accessory kits. With optional piano lacquer interior bits, the sports cars followed the trend set by smaller sedans. Another new alternative was light elm veneer. With cleverly combined equipment packages, further price reductions were possible.

On March 10, 2005, Jaguar surprised the public at the Leipzig Auto Mobil International show with a limited XKR 4.2 S convertible called Celebration. The name had been used 10 years before for an XJS special celebrating 60 years of Jaguar. Like the XJS Celebration, this limited-edition XKR was separated from its normal siblings by a more complete level of equipment, including Bluetooth interface for the mobile phone. Only the cruise control, the alarm system with interior and broken glass sensors, and leather-colored ivory were extras, which further increased the price of 95,500 deutsche marks (in Germany). Only 50 examples of the Celebration were produced; it was the swan song of the XK in that form.

In Europe the XK had a reputation for being an elegant boulevard rider, while Jaguar was represented in racing by a sort of dinosaur. Warren Pearce, well known from his XJ-S Le Mans conversion, had in 1993 installed an XJR-12 engine in a GT prototype of his own design. With kind permission from Brian Lister, he was allowed to call this car the Lister Storm. It was an alloy sandwich design with the engine mounted in the front but very close to the cabin. Transmission was via a five-plate racing clutch with a sequential Hewland six-speed gearbox attached to the rear differential. Although weighing in at 1,270 kilograms (2,806 pounds) initially, Pearce managed to bring weight down to 900 kilograms (1,989 pounds) so that for homologation more weight could be added selectively to enhance handling. The car's debut coincided with the XJ 220 C's last start at Le Mans in 1995, but it retired. The two following years were also full of setbacks. In 1998 however, after retiring unluckily at the season's first race, the Daytona 24 Hours, some remarkable wins were achieved in the British GT championship, one in the final race at Silverstone. In 1999, under Julian Bailey and David Warnock/Rob Schirle, the Storm gained the well-deserved British championship with six wins each in the new GT1 and GT2 classes. In 2000, Julian Bailey/Jamie Campbell-Walter achieved 5 wins out of 10 races and the international FIA GT championship. In 2001 Lister again had to be content with the British championship and a third in the FIA championship. During both years, German Nikolaus Springer drove a second Lister Storm in the British series, with Swiss Philippe Favre, and in 2001 with Bailey as co-driver. From 2002 onward Pearce and his team were occupied with development of the 4-liter V-8. So Lister dropped behind and in 2004 was only represented by a private team, Creation Autosportif.

America had a different view of the Jaguar XK: While Jaguar enjoyed increasing sales of the XK, in the Trans-Am series, Paul Gentilozzi and his Rocketsports team twice won the championship with a Jaguar. The Jaguar XK, with its aerodynamic shape was the right car for Gentilozzi. The body itself was a fiberglass copy, and the mechanical components were totally different from Jaguar. The tube frame required by the regulations, with a solid rear axle and V-8 engine, came from the previous year's Mustang. In 2003 Gentilozzi won the Trans-Am championship and repeated in 2004. For 2005 Gentilozzi aimed at using Jaguar's own V-8, an improvement that Tommy Kendall already had carried out for 2004, and he was successful with his driver Klaus Graf.

The XK 8 and its rear end as revised for the millennium. *(J)*

21
INCREASE BY DECREASE

The S-Type (not to be mixed up with the XJ-S, which in some countries was unofficially called S-Type) was a more compact sporting sedan and part of the strategy aiming at sales of 200,000 per year for Jaguar. This figure was announced soon after the Ford takeover, but it was clear even for Jaguar management that such a figure could not be achieved without expanding to new segments of the market. A more compact Jaguar was the obvious solution, and on August 14, 1995, the project got a green light from Ford management. A project aiming at the same market had been started back in the 1960s, with a V-8 of less than 2-liter capacity supplied by Coventry Climax, then a company wholly owned by Jaguar. The prototype was Doug Thorpe's and Eric Winterbottom's brainchild, inspired by Alfa Romeo Giulia Sprint. However, as part of the BLMC concern, Jaguar had to avoid conflict with Rover and Triumph.

This new premium middle-class project of the 1990s raised concerns about whether a Jaguar-badged Ford might emerge. These concerns were to be destroyed most convincingly. Early in 1995, Britain's government had already announced that it would subsidize Jaguar with about £60 or £80 million if the new S-Type would be produced in England. This is what did happen, although to the chagrin of Jaguar traditionalists, assembly would take place at Castle Bromwich, where the body shells of the other models were made as well, not at the traditional Browns Lane plant. Browns Lane was fully occupied with the assembly of the existing models, so that there simply was no alternative.

As with the XK 8, the S-Type was introduced in several steps, starting with glimpses at the styling, which was both traditional and dynamic. As a surprise to the guests of the new visitor's center at Castle Bromwich, a first look at the lines of the S-Type was allowed on the eve of the official unveiling. Similar to the first XJ 6, this took place in a darkened room, the gleaming car gracefully rolling in with the limelight focused on it. The official unveiling took place on October 20, 1998, simultaneously at the Birmingham Motor Show and at the AAA show at Berlin, this owing to the special significance Nick Scheele saw in the German market for the premium segment.

By this occasion very detailed technical specifications were published, among which the use of a V-6 engine was most significant. This engine was basically what Ford used for some of its own Taurus and Windstar models. A smaller variant with a 2.5-liter capacity was better known in Europe from the Ford Mondeo and Cougar models. However, Jaguar engineers found quite a few details to improve on the already very advanced Duratec engine concept. They managed to further improve its smoothness and raise power output of the 3-liter to no less than 238 horsepower by the use of variable timing, a three-stage variable-length intake manifold, and other tricks from Jaguar's own V-8. All this was transformed into impressive performance via a Getrag five-speed gearbox weighing in at no more than 33 kilograms (73 pounds), or a five-speed automatic.

The automatic was made by Ford in the United States, as was the six-cylinder engine, but Jaguar engineers had the last word in the design, as they knew the automatics of competing companies like Mercedes-Benz, ZF, and GM quite well. The electronic engine management integrated with the automatic so that a particularly smooth gearchange could be assured. The specific power output of this engine (80 horsepower per liter) was remarkable indeed! The durability of the engine had been proven in endurance tests, in which the engine ran at 6,000 rpm for no less than 180 hours. No wonder that this engine turned the S-Type into a wonderful sporting sedan!

It was hardly imaginable that further improvement was possible with the by then well-introduced 4-liter V-8 (without supercharging), although only a five-speed automatic transmission was available. The V-8 had variable camshafts, and an air injection system helped optimize fuel atomization. Interestingly there was no return pipe back to the fuel tank. Earlier cars could incur damage to the fuel pump caused by the circulating fuel getting warmer and warmer.

The chassis layout had been designed by Lincoln engineers, which helps explain why the drive shafts no longer acted as transverse control arms. The position of the outer end of the lower transverse arm exactly below the center of the wheel was patented. Jaguar engineers found ways to ensure that the typical Jaguar roadholding and riding comfort were achieved. Part of the suspension is not attached to one of the two (for weight-saving) rear subframes, but is attached directly to the body via rubber elements. This did not affect

S-Type styling clay of 1995. *(J)*

S-Type and its illustrious forebears. *(J)*

noise levels in the car, while handling became much more precise. The electronically adjustable dampers (CATS), which had been introduced with the XK, were also available at extra cost for the S-Type.

All S-Types used the same bodyshell, the platform of which had been developed in conjunction with Lincoln, who used it for their LS models, cars of a much different character than the Jaguar. Later it was also adopted for Ford sports cars with traditional names like Thunderbird and Mustang (in both cases with different engines). Despite this commonality, the S-Type had the air of a true Jaguar, as mother Ford wisely refrained from commanding in questions of style and ambience. This was left with Jaguar chief stylist Geoff Lawson, who sadly died from a stroke on June 24, 1999, at only 54. His successor was Ian Callum, who already had designed the Aston Martin DB 7. In effect the S-Type adopted many of the typical Jaguar styling clues of the 1960s. This included the leaper hood mascot, although it was restricted to North America.

Again, several clay models had been made for evaluation, among them one with the XK 8 mouth, one

Above: This view clearly shows the influence from the Mark II. *(J)*

Right: Navigation system in the 1999 S-Type. *(J)*

with heavily chromed bumpers like the Mark II, and one with the grille of the XJ. Interior designs were much more modern; only the choice of wood and leather followed Jaguar tradition. So there was some parallel with the XJ 40 and its electronic monitor, but in this case the useful navigation system made the screen acceptable even for old Jaguar fans. Soon after introduction, however, criticism emerged that the interior reflected Ford's style too much, particularly with regard to the half-circle center console. The car was loaded with electronic playthings, and it would be only a year before steering wheel knobs for radio and phone had been introduced, and Jaguar dared to offer voice-activated systems.

Interior space was generous, and was at least similar to the existing short wheelbase sedan. Little wonder that the S-Type was acclaimed by the press, over the similarly stylish but less powerful, inexpensive Rover 75 that debuted at the same time.

Testers were delighted with the sporting, elegant appearance of the S-Type, which despite its rather high and somewhat unusual waistline was as much a thing of beauty as the Jaguar name suggested. Roadholding and riding comfort were much praised, as were the level of equipment and the price, but the 3-liter engine lacked some low-speed torque in direct comparison with its competitors. This was somewhat balanced by the light, short-travel gear lever and the smoothness of the engine, which is so difficult to achieve in a V-6 configuration. *Auto Motor und Sport* summed up: "The established competitors will have to worry about their territory." The advantages of the S-Type showed clearly if compared with the XJ sedan, which with its larger dimensions and higher level of equipment could hardly make up for the modernity and functionality of the S-Type.

In Germany a single S-Type 3.0 took part in some long-distance races, a courageous effort by the Bamberg Jaguar dealer Sauer, who in the Nürburgring 24 Hours scored fourth in class. Two years later a mishap dropped them to eighth in class. In both cases Wolfgang Schuhbauer was among the drivers. He had worked for Jaguar Deutschland for many years; among his duties were questions of technical homologation.

Design chief for the millennium: Ian Callum. *(J)*

Ford chief Jacques Nasser. *(J)*

The original S-Type interior was not widely accepted. *(J)*

At Jaguar in Coventry in the meantime, rumors about a possible merger of Ford and BMW were discounted by BMW. Ford turned to the automobile business of Volvo in Sweden, after a take-over by Renault had failed. Volvo is said to have been happy to take on its new parent—the Swedes were impressed with Ford's ten years of management of Jaguar.

Jaguar chief Nick Scheele had in the meantime become president of Ford of Europe. His successor at Jaguar, directly reporting to Ford chief Jacques Nasser, was Dr. Wolfgang Reitzle, appointed on March 19, 1999. Born March 7, 1949, he had served BMW faithfully for more than 23 years. However, he could not become chairman at BMW. When chief Bernd Pischetsrieder was forced out in a management shakeup in 1998, the representatives of the workforce voted against Reitzle on February 5, 1999. So he moved to the marque that was the nearest in style to BMW. A German in the Jaguar chair—this had always been unthinkable but now it was true. England captured one of the most

S-Type prepared for racing by Autohaus Sauer at Bamberg in Germany. *(J)*

gifted managers in the automotive industry only a few months after Germany had acquired the British icons Rolls-Royce and Bentley.

Similar to the disastrous JRT in the British Leyland era, Jaguar now was combined with some prestige makes of the Ford group in the Premier Automotive Group (PAG). These were Aston Martin with its ultra-expensive sports cars, Lincoln with its American luxury sedans, and Volvo with its practical premium sedans, station cars, and sports utility vehicles.

At the upper echelons of Jaguar management, Ford people became more and more present. At Jaguar Deutschland, chief Jeffrey L. Scott after only two years moved on to even more important functions in the Ford hierarchy at Cologne, being replaced at Kronberg am Taunus in October 2000 by Wolfgang Steib, who came from Peugeot Deutschland.

Owners of older Jaguars were most pleased when Coventry decided that spares supply for the more than 10-year-old XJ and XJ-S would now be organized by the Jaguar Daimler Heritage Trust in the "Jaguar Classic Parts" scheme via selected Jaguar dealers. In January 2000 Anders Ditlev Clausager, coming from the British Motor Industry Heritage Trust (BMIHT), became chief archivist at the JDHT.

At the same time early in 2000, 38-year-old Julian Thompson came to Jaguar from the Volkswagen Design Center in Spain. He had a master's degree from the Royal College of Art and joined the development center at Whitley, where Jaguar established its Advanced Design Studio in a new facility that was called Lawson Building. Soon a crew of up to 30 experts—all free from the necessities of day-to-day design work on the

Above from left: Dr. Wolfgang Reitzle, the first German chief of Jaguar.

Mike Beasley became executive director in 1999.

Joe Greenwell became Jaguar chief in 2003. *(all J)*

Eddie Irvine (above) in the Jaguar R1. *(J)*

Formula 1 engineering chief Neil Ressler. *(J)*

now rather numerous Jaguar models—planned the long-term development of Jaguar styling. In parallel, Jaguar also created a Geoff Lawson Jaguar Stipendium for the advancement of particularly talented students at the Royal College of Art.

The traditional administration building at Browns Lane was again renovated. A customer center was added to the north corner, where the latest models were exhibited and Jaguar's research and development activities were described. It included a Formula 1 driving simulator, featuring a true Jaguar R-1. At the opposite side toward the JDHT building, an elegant coffee bar was added. However, Dr. Reitzle was a rare sight at Browns Lane. He usually worked from London, as he also was head of PAG, to which Land Rover was added when Ford took it over (from BMW, by the way). This included the integration of BMIHT with its famous museum at Gaydon and the license for some old makes. Mike Beasley became executive director at Jaguar. Born on July 18, 1943, he had joined Ford in 1966, but moved to BLMC in 1974, where he became chief of the Browns Lane factory in 1977 and a Jaguar board member in 1985. Jaguar's new managing director was Jonathan Browning, former Ford marketing director.

By the end of 2001 Browning had departed, and Mike Beasley took over his duties as well. Mike himself retired in March 2003, succeeded by Mike Wright, while Joe Greenwell became Jaguar and Land Rover chief, following Bob Dover. Greenwell had had a hand in reorganizing Jaguar's sales and marketing in 1983 and was a dyed-in-the-wool Jaguar man, although he had a three-year episode at Dearborn, where he worked for Nick Scheele.

In the meantime Jaguar celebrated the millennium by entering Formula One. Jaguar had never raced in that class but always followed it attentively. In the C-Type days, Jaguar felt challenged by the BRM disaster to save Britain's honor with a monoposto made from C-Type parts. This did not materialize, nor did a Jaguar Formula One racer to prevent Mike Hawthorn from moving to Ferrari. As late as in the 1960s, technical director William Heynes proposed a Formula One racing car, which also was dumped. After Ford had taken over Jaguar, Tom Walkinshaw could have joined Jaguar on its way to Formula One instead of setting out on his own financial adventure with Arrows, but he found no one at Jaguar to support his idea.

Jackie Stewart, 1969, 1971, and 1973 F1 champion, and his family were closer to Formula One. Since 1988 Jackie's son Paul had his own racing team called Paul Stewart Racing. This fully occupied Paul so that he had to abandon his own racing career. Paul Stewart Racing

Johnny Herbert (below) enjoying the sunshine in Jaguar's Formula 1 racing car. *(J)*

earned 130 wins and 13 championship titles in lower formulae. In 1996, Jackie established a Formula One team, which early in the 1997 season had its first podium place with Rubens Barrichello finishing second in Monaco. The team was successful in other races as well and in 1999 finished fourth in the constructors' championship.

Jackie Stewart had been associated with Ford since his own Formula One days using Ford-Cosworth engines. Stewart offered Dearborn a takeover of his team in order to ensure sufficient financial backing. Ford management grasped at the chance, of course, and took over the Stewart Formula One team. It was soon decided that, despite the marque's lack of tradition in Formula One, the team would be renamed Jaguar. The team stayed at Milton Keynes and was increased to 70 employees under Chief Neil Ressler, technical director Gary Anderson, and chief engineer John Russell. They designed the first Jaguar Formula One racing car for 2000, with more than two-thirds of its parts being made in-house (which is an unusually high proportion). Trevor Crisp came over from Jaguar engine development to (also Ford-owned) Cosworth, where he had a hand in the engine of the Jaguar R-1. In Stewart's tradition this CR2 engine was a 72-degree V-10 weighing-in at only 97 kilograms (214 pounds) with a power output of around 820 horsepower at 18,000 rpm. The R-1's debut was January 25, 2000. The metallic green finish had been specially mixed according to specifications from Ian Callum and his assistant Fergus Pollock. A liter of it is said to have cost £600.

Drivers were Michael Schumacher's former Ferrari teammate and championship runner-up Eddie Irvine and the much-loved Johnny Herbert, who after three years with Sauber had joined Stewart for the 1999 season and won the Nürburgring race. Race organizer was Andy Miller, who had Brazilian test driver and 1999 Formula 3 runner-up Luciano Burti at hand if one of the drivers was not available.

The 2000 season was not as glorious as Jaguar's enthusiastic fans might have wished. Both cars retired early in the first races. When the cars had become

From top: Trevor Crisp, racing team leader Bobby Rahal, and Niki Lauda at Jaguar's wind tunnel. *(all J)*

Left: JP1 monoposto with Cosworth-tuned 3-liter engine from the X-Type. *(J)*

sufficiently reliable they came in far behind the quickest, and even the return to the previous year's engine could not change this. Less than helpful was Paul Stewart's ill health, which forced him to retire from his managing posts. While Eddie Irvine had expected a race win at the beginning of the season, less optimistic statements became prevalent as the schedule wore on. Although Jaguar's Formula One activities were said to be aimed at a long-term success, the team's third-from-the-bottom finish in the constructors' championship was a great disappointment.

For 2001 much was changed. The car was designed by chief engineer John Russell and aerodynamicist Mark Handford (formerly of Lola). With 820 horsepower at "only" 17,300 rpm, the Cosworth CR3 was again among the most powerful engines in Formula One. The seven-speed gearbox now had its own oil circulation, which was expected to avoid some of the previous year's problems. The rear suspension was less innovative than before. So much was renewed that the first tests involved a modified R-1 equipped with the transmission and suspension of the revised model. Following the latest

Jaguar R5 for 2004. *(J)*

homologation regulations, downforce had to be reduced for the R-2, a handicap for cornering.

The team was completely restructured with the appointment of another former Formula One champion, Niki Lauda. He chaired the Premier Performance Division, which governed Jaguar Racing under its director, Indy 500 Champion Bobby Rahal with 320 employees, Cosworth Racing under Trevor Crisp with 720 employees, and Pi Research with 300 employees, who under Mike Purnell looked after electronics.

Stewart's Formula 3 team now also was renamed Jaguar. The season was entered with drivers André Lotterer from Germany and James Courtney from Australia. Courtney finished fourth and Lotterer fifth in the drivers' championship that year, upon which the team was sold to a consortium formed by John Uprichard (Van Diemen), Roly Vicini (P1 Motorsport), and John Sweeney (Sweeney Racing).

Beginning December 1, 2000, Bobby Rahal was Jaguar's new team leader. The drivers were Eddie Irvine and Luciano Burti; Johnny Herbert had ended his racing career. Test driver Narain Karthikeyan was the first Indian at the wheel of a Formula One racing car. Technical chief was Steve Nichols, born in 1947 in the United States, who had gained Formula One experience with Jordan and McLaren. Disappointment was great when despite Niki Lauda's consultancy, the 2001 season was not more successful than before. The fall guy was Luciano Burti, who was replaced with another Brazilian, Pedro de la Rosa, the former test driver. He was replaced in that position by Thomas Scheckter. Results did not improve, however. Aerodynamics may have been the reason, as there was not sufficient wind tunnel capacity for testing. Jaguar finished eighth in the constructors' championship in 2001; the poor showing was mainly credited to the use of Michelin tires.

Under the new managing and technical director, Günther Steiner, 2002 was a year of technical continuity. The higher-revving CR4 engine was available from the Nürburgring race onward. The R-3, which had lost 30 kilograms (66 pounds) in weight, at first gained a reputation of not being faster than its predecessor. Finally, a wind tunnel in nearby Bicester was purchased so that the time-consuming transport of parts to and from Ford's wind tunnel in America could be avoided. This new wind tunnel was only available from the spring of 2002. Toward the end of the season at least, Eddie Irvine was in a position to more regularly finish in the middle of the pack. With an improved front suspension, the car reacted more quickly when entering tight bends. But when all the points were added up at the end of the season, no progress had been achieved. Jaguar still ranked seventh in the constructors' championship.

Ford chiefs began to lose patience, making many changes to attempt to improve performance and save money. Among the victims were Rahal, Lauda, and Irvine. The changes were so extensive that practically a new team was formed. The wheelbase of the new R4 was reduced by 6 inches and thus was somewhat more compact than the previous racing car. Under Tony Purnell, two young drivers were contracted: 26-year-old Australian Mark Webber, who had his first Formula One experience with Minardi, and 22-year-old Antonio Pizzonia, who had shown his considerable talent as BMW-Williams test driver.

The course now seemed to have been set right for the Jaguar team. It still suffered many retirements, but remarkably often, quite good results were achieved. The dismissal of Pizzonia seemed to be a bit quick, but he was successfully replaced for the Hockenheim race with tall Australian Justin Wilson, who demanded no pay for his driving for Jaguar. The season nevertheless ended disappointingly. Jaguar only had managed to beat Minardi, who had not entered the last races; the Jordan with its less powerful Cosworth engine; and outsiders Toyota. This was not easy to explain to Ford.

Jaguar Racing still continued everyday work and announced the purchase and revamp of the DERA wind tunnel in Bedford in October 2003, which made

Above: Mark Fields. *(S)*

Below: The dark interior of an early S-Type Sport. *(J)*

Under Rainer Landwehr, Jaguar and Land Rover Deutschland were unified. *(J)*

With the Red Bull badge massive change would come, but Jaguar F1 driver Mark Webber could not foresee this early in 2004. *(J)*

quicker aerodynamic testing possible. Christian Klien from Austria replaced Justin Wilson. In 2004 Jaguar was among the teams with the tightest budgets, but again Mark Webber gave his best, particularly in qualification runs. At Malaysia the R-5 started from the first row, but Webber lost the advantage in the race. The season continued without further highlights for Jaguar, so that the end result was similar to the previous years. Quite a few Jaguar aficionados sighed with relief when Jaguar left Formula One at the end of 2004 and sold the team to Red Bull chief Dietrich Mateschitz, while Cosworth was sold to Kevin Kalkhoven and Gerry Forsythe from the U.S. Champ Car series.

The initiators of Jaguar's Formula One adventure, particularly Jac Nasser and Wolfgang Reitzle, had left the Ford group already, Nasser in October 2001. Nick Scheele, who still benefited from his success with Jaguar in the late 1990s, became Ford's CEO. Wolfgang Reitzle, to whom this job had not been offered, moved in April 2002 to Linde, a German company that made gases for different purposes as well as fork-lift trucks. Mark Fields, only 41 years old and working for Ford since 1989, had done a remarkable job in reviving Mazda and giving it a sporty, elegant image. He became the new PAG chief, which now comprised Aston Martin, Jaguar, Land Rover, and Volvo.

On December 5, 2000, at the Bologna show, Jaguar unveiled the Sport version of both S-Type variants with a darker interior, reduced chrome on the outside, and 18-inch Monaco wheels, dynamic stability control, and—in the case of the 4.0—the CATS system, more or less following the style of the XJR.

Particularly in the United States, the S-Type had a consistent following. Jaguar North America, until then at Mahwah, New Jersey, in mid-2001 moved to faraway Irvine, California, where most of its customers lived, together with Aston Martin and Land Rover, both Premier Automotive Group partners. The move was directed by Mike O'Driscoll; general manager of the Jaguar Division was Sue Callaway.

Little wonder that Jaguar Deutschland soon went the same route. The newly established Land Rover Deutschland GmbH had erected a new building at Schwalbach in Jaguar's neighborhood. Early in 2003 Jaguar Deutschland moved in there as well, as its chief since August 2002, Reinhard Künstler, also chaired Land Rover Deutschland. Germany became ever more important for Jaguar, as a new test center was created at the Nürburgring for suspension testing, replacing provisional premises near the Brünnchen and Karussell corners of the circuit. This test center was directed by Wolfgang Schuhbauer, the competent homologation expert and hobby racing driver. In August 2003 Künstler moved on to become director of European operations for Land Rover. His post at Schwalbach was taken over by Dr. Rainer Landwehr, who had worked for the Ford group since 1987. He, however, left on December 1, 2004, so Jeffrey L. Scott had to return to Jaguar.

At home in England the PAG marques worked together more closely in areas well-hidden from customers. PAG now created a common panel for purchasing, financial, and legal matters. Nick Barter took over Jaguar and Land Rover development, so commonalities were to be expected in areas, such as platforms, wiring harnesses, and basic engine design.

The Jaguar range of models was supplemented by a quite revolutionary compact: The X-Type, unveiled late in 2000, became available in June 2001. It was even smaller than the S-Type. The X-Type's exterior was all but revolutionary in that it closely resembled the XJ sedans but with slightly smaller dimensions. The X-Type was only about 12 inches shorter than the XJ sedan. The most significant difference was the shorter, more sloped hood. All in all the X-Type was so typically Jaguar that it was hardly recognized as a novelty in traffic. This effect diminished its sales success, at least abroad.

The interior mirrored Jaguar's typical quality of style, not repeating the S-Type's unusual design but sharing its birds-eye maple veneer, while walnut remained the reserve of XJ and XK. The liquid-damped grab handles over the doors folded neatly and gently away when not used. Hidden behind the dashboard was a strong steel tube for further stiffening of the bodyshell. A novelty was the 7-inch monitor with a touch control function that also served as a video monitor. This monitor was again used for the navigation system that could direct drivers around traffic jams and other obstacles. A refined version of voice control was also available for the X-Type. In fact, the X-Type's interior, with the shining growler on the steering wheel boss, was to become the pattern for future

The Jaguar X-Type was timeless and elegant. It was the first Jaguar with all-wheel drive as standard. It started production with 2.5- or 3.0-liter V-6 engines. The quality interior impresses with traditional materials and modern technology. *(J)*

Jaguar sedans. The Sport variant could be ordered with two-tone leather.

The interior dimensions made one forget about the decreased exterior ones. With 16 cubic feet, the trunk was larger than any other Jaguar's. It could be enlarged further by folding down the asymmetrically separated rear backrest with its three headrests. The four airbags—with ARTS at extra cost—were joined by side curtain airbags on each side, another first for Jaguar. An air conditioning unit with a pollen filter was standard, while automatic temperature adjustment was standard only with S.E. models, which in some countries were called Executive.

Under the hood, Jaguar's first transversely mounted engines were remarkable. The V-6 unit itself was similar to the S-Type in its 3-liter form, but in the X-Type also was offered as a 2.5-liter with 198-horsepower. Ceramic catalysts made warming up quicker so that in the testing cycle better emissions were achieved.

The X-Type had all-wheel drive, and this explains its name. The only other Jaguar to have all-wheel drive had been the XJ 220 prototype. The reason for this conception lies in its platform, which also was used for the front-wheel drive Ford Mondeo. The Jaguar engine's power output was such that front-wheel drive would often cause wheelspin, and so the Whitley engineers

X-Type Sport. *(J)*

took the same route that Audi engineers had taken 20 years before with their Quattro system. In order to maintain the traditional Jaguar feeling, 60 percent of the power went to the rear wheels under normal circumstances. This was automatically varied by a viscous coupling in the epicyclic central differential, if required. The system was called Traction 4. The gearbox was situated below the engine, the manual box being Ford's renowned MTX 75, the automatic being made by Jatco, with Jaguar's typical J-gate.

While the fine Special Equipment (or Executive) and Sport versions could be combined with both engines, the standard equipment was limited to the 2.5-liter variant. Jaguar aimed at young, successful businessmen as their new clients, but many X-Type customers were well-to-do older people who no longer needed the spaciousness of a large sedan but preferred a shorter car for ease of parking.

The X-Type was not made in the Midlands but at Halewood, near Liverpool on England's northwest coast. After production of the Ford Escort had ceased in July 2000, the large plant there, which had been in use since 1962, and lots of personnel had nothing to do. So Jaguar came in, practically reconstructing the whole site and bringing it up to the standard of the other Jaguar plants. The work was carried out under the guidance of David Hudson, who had been Jaguar's production director at Browns Lane. The workforce had to adapt from building an inexpensive, mass-production car to a premium-class car. Visits to Castle Bromwich and endless training were inevitable, as was a drastic reduction of personnel. All in all, the Jaguarization of Halewood may have cost $450 million. It was believed that 100,000 to 140,000 X-Types would be produced there in 2004 with only 3,000 employees.

The X-Type did not fulfill the sales targets as naturally as the S-Type did. The U.S. market was particularly difficult, and sales did not achieve the targets. Luckily the English and Italian markets responded to the car, while in Germany it was hardly noticed. All in all, the production facility was somewhat larger than needed. Already in 2001, it was clear that there would be no work for about 500 employees. The hourly production rate was reduced from 39 to 29 units. In early 2002, Colin Tivey became David Hudson's successor at Halewood.

Thus, great hopes were attached to the X-Type 2.0 launched early in 2002. The stroke of the engine had been reduced from 79.5 to 66.8mm, resulting in a capacity of 2.1 liters and 156 horsepower. As the six-cylinder concept remained, the smoothness of the engine was guaranteed. For this lower-powered variant front-wheel drive was sufficient, so the heavy and expensive differential and driveshaft delivering power to the rear wheels could be abandoned, which helped performance. External differences were minimal, and the equipment was similar to the 2.5-liter models.

Jaguar's development team had put some effort into achieving precise steering with sufficient feel despite the front wheel drive. The X-Type already had two equal-length driveshafts with particularly low-friction outside links. Thanks to a specially tuned suspension and electronic traction control as standard, a particularly well-balanced compromise was achieved. Dynamic stability control was available at extra cost only.

At the 2002 Motor show, Jaguar unveiled the limited X-Type 2.5 and 3.0 Indianapolis with 18-inch wheels, a mesh grille *à la* the XJR, black alcantara seats, new veneer interior panels, and Xenon headlights, but both models were restricted to the British market. The X-Type 2.0 S, introduced in April 2003, was also meant to offer value for the money and slotted somewhat

R-Coupe concept gave an idea of what might come from Jaguar under Ian Callum's direction. *(J)*

Classical elements newly presented on R-D6. *(J)*

between Sport and S.E. It featured 17-inch wheels, elegant chrome, automatic climate control, a metallic finish, a reverse parking aid, electric exterior mirrors, divided rear backrests, a Premium sound system, and cup holders in the front compartment. Being only £1,000 more expensive than the standard model, it was a lot of car for the money.

Nevertheless, demand for the X-Type did not increase. Jaguar also announced that about 500 employees from all three sites would have to face layoffs. Jaguar may have incurred losses of about $500 million in 2002. Following demand, Jaguar decided that from model year 2004 onward the 3.0 would be the only X-Type to be offered in North America, the smaller models obviously spoiling Jaguar's image there.

Browns Lane hoped that X-Type sales would rise with the help from a territory yet unexploited by Jaguar—the diesel engine! Jaguar did investigate several diesel possibilities in the 1980s, but now a Jaguar diesel was to become reality. This happened, again, with the help of the Ford Mondeo, which had a tried-and-tested 2-liter TDCI engine. This engine offered state-of-the-art diesel technology with four valves per cylinder, turbocharging with an intercooler, and direct injection via common rail under extremely high pressures of around 1,600 bar. This form of injection resulted in an effective microspray of fuel, which ensured effective and complete combustion. With some tricks, Jaguar engineers found some extra horsepower in the engine and employed two-stage injection to achieve smoother running. This made one forget that the engine only had four cylinders, unlike any Jaguar since 1948—55 years before.

Although some fastidious Jaguar drivers may not have been overwhelmed by the performance of this youngest and smallest Jaguar, it was well ahead of its competitors and could boast of running costs lower than with any previous Jaguar. Together with the diesel, revised 2004 X-Types were introduced with chrome bars in the grille and under the side windows of the S.E. models, a less rounded trunk plinth and a new release knob, cup holders with a fine chrome ring, a wider range of adjustment for the front seats and the choice of alcantara, a more powerful audio system with six

2003 X-Type diesel with front-wheel drive. *(J)*

instead of four speakers, softer molded parts for the central console, and a choice of new alloy wheels. The front bumper bracket was redesigned to facilitate repair by being screwed to the body instead of being an integral part of it.

Only three months later, Jaguar introduced the X-Type estate, which resembled the Volvo V40 and BMW 3 Touring. The rear window could be opened independent of the whole rear door. The cargo capacity was 50 cubic feet, larger than competition, without any loss to the external appearance of the car. With four engines and three lines of equipment (similar to the sedan) this car really entered Ford, Mazda, and Volvo territory, and the question was whether the more expensive but noble car would gain sales in this market. This turned out to be the case, and convincingly so. Jaguar even decided, against its previous strategy, that the X-Type estate should be offered as the "Sportwagon" in the United States.

At the end of 2002 the Japanese were offered a series of 200 X-Type 2.0 S.E. Limiteds with an automatically dimming rear mirror, cruise control, electric seats, auto headlights, and rain-sensing wipers priced at 4.25 million yen. In June a series of 300 X-Type 3.0 Sovereigns was added with additional chrome, walnut instead of maple veneer, a wood/leather steering wheel, heated seats stitched in contrasting colors, 70/30 folding backrest and lambswool mats at 5.58 million yen, 200,000 more than the 3.0 S.E. This was a mixture that also would have been appreciated elsewhere.

In March 2005 Jaguar announced an enlarged 2.2-liter diesel engine with electronically adjustable valve timing, 155 horsepower, and 360 Nm. (The torque could increase to 400 Nm for short bursts.) This extraordinarily dynamic diesel vehicle had a particle filter on board in order to ensure clean emissions, and on country roads an astonishing 50 miles per gallon was the norm. Equipment was upgraded and the smallest V-6 was deleted. In Germany the 2.0 diesel was dropped as well. For the 2006 model year the S.E. had even more chrome and Sapelli mahogany instead of birds-eye maple. The Sport was no longer exported to Europe. England got a limited series of 1,000 XS 2.0 diesels or 2.5 V-6. A body kit from Jaguar's latest Sports Collection made the car look sportier than typical British restraint would allow. Eighteen-inch Proteus wheels (Aruba wheels on the sedans) underlined the dynamic appearance. More akin to British tradition was the new Sovereign, with walnut veneer and more chrome, a model preserved for the U.K. A Sport Premium variant with a more aggressive appearance was offered at the same price as the Sovereign, both in conjunction with the 2.2- and 3.0-liter engines.

X-Type diesel with common rail direct injection. *(J)*

While the X-Type represented a classical Jaguar line, Ian Callum presented an alternative direction for Jaguar design. As a trial balloon he presented the R-Coupe at the 2001 Frankfurt show, a four-seater with unusually flat body panels and some bold edges, not dissimilar to Ford's then prevailing design. The car was hardly reminiscent of earlier Jaguar models, with the exception of the S-Type grille filled with mesh as on the XJR. It did have the typical hump over the rear wheels, but it was more reminiscent of a 30-year-old Corvette Stingray. Door handles were left off completely, which saved design work; an electronic remote control would open the doors. The side vent for the engine bay had an interesting Union Jack grille. Lighting with Xenon at the front and LEDs at the rear was well advanced.

The interior surprised with a dark brown dashboard with no wood. Wooden panels of Macassar

Top: Dynamic styling of R-D6 concept car. *(J)*

Above: Rear "suicide" doors on R-D6. *(J)*

ebony instead of mahogany were used for the lower door panels and transmission tunnel sides, the latter continuing at unchanged level right to the back seats, providing a center console in the rear. The whiskey bottle that integrated neatly into that console was not very politically correct. The instruments with red lights did not mirror the old British style despite their silver coating—which they shared with all bright external parts, including the fuel filler—but the steering wheel with its small round boss would have suited standard Jaguar models, as would have the paddles behind it for shifting gears.

Two years later, in September 2003, the Frankfurt show again had an astounding Jaguar concept car to view. This was the R-D6, an R-Coupe taken a bit further. Front and rear overhangs were much shorter, and behind the front doors were two rear suicide doors—similar to Mazda's RX-8, which in most other respects was very close to the R-D6. The engine, however, was Jaguar's reserve: a new six-cylinder diesel, as suggested by the name. This was the 2.7-liter V-6 with more than 200 horsepower that was still under development at Jaguar and Peugeot, but which had been announced for the S-Type. Despite large door panels, no wood was used in the interior, which was somewhat more conservative than in the R-Coupe. It again boasted separate rear seats, covered in dark brown saddle leather and again separated by a central console. The bright red interior lights produced something other than the typical Jaguar aura.

The modifications made to the S-Type early in 2002 were less radical. Of course, the front and grille were slightly revised while at the rear only the reverse lights with clear glass lenses and badges were changed. The 2.5-liter engine from the X-Type now also was available for the S-Type, providing adequate performance. The 3.0 benefited from the refinements that had been introduced when it was first installed in the X-Type. With a

Above: On the X-Type estate the rear window could be opened separately. *(J)*

Right: With elegance the X-Type estate occupied a fine niche. *(J)*

Above: S-Type as revised in 2002. *(J)*

Left: Brand-new 4.2-liter engine for S-Type. *(J)*

Below: The much-revised interior of the 2002 S-Type. *(J)*

Top: From 2004 the hood of the S-Type was made of aluminum. *(J)*

Above: For 2004 the rear end of the S-Type was restyled. *(J)*

stroke increased to 90.6mm the V-8 was enlarged to 4.2 liters, a classical format for Jaguar, and 298 horsepower. Even more powerful was the new variant S-Type R, with 395 supercharged horsepower, recognizable by the mesh grille. All models benefited from the completely new six-speed automatic from ZF, which provided quick gear changes without the slightest jerk, particularly in the supercharged model. Unfortunately the J-gate, with its manual detents, now became somewhat complicated! The gearbox consisted of only 470 instead of 660 parts and was eight kilograms (17.7 pounds) lighter than the previous five-speeder. The manual gearboxes of the six-cylinder variants still made do with five speeds.

The occasionally criticized front suspension and front subframe had been revised more thoroughly than would be expected for such a young model. The car's handling now was even more agile. At the rear, some fine tuning had been carried out; for example, the joints for the subframe went more outboard. The S-Type R had even further enhanced suspension at both ends.

Many opinions said that the interior had been the original S-Type's greatest disadvantage, and so this was replaced by a near-copy of the X-Type's. For the first time an electronic hand brake was added so that the old lever could be replaced with one not dissimilar to a flush-fitting door handle. Brake assist provided added braking power in panic braking situations. The electric windows were improved with a device to prevent pinching fingers, and they opened and closed completely with a short push on the switch. The adjustable pedals were a remarkable feature, operated with the same lever as the electrical steering-wheel adjustment. Magnesium reinforcements under the seats and gearbox brackets helped save weight, as did the further use of aluminum for suspension elements. The ARTS system for the airbags was now available for the S-Type, as were two side-curtain airbags.

Testers were delighted with the improvements. "Couldn't they have made it that way from the beginning?" was the implicit question particularly in the enthusiastic reports about the S-Type R, which now with its more than complete electronic package was well ahead of the competition. However, in October 2003 Jaguar felt compelled to help sales with a limited S-Type Plus, a 3.0 S.E. with automatic air conditioning, 17-inch alloys, metallic finish, cruise control, rear parking aids, a heated windshield, and a CD-player storing six CDs at just £30,250.

Jaguar designers saw further opportunities to creatively improve the S-Type and undertook another remarkable redesign in March 2004. These changes included a more pronounced hood made from aluminum with a more upright grille, a revised rear end with the restyled taillights being positioned higher. The straighter trunk plinth was changed according to the style introduced shortly before on the X-Type. The interior was enhanced in detail, again in accordance with other models, particularly in the sporting models with bright aluminum in place of wood. The dials, which had become dark green with the 2002 model changes, now were black again.

Mechanically nothing was changed apart from suspension details. Nevertheless, under the hood of the S-Type a most noticeable innovation took place with the availability of a completely new diesel engine designed in cooperation with Peugeot. Unlike the diesel in the X-Type, this was a unit for the sporty Jaguar driver: with four camshafts, 24 valves, and two electronically controlled turbochargers, it turned out 207 horsepower and 435 Nm, no less a masterpiece of engineering than Jaguar's gasoline units. Thanks to efficient sound-deadening and a carefully controlled combustion process (with the help of high-pressure piezo valves for the injection system), hardly any difference could be heard in the interior versus the available gasoline engines. The engine block was made of cast iron and vermicular graphite so that the whole engine was just 15 kilograms (33 pounds) heavier than the gasoline V-6. Its sensational low-speed torque—thanks to well-chosen gears in the (automatic or manual) gearbox—and fuel economy (33 miles per gallon) were convincing in every respect. In Germany the automatic version initially did not receive a very good emissions rating but this would soon be changed, so that a reduced road tax to D4 standard became applicable.

In June 2004 the S-Type diesel took part in the Nürburgring 24 Hours, generating a good bit of attention. Starting from position 186 the car had moved forward to 73rd when, while making an evasive maneuver the car spun around, damaging not only the body but the front suspension as well and requiring 1½ hours of repair. Although a good position could not be achieved, the car returned to the race, proving its reliability.

The 2.5-liter variant was upgraded by the Plus model for Great Britain early in 2005. Extras like cruise control, automatic air conditioning, ESP+T traction control, an automatic gearbox, 17-inch Aurora wheels, and rear parking aid were standard. In Sport and S.E. models a navigation system, phone with Bluetooth interface, voice control, front parking aid, rain-sensing wipers, automatically dimming interior and door mirrors, heated seats and windshield were also included. The 2.5-liter engine was then deleted from the S-Type range for the 2006 model year. The diesel, now with a particle filter, had been well accepted by customers. From late 2004 British customers could order Sports Collection bumpers and skirts, a concession to the tastes of younger customers who bemoaned the demise of the M.G. sports sedans.

The S-Type introduced a completely new six-cylinder diesel with twin turbocharging. *(J)*

The S-Type diesel for the 2004 Nürburgring 24 hours. *(J)*

22
AIRY LIGHTWEIGHT

For a long time, rumors had circulated that Jaguar planned to replace the steel body panels of its cars with aluminum, the material used in the early Swallow days. Such a major step was of course reserved to the flagship, and so Jaguar on September 26, 2002—exactly 34 years after the debut of the first Jaguar XJ—unveiled the completely new third generation of the large sedan. Aluminum panels are less stiff than steel, and so it was to be expected that Jaguar—like its competitors—would use extruded aluminum sheaths. But Jaguar chose another route, as with the aluminum D-Type and Lightweight E-Type: Nearly all parts contributing to stiffness were formed from aluminum sheets; only the front spring towers were cast-aluminum parts, while behind the dashboard a magnesium strut was used—similar to the S-Type. Patented slim rivets were used to connect panels, with a special adhesive giving additional strength so that the stiffness of the preceding body shell was bettered by no less than 60 percent.

Breaking new ground always bears a risk. Thus, Jaguar first built some experimental S-Types with aluminum bodies. In endurance tests, these showed their weak points and Jaguar learned valuable lessons on how to eliminate them. One concern with aluminum bodies is to make sure that repairs can be carried out at reasonable cost. Jaguar tried to achieve this with a modular design that would allow whole parts of the structure to simply be replaced when damaged. The structure beneath the front bumper was screwed to the body, so that it could be replaced with little effort and expense. Doors and the hood were other modules that could easily be separated from the main body. Despite its light body, the XJ was one of the first cars to pass the newly tightened U.S. crash standard FMVSS 208. Of course the body shop at Castle Bromwich had to be modified considerably for the new technology. Although the cost was high, Jaguar was determined to go ahead, and Ford generously financed the improvements. This may not have happened in later years, as Ford's economical situation worsened.

The aluminum body was presented boldly, with a polished, unpainted example of the body shell gleaming in the limelight like silver. Weighing in at only 1,545 kilograms (3,414 pounds), the basic XJ matched the weight of its smallest sibling, the X-Type, with the same engine and automatic gearbox!

The second technical stroke of the XJ was brought in from German Thyssen-Krupp (which also supplied Mercedes-Benz): This was the air suspension, which ensures good springing even for lighter cars. In the XJ,

Above: The featherweight aluminum structure of X 350. *(J)*

Below: The third generation XJ 6. *(J)*

Above: 2003 XJ 8 4.2. *(J)*

Right: The rear end of the X 350 with styling cues taken from XJ Series 3. *(J)*

Below: The dashboard of the X 350 was particularly elegant. *(J)*

electronic aids also helped avoid excessive roll in corners. Its most important advantage was that heavy loads could not spoil springing, as the system incorporated automatic level control. This system was integrated into a new suspension configuration that was very similar to the S-Type—another major mechanical item that was shared among different ranges of Jaguar cars.

In contrast to the technical advances, the styling of the new XJ was very traditional. The considerable height of the car (nearly 57 inches, more than with any Jaguar since the Mark II) was well hidden, while the interior offered generous space. The far-forward position of the front suspension allowed more legroom.

The interior was similar to the S-Type but with additional chrome, 16-way electrically adjustable seats, two- or—at extra cost—four-zone climate control, TV and DVD player, and other electronic gadgets. Even the "piano lacquer" fashion for the dashboard, which Volkswagen had introduced for its Phaeton, was available on request. The chromed knob for the glove box lid and its hydraulic-dampened hinge were further niceties that supported the fine ambience of the car.

Transmission also was very similar to the S-Type, but wisely the smaller V-6 was not offered. Instead a 3.5-liter V-8 with 258 horsepower was added, an exact copy of the 4.2 but with the stroke reduced to 76.5mm.

British traditionalists regretted that Jaguar had no Daimler variant to offer. The Super V-8 was now a Jaguar, although a Jaguar XJR with the same supercharged engine was offered. The XJ 6 was offered in the U.K. in a basic version with steel springs, and Sport variants were available in conjunction with the 3.5 and 4.2 nonsupercharged V-8s. For export only a single level of equipment was offered, with the option to combine extras to personalize the car. In literature and advertising, the leaper had been restyled, now seemingly three-dimensional. The latest motto was "Born to perform."

Customers had to be patient, as supplies of the XJ only became available in the spring of 2003. It had been difficult to make pressing tools that supplied panels guaranteeing both the desired door gaps and continuous curves along the whole body. When aluminum panels leave the pressing tool, the shape is slightly less pronounced than it would be with a steel panel. The tool

Above: Space and luxury in the X 350 LWB. *(J)*

Below: Concept Eight concept car with large vent just in front of the doors. *(J)*

thus has to overdo things a little in order to compensate for that effect—it is a matter of patience and a good eye to ensure that an excellent result is achieved. Jaguar must have done a perfect job as the finish of the bodies was excellent. According to the judgment of the motoring press, Jaguar had made a large leap forward. The XJ garnered the well-deserved title of "best car in the world," despite considerable efforts from the competition.

Some customers wished for even more generous legroom in the back than the new XJ offered, and a long-wheelbase version of the V-8 models was announced on April 4, 2004, with an additional weight of just 20 kilograms (44 pounds). The grille surround was chromed or color-coded according to the taste of the customer. The previous picnic tables were revived, now as business trays in a size suitable for a laptop. Interior dimensions also benefited from the roof being a further 7mm higher. From the outside, the long wheelbase was hardly recognizable, although larger wheels helped spotters.

Chief Stylist Ian Callum used the debut of the long-wheelbase XJ to showcase his Concept Eight derivative: No electronic gadgets, no multimedia show, but including the finest materials like thick ox hide, two separate seats in the rear, and a massive wooden rail below the side windows—not seen in a Jaguar for more than 30 years. The roof panel was tinted glass fashionably surrounded by a row of red lights—not exactly what the normal customer would desire for his everyday transport, but eye candy for the Motor Show. Large wheels, a vertical vent for the engine bay behind the front wheels (similar to the Range Rover), dark cherry red paint, and the XJR mesh grille made this car unique. Americans at the New York Auto Show were particularly impressed by the all but traditionally British style of this concept car.

The most longstanding Jaguar clients would have wished for a revival of the Daimler name with this model, but this was not yet to happen. Jaguar stated that it would think about creating a Daimler that looked much different from the Jaguar. A year later, Callum's Concept Eight was offered to North American customers as the Portfolio limited edition, and very similar cars were offered in other countries as the Super-Eight, reviving the Daimler name, at last! This Super-Eight was introduced in Britain, Europe, and the Far East in November 2005. It was similar to the previous Jaguar Super V-8 with a long wheelbase, 18-inch Rapier wheels, and typical Daimler insignia like the crinkled grille and trunk plinth, additional chrome, figured walnut veneer with a boxwood inlay, and the curved D on the steering wheel boss and stitched into the headrests. Of course, picnic tables and lambswool rugs were on board, and the standard equipment also comprised voice-controlled four-zone automatic air conditioning, a multimedia information system, and adjustable rear seats instead of the bench. The range of colors included new—and exclusive to the Daimler—shades of Garnet Red and Westminster Blue, while the interior colors of Ivory, Champagne, and Charcoal were less extravagant. The 4.2-liter supercharged engine and transmission remained unchanged.

Naturally, this flagship benefited from the improvements introduced for the 2006 model year XJ series, including sound-deadening laminated glass for the side windows and further sound-deadening in the engine bay. All in all, the noise in the interior was again reduced by up to 5 decibels. With regard to future legislation, a tire pressure warning system was installed (standard for XJR). The Brembo brakes of the XJR were replaced with even better ones from Conti-Teves, and a Bluetooth interface was added to the telephone system.

2005 Jaguar advanced lightweight coupe. *(J)*

The deletion of the windshield frame and the side rubbing moldings was intended to make the car more attractive. In Germany, the Executive was reintroduced with a higher level of equipment (soft grain leather, heated seats with a memory package for the driver's seat, walnut veneer, leather-wood steering wheel, and more chrome). The Jaguar long-wheelbase models were all called Sovereign in Europe—a return to familiar names.

One revolution was the transplant of the fabulous 2.7-liter twin-turbo diesel engine with 207 horsepower that had been introduced in the S-Type. In this car it ran even smoother and accelerated the car to 60 miles per hour in just six seconds, allowing a maximum speed of 138 miles per hour. With a particle filter, the car fitted the tightest emission standards in Europe. For country roads, the average fuel consumption was 36 miles per gallon. This made the new XJ 6 diesel a worthwhile proposition for frequent drivers, particularly in the less expensive Classic guise.

Everyday life for Jaguar was less bright than the appearances at motor shows might suggest. During 2004 it was apparent that the planned sales increases had been too ambitious, so a moderate reduction caused by the generally weak economy turned into a hard setback. The devaluation of the U.S. dollar against the pound also was less than helpful for Jaguar (and Land Rover) accounts, so that losses soon rose into the millions. Saving money became the order of the day, and the consequences were strict: Jaguar left the Formula One circuit and had to abandon one of its three plants as these were too many for a yearly production of 120,000 cars. Unfortunately it was the traditional Browns Lane plant with its XK and XJ assembly that saw the axe: The bodies were being brought there by trucks from Castle Bromwich just for assembly, even though Castle Bromwich was large enough to house this assembly as well.

Assembly for the XJ sedans took place from July 1 through August 15, 2005. With respect to tradition, the Jaguar-Daimler Heritage Trust (JDHT) museum, the veneer shop, and Jaguar headquarters remained at Browns Lane. The large factory area was intended to be sold as a specific land-use area.

Beginning in July 2004, Bibiana Boerio became the chief of Jaguar. She had served Jaguar in the 1990s as finance director. Boerio's predecessor, Mike Wright, was the board member responsible for a more effective sales structure that would eliminate some administration costs.

Following the idea of cost-saving, the transfer of XK assembly to Castle Bromwich coincided with the introduction of its aluminum replacement, which had long been scheduled for 2005. After the U.S. Limited and U.K. 4.2 S gave sales one last boost, the last XK 8 was completed on May 27, 2005, ready for the JDHT museum. An identical example was made for JDC director Brian Ekin. With a yearly production average in excess of 10,000, the XK had been Jaguar's most successful sports car.

Jaguar revealed the general direction for the new XK with a concept car called the Advanced Lightweight Coupe at the Detroit Motor Show on January 10, 2005. The marketing materials highlighted the aluminum construction of the two-plus-two, which had been an important advance for the XJ and now also would be used for the sports car. With aluminum frames around interior vents and brushed aluminum replacing the traditional wood, the car made a statement about its new construction material. The car's oval mouth was a

Top: After a three-year break the crinkled Daimler grille returned with the Daimler Super-Eight, a variant of the X 350. *(J)*

Above: The exquisite interior of Daimler's Super-Eight. *(J)*

Early drawings for the new XK of 2005. *(J)*

wonderful citation from the E-Type, as was the tailgate, although it was hinged at the top.

The Advanced Lightweight Coupe explained much about Jaguar's latest design philosophy, and that was greeted with a warm reception. With its increased wheelbase and shorter overhangs, the coupe seemed to be more compact than the old XK 8. The rear "seats" offered some more headroom. Wheels had grown to up to 21 inches. Paddles behind the steering wheel for the gear change were inspired by (still) sister Aston Martin and served the same function as the former J-gate shifter. The mechanical package was similar to the XKR, thus promising a top speed of 180 miles per hour and acceleration from standstill to 60 miles per hour in less than five seconds!

The official successor to the XK 8 was introduced alongside the Daimler and the XJ 6 diesel at the 2005 Frankfurt show. It was very similar to the Advanced Lightweight Coupe. The most significant changes were the replacement of brake cooling ducts at the front skirt with round fog lights, and a more pronounced vertical engine bay vent with an integrated Jaguar logo. The pointed ends of the front indicators and taillights, together with the curved edge above the rear wheels, were departures from earlier designs. The headlights pivoted to shed light into corners, as the Citroën DS had once done. Round elements in the taillights recalled the E-Type, and more than one Jaguar enthusiast was relieved that the styling of the Jaguar sports car had not been changed too radically, although its air was now cooler, more functional.

The coupe, at 1,595 kilograms (3,525 pounds) was indeed a lightweight (as had promised the concept car's name), but more cast-alloy elements had been integrated into the structure than in the XJ sedan. This made it possible for the convertible to offer the same stiffness as the coupe. Thanks to the increased wheelbase, the interior was much more spacious, although the rear seats still were not adequate for adults on a long journey. The trunk, in the case of the coupe accessible via a large tailgate, offered the same spaciousness as before. The cover for the convertible top, for the first time on a production Jaguar, had been replaced with a metal cover that was integrated in the electronic opening cycle—as had been tried with the Daimler Corsica concept car.

The dashboard was a relief for Jaguar enthusiasts in that it returned to wood, which had been abolished from the Lightweight concept car. The veneer now covered a smaller area than in the previous XK 8, which helped give the interior a more spacious air. A small monitor for the most important information was fitted neatly between the two classic round instruments behind the steering wheel. The standard 7-inch monitor in the center console was made foolproof, and touch elements grew larger as soon as a finger came near them. It allegedly reacted 16 times as fast as the earlier one.

The gearlever indeed dispensed with the J-gate, as the gears could be changed manually with paddles (Bosch Mechatronic) behind the steering wheel. These allowed a gear change at record speed without any jerk even under extreme conditions. Thanks to a smart key system and keyless entry, no ignition key was used; a red starter button alongside the gearlever is the telltale.

Engine and transmission remained nearly the same, but now conformed to the latest Euro 4 emissions standard. The new car approached the performance of the earlier XKR (standstill to 60 miles per hour in six seconds, maximum speed limited to 155 miles per hour), showing how the weight advantage worked. Brakes were optimized in many respects, with larger discs and improved hydraulic valves for better stability in an emergency. Pedestrians benefited in case of a collision from a hood that could rise in one-thousandth of one second to soften the impact.

Full of determination and enthusiasm, Bibiana Boerio arrived in 2004 as Jaguar's new chief. *(J)*

A wonderful face with an ideally positioned "mouth" on Jaguar's 2005 XK. *(J)*

Overleaf: The hump above the rear wheels and round backlights recall the unforgettable E-Type. *(J)*

AHO 108

An electronic tire pressure warning device added to the vehicle's safety.

The XK convertible had a self-extending rollover bar hidden behind each tiny back seat. With the top closed, the bars would extend through the back window; otherwise the intended low roofline would have been affected.

The sports car, vital for Jaguar's image, was promoted with a new style of advertising under the "Gorgeous" theme, created by Euro RSCG/Fuel, which at first left unclear what product it was for. The first production vehicle was ready on December 20, 2005—a silver coupe for the JDHT museum. Even the prototypes, thanks to computer-aided design and development, had been of first-class quality, despite a development period of only two years. In mid-January 2006, the press was invited to Stellenbosch in South Africa for evaluation, and indeed the car was much acclaimed. As promised by Chief Stylist Ian Callum, the car was still more elegant on the road than it was on a show stand or in the advertising photos.

Everyone was keen to learn how the XK drove, and there was no disappointment. The seating position ensured good visibility and generous space, particularly for shoulders and feet. The car produced smooth power, which was ferocious in the lower gears. Reviewers liked the good accelerator pedal feel (despite the "drive-by-wire" system, a first for Jaguar), the sensible steering, the car's exceptionally neutral behavior in fast corners (CATS now regulating each damper separately), and the excellent brakes, all of which were to the enthusiast's taste.

Spacious, cozy, modern—the interior of Jaguar's 2005 XK. *(J)*

Below: The XK coupe on its debut with Ian Callum. *(J)*

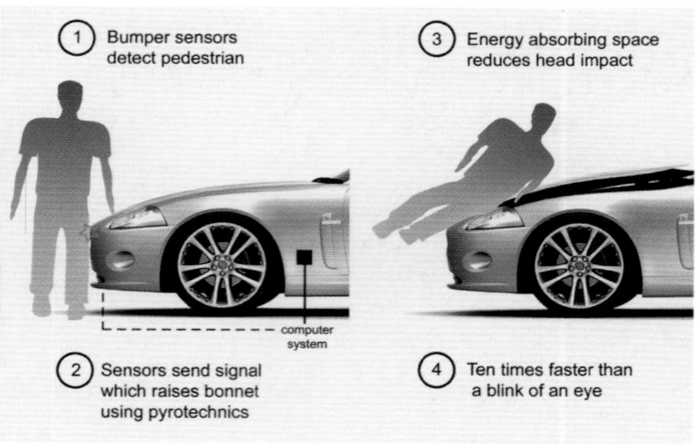

Exemplary pedestrian protection with the help of a hood that could lift several inches within a fraction of a second upon impact. *(J)*

The carefully composed exhaust note was a particular delight at full throttle or when the engine was used to assist braking. A bypass valve in the silencer enabled an imposing trombone sound when it was desired, while at low revs it kept the engine nearly inaudible.

Jaguar's development team was little surprised that the initially low demand rose quickly as soon as XK test cars were available in March 2006.

During the first quarter of 2006, PAG—thanks also to some seasonal influence—achieved a profit of $163 million, while the previous year $100 million in losses had been incurred. Was this an early result of PAG chief Mark Fields having been replaced by Lewis Booth? At nearly the same time, on September 1, 2005, Geoff Polites had taken over from Joe Greenwell as Jaguar's chief executive officer. The money spent on advertising was not lost and even helped raise sales of the XJ range, which had been a bit sluggish. From July 2006 the limited edition XJR Portfolio was offered with the side vents, large wheels, and mighty exhaust of the Concept Eight, and the price was £62,040. The diesel now also was available on the long-wheelbase car.

In the meantime a buyer had been found for Browns Lane: The Delamar Company, which made standardized parts for houses. They required that JDHT, the wood shop, and headquarters be moved near the development center at Whitley.

The new XKR was introduced in London on July 20, 2006. Like its predecessor it was recognizable by the supercharger. Further development of the engine—including variable valve timing—made power output increase to 416 horsepower. The front end bore another variant of the mesh grille, the brake calipers now were finished black, and the side vents were aluminum-colored.

Driving, particularly with Dunlop's Sport Maxx tires (285mm wide on 20-inch wheels at the rear) was just a dream! Even the supercharger noise had been reduced by 5 decibels thanks to improved sound-deadening—although the engine now was hidden behind plastic panels.

No other vehicle combined noble style and athletic power in the way Jaguar did with this latest sporting flagship. The return to old virtues led back to success, which so many pessimists thought was lost. Enthusiasts all over the world look forward to further surprises that Jaguar has in store.

The XK convertible is harmonic with either an open or closed top—since the E-Type, it was the first Jaguar that was not derived from an enclosed model. *(J)*

Above: No less than four vents help keep the XKR's engine bay cool. *(J)*

Left: The 2006 XKR. *(J)*

Below: Jaguar deliberately chose to retain the classic fabric folding top. *(J)*

APPENDICES

CHRONOLOGY

Summer 1892
Birth of William Walmsley

September 4, 1901
Birth of William Lyons

1920
Completion of William Walmsley's first motorcycle sidecar

June 1921
Walmsley family moves to Blackpool

November 21, 1922
Establishment of the Swallow Sidecar Company by Walmsley and Lyons, effective September 11, 1922

1923
First automobile body for own use

1926
Move of the renamed Swallow Sidecar & Coach Building Company to Cocker Street in Blackpool; first exports to Emil Frey in Switzerland

May 1927
Completion of the first Austin-Swallow Seven

January 1, 1928
Effective date of the order of 500 Austin-Swallows from London dealer Henlys (first car being delivered on January 21, 1928)

September 1928
First Austin-Swallow sedan completed

October 8, 1928
Rental of one of four workshop blocks by Lyons and Walmsley from Whitmore Park Estate Company near Holbrook Lane, Foleshill, near Coventry, at a yearly rate of £1,200, with an option to purchase the premises; move lasted until November 1928

Around 1929
Company name changed to Swallow Coachbuilding Company (presumably with a subsidiary Swallow Sidecar Company)

1929
First Standard-Swallow

September 29, 1929
Purchase by Lyons and Walmsley of the rented and an adjacent workshop block (both covering 1.85 acres in all) from Whitmore Park Estate Company at £18,000 (mortgage by Coventry Permanent Building Society), the deal having been arranged by solicitor Gillitt.

October 1929
Sir John Black made chief at Standard

January 1931
First Swallow body for a six-cylinder chassis (Wolseley Hornet)

May 1931
First six-cylinder Standard-Swallow

October 1931
First SS with exclusive chassis

May 5, 1932
First Annual General Meeting (AGM) of Swallow Coachbuilding Company

December 9, 1932
Purchase of two further blocks, including the sawmill, by Lyons and Walmsley for £8,000; company bank became Lloyds Bank instead of William's and Deacon's Bank

1933
First SS in an internationally recognized event (Monte Carlo Rally)

October 10/26, 1933
Establishment of SS Car Company as a subsidiary of Swallow Sidecar Company, taking over the business, and registration under No. 280990

January 11, 1934
Floating of 100,000 nominal £1 preference shares by SS Car Company (yearly profit 6.5 percent) and 140,000 voting nominal £1/4 shares sold at £1.075 and £0.525 (thus £135,000 authorized capital, Lyons holding the majority of the voting shares, Walmsley leaving the company)

Mid-1934
Establishment of the SS Car Club

November 20, 1934
First AGM of SS Car Company Limited

1935
Reestablishment of the Swallow Coachbuilding Company (1935) as subsidiary of the SS Car Company Limited with an authorized capital of £10,000

September 21, 1935
Debut of the SS Jaguar with a Standard-built OHV engine exclusive to SS

October 11, 1935
Second AGM of SS Car Company Limited

October 1936
Third AGM of SS Car Company Limited

1937
First overseas win of an SS 100 at Vila Real in Portugal

March 1937
Purchase by SS of 19 acres adjacent to its site on which until 1940 further production facilities are to be erected

October 1937
Adoption of all-steel body construction, larger panels made by Pressed Steel

November 11, 1937
Registration of a Jaguar Cars Limited for SS under No. 333482

1938
Adoption of the leaper mascot

1939
Purchase of Motor Panels Company at a little over £20,000 from Mulliners in Birmingham

July 1939
1,500 employees at SS

November 30, 1939
Sixth AGM at SS Car Company Limited

1940
Production changed to war requirements (airplane parts, motorbike trailers, and sidecars)

December 12, 1940
Seventh AGM of SS Car Company Limited; loss announced following the loss of an order for the canceled Manchester bomber project

Autumn 1942
Purchase of the production facilities for the six-cylinder engines from Standard at £6,000 (accounting value more than £16,000)

1943
Sale of Motor Panels to Rubery Owen to improve capital stock by about £50,000 (price per share: £2)

May 1944
AGM of SS Car Company Limited; return to peace production announced

November 1944
Purchase of the Triumph automobile works by Standard in order to develop it into an SS competitor after the war

April 9, 1945
Exchange of names between SS Car Company Limited and Jaguar Cars Limited, making the Jaguar name a marque

1945
Authorization in the AGM of additional 150,000 preference shares at nominal £1 with 5.5 percent profit (subsequently only 100,000 such shares were floated, the authorized capital then being £500,000)

October 1945
Sale of Swallow Sidecar Company (1935) Limited to Helliwell at Stratford-upon-Avon, who earlier had offered £10,000 in December 1944

Summer 1946
Replacement of Australian importer Tozer, Kemsley & Millbourn after contenting themselves with 100 Jaguar sales per year, with Jack Bryson, who promises 2,000 sales per year

September 1946
Approximately 1,400 employees at Jaguar

October 1946
First issue of in-house magazine, *Jaguar Journal*

January 31, 1947
Fire at the felt store destroys an area of nearly 900 square feet

1947
Start of Joska Bourgeois as Belgian Jaguar importer

August 1947
Shipping of the first left-hand drive (LHD) Jaguar

1947

March/April 1948
Nomination of Max Hoffman, 487 Park Avenue, New York instead of Inskips (already importing Rolls-Royce and Bentley) as importer for the U.S. East Coast and Charles "Chuck" Hornburg, 9155 Sunset Boulevard, Los Angeles (prevailing over Roger Barlow's International Motors) for the West Coast

May 6, 1948
Jaguar AGM

July 1948
Class win at the Alpine Rally for SS 100 and Ian Appleyard

August 1948
Clearance sheets for every vehicle now to be signed by inspection personnel

October 27 until November 6, 1948
Thirty-third Motor Show, unveiling of the Jaguar XK 120 prototype at Stand 146 (press had seen the car some days before on press day); Rankin arranges Jaguar advertisements at all London underground stations and on 750 buses

February 1949
First "International Automobile Exhibition" in New York, XK 120 on display

1949/1950
Abbey Panels & Sheet Metal Company supplies XK 120 aluminum bodies (and continues to do so for other prototypes like E-Type Lightweight and XJ 220, Ted Loades buying out his three partners step-by-step)

May 6, 1949
Jaguar AGM, further new production facilities completed

1950
Tooling-up at Pressed Steel for the Mark VII body (debut in October) costs Jaguar £250,000

1951
Permission refused for further expansion at Foleshill; rental by Jaguar from British government of Daimler's Shadow Factory No. 2 at Browns Lane, Allesley, Coventry (approximate 23 acres, yearly rental is £30,000) for five years with a most-favored clause for Jaguar; sale of Foleshill to Dunlop at £433,000

June 1951
First Jaguar victory at Le Mans (XK 120 C, Whitehead/Walker)

June 1952
First victory of a disc-braked car (Reims, XK 120 C, Stirling Moss)

November 1952
Completion of move to Browns Lane, the delays having been caused by Daimler's delayed end of Ferret production

December 31, 1952
Announcement by Lyons at a directors' meeting of a 2-liter car at £695

1953
Establishment of Jaguar Cars North America with Eerdmans in the same building as Hoffman; reorganization of U.S. distribution (during 1953 and 1954 imports into the U.S. of no other car company are higher than Jaguar's)

April 1953
Borg-Warner automatic available in Mark VII

1953
Tooling up for the 2.4-liter body at Pressed Steel costs Jaguar £360,000, preparation for 2.4-liter production costs a further £300,000

May 1954
Twentieth Jaguar AGM; dividend is 30 percent after having been raised in 1950, 1952, and 1953 by five percentage points

October 1954
Price of a £1/4 share rises from £2.5 to £3.5 at the London Stock Exchange

January 1955
Dispute with Hoffman about his preference of Mercedes-Benz makes him lose his status as importer (According to arbitration he will continue for years to gain from each Jaguar sold east of the Mississippi, and he gets $600,000 for his spares store.) Briggs Cunningham will become New York Jaguar dealer from 1955 on. Despite his tendency not to reinvest profits, Hornburg retains his status, even after a dispute about the repayment of customs refund

1955

1954
Just 21 new Jaguars registered in Germany

June 6, 1955
Death of Lyons' only son, John Michael, on his early evening drive to Le Mans in an accident 30 miles south of Cherbourg, driving into an oncoming American military bus (the reason for the accident is unclear with regard to good visibility and Lyons' familiarity with driving on the right side; Lyons had only joined Jaguar in March 1955)

1955
Issuance of new shares of Jaguar Cars Limited spread among shareholders in accordance with their previous share

January 1, 1956
William Lyons knighted

January 1956
Victory at Monte Carlo Rally (the only one for Jaguar, Mark VII M, Adams/Bigger)

March 22, 1956
Royal visit (Queen Elizabeth II and Prince Philip) at Browns Lane

November 29, 1956
Following the Suez crisis, Jaguar production cut for two months to four working days per week

February 12, 1957
Destruction of the northern part of the assembly hall (17,500 square yards) by fire; normal work resumed on June 8, 1957

April 1957
Dismissal of Works Director Ted Orr after a dispute about wage negotiations; successor is Bob Grice, who has just returned to Jaguar from BMC

August 1, 1957
A new bonus system allows wage increases of up to 40 percent without effect to the sum of all wages at Jaguar

August 1957
Start of assembly of 214 2.4- and 3.4-liter in Mexico, which ends in July 1960

January 1958
Jaguar Cars North American Corporation renamed Jaguar Cars Incorporated (delayed delivery of Mark VIII with power steering makes sales of that model fall from 602 to 363)

January 1958
Quickly expanding Peter Lindner becomes importer for Germany along with Fendler & Lüdemann

June 26, 1958
Jaguar AGM, dividend now 40 percent

1958
Employment of Pat Appleyard after her divorce from Ian at London Jaguar service, where Americans on holiday collect their new Jaguars (20 percent of Jaguar sales in the United States are followed by such an arrangement)

Early 1959
Purchase of the Browns Lane plant inclusive of the building formerly used by General Electric Corporation at £1.25 million

1959
Establishment of a committee for improved quality

June 1959
Jaguar AGM, dividend raised from £36,225 to £158,175 (directors' wages traditionally are higher, now amounting to £205,000 despite Lyons' waiver of part of his commission)

October 1959
Cost of production of a Mark II is £681, £60 more than for the predecessor; overhead and distribution cost are calculated at £358, the car is sold in Britain at £1,082 (pretax)

Late March 1960
Jaguar AGM

May 26, 1960
Purchase of Daimler Motor Company from BSA inclusive of its 23-acre production facility at Radford, Coventry, and more than 1,700 employees at £3,240,000 (Production of the Major is just ending in favor of the Majestic Major, of which initially 10 per week are made)

September 1960
Start of Mark II assembly in South Africa

Early 1961
Purchase of lorry manufacturer Guy (est. 1914) at Wolverhampton with 23 acres of production facilities and 825 employees, from the receiver at £800,000 (the company being taxed at £2.22 million)

March 15, 1961
Unveiling of the Jaguar E-Type after Bob Berry's breakneck drive to Geneva at a SMMT meeting at the Parc des Eaux Vives

March 1961
Jaguar AGM

April 1961
Introduction of the E-Type at the 5th International Automobile Show, now at the New York Coliseum

April 1961
Victory for the E-Type at its first race at Oulton Park, the two participating cars having been completed only the Thursday before

1961
A Jaguar share costs £3.94 (a 1952 share that cost £1.20 would have grown to nine shares by then)

1961
First wins of Lindner's team at the Nürburgring

1962
Jaguar's weekly sum of wages is £150,000

July 1962
Jaguar honored by Queen Elizabeth II with the Royal Warrant of Appointment as Motor Car Manufacturer

March 7, 1963
Purchase of engine and fork-lift truck manufacturer Coventry Climax Engines Limited (exchange of shares for which Jaguar issues 428,572 new voting shares, the first time that Lyons' share of the votes is reduced)

May 1963
End of takeover negotiations with Lotus (who use Coventry Climax engines) without result

July 1963
Purchase of Paget works with approximately 35 acres of land adjacent to Guy

Late April 1964
Establishment of Jaguar-Cummins Limited, a 50/50 joint venture between U.S. engine manufacturer Cummins and Guy; due to insoluble technical problems, Jaguar will sell its share to Cummins in 1967 at £1 per share

1964
Distribution cooperation with BMW considered (ended by Lyons when he learned that BMW owner Quandt's family held a 14 percent stake in German Daimler; negotiations about a Maserati takeover are also ended without result)

1965
Purchase by Jaguar of 1919-established engine manufacturer Henry Meadows from Quinton Hazell Limited, with nearly 90 acres land adjacent to Guy, at £212,500

January 1966
Fendler & Lüdemann give up their status as one of the importers to Germany

1966
12,000 employees at Jaguar; the number of Jaguar preference shares is 3.5 million, the number of Jaguar voting shares is 450,000, of which 260,000 are held by Sir William Lyons

July 12, 1966
Merger with BMC (Austin and Morris) to establish BMH (British Motor Holdings), which cost BMC £17,485,000 (£1.7 million for Lyons); George Harriman to become BMH chairman, Lyons to become director with a maximum of autonomy for Jaguar (Lyons had not analyzed the financial situation of BMC, relying on the company's strong impression; losses in the second half of 1966 amount to £7.5 million after £5.8 million profit in the second half of 1965)

1967
Queen's Award for Export Achievement given to Jaguar

1967
Transfer of £900,000 dividend from Jaguar to BMH for the last three months of 1966 and the first three months of 1967

1967
Merger of Jaguar Cars Incorporated with BMC-Hambro to form British Motor Holdings (USA) under Graham Whitehead, with Eerdmans and Lyons as lifelong directors

January 17, 1968
Announcement of the merger between BMH and Leyland to form (with effectiveness from May 13, 1968) BLMC; Jaguar to become part of Specialist Car Division (during the ensuing negotiations Lyons mediates between Stokes and Harriman, who has no chance to become BLMC chief; Stokes guarantees Lyons Jaguar autonomy under the BLMC umbrella, Stokes to become Jaguar director, Lyons to become BLMC deputy chairman)

September 1968
Loss of the prosperous South African import organization to BLMC

1968
BLMC to receive £1,011 million dividend from Jaguar for the 14-month business year 1967-1968

1969
Truck manufacturers Henry Meadows transferred against financial compensation to Leyland Truck and Bus Division

1969
9,000 employees at Jaguar group

1969
Plans to extend Jaguar fabrication at Browns Lane, birth of the idea of a Coundon Wedge Road with a gate at the former back side of Jaguar's plant (both only being completed in 1991)

1970
BLMC to receive £3.3 million dividend from Jaguar for the 1970 business year

April 1971
Rover Deutschland named temporary importer for Jaguar in Germany

July 1971
According to Lyons he had made £20 million Jaguar assets out of £350,000 in borrowed capital

1971
BLMC to receive £3.68 million dividend from Jaguar (the whole profit) for the 1971 business year

Late 1971
Brüggemann new exclusive Jaguar importer to Germany

March 3, 1972
Retirement of Sir William Lyons, successor is Lofty England

1972
Loss of importer status for Chuck Hornburg, who becomes a normal dealer

July 7, 1972
Announcement that all BLMC companies will be merged into the new British Leyland UK Limited

October 1972
Jaguar reduced to a Division within BLMC

September 1973
Geoffrey Robinson becomes new managing director at Jaguar, England remains chairman until retiring in late January 1974

Early 1974
British elections won by Labour Party, Harold Wilson new prime minister

July 1974
BLMC—after £50 million profits in 1973—fully exploits its line of credit and applies for a state guarantee for another £50 million, which minister for industry Anthony Wedgwood Benn, a strong trade unionist, grants under the condition that the situation of BLMC be analyzed by the industrial adviser to the prime minister, Sir Don Ryder; his commission starts on December 18, 1974. Furthermore, government via the National Enterprise Board becomes BLMC shareholder

December 27, 1974
Jaguar board replaced with a management board of seven persons nominated by Robinson until mid-1975

April 23, 1975
Submission of the fateful Ryder report, which leads to the dissolution of the Jaguar management board; two weeks later Geoffrey Robinson resigns under protest against the integration of Jaguar into the ailing BLMC

May 1975
Tony Thompson chairs an operating committee for the concerns of Jaguar that now is part of Leyland Cars division, but has little influence

August 1977
Sir Don Ryder resigns from the National Enterprise Board; end of 2½ years of inactivity within BLMC

November 1977
Michael Edwardes is new BLMC chief; he also becomes member of the NEB

1978
Unveiling of Pininfarina's Jaguar Spyder concept car at the Motor Show; the car inspires later Jaguar styling

1978
Reestablishment of Jaguar in the Jaguar Rover Triumph Division (headed by William Pratt Thompson, dissolved in 1979); Jaguar headed by Robert Knight, who retires in 1980; his successor is Percy Plant

1979
British elections won by Conservatives. "Iron Lady" Margaret Thatcher becomes prime minister; the consequent upward revaluation of the pound makes life harder for BLMC

1980
Nearly 10,000 employees at Jaguar

April 26, 1980
Retirement of Knight, successor is John Egan; from the start of a serious strike on April 9, 1980 until 1981, BL seriously considers closing down Jaguar production

1982
7,200 employees at Jaguar

February 15, 1982
Registration of Jaguar Cars Limited under No. 16720070 and of Jaguar Cars Holdings Limited under No. 16720066

1982
Reestablishment of Jaguar Cars Incorporated at BL's site at Hudson River with Graham Whitehead as president and vice president Michael Dale; John Egan to become chairman in May 1984 (at the same time establishment of Jaguar Canada Incorporated under Whitehead)

1983
Purchase of plants at Browns Lane, Radford, and Castle Bromwich where, after cessation of Triumph TR 7 production, only Jaguar bodies are made

December 1, 1983
Announcement of privatization of Jaguar and spares organization UNIPART by Industry and Trade Secretary Norman Tebbitt

January 1, 1984
Start of Jaguar import to Germany by Jaguar Deutschland GmbH, established in the previous year by Jaguar Cars Limited and Emil Frey

February 1984
Browns Lane visit of Prince Charles and Lady Diana

May 1984
Name of Jaguar Cars Holdings Limited changed to Jaguar plc, with board members Hamish Orr-Ewing as chairman, Raymond Horrocks, and Edward Bond

August 3, 1984
Privatization of Jaguar plc by flotation of 177,880,000 nominal £1/4 shares via London Stock Exchange at £1.65 each arranged by Hill Samuel & Company Limited (Board members are Egan, Beasley, Whitehead, and both Edwards; honorary president is Sir William Lyons)

1984
Touring car championship for Jaguar XJS-TWR

1985
Again 10,000 employees at Jaguar

February 8, 1985
Death of Sir William Lyons

June 1986
Egan knighted

February 10, 1988
Announcement by Jaguar and GKN-Sankey of a 50/50 joint venture called Venture Pressings Limited for the pressing of XJS body panels (Jaguar represented in the six-person board by Mike Beasley, Gerry Lawlor, and Mike Kinski)

May 9, 1988
Announcement by Jaguar and TWR (Tom Walkinshaw) of a 50/50 joint venture called Jaguar Sport Limited, with Egan as chairman

May 23, 1988
Opening of the new development center at Whitley near Coventry (in part use since 1987) making the GEC building at Browns Lane free for production purposes

June 12, 1988
First win of a TWR-Jaguar at Le Mans (XJR-9, Lammers/Dumfries/Wallace)

September 14, 1989
Announcement of a half-year loss of £1.1 million

September 19, 1989
Announcement by Ford of its intention to take over 15 percent (the highest proportion not requiring permission from the British government) of Jaguar

October 25, 1989
Application by Ford at the U.S. Securities & Exchange Commission for the 100 percent takeover of Jaguar

October 31, 1989
Annullment of the "Golden share" (expiration previously set at the end of 1990), allowing the takeover of Jaguar

November 1, 1989
Offer by Ford to take over all Jaguar shares; Jaguar board manages to lift the price per share to £8.50 during night-time negotiations and then recommends shareholders to accept this offer; GM withdraws its offer

December 1, 1989
Jaguar AGM; deletion of "Golden share" clause; all in all the takeover of Jaguar (effected via S. G. Warburg & Company Limited and Goldman Sachs International) costs Ford more than £1.5 billion

March 22, 1990
William Hayden, CBE, new Jaguar chief executive (succeeding Egan); from July 1, 1990, he is Jaguar chairman

June 8, 1990
Removal of Jaguar Cars Incorporated from Willow Tree Road, Leonie, New Jersey, to MacArthur Boulevard, Mahwah, New Jersey; opening by the Duke and Duchess of York

June 1990
Establishment of Jaguar Australia by Inchcape Group (already Jaguar importer to Hong Kong and owner of former coachbuilder Mann Egerton)

October 1990
Mike Dale new chief of Jaguar Cars Incorporated after Whitehead's retirement

1992
Only 8,000 employees at Jaguar

April 1, 1992
Nicholas V. Scheele becomes the new Jaguar chairman after Hayden's retirement

Summer 1993
Replacement of the complete assembly tracks at Browns Lane during the three weeks summer holidays under the direction of Jim Padilla

March 1999
Dr. Wolfgang Reitzle becomes new Jaguar chairman and head of newly established Premier Automotive Group (PAG) with Aston Martin, Jaguar, Lincoln, and Volvo

2000
Ailing Land Rover taken over by Ford and integrated into PAG

April 2002
Mark Fields becomes new PAG chief

2002
Separation of Lincoln from PAG

October 2003
Joe Greenwell becomes new Jaguar chief

July 2004
Bibiana Boerio becomes new Jaguar managing director

2005
Relocation of final assembly of XJ and XK models to Castle Bromwich; Lewis Booth becomes new PAG chief

September 2005
Geoff Polites becomes new chief executive officer at Jaguar

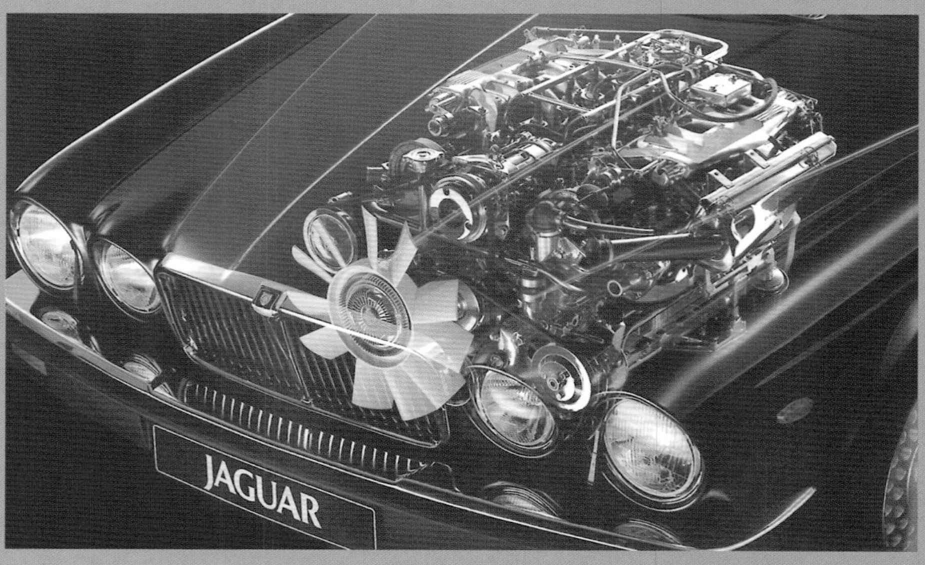

JAGUAR ENGINEERING

This appendix may help readers who, for their own restoration, want detailed information that was not provided earlier in the book. The appendix provides details about the technical evolution at Jaguar.

It is surprising how closely related the very different Jaguar models are and how continuously they developed from the very first SS to beyond the turn of a millennium—a true evolution! This is all the more surprising as William Lyons' first cars were based on chassis sourced elsewhere, a process through which Standard was to grow into the most important role. This appendix addresses each mechanical unit and describes the development step by step, following its own logic.

In order not to get lost, racing cars and their derivatives for road use (XK-SS, XJ 220, and XJR-15) have been kept outside the scope of this appendix. Although they influence the standard models, they often deviate extensively in their technical specifications. In many respects the X-Type has its individual mechanical solutions, most of which are not compatible to other models. It is technically more akin to other makes in the Ford group, thus helping Jaguar save development cost and resources.

XK Engine

With regard to engines, Jaguar always has been remarkably conservative. For example, its efforts in diesel technology only bore fruit in 2003. According to good British tradition, engines usually are mounted longitudinally in the front of the chassis. Jaguar's early engines were not developed from a clean sheet of paper but were derived from the six-cylinder engine found in the Standard chassis (the smaller four-cylinder would not play any role in Jaguar's heyday). This engine was particularly smooth, reliable, and inexpensive with about 2- or 2.5-liter capacity. This was unusually progressive with its seven main bearings of 2.25-inch diameter. The crankshaft had been statically and dynamically balanced at Standard.

In order to decrease the weight of parts moving in the engine, pistons and con-rods were made of light alloy. These expanded more when heated than the steel crankshaft. Due to the expanding big ends of the rods, a drop of oil pressure could result, this being the Achilles' heel of the engine. The electric sparks were provided with energy via a conventional battery-fed coil.

While the carburetor was situated at the right side of the engine block, the side valves were at the left. The gas was directed to them passing between the third and fourth cylinder. Given this complicated arrangement, it is hardly surprising that SS looked at this arrangement first when optimizing the engine for the second series of the SS One, which was unveiled after only one year in the autumn of 1932. Courageously, SS decided in favor of a light alloy cylinder head made exclusively for SS at the Coventry Motor Cylinder Company. SS also

Opposite: XJ 12 H.E. with its engine. *(J)*

Below: SS Jaguar 2.5-liter engine. *(J)*

The engine of the SS 100. *(Schön)*

chose a horizontal carburetor with a float chamber (M-Type) made by RAG. The fuel tank was enlarged from 9 to 12 imperial gallons.

In autumn 1933, Standard made a more conventional effort in increasing power output and extended the stroke of the engine from 101.6 to 106mm, a standard for Jaguar over nearly 60 years! The engine was further refined with an oil pump situated in the oil reservoir and a timing chain tensioner made of spring steel. The exhaust manifold was revised, collecting the hot gases further forward and directing less heat to the cabin. In 1934 the first electric (instead of mechanically driven) fuel pumps were used.

In the autumn of 1934, Harry Weslake redesigned the cylinder heads and changed the cam profile to increase valve lift. Twin carburetors became an option, still made by RAG.

A year later, for the first Jaguar models, Weslake again revised the cylinder heads. These were more radical in that the previously side valves were relocated overhead and operated by the side camshaft via long rods hidden under an attractive polished aluminum cover (seemingly hiding an overhead camshaft). Inlet and exhaust manifolds now were much straighter, and the combustion chamber became much more compact. These changes, with the help of two S.U. H3 carburetors, helped boost power output from 55 horsepower in the first SS One to more than 100 horsepower. The number in the carburetor designation stood for the inlet port diameter, reduced by 1 inch, in eighths of an inch. With this, engine ignition timing could be chosen manually with a lever at the steering wheel boss.

The fuel tank, again situated under the trunk, held 12 gallons. The electrical S.U. fuel pump was standard. (The 1.5-liter four-cylinder got its fuel via a mechanical A.C. pump).

It is hardly surprising that this bold step was followed by minor improvements only. In May 1936 the adjustment of tappet clearance was changed. In the autumn of the same year, a Tecalemit oil filter was introduced in the bypass flow. Block and pistons grew by slightly more than 0.6mm when a Corrujoint cylinder head gasket from copper and nickel was introduced. This invention from the United States was designed to prevent cylinder head distortion and leaks at great heat. Additionally, a new cold-start device was chosen, and the fuel tank was enlarged to more than 13 gallons. From the autumn of 1939 onward the con-rods were made from steel in order to avoid oil pressure drops at heat.

In the autumn of 1937 a 3.5-liter variant with enlarged bore and stroke was introduced. With the exception of its cast-iron cylinder head and its larger H4 carburetors, it was similar to the earlier engine. For obvious reasons, it had steel con-rods from the outset.

With regard to deteriorating fuel quality, metal sheets were put under the head gaskets to reduce the compression ratio. For export these sheets were deleted soon after the war. The relocation of engine assembly from Standard to Jaguar had hardly any effect on the engines' technical specification, as all the tooling was taken over from Standard. The clutch and flywheel were integrated in the balancing process. A Metalastik vibration damper was added to the crankshaft.

The smaller four-cylinder was similar to the six-cylinders, but it retained the cast-iron block. Its side valves were even continued until autumn 1937. After the war, the inlet manifold was water tempered, which allegedly helped raise performance output by

10 percent. However Jaguar, who still bought-in the completed four-cylinder engine from Standard, saw no reason to alter the performance data given in the vehicle specifications.

Early in 1946 the single timing chain in the six-cylinders was replaced with one of the duplex type, and the con-rods reverted to light alloy, as steel was not available in sufficient quantity. For the 2.5-liter engine, the cylinder head became slightly higher, so that the lower compression ratio was maintained, and the steel spacer below the head gasket could be deleted.

By the end of 1947, the manual ignition timing adjustment at the steering wheel, which was of little help for the normal driver, was replaced with an automatic device using vacuum and centrifugal forces. In autumn 1948, when the Mark V was introduced, it included a camshaft with less power-oriented cam profiles and a 15-gallon fuel tank located between the trunk and spare wheel. From January 1950 steel con-rods were universally used again, as the light alloy tended to become brittle with age.

In the autumn of 1948 the famous XK engine was introduced. It had been developed by Jaguar itself. The block was so strongly influenced by the earlier Standard engine that it still could be made on the existing tooling. The cylinder head, made of RR50 aluminum, was 66 pounds lighter than the iron head, and it dissipated heat better. The casting was made at William Mills Limited. The valve seats were surrounded by cooling liquid. With a gallery collecting water along the cylinder head, hot spots were avoided. Valve seat rings were made from steel austenited with nickel (Brimol) and were inserted with the head heated up to 232 degrees Celsius in order to ensure a tight fit. The cast-iron valve shaft guides were set at a 35 degree angle to the cylinder axis; they were inserted when the head still was hot. The inlet valves were made of EN 52 chrome silicon steel, the outlet valves of austenite steel. The camshaft was driven from the crankshaft via two-stage duplex chains. A single duplex chain would have caused audible oscillation, which Jaguar was not able to avoid. Spring steel chain tensioners again helped the lower chain. By adjusting the sprockets at the ends of the camshafts, the valve timing could be fine-tuned.

The double overhead camshafts turned in four white metal bearings and initially lifted the valves by only 5⁄16 of an inch. At the time, incautious mechanics had to be considered because after decarbonizing they might wrongly adjust the camshafts, in which case higher-lift valves might touch the piston and bend. With improving fuel quality decarbonizing was no longer necessary, so soon 3⁄8-inch-lift camshafts were optional and from the autumn of 1954 onward, they were standard. The inlet valves had a diameter of 1 3⁄4 inches; the exhaust valves still were 1 7⁄16 inches. Again the (now real) camshaft covers were made of polished aluminum.

Carving a cylinder head for an XK engine. *(J)*

XK engine with a C-Type head. *(Schönborn archive)*

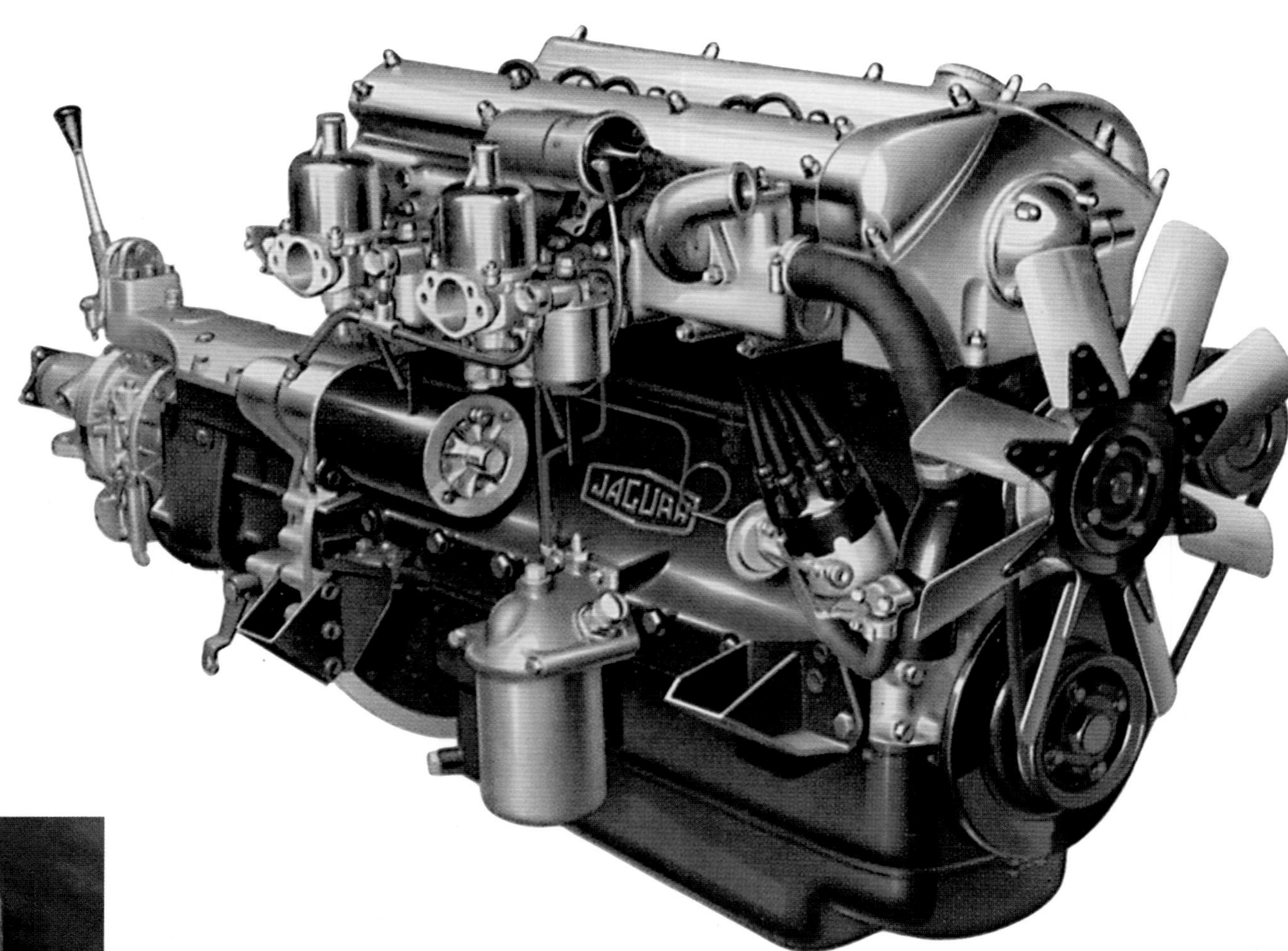

An early S.U. H6 carburetor. *(S)*

The spark plug had to be screwed directly into the cylinder head. Thanks to the inclined valves, the combustion chamber had a hemispherical shape, which was thought ideal at the time. For good looks the exhaust manifolds were black enameled. The light alloy pistons ran in dry chrome steel liners. A chromed upper piston ring reduced wear on the liners. The forged steel for the con-rods was particularly tensile. The crankshaft ran in seven main bearings, each with a diameter of 2¾ inches. The distance between the cylinder axes was 7½ inches. Toward the rear, no oil seal was provided. Instead, the crankshaft had a thread that "screwed" the oil back to the sump as long as the engine ran. However, this did not work when the bearings were worn or when the car was parked uphill. The flywheel had a ring of 132 teeth.

The engine block castings were sourced from Leyland. The oil sump was made of DTD 424 aluminum. In original guise the engine had two S.U. H6 carburetors with an automatic cold start enrichment that tended to switch off too late, so enthusiasts preferred to replace it with a manual switch. Until August 1950 the XK 120 had no air filter. The "church towers" on the carburetors for the needles were less prominent from April 1950 onward.

The engine for the Mark VII was similar in most respects to that in the XK 120. For the first time two fuel tanks were provided, one in each rear fender, with a total capacity of 18 gallons. This arrangement was typical for the large Jaguar sedans up to the Mark X and its descendants as well as for the XJ Series 1 to 3.

From 1951 onward a Special Equipment variant was available with the higher-lift camshafts; for most export markets the engine now was built to the higher compression ratio of 8:1. A lighter flywheel, a special vibration damper, and stronger valve springs completed the specification of this high-performance engine.

In 1952 three bolts were added to the front of the cam covers to make them oil-tight, and the valve guides were changed to accommodate the higher-lift camshaft. In 1953 further innovations were a larger water pump with a Hoffman bearing and carbon gasket, together with a revised inlet manifold.

From April 1953 the cylinder heads for the racing engines—called the C-type head—became optional for the normal Jaguars. The XK 140 with C-head had larger exhaust valves ($1\frac{5}{8}$ instead of $1\frac{7}{16}$ inches diameter). A lighter flywheel and a high-performance crankshaft added to the power output, which—slightly exaggerated with a view to the horsepower race in the United States—was stated as 210 horsepower. Two months later a deep, stamped oil sump was added.

From the autumn of 1954, oil-tight ignition coils were used. For the standard XK 140, the two air filters were combined into a single, much larger unit.

From the spring of 1955, a new casting for the engine block was used, designated C 8610 instead of C 4820. Instead of a traditional toothed oil pump, a Hobourn-Eaton oil unit was employed. The two half-circle asbestos cord seals were replaced with a retaining ring at the front end of the crankshaft. A smaller, less expensive oil sump with partitions to prevent oil being forced away from the pump during cornering was now used.

In September 1955 the spring-steel chain tensioner was replaced with a hydraulically sprung Reynolds unit, and a nylon damper replaced the former guide.

The four-cylinder variant of the XK unit has been mentioned already, particularly its disadvantages with regard to cost and spares storage. It was obvious that a smaller variant of the six-cylinder would be preferable. The first design, called X 102, was made in 1952 with a stroke of 77mm and a capacity of 2,299cc. Its performance was disappointing. The next step was slightly smaller. Called EXP 1, this evolution clearly showed its advantages over the four-cylinder XK (then called EXP 2). So the 2.4-liter was introduced with the unitary sedan in 1955. It was similar to the larger six-cylinder with the exceptions of the stroke; the reduced valve lift of $\frac{5}{16}$ inch; the Metalastik vibration damper only being supplied from June 1956 onward; the shorter con-rods (for better smoothness it had to be 1.87 times as long as the stroke); and the engine block more than 2 inches lower, which saved 45 lbs in weight. In addition, the usual S.U. carburetors were replaced with Solex units, which were renowned for economy.

The flywheels for engines in the compact sedan, from the 3.4 and 3.8 S up to the 240/340 and the 2.8-liter XJ 6 all had only 104 teeth.

With the Mark VIII in the autumn of 1956, an improved B-Type head was introduced. The exhaust valves now were $1\frac{5}{8}$ inches in diameter, as in the C-Type engine for the XK 140. A new inlet manifold with the water gallery screwed on was employed. The B-Type head was combined with the latest S.U. HD 6 carburetors. Their peculiarity was the diaphragm (hence the D in the name) holding the needle. All in all, this engine had better low-rev torque but did not quite achieve the maximum power of its C-Type sibling.

From about the same time Jaguar itself offered tuning kits for the 2.4 engine, which was criticized for its lack of power. The most advanced had the B-Type head with a power output of 150 horsepower. In 1956

The straight-port head had six equally long ports. *(S)*

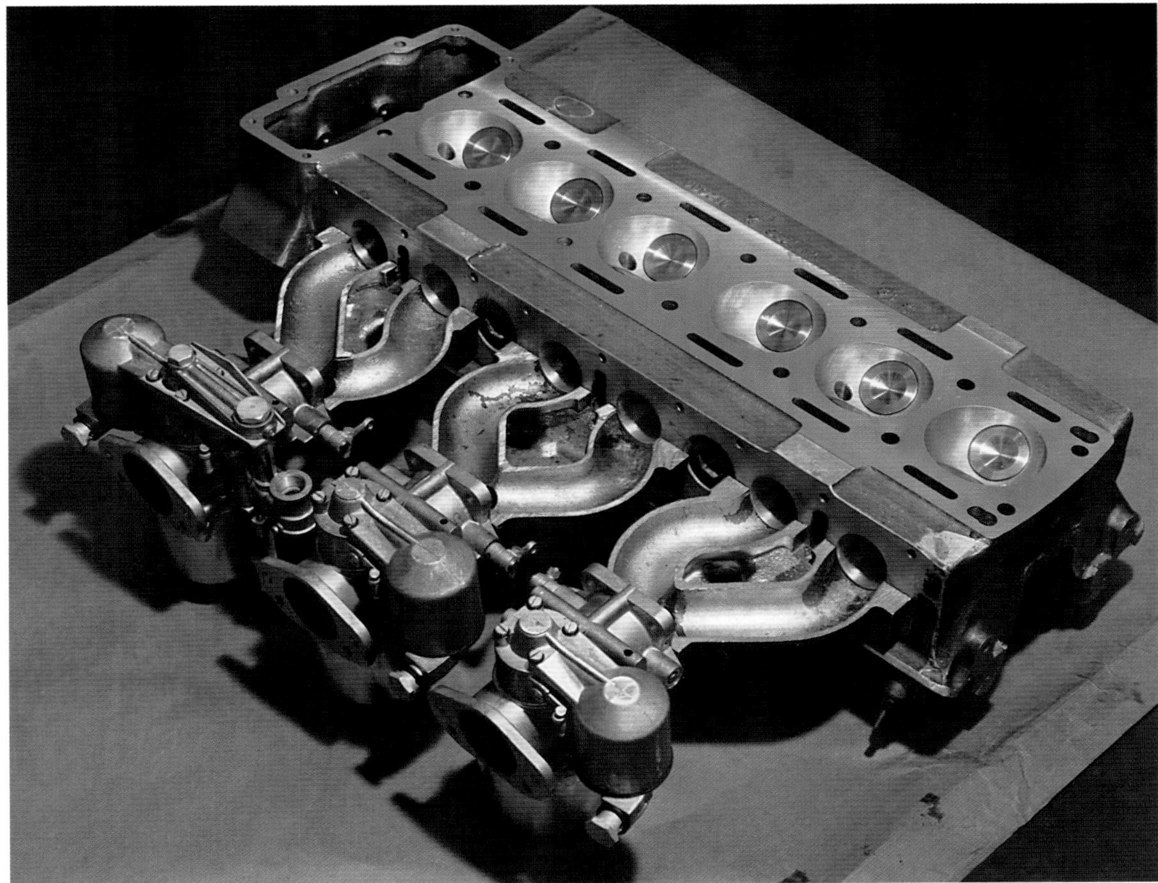

4.2-liter XK engine with two carburetors. *(J)*

an oil sump made from cheaper steel instead of aluminum was employed.

From early 1957 the camshafts were drilled for a quieter cold start.

From 1958 the Mark IX and XK 150 could be ordered with the 3.8-liter engine. The increase in displacement had been achieved by boring-out the engine by another 4mm. As the distance between the cylinder liners now became too tight for a cooling water passage, this was replaced with a smaller passage at the upper end of the liners, thus preventing heat cracks in the block. This solution had been patented for Jaguar. The cold-start unit had been revised, now guaranteeing a better distribution of the rich mixture. Lead-bronze alloy main bearings were coated with indium to help their longevity. The underside of the pistons now had a stronger profile for better heat dissipation. The second piston ring was slightly inclined and an oil scraper ring was added. The oil feed for all crankshaft bearings was improved.

With the XK 150 S, the Straight Port cylinder head was introduced, which again was developed by Harry Weslake. With its straighter one-into-two ports, all of exactly the same length, it produced less turbulence and improved volumetric efficiency—not the least thanks to its three S.U. HD 8 carburetors of 2 inches in diameter. A higher compression ratio of 9:1 was the norm, and a lighter flywheel made the engine rev more freely. Additionally, larger exhaust valves of 1⅝-inch diameter were employed. In the case of the larger engine, power output was nominally 265 horsepower; even under the then-usual SAE standard recorded without air filter, exhaust, and auxiliaries, this was an optimistic figure. Rarely would such an engine turn out more than 190 horsepower by Economic Commission for Europe (ECE) standards.

In the Mark II, even the small six-cylinder was provided with the approved B head and the ⅜-inch lift cams, resulting in an alleged power output of 120 horsepower. Nevertheless, the car was not quite able to equal the previous 2.4-liter's performance.

Early in 1960 a revised water pump, a different connection with the radiator, and an improved oil sump seal were employed. The oil-bath air filter was replaced with a paper element at the same time. In the following years the oil tightness of the engine was continually improved, particularly the seal at the rear end of the crankshaft. From May 1960, a crankcase breather was added, which according to a California law had to end at the inlet ports from 1961 onward.

The flywheel for the E-Type 3.8 and Mark X 3.8 only had 104 teeth; the E-Type's was of the lightweight type, as had been the XK 150's. The two fuel tanks at the rear of the Mark X had a capacity of 20 gallons.

From June 1960 the oil pump and oil sump were enlarged, and the oil dipstick sat in a larger pipe for ease of maintenance. From September 1962 BRICO Maxiflex oil scraper rings were used. They operated very well, so that additional oil had to be squirted to the liners. In April 1963 a new ignition distributor was introduced.

From September 1963 the exhaust valves benefited from an improved alloy, and in May 1964 the timing chain tensioner was improved. As with the large sedans, the 3.4- and 3.8-liter S had one fuel tank on each side of the trunk, although the capacity was only about 14 gallons.

In 1964 the XK engine was further enlarged to 4.2 liters. While the straight-port head remained unchanged, the block below was much different, with only cylinders 2 and 5 staying at their previous position. The others had been moved further apart so that the engine could be bored out by ⅕-inch to 92.07mm. The cooling water slot at the upper end of the liners was maintained. Thus, most cylinders were no longer on the same axis as the combustion chamber, but this seemed to matter little. The engine caused headaches, as the head gaskets were too weak where they filled the gap between the cylinders. Cooling was another difficult subject. The crankshaft had to be adapted and reinforced, of course. Its newly designed counterweights now were lighter, putting less stress on the crankshaft, with its equally new vibration damper at its front end. The flywheel now had 133 teeth. Again, the lightweight type was used in the E-Type. The water-jacketed inlet manifold now was cast in one piece.

In 1966 the 420 was equipped with the 4.2-liter engine and straight-port head, which for reasons of space was equipped with two instead of three carburetors.

In the autumn of 1967 Jaguar engineers made the 2.4-liter somewhat livelier. For the introduction of the 240, the cylinder head was replaced with a straight-port, with two S.U. HS 6 carburetors and paper element air cleaners, the latter shared with the 340.

In 1968 safety and emissions regulations began to bite in the United States. Jaguar was forced to replace the approved S.U. carburetors with Zenith-Stromberg 175 Cds and to divert the mixture near the exhaust en route to the cylinder head in order to warm it up. At full throttle, the intake charge took the direct route, so that maximum power output was not affected. The camshaft covers were now black with bright, raised strips. Development and tooling-up for the preheating intake system amounted to £250,000. This device, although proudly presented to the Americans as a simplistic solution to the emissions problem, did not last much longer than one year. Soon it became evident that it was easier to simply draw warm air from the exhaust area into the air filters instead of the complicated diversion.

The nonemissions versions received the revised camshaft covers late in 1968 only. The 4.2 also had new S.U. HS 8 carburetors. Soon the power of these engines was rated at 186 DIN horsepower, and after the higher-compression variant disappeared, 172 DIN miles per hour. The DIN figures always were considerably lower than the SAE figures that had been quoted before.

From July 1968 the higher-compression engines (9:1) had Hepworth Grandage pistons. At the same time a new inlet manifold was employed for the XJ 6, which was not compatible with the one for other two-carburetor models. The front engine supports were relocated from the body to the front subframe, which necessitated a further modification to the engine block. Cylinder head bolts in the 4.2 now, and later in the 3.4 as well, reached further down in the block, where the main bearings were supported. This again helped combat cylinder head distortion. A larger oil filter and revised oil pipes made sure that all oil passed through the filter. Additional bores through the cylinder head gasket allowed an exchange of cooling water; for a better temperature balance these bores were larger on the exhaust side.

For the XJ Jaguar introduced the 2.8-liter variant of the XK engine. Already on November 20, 1961, Weslake had reported to Heynes that he had designed an inlet port that resulted in a power output of 170 horsepower for the 2.4-liter. This development was put aside until a modern power plant was required for the XJ 6. First ideas were in the direction of a 2.6-liter in combination with a powerful 3.0-liter, as tested by Norman Dewis in 1965. Dewis found it gave the E-Type good low-speed torque, economy, and quiet running. But the torque was not sufficient to replace the mighty 4.2, which made the 3.0 superfluous.

The 2.8, to which the 2.6 grew in the end, was similar to the 240 engine, including the 104-tooth flywheel. It retained the 2.4 liter's engine block with the cylinders at their original position. The cylinder head with its two carburetors was similar to the 4.2, however. The two fuel tanks of the XJ had a capacity of 23 gallons, but they soon had to be reduced to 20 gallons because they reached well into the crush zone of the car.

In June 1969 the oil-drain tap was replaced with a screw. Four months later, for manual models, the rear engine mount was revised. From November, smoother running cams with a different profile were adopted so the tappets had to be adjusted less frequently.

From January 1970 the exhaust cam cover was provided with a warm air duct. From March the exhaust manifold of the variant with the preheating device was standardized. In June 1970 the screen in the oil sump was changed to avoid deforming under vacuum caused by suddenly dropping revs. From October the preheating device was only combined with 7:1 and 8:1 engines, the high-combustion ratio version being deleted. The rear engine mount was again revised. In order to reduce oil consumption, the bore at the rear end of the exhaust camshafts disappeared. In December the camshaft drive was improved and the oil return pipe was better protected against breaking at the oil pump joint. From now on the compression ratio was indicated with a letter as a suffix to the engine number instead of the former digit (H for high, S for standard, L for low instead of 9, 8, or 7).

From March 1971, improved HS 8 carburetors with a new cold-start enrichment feature were used. In April the rear crankshaft seal was again changed; in December the oil pump housing changed.

The 2.8 in everyday use tended to melt its pistons, particularly on fast motorway drives following longer city traffic. Such damage could not be simulated in tests, so that the cause remained unclear. As a precaution, Jaguar recommended in July 1972 that the ignition be retarded by six degrees. Faults in the material could not be excluded. At last, metallic ashes were found in the combustion chamber walls in damaged engines, which might have caused self-ignitions. Obviously the open exhaust valves were too close to the pistons. Another explanation came from the very thick cylinder liners, which were less than helpful for heat dissipation. All in all, the problem could not be solved, and as the smaller engine featured only slightly lower fuel consumption, it was easy to dispense with the 2.8, at least on the domestic market.

In November 1972 a solenoid was introduced to cut out fuel supply in the case of an accident, thus helping to avoid the danger of fire. From February 1973 new camshafts were introduced with a plug at the rear end. In March the seal at the rear end of the crankshaft was conformed to that of the V-12, and the valve guides were improved. In the meantime the intake system that ducted in preheated air from the exhaust manifold had been standardized.

In August 1974 the oil filler cap on the camshaft cover was standardized with the V-12. From October revised con-rods were used with a slightly roof-like profile at the sides instead of the central bulge. From November new tappets were used.

4.2-liter XK engine with injection—certainly the most powerful production XK engine. *(S)*

In January 1975 the oil feed to the main bearings was improved. In December the water pump and its drive were standardized with the V-12.

In April 1975 another 3.4 engine was introduced. It was not similar to the one last used in the 340, but was closely related to the latest 4.2, although with the compression ratio reduced. It also had the straight-port head with two carburetors (although only S.U. HS 6s) and—presumably for reasons of rationalization—the combustion chambers were not flush-fitting on four of the cylinders. The compression ratio was set at 8.8:1.

From May 1975 the ignition coil had a plastic housing. From January 1976 sintered valve seats were used. This was necessary as in the United States the use of leaded fuel was soon to be prohibited. From February 1976 a canister oil filter was employed for all models without an oil cooler, and it was mounted horizontally from February 1978 onward. From May 1976 new S.U. HIF 6 or 8 carburetors came into use with an integral float chamber. From the same time the power output of the 4.2 was rated at 168 horsepower. In January 1977 the seal at the front end of the crankshaft was improved again.

From early 1978 the U.S. six-cylinder models benefited from the new Bosch-Lucas L-Jetronic injection system. This electronic system measured the quantity of air passing through the inlet manifold. A Lambda (oxygen) sensor and three-way catalytic converters were also included. The compression ratio, reduced previously to 7.4:1, now could be raised to 7.8:1. American emissions limits were so tight that they could not be achieved any longer with carburetors. Now each cylinder had its own solenoid valve fed with fuel via a ring line with a pressure-relief valve to provide constant pressure. A central fuel injector for automatic cold-start enrichment was also provided. As once with the D-Type, the inlet valves were enlarged to 1⅞ inches. All this added up to 176 horsepower (instead of 161 before) at 4,750 rpm! This engine was suitable for all North American states, while before a special variant was necessary to fulfill California legislation. In July heat dissipation via the exhaust valve shafts was improved. In October a bracket between the oil sump and torque converter was introduced. From November a new water pump with single-belt instead of twin-belt pulley was employed.

Since the introduction of the Mark X, Jaguar had dispensed with slightly out-of-round big-end bearings (previously they had deviated by 0.007mm) in order to save cost. This hampered big-end lubrication, but was nevertheless generally used from 1978 onward, despite the adverse effect on longevity. The problem was solved in 1983 with hardened big-end bearings.

With the XJ Series 3, fuel injection became integral part of the 4.2 package all over the world. In Europe the compression ratio was set at 8.7:1. The former 9:1 pistons were used; the deviation in ratio was caused by the larger inlet valves. No catalytic converter was necessary yet, but an overrun fuel cut-off above 1,200 rpm helped save fuel. A further novelty was the Lucas Oscillating Pick-Up System (OPUS) ignition system from the V-12. The Anglo-European variant of the 4.2 turned out 205 horsepower at 5,000 rpm—a peak value among standard XK engines.

In December 1979 further cooling slots between block and head were introduced as additional water passages. The new block needed to be combined with a new cylinder head; older ones would need to be modified to match the new block. The new head gaskets could be used for the previous engine, but not the old ones for new engines. From January 1980 a revised water pump was used. At the same time, the electronic ignition system called AB 14 Constant Energy, developed by Lucas, was introduced. With magnetic force, a breaker impulse was generated at the distributor. In June 1983 a new camshaft cover was employed to avoid a groaning noise under fast cornering. This cover could be identified with its more prominent bright stripes. In November 1984 the ignition system was further improved with a Ducellier coil.

The XK engine survived in the XJ 6 until May 1987 and in Daimler's limousine until 1992—no less than 44 years after its introduction with the XK 120. This alone shows the unique abilities of the engine. As a Le Mans winner, it gained the highest acclaim, and it still served well decades later with its magnificent low-speed torque.

The above description has shown some difference between similar XK engines for different models. In order to identify from which model an XK engine comes, a prefix is set in front of the engine number.

E-Type V-12 with four carburetors. *(S)*

These prefixes were:

- XK 120: W, later F
- XK 120 C: E
- D-Type, XK-SS: E or EE
- Mark VII: A, B, D
- Mark VII M: D, N
- XK 140: G (Cylinder head painted red, if C-Type)
- 2.4-liter: BB, BC, BE
- 3.4-liter: KE, KF (head painted light green or light blue)
- Mark VIII: N, NA (head painted light green or light blue)
- XK 150: V (head painted light green or light blue)
- XK 150 S: VS (head painted pumpkin)
- XK 150—3.8-liter: VS (head painted metallic blue)
- XK 150 S—3.8-liter: VAS (head painted pumpkin)
- MK IX: NC, NE (head painted metallic blue)
- Mark II—2.4-liter: BG, BH, BJ (head painted light green or light blue)
- Mark II—3.4-liter: KG, KH, KJ (head painted light green or light blue)
- Mark II—3.8-liter: LA, LB, LC, LE (head painted metallic blue)

V-12 engine with fuel injection. *(J)*

- 240 and 340: 7J
- E-Type 3.8: R, RA (head painted gold, if not "Lightweight")
- E-Type 4.2 Series 1 and 1½: 7E (head painted gold)
- E-Type Series 2: 7R (head not painted)
- Mark X 3.8: ZA, ZB (head painted golden)
- Mark X 4.2 and 420 G: 7D
- 3.4 S and 3.8 S: 7B (head painted light green or light blue)
- 420: 7F
- Daimler Sovereign: 7A
- XJ 6 2.8 and Daimler Sovereign: 7G
- XJ 6 3.4 and Daimler Sovereign: 8A
- XJ 6 4.2 and Daimler Sovereign: 7L
- XJ 6 4.2 etc. Series 2 and 3: 7L, 8L
- Daimler DS 420: 7M

The engine numbers of XK 120 Special Equipment, XK 140 with C-Type head, and E-Type Lightweight have a suffix "S."

V-12 engine

The idea of a Jaguar V-12 goes back to the early 1950s and on a complicated route found its way into the mid-engined XJ 13 sports prototype. Its two banks of cylinders formed a 60-degree angle, with a bore of 87mm and a stroke of 70mm, resulting in a capacity of 4,991cc, well within Le Mans limitations. The engine had four camshafts and dry-sump lubrication. Its cylinder heads were similar to the XK engine, but the valves were set at an angle of 30 degrees from the cylinder axis, and the inlet ports had to be adapted to this quite different environment. In its most powerful guise it was rated at 502 horsepower at 7,600 rpm, while the final version may have turned out about 475 horsepower. The engine first ran in August 1964, but it never started in a race.

Instead, Jaguar adapted the engine to its standard models for everyday use, returning to wet-sump lubrication. William Heynes and Claude Baily did the first drawings. With Coventry Climax being taken over in 1963, Walter Hassan completed the team that had proven itself with the XK engine. A head with a single camshaft for each bank was designed, tooling up for which cost only £420,000 instead of £491,000 for the DOHC (dual overhead camshaft) heads. The anticipated power output of 330 horsepower was quickly reached with the DOHC engine. In May 1965 both engines were tested in Mark X prototypes, together with V-8 and even V-10 alternatives. The simple single overhead camshaft (SOHC) V-12 was superior to the DOHC V-12. It was less expensive, saved 30 pounds in weight, and the camshaft drive needed only one chain and four sprockets instead of four chains and twelve sprockets. In particular, the single-camshaft heads ran smoother. The SOHC V-12 required less space under the hood and offered better torque up to 5,000 rpm. It was decided before the XJ 6 debut that the SOHC V-12 would be the way to go.

For Coventry Climax, Walter Hassan had developed an engine with a flat cylinder head and the combustion chamber in the piston crown. This solution was tested in a one-cylinder engine, as was a wedge-shaped combustion chamber. As the results were promising, the Heron (in-piston) combustion chamber was regarded as a suitable alternative for the V-12, and in direct comparison it was superior to the hemispherical shape up to 5,000 rpm. As the Le Mans limit was no longer important, the bore was extended to 90mm, resulting in a capacity of more than 5.3 liters.

The first production prototypes of this V-12 had a mechanical Lucas injection system, which was not able to cope with the latest U.S. emissions standards; fuel metering still was inadequate. An electronic device from BRICO was the solution and worked perfectly in tests. But as BRICO decided against producing this system, another solution had to be found. So Jaguar had to return to its familiar carburetors. Downdraft carburetors were not available from British sources in the right dimensions, and the space inside the V was not sufficient for horizontal carburetors. So the Stromberg 175 CD 175 SE was located outboard, with inlet manifolds extending above the cylinder heads to reach the inlet valves on the inside of the V.

Optimizing of the combustion chamber shape and changes needed to meet emissions requirements delayed development for two years. The compression ratio was initially set at 10.6:1, but for production 9:1 was chosen as the legendary high-octane five-star fuel was disappearing from the pumps. Countries with even lesser fuel quality had to make do with a 7.8:1 ratio. The valve lift was set at ⅜ inch. The valve diameters were 1⅝ inch for the inlet and 1⅜ inch for the exhaust, smaller than on the XK engine. The camshafts had seven bearings and were driven via a single duplex chain, but without a chain tensioner, specially developed in cooperation with Morse. Instead of the usual distributor, with contacts being prone to wear, Jaguar chose Lucas' new Oscillating Pick-Up System (OPUS) with more accurate electro-magnetic switching of the igniting spark.

The engine block was made from light alloy; only a few XK units for racing were made this way. The loss in weight compared with cast iron was more than 110 pounds, without disadvantages in noise suppression, which had spoiled the aluminum XK unit. Only the seven main bearing supports were made from cast iron. The block extended 4 inches below the crankshaft axis, which was good for additional noise deadening. In order to avoid contacting the front subframe, the oil cooler had to be relocated below the water radiator. The crankshaft was made of EN 16 T steel, and the main bearings were manufactured to tolerances of 0.01mm. The exhaust manifold was double-skinned for better noise deadening. The weight of the dry engine was 680 pounds, less than 100 pounds more than the six-cylinder. The U.S. variant had air injection into the exhaust manifolds to help burn the remaining hydrocarbons, as well as an exhaust gas recirculation system, so that only 241 horsepower was achieved. These systems generated additional heat in the engine bay. The XJ 12 had a different crankshaft from the E-Type's; the XJ's was standardized in May 1973.

From October 1972, N9Y instead of N10Y spark plugs were used, and the bore at the back end of the camshafts disappeared. From December 1972 different main bearings with new linings came into use. From March 1973, engines destined for Germany were modified to Economic Commission for Europe (ECE) standard. From October this specification was standard for all markets other than North America and Japan. Despite the many changes, power output had decreased to 253 horsepower.

In June 1973 an improved oil pump housing and a larger oil sump (holding 19 instead of 16 pints) were employed for better oil supply under hard cornering. This change was made obvious by the blue oil dipstick. Additionally, oil filler caps were placed on the camshaft covers of both sides of the engine. From October 1973 a revised camshaft profile was employed for North American vehicles. In February 1974 the ignition system and coil were reinforced, and in November 1974 the valve seats were revised.

The injection system for the V-12 had not been forgotten. Behind the scenes the company prepared for stricter emissions regulations, which the V-12 could no longer meet with its carburetors. Jaguar eventually offered the Bosch D-Jetronic (D for depression, or vacuum) system that initially had been developed by Bendix. Until then the device had been suitable for only up to eight cylinders, but Lucas adapted it for the V-12. Electronic metering via solenoid valves considered parameters like air and cooling water temperature, inlet vacuum, and revs. For the United States, a compression ratio of 8:1 was used with air injection, exhaust gas recirculation, and oxidation catalysts, limiting power output to 244 horsepower. The catalysts, a Swedish invention, still had some teething problems to cope with and the lifetime of one of these units usually was limited to 25,000 miles; this life cycle was doubled by 1976. For markets with less stringent emissions regulations, the 9:1 compression ratio could be maintained, so that power output was 287 horsepower, despite exhaust gas recirculation. Early in 1976 the V-12 received sintered valve seats. In October 1976 the injection system was revised, and finally the V-12 got its automatic cold-start enrichment, which had to be revised only two months later.

From September 1976 a canister oil filter was used. In the following month the oil pump was changed, and in May 1978 the air filter housing changed. From October 1978 alternative ignition distributors and amplifiers (Millard) were used, the amplifier being relocated from the center of the engine to above the radiator. From early 1979 two injection valves per inlet manifold were used, and instead of the earlier wax capsule, the cold-start enrichment system was activated with

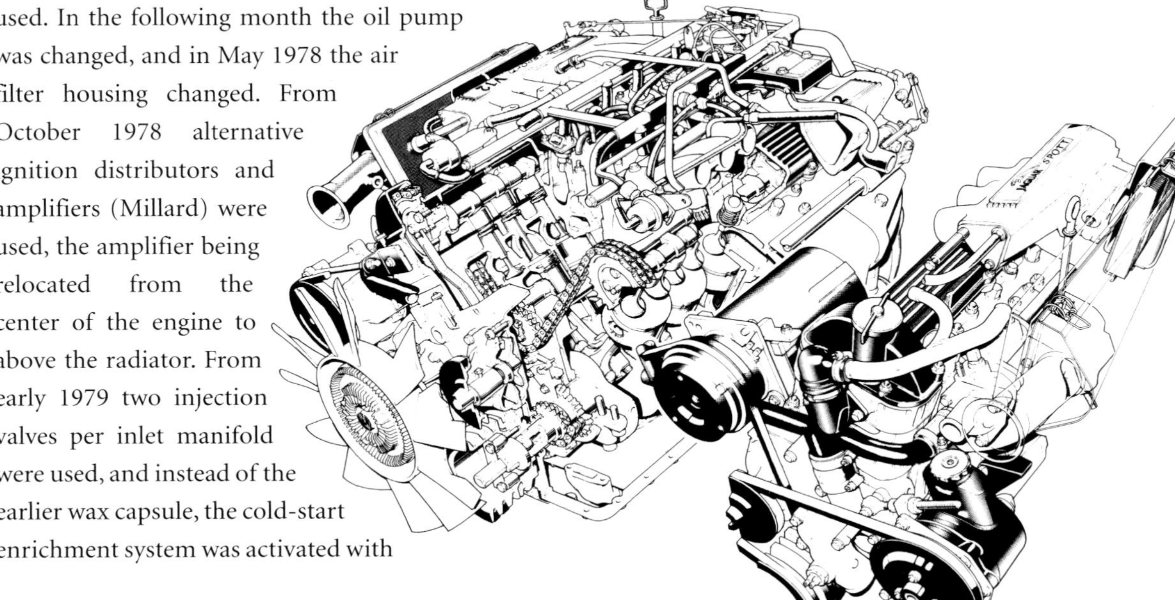

A view into the Jaguar Sport 6-liter V-12. *(J)*

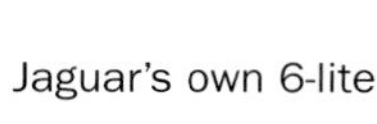

Jaguar's own 6-liter V-12. *(J)*

a bimetal spring. In September 1979 an electronic amplifier was introduced; it helped overcome the traditional ignition weakness of the V-12.

In mid-1980 the Anglo-European variant of the XJ-S—and more secretly the XJ sedans as well—received a higher compression ratio of 10:1, supported by more precise pressure regulation in the now single instead of twin fuel ring line, in combination with the latest P-Jetronic system from Bosch. The air-flow meter replaced the pressure sensor in the inlet manifold, and a lambda sensor was integrated. This engine achieved 299 horsepower at 5,400 rpm. At the same time exhaust gas recirculation and air injection were dispensed with for the North American version in favor of a system with a lambda sensor and a three-way catalyst. Power output thus was 262 horsepower. In November 1980, the oil drain screw was relocated for better accessibility, while the engine mounts and front subframe were reinforced.

In June 1981 the Michael May designed Fireball combustion chambers were introduced, with the chamber's shape concentrated around the exhaust valve, which now was situated somewhat higher. The piston crown now was nearly flat again. During the intake cycle, the gas entered the cylinder at a tangent, thus inducing a swirl that helped prevent preignition on hot spots in the chamber, even with lean mixtures. Thus the compression ratio was raised to an unusually high 12.5:1. Wise Harry Weslake had patented a similar idea as early as 1943.

The injection system was modernized (Bosch L-Jetronic with an air-flow meter and one injection impulse per rotation of the crankshaft, instead of individual ones for each cylinder) and calibrated for the leaner required mixture. Good ignition now was even more essential, and the choice was the powerful AB 14 amplifier as used in the 4.2 with a new double coil system. The mechanism regulating the ignition timing fortunately worked better than it looked. The lead-free fuel used in North America required a lower compression ratio of 11.5:1, resulting in only 264 horsepower.

A revised injection system for low-octane fuel was used from 1986 and is said to have cost 4 horsepower from maximum power. At the same time the amplifier was revised and different spark plugs were specified. From 1989 a new solid-state coil was used. With tighter emissions regulations in the European Union, the North American catalytic converter-equipped version, with its changes to engine block, crankshaft, and air filters to incorporate sensors, was used here as well. At the same time the rear crankshaft seal was replaced with a shaft seal and a new starter motor was employed.

In August 1989 the XJR-S became the first 6-liter V-12 with a stroke extended to 78.5mm. For the first time, Zytec engine management was used and the valve mechanism was changed considerably by TWR.

From December 1989 the normal XJS received Marelli engine management, which raised power output to 280 horsepower after a drop to less than 270 due to the catalysts. These were soon recalled in order to make sure that no short-circuit would occur. Possibly, some of these engines found their way under XJ hoods. From May 1991 the inlet manifolds were decorated with a red "Jaguar V-12" badge and (in the case of the XJS) the latest Lucas 26 CU engine management, which ensured smoother starting and cold running. It replaced the former 16 CU, which before had superseded the 6 CU. The 26 CU system remained in service until being replaced by 36 CU, which lasted until 1994. The latter two had an on-board diagnosis system that soon would be obligatory for California.

In September 1991, in conjunction with the XJR-S facelift, the power output of the 6-liter engine was raised again. The assembly of one engine cost two-man week's time, which made it inappropriate for production in larger series. Nevertheless, Jaguar used the same basic dimensions when introducing its own 6-liter V-12 for the XJ 8 in February 1993, but it revised the cylinder head to save assembly cost. The camshaft profile was revised for smoother running, as were the flat head pistons, the cylinder liners, and the forged crankshaft. The compression ratio was reduced to 11:1. The engine was just two pounds heavier than the 5.3. In 1994 a new Programmable Electronic Control Unit Systems (PECUS) engine management system was introduced, integrating the control over ignition.

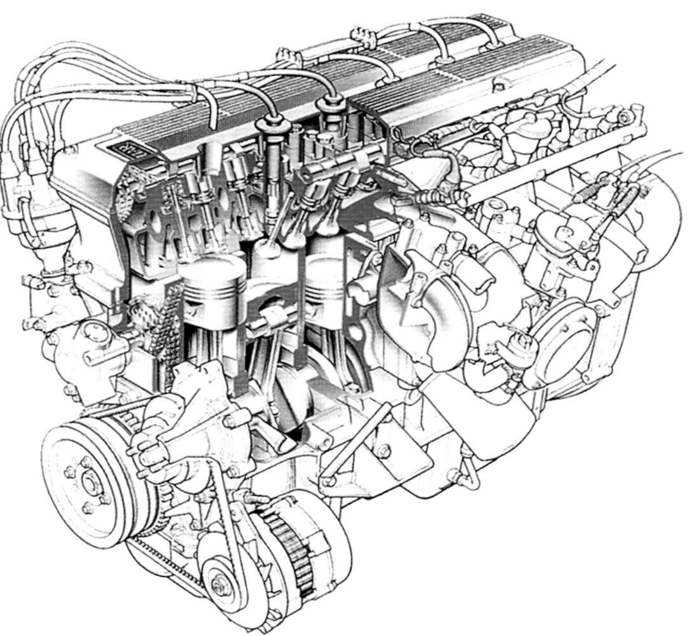

AJ6 3.6-liter. *(J)*

Four-liter six-cylinder—very robust and very refined. *(S)*

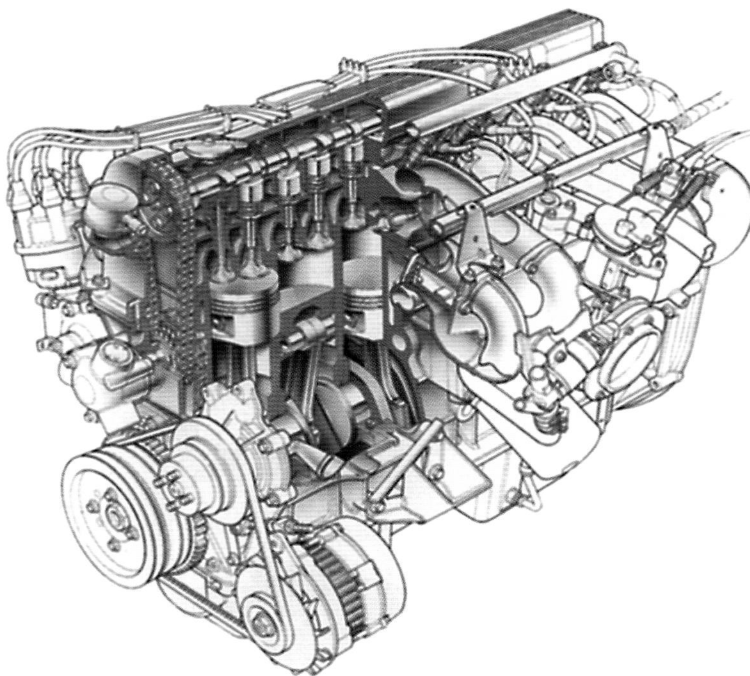

AJ6 2.9-liter. *(J)*

AJ6 3.2 engines in the XJ 40. *(J)*

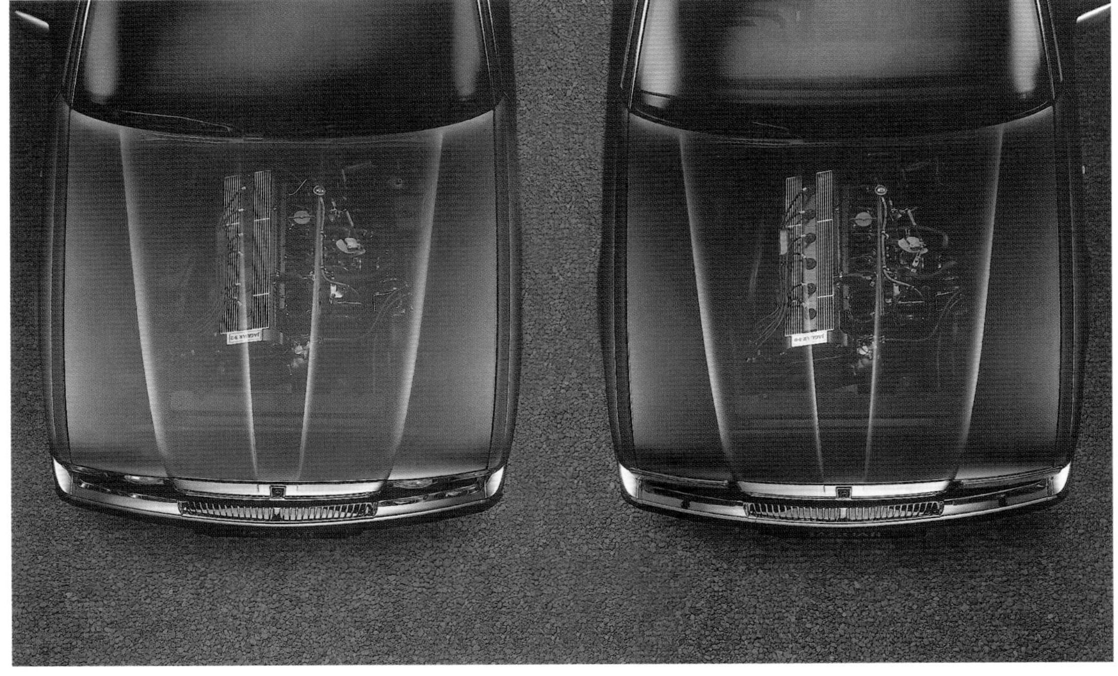

Top: The ultramodern V-8 engine. *(J)*

Above: The supercharger for the AJ V-8. *(J)*

AJ 6 and 16 Engines

With the 1984 XJ-S 3.6, Jaguar for the first time since 1948 brought out a completely revised six-cylinder unit. Its two-stage camshaft drive with duplex chains remained faithful to the XK, as did the double camshafts on the four-valve 3.6, while the 2.9 shared its SOHC head with the V-12. In both cases the engine block was a close relation to the V-12 but had thin, closed-deck, dry liners (Series 3000 instead of the earlier Series 2000), as this saved tooling cost and 3.8 kilograms (8.4 pounds) of weight. The block was sand cast from LM 25 light alloy and, as with the V-12, its skirt reached well below the crankshaft axis.

The diameter of the main bearings was the same as in the XK engine; the cast-iron crankshaft was 9 kilograms (19.9 pounds) lighter than the forged one of the V-12. The loss in stability was justifiable and helped keep down manufacturing cost. The con-rods still were forged. Much know-how from the Cranfield Institute of Technology was used for the design of the camshaft profile. In the 3.6 the 1.39-inch inlet valves were set at an angle of 24 degrees to the cylinder axis, and the 1.17-inch exhaust valves at 23 degrees. The valve lift remained ⅜-inch. The camshafts ran directly into the cylinder head without any bearings. Long inlet manifolds were intended to improve low-speed torque. The pentroof combustion chamber in the light alloy cylinder head had been chosen to maximize valve dimensions. The compression ratio was 9.6:1. The 3.6-liter was equipped with a Lucas digital injection with overrun fuel cutout above 800 rpm. This saved about 3 percent in fuel economy but caused a jerk when fuel supply was resumed. For this reason, for some time the system was not available in combination with manual gear change. Reprogrammed electronics solved the problem with a smoother cut-in. The 2.9 was equipped with Bosch LH Jetronic. Weighing less than 200 kilograms (4.4 pounds), the Advanced Jaguar Six (AJ 6) was more than 25 percent lighter than the XK unit.

During the first three years of production much was done to improve smoothness of the engine, like tighter tolerances in the main bearings, different chain tensioners, stiffer camshafts, and lightweight tappets made from pressed steel instead of cast iron. From January 1987 a new starter motor was used, and in March 1987 a fully electronic ignition system arrived.

For North America—the AJ 6 engine arrived in 1987 with the late introduction of the XJ 40—the power output was 181 horsepower at 4,000 rpm with a compression ratio of 8.5:1 For the 1988 model year this was increased to 9:1 and 195 horsepower at 5,000 rpm. From March 1989 onward even engines with a 9.6:1 compression ratio (i.e., nonemission) accepted the latest 95 octane fuel.

In autumn 1989 the capacity was raised to 4 liters with a longer stroke. A two-mass flywheel and a new, cast-steel crankshaft further helped smoothness. A year later the smaller engine was increased to 3.2 liters. It was now offered in Europe as well and used the same cylinder head as the 4-liter engine instead of the Fireball design.

From September 1993 a new camshaft cover was used with an integrated oil filler cap, crankcase breather, and 13 bolts. The extra long inlet manifold was now made in one piece.

A year later the engine was substantially revised again so that it was renamed the AJ 16 (although it still was a six-cylinder, of course). The engine block was new and much stiffer than before. The cylinder head, with its still longer inlet ports and slimmer valve shafts, further improved gas flow. New camshaft profiles, a higher compression ratio, new aluminum pistons, and engine management with an On-Board Diagnosis system (OBD 2 as required in America), sequential fuel injection, a new throttle cable, and catalysts with less resistance made the unit superior. Its external telltale was the camshaft cover made from magnesium, which helped sound deadening. A traction control system was incorporated into the engine management electronics and used the car's ABS sensors to detect wheelspin.

The 4-liter engine was available in combination with an Eaton M 90 Roots supercharger—as was the 3.2-liter in the Aston Martin DB 7. This was the first-ever supercharged Jaguar. With an intercooler, which for reasons of space was located adjacent to the supercharger and not to the radiator, a maximum power of 325 horsepower was reached. This was more than the V-12, but acceleration was much less refined because of the noise of the supercharger.

AJ V-8 Engine

Jaguar's first V-8 engine was completely new when it debuted in 1996. Within months it had replaced all previous 6- and 12-cylinder units, thus becoming Whitley's engineering nucleus. Particularly advanced was the variable length inlet manifold made of polyamide material with a valve joining the different runners. A five-valve unit was tested but showed no advantage. As with the AJ 6, the combustion chamber was of pentroof shape, with the valves set at a slightly larger angle of 28 degrees. Thanks to still slimmer valve shafts, the width opened by the valves in relation to the piston surface was much higher than with other engines. This resulted in a particularly high power output. The inlet camshaft timing was variable in order to ensure good low-speed torque without spoiling maximum power. It was driven by a chain requiring less space than a tooth belt and offering better longevity. With Nippondenso engine

Above: Supercharged V-8 in XJR. *(J)*

Left: Three-liter V-6 of the S-Type. *(J)*

management, the engine produced the best brake mean effective pressure of its class. The throttle was electronic and incorporated the traction control system.

The cylinders were not surrounded by liners; rather, the pistons were in direct contact with the engine block's light alloy, which was reinforced with a Nikasil process. The flat-head pistons were made of aluminum. The development of the engine had cost £240,000,000. It was 12 inches shorter and 40 kilograms (88 pounds)lighter than the AJ 16. For the first time Jaguar specified hydraulic engine mounts. The exhaust note had been specially composed by supplier Arvin Cheswick according to Jaguar's requirements, and indeed it hardly resembled the typical burbling sound of large V-8s.

A smaller variant of the engine with 3.2-liter capacity had a shorter stroke, while the 4-liter engine in the XJR again was accompanied by a supercharger, now the longer Eaton M 112. Rotating at double engine speed, this blower put 24 percent more air through the engine, again with an intercooler. For this variant, head gaskets with stainless steel rings around the cylinder bores were used, as were pistons with a lowered crown for a reduction of compression ratio to 9:1. The 3.2 and supercharged engines had no variable camshafts, and yet their emissions were very clean, so this mechanical gadget was restricted to the normally aspirated 4-liter.

For the 1999 model year, the engine was thoroughly revised, and now was called AJ 27 instead of AJ 26. The knock sensors were improved and low-speed torque was increased with some loss of maximum power. The spark plugs had a lifetime of 60,000 miles. The innovative Nikisil process, however, made the cylinder walls not as durable when using fuel including a certain amount of sulfur—a problem BMW also was confronted with. At the end of the 1999 model year, Jaguar reverted to cast-in liners (VIN 812256 to 878717 for XJ 8 and 001036 to 042775 for XK 8, in both cases ending together with the usual six-figure counting number). Many engines had to be exchanged—the telltale sign is a green sticker behind the right-hand side cylinder bank.

Just in time for the X 350, both the smaller and bigger engines were enlarged by a longer stroke to 3.5 liters (258 horsepower, 76.5mm stroke) and 4.2 liters (90.3mm stroke). These were introduced in the S-Type early in 2002, and in the XK in late 2002. The smaller engine in particular benefited from this increase, while the supercharged 4.2 delivered—according to DIN standard—400 horsepower. According to ECE standard, the power output of the two 4.2 variants was 298 and 395 horsepower (for the 2007 XKR, 416 horsepower). Cold-start ignition was retarded so the catalyst could become active earlier. An exhaust gas recirculation system helped reduce emissions.

Exhaust System

Under the Standard chassis taken over by Lyons, a simple exhaust pipe with a silencer was found. Presumably for visual reasons the six-cylinder models for the 1938 season (which started in the autumn of 1937) were equipped with double exhaust pipes, which disappeared when the Mark V came out but returned with the XK 120 Special Equipment. Even in this car it, was replaced with a single pipe toward the end of its production cycle, while the XK 140 Special Equipment had two full-length pipes, each with its own silencer. The XK 140 was the first Jaguar with chromed exhaust pipe ends. When the XK 140 went out of production, only the standard 2.4-liter and the smallest Mark II had single-pipe exhaust systems; the latter seems to have received a twin system only when it was re-named 240 in 1967. The exhaust manifolds of Mark V up until XJ Series 3 were black enameled, the standard 2.4-liter being the exception for cost reasons.

From autumn 1964, with the introduction of the 4.2 engine, the silencers were made from aluminum, which increased their lifetime considerably. The XJ 6 had two exhaust pipes again. For noise suppression, each had one silencer before and one after the rear wheel suspension. With the Series 2 the flexible connection between the exhaust manifold and pipe was modified. In 1975 stainless steel silencers were introduced. These had an expected lifetime equal to that of the whole car. Early in the 1980s the whole exhaust system was changed to stainless steel, with the exception of the rear ends. Catalytic converters already were standard equipment for North American cars, while in most European countries they became standard only in the late 1980s.

Cooling System

Along with the engine they inherited, Walmsley and Lyons also took over Standard's cooling system with its centrifugal water pump. Only the fan had to be adapted to the new body, and of course the radiators were

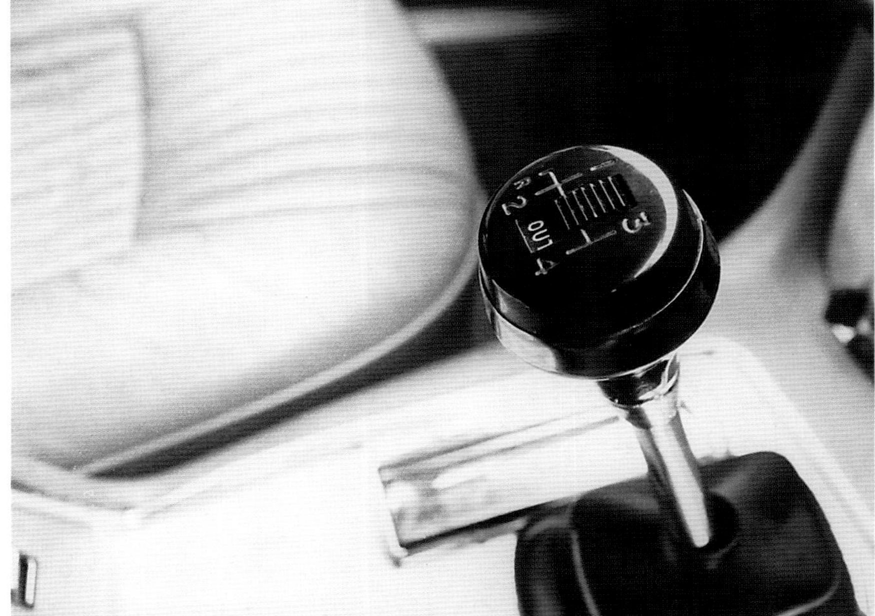

enclosed in a neat shell and grille. Instead of a muffler or the adjustable bars of the Rolls-Royce, a thermostat and bypass were used to regulate cooling. The revised SS One of October 1932 had a new Marston radiator and a broader grille. This was too much cooling for England, so the efficiency of the radiator was reduced in autumn 1934. In autumn 1936 the water distribution in the radiator was changed. The fan for the Mark VII had steel instead of cast-aluminum blades and rotated more quickly. For colder climates, a plug for a cooling water heater was introduced. In 1953 an eight-blade fan was introduced. With expansion tanks on both sides of the filler, a larger bypass, and a more efficient water pump with a slimmer V-belt, the cooling system was modernized. With the Mark VII M in the autumn of 1954, the expansion tank was reunified with the radiator. From 1955 the header tanks were crinkled to help cooling. From July 1957 the radiator surround—it was much broader in the XK 150 than in its predecessors—was made of aluminum instead of brass, but this turned out to be prone to corrosion.

The XK 150 S had a horizontal-flow radiator. In 1959 the V-belt was again changed, while the water pump was improved early in 1960 and again in September 1963. With the E-Type in March 1961, an additional thermostatically controlled electric fan was introduced, but the header tank was again revised in summer 1961. In 1963 the pressure cap was adjusted to release at 9 psi, from September to 7 psi, and finally from May 1964 to 4 psi.

From January 1964 the Mark X had a separate expansion tank and modified pipes to avoid bubbles. The 4.2 was introduced with new radiators with thin pipes and corrugated cooling fins. The fan was operated via a Holset viscous coupling that cut out at higher revs and thus added up to 15 horsepower to maximum power. The radiator was enlarged again in April 1966.

The E-Type Series 2 had a horizontal-flow radiator with two fans, and the XJ 6 automatic that appeared at the same time had an additional oil cooler at the lower part of the radiator. The water pump now rotated 25 percent faster than the engine and, in combination with the larger bypass, helped improve cooling efficiency. The fans now were made of plastic and had 12 blades. The Holset viscous coupling now was set to cut off at 2,500 rpm. From March 1973 the pressure cap was set at 13 psi.

The radiator of the XJ 12 was horizontally divided with 36 upper and 80 lower pipes, as well as an oil cooler integrated below and an additional electric fan. XJ 6 Series 2 had a new Clayton-Dewandre single-pipe oil cooler at the side of the radiator. In March 1978 a special radiator for air-conditioned cars was introduced. In October the radiator assembly, and in November the water pump drive, were improved. From November 1980 completely new fans were used. Mid-1981, the 4.2 got an engine oil cooler for the first time, as well as the

Left: The overdrive switch in the XK 150 between the ashtray and gear lever. *(S)*

Right: Gear lever with overdrive switch on XJ Series 1. *(S)*

Below: Moss gearbox and Laycock overdrive. *(S)*

V-12 fan and an expansion tank of light plastic that was positioned higher to help water flow. From March 1987 the pump drive for the AJ 6 engine was modified. In September 1987 the V-12 water pump was revised. The V-8 models introduced in the second half of the 1990s had a patented and particularly effective cooling system.

Clutch and Manual Gear Change

For the SS One and Two the Standard gearboxes were used. Standard had a single-plate dry clutch and a reasonably geared four-speed gearbox (in the case of the early SS Two, a three-speed). The Wilson preselector that was available at Standard from 1932 was not used for SS, although Alice Fenton had promised this to one client, Colonel Rixon Bucknall. Later experiments with a Cotal preselector also bore no fruit for series production.

From autumn 1934 the gearbox was synchronized on second through fourth gears. The bearings were modified and teeth now were of the more silent double helical type, as had been so typical for the Citroën. But in 1946 Jaguar returned to single helical. Development was carried out at Jaguar, and as of the JH variant, the gearbox was even manufactured there. The SH variant was made at Moss, and soon a close-ratio version was added. In 1949 the reverse lock was strengthened. The power of the new XK engine required the Borg & Beck single-plate dry clutch to be enlarged to 9⅞ inches in diameter. Its hydraulic operation was introduced only shortly after the Mark VII debut. From February 1952 new, shorter gearboxes were employed, called "short-shaft." These were called JL or SL (depending on where they were made), and had to be combined with a longer driveshaft.

From January 1954 an electric Laycock de Normanville overdrive was optional. In fourth gear this reduced engine speed by 22 percent. The chassis numbers of cars so equipped had a suffix "DN." For the sporting models a manual (or, in some cases, electrical) overdrive with a corresponding lever on the gearbox tunnel was available.

The 2.4-liter of 1955 had a 9-inch clutch. The most powerfully tuned variant retained the larger clutch, as did the 3.4-liter.

The long-serving and often criticized (for its long and stiff throw), but very reliable Moss gearbox was replaced in October 1964 with a fully synchronized unit developed at Jaguar. The development of this unit had already started in 1961. A Porsche-style synchronization would have been too expensive, so the Borg-Warner system was chosen, with the largest possible diameter for the synchro rings. The shaft driven by the engine had ball bearings, and the one driving the driveshaft had needle bearings. The gearwheels were made of hardened steel and the teeth again were set at an angle. The throw was somewhat shorter than before. The housing of the gears was made of cast iron, and all gearboxes now were made at Jaguar. The new Haussermann clutch with its 9.5-inch diameter (8.5 inches for the 2.4 and 9 inches for the 2.8) had a spring cup for ease of operation. The clutch continued to be hydraulically operated, with a self-adjusting slave cylinder.

For XJ 6 the angle at which the teeth were set on the permanently engaged gearwheels at the front end of the gearbox was increased to 34 degrees. In the Daimler Sovereign, the overdrive was standard, as with the other XJ models from 1974 onward. It is possible that the cars without overdrive were in reality not available for some time, but were included in sales brochures to suggest lower prices.

For the XJ-S the Jaguar four-speed was offered as an alternative to the automatic, but because of the power of that engine, it had to be reinforced, and from mid-1977 a stiffer gear change mechanism was employed. When gearbox production ended at Jaguar in 1979, the XJ-S was no longer available with manual gear change. (It had been the only V-12 Jaguar with this option apart from the E-Type.)

When the E-Type V-12 was under development, Jaguar also developed a five-speed gearbox, the manufacture of which, at £65,000, would have been too costly. Designed by Harry Mundy, it ended up being used by Rover, albeit with a 77mm instead of 88mm main shaft. Jaguar then turned to a two-speed differential, which again did not make it to production. XJ-S drivers could see one sign of it—the large control lamp on the instrument panel—but of course, they did not know what it had been intended for. Not before 1981, after two years without any manual cars, did the Rover gearbox finally return to Jaguar, although the 4.2 was only just within its torque limits. Vanden Plas and 12-cylinder cars continued to be supplied with automatics only.

For the modern six-cylinder engines, the Rover gearbox was hardly strong enough, and so John Egan opted for the German Getrag five-speed box, Model 265, shortly before the introduction of the XJ-S 3.6.

The 4-liter engine was combined with the same manufacturer's Model 290, with the gears being positioned in three gates instead of four. From 1993 the manual box was also offered in the United States, where Jaguar had supplied only automatic cars since the days of the E-Type. Repair and overhaul considerations for the Getrag boxes were not well planned; the necessary spares were not available. Indeed the boxes have turned out to be very durable. With the end of 6- and 12-cylinder engine production, no more manual boxes were used for the larger Jaguars.

Automatic Gearbox

From March 1953 an automatic transmission was available in the Mark VII for buyers paying with dollars, who nearly always wanted these automatic Jaguars. The Borg-Warner three-speeder had the gear change points chosen to suit the XK engine. The torque converter more than doubled the engine's torque. The Borg-Warner automatic was superior to other automatics developed in the United States (Hydra-matic and Dynaflow) in that it had a fuel-saving torque converter bypass in direct gear, but that had to be given up during the first year. The quadrant with P, N, D, L, and R positions was mounted on the steering wheel column, and a kick-down switch was located beneath the accelerator pedal. L held first gear. Braking bands prevented rolling backward; in P, rolling forward was prevented as well. Creeping at idle was avoided by hydraulically activated rear brakes. Longer-distance towing was possible, thanks to an oil cooler. On the first Mark VIIs the car started in second instead of first gear. Automatic cars (even if not supplied from Borg-Warner) had a "BW" suffix added to the chassis number.

With the Mark VIII in 1956, a patented brainchild of Jaguar engineer Tom Jones was introduced: the intermediate speed hold. With this switch at the outer side of the dashboard, change to third gear could be made impossible. From the autumn of 1956, the XK 140 fixed head and drophead coupes were also available with automatics.

The 3.4-liter had the automatic as an option, but these were equipped with a horizontal lever located centrally below the dash. In late 1958, the automatic was introduced for the 2.4-liter, with the same quadrant. The automatic now was supplied from Borg-Warner's Detroit factory instead of the previous British manufacture. The Mark II returned to the more familiar quadrant on the steering wheel column.

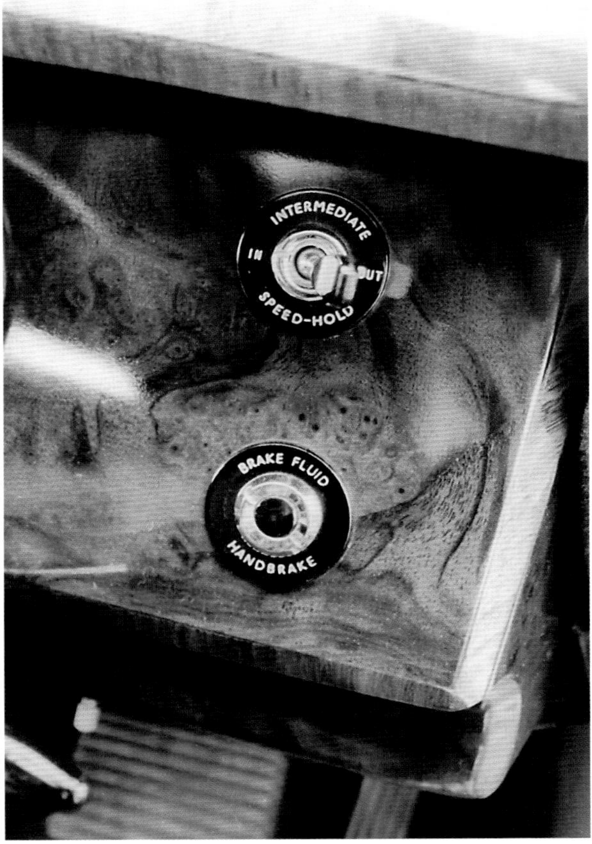

Intermediate speed hold forced the automatic to retain second gear. *(S)*

The Mark X again had the Borg-Warner DG automatic with intermediate speed hold and, from October 1963, a modified counterbalance valve for a better gear change.

With the Mark X 4.2n Jaguar introduced Borg-Warner's latest model 8, a larger-dimensioned sibling to the Type 35 used since 1962 in the Daimler 2.5-liter V-8. Both had an additional D2 position instead of the speed hold. It had an oil cooler that was assisted by the cooling water of the engine.

The Model 8 was also used for the E-Type 2+2 and V-12, Mark II, 3.4 S, 3.8 S, and 420, while the Model 35 was adopted for the 240. Cars with these boxes could not be towed with the engine off because of a lack of lubrication to the transmission. The XJ 6 4.2 inherited the Model 8, and the 2.8 got the Model 35.

In June 1970 the Model 8 was replaced with the Model 12, with lever positions of 1 and 2 instead of D1 and D2. In these positions the transmission would hold the selected gear. This gearbox was suitable for engines with 40 percent more torque than before and changed to a lower gear even under part-throttle, actuated with a vacuum signal that was combined with a barometric height compensation. Gear ratios and performance remained unchanged.

From October 1970 the smaller gearbox was equipped with a self-adjusting servo that needed no regular maintenance. The throttle cable for both boxes and the kick-down switch were changed. As a preparation for use in connection with the V-12 engine—for which the Model 12 was the appropriate choice not only in name—the vacuum tank was changed.

From December 1973 the six-cylinder models used Borg-Warner's new Model 65, successor to Model 35, with an even smoother gear change. In June 1979 it was further refined, now being called Model 66. The driving element in the torque converter now was crinkled in shape.

The V-12 was combined with a new automatic only from April 1977, the choice now being General Motors' Turbo Hydra-matic 400, which already had been chosen by Rolls-Royce. This shifted down more willingly than the previous Model 12, and at full throttle the lower gears were retained until nominal engine speed was reached. Shifting down into first below 30 miles per hour had to be prevented in order to comply with Swiss noise emission regulations. This automatic is recognizable by its wide space between the P and R positions. In January 1980 its torque converter was modified.

About mid-1981 the detent between N and D was, after much criticism from car testers, relocated to a more suitable place between D and 2; operation of the gearlever now was much easier indeed. In September 1985 the diameter of the dipstick pipe was enlarged and by the end of 1988 the box reacted more quickly to full throttle.

With the 318-horsepower 6-liter, an improved Turbo Hydra-matic called 4L80E was introduced. The torque converter bypass was new, as was a fourth gear. This latest development of the Americans had sport and standard modes to choose from, thus catching up with the competition after many years. This automatic was used exclusively for Jaguar's 6-liter V-12s and (as an alternative to a manual) in the supercharged six-cylinder XJR.

From September 1992 for safety reasons—in the United States, litigation about unintended acceleration from automatic-transmission cars had drawn public concern—changing from P to R was only possible as long as the brake pedal was pushed.

Above: ZF five-speed automatic for the X 308. *(J)*

Right: ZF four-speed automatic in the XJ 40. *(J)*

The AJ 6 engine was combined with the 4 HP 22 of Zahnradfabrik Friedrichshafen (ZF). Like the later GM unit, this was a four-speed epicyclic gear with hydraulic torque converter that could be bypassed. Control was electronic instead of hydraulic. The gear lever gate had two turns, and was thus called the J-gate. These turns helped to avoid inadvertent changes to neutral or rear. This gate was an invention of Jim Randle, thus for some it was called the Randle handle. From 1986 the J-gate was used in all models with the exception of Series 3 and XJS.

The improved 4 HP 24 was combined with the 4-liter engine for 1989. The 4 HP 24 now could bear 30 percent more torque than the previous model. It also had sport and economy modes. From the autumn of 1994, its torque converter was still more effective.

For the XJ 8 and XK 8, only the 5 HP 24 was used, specially developed for this purpose by ZF. This was the first five-speed automatic used by Jaguar for better acceleration from standstill. The torque converter, with an electronically controlled bypass, was particularly effective, but it allowed some slip at low revs to avoid jerks. The automatic could choose from seven shift programs and was integrated with the engine management system; this connection with the throttle improved the smoothness of the car's operation. The box could not cope with the torque of the supercharged engine, so the latest five-speed automatic from Mercedes-Benz (W5A580) was chosen for this task. This transmission was superior in weight and response, but was also combined with the J-gate.

The S-Type of 2002 was chosen for the debut of ZF's 6 HP 26, a six-speeder with fewer parts and less weight. Together with the 4.2-liter engine, it was also used in the XJ and XK. One problem was that it theoretically could reverse itself inadvertently, but this was cured in 2004 with the new programming of 14,284 vehicles that were recalled.

Driveshaft and Axle

All SS cars used Hardy-Spicer driveshafts with needle bearings and a helical differential. From autumn 1939 ENV hypoid bevel differentials were used in the 1.5-liter, enabling a lower position of the driveshaft. It worked well, and after the war it was used universally until 1953—it was made in part by Salisbury from 1951 onward. With the Mark V the tradition of a divided driveshaft with a universal joint was established, allowing a still lower driveshaft tunnel. Soon after this the central bearing was isolated from the body by a spring.

From summer 1958 the limited slip option made by Spicer under license from American Thornton became available. As "Powr Lok," it was used in XK 150 3.8-liter, E-Type, Mark II 3.8-liter, Mk X, XJ 12, XJ-S, and XJR 4.0. With the advent of the X 300, electronic devices could perform a similar function, using engine management and antilock brakes. With the V-8, no more limited slip differentials were used.

From February 1961 onward the central mount of the driveshaft was improved with thick rubber, so that no vibrations could be transmitted to the body. With the brakes moving inboard with the E-Type and other IRS models, the differentials were exposed to much heat, which affected the seals, eventually causing them to leak. From September 1963 the driveshaft bearings were maintenance-free.

In September 1975 the central driveshaft mount was again improved for six-cylinder models. Between 1985 and 1988 some Dana differentials with a flat underside and brake caliper mounts at their sides were used, for which no spares are available. Salisbury, once a branch of a company established 1901 in New York, had before World War I invented a universal joint upon which the whole automobile industry became dependant. However, in a period of near-bankruptcy a lawyer named Charles Dana gained control over Spicer, which in 1919 took over its former joint venture partner, Salisbury. Dana managed to establish Hardy Spicer & Co. Ltd. together with Edward John Hardy, who had invented the flexible Hardy joint. From 1939 differentials were made for the whole industry under the Salisbury name. Shortly after World War II, the British company gained independence from its American mother and co-operated with Laycock from Sheffield, which supplied Jaguar with differentials. This new group was swallowed by GKN in 1967, which in turn was taken over in the 1980s by the American Dana Corporation. With regard to the differentials, despite ever-changing names, the supplier always remained the same.

With the XK 8 and XJ 8, Jaguar tried new differentials from GKN, called 14 HU. Like with the oldest types, the driveshaft and drive pinion were at the same level. The higher position of the driveshaft necessitated an equally higher tunnel along the floor, but this location also promised better protection from vibrations. In the XK 8 the driveshaft was a single 100mm tube and no longer divided.

The XJ 8 retained the divided driveshaft, but the central mount went further forward as did the engine, which again helped against noise and vibration. New welding technology helped make the driveshaft still thinner and reduced its weight by 44 percent—thus facilitating the balancing of the unit.

Steering

While the SS One had a Marles & Weller cam and lever steering, the SS Two made do until autumn 1933 with a Burman spindle. The SS Jaguar also had spindle steering with a Bluemel steering wheel and just 2½ turns from lock to lock. The need for greater ease of operation and increasing weight of vehicles forced cars to offer more and more indirect steering until, with Mark VII, nearly five turns lock-to-lock were reached. Like Mark V and XK 120, it had a lighter recirculating ball steering. Rubber elements between the steering column and steering gear helped suppress noise and vibration.

The XK 120 C was the first Jaguar with rack and pinion steering, and this was used from then on in all sporting models. In the XK 140 it was combined with a divided steering column and a universal joint—the more vertical steering wheel allowed a more relaxed seating position. The 2.4-liter had two universal joints in its steering column to guard against vibrations. These joints also helped the steering column collapse in case of a frontal collision.

From April 1958 Burman power steering could be ordered with a Hobourn-Eaton eccentric rotor pump at the dynamo shaft. This reduced steering wheel turns to just over three from lock to lock. In the Mark IX the servo was standard equipment.

The Mark II had a new two-spoke steering wheel with a horn ring. As with the XK models, a wooden or ivory steering wheel was optional. A variety of ratios were available, as was (at least in later years) servo assistance. Upon its introduction the steering gear had been modified for better precision. In April 1963 a variable servo was introduced for the Mark X, servo assistance decreasing with higher engine revs. One year later, with the introduction of the Mark X 4.2, the Varamatic servo had its world premiere. This had been developed by Arthur Bishop in Australia, adopted in 1958 by Bendix in the U.S., and perfected by Adwest Engineering in Reading. The gearing increased toward the locks so that less than three turns of the steering wheel were necessary. The system was activated by a torsion bar at the steering column and a rotor valve. Step by step this system became available for the smaller models as well.

The rack and pinion steering of the XJ 6 was—contrary to the one in the E-Type—supplied by the manufacturers of the servo, Adwest Engineering. The rack was mounted behind the front subframe in Metalastik rubber bushings that could absorb impacts from road undulations. The telescopic Saginaw steering column had a flexible joint at its lower end so that no movements of the steering rack filtered through. Again, the Varamatic power system was included, with the exception of the (very, very rare) 2.8-liter standard model. It was modified in December 1972 to counter a tendency of the whole front suspension to self-steer under certain conditions. From May 1973 a new steering column was used. In spring 1975 the steering gear was changed so that the pinion had no more than eight teeth. At this opportunity the steering geometry was optimized. Obviously as a reaction to testers' complaints about a lack of "feel," the XJ-S was equipped with a seven-tooth pinion and a more direct ratio.

From June 1977 until October 1978 the Adwest steering gear was replaced with one of Alford & Alder manufacture. In April 1978 steering column and brackets were standardized with other Leyland products. In May 1980 the steering was revised again for better directional stability. A new Saginaw pump was used for the servo, and hydraulic pipes got better protection against leaks. In June 1983 new Shamban steering gear seals were employed. In November 1984 the grease nipple at the steering gear was deleted. Beginning with the XJ-S 3.6, which from its start had a stiffer torsion bar in the servo unit to provide less power support and stiffer mounting for the steering rack, the sporting models were equipped with steering systems offering more feel.

The XJ 40 retained the proven steering system, but with a different servo pump. From May 1993 the XJS had a more durable and reliable steering gear made at Zahnradfabrik Friedrichshafen (ZF).

Left: Adjustable André Hartford shock absorbers on an SS One Airline. *(Schön)*

Below: Chassis for the XK 120. *(S)*

Bottom left: Independent front suspension for the Mark V. *(S)*

Bottom right: Front suspension of the XK 150 with the steering rack clearly visible. *(S)*

The XK 8 and XJ 8 had a completely new ZF Servotronic steering system. The distance between the teeth on the rack increased toward its ends, thus increasing the ratio. This also helped reduce the turning circle. Around the center, servo support was reduced nearly to nothing, so that the driver had better feel. For the 1999 model year (and the XKR from its introduction) the whole system was replaced with the new Servotronic II, which the S-Type adopted from the 2001 model year.

Front Suspension

All SSs had a live front axle with half-elliptic springs in a chassis that, in the case of the SS One, had been supplied by Rubery Owen to Standard, where it was combined with engine, transmission, and wheel suspension. Contrary to the version used by Standard for its own models like the Ensign, the U-section longitudinal and the transverse joints had been lowered below the cabin but still ran above the rear axle. At the front, flat half-elliptic nine-leaf springs were mounted on the outside of the frame. The split hubs were made by Rudge Whitworth. In order to achieve the desired proportions, the position of the engine was 7 inches further back than in Standard's own models.

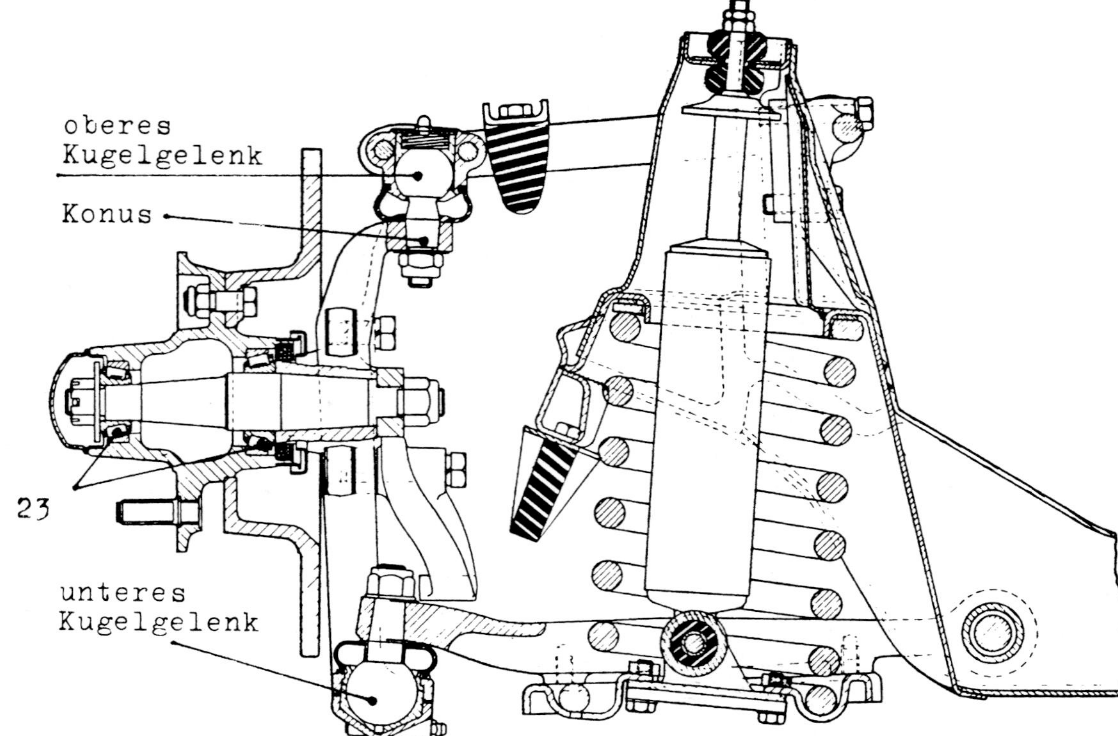

Sectional drawing of the 2.4-liter's front suspension. *(JAGMAG archive)*

The second version of the SS One had a new chassis that had been designed by Standard and was made by Thompson Pressings Limited exclusively for SS. This had X bracing under the cabin and near-parallel longitudinal members running below the rear axle ("underslung"). André Hartford friction dampers also were specified.

From September 1933 the engine was mounted in rubber at the front and in silent bushings at the rear. In advertising this was somewhat appropriately called "buoyant power." Track width was increased and the chassis X was reinforced and put further forward, thus creating more legroom in the back. Broader springs in maintenance-free silent bushings at the rear ends improved riding comfort. A year later, the chassis was further stiffened; at the front two transversely mounted dampers were added. For the SS 90 standard chassis were shortened to the SS Two's wheelbase in Jack Beardsley's smithy. After 1938 AC benefited from Standard's development work for lower chassis for their 16/80 and 16/90 types.

The SS Jaguar had boxed underslung longitudinals with X braces, the chassis having been designed by William Heynes for SS and made at Rubery Owen. The rear ends of the front leaf springs had sliding bearings instead of shackles. The springs were assisted by LUVAX hydraulic lever shock absorbers. The SS 100 added friction dampers to them.

In the autumn of 1936 the frame became broader at the rear, with larger shock absorbers and a more solid bracket for the steering gear. In the following year the chassis was adjusted to the new all-steel bodies. The longitudinals now were 6 inches high and the X bracing had been replaced with transverse links, increasing stiffness by more than 30 percent.

With the Mark V and XK 120, Jaguar introduced its first independent front suspension. It had been developed by William Heynes. He decided on double wishbones, the lower ones being lighter and extending to a long torsion bar that replaced the spring. The design was notable for its upper and lower ball joints for the axle legs, enabling movement for both steering and springing. The sockets were prone to wear and had to be modified several times until sufficient longevity was achieved. From the 1951 model year, grease nipples were added to them. All suspension parts were

FEATURES OF THE JAGUAR "S"

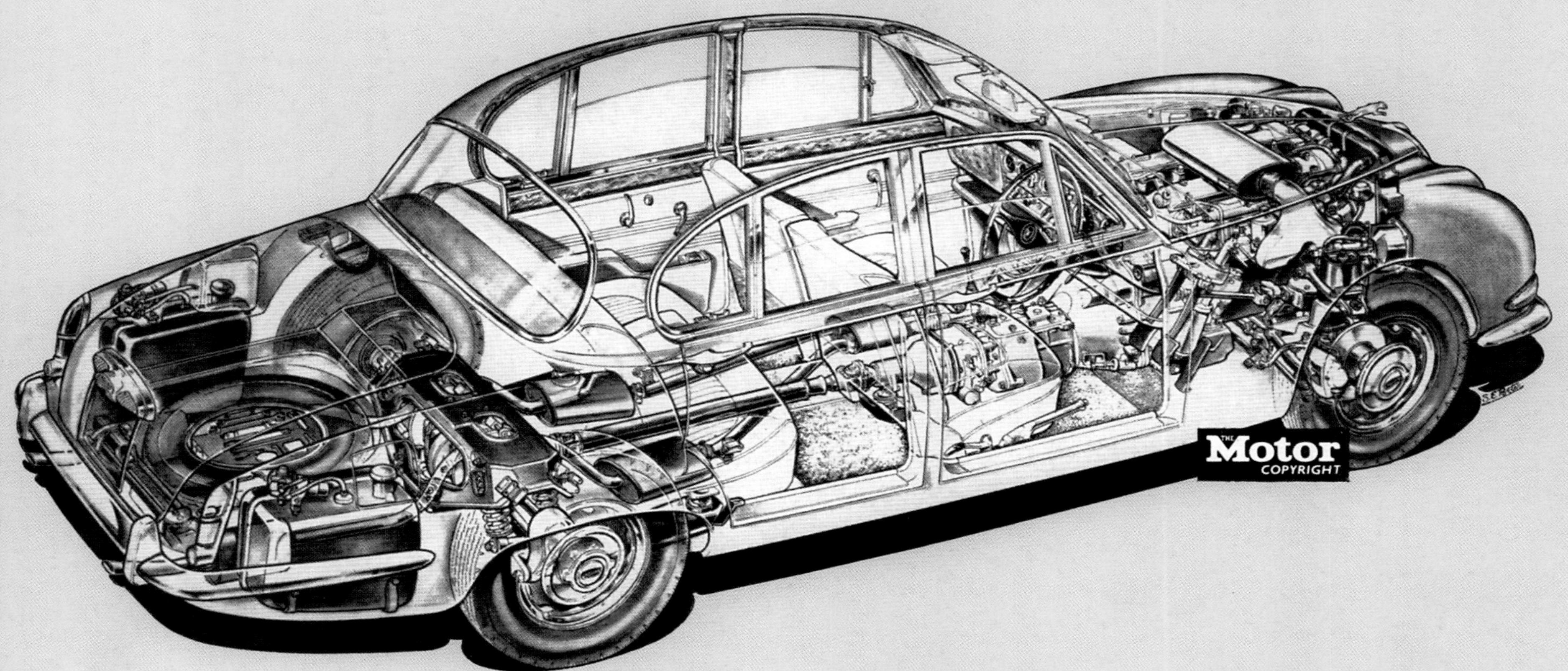

- Comfortable five-seat sedan luxuriously equipped with outstanding workmanship
- Independent suspension, four-wheel disc brakes
- Front seats with combined adjustment for height and width, reclining backrest, and foldable armrests
- Anatomically-shaped back seats with a central armrest, offering maximum comfort for two or three people
- High-performance heating and ventilation systems with gradual regulation
- Large trunk with 532-liter capacity
- Choice of 3.4- or 3.8-liter engine
- Choice of fully-synchronized four-speed manual transmission with overdrive or fully-automatic transmission
- Two independent fuel tanks with a total capacity of 64 liters
- Generous instrumentation

Every technical detail of the 3.4 and 3.8 S made visible. *(Schönborn archive)*

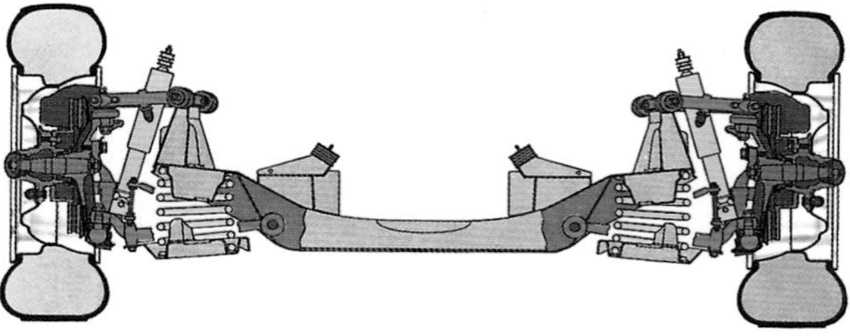

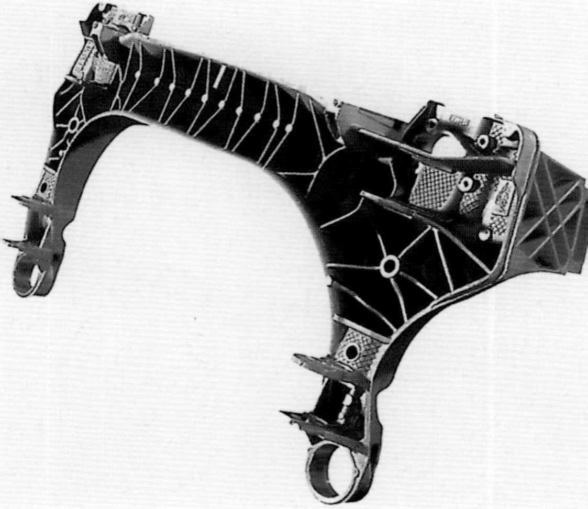

Top: Front suspension for the XJ 12 Series 1. *(S)*

Above: Sectional drawing of the front suspension for the 1968 XJ 6. *(J)*

Right: Aluminum front subframe of the 1996 XK 8. *(J)*

borne in Metalastik silent blocks. The new chassis had straight longitudinal members, up to 6½ inches high and 3½ inches wide with a sharp upturn before the rear axle and solid transverse links in the middle, at the front, and at the rear. This ensured longer wheel travel and higher ground clearance at the same time. At the front a stabilizer was employed and—for the first time at Jaguar—telescopic Girling dampers. From January 1950 maintenance-free rubber bushings were used instead of the former, while threaded bushings were used at the tie rod. For the Mark VII, firmer dampers could be ordered. The Mark VII M's torsion springs were slightly stiffer, which resulted in still more ground clearance. From April 1955 the wheels were situated further to the inside of the hub, but the track remained unchanged.

The 2.4-liter retained the IFS principle but with coil springs attached to the lower wishbone. The dampers were situated inside the coil springs, and both attached to a front subframe, as the body construction was unitary. The subframe also supported the steering gear and was attached to the body via V-shaped rubber bushings at the rear end and vertical rubber blocks at the front. The rubber material was selected to better absorb road noise. Even the stabilizer was supported in rubber.

Shortly after Mark IX went into production, new ball joints were used that allowed an increased steering angle. For Mark II the wishbones were aligned slightly transversely with an intention to lift the body roll center by 100mm and thus reduce roll under fast cornering. The body roll center is the axis around which the body would turn if pushed down on one side. At the time it was a much-discussed technical feature. In the ensuing years dampers and springs would often be changed in search of optimum ride comfort and roadholding. In February 1961 the Mark II was equipped with cast instead of pressed upper wishbones. The Daimler 2.5-liter V-8 had softer springs, as its engine was considerably lighter than the XK unit.

The E-Type had torsion springs for the front suspension, which otherwise remained faithful to the XK principle as well. Mark X's front suspension was similar to the Mark II's, but the springs were attached to the upward ends of the forged steel subframe, which bore the body via V-shaped Metalastik elements. The front suspension parts were supplied from Alford & Alder, the telescopic dampers from Girling.

From March 1964 the grease nipples at the ball joints were improved. Nylon discs were employed to help excessive grease leak out. The wheel bearings now also had grease nipples.

The XJ 6 remained faithful to the now well-approved IFS, but in a further refined version. According to an idea of Derek White for Graham Hill's E-Type, the upper and lower wishbones were slightly inclined, which reduced dive under braking by 50 percent. A further decrease would have been possible but the usual brake feeling would have suffered. This anti-dive effect allowed the use of softer springs. The shock absorbers were positioned outside the coil springs to the very outside of the lower wishbone, where they could control wheel travel even better. Their upper ends were carried in Microvon plastic bushings. The wishbone's inner ends were carried in Slipflex bushings, which allowed easier turning. A stabilizer was again attached to the lower wishbones. The suspension bushings were stiffer, so that the tendency of the whole subframe to turn under load, for example when driving over a hump on one side of the car, was reduced.

The subframe was no longer a simple forged transverse link but a complex box section with two 45-degree V-shaped natural rubber bushings near the hub axis bearing the body, and horizontal-cylindrical rubber elements at the ends of the front legs. The latter elements were made of synthetic SBR rubber in six different degrees of hardness, which helped reduce noise transmission. Eighty percent of the weight of the engine now was put directly on the subframe, helping to keep it quiet, a system that was copied for the 420 G.

In May 1969 still stiffer front springs were employed with different upper sockets. This resulted in increased ground clearance, and the front wheels in sharp turns would no longer scrape the inner wheel arches. In the spring of 1975 the front suspension geometry was revised, and for Jaguar's first light alloy wheels the hubs had to be modified. From February 1978 larger wheel bolts were used. From 1988 German Boge dampers were used, and from 1993 Bilsteins.

The XJ 40 also remained faithful to IFS, but with a multitude of detail changes. This included maintenance-free wheel bearings, which were later also seen on other models. For different variants the suspension settings changed ever more in order to underline each version's specific character.

For the XK 8, the front subframe was an aluminum casting, which for the relatively small series was the cost-efficient solution, and in addition saved more than 7 kilograms (15½ pounds) compared to steel. The wishbones had been redesigned, although the general layout was not changed. The anti-dive effect was increased and the steering geometry improved with a halved roll radius—a dimension that had remained unchanged since Mark X days. This improved directional stability under braking. For the XK coupe with 18-inch wheels the dampers could be varied electronically—this option was called Computer Active Technology System (CATS). Out of two damper modes the computer chose the more appropriate one based on the evaluation of a variety of data, including two measures of vertical acceleration and one for horizontal. The XK 8 front suspension proved itself and was adapted for the XJ 8 with a variety of stabilizers, but not the light alloy subframe, as this would have necessitated too many changes to the body.

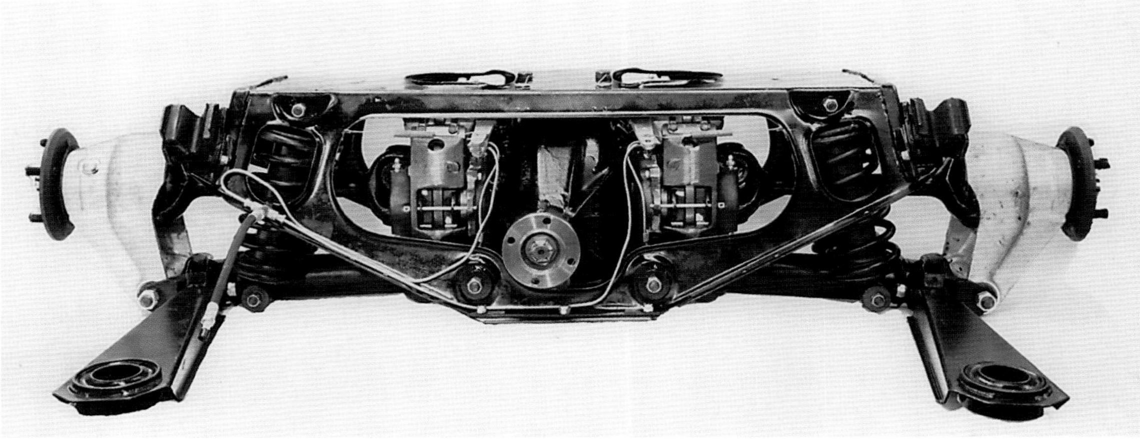

The secret of Jaguar's fabulous roadholding and ride comfort lies in its complicated rear suspension. *(S)*

The suspension of the S-Type was developed in parallel to Lincoln's LS, which debuted at the same time using the same platform. Design was not yet perfect, as late in 2000 all cars produced were recalled because of excessive wear at the lower ball joint. The revised joints were used in production right from the beginning of the 2001 model year. For 2002 the front suspension was revised substantially, and it was further refined for 2004.

The X 350 chassis showed with its front suspension that Jaguar aimed at using similar components for its middle and large sedans. It used the suspension and subframe of the S-Type, which after all changes was quite good. With the exception of the basic model for the British market, X 350 chassis had springs and dampers replaced with air suspension elements supplied by German company Thyssen-Krupp.

Rear Suspension

With the exception of the X-Type, all Jaguars have had rear-wheel drive, so the quality of rear suspension was vital. According to the state-of-the-art of the time, SS inherited from Standard a live axle with half-elliptic leaf springs, without any control links. With the SS Jaguar, the leaf springs went to the inner sides of the longitudinal chassis members, and for the first time LUVAX hydraulic lever shock absorbers were used.

Thanks to the new chassis design, the Mark V offered much longer wheel travel, the springs being 6 inches longer than before. In August 1953 telescopic dampers were added to the rear suspension of the Mark VII, while the XK received them only when the 140 was introduced more than a year later.

Due to the lack of the familiar chassis frame, the 2.4-liter had a completely different rear suspension in that the live axle was attached to the rear ends of the leaf springs that were attached to the underside of the body at the front and in the middle, making them work as quarter-elliptic springs. They were fixed to the body with bolts and rubber blocks above and below the springs. A link was fixed to the top side of the axle on both ends, so that turning of the axle under heavy acceleration or braking was impossible. A Panhard rod was added to avoid sideways movement. Due to the spats the rear track was unusually narrow; this made the car look spectacular under fast cornering. Not only for this reason, the Mark II had a wider rear track that necessitated a recess in the spats. In June 1956 stiffer Girling dampers were introduced.

In May 1957 Mark VIIIs were improved with rubber layers between the spring leaves; after July 1957 the layers were made of nylon.

The E-Type was the first Jaguar produced in real series with an independent rear suspension. In principle it worked like two transverse links, with the driveshafts acting as the upper links. This made it similar to a design Georges Roesch patented for Talbot in 1935, but with the lower link being left out. Lotus used a similar design for the Elite sports car, but Jaguar's, with its two coil springs and dampers at each side, was much more impressive. In addition Knight attached a trailing link to the lower transverse links. The front end was attached to the underside of the body via rubber pads with layers of different hardness. Transverse links, differential, springs, and dampers were attached to a subframe, which itself was attached to the body via four V-shaped Metalastik rubber blocks, two on each side positioned at a 90-degree angle to each other.

The flexibility caused by all the rubber elements allowed the whole suspension to turn around an axis just in front of that of the drive shafts. The torque of the differential was taken up by two links attached to the subframe. The differential remained unchanged, with the exception that its housing had to be adapted to the needs of this independent rear suspension and was now called 4HU instead of 4HA. The axle leg was made of aluminum. In order to reduce unsprung weight, the brakes had been moved from their normal position just behind the wheel to just outboard of the diff housing. The design was further improved in January 1963 when telescopic dampers filled with gas were introduced.

From January 1964 the often-neglected grease nipples at the universal joints of the drive shafts were deleted. These were replaced with rubber grommets.

The XJ 6 was intended to live without the rear subframe and the trailing links; the latter were to be replaced with a torsion tube. This suspension, developed by Knight, was quite similar to what the XJ 40 would have. Test driving at MIRA made the dampers run dry and hot. So for further testing they were provisionally covered with wool, which was kept damp with water from a reservoir in the trunk. But as soon as the tank ran empty the wool caught fire, nearly setting the whole car aflame! Roadholding was perfect, but directional stability was somewhat imprecise, which could be traced down to a small mistake in front suspension geometry. The lack of the subframe resulted in noise and vibration being transferred to the body. Initially it was thought the exhaust might be the cause, but changes to its mounting provided no cure. So it seemed worthwhile to stick with the approved system, which later was used in the XJ-S and even the Aston Martin DB 7, which survived until 2003.

The rear of the XJ 40 included some of the ideas that had been discarded for the first XJ 6. A subframe was used, however, and due to wider spread ends of the transverse links, neither a second pair of springs and dampers nor trailing arms were necessary. A Bilstein Nivomat self-leveling shock was available on request or from 1988 as standard in the Sport variants. Due to its high pressure, it was prone to damage and was not retained for the X 300. The many different variants of the XJ 40 and its successors had different settings for springs and dampers to underline the specific character of each model. The X 300 was the first Jaguar with electronic traction control, which prevented wheelspin by automatically activating a single brake. It was standard equipment on all X 300s with more than 300 horsepower.

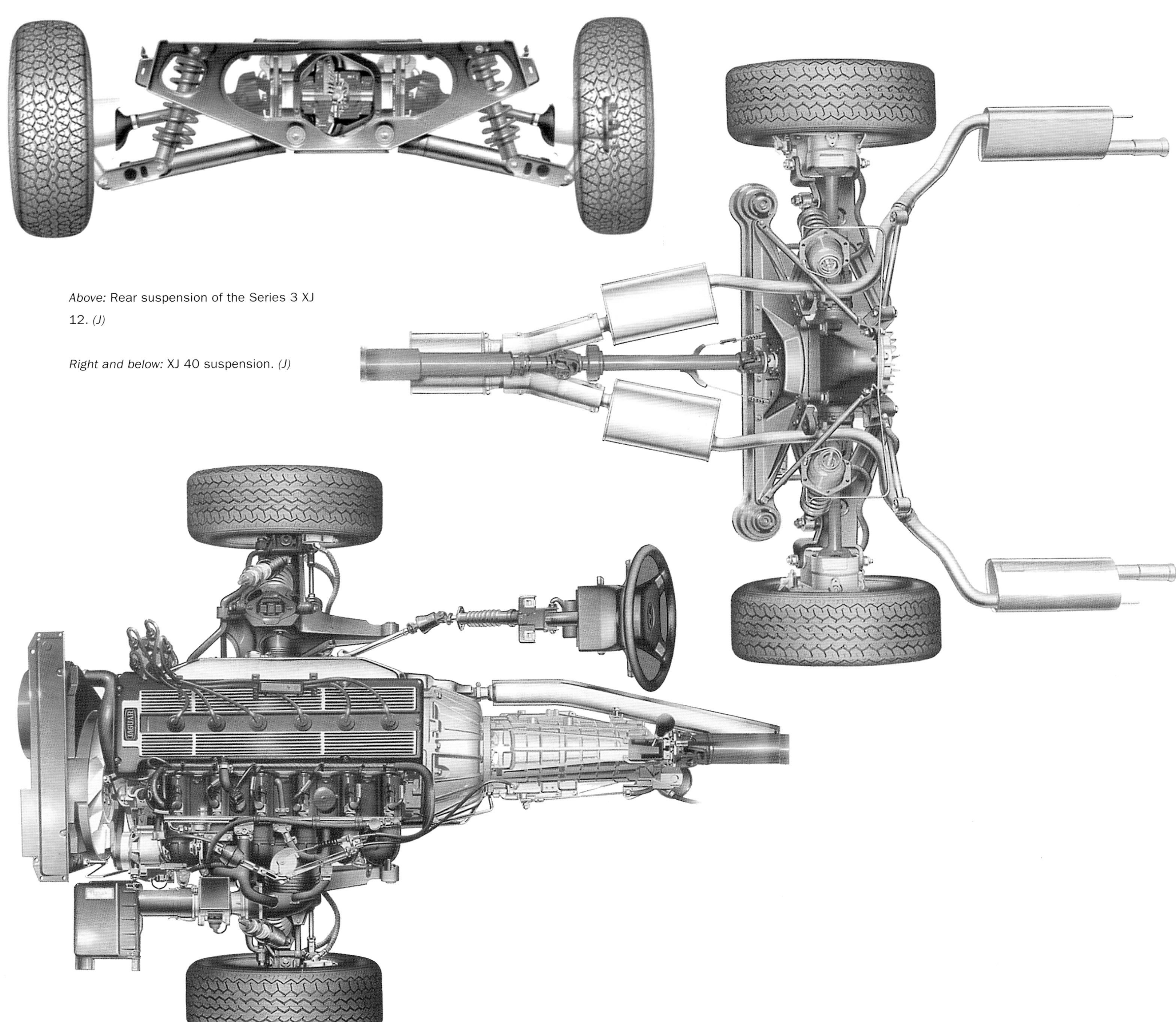

Above: Rear suspension of the Series 3 XJ 12. *(J)*

Right and below: XJ 40 suspension. *(J)*

The XK 8 was intended not only to inherit the XJ-S' platform but also its rear suspension, with the brakes in the meantime having moved outboard. The first major change to the vehicle concept, however, resulted in this item being replaced with the one from the XJR. The underside of the body had to be adjusted to the links of this subframe. The idea behind this certainly was to have more uniform parts for easier production and spares storage. The XJ 8 also used this suspension with all the variations for different requirements of comfort and roadholding. Quite remarkably, a Nivomat was again available for XJ 8, but it was not compatible with CATS dampers.

The S-Type was remarkable for introducing double wishbone suspension to the rear of a Jaguar, in a subframe consisting of two parts. This meant that the driveshafts were of no influence to suspension geometry for the first time in a Jaguar IRS. The theme was continued in the X 350, albeit almost universally in combination with air springs.

Brakes

SS One used Bendix-Perrot drum brakes on all four wheels. These had an easy-to-maintain duo-servo control wire that Standard had chosen for its six-cylinder models. From October 1932 the handbrake also worked on all four wheels. In autumn 1933 the brake diameter was increased to 12.5 inches. In the following year the rod-operated Girling brake with 13-inch drums was introduced.

The SS Jaguar continued with these, but the 1.5-liter only had 12-inch drums with Girling transverse-wedge rods, which soon were taken over by the six-cylinders. After only a year, the drums were further increased to 14 inches and those of the 1.5-liter were widened. Before World War II again, for a short time, a four-wheel handbrake was used.

Immediately after the war, the Girling 2 LS with two leading shoes was introduced, while the hydraulic operation—it had been invented by Lockheed in 1914– was reserved for the Mark V and XK 120. The handbrake lever was now mounted beneath the dashboard instead of on the driveshaft tunnel, acting via a control wire. Because of the smaller wheels, the drums had to be reduced to 12 inches and the disc wheels (wires were no longer available) further impeded brake cooling.

In January 1950 the brake shoes were provided with sliding journals. At the rear one shoe of each pair was no longer a leading one.

Mark VII front brakes surprised experts in that no more leading shoes were employed, but all were self-adjusting. As a consequence, the driver had to push harder to obtain reasonable slowing. This was compensated for by a brake servo as invented in the 1920s by Belgian Dewandre that reduced pedal effort by half with vacuum from the inlet manifold. The system was supplied by Clayton. The general opinion was that this system provided more precise control of braking power and greater immunity from fade. The handbrake lever returned to the driveshaft tunnel, but the front bench of the automatic version meant that the lever would move under the dash again.

The 2.4-liter had Lockheed Brakemaster drum brakes with a diameter of 11⅛ inches, and these were self-adjusting at the front.

In 1957 disc brakes, which by now had been sufficiently tried and tested in racing, were introduced in the XK 150. The system had round pads, 12-inch discs front and rear, and a vacuum servo. To change brake pads, the whole caliper had to be taken off. The system also became available in the 2.4- and 3.4-cars, but with smaller discs, which for the Mark II were enlarged to 11 inches. From the first half of 1958 several changes were made to avoid long pedal travel, including master cylinders made of cast iron instead of aluminum and better seals.

The Mark IX used the same system as the sports car, but with slightly larger discs, thicker brake pads, and a Lockheed servo with a vacuum reservoir that retained brake pressure after the engine stopped. In January 1959 pad changes were made easier; the pads now were nearly square. With the Mark II, a brake fluid and handbrake warning light was introduced, which soon also appeared on other models. From early 1960 the brake fluid reservoir was plastic, not glass.

With the E-Type a twin-circuit system was introduced, with one circuit for each axle. A leak in one did not affect the function of the other. All subsequent new models also had twin circuits, with the exception of Mark II 240, 250 V-8, and 340. The position of the rear brakes adjacent to the differential housing was less than ideal for cooling or maintenance. The rear brakes incorporated the self-adjusting handbrake with its own Dunlop caliper. The brake servo now was supplied by Kelsey-Hayes, based on an American invention made under license by Dunlop in Britain. It had a bellows that contracted by vacuum and acted on both master cylinders. The assistance was not particularly effective, but the system reduced brake feel considerably.

The huge Mark X, with its small 14-inch wheels, could not benefit from the large braking system of its predecessors. Its discs were 10½ inches (front) and 10 inches (rear). Otherwise its brakes were copied from the E-Type, but the handbrake lever was again positioned under the dashboard, not on the driveshaft tunnel.

In July 1962 the brake calipers were enlarged; in January 1963 the discs became thicker. The 3.4 and 3.8 S had Dunlop's Mark III disc brakes with cast-iron instead of forged brake cylinders and larger pads. In the following year, with the advent of the 4.2-liter engine, the Kelsey-Hayes servo was replaced with a conventional vacuum unit. This helped avoid boiling brake fluid, from which early E-Types in particular suffered.

The 420 of 1966 was the first Jaguar with Girling disc brakes (type 72/13) which also were used for the E-Type Series 2 and the XJ 6. Their diameters were 11.8 inches front and 10.4 inches rear. For reduction of wear, the front calipers had three pistons, with two smaller pads on the outside and a larger one on the inside. The area on the discs covered by the pads remained the same, as did the design of the rear calipers. The tandem master cylinder was now directly operated by the brake pedal.

From July 1969 the brake fluid reservoir was positioned alongside, not behind the servo, and from August 1970 the front discs had protective shields.

For V-12-engined cars, ventilated brake discs were introduced at the front; the discs were 11.18 inches in diameter. The XJ 12 also had a Kelsey counterbalance valve to prevent early rear wheel lock; with increasing pedal pressure a larger proportion of the brake power was diverted to the front brakes. The servo now was of Girling Supervac 100 type and was installed on the pedal box, with an additional polypropylene vacuum reservoir under the right front fender.

In August 1972 the brake pads were grooved for easier running in. From May 1973 the left-hand side inlet manifold of the V-12 also contributed vacuum to the brake servo. From the introduction of Series 2, the XJ 6's front discs also were of 11.18 inches diameter. From January 1974 a new master cylinder and four-piston calipers were used. The XJ-S had the same brake system as XJ 12, but with a handbrake lever at the outer side of the driver's seat that folded down to the floor after use—a system from Guy trucks of the 1960s, when Jaguar reigned there. To apply the handbrake the lever was pulled upward as usual and then put down; to release, the brake lever had to be lifted and then pushed down while depressing the button at the lever's front end. The mechanism was further refined in September 1979. The front calipers were adapted for the rear soon after introduction of the XJ-S.

In November 1975 the XJ 6 received XJ 12 calipers so that light alloy wheels could be mounted. In May 1977 a new servo was introduced, and the brake fluid reservoir was attached to the master cylinder. In July 1980 improved discs were introduced, with a reduced tendency to judder. From summer 1982 the front brake pipes were changed and the system was converted to green anticorrosive fluid. As mentioned, the XJ-S brakes were identical to the XJ 12's, but in May 1993, when Series 3 had gone out of production, the rear discs were moved away from the diff to the outside just behind the wheels. It is not difficult to change the brake position on older cars as well—even the sedans.

XJ 40 had 11.6-inch ventilated discs at the front and 10.6-inch outboard rear discs with separate handbrake drums instead of the additional calipers acting on the rear discs, which were less suitable for cable operation. The servo became independent of the inlet manifold, getting its own hydraulic pump. New for Jaguar was the antilock system imported from Girling/Bosch in Germany. (A similar device had been developed by Jaguar and Dunlop in the 1960s.)Two years later, on introduction of the 4-liter engine, it was replaced by a Teves system that was also used as standard equipment in the XJ 12 and XJ-S from the 1989 model year onward. For the X 300 electronic traction control was integrated to activate a rear brake in case of wheelspin.

The XK 8 continued with these brakes, while the antilock system was further developed and used as signal for the electronic stability control. The XJ 8 took over all these refinements, combined with a Teves Mark XX system. The supercharged version had larger brakes

Above: Kent alloys were the first alloy wheels for production cars from Jaguar. *(J)*

Right: Classic style enhanced by chromed wire wheels on a Mark II. *(Schön)*

from the 1999 model year onward. Brake distribution between front and rear was electronically controlled. For the 2000 model year, the sports cars could be supplied with Brembo four-piston brakes called "R-Performance."

In 2001 the S-Type became the first Jaguar with a true computer-controlled dynamic stability control. A brake assist that could reinforce the pedal pressure under sudden braking was added for the 2003 model year, starting with the XK.

Wheels and Tires

Most Swallows—the Morris-Swallow and some unsalable FIAT-Swallows excepted—had painted wire wheels instead of the more old-fashioned wooden wheels. A then-fashionable Ace wheel cover was an available option. SS One and Two had Rudge-Whitworth racing-type 18-inch wire wheels, the outer edge of which were chromed from around 1934. Some few cars had fully chromed wire wheels. The SS Jaguar had the same wheels, but without the chromed edges. From 1937 the Ace wheel disc was available fully chromed.

With the Mark V and XK 120, the wheel size was reduced to 16 inches and the wires replaced with steel disc wheels held by five bolts instead of the prior central nut. These bolts were hidden behind hubcaps with the Jaguar name on them. Additionally, rim embellishers would be delivered on special order. The Mark V and XK 120 were the first cars with Dunlop Super Comfort tires. Wire wheels painted in body color or silver were reintroduced for the XK 120 in March 1951. From 1953 wholly chromed wire wheels were available. Wire wheels were part of the XK Special Equipment package.

From late 1952 the rim width for the XK 120 and Mark VII was increased from 5 to 5½ inches. The Mark VII M came with rim embellishers as standard equipment and—initially as an optional extra only—tubeless tires.

For the XK 140 and 150, painted or chromed Dunlop wire wheels with a central nut remained available instead of the standard disc wheels; from June 1958 they had 60 instead of 54 spokes. For the XK 140 and Mark VII M the hubcaps changed design, doing away with the painted body-color ring. Whitewall tires remained an optional extra that was particularly sought-after in the United States.

The D-Type, XK-SS, and E-Type had special magnesium disc wheels with holes for better brake cooling.

The 2.4-liter had 15-inch wheels, 4½ inches wide. The 3.4-liter was equipped with new Dunlop Road Speed RS3 tires and was also available with painted or chromed wire wheels with 60 or, from 1958, 72 spokes. For export to Germany the "ears" for knocking off the wheel nuts had to be cut off in order to comply with latest legislation. From 1958 Dunlop RS4 tires were optional.

For the Mark II chromed rim embellishers were available; from September 1960 the disc wheel was 5 inches wide as well. The E-Type was introduced with further improved Dunlop RS5 tires on 75-spoke wire wheels.

Mark X, the largest Jaguar ever, was supplied with 14-inch wheels only. From November 1963 Dunlop SP radial ply tires of 205 x 14 size were available as an extra; these required the speedometer to be recalibrated.

The 3.4 and 3.8 S of late 1963 were introduced with disc wheels and chromed rim embellishers or 72-spoke painted or chromed wire wheels, each with the SP radial as an optional extra (also available on the E-Type). The E-Type Series 2 had wire wheels of the same size with 96 spokes.

For the XJ 6, launched at the same time, no wire wheels were available, although during development these had been considered and tested on Heynes' prototype. Instead, 15 x 6 steel disc wheels were used with hubcaps and rim embellishers made from bright stainless steel. The wheels were normally painted silver, not body color. They wore Dunlop SP Sport radials that had been specially developed for XJ 6. With a slightly irregular tread pattern they avoided some noise and their Aquajet drainage system helped prevent aquaplaning. The suspension with its subframes and lots of rubber effectively suppressed the higher noise level that was so typical of this type of tire. In 1970 the latest chromed disc wheels with larger ventilating holes were available on special order, an extra particularly appreciated in the United States.

The E-Type V-12 had the disc wheels with the enlarged holes or chromed wire wheels, both wearing the same tires as the sedan. No change again with XJ 12, with the exception of additional steel threads in the tires. The disc wheels had the larger holes but were chromed only to special order. Normally painted silver, they were gunmetal on Vanden Plas models. With the start of Series 2, the XJ 6 used the same wheels as the XJ 12.

From April 1975 GKN light alloy wheels called Kent were available for V-12 models; for export they were standard equipment. Vanden Plas models now had the chromed wheels as standard on the home market. Tires now were Pirelli P5; the Dunlops were available to special order only. The tires for the XJ-S, which appeared in September 1975 were even further reinforced.

The Series 3 XJ had new stainless steel wheel covers on which the wheel nuts remained visible. Hubcaps that covered this less clean area were employed only from November 1982. Home-market Vanden Plas models retained the traditional chromed wheels for some while, until the Kent alloys became standard here as well.

XJ 12 H.E. had Dunlop D7 or Pirelli P5 tires on light alloy (Jaguar and Vanden Plas) or steel (Double-Six) wheels. The Kent alloys were completely painted silver without the five black sectors that were retained for Daimler and Vanden Plas only. The XJ-S H.E. had new five-spoke Starfish alloys.

For the 1983 model year, Sovereign and export Vanden Plas models were shod with pepper pot alloys with two rings of holes for ventilation.

The XJ-S 3.6 took over the pepper pots while the cabriolet and XJ-S H.E. had lattice alloys. The XJ-S started to be offered with a variety of different sizes and designs of wheels.

The XJ 40 had Michelin TD wheels that allowed being driven for some miles even with a flat tire. A hump in the rim made it nearly impossible for the tire to be lost, and a gel prevented overheating of the tire. The wheels were very expensive and thus did not become popular. They were covered with rather bland plastic hubcaps, and even the alloys, with their rather uninspiring design, were all but eye candy, but they were easily cleaned, thanks to their flat face. For the 1993 model year they were replaced with conventional wheels (and Dunlop SP 2000 tires, with Pirelli P 4000s for Daimlers). For the U.S. nothing changed, as they had retained the conventional wheels from the beginning.

From the autumn of 1994 the sedans also started to have a wider range of wheel sizes and dimensions as a choice. The XK 8 had an ultramodern asymmetrical tread. Its rims were up to 20 inches in diameter, with the tires becoming ever more low-profile, to the detriment of riding comfort but offering more precise handling.

Body

Coachwork was how William Lyons' work on cars started when he—with help from Cyril Holland—turned dull Sevens into gleaming Austin-Swallows. As with the Swallow sidecars, work started with ash frames. Aluminum and later steel sheets were nailed onto these frames after their edges had been flanged. More complicated parts like fenders were supplied by Cooke and Sons at Nottingham. Other large formed sheets were made at nearer-by Motor Panels. Chromed Wilmot-Breeden bumpers had been standard equipment of the first SS Ones, as was the Pytchley sliding roof that, contrary to usual designs, fitted flush with the roof panels when closed. The radiator cap was adorned with wings (referencing the Swallow name?) with the SS insignia on both sides. The wings in different designs would remain on SS and Jaguar radiator grilles until as late as 1970, when the 420 G went out of production. The steel housings for the spare wheel, which were available on special order, also had a chromed SS badge.

As with the Swallows since early 1930, the SS was painted with nitro-cellulose paint instead of oil-resin mixtures. The paint was applied in two layers wet-in-wet and a final very thin coat. This paint was chosen for its relatively quick drying, but it had to be polished thoroughly in order to achieve the intended

Top: Stainless steel hubcaps were reintroduced late in 1982. *(J)*

Middle: "Pepper pot" wheels for Jaguar's first Sovereign. *(J)*

Bottom: Plastic hubcaps for the early XJ 40. *(J)*

shine—and later the chauffeur had to repeat this sudatory procedure every three months. All Austin-Swallows had duotone paint, while the SS examples were usually monochrome.

For the second SS One, which debuted in October 1932, the main change was the longer body, with its wonderfully flowing fenders that formed one part with the running boards. Thanks to the elongated chassis it now became a full four-seater. The badge bar between the front fenders disappeared. The hood had more louvers (thus suggesting more power), and each door hinge had its own grease nipple. The interior was now better isolated from the engine bay.

In autumn 1933 quick-release fuel filler caps were employed and a painted steel cover for the spare wheel now was standard on the coupe. A hydraulic D.W.S. four-wheel jack could be specified, and the Airline was the first SS with an impressive tool tray in the trunk lid. It also was the first SS with skirted front fenders as they were just becoming fashionable.

With the 1935 Jaguar, SS presented its first four-door car. The badge at the top of the radiator now read "SS Jaguar." The trunk was fully integrated in the body and—following the example of the Airline—was accessible via a trunk lid with the tool tray. The broad chromed molding at the sides was quite obtrusive.

After just a year the styling of the SS Jaguar was slightly altered with a mighty radiator grille and broader bars, quite similar to the Bentley. The marker lamps on top of the front fenders of the six-cylinder cars were now integrated into these fenders. In the autumn of 1937, the company made the bold step to all-steel bodies. All wooden frames were replaced with reinforcing steel panels on the inside of the body panels. Only the drophead coupe still had wood in its doors and rear end. Although the cars appeared to be more or less unchanged—the front fenders now extended down nearly to the front bumpers—the interior was roomier. The paint now consisted of four coats, one being a clear coat. The spare wheel now was in the trunk lid. This made the lid too heavy, so in May 1938 it was moved into its own compartment below the trunk, which was slightly enlarged for the 1940 model year.

In the autumn of 1945 production of the 1940 model year sedans was resumed, but with some additional changes because of the lack of material. The SS badges disappeared, and a large "J" on a rectangular chromed badge adorned the center of the rear bumpers.

The Mark V and XK 120 had their headlamps integrated into the front wings, and the rear wheels were covered with spats. The filler cap was hidden behind a heavy, somewhat complicated flap, which initially tended to spring open. The slim chromed door window frames were to become a Jaguar hallmark but they had to be reinforced, particularly the rear ones with their D-shape to the back. For the first time, press-button door locks were used; only the drophead coupe retained the traditional door handle. Following American taste, both had thicker, profiled double bumpers of solid, not spring steel. For the Americans' less cautious parking, large overriders were added to the front as well as to the rear. The rear bumper could be folded down, giving access to the spare wheel. It had lost its "J" badge. In 1949 the rubber lip seals around doors and trunk lid were replaced with hose-style seals.

The XK 120 had been intended to be built in a small series and thus was made in the traditional way with ash and aluminum. Its longitudinal oval grille with a round "growler" badge above it became a typical Jaguar styling element in the following years. The change to all steel in April 1950 did not affect doors, hood, or trunk lid, which were still made of aluminum, but the drophead coupe started with steel doors over a wooden frame in December 1953. From February 1951, cooling flaps for the front were included in the front fenders, as had been introduced with the Mark VII. The spare wheel compartment had to be made an inch higher when wire wheels, with their larger hubs, were introduced—at the cost of trunk space. The XK 140 had much larger bumpers and a grille with broader bars cast in one piece. Chromed strips were added along the middle of the hood and trunk lid. The radiator badge was red and orange, listing the manufacturer, model name, and place of manufacture. On the trunk lid a similarly colored badge told of the Le Mans victories. For the XK 140 drophead coupe, push-button door handles were introduced. With the engine moved forward, more space was made available for the interior. Fixed head and drophead coupes had steel doors from mid-1956. The three variants of XK 140 had many more differences than was visible at first glance, particularly with regard to interior space, which was largest in the fixed head coupe, benefiting most from the engine having been moved further to the front of the chassis.

The Mark VII body with its integral fenders and large body panels seemed to be much more modern than its predecessor. Following the example of the XK 120, its doors were all hinged at the front. Instead of the double bumpers, single ones imitating the previous style were employed, initially with a third smaller bulge between two large ones. The much longer rear end contained a very large trunk with a square number plate. At the side, vertical lockable trunk lid handles were an impressive pair. While the tools had moved to the lower part of the Mark VII driver's side door trim, the spare wheel stood at the right side of the trunk. Now there was a step for the axle in the much lower trunk floor. The trunk lid was hinged at its front, no longer at its lower end, which had been so practical for wardrobe trunks, which now were no longer popular.

By the end of 1952, with the move to Browns Lane, a new paint shop was opened. Instead of nitro-cellulose, modern synthetic enamel, invented in the 1930s, was used. Its shine was more persistent without polishing. The D of the color code, which had indicated supplier British Domolac, was now changed to Q, while "J" was for Pinchin Johnson, and "ICI" for Imperial Chemical Industries, particularly known for its "opalescent" shades of the 1960s.

In 1954 the Mark VII M was the first Jaguar with fenders mirrors, although for some export markets only, as such equipment was not mandatory for Britain. It also had higher overriders and longer rear bumpers that nearly reached the spats. The fog lamps were now mounted on the bumper while their earlier position now was occupied by two round horn grilles.

More revolutionary than the all-steel body was its chassis-less, unitary body construction. This construction was tested in a smaller scale, in a sort of successor to the old 1½. The stiffness formerly provided by the chassis now had to come from the body itself, which incorporated boxes made from sheet metal that extended from the front bumper brackets along the floor to the rear leaf springs. Between the inner fenders and bulkhead, further boxed sections were welded in. In order to avoid a weak spot, Lyons dispensed with the sunroof for the first time on an enclosed sedan. Soon, however, Webasto folding roofs became available. For the same reason the pillars were rather thick, if not cumbersome. The bodyshell was completely manufactured at Pressed Steel Company Limited, who also had calculated the body structure. The body styling was heavily influenced by the XK 140, particularly the front, although the grille was wider. The longitudinal side windows and indicators at the front ends of the fenders were of an unusual shape.

As a remainder of old times the Special Equipment version of the 2.4-liter had a leaping jaguar on its hood, while the Mark VII had a jaguar head mounted between two wings above the radiator grille. From Mark VIII the leaper on the chromed strip along the hood took over, and it was available as an extra even for the XK 150. The "new" leaper had its rear legs extended, which had not been the case with the earlier ones that had been mounted on the radiator caps. There they had needed a more solid base so that they would not be broken off by less cautious mechanics when adding cooling water. The spare wheel and tools were placed under the trunk in the unitary bodies. The trunk lid had a chromed "Jaguar" badge, at least since the 3.4-liter was introduced. The rear mount of the gearbox was quite elaborate, with a very soft spiral spring that—mounted between two polyurethane bushings—transmitted neither vibration nor noise. The new car was shorter in height than the larger Mark VII, which made entering the car a bit difficult—something people had to get accustomed to.

The Mark VIII trunk was completely lined in Hardura, and even the spare wheel had its hull. The inner side of the trunk lid was also partly lined.

The XK 150, although a transition model, had quite a few improvements to the body. One of them was the door hinges, which from mid-1958 were drop-forged, but the pressed steel items returned shortly before the end of production. Springs were added to the trunk lid bars, which held the lid open. Shortly after introduction the rear number plate was mounted in a more inclined position. For the first time the roadster boasted external door handles.

For the Mark II a lockable fuel filler cap was available at extra cost. Customers could also order a tow bar, child-proof rear door locks, and the Webasto sunroof. Like the Mark IX, it had its model name indicated at the lower end of the trunk lid in chromed letters, while similar to the XK 150 its front bumper had a sort of cutout so that the lower end of the radiator grille remained visible. From July 1960 nylon fuel pipes were used.

The E-Type also was, from the bulkhead back, made of unitary construction, with a tubular frame beneath its large hood. Its oval mouth was divided by a horizontal chromed bar with the growler motif in the middle on a round badge. The hood and panels for the bodyshell were supplied by Abbey Panels, but were assembled and lead-loaded at Jaguar only. The E-Type was the first Jaguar with brackets for safety belts.

The Mark X brought the unitary all-steel system into Jaguar's big class, combined with a particularly low roofline. The body-in-the-white again came from Pressed Steel Company Limited, this time from its Swindon, Wiltshire works. Two box profiles were welded transversely onto the floor between the driveshaft tunnel and the sills, which were 7 inches high and wide and made access to the car even more awkward. The bulkhead and the boxed-in front footwell also reinforced the structure, and again reinforcing structures were added between the bulkhead and inner wheel arches. At the rear the seat pan and wheel arches had deep profiles in order to improve stiffness. Along the trunk floor the boxed structures extended right to the rear bumpers. The body had been further strengthened where the front and rear suspensions were attached. The roof contributed little to the stability—for some time a "hardtop" variant without a B pillar had been considered. The chassis could take 3½ tons of twisting force before yielding one degree of distortion.

The hood was now hinged at the front and integrated the inner headlamps. The completely new front, with its dramatically inclined grille and twin headlamps of different sizes, were to become typical for Jaguar sedans in the following decades. The leaper above the grille was somewhat smaller than before, as the height of the radiator had been reduced. The bumpers were much slimmer than on earlier cars, but again had overriders—the front ones inclined forward. The trunk lid handle was now integrated into the plinth. The spats had disappeared, but the cutout for the rear wheels was not very large. The bulbous side panels were clearly influenced by the E-Type. The front wheels in particular looked somewhat lost in their large wheel arches. Painting had grown into a complicated process: After cleaning in a TRICO solvent, the body was phosphated six times with a high-pressure jet. Then anticorrosion paint was applied in a dipping bath. The bodies were then heated up to 320 degrees, which was necessary for application of bituminous underbody sealant. The process was finished with two coats of paint.

The 3.4 and 3.8 S retained the Mark II structure but the rear box sections were extended from over the rear suspension to the rear end. The double-layer trunk floor was deeply profiled. As on Mark II, the hood could be adorned with the larger leaper if requested. The 420, with its face taken from the larger Mark X and its smaller leaper, was the first Jaguar with rectangular horn grilles at both sides of the radiator grille—since their introduction on the Mark VII M, they had been round.

Daimler's DS 420 was based on the Mark X structure, which had been extended by 21¼ inches in front of the rear seats. The sills were reduced in height by more than 1½ inches in order to make entry and exit easier for the noble passengers.

The XJ 6 was another fresh start. Incorporating the latest findings of accident research, the unitary body included crush zones at both front and rear. The grille had no thick chromed frame. For the first time a second grille was visible below the front bumper. Here and on the E-Type V-12, the grille had vertical and horizontal bars of doubtful elegance. On the upper end of the central vertical bar, a round growler emblem was mounted. The bodyshell again came from Pressed Steel Fisher. The drag coefficient was figured as 0.48, 0.46 for Series 2, and Series 3 recorded a hard-to-believe 0.412. With nearly 4 tons of force needed to yield 1 degree of torsion, the body was even stiffer than Mark X, although the roof now helped. The very stiff bulkhead was made in two layers and reduced noise transmission five times more efficiently than the one-layer unit of its predecessor. The air ducts for heating and ventilation were integrated between these two layers. In addition to the bulkhead, the massive sills, the driveshaft tunnel, a box section beneath the front seats, and a deeply profiled floor made the car stiffer and protected from drumming noise. The space between the supporting box sections increased toward the front in an attempt to reduce reflections from its sides to the cabin. Under the radiator, a transverse link stabilized the structure, but it was prone to corrosion. The front fenders and rear side skirts under the bumper were screwed instead of welded to the body, which made them easily exchangeable. The trunk floor again consisted of two layers of sheet metal.

From August 1969 mud flaps could be ordered directly from Jaguar. From November 1969 additional heat shields were introduced under the floor where the exhaust pipes passed below the front seats.

In October 1969 the Daimler Sovereign was introduced as a variant of the XJ 6, with a thicker chromed grille frame and the typical Daimler crinkles. The grille itself consisted of traditional vertical bars only. The trunk lid plinth was also crinkled. Badges were revised where appropriate; the ones at the lower end of the front fenders showing a leaping Jaguar on the XJ 6 were completely discarded.

In April 1970 the rear door locks were changed so that they could not be opened from the inside when the childproof lock was activated. The grille in front of the windshield was finished matte silver instead of bright; in August 1970 a larger fly screen was added beneath it. From October 1970 the flanges at the front wheel arches were changed so that they were no longer within reach of the wheels. The aluminum kick plates now bore Jaguar signs, as the Daimler variant's make was embossed there since its introduction.

From March 1971 the rear bumpers consisted of three parts, invisibly linked to each other behind the overriders. In November 1971 new door locks were introduced. Locking the key inside the car was impossible, for the key had to be used to lock the car from the outside.

The Vanden Plas, which was introduced in 1972, had been painted at Kingsbury, which secured it an individual choice of colors until painting was relocated to Castle Bromwich in 1979. All Vanden Plas models had a golden coachline applied by hand along the chromed molding, which also remained reserved for the Vanden Plas.

For 1974 it became mandatory that bumpers be positioned at a 16-inch height in the United States. So in September 1973 the XJ Series 2 was introduced with higher front bumpers, a lower grille above, and a larger one below. The leaper was placed on the bright grille surround that had returned to the Jaguars as well; it was now a rectangular shape. As on late Series 1s, a special badge in the upper center of the grille indicated the V-12 engine. The Nordel rubber overriders for the United States were replaced with thick rubber elements along the width of the bumper, which also was set slightly higher at the rear. In March 1975 these elements were further enlarged, being practically identical to what the original XJ-S was equipped with all over the world. For the rest of the world, the XJ had straight underriders along the sides of the lower grille, while the bumpers themselves remained their well-known shape, to which a rubberized knob was added at each side.

The redesigned bulkhead now only had one layer of metal. In the engine bay it was covered with asbestos; on the cabin side it was covered with Oldfield bitumen, felt for noise reduction, and Hardura PVC foam beneath the carpets. At the same time a new light alloy pedal box was introduced, with all openings carefully sealed. All electrical and other connections through the bulkhead were separated by multiple plugs, which facilitated assembly, avoided unreliable grommets, and again helped against heat transfer and noise transmission. The V-12 models now had a coachline glued to the sides. Later the 4.2 had this as well. Additional panels inside the doors protected against side intrusion in an accident. When the injection system was introduced on V-12 models, this was designated by chromed letters on the left-hand side of the trunk lid. For these models, a Vanden Plas style vinyl roof and chromed side moldings were available as extras, but only until the Series 3 was introduced. The XJ coupe was based on the sedan with the original wheelbase. Its doors had been elongated by 4 inches; the B pillars were moved accordingly and were cut off below the windows. The C pillars were broadened and were covered with elegant black vinyl together with the whole roof. Rumor has it that vinyl was chosen to make slight irregularities on the C pillar invisible.

The XJ-S used the XJ floorpan shortened by 5½ inches, with lower sills and a shorter rear bench. The trunk was completely different, as the 20-gallon fuel tank had been relocated over the rear axle with the spare wheel screwed to its rear side. For reasons of space and weight distribution, the battery was put into the trunk alongside the spare wheel. The fuel line had a

Welding of the E-Type's subframe was handled by Jaguar itself. *(S)*

spiral section encased by foam so that the fuel pump became inaudible. The inner wheel arches ended further outside at the front and were reinforced. The drag coefficient was said to be 0.39, so the XJ-S, despite its larger, more sedan-like frontal area, was more aerodynamically efficient than the E-Type!

Noise suppression of the XJ-S was at the sedan's level. With its shorter dimensions, stiffening at the bulkhead, and only two doors, the XJ-S was much stiffer than the sedan, despite its smaller sills. The body-in-the-white weighed in at just over 700 pounds. Most parts were formed from steel sheets, which as usual were somewhat thicker than with other makes. The bumpers were attached to MENASCO elements from America. These devices were cylinders filled with wax, in which a sort of sieve was pressed by the bumper in the case of a collision. This would make the wax fluid and allow a controlled compression of the bumper. After a short while the wax pushed the bumper back to its initial position so that no damage occurred from collisions up to 5 miles per hour. The XJ-S was the only Jaguar made for European markets with these heavy, cumbersome bumpers. The body-in-the-white was made at Pressed Steel Fisher's Castle Bromwich factory in the north of Birmingham.

In the autumn of 1977, the black grille in front of the windshield of the XJ-S became chromed while the B post lost its bright strip and was now black, which underlined the length of the car. The panel between the taillights now was painted body color instead of black, and the Jaguar badge above the number plate now had a black instead of silver background.

From March 1978 all XJs and XJ-Ss got larger external mirrors with remote control via cables. Remote control had been an optional extra for years. The side intrusion reinforcements were deleted from vehicles not destined to the U.S. or Japan. From April 1978 cars without vinyl roofs were equipped with different stainless steel gutter moldings.

From about July 1978, the traditional chassis numbers were replaced with Vehicle Identification Numbers (VIN) according to international standard. Each car's specification was coded with 14, and later 17, digits. This is explained in more detail in the appendix to this book.

From August 1978 a seal between bulkhead and wiper motor box was added to prevent water ingress, which could cause short circuits that would activate the horn without giving the driver a chance to stop the horn blowing—not a very comfortable situation!

The XJ Series 3, which debuted in March 1979, had a different glasshouse with more headroom, particularly over the rear seats. The roof was slightly slimmer, and as an option, an electrically operated steel sunroof could be ordered for the first time in many years. The electric motors were hidden beneath the rear parcel shelf. The sunroof was part of the Vanden Plas' standard equipment and had a wind deflector that folded out as soon as it opened. In the middle the deflector was broader in order to avoid buffeting. Behind the sunroof the mold for the headliner had a bulge to give rear passengers more headroom. Strong bumpers with full-width rubber elements were now supplied to all markets. The United States got a larger variant with the MENASCO buffers. These buffers were now mounted on an aluminum assembly. According to the latest fashion, the practical door handles were replaced with flush-fitting ones. Pininfarina had inclined the A posts by a further 3 inches and lifted the rear end of the roof, doing away with the more rounded end. V-12 models had twin coachlines, one of which was replaced with a chromed molding on Vanden Plas models. The 4.2 could be recognized by its single coachline, although this coachline was added to the 3.4 as well from the 1982 model year onward. Even on the Vanden Plas the coachline was glued on, not painted by hand. With the new paint shop, many new colors were introduced, which were similar for all models including the Vanden Plas.

A “naked” E-Type reveals much of its supporting structure. *(S)*

The less prominent trunk plinth now was slightly wider than the number plate. The tools were put in a neat attaché case at the side of the trunk, which replaced the cloth roll. Further sound-deadening mats at doors, bulkhead, and gearbox tunnel helped improve noise insulation. At last the hollow spaces of structural parts were rust protected (complete rust protection was applied from autumn 1982). The Daimler had a reversible carpet with a rubber mat on the opposite side on its trunk floor. The bodies were made in a completely new assembly hall at Castle Bromwich.

From October 1979 difficulties with the new paint forced a temporary return to cellulose for dark green shades. The new technique was not fully implemented until 1981. From January 1980 the windshield washers were bright instead of matte silver. In November 1980 a badge with the Daimler "D" was added at the lower parts of the front fenders on all Daimlers.

The XJ-S H.E. returned to black grilles in front of the windshield and double coachlines that unified at both ends. The bumpers had a chromed upper element and looked similar to the Series 3. A new bronze growler was put on the hood, while in the trunk the spare wheel and battery covers were now carpet.

From mid-1981 all Jaguars had electrical remote-control mirrors on both sides, and the door handle surrounds were black, not chromed. From February 1982 the recesses for the inside door handles were also black instead of chrome.

From the 1983 model year onward the XJ 12 had silver growlers on black backgrounds as grille badges instead of gold over amber. The badges on the front fenders were also changed. Daimlers no longer had a chrome strip along their hoods, which necessitated a change to the grille surround.

The XJ-SC used the XJ-S body with the roof cut off, a reinforced gearbox tunnel, and additional cross bracing at the rear axle. Over the front seats were two glass-reinforced plastic (GRP) panels; a large case for storing them in the trunk was provided as well. Behind them a roll-over bar was added with a small top attached. The rear seats had been replaced with lockable cases. The roof rails remained in place when the top was folded down, and the rear side windows could not be opened. The transformation was carried out at Park Sheet Metal at Exhall, where bodies without the roof or the panel between rear window and trunk lid arrived from Castle Bromwich. The C posts were cut off there and reinforcing panels were welded in. Painting was carried out at Castle Bromwich and further assembly at Browns Lane. The top mechanism was assembled at Aston Martin's Tickford at Bedworth, while quality control and dispatch were carried out at Browns Lane again. Only in 1985, when the V-12 was introduced, was

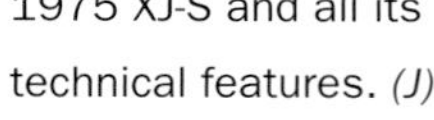

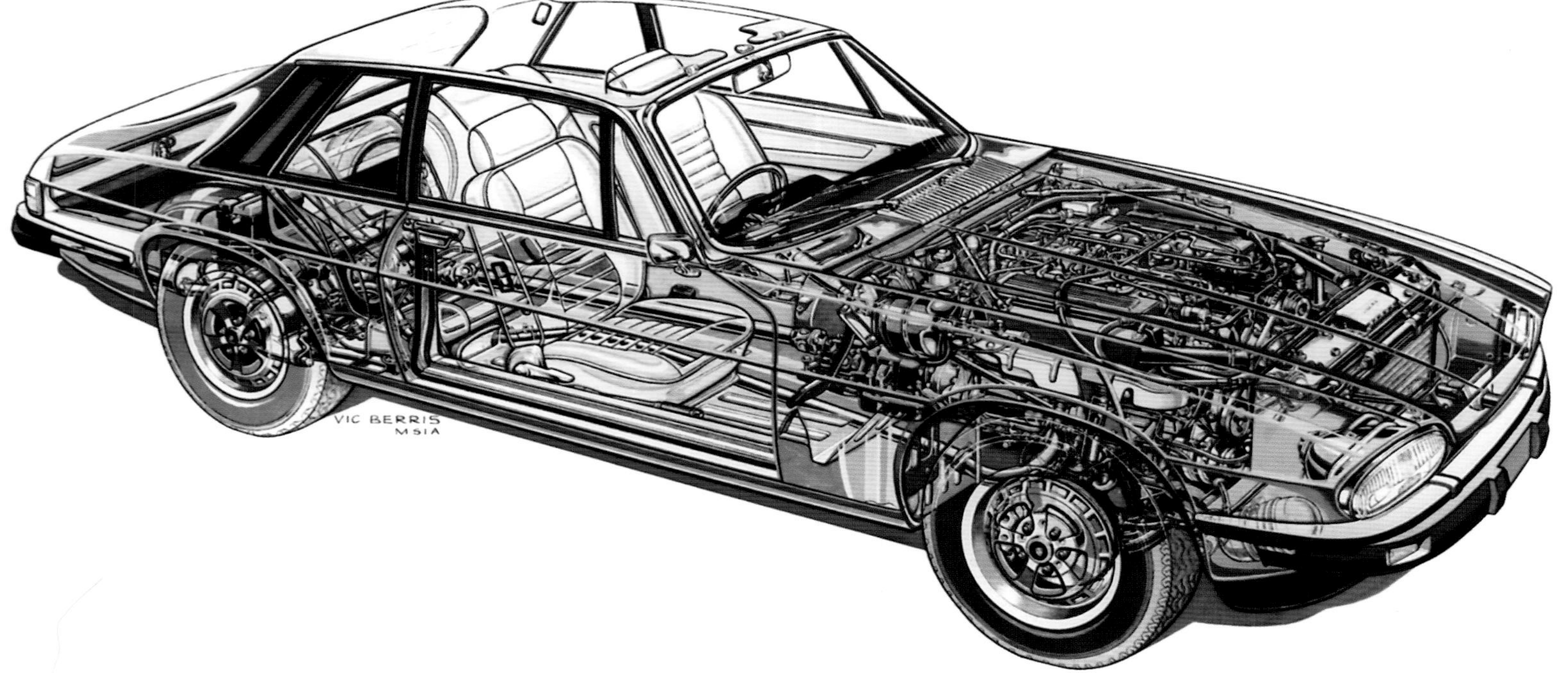

1975 XJ-S and all its technical features. *(J)*

the process simplified. At that time a solid hardtop to replace the rear top had been introduced.

For the 1987 model year, a new clear-over-base paint technology was employed for all models. Again new colors were introduced, now more often changing their names. Shades with particularly fine metallic particles were called Micatallic, and they gave a silky, deep shine. Critical parts were zinc covered, and finally even the smallest cavity had rust prevention. The paint was now applied in two coats with two further clear coats. In 1987 the XJ-S got a lockable filler cap (the SC already had one), and red and silver coachlines instead of two silver ones.

The XJ 40 had a completely new body with large panels pressed in one piece, facilitating assembly and avoiding opportunities for bad quality. The body-in-white weighed in at 650 pounds instead of 740 for the previous XJ. It consisted of 425 instead of 558 parts. Rust protection was further improved with zinc coats and a thick undercoat. The drag coefficient was 0.38, which resulted in an air resistance factor of 0.762 versus 0.849 for Series 3.

During the 1987 model year bright stainless steel tread plates were introduced, which were more robust than they looked. For the 1990 model year the XJ 40 was transferred to a single-key system. For the 1993 model year the skirts under XJ 40 bumpers were revised. For all Jaguar and Daimler models, special insignia colors and equipment were available from Special Vehicle Operations.

In May 1991 the grille on the revised XJS was black as it had been when the XJ-S was introduced. This time a broad chrome strip was added to the top. Panels hiding the sills made the car look lower. Of the 490 body parts, 180 had been changed or deleted. Nevertheless, the body style remained unaltered with the exception of the rear side windows and the taillights. Manufacture now was much easier, and corrosion had even less of a chance. The grille in front of the windshield was now painted body-color. The door window frame now was deleted on the coupes as well. In May 1992 crossbracing was added below the engine box of the convertibles, which increased body stiffness by a remarkable 25 percent. Nevertheless, in September 1992 the floor of the convertible was further reinforced.

From May 1993 all XJSs had large body-colored bumpers that also covered the front and rear skirts. In July 1994 a V-12 badge was added to the front fenders of the 6-liter XJS, as were silver and red coachlines. The six-cylinder XJS now had body-colored grille, headlamp surrounds, and mirrors, but only until 1995 when the growler badges on all XJSs became green.

In September 1994 the revised XJ 40, now called X 300, was introduced—an excellent face-lifting exercise that, without deeper changes to the body structure, totally changed the appearance of the car. Following the changes the year before to the XJS, the bumpers now were body-colored, covering the former skirts as well. At the sides just below a corrugation that was taken over from XJ 40, a slim rubbing strake was added. Painted body color, this may not have been overly practical, but it remained a feature for many years.

Although the XJS was one of the stiffest convertibles on the market, the XK 8 was destined to be another 10 percent stiffer, as the requirements of the open car could be considered from the very beginning of its development. Starting from the coupe platform, the stiffness was calculated completely anew for the convertible. The results were considered even for the panels that the coupe would share with the convertible which helped reduce welding work on the body by one-third. The top mechanism was designed and built in Germany at Karmann, as were some body panels that were unique to the convertible.

The XJ 8 of 1997 looked very similar to its predecessor, betraying all the changes that had been carried out under the skin for the implementation of the new V-8 engine and revised front suspension, which also was taken from the XK 8. Due to the longer supercharger and more forward position of the engine, the radiator mounting had to be adapted as well. The chrome strip on the bumpers was reduced to the corners of the car, a styling cue that soon would be seen on other Jaguar sedans, while the sports car continued to live without chrome on its bumpers.

From 1995 until 1998 the paint shop at Castle Bromwich was changed to water-soluble two-component acrylic paint, from which all models benefited. The appendix to this book shows which colors were available at what time. Jaguar always supplied special shades to the customer's order at additional cost.

With the S-Type, Jaguar returned to more compact dimensions. With its fashionable rounded lines, particularly the oval grille, the S-type recalled the Mark II, which was Jaguar's most appreciated sedan among enthusiasts. From a technical point of view the design was surprising in that no front subframe was used; the suspension instead was directly attached to the body. At the side, slim rubber strips painted body color would help prevent small dents, but this was nevertheless deleted for visual reasons from the 2001 model year onward.

A true milestone for the whole automobile industry was the X 350 range that was introduced in 2002. Its body consisted of aluminum instead of steel panels. Aluminum, only one-third the weight of steel, had been used by Jaguar for its postwar racing cars. Aluminum panels are less stiff than steel ones, and so it was quite an achievement to nearly completely avoid cast items. German competitor Audi used such extruded aluminum sheaths quite extensively. The Jaguar only had two at the upper ends of the front coil springs. This made the X-Type the lightest car in its class, weighing in at only 3,400 pounds.

Windows

According to general practice in classic times, the SS One had a laminated one-piece Protecto windshield. It was hinged at the top, so it could be opened for better ventilation. Wind-down windows filled the doors. From autumn 1932 the rear window was hinged, and thus could also be opened. It had a chromed frame and one year later a roller blind was added, which could be operated from the driver's seat. The rear side windows of the sedan and Airline could not be opened.

The SS Jaguar also had wind-down windows in the rear doors. From late 1936 front quarter windows were added, which could be opened, and for the Mark V the same were introduced in the rear doors, where they were D-shaped. The front quarter windows were soon improved with rounded instead of pointed front ends. The Mark V was also acclaimed as the first Jaguar with a windshield that could not be opened, so that no dust could find its way into the interior past the gap along the window frame.

With the Mark VII and XK 120, Jaguar tried the split windshield again, but with Mark VIII and XK 150 one-piece windshields returned, although they now were curved. The relatively thick rubber blocks at the lower corners of the windshield frame are a good telltale for the aluminum-bodied XK 120, while the steel cars had much slimmer rubber pieces. From February 1951 the rear windows in the tops could be zipped out. The XK 140 drophead coupe was the first with a Perspex rear window, and the XK 150 was the first Jaguar roadster with wind-down windows in the doors.

The Mark II continued with the curved windshield of its predecessor in a larger format, and it had a heated rear window as an option. From April 1962 this switched off automatically with the ignition. From then on, tinted glass was available at extra cost. Tinted glass was the latest fashion, and it helped keep temperatures in the car down.

The Mark X was the first Jaguar with electric windows, which initially tended to jam. This is why from early 1963 nylon rubber hoses were fitted into the window rails.

For the XJ 6 the engineers had a nice idea of how to open and close the front quarter window: a small knurled wheel was chosen, which looked much neater than the previous toggle. The rear quarter windows could not be opened; forced ventilation via the rear parcel shelf did the job.

From March 1970 new rubber seals for the front and rear windows were used, with a thinner chromed strip from late 1970. After June 1970 laminated front windshields became standard for European-specification cars. From October 1970 the lamination was vaporized and sprayed rather than glued to the rear screen.

On the Series 2 XJ, the front quarter windows could no longer be opened. The XJ-C had none at all, but its rear side windows could be electrically lowered. If closed, the coupe's side windows were tensioned, but increased pressure in the interior caused by the airstream still forced them to bend outward, which caused wind noise. Even a later revised window mechanism could not cure this.

The XJ Series 3 was ultramodern with front and rear windows being glued in instead of held by their rubber seals. The rear window was laminated, and the side windows were curved as they had been in the XJ-C. The sedan dispensed with the front quarter windows.

For the XJ-S, power windows were standard. The SC had a Perspex rear window, while the convertible had a heated glass window. When the two additional seats were installed, the window had to be reduced in size. In 1991 the front quarter windows of the XJ-S disappeared on introduction of the XJS.

Upon the Ford takeover, heated windshields became an optional extra. The nearly invisible heater filaments did cause minor irritating reflections in the dark. Starting with the S-Type in 2002, the electric windows had an antipinch safety function when closing. With a short push on the switch, they could be fully opened or closed. With the X 350, elegant blinds could be ordered for the rear door windows and quarter windows.

Heating and Ventilation

Until World War II drivers needed to open a window if fresh air was desired. If it was cold, a thick coat would need to be worn, because the heat dissipating from the engine would not sufficiently warm up the interior. A heating arrangement would only be found in the most expensive of limousines. So it is not surprising that it was 1939 before the first Clayton-Dewandre radiator used hot water from the cooling system to send warm air into the front footwells and toward the windshield of a Jaguar. In the case of the four-cylinders and again the 2.4-liter, this was an extra-cost option. In 1945 the air duct in front of the windshield was enlarged, and the warm-air ducts were larger from 1954 onward. For the XK 120 a less elaborate heater that recirculated air from the interior and blew it back after warming it up a bit was an optional extra, until in September 1951 it became standard equipment. In fixed head and drop-head coupes, some of the warm air was directed to the windshield. It was the summer of 1958 before the heating system was integrated into the XK's dashboard (this was already the case in the sedans) instead of being mounted under it.

The Mark IX had a more powerful heating system, and the ventilation system was supported with a fan. This was also the case in the Mark II, which had a separate warm-air duct to the rear footwells.

As previous Jaguars all had been criticized for their heating, the Mark X was equipped with a completely new system developed in conjunction with Marsten Excelsior, who also supplied the radiator. Two separate ducts led to the windshield and the sides of the center console, and one to the rear footwells. Two electric fans supported the system, which was adjusted with a mechanism utilizing the vacuum at the inlet manifold. The same mechanism opened the air duct in front of the windshield, which from March 1963 onward was possible even when the heating was switched off. Unfortunately, no temperature regulation was possible until autumn 1964; the only choice was to switch the heating on or off.

From October 1965 a true air conditioning unit could be specified for the Mark X at an additional £275. American customers urgently requested these; quite a few aftermarket units had been mounted before Jaguar incorporated them. Via the rear parcel shelf, air was extracted from the interior and then cooled and dehumidified by a radiator. The Freon 12 coolant—containing chlorofluorocarbons (CFCs) that were later legislated out of use—was cooled in a radiator, compressed, and liquified. The unit had only three switches, one for on and off, another for the temperature, and a third one for the fan speed. As the engine now had to work harder (driving the compressor) when it was hot, a larger radiator was employed. Air conditioning was also available for the 420.

The XJ 6 had another completely new heating and ventilation system from Delaney Galley in Barking. With a temperature difference of 180 degrees Fahrenheit between ambient and cooling water temperatures, its heating power was 5.5 kilowatts. Within one minute, more than 140 cubic feet of air could be exchanged. After setting a temperature, the system automatically regulated the heating with the help of temperature sensors. Ventilation could be adjusted independently for both sides of the car and the rear compartment. Air was extracted via the rear parcel shelf and the gap between the body and trunk lid below the rear window. The air conditioning unit, which was an optional extra, was integrated into the heating system with its radiator, working more or less the other way around. In the process water would inevitably condense and leave the radiator box via small hoses, which with age tended to become blocked. From January

1973 Frigidaire compressors were used—this supplier was a General Motors company.

From March 1971 additional air ducts above the main headlights were introduced to bring fresh air to the front footwells. The disadvantage was that the airstream could push open its flaps at high speed and thus let cold air in.

The XJ Series 2 had another completely new heating and air conditioning system, which produced the right temperatures by mixing hot and cold air, not by regulating the amount of water passing through the radiator. This system reacted more quickly to a change of temperatures or settings. The control was supported by electric motors, which automatically held interior temperature constant. Only the water valve and the air flaps were moved with vacuum derived from the engine. The air conditioning unit was much more powerful, as had been shown during tests in Arizona, and was up to the standard of the acclaimed Cadillac system.

From February 1980 a lever for temperature distribution between upper and lower parts of the cabin was added. From October 1985 the system was computer-controlled; this system is easily distinguished by the addition of a lever on the left that could be pulled out to choose between manual and automatic modes.

The XJ 40 had another new heating and air conditioning system, with only electric motors as servo units. From September 1992 the switches were changed, including recirculation air, defroster, and on/off switches. The air conditioning unit soon was supplied exclusively by Nippondenso, and now was CFC-free. Jaguar delayed introducing separate adjustment of heating and air conditioning for the front passenger and rear passengers until the X 350 in 2002, but then also offered as an option separate regulation for the front and rear compartment on each side.

Interior

The SS One was equipped with a front and a rear bench, both leather-covered. The sunbeam ornament on the artificial leather door trim became typical for SS. Dash and window sills were made of wood, not yet veneered but painted to give the impression of dark sycamore or birds-eye maple. The Watford speedometer showed up to 80 miles per hour. There was an electric fuel gauge and an Empire clock as well, but instead of a true rev counter, rpm markings for third and fourth gear were added on the speedometer, but only from March 1933 onward. In October 1932, British Jaeger instruments on walnut veneer came into use.

For the 1934 model year the instruments had hexagonal surrounds and were placed on a matte-chromed metal panel that carried the speedometer, clock, ammeter, fuel, oil pressure, and water temperature gauges. The tourer's dashboard in the main consisted of painted metal; only the central part with the instruments was chromed or wooden.

For the 1933 model year the bench seat was replaced with bucket-like seats with fold-down backrests covered with Connolly's finest Vaumol leather. It was said that these seats had been inspired by the chief chairs at Henlys. In the dark rear compartment the narrow bench was mounted so low that a bulge in the middle for the differential was unavoidable—this was hidden by a central armrest. In the trim two little compartments were hidden by a lid. Even an ashtray on the dash and a make-up set in the glove box were part of the equipment. The colors of the carpet and headliner were coordinated to the exterior paint.

The 1934 Airline was particularly well equipped, with seats covered in plain leather and mounted more forward. It had map pockets in the doors, which continued the sunbeam theme. Compared with the coupe, the dash was even more complete and veneered with walnut. It is likely that there were folding picnic tables at the rear of the backrests.

The SS Jaguar was just as lavish as the Airline, but with a folding armrest in the middle of the rear bench. For open models, Connolly's more robust Celstra leather was now used. The speedometer read to 100 miles per hour, and at last a rev counter was added, within which the clock was integrated. The instruments were made by Smiths, with a small SS symbol on the dials. Only the ammeter was made by Lucas and had no SS symbol. The Bluemel steering wheel, again with leaf springs, was now adjustable in reach.

From autumn 1936 a Dunlopillo foam layer was put over the coil springs of the seat cushions. The passenger now had his own armrest on the door trim. On the newly styled walnut dash the two smaller instruments were now encased by the larger ones; until then the larger ones had been between the smaller ones. From autumn another change occurred to the dashboard, which now had straighter lines and edges instead of the previous more rounded design. The instruments were now directly surrounded by walnut veneer, and the rear doors now also had armrests.

From autumn 1939 the dials were black with white letters. The seats were covered with plain leather with folding picnic tables at the rear of the backrests, the door trim had a new style, and the driver's seat height was adjustable with a crank. After the war, the seats themselves were again covered with the more familiar pleated leather, and the picnic tables had also disappeared. In 1946 the rubber knob on the gear lever was replaced with a plastic one.

The Mark V returned to plain leather and had a new dashboard with art deco letters on the dials, which were illuminated with black light at night. The sedan doors could be locked with a chromed lever on the inside. The dimmer switch was no longer on the steering wheel but near the clutch pedal. The central section of the dashboard could be folded forward to make the electrics behind it accessible—a very useful idea of William Heynes.

The XK 120 had a much more practical interior with the dash covered in vinyl and a 120-mile-per-hour speedometer. In the first years a duotone interior was offered at extra price. For cars with the higher compression ratio, a plaque on the dash indicated that this was an exact replica of the 1949 Jabbeke record car. Fixed head and drophead coupes had a parcel shelf behind the seats. Their XK 140 successors had a flap at the rear so that this section could become part of the trunk. All these coupes had lavish interiors with walnut veneer, even on some components of the top mechanism.

The Mark VII, with its wide body *sans* runningboards, had a much larger interior than its predecessor, although the rear bench had been moved forward. The seats again had pleated leather, but with a horseshoe element around them on the seat and backrest. Automatic cars with the quadrant at the steering column had a bench instead of separate front seats, so that the place of the gear lever could be taken by another passenger. The horn button was pointed like a bullet. The instruments had returned to conventional letters. The Mark VII M rev counter had its red sector at 5,500–6,000 rpm instead of 5,250–5,500—the new camshaft allowed higher engine speeds. In order to avoid irritating reflections on the windshield—this was the explanation given by the works—a flat horn button was now used, again showing the profile of a Jaguar head. The same horn button was used for the XK 140. The seats now were completely filled with Dunlopillo foam.

The 2.4-liter had conventional instrument lights with a nonadjustable intensity. The rev counter was left out of the standard model; from July it was provided with an electrically driven counter, rather than a mechanical one.

The XK 150 is a sin for Jaguar enthusiasts in that its coupe variants had no veneered wood in them, the dash being covered with vinyl that was functional and soft. But even this was left out of some of the first cars, which incorporated brushed aluminum instead.

The Mark VIII's rear backrests were styled so that with the armrest folded down they looked like separate seats. The automatic variant was supplied with picnic tables for the first time in many years; this car also had another clock and small case in the armrest. The armrest was even better padded, and each of the rear doors had an ashtray. From July 1958 the backrests were adjustable using the Reutter system from Germany; the company is now better known for its Recaro seats.

The Mark IX was the first Jaguar limousine, in that it could be delivered with a partition. Its military variant, which had no power steering, was called the Mark VIII b.

The Mark II was remarkable for its newly arranged dash with speedo and rev counter right in front of the driver and a lockable glove box. The front seats were new, with thicker cushions. The lateral support they offered was slight, but small picnic tables for the rear passengers were included. The central console was also new; it was made possible by moving the shifter quadrant to the steering column. From March 1960 the oil pressure gauge was recalibrated, as the normal 40 psi pressure had been positioned too far away from the safe middle of the scale. Around the same time the hinges of the sun visors were given a swivel so that they could be

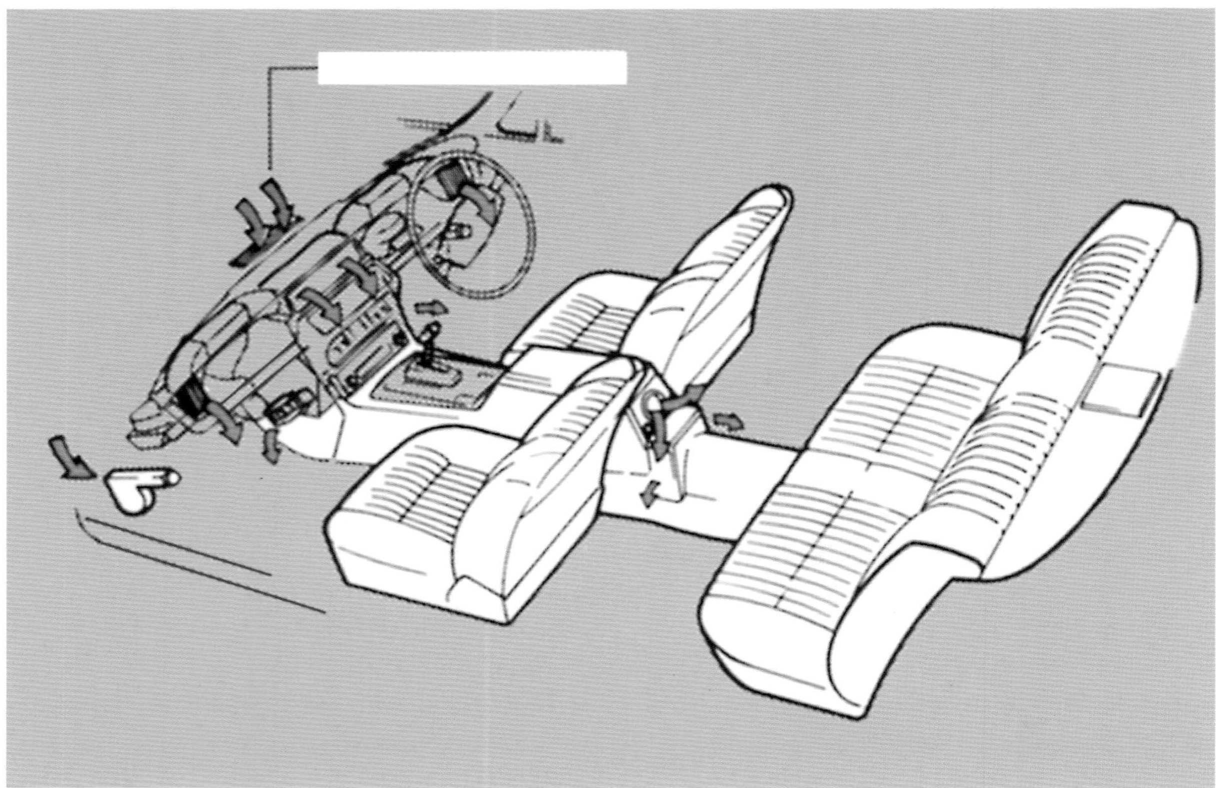

Functional diagram of the 1973 XJ 12's air conditioning. *(J)*

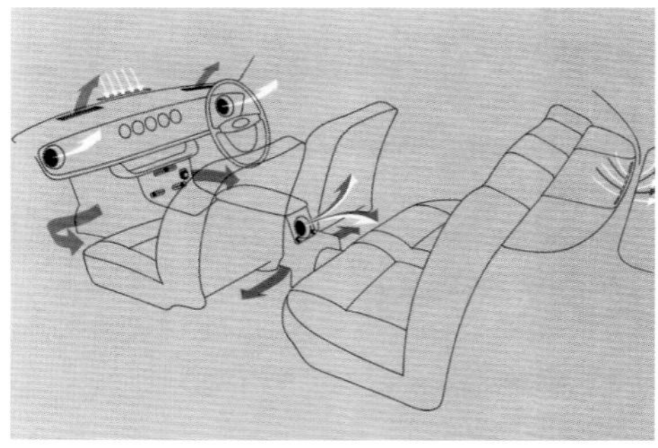

Arrangement of the 1968 XJ 6's heating and ventilation. *(J)*

Rear air ducts in the Mark X. *(S)*

turned to the side window. Indicator and overdrive switches also changed their positions.

The E-Type's interior continued the functional theme of the XK 150, without any wood . The center console panel was bright metal and reminded one of an aircraft cockpit. With the introduction of the 4.2-liter engine, its seats became much more comfortable; the dash and central console were covered by black vinyl.

The Mark X had a dash similar to the Mark II, but with a small tray along its width and a more rounded center console with a wood panel. Its speedometer scale ended at a lofty 140 miles per hour. Even the automatic now had separate front seats but with their width they offered little lateral support. Some Mark Xs and 420 Gs had partitions, and these again were called limousines.

The Daimler V-8 2.5-liter had to make do without picnic tables. Its split bench at the front had two folding central armrests and a smaller center console that housed the radio and two heating levers.

From early 1963 a cutout in the front backrests gave much more space for the toes of the rear passengers—a small change, but a great improvement for long travels.

In September 1966 the level of equipment in the Mark II was reduced in order to save cost. Even the leather, if not ordered at additional cost, was replaced with Boyriven Ambla.

Daimler's 250 V-8 and Sovereign had black padding above and below the dashboard and at the upper ends of the door trim, with only a thin wooden strip remaining.

From October 1966, the 420, Sovereign, and 420 G had the same padding and perforated leather of a more standard quality, which was soon to be used in other models as well. The electric clock was moved away from the rev counter to its own rectangular housing in the center of the padding above the dashboard.

The E-Type Series 2 was the first Jaguar with headrests. The old toggle switches were thought to be dangerous in case of an accident and were replaced with flush rocker switches.

The XJ 6 had leather seats again, with particularly slim flutes over more profiled cushions of a special material developed by Slumberland, which supported a healthful posture and saved 10 percent in weight over the previous cushions. As in the E-Type, the leather was perforated in order to prevent a sweating back in hot weather. Another glove box was hidden in the central armrest, while the rear folding armrest was conventional. As usual, door trim and the sides and rears of the seats were covered with vinyl. Over the map cases in the backrests, two concentric rectangles and, in the door trim, groups of horizontal lines had been embossed. The front door trim had short armrests with map boxes in front of them. At the rear were longer armrests with an opening that could be used for map storage as well. A pile carpet with thick felt beneath and a nylon headliner made the interior more silent and noble. The dash was walnut veneer, surrounded by the now well-known padding. The instruments were similar to the ones used previously, but they now had chromed rings, as did the ventilation outlets at the sides of the dash. These rings were matte black again from September 1970. A row of control lamps for oil pressure, ignition, brake, and hazard warnings was put between the speedo and rev counter. The make-up mirror was placed in the glove box lid. The optional automatic safety belts no longer reacted to quick extraction but to the abrupt slowing of the vehicle.

From August 1969 the backrests of the XJ 6 were prepared for head restraints, but the opening for them was usually hidden by a plastic plug. The Daimler Sovereign variant of the XJ 6 had plain door trim with a black upper section, which also surrounded the interior handle. A chromed bar was positioned in the upper section.

The XJ 12 interior was similar to the Sovereign's, but the upper part of the door trim had the same color as the rest of the door trim. The chromed bar was left out, but some carpet was added to the lower part of the door trim in order to avoid shoe marks. If ordered, the loudspeakers would be positioned in that section as well. The seats were similar to the XJ 6. Below the dashboard were the choke lever and trays on both sides. The panels on the center console and gearbox tunnel were black instead of bright, with a V-12 emblem behind the transmission selector lever. The speedometer scale ended with 160 miles per hour and the red sector on the rev counter started at 6,500 rpm. The Double-Six shared the interior of the XJ 12, but with Sovereign door trim. It was even more completely equipped.

The Vanden Plas was even more lavish, with separate seats in the back, reading lights at the top of the C-posts, red warning lights under the door locks, and whitewood inlays in the burl walnut veneer of the doors and dashboard. The door trim had special styling with the armrests set at an angle and separate map boxes in front of them, in which the loudspeakers were housed as well. The floor was covered with deep lambswool mats and better-quality carpets supplied by Birstall Evlan. For the interior, among other colors, a chamois shade was available that had been created for the society rooms on board the *Queen Elizabeth II* ocean liner.

The XJ Series 2 had a new dashboard. The line of rocker switches and the dimmer switch were moved to steering column levers and a new combined light switch. The small instruments were grouped in pairs along the main instruments. The row of control lights between them was now much larger. Instruments, rectangular air ducts, and switches had a printed silver streak around them, which was not very elegant and disappeared in 1977. A further silver streak extended along the lower edge of the dash, while the whitewood inlay of the Vanden Plas models at the same place had disappeared. The trays beneath the dash also disappeared, but the glove box grew in size. The V-12 had a black panel only on the gearbox tunnel, the rest being

Dashboard of the 1934 SS One sedan. *(J)*

standardized with the six-cylinder models. The doors of short-wheelbase XJ now showed two concentric trapezoids instead of the horizontal lines. In the rear, the ashtrays were moved away from the air ducts, which blew the ash away from the cigar just before the ashtray was reached—they now moved under the rear door handles. Only Vanden Plas models, with their window switches between ashtray and air duct, remained unchanged. A new steering wheel with a very large padded horn push was introduced on all models—no more horn ring. A fiber optic cable provided light to all switches at night. This was called Opticell, and Jaguar was the first to use this development of Lucas and Scan Ltd. at Solihull. The usually visible safety belt reels were hidden in the door panels of the coupe.

In 1975 the XJ 3.4 and Sovereign 3.4 were the first Jaguars to be delivered with cloth trim, a polyester velour material. Leather remained an extra-cost option for the 3.4. All other models could be delivered with cloth instead of leather, but no reduction in price was granted. The XJ 12 C had broader leather piping, as usual for the Daimler.

Interior trim was one of the few areas where the XJ-S remained faithful to the E-Type. However, being much darker, it did not compare favorably with the luxurious trim of the XJ coupes. The dash was black vinyl as was most of the trim, and the many items borrowed from XJ looked somewhat lost. The new seats with their slim backrests with horizontal pleats were much more comfortable than they looked. The carefully trimmed back seats still were much too small for an adult. Less tasteful was the instrument panel, with its unusual surrounds for the speedo and rev counter that was separated from the rest of the dashboard. An impressive row of 18 control lights was integrated into it, one reserved for the two-speed axle that never became available. In June 1976 the instruments were slightly revised; the speedometer now also had a small kilometers-per-hour scale.

The XJ Series 3 boasted new seats with backrests 1½ inches higher. These extended over the bottom of the window glass—Sir William never would have accepted that! A knob on the insides of these backrests indicated the addition of adjustable lumbar support. A further switch on the front of the seat cushion activated the height adjustment, which returned after several decades, but this time it was accomplished by an electric motor. New headrests reached further forward. As with the XJ-S, the seat belt reels were hidden behind the trim. Rear seat belts were provided where legislation demanded. New deep-pile carpets added comfort. The column levers changed position on right-hand drive cars in order to achieve commonality with other manufacturers. Instruments and levers were labeled with internationally recognizable symbols instead of English words. A new lock system provided an ignition key; one for doors, fuel filler, trunk, and glove box; and a third one for doors and filler cap only, the latter intended for chauffeurs and mechanics. A new leather-covered steering wheel had a less obtrusive horn button but retained the thin rim. (For many drivers, too thin.) Control lights indicating a lack of coolant, activation of the rear fog light, and malfunction of rear or braking light were added to the already impressive collection.

From the 1980 model year, the driver's side mats bore the Jaguar or Daimler name and were similar in color to the carpet. From November 1980 the thick Vanden Plas footwall rugs, rear headrests, reading lights, and wooden panels in the door trim (although without the inlays) became standard on all Daimler variants. All XJs now had red courtesy lights placed into the door trim and coupled to the interior lights. The gearbox tunnel panel now became black on all models.

The XJ-S H.E. finally had veneered wood on its dashboard, center console, and door trim; it also copied the Series 3 steering wheel. Front armrests were leather-covered. New interior colors and more details shared with the sedans helped create a friendlier, luxurious ambience, which was most appropriate for a grand tourer.

Dashboard of the 1950 Mark V drophead coupe. *(Schön)*

Dashboard of the 1954 XK 140 drophead coupe. *(Schön)*

From mid-1982, more reliable Veglia instruments were used. The 1993 model year XJ was recognizable by its revised center console with wood veneers, which, according to Rolls-Royce practice, were directly laminated onto metal panels. Instead of the clock, a trip computer could be supplied; it showed time, distance covered, average speed, and time elapsed since last setting, and average and instantaneous consumption—in British and metric units! The selector lever had been moved backward so that the radio became more accessible. The leather-covered steering wheel rim had become thicker, and the horn button on the Daimler was plainer. The front seats had stiffer cushions.

From 1983 new Raschelle cloth (woven velour) was used. Sovereign models took over the Vanden Plas door trim, but not the wood inlays. The headliner was limestone in color, irrespective of the interior trim—not always an ideal combination. In March 1983 the speedometer signals were changed from mechanical to electrical, which made it usable for the trip computer and cruise control as well, but this necessitated a change to engine management.

The XJ-SC had a case instead of the rear cushions, the lid of which was divided in two parts. Both were provided with a chromed bar to prevent items put on it from slipping down.

For the 1986 model year all XJ models had wooden panels on the door trim and wooden panels on the gearbox tunnel. The A, B, and C posts were trimmed with the interior color instead of black. The levers

The interior of an XK 150; the vinyl on the central panel has been replaced with wood veneer. *(Balken)*

Adjustable backrest of the Reutter system. *(S)*

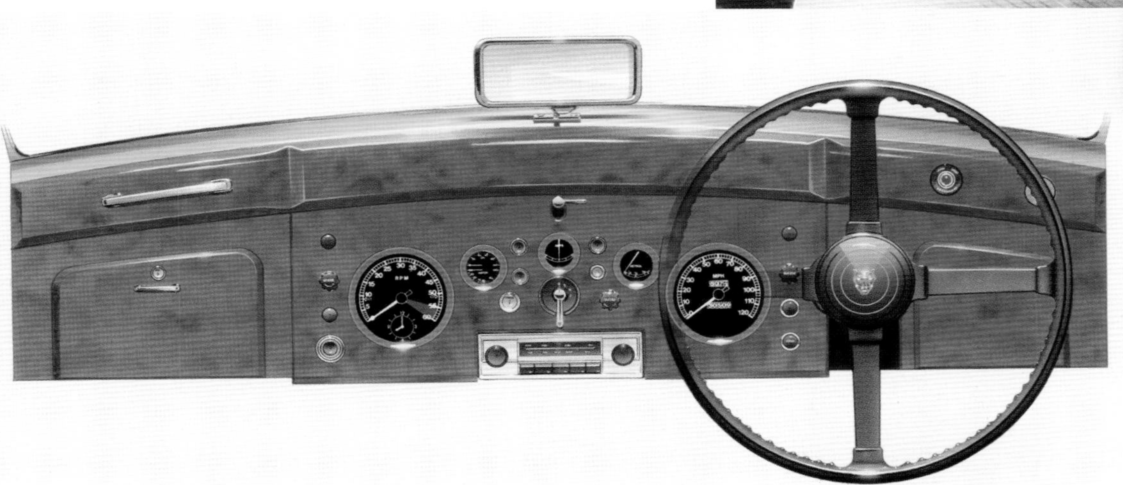

Dashboard of the 1958 Mark IX. *(J)*

for seat position and the loudspeaker frames now were chromed. In the XJ-S V-12 the walnut veneer was replaced with lighter elm. Cloth now was a traditional tweed.

The XJ 40 was disappointing for aficionados, particularly from America, with its ultra-modern dashboard featuring horizontal scales for the smaller instruments and a monitor for controls. In the autumn of 1989 Jaguar reverted to six traditional round instruments with wood veneer around them. With some delay, the XJ-S benefited from new switches that had been introduced for XJ 40.

From December 1988 the steering wheel became adjustable in height, but no longer in reach; the steering column levers were changed as well. The ignition lock was moved from the dashboard to the steering column. From the 1990 model year the XJ 12 adopted the steering wheel that had been in the XJ-S since 1988; it had two thicker sections on the rim. In the XJ 40 the color of the dash padding was changed from black to interior color, but some color choices were doubtful. Even the safety belts now were in the trim color.

From May 1991 the revised XJS boasted traditional round instruments, a change much acclaimed by enthusiasts. For 1992 the map cases at the backrests, armrests, map boxes in the doors, and sunblinds in the XJ 40 were leather-covered. Door trim was styled with more verve.

Above: 1961 Mark X interior. *(J)*

Right: Spacious rear compartment in the Mark X. *(J)*

Above and left: 1966 420 G interior. *(Schönborn archive)*

Top: E-Type 4.2 interior. *(Schön)*

Middle: 1971 E-Type V-12 dashboard. *(Schön)*

Bottom: 1968 XJ 6 dashboard in its original guise. *(J)*

Right: Dashboard of the 1966 420. *(Schönborn archive)*

Above and above right: Interior of a 1973 Daimler Double-Six Series 2. *(J)*

Right: Rear compartment of a 1972 Daimler Double-Six Vanden Plas. *(J)*

The lumbar supports now were electrically inflatable, and real lambswool mats replaced the former deep mats of artificial material in the Daimlers.

From September 1992 the seats could be adjusted further backward by 20mm in the sedans. The XJS selector lever grew in size and was cylindrical instead of conical. The XJS was available with an airbag supplied by Breed Automotives. The following year the passenger side also received an airbag, for which the glove box had to disappear; a map case was added to the front of the passenger's seat cushion to compensate. The same happened with the X 300 on its introduction. It continued the airbag steering wheel of the XJ 40.

For the 1997 model year, wooden gearbox and selector levers were introduced. The rear seat cushion was changed to offer better comfort to the passenger in the middle, who now also had an automatic seat belt instead of a static one.

The XK 8 and XJ 8 had large wooden dashboards. In the case of the XK, this was reminiscent of a Spitfire plane. The instruments were sunk into deep holes, but intense permanent illumination and different dials helped readability. Safety fanatics had noticed

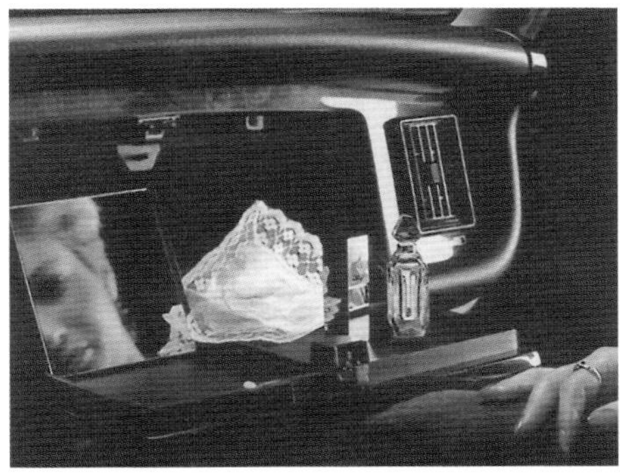

Above left: Dashboard of a 1979 Daimler Double-Six Vanden Plas Series 3. *(J)*

Top: Interior of a 1979 Daimler Double-Six Vanden Plas. *(J)*

Above: Glove box with mirror—a specialty of all XJ Series 1-3 cars. *(J)*

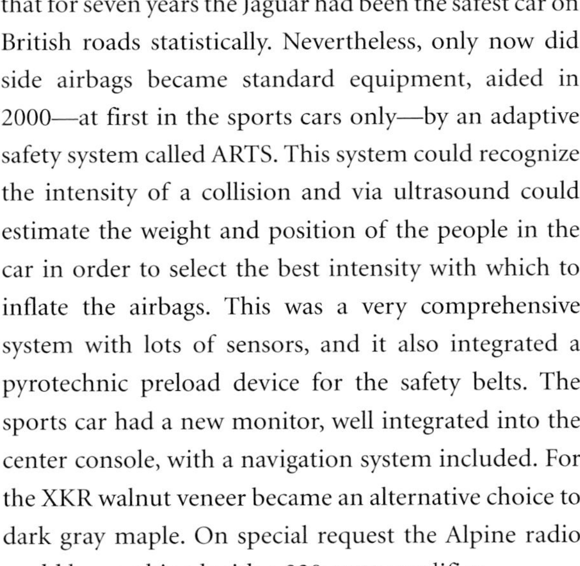

that for seven years the Jaguar had been the safest car on British roads statistically. Nevertheless, only now did side airbags became standard equipment, aided in 2000—at first in the sports cars only—by an adaptive safety system called ARTS. This system could recognize the intensity of a collision and via ultrasound could estimate the weight and position of the people in the car in order to select the best intensity with which to inflate the airbags. This was a very comprehensive system with lots of sensors, and it also integrated a pyrotechnic preload device for the safety belts. The sports car had a new monitor, well integrated into the center console, with a navigation system included. For the XKR walnut veneer became an alternative choice to dark gray maple. On special request the Alpine radio could be combined with a 320-watt amplifier.

The S-Type's interior, in its original guise, was not exactly to the taste of Jaguar enthusiasts, who particularly disliked the design of the center console and the not-always-tasteful color shades. For the 2001 model year a dead pedal for the left foot was introduced. Stylists integrated telephone dials into the central console and the CD player was moved from the glove box to the trunk. The revised edition of 2002 was the first Jaguar with pedals adjustable in reach, using the same lever as the steering height and reach adjustment. Magnesium elements under the seat cushions helped save weight.

The X 350 impressed with a more lavish use of chrome in the interior, but otherwise remained faithful to the style that had been introduced with the X-Type and face-lifted S-Type. The wooden panels could be replaced with black piano lacquer. Other niceties were the chromed knob for the glove box and its hydraulically dampened opening mechanism. With the long-wheelbase version, the picnic tables returned, now being called business trays and no longer as feudal as once in the Daimler.

Electrics

At the times of the early SS cars, wiring harnesses were quite simple. Only starter, ignition, horn, and lights were operated electrically. So William Lyons had little to bother about electrics. The most prominent electrical items were the P 170 headlights. The electrical wipers were very useful, particularly in the British climate. Electricity was provided by a 12-volt dynamo, which was moved by the timing chain and served as its tensioner. Only in September 1933 was this

Interior of a 1981 XJ-S H.E. *(J)*

replaced with a conventional V-belt. Dipping headlights also were available, as were two Lucas horns on the bumper, self-canceling directional indicators, and a backup light.

Soon after its presentation in autumn 1935, the SS Jaguar was admired for its mighty P 100 headlights. These used to be reserved for Rolls-Royce and gave wonderful light, while before the smaller QK 596 had been used, which were continued for the 1.5-liter and SS 100. The latter had chromed stone guards as an optional extra. In the following year, the side markers on the front fenders started to become integrated into them for the six-cylinder sedans and tourers. Another year later a radio could be ordered from SS directly. It was of Philco manufacture, while after the war Radiomobile was preferred.

In autumn 1939 a new Mellowtone horn was hidden behind the radiator. The Mark V and XK 120 were the first Jaguars with integrated headlamps. Thus, the large headlights of the earlier models disappeared. The side markers on the XK 120 open two-seater had their separate chromed housings on the fenders until September 1952. Afterward they were integrated into the fenders, with translucent red plastic telltales that showed the driver that the lamp was working. The more vertical face of the plastic item should be to the front when mounted correctly. Only on the 240, 250 V-8, and 340 was it was mounted more aerodynamically the other way around. In 1952 so-called tripod headlights were introduced. They were named after the three bars visible behind the glass. For the United States sealed-beam headlights already were required by legislation. Being slightly smaller, broader chrome rings were put around them. The XK 120 had two six-volt batteries behind the seats and used no more than four fuses!

The Mark VII was the first Jaguar with the back-up lights integrated into the number plate plinth. From late 1952—shortly after introduction of a second wiper speed—TRICO windshield washers became an optional extra. Soon they were standard equipment, but for some considerable time they retained pneumatic function, rather than electric. From August 1953 duotone horns were employed.

The XK 140's batteries were moved to the front fenders, just behind the wheels. The open variants had just one 12-volt battery. The Mark VII M had the fog lamps mounted on the bumper instead of being integrated into the body, and indicators were added to the front bumpers. These indicators started with clear lenses before changing to amber from February 1955 for all but the American markets. Its headlights were Lucas J 700 with modern glass. In some countries the headlights were PF 770s, which were called "special Le Mans-type" in advertising. The taillights had integrated indicators and reflectors, which now were required by legislation. In summer 1959 (September for XK 150) taillights were enlarged and the indicators were separated from them; the indicator sector was provided with amber lenses for all countries except America. On the XK 150, the over-riders had to be relocated closer to each other.

The Mark II was the first Jaguar with a headlamp flasher. Since early 1962 for reason of legislation the ignition lock was relocated at the steering column for cars destined to Germany. On the Mark X the side markers and indicators moved close to each other, but retained separate housings.

In October 1964 the electrical system was thoroughly revised, with alternators replacing the dynamos.

Far left: Tweed cloth for the basic 1985 models. *(J)*

Left: Dashboard of a 1989 XJ 6 4.0. *(J)*

Below: Dashboard of a 1990 XJ 6 3.2. *(J)*

They ran at double engine speed; drive was transmitted via the vibration damper and V-belt. Finally, following international standard, the negative earth system was adopted. The new starter could no longer be thrown out of engagement by backfire.

The XJ 6 had a combined starter-and-ignition lock, dispensing with the traditional starter knob. It also continued the hazard warning switch that only a year before had been introduced for America. Indicators and side markers finally were integrated into a common housing, which was also used for the E-Type Series 2 and 3. Cars destined for America had the side markers integrated into the sealed beam headlights, however, thus leaving the combined housing with one amber lens for the indicator.

The XJ Series 2 had a central locking system for the doors with a switch on the gearbox tunnel. From autumn 1977 Philips radio/cassette players were used; stereo sound for the audiophile enthusiast was available at extra cost. In February 1978 the side markers were relocated to the headlights, as was the practice for American and XJ-S cars already. The XJ-S' huge oval headlights were produced exclusively for Jaguar at Cibie in France; they were much-acclaimed for their good light. The American XJ-S had small double headlights set into the oval, as only sealed-beam units of a particular size were admissible there. In these the bulbs could only be replaced in conjunction with the reflectors.

With the better-equipped versions of the XJ Series 3, a pair of rear fog lights was integrated into the rear bumper. They had to be switched on and off by the main light switch, which had become a bit over complicated. The larger rear taillights now included the backup lights. The fog lamps and the front indicators were no longer provided with a chromed surround. From as early as 1978, automatic cars had cruise control as an optional extra. The cruise control system was only operable in the upper gear. A further modernity was the intermittent setting for the wipers, which however did not prevent the wipers from doing their funny dance before reaching parking position. A headlamp washer was also available, requiring a larger water reservoir in the nearside front fender. The electric aerial—flush-fitting from 1979 or spring 1981 at the latest—now had a standard retarding relay for retracting. Interior lights also remained alight for some seconds after the last door was closed. The heated rear window switched off automatically after 15 minutes. The central locking system was now controlled from the driver's door, locking the trunk but not releasing it. The switch on the gearbox tunnel was discarded. The mirrors' remote control now was electric, not via cables.

Dashboard inspired by Spitfire wings in the 1996 XK 8. *(J)*

Dashboard of the 1991 XJS. *(J)*

Luxuriously appointed interior of the limited-edition 1996 Daimler Double-Six Century. *(J)*

From November 1980 Merlin aerials were used, as these had a reputation for better reliability. From mid-1981 maintenance-free batteries were used, and from June 1984 more reliable mirror motors were provided from Kienzle. From November 1984 Clarion radios were used exclusively, and the trip computer was revised. From February 1985 single-part Hirschmann aerials were used. From September a completely new central locking system with electric motors instead of solenoids was used.

The XJ 40 was infamous for its unique square headlamps on Sovereign and Daimler models and for vehicles destined for America. Nice amenities were heated windshield washers, door locks, mirrors, and seats. The central locking system incorporated the windows and sunroof. Signaling wires were operated with low-voltage electricity, so they could be smaller in diameter and save cost and weight. More durable relays and connectors were very helpful and thus were transferred to the XJ-S as well. Cruise control soon was supplied from Hella in Germany, and the central

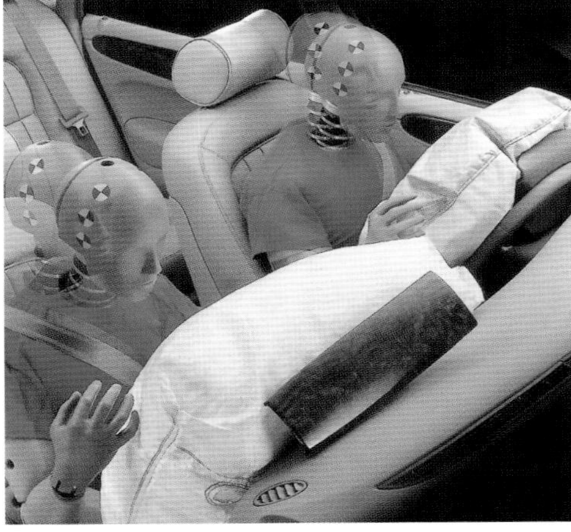

Above: Airbags in the XJ 8. *(J)*

Left: Plush interior of a 1997 XJ 8. *(J)*

locking system from May 1998 was supplied by Keikert instead of Lucas. From July 1988 the cruise control system worked in the upper two gears of the automatic gearbox. From August 1989 the wiper motors, which here had to move only one wiper arm, came from Electrolux instead of Lucas; their parking position was moved to the opposite side.

From 1987 the XJ-S had heated seats as well. From September 1992 a remote-control (infrared beam) central locking system with immobilizer was introduced but was replaced with another design only one year later. As requested from America, interior lights were added to the undersides of the sun visors in the XJS, as was an electronic immobilizer. For the X 300 a

The XJ 8 dashboard is intended to be shaped like a propeller. *(J)*

Despite its more compact exterior dimensions, the S-Type had a generous interior. *(J)*

thoroughly revised electric system was employed that included electrically folding mirrors. An electronic immobilizer became standard as well. On special request an electronic parking aid warned of obstacles that had been overlooked when reversing. Shorter and shorter intervals gave an indication of distance to the obstacle.

The XK 8 had a multiplex electric system in which each wire had a multitude of functions, which helped keep the wiring harness smaller. This technology and the common electronic "brain" of engine, transmission, and suspension, which was hidden beneath the dashboard, was adopted for the sedans. The long-wheelbase variants (X 330) had adjustable rear seats and a switch in the rear to move the front passenger's seat forward. This hobby-horse for directors was standard equipment on Daimlers. For the 1997 model year an electrically adjustable interior mirror was introduced, this being justified by its integration into the seat memory functions.

The XK 8 lowered its door windows by 15mm when the doors opened and returned them to their previous position after the door had been closed, thus pressing it securely into its seal. This helped avoid wind noise caused by the window being flexed outside by the rise in air pressure of a closing door.

The S-Type was introduced with a DVD-based navigation system that had a storage capacity eight times as high as before. The electronic immobilizer was further improved and programmed to a new code each time the ignition key was taken off the lock. The XKR was available with a new adaptive cruise control that automatically kept the right distance to the car in front, helped by a 77 gigahertz radar sensor made by Delphi Automotive Systems. One year later this system used 40 radar beams for measuring and its "brain" became lighter and more compact. A control light warned if the system was inoperative due to dust or snow. At the same time the XK and XJ were the first cars in the world equipped with a dual-band (900 and 1,800 megahertz) telephone system made by Motorola. It offered a voice-controlled choice of 20 programmable numbers and could also be operated with the approved switches at the steering wheel.

The 7-inch monitor introduced with the X-Type soon was found in other models as well. It incorporated touch-screen functions, a navigation system with traffic information and normal TV function. Voice control was continually improved and information technology inclusive of the dual-band telephone operated via digital data bus systems.

The bi-xenon headlights on the 2003 XK 8 automatically switched on and off and adjusted height automatically. The X 350 used the same system and had optional electrically heated and folding door mirrors; automatically dimming mirrors; rain sensors for the wipers; parking aids at front and rear; variable seat heating; audio systems with at least eight loudspeakers and 140-watt amplifiers; automatic loudness adjustment; a CD-player storing six CDs; separately operating monitors in the backrests of the front seats; 16-way seat adjustment for the front seats with threefold memory; six-way seat adjustment in the rear; an electric blind for the rear and rear side windows; a trip computer with two memories; switches on the steering wheel for cruise control; audio system; hands-free telephone system; and voice control of audio system, air conditioning, telephone, navigation system, and TV.

This was a far cry from Austin-Swallow times when even a horn and electric starter were deemed to be luxury items. This chapter about electrics in particular shows how much Jaguar has advanced since its early years. What started as a solution to existential demands (ignition and lighting) made many a dream come true. The number of switches, once a symbol of lavish equipment, is now being reduced while evermore complicated systems listen to or even take away decisions from the driver. For many years the electrical system was a source of trouble for drivers; now computer technology is so advanced that the most complicated systems are being deployed without detriment to reliability.

Top: Headlamp washer and wiper for the XJ Series 3. *(S)*

Above left and right: The mechanically operated, remote-controlled door mirror of 1978. *(J)*

Shortly after the introduction of the XJ Series 3, Jaguar introduced electric mirrors. *(J)*

JAGUAR CATALOG

This appendix contains the most important technical data of Jaguar and other cars made under Sir William Lyons. The one-off Swallow bodies for works use on Austro-Daimler, Talbot-Darracq, and Clyno chassis have been omitted, though.

For reasons of simplicity the Swallow, SS, Jaguar, and Daimler cars have been sorted by their model ranges, which are listed in the chronological order of their first appearance. In some cases the grouping is debatable, but the following scheme with 35 model ranges seemed sensible enough.

The first group are Swallow bodies on more or less unchanged bought-in chassis. These were the following ranges:

- Austin-Swallow, based on the Austin Seven (1928–1932)
- Morris-Swallow, based on the Morris Cowley (1928 only)
- Alvis-Swallow, based on the Alvis 12/50 (1928 only)
- Morris-Swallow, based on the Morris Minor (1930 only)
- FIAT-Swallow, based on the FIAT 509 A (1930 only)
- Swift-Swallow, based on the Swift 10 HP (1930 and 1931)
- Standard-Swallow, based on the Standard 9 HP (1930–1933)
- Wolseley-Swallow, based on the Wolseley Hornet (1931–1933)
- Standard-Swallow, based on the Standard 16 HP (1931 and 1932, see Standard-Swallow 9 HP)

With SS, the production of cars recognized as a brand started. Again the cars are listed in the context of their model ranges, which are as follows:

- SS Two (1932 and 1933)
- SS One (1932)
- New SS One (1933-1936, including 1935 SS 90)
- New SS Two (1934 and 1935, see original SS Two)
- SS Jaguar four- and six-cylinder cars (1936–1949 and 1936–1940 SS 100)
- Jaguar Mark V (1949–1951), Mark VII-IX (1951–1961)
- Jaguar Mark X-420G (1962–1970 and 1968–1992) Daimler DS 420

Produced in parallel and technically closely related were the sports cars, which are grouped in the following ranges:

- XK 120 (1949–1954), XK 140 (1955–1957), XK 150 (1957–1961)
- E-Type (1961–1970 and long wheelbase 1966–1975)
- XJ-S (1976–1991), XJS (1991–1996), Aston Martin DB 7 (1994–2003)
- XK 8 and XKR (1997–2005)
- XK 4.2 and XKR (2006 onward)

For racing the following groups of cars were built:

- XK 120 C (1951–1953)
- D-Type, XK-SS, E1A, and E2A (1954–1960)
- XJ 13 (1966 one-off)
- Group 44 and TWR prototypes (1982–1991), XJ 220 (1989–1993)
- Formula 1 racing cars R1-R5 (2000–2004)

The smaller sedans originally more aimed at the owner-driver were:

- 2.4-liter-340 (1956–1969), 3.4 and 3.8 S, 420, Daimler Sovereign (1964–1969)
- XJ Series 1 (1969–1973, lwb 1973), Series 2 (1974–1978, lwb 1974–1979), Series 3 (1979–1992)
- XJ 40 and 81 (1987–1994, lwb 1993–1994), X 300 and 330 (1995–1997, lwb 1996–1997), X 308 (1998–2002)
- X 350 (2003 onward, lwb 2005 onward)

With Daimler, Jaguar inherited these models:

- Majestic (1959–1960), Majestic Major, and DR 450 (1960–1968)
- SP 250 (1960–1964)

As the more traditional sedans had grown in size, more compact models were added:

- S-Type (1999–2007)
- X-Type (2001 onward, Estate 2003 onward)

The Group 44, TWR, and Jaguar Sport specials, including the XJR-15, have been included with respect to their proximity to Jaguar and the fact that Jaguar held a share in the latter company. The Aston Martin DB 7 has been included because it is so closely related to the XJS, and as both companies were then under Ford's umbrella. The last reason also made it seem worthwhile to add the Formula 1 cars.

British singularity—or just the belief in tradition—was the reason why technical data often were given in now outdated units. For reasons of comparability these have been converted into the units used most. Rounding differences have been accepted to some extent in order to avoid unreadable figures. These differences

may be one reason for different figures being found in literature as technical data for one and the same model. Often, decision-making in these cases was quite difficult.

Many collections of technical data suffer from some data being mixed up, and particularly with regard to production figures considerable deviations have occurred. The reason may be that, arguably, prototype examples can be added to the production figure. The number of cars dispatched from Jaguar is smaller than the number of cars made, and the number of cars actually registered for use in traffic is still smaller. Some differences result from sources just counting the difference between first and last chassis number. Production figures given here are the result of careful counting by Anders Ditlev Clausager since the 1980s. Production figures of the younger models are derived from information made publicly available by Jaguar.

A 1928 Austin-Swallow roadster in front of an equally cherished house in the center of Coventry. *(J)*

Make, range	**Austin-Swallow**			**Morris-Swallow Cowley**	
Type	*Roadster*	*Coupe*	*Sedan**	*Roadster*	*Coupe*
Public debut	20/5/1927	9/1927	9/1928	19/8/1927	19/8/1927
End of production	20/10/1932	29/2/1932	2/7/1932	1928	1928
Production figure	800		1700	10	
First, last chassis number RHD	As Austin Seven			As Morris Cowley	
First, last chassis number LHD n/a	n/a				
Body type	Aluminum panels on wooden frame, 2 doors, 2 (sedan 4) seats			Aluminum panels on wooden frame, 2 doors, 2 seats	
Weather protection, top mechanism	As Morris-Swallow (Sedan enclosed-drive with vent)			Manually operated top (coupe with detachable steel hardtop)	
Length, width, height (mm)	2692 (from 10/30 2800) x 1168 x 1350 (Sedan 1500)			3600 x 1450 x 1400	
Length, width, height (inches)	106 (from 10/30 110) x 46 x 53 (Sedan 59)			141 3/4 x 57 x 55	
Wheelbase, front, rear track (mm)	1905 x 1016/1030 (from 10/30 2025 x 1016/1090)			2616 x 1219/1219	
Wheelbase, front, rear track (inches)	75 x 40/40 1/2 (from 10/30 79 3/4 x 40/43)			103 x 48	
Ground clearance, turning circle, curb weight	170mm, 10m, 500kg			170mm, 11m, 750kg	
Max speed, acceleration 0-60 mph	60 (from 10/30 70) kph, n/a			80kph, n/a	
Max power, standard, revs	12 SAE-HP/2400 (from 10/30 15 SAE-HP/2400)			35 SAE-HP/3000	
Max torque, revs	Unknown			Unknown	
Engine type, position, number and configuration of cylinders	Four-stroke gasoline, front longitudinally, 4 cylinders straight			Four-stroke gasoline, front longitudinally, 4 cylinders straight	
Bore x Stroke (mm), capacity (cc), compression ratio	56 x 75.2, 747cc, 5.6 : 1			75 x 102, 1802cc, 6 : 1	
Designation of engine and cylinder head	Engine and head "Austin Seven"			Engine and head "Morris Cowley"	
Engine block and cylinder head material, number of main bearings, type of liners	Block and head cast chrome-iron, 2 main bearings, n/a			Block and head cast chrome-iron, 2 main bearings, n/a	
Number of valves per cylinder, configuration, valve gearing, timing variants	2 side valves, directly, 1 side camshaft, sprocket, fixed			2 side valves, directly, 1 side camshaft, sprocket, fixed	
Air supply, type of inlet manifold, air tempering	Normally aspirated, one-stage inlet manifold, n/a			Normally aspirated, one-stage inlet manifold, n/a	
Type, position, make, and designation of mixture preparation	1 horizontal carburetor, Solex or Zenith			1 carburetor, unknown	
Energy source, type, make, and designation of ignition system	Magneto, breaker, Lucas			Battery, breaker, Lucas	
Make of alternator, voltage, earthing	DC dynamo, 6V, positive			DC dynamo, 6V, positive	
Engine coolant, drive, regulation of cooling	Liquid, gravitation, n/a			Liquid, unknown, unknown	
Type of clutch, number of gears in manual box, synchronized gears	Single-plate dry clutch, 3 (from 10/30 4), none			Wet, cork-lined clutch, 3, none	
Gear ratios in manual box	3.25, 1.82, 1 (from 10/30 4.30, 2.64, 1.62, 1) : 1			Unknown	
Make, type, ratio of overdrive	n/a			n/a	
Type of clutch, number of gears, make and model of automatic box	n/a			n/a	
Gear ratios in automatic gearbox	n/a			n/a	
Driven axle, type of diff, traction control	Rear, spiral bevel, n/a			Rear, spiral bevel, n/a	
Axle ratios	4.9 (from 10/30 5.25) : 1			Unknown	
Type of chassis	Separate A chassis			Separate chassis	
Suspension, springing front	Live axle, half-elliptic transverse leaf spring			Live axle, half-elliptic leaf springs	
Suspension, springing rear	Live axle, quarter-elliptic cantilever leaf springs			Live axle, half-elliptic leaf springs	
Reduction of roll	n/a			n/a	
Type of shock absorbers	n/a			n/a	
Type and dimensions of wheels	Steel spokes, painted, 2.75 J x 18			Artillery, painted, unknown	
Type, dimensions, make of tires	Dunlop, 26 x 3.50			Dunlop, unknown	
Type of braking front	Drums, unknown			Drums, unknown	
Type of braking rear	Outboard drums, unknown			Outboard drums, unknown	
Braking mechanism, number of circuits, servo assistance, electronic aids	Cable, n/a			Cable, n/a	
Steering gear, make and model of power steering	Worm, n/a			Worm, n/a	

* 1 van of 17/08/1932 for works use

Swallow

Make, range	**Alvis-Swallow**	**Morris-Swallow Minor**
Type	*Sedan*	*Sedan*
Public debut	1928	1930
End of production	1928	1930
Production figure	1	1
First, last chassis number RHD	As Alvis 12/50	As Morris Minor
First, last chassis number LHD	n/a	n/a
Body type	Aluminum panels on wooden frame, 2 doors, 4 seats	Aluminum panels on wooden frame, 2 doors, 4 seats
Weather protection, top mechanism	Enclosed-drive with vent	Enclosed-drive with vent
Length, width, height (mm)	3886 x 1511 x 1500	3200 x 1350 x 1400
Length, width, height (inches)	153 x 59 1/2 x 59	126 x 53 x 55
Wheelbase, front, rear track (mm)	2860 x 1270/1270	2184 x 1067/1067
Wheelbase, front, rear track (inches)	112 1/2 x 50/50	86 x 42/42
Ground clearance, turning circle, curb weight	170mm, 11m, 850kg	170mm, 10m, 700kg
Max speed, acceleration 0-60 mph	110kph, 50 sec	70kph, n/a
Max power, standard, revs	50 SAE-HP/4000	20 SAE-HP/4000
Max torque, revs	Unknown	Unknown
Engine type, position, number and configuration of cylinders	Four-stroke gasoline, front longitudinally, 4 cylinders straight	Four-stroke gasoline, front longitudinally, 4 cylinders straight
Bore x Stroke (mm), capacity (cc), compression ratio	69 x 100, 1496cc, unknown	57 x 83, 847cc, unknown
Designation of engine and cylinder head	Engine and head "Alvis 12/50"	Engine and head "Morris Minor"
Engine block and cylinder head material, number of main bearings, type of liners	Block and head cast chrome-iron, 3 main bearings, n/a	Block and head cast chrome-iron, 2 main bearings, n/a
Number of valves per cylinder, configuration, valve gearing, timing variants	2 overhead valves, pushrod/rocker, 1 side camshaft, sprocket, fixed	2 overhead valves, bucket tappets, 1 overhead camshaft, chain, fixed
Air supply, type of inlet manifold, air tempering	Normally aspirated, one-stage inlet manifold, n/a	Normally aspirated, one-stage inlet manifold, n/a
Type, position, make, and designation of mixture preparation	1 carburetor, unknown	1 carburetor, SU
Energy source, type, make, and designation of ignition system	Battery, breaker, Lucas	Unknown, breaker, Lucas
Make of alternator, voltage, earthing	DC dynamo, 6V, positive	DC dynamo, 6V, positive
Engine coolant, drive, regulation of cooling	Liquid, gravitation, n/a	Liquid, gravitation, n/a
Type of clutch, number of gears in manual box, synchronized gears	Single-plate dry clutch, 4, none	Single-plate dry clutch, 3, none
Gear ratios in manual box	Unknown	Unknown
Make, type, ratio of overdrive	n/a	n/a
Type of clutch, number of gears, make and model of automatic box	n/a	n/a
Gear ratios in automatic gearbox	n/a	n/a
Driven axle, type of diff, traction control	Rear, spiral bevel, n/a	Rear, spiral bevel, n/a
Axle ratios	4.77 : 1	5.37 : 1
Type of chassis	Separate boxed-in chassis	Separate chassis
Suspension, springing front	Live axle, half-elliptic transverse leaf spring	Live axle, half-elliptic leaf springs
Suspension, springing rear	Live axle, half-elliptic leaf springs	Live axle, half-elliptic leaf springs
Reduction of roll	n/a	n/a
Type of shock absorbers	Friction, manually adjustable	n/a
Type and dimensions of wheels	Steel spokes, painted, unknown	Artillery, painted, 19 x 3
Type, dimensions, make of tires	Dunlop, unknown	Dunlop Cord, 27 x 4.00
Type of braking front	Drums, unknown	Drums, unknown
Type of braking rear	Outboard drums, unknown	Outboard drums, unknown
Braking mechanism, number of circuits, servo assistance, electronic aids	Unknown, n/a	Cable, n/a
Steering gear, make and model of power steering	Cam and lever, n/a	Unknown, n/a

Swallow

Make, range	**FIAT-Swallow**	**Swift-Swallow**
Type	*Sedan*	*Sedan*
Public debut	7/1929	10/1929
End of production	1930	6/1931
Production figure	60	150
First, last chassis number RHD	As FIAT 509 A	As Swift Ten
First, last chassis number LHD	n/a	n/a
Body type	Aluminum panels on wooden frame, 2 doors, 4 seats	Aluminum panels on wooden frame, 2 doors, 4 seats
Weather protection, top mechanism	Enclosed-drive with vent	Enclosed-drive with vent
Length, width, height (mm)	3700 x 1420 x 1500	3700 x 1420 x 1500
Length, width, height (inches)	146 x 56 x 59	146 x 56/56
Wheelbase, front, rear track (mm)	2550 x 1200/1200	2515 x 1200/1200
Wheelbase, front, rear track (inches)	100 1/4 x 47 1/4/47 1/4	99 x 47 1/4/47 1/4
Ground clearance, turning circle, curb weight	180mm, 10m, 800kg	180mm, 10m, 820kg
Max speed, acceleration 0-60 mph	75kph, n/a	85kph, n/a
Max power, standard, revs	22 SAE-HP/3400	22 SAE-HP/3000
Max torque, revs	Unknown	Unknown
Engine type, position, number and configuration of cylinders	Four-stroke gasoline, front longitudinally, 4 cylinders straight	Four-stroke gasoline, front longitudinally, 4 cylinders straight
Bore x Stroke (mm), capacity (cc), compression ratio	57 x 97, 990cc, 5.35 : 1	62.5 x 97, 1190cc, 6 : 1
Designation of engine and cylinder head	Engine and head “FIAT 509 A”	Engine and head “Swift Ten”
Engine block and cylinder head material, number of main bearings, type of liners	Block and head cast chrome-iron, 2 main bearings, n/a	Block and head cast chrome-iron, 3 main bearings, n/a
Number of valves per cylinder, configuration, valve gearing, timing variants	2 overhead valves, bucket tappets, 1 overhead camshaft, chain, fixed	2 side valves, directly, 1 side camshaft, sprocket, fixed
Air supply, type of inlet manifold, air tempering	Normally aspirated, one-stage inlet manifold, n/a	Normally aspirated, one-stage inlet manifold, n/a
Type, position, make, and designation of mixture preparation	1 carburetor, Solex	1 carburetor, unknown
Energy source, type, make, and designation of ignition system	Magneto, breaker, Lucas	Battery, breaker, Lucas
Make of alternator, voltage, earthing	DC dynamo, 6V, positive	DC dynamo, 6V, positive
Engine coolant, drive, regulation of cooling	Liquid, gravitation, n/a	Liquid, gravitation, n/a
Type of clutch, number of gears in manual box, synchronized gears	Single-plate dry clutch, 4, none	Single-plate dry clutch, 3 (optional 4), none
Gear ratios in manual box	Unknown	Unknown
Make, type, ratio of overdrive	n/a	n/a
Type of clutch, number of gears, make and model of automatic box	n/a	n/a
Gear ratios in automatic gearbox	n/a	n/a
Driven axle, type of diff, traction control	Rear, spiral bevel, n/a	Rear, spiral bevel, n/a
Axle ratios	6.1 : 1	5.4 : 1
Type of chassis	Separate chassis	Separate chassis
Suspension, springing front	Live axle, half-elliptic leaf springs	Live axle, half-elliptic leaf springs
Suspension, springing rear	Live axle, half-elliptic leaf springs	Live axle, quarter- (from 10/30 half-)elliptic leaf springs
Reduction of roll	n/a	n/a
Type of shock absorbers	n/a	Friction at rear only
Type and dimensions of wheels	Artillery, painted, unknown	Steel spokes, painted, unknown
Type, dimensions, make of tires	Unknown	unknown
Type of braking front	Drums, unknown	Drums, unknown
Type of braking rear	Outboard drums, unknown	Outboard drums, unknown
Braking mechanism, number of circuits, servo assistance, electronic aids	Cable, n/a	Rods, n/a
Steering gear, make and model of power steering	Worm and bevel, n/a	Worm, n/a

Swallow

Make, range	**Standard-Swallow 9 HP**	**Standard-Swallow 16 HP**
Type	*Sedan*	*Sedan*
Public debut	9/1929	5/1931
End of production	29/4/1933	24/8/1932
Production figure	200	56
First, last chassis number RHD	As Standard 9 HP (-188254)	As Standard 16 HP (118000-119888)
First, last chassis number LHD	n/a	n/a
Body type	Aluminum panels on wooden frame, 2 doors, 4 seats	Aluminum panels on wooden frame, 2 doors, 4 seats
Weather protection, top mechanism	Enclosed-drive with vent	Enclosed-drive with vent
Length, width, height (mm)	3500 x 1350 x 1500	4200 x 1400 x 1500
Length, width, height (inches)	138 x 53 x 59	165 x 55 x 59
Wheelbase, front, rear track (mm)	2515 x 1143/1143	2800 x 1200/1200
Wheelbase, front, rear track (inches)	99 x 45/45	110 x 47/47
Ground clearance, turning circle, curb weight	180mm, 11m, 750kg	180mm, 11m, 1100kg
Max speed, acceleration 0-60 mph	75kph, n/a	110kph, 50 sec
Max power, standard, revs	25 SAE-HP/unknown	45 SAE-HP/unknown
Max torque, revs	Unknown	Unknown
Engine type, position, number and configuration of cylinders	Four-stroke gasoline, front longitudinally, 4 cylinders straight	Four-stroke gasoline, front longitudinally, 6 cylinders straight
Bore x Stroke (mm), capacity (cc), compression ratio	63.5 x 10..6, 1287cc, 4.8 : 1	65.5 x 101.6, 2054cc, 6 : 1
Designation of engine and cylinder head	Engine and head "Standard 9 HP"	Engine and head "Standard 16 HP"
Engine block and cylinder head material, number of main bearings, type of liners	Block and head cast chrome-iron, 3 main bearings, n/a	Block and head cast chrome-iron, 7 main bearings, n/a
Number of valves per cylinder, configuration, valve gearing, timing variants	2 side valves, directly, 1 side camshaft, sprocket, fixed	2 side valves, directly, 1 side camshaft, sprocket, fixed
Air supply, type of inlet manifold, air tempering	Normally aspirated, one-stage inlet manifold, n/a	Normally aspirated, one-stage inlet manifold, n/a
Type, position, make, and designation of mixture preparation	1 carburetor, unknown	1 carburetor, unknown
Energy source, type, make, and designation of ignition system	Battery, breaker, Lucas	Battery, breaker, Lucas
Make of alternator, voltage, earthing	DC dynamo, 6 V, positive	DC dynamo, 6 V, positive
Engine coolant, drive, regulation of cooling	Liquid, gravitation, n/a	Liquid, gravitation, n/a
Type of clutch, number of gears in manual box, synchronized gears	Single-plate dry clutch, 3, none	Single-plate dry clutch, 4, none
Gear ratios in manual box	Unknown	3.455, 2.09, 1.32, 1, unknown : 1
Make, type, ratio of overdrive	n/a	n/a
Type of clutch, number of gears, make and model of automatic box	n/a	n/a
Gear ratios in automatic gearbox	n/a	n/a
Driven axle, type of diff, traction control	Rear, worm gear (from 1931 spiral bevel), n/a	Rear, spiral bevel, n/a
Axle ratios	Unknown	Unknown
Type of chassis	Separate chassis	Separate chassis
Suspension, springing front	Live axle, half-elliptic leaf springs	Live axle, half-elliptic leaf springs
Suspension, springing rear	Live axle, half-elliptic leaf springs	Live axle, half-elliptic leaf springs
Reduction of roll	n/a	n/a
Type of shock absorbers	n/a	n/a
Type and dimensions of wheels	Steel spokes, painted, unknown	Steel spokes, painted, unknown
Type, dimensions, make of tires	Dunlop, unknown	Dunlop, unknown
Type of braking front	Drums, unknown	Drums, unknown
Type of braking rear	Outboard drums, unknown	Outboard drums, unknown
Braking mechanism, number of circuits, servo assistance, electronic aids	Cable, n/a	Cable, n/a
Steering gear, make and model of power steering	Cam and lever, n/a	Cam and lever, n/a

Swallow

Make, range	**Wolseley-Swallow**		**Wolseley-Swallow Special**	
Type	*Roadster*	*Tourer*	*Roadster*	*Tourer*
Public debut	1/1931	10/1931	4/1932	4/1932
End of production	22/7/1932	13/7/1933	7/7/1933	17/8/1933
Production figure	150	220	22	181
First, last chassis number RHD Model year	1932 2/51-847/51, then 6/78-1146/78		Model year 1932 1/65-858/65, then 6/78-1146/78	
First, last chassis number LHD n/a	n/a		n/a	
Body type	Aluminum panels on wooden frame, 2 doors, 4 (roadster 2) seats		Aluminum panels on wooden frame, 2 doors, 4 (roadster 2) seats	
Weather protection, top mechanism	Manually operated top		Manually operated top	
Length, width, height (mm)	3073 x 1295 x 1350		3073 x 1295 x 1350	
Length, width, height (inches)	121 x 51 x 53		121 x 51 x 53	
Wheelbase, front, rear track (mm)	2337 x 1007/1007 (from 10/31 2337 x 1080/1080)		2337 x 1080/1080	
Wheelbase, front, rear track (inches)	92 x 39 3/4/39 3/4 (from 10/31 92 x 42 1/2/42 1/2)		92 x 42 1/2/42 1/2	
Ground clearance, turning circle, curb weight	180mm, 12m, 750kg		180mm, 12m, 750kg	
Max speed, acceleration 0-60 mph	110kph, 50 sec		120kph, 30 sec	
Max power, standard, revs	32 SAE-HP/4300		43 SAE-HP/4500	
Max torque, revs	Unknown		Unknown	
Engine type, position, number and configuration of cylinders	Four-stroke gasoline, front longitudinally, 6 cylinders straight		Four-stroke gasoline, front longitudinally, 6 cylinders straight	
Bore x Stroke (mm), capacity (cc), compression ratio	57 x 83, 1271cc, 5.9 : 1		57 x 83, 1271cc, 6 : 1	
Designation of engine and cylinder head	Engine and head "Wolseley Hornet"		Engine and head "Wolseley Hornet"	
Engine block and cylinder head material, number of main bearings, type of liners	Block and head cast chrome-iron, 4 main bearings, n/a		Block and head cast chrome-iron, 4 main bearings, n/a	
Number of valves per cylinder, configuration, valve gearing, timing variants	2 overhead valves, bucket tappets, 1 overhead camshaft, chain, fixed		2 overhead valves, bucket tappets, 1 overhead camshaft, chain, fixed	
Air supply, type of inlet manifold, air tempering	Normally aspirated, one-stage inlet manifold, n/a		Normally aspirated, one-stage inlet manifold, n/a	
Type, position, make, and designation of mixture preparation	1 carburetor, SU		2 carburetor, SU	
Energy source, type, make, and designation of ignition system	Battery, breaker, Lucas		Battery, breaker, Lucas	
Make of alternator, voltage, earthing	DC dynamo, 6 V, positive		DC dynamo, 6 V, positive	
Engine coolant, drive, regulation of cooling	Liquid, gravitation, n/a		Liquid, gravitation, n/a	
Type of clutch, number of gears in manual box, synchronized gears	Single-plate dry clutch, 3, none		Single-plate dry clutch, 4, none	
Gear ratios in manual box	Unknown		Unknown	
Make, type, ratio of overdrive	n/a		n/a	
Type of clutch, number of gears, make and model of automatic box	n/a		n/a	
Gear ratios in automatic gearbox	n/a		n/a	
Driven axle, type of diff, traction control	Rear, spiral bevel, n/a		Rear, spiral bevel, n/a	
Axle ratios	4.77 : 1		4.89 : 1	
Type of chassis	Separate chassis		Separate chassis	
Suspension, springing front	Live axle, half-elliptic leaf springs		Live axle, half-elliptic leaf springs	
Suspension, springing rear	Live axle, half-elliptic leaf springs		Live axle, half-elliptic leaf springs	
Reduction of roll	n/a		n/a	
Type of shock absorbers	n/a		n/a	
Type and dimensions of wheels	Steel spokes, painted, unknown		Steel spokes, painted, unknown	
Type, dimensions, make of tires	Dunlop, unknown		Dunlop, unknown	
Type of braking front	Drums, unknown		Drums, unknown	
Type of braking rear	Outboard drums, unknown		Outboard drums, unknown	
Braking mechanism, number of circuits, servo assistance, electronic aids	Hydraulics, 1 circuit, n/a		Hydraulics, 1 circuit, n/a	
Steering gear, make and model of power steering	Worm, n/a		Worm, n/a	

Swallow

Make, range	**Early SS Two**	**Late SS Two**		
Type	*Coupe*	*Coupe 10 (12) HP*	*Sedan 10 (12*) HP*	*Tourer 10 (12) HP*
Public debut	9/10/1931	10/1933	10/1933	3/1934
End of production	9/1933	1934	1936	1935
Production figure 549 154 905 184				
First, last chassis number RHD	As Standard 9 HP	300001-301250	300001-301250	300001-301250
First, last chassis number LHD	n/a	n/a	n/a	n/a
Body type	Steel panels on wooden frame, 2 doors, 2 seats	Steel panels on wooden frame, 2 doors, 4 seats		
Weather protection, top mechanism	Enclosed-drive, manually operated sunroof	Enclosed-drive, manually operated sunroof (tourer manually operated top)		
Length, width, height (mm)	3658 x 1373 x 1372	4166 x 1422 x 1372		
Length, width, height (inches)	144 x 54 x 54	164 x 56 x 54		
Wheelbase, front, rear track (mm)	2286 x 1122/1122	2642 x 1181/1181		
Wheelbase, front, rear track (inches)	90 x 44/44	104 x 46 1/2		
Ground clearance, turning circle, curb weight	180mm, 11m, 800kg	180mm, 11m, 1000kg		
Max speed, acceleration 0-60 mph	95kph, n/a	100kph, n/a (12 HP 105kph, 50)		
Max power, standard, revs	28 SAE-HP/4000	32 (12 HP 38) SAE-HP/4000 (10 or 12 HP with twin carb unknown)		
Max torque, revs	Unknown	Unknown		
Engine type, position, number and configuration of cylinders	Four-stroke gasoline, front longitudinally, 4 cylinders straight	Four-stroke gasoline, front longitudinally, 4 cylinders straight		
Bore x Stroke (mm), capacity (cc), compression ratio	60.25 x 88, 1004cc, 6 : 1	63.5 x 106, 1343cc (12 HP 69.5 x, 106, 1608cc), 6 : 1		
Designation of engine and cylinder head	Engine and head "Standard Little 9 HP"	Engine and head "Standard 10 (12) HP"		
Engine block and cylinder head material, number of main bearings, type of liners	Block and head cast chrome-iron, 2 main bearings, n/a	Block and head cast chrome-iron, 3 main bearings, n/a		
Number of valves per cylinder, configuration, valve gearing, timing variants	2 side valves, directly, 1 side camshaft, sprocket, fixed	2 side valves, directly, 1 side camshaft, sprocket, fixed		
Air supply, type of inlet manifold, air tempering	Normally aspirated, one-stage inlet manifold, n/a	Normally aspirated, one-stage inlet manifold, n/a		
Type, position, make, and designation of mixture preparation	1 carburetor Stromberg	1 (from 10/34 optional 2) horizontal carb. RAG T-Type		
Energy source, type, make, and designation of ignition system	Battery, breaker, Lucas	Battery, breaker, Lucas		
Make of alternator, voltage, earthing	DC dynamo, 12 V, positive	DC dynamo, 12 V, positive		
Engine coolant, drive, regulation of cooling	Liquid, gravitation, n/a	Liquid, gravitation, n/a		
Type of clutch, number of gears in manual box, synchronized gears	Single-plate dry clutch, 3, none	Single-plate dry clutch, 4, 2–4		
Gear ratios in manual box	3.6, 2.11, 1.37, 1, unknown : 1	3.6, 2.11, 1.37, 1, unknown (from 10/34 3.81, 2.45, 1.39, 1, unknown) : 1		
Make, type, ratio of overdrive	n/a	n/a		
Type of clutch, number of gears, make and model of automatic box	n/a	n/a		
Gear ratios in automatic gearbox	n/a	n/a		
Driven axle, type of diff, traction control	Rear, spiral bevel, n/a	Rear, spiral bevel, n/a		
Axle ratios	5.25 : 1	5.43 (from 1935 5.25, 12 HP 5.5, from 1935 5.25) : 1		
Type of chassis	Separate boxed-in chassis	Separate boxed-in chassis		
Suspension, springing front	Live axle, half-elliptic leaf springs	Live axle, half-elliptic leaf springs		
Suspension, springing rear	Live axle, half-elliptic leaf springs	Live axle, half-elliptic leaf springs		
Reduction of roll	n/a	n/a		
Type of shock absorbers	n/a	Friction, manually adjustable		
Type and dimensions of wheels	Steel spokes, painted, unknown	Steel spokes, painted, unknown		
Type, dimensions, make of tires	Dunlop, 27 x 4.75 (from 10/32 balloon 4.75 x 18)	Dunlop, balloon 4.75 x 18		
Type of braking front	Drums with two leading shoes	Drums with two leading shoes		
Type of braking rear	Outboard drums with two leading shoes	Outboard drums with two leading shoes		
Braking mechanism, number of circuits, servo assistance, electronic aids	Cable, n/a	Cable, n/a		
Steering gear, make and model of power steering	Cam and lever, n/a	Cam and lever, n/a		

*1935: 2 vans for work use

SS

Make, range	**Early SS One**		**Revised SS One**		
Type	*Coupe 16 HP*	*Coupe 20 HP*	*Coupe 16 HP*	*Coupe 20 HP*	*Tourer 16 (20) HP*
Public debut	9/10/1931	15/10/1931	30/9/1932	30/9/1932	3/1933
End of production	12/7/1932	22/6/1932	25/9/1933	7/8/1933	12/7/1933
Production figure	434*	61	933	165*	114 (31)
First, last chassis number RHD	135001-135502	135021-135487	135503-136752	135598-136735	135988-136734
First, last chassis number LHD	n/a	n/a	n/a	n/a	n/a
Body type	Steel panels on wooden frame, 2 doors, 2 + 2 seats		Steel panels on wooden frame, 2 doors, 4 seats		
Weather protection, top mechanism	Enclosed-drive, manually operated sunroof		Enclosed-drive, manually operated sunroof (tourer manually operated top)		
Length, width, height (mm)	4420 x 1524 x 1397		4724 x 1613 x 1397		
Length, width, height (inches)	174 x 60 x 55		186 x 63 1/2/55		
Wheelbase, front, rear track (mm)	2845 x 1245/1245		3023 x 1295/1295		
Wheelbase, front, rear track (inches)	112 x 49/49		119 x 51/51		
Ground clearance, turning circle, curb weight	200mm, 12m, 1100kg		200mm, 12m, 1300kg		
Max speed, acceleration 0-60 mph	110kph, 32 sec (20 HP 120kph, 30 sec)		120kph, 28 sec (20 HP 130kph, 22 sec)		
Max power, standard, revs	45 (20 HP 55) SAE-HP/3800		48 (20 HP 62) SAE-HP/3600		
Max torque, revs	Unknown		Unknown		
Engine type, position, number and configuration of cylinders	Four-stroke gasoline, front longitudinally, 6 cylinders straight		Four-stroke gasoline, front longitudinally, 6 cylinders straight		
Bore x Stroke (mm), capacity (cc), compression ratio	65.5 x 101.6, 2054 (20 HP 73 x 101.6, 2552) cc, 5.8 : 1		65.5 x 101.6, 2054 (20 HP 73 x 101.6, 2552) cc, 6 : 1		
Designation of engine and cylinder head	Engine and head "Standard 16 (20) HP"		Engine and head "Standard 16 (20) HP"		
Engine block and cylinder head material, number of main bearings, type of liners	Block and head cast chrome-iron, 7 main bearings, n/a		Block cast chrome-iron, head aluminum, 7 main bearings, n/a		
Number of valves per cylinder, configuration, valve gearing, timing variants	2 side valves, directly, 1 side camshaft, sprocket, fixed		2 side valves, directly, 1 side camshaft, sprocket, fixed		
Air supply, type of inlet manifold, air tempering	Normally aspirated, one-stage inlet manifold, n/a		Normally aspirated, one-stage inlet manifold, n/a		
Type, position, make, and designation of mixture preparation	1 horizontal carb., RAG M-Type		1 horizontal carb., RAG M-Type		
Energy source, type, make, and designation of ignition system	Battery, breaker, Lucas		Battery, breaker, Lucas		
Make of alternator, voltage, earthing	DC dynamo, 12 V, positive		DC dynamo, 12 V, positive		
Engine coolant, drive, regulation of cooling	Liquid, gravitation, n/a		Liquid, gravitation, n/a		
Type of clutch, number of gears in manual box, synchronized gears	Single-plate dry clutch, 4, none		Single-plate dry clutch, 4, none		
Gear ratios in manual box	3.455, 2.09, 1.32, 1, unknown : 1		3.455, 2.09, 1.32, 1, unknown : 1		
Make, type, ratio of overdrive	n/a		n/a		
Type of clutch, number of gears, make and model of automatic box	n/a		n/a		
Gear ratios in automatic gearbox	n/a		n/a		
Driven axle, type of diff, traction control	Rear, spiral bevel, n/a	Rear, spiral bevel, n/a			
Axle ratios	4.66 : 1		4.66 : 1		
Type of chassis	Separate boxed-in chassis		Separate boxed-in chassis		
Suspension, springing front	Live axle, half-elliptic leaf springs		Live axle, half-elliptic leaf springs		
Suspension, springing rear	Live axle, half-elliptic leaf springs		Live axle, half-elliptic leaf springs		
Reduction of roll	n/a		n/a		
Type of shock absorbers	n/a		Friction, manually adjustable		
Type and dimensions of wheels	Steel spokes, painted, unknown		Steel spokes, painted, unknown		
Type, dimensions, make of tires	Dunlop, 28 x 5.50		Dunlop, balloon 5.50 x 18		
Type of braking front	Drums with two leading shoes		Drums with two leading shoes		
Type of braking rear	Outboard drums with two leading shoes		Outboard drums with two leading shoes		
Braking mechanism, number of circuits, servo assistance, electronic aids	Cable, n/a		Cable (Bendix), n/a		
Steering gear, make and model of power steering	Cam and lever, n/a		Cam and lever, n/a		

* Each plus two chassis without body

Make, range	Late enclosed-drive SS One			Late open SS One		
Type	*Coupe 16 (20) HP*	*Sedan 16 (20) HP*	*Airline 16 (20) HP*	*Tourer 16 (20**) HP*	*DHC 16 (20) HP*	*SS 90 20 HP*
Public debut	1/1934	10/1933	9/1934	1/1934	19/3/1935	22/3/1935
End of production	9/1934	2/1936	7/1936	7/1935	10/1935	5/1935
Production figure	209	1144*	624	401	100	24
First, last chassis number RHD	247001-249500	247001-249500	248291-249500	247001-249500	248559-249500	248436, 249476-249498
First, last chassis number LHD	n/a	n/a	n/a	n/a	n/a	n/a
Body type	Steel panels on wooden frame, 2 doors, 4 seats			Steel panels on wooden frame, 2 doors, 4 (SS 90 2) seats		
Weather protection, top mechanism	Enclosed-drive, manually operated sunroof			Manually operated top		
Length, width, height (mm)	4724 x 1664 x 1397 (Airline 4670 x 1664 x 1435)			4724 x 1664 x 1397 (SS 90 3810 x 1600 x 1372)		
Length, width, height (inches)	186 x 65 1/2 x 55 (Airline 184 x 65 1/2 x 56 1/2)			186 x 65 1/2 x 55 (SS 90 150 x 63 x 54)		
Wheelbase, front, rear track (mm)	3023 x 1346/1359			3023 (SS 90 2642) x 1346/1359		
Wheelbase, front, rear track (inches)	119 x 53/53 1/2			119 (SS 90 194) x 53/53 1/2		
Ground clearance, turning circle, curb weight	200 (Airline 170)mm, 12m, 1300kg (Airline 1500kg)			200mm, 12m, 1300kg (SS 90 150mm, 11m, 1150kg)		
Max speed, acceleration 0-60 mph	120kph, 29 sec (20 HP 130kph, 21 sec)			120kph, 29 sec (20 HP 130kph, 21 sec, SS 90 140kph, 17 sec)		
Max power, standard, revs	53 SAE-HP/3600 (twin carb 62 SAE-HP/4000, 20 HP, tourer)			Coupe (20 HP 68 SAE-HP/3600, 20 HP twin carb 70 SAE-HP/4000)		
Max torque, revs	Unknown			Unknown		
Engine type, position, number and configuration of cylinders	Four-stroke gasoline, front longitudinally, 6 cylinders straight			Four-stroke gasoline, front longitudinally, 6 cylinders straight		
Bore x Stroke (mm), capacity (cc), compression ratio	65.5 x 106, 2143 (20 HP 73 x 106, 2663) cc, 6.2 (twin carb 7) : 1			65.5 x 106, 2143 (20 HP 73 x 106, 2663) cc, 6.2 (twin carb 7) : 1		
Designation of engine and cylinder head	Engine and head "Standard 16 (20) HP"			Engine and head "Standard 16 (20) HP"		
Engine block and cylinder head material, number of main bearings, type of liners	Block cast chrome-iron, head aluminum, 7 main bearings, n/a			Block cast chrome-iron, head aluminum, 7 main bearings, n/a		
Number of valves per cylinder, configuration, valve gearing, timing variants	2 side valves, directly, 1 side camshaft, sprocket, fixed			2 side valves, directly, 1 side camshaft, sprocket, fixed		
Air supply, type of inlet manifold, air tempering	Normally aspirated, one-stage inlet manifold, n/a			Normally aspirated, one-stage inlet manifold, n/a		
Type, position, make, and designation of mixture preparation	1 (from 10/34 optional 2) horizontal carb., RAG M-Type			1 (from 10/34 optional, SS 90 always 2) horizontal carb., RAG M-Type		
Energy source, type, make, and designation of ignition system	Battery, breaker, Lucas			Battery, breaker, Lucas		
Make of alternator, voltage, earthing	DC dynamo, 12 V, positive			DC dynamo, 12 V, positive		
Engine coolant, drive, regulation of cooling	Liquid, gravitation, n/a			Liquid, gravitation, n/a		
Type of clutch, number of gears in manual box, synchronized gears	Single-plate dry clutch, 4, 2–4			Single-plate dry clutch, 4, 2–4		
Gear ratios in manual box	3.455, 2.09, 1.32, 1, unknown (from 10/34 3.94, 2.42, 1.45, 1, unknown) : 1			3.455, 2.09, 1.32, 1, unknown (from 10/34 3.94, 2.42, 1.45, 1, unknown) : 1		
Make, type, ratio of overdrive	n/a			n/a		
Type of clutch, number of gears, make and model of automatic box	n/a			n/a		
Gear ratios in automatic gearbox	n/a			n/a		
Driven axle, type of diff, traction control	Rear, spiral bevel, n/a			Rear, spiral bevel, n/a		
Axle ratios	4.75 (from 1935 4.5, 20 HP from 1935 4.25) : 1			4.75 (from 1935 4.5, 20 HP, from 1935 4.25, SS 90 4.25, SS 90 optional 3.75) : 1		
Type of chassis	Separate boxed-in chassis			Separate boxed-in chassis		
Suspension, springing front	Live axle, half-elliptic leaf springs			Live axle, half-elliptic leaf springs		
Suspension, springing rear	Live axle, half-elliptic leaf springs			Live axle, half-elliptic leaf springs		
Reduction of roll	n/a			n/a		
Type of shock absorbers	Friction, manually adjustable			Friction, manually adjustable		
Type and dimensions of wheels	Steel spokes, painted, unknown			Steel spokes, painted, unknown		
Type, dimensions, make of tires	Dunlop, balloon 5.50 x 18			Dunlop, balloon 5.50 x 18		
Type of braking front	Drums with two leading shoes			Drums with two leading shoes		
Type of braking rear	Outboard drums with two leading shoes			Outboard drums with two leading shoes		
Braking mechanism, number of circuits, servo assistance, electronic aids	Cable, n/a			Cable, n/a		
Steering gear, make and model of power steering	Cam and lever, n/a			Cam and lever, n/a		
	* Plus one chassis 20 HP without body			** Incl. 1 or 2 close-coupled with Roadster body		

Make, range	**Early SS Jaguar 1.5-Liter**		**Late SS Jaguar 1.5-Liter**	
Type	*Sedan '36*	*Sedan '37*	*Sedan (S.E.)*	*DHC (DHC S.E.)*
Public debut	6/10/1935	10/1936	10/1937 (10/1939)	10/1937 (10/1939)
End of production	1936	3/1938	1940	10/1939
Production figure	2250		4408	677
First, last chassis number RHD	20001-22250		50001-53754, 70001-688	56001-56660, 70001-70688
First, last chassis number LHD	n/a	n/a	n/a	n/a
Body type	Steel panels on wooden frame, 4 doors, 4 seats		All-steel, 4 doors (DHC doors and rear steel panels on wooden frame, 2 doors), 4 seats	
Weather protection, top mechanism	Enclosed-drive, manually operated sunroof		Enclosed-drive, manually operated steel sunroof (DHC manually operated top)	
Length, width, height (mm)	4242 x 1562 x 1524		4394 x 1664 x 1524	
Length, width, height (inches)	167 x 61 1/2 x 60		173 x 65 1/2 x 60	
Wheelbase, front, rear track (mm)	2743 x 1219/1219		2858 x 1321/1397	
Wheelbase, front, rear track (inches)	108 x 48/48		112 1/2 x 52/55	
Ground clearance, turning circle, curb weight	180mm, 12m, 1100kg		180mm, 12m, 1350kg	
Max speed, acceleration 0-60 mph	110kph, 40 (Sedan '37 33) sec		120kph, 25 sec	
Max power, standard, revs	40 SAE-HP/4000 (Sedan '37 52 SAE-HP/unknown)		65 SAE-HP/4600	
Max torque, revs	Unknown		130 Nm/2500	
Engine type, position, number and configuration of cylinders	Four-stroke gasoline, front longitudinally, 4 cylinders straight		Four-stroke gasoline, front longitudinally, 4 cylinders straight	
Bore x Stroke (mm), capacity (cc), compression ratio	69.5 x 106, 1608cc, 6 (Sedan '37 7) : 1		73 x 106, 1776cc, 7.2 (from 10/39 optional 7.6) : 1	
Designation of engine and cylinder head	Engine and head "Standard 14 HP"		Engine "Standard 1.5-Liter," head "Weslake"	
Engine block and cylinder head material, number of main bearings, type of liners	Block cast chrome-iron, head aluminum, 3 main bearings, n/a		Block and head cast chrome-iron, 5 main bearings, n/a	
Number of valves per cylinder, configuration, valve gearing, timing variants	2 side valves, directly, 1 side camshaft, sprocket, fixed		2 overhead valves, pushrod/rocker, 1 side camshaft, sprocket, fixed	
Air supply, type of inlet manifold, air tempering	Normally aspirated, one-stage inlet manifold, n/a		Normally aspirated, one-stage inlet manifold, n/a	
Type, position, make, and designation of mixture preparation	1 horizontal carb., Solex 35 FIL (Sedan '37 35 FI, from 10/37 35 HBFD)		1 horizontal carb., SU 35 HBFD	
Energy source, type, make, and designation of ignition system	Battery, breaker, Lucas		Battery, breaker, Lucas	
Make of alternator, voltage, earthing	DC dynamo, 12 V, positive		DC dynamo, 12 V, positive	
Engine coolant, drive, regulation of cooling	Liquid, gravitation, n/a		Liquid, pump, thermostat	
Type of clutch, number of gears in manual box, synchronized gears	Single-plate dry clutch, 4, 2–4		Single-plate dry clutch, 4, 2–4	
Gear ratios in manual box	3.81, 2.45, 1.39, 1, unknown : 1		3.81, 2.45, 1.39, 1, unknown : 1	
Make, type, ratio of overdrive	n/a		n/a	
Type of clutch, number of gears, make and model of automatic box	n/a		n/a	
Gear ratios in automatic gearbox	n/a		n/a	
Driven axle, type of diff, traction control	Rear, spiral bevel, n/a		Rear, hypoid bevel, n/a	
Axle ratios	4.86 : 1		4.86 : 1	
Type of chassis	Separate boxed-in chassis		Separate boxed-in chassis	
Suspension, springing front	Live axle, half-elliptic leaf springs		Live axle, half-elliptic leaf springs	
Suspension, springing rear	Live axle, half-elliptic leaf springs		Live axle, half-elliptic leaf springs	
Reduction of roll	n/a		n/a	
Type of shock absorbers	Lever		Lever	
Type and dimensions of wheels	Steel spokes, painted, unknown		Steel spokes, painted, unknown	
Type, dimensions, make of tires	Dunlop, balloon 4.75 x 18		Dunlop, balloon 5.25 x 18	
Type of braking front	Drums with two leading shoes		Drums with two leading shoes	
Type of braking rear	Outboard drums with two leading shoes		Outboard drums with two leading shoes	
Braking mechanism, number of circuits, servo assistance, electronic aids	Rods, n/a		Rods, n/a	
Steering gear, make and model of power steering	Cam and lever, n/a		Cam and lever, n/a	

SS

Make, range	**Early SS Jaguar 2.5-Liter**		**Late SS Jaguar 2.5-Liter**	
Type	*Sedan*	*Tourer*	*Sedan*	*DHC*
Public debut	21/9/1935	24/9/1935	10/1937	10/1937
End of production	1937	1936	1940	1939
Production figure	3444	105	1579	279
First, last chassis number RHD	10001-13445	19001-105	40001-41450, 80001-80135	46001-46273, 80001-80135
First, last chassis number LHD	n/a	n/a	n/a	n/a
Body type	Steel panels on wooden frame, 4 (tourer 2) doors, 4 seats		All-steel, 4 doors (DHC doors and rear steel panels on wooden frame, 2 doors), 4 seats	
Weather protection, top mechanism	Enclosed-drive, manually operated sunroof (tourer manually operated top)		Enclosed-drive, manually operated steel sunroof (DHC manually operated top)	
Length, width, height (mm)	4521 x 1702 x 1549		4724 x 1676 x 1549	
Length, width, height (inches)	178 x 67 x 61		186 x 66 x 61	
Wheelbase, front, rear track (mm)	3023 x 1372/1422		3023 x 1372/1422	
Wheelbase, front, rear track (inches)	119 x 54/56		119 x 54/56	
Ground clearance, turning circle, curb weight	180mm, 12m, 1600kg		180mm, 12m, 1650kg	
Max speed, acceleration 0-60 mph	140kph, 17 sec		140kph, 17 sec	
Max power, standard, revs	102, from 10/36 104 SAE-HP/4600		105 SAE-HP/4600, with low compression 102 SAE-HP/4600	
Max torque, revs	181 Nm/2500		181 Nm/2500	
Engine type, position, number and configuration of cylinders	Four-stroke gasoline, front longitudinally, 6 cylinders straight		Four-stroke gasoline, front longitudinally, 6 cylinders straight	
Bore x Stroke (mm), capacity (cc), compression ratio	73 x 106, 2663cc, 6.4 (from 10/36 6.8) : 1		73 x 106, 2663cc, 7.6 (from 10/39 optional 6.9) : 1	
Designation of engine and cylinder head	Engine "Standard 2.5-Liter," head "Weslake"		Engine "Standard 2.5-Liter," head "Weslake"	
Engine block and cylinder head material, number of main bearings, type of liners	Block and head cast chrome-iron, 7 main bearings, n/a		Block and head cast chrome-iron, 7 main bearings, n/a	
Number of valves per cylinder, configuration, valve gearing, timing variants	2 overhead valves, pushrod/rocker, 1 side camshaft, sprocket, fixed		2 overhead valves, pushrod/rocker, 1 side camshaft, sprocket, fixed	
Air supply, type of inlet manifold, air tempering	Normally aspirated, one-stage inlet manifold, n/a		Normally aspirated, one-stage inlet manifold, n/a	
Type, position, make, and designation of mixture preparation	2 horizontal carb., SU H3		2 horizontal carb., SU H3	
Energy source, type, make, and designation of ignition system	Battery, breaker, Lucas		Battery, breaker, Lucas	
Make of alternator, voltage, earthing	DC dynamo, 12 V, positive		DC dynamo, 12 V, positive	
Engine coolant, drive, regulation of cooling	Liquid, pump, thermostat		Liquid, pump, thermostat	
Type of clutch, number of gears in manual box, synchronized gears	Single-plate dry clutch, 4, 2–4		Single-plate dry clutch, 4, 2–4	
Gear ratios in manual box	3.94, 2.42, 1.45, 1, unknown : 1		3.94, 2.42, 1.45, 1, unknown : 1	
Make, type, ratio of overdrive	n/a		n/a	
Type of clutch, number of gears, make and model of automatic box	n/a		n/a	
Gear ratios in automatic gearbox	n/a		n/a	
Driven axle, type of diff, traction control	Rear, spiral bevel, n/a		Rear, hypoid bevel, n/a	
Axle ratios	4.25 (from 10/36 4.5) : 1		4.5 : 1	
Type of chassis	Separate boxed-in chassis		Separate boxed-in chassis	
Suspension, springing front	Live axle, half-elliptic leaf springs		Live axle, half-elliptic leaf springs	
Suspension, springing rear	Live axle, half-elliptic leaf springs		Live axle, half-elliptic leaf springs	
Reduction of roll	n/a		n/a	
Type of shock absorbers	Lever		Lever	
Type and dimensions of wheels	Steel spokes, painted, unknown		Steel spokes, painted, unknown	
Type, dimensions, make of tires	Dunlop, balloon 5.50 x 18		Dunlop, balloon 5.50 x 18	
Type of braking front	Drums with two leading shoes		Drums with two leading shoes	
Type of braking rear	Outboard drums with two leading shoes		Outboard drums with two leading shoes	
Braking mechanism, number of circuits, servo assistance, electronic aids	Rods, n/a		Rods, n/a	
Steering gear, make and model of power steering	Cam and lever, n/a		Cam and lever, n/a	

Make, range	**SS Jaguar 100**			**SS Jaguar 3.5-Liter**	
Type	*2.5-Liter Roadster*	*3.5-Liter Roadster*	*3.5-Liter Coupe*	*Sedan*	*DHC*
Public debut	24/9/1935	10/1937	10/1938	10/1937	10/1937
End of production	1940	1940	10/1938	1940	1939
Production figure	191	117	1	1067	241
First, last chassis number RHD	18001-18126, 49001-49065	39001-39118	39088	30001-31003, 90001-90068	36001-36238, 90001-90068
First, last chassis number LHD	n/a	n/a	n/a	n/a	n/a
Body type	Steel panels on wooden frame, 2 doors, 2 seats			All-steel, 4 doors (DHC doors and rear steel panels on wooden frame, 2 doors), 4 seats	
Weather protection, top mechanism	Manually operated top (coupe enclosed-drive)			Enclosed-drive, manually operated steel sunroof (DHC manually operated top)	
Length, width, height (mm)	3810 x 1600 x 1372			4724 x 1676 x 1549	
Length, width, height (inches)	150 x 63 x 54			186 x 66 x 61	
Wheelbase, front, rear track (mm)	2642 x 1372/1422			3023 x 1372/1422	
Wheelbase, front, rear track (inches)	104 x 54/56			119 x 54/56	
Ground clearance, turning circle, curb weight	140mm, 11m, 1150kg			180mm, 12m, 1650kg	
Max speed, acceleration 0-60 mph	155kph, 12 sec (3.5-Liter 165kph, 11 sec)			150kph, 14 sec	
Max power, standard, revs	102 (from 10/36 104, 10/37 105, 10/39 optional 102 SAE-HP/4600, 3.5-Liter 125 SAE-HP/4250)			125 SAE-HP/4250	
Max torque, revs	181 Nm/2500 (3.5-Liter 247 Nm/2000)			247 Nm/2000	
Engine type, position, number and configuration of cylinders	Four-stroke gasoline, front longitudinally, 6 cylinders straight			Four-stroke gasoline, front longitudinally, 6 cylinders straight	
Bore x Stroke (mm), capacity (cc), compression ratio	73 x 106, 2663cc (3.5-Liter 82 x 110, 3485cc), 6.4 (from 10/36 6.8*) : 1			82 x 110, 3485cc, 7.2 (from 10/39 optional 6.6) : 1	
Designation of engine and cylinder head	Engine "Standard 2.5- (3.5) Liter," head "Weslake"			Engine "Standard 3.5-Liter," head "Weslake"	
Engine block and cylinder head material, number of main bearings, type of liners	Block and head cast chrome-iron, 7 main bearings, n/a			Block and head cast chrome-iron, 7 main bearings, n/a	
Number of valves per cylinder, configuration, valve gearing, timing variants	2 overhead valves, pushrod/rocker, 1 side camshaft, sprocket, fixed			2 overhead valves, pushrod/rocker, 1 side camshaft, sprocket, fixed	
Air supply, type of inlet manifold, air tempering	Normally aspirated, one-stage inlet manifold, n/a			Normally aspirated, one-stage inlet manifold, n/a	
Type, position, make, and designation of mixture preparation	2 horizontal carb., SU H3 (3.5-Liter H4)			2 horizontal carb., SU H4	
Energy source, type, make, and designation of ignition system	Battery, breaker, Lucas			Battery, breaker, Lucas	
Make of alternator, voltage, earthing	DC dynamo, 12 V, positive			DC dynamo, 12 V, positive	
Engine coolant, drive, regulation of cooling	Liquid, pump, thermostat			Liquid, pump, thermostat	
Type of clutch, number of gears in manual box, synchronized gears	Single-plate dry clutch, 4, 2–4			Single-plate dry clutch, 4, 2–4	
Gear ratios in manual box	3.94, 2.42, 1.45, 1, unknown (3.5-Liter 3.165, 1.86, 1.205, 1, unknown) : 1			3.165, 1.86, 1.205, 1, unknown : 1	
Make, type, ratio of overdrive	n/a			n/a	
Type of clutch, number of gears, make and model of automatic box	n/a			n/a	
Gear ratios in automatic gearbox	n/a			n/a	
Driven axle, type of diff, traction control	Rear, spiral bevel, n/a			Rear, hypoid bevel, n/a	
Axle ratios	4.25 (from 10/36 4.5, 3.5-Liter 4.25) : 1			4.25 : 1	
Type of chassis	Separate boxed-in chassis			Separate boxed-in chassis	
Suspension, springing front	Live axle, half-elliptic leaf springs			Live axle, half-elliptic leaf springs	
Suspension, springing rear	Live axle, half-elliptic leaf springs			Live axle, half-elliptic leaf springs	
Reduction of roll	n/a			n/a	
Type of shock absorbers	Lever, at front also manually adjustable friction			Lever	
Type and dimensions of wheels	Steel spokes, painted, unknown			Steel spokes, painted, unknown	
Type, dimensions, make of tires	Dunlop, balloon 5.50 x 18			Dunlop, balloon 5.50 x 18	
Type of braking front	Drums with two leading shoes			Drums with two leading shoes	
Type of braking rear	Outboard drums with two leading shoes			Outboard drums with two leading shoes	
Braking mechanism, number of circuits, servo assistance, electronic aids	Rods (Girling), n/a			Rods (Girling), n/a	
Steering gear, make and model of power steering	Cam and lever, n/a			Cam and lever, n/a	

* From 10/37 7.6, from 10/39 optional 6.9 (SS 100 3.5-Liter as Jaguar 3.5-Liter)

SS

Make, range	**Jaguar Mark IV 1.5-Liter**		**Jaguar 2.5- and 3.5-Liter**		
Type	*1.5-Liter Sedan*	*1.5-Liter Sedan S.E.*	*2.5-Liter Sedan (DHC)*	*3.5-Liter Sedan*	*3.5-Liter DHC*
Public debut	21/9/1945	21/9/1945	21/9/1945 (12/1947)	21/9/1945	12/1947
End of production	3/1949	3/1949	3/1949 (12/1948)	3/1949	9/1948
Production figure	5761		1749 (101)	3860	498
First, last chassis number RHD	410001-415450		510001-511682*	610001-613606	617001-617184
First, last chassis number LHD	430001-430311		530001-530075*	630001-630254	637001-637376
Body type	All-steel, 4 doors, 4 seats		All-steel, 4 doors (DHC doors and rear steel panels on wooden frame, 2 seats), 4 seats		
Weather protection, top mechanism	Enclosed-drive, manually operated steel sunroof		Enclosed-drive, manually operated steel sunroof (DHC manually operated top)		
Length, width, height (mm)	4394 x 1664 x 1524		4724 x 1676 x 1549		
Length, width, height (inches)	173 x 65 1/2 x 60		186 x 66 x 61		
Wheelbase, front, rear track (mm)	2858 x 1321/1397		3023 x 1372/1422		
Wheelbase, front, rear track (inches)	112 1/2 x 52/55		119 x 54/56		
Ground clearance, turning circle, curb weight	180mm, 12m, 1350kg		180mm, 12m, 1650kg		
Max speed, acceleration 0-60 mph	120kph, 25 sec		140kph, 17 sec (3.5-Liter 150kph, 14 sec)		
Max power, standard, revs	65 SAE-HP/4600		105 SAE-HP/4600 (6.9 : 1 102/4600, 3.5-Liter 125 or 120 SAE-HP/4250)		
Max torque, revs	130 Nm/2500		181 Nm/2500 (3.5-Liter 247 Nm/2000)		
Engine type, position, number and configuration of cylinders	Four-stroke gasoline, front longitudinally, 4 cylinders straight		Four-stroke gasoline, front longitudinally, 6 cylinders straight		
Bore x Stroke (mm), capacity (cc), compression ratio	73 x 106, 1776cc, 7.2 (optional 7.6) : 1		73x106, 2663, 7.6, optional 6.9 : 1 (3 1/2 L. 82 x 110, 3485cc, 7.2, optional 6.6 : 1)		
Designation of engine and cylinder head	Engine "Standard 1.5-Liter." head "Weslake"		Engine "Standard 2.5- (3.5) Liter," head "Weslake"		
Engine block and cylinder head material, number of main bearings, type of liners	Block and head cast chrome-iron, 5 main bearings, n/a		Block and head cast chrome-iron, 7 main bearings, n/a		
Number of valves per cylinder, configuration, valve gearing, timing variants	2 overhead valves, pushrod/rocker, 1 side camshaft, sprocket, fixed		2 overhead valves, pushrod/rocker, 1 side camshaft, sprocket, fixed		
Air supply, type of inlet manifold, air tempering	Normally aspirated, one-stage inlet manifold, n/a		Normally aspirated, one-stage inlet manifold, n/a		
Type, position, make, and designation of mixture preparation	1 horizontal carb., SU		2 horizontal carb., SU H3 (3.5-Liter H4)		
Energy source, type, make, and designation of ignition system	Battery, breaker, Lucas		Battery, breaker, Lucas		
Make of alternator, voltage, earthing	DC dynamo, 12 V, positive		DC dynamo, 12 V, positive		
Engine coolant, drive, regulation of cooling	Liquid, pump, thermostat		Liquid, pump, thermostat		
Type of clutch, number of gears in manual box, synchronized gears	Single-plate dry clutch, 4, 2–4		Single-plate dry clutch, 4, 2–4		
Gear ratios in manual box	3.81, 2.45, 1.39, 1, unknown : 1		3.94, 2.42, 1.45, 1, unknown (3.5-Liter 3.165, 1.86, 1.205, 1, unknown) : 1		
Make, type, ratio of overdrive	n/a		n/a		
Type of clutch, number of gears, make and model of automatic box	n/a		n/a		
Gear ratios in automatic gearbox	n/a		n/a		
Driven axle, type of diff, traction control	Rear, hypoid bevel, n/a		Rear, hypoid bevel, n/a		
Axle ratios	4.875 : 1		4.55 (3.5- Liter 4.27) : 1		
Type of chassis	Separate boxed-in chassis		Separate boxed-in chassis		
Suspension, springing front	Live axle, half-elliptic leaf springs		Live axle, half-elliptic leaf springs		
Suspension, springing rear	Live axle, half-elliptic leaf springs		Live axle, half-elliptic leaf springs		
Reduction of roll	n/a		n/a		
Type of shock absorbers	Lever		Lever		
Type and dimensions of wheels	Steel spokes, painted, unknown		Steel spokes, painted, unknown		
Type, dimensions, make of tires	Dunlop, balloon 5.25 x 18		Dunlop, balloon 5.50 x 18		
Type of braking front	Drums with two leading shoes		Drums with two leading shoes		
Type of braking rear	Outboard drums with two leading shoes		Outboard drums with two leading shoes		
Braking mechanism, number of circuits, servo assistance, electronic aids	Rods, n/a		Rods, n/a		
Steering gear, make and model of power steering	Cam and lever, n/a		Cam and lever, n/a		

* DHC 517001-517073 and (LHD) 537001-537031

Mk IV

Make, range	**Jaguar Mark V 2.5-Liter**		**Jaguar Mark V 3.5-Liter**	
Type	*2.5-Liter Sedan*	*2.5-Liter DHC*	*3.5-Liter Sedan**	*3.5-Liter DHC*
Public debut	1/10/1948	9/1949	1/10/1948	9/1949
End of production	12/1950	5/1950	12/1950	6/1951
Production figure	1674	29	7828	971
First, last chassis number RHD	520001-521481	540001-540017	620001-625926	640001-640395
First, last chassis number LHD	527001-527190	547001-547012	627001-628905	647001-647577
Body type	All-steel, 4 doors (DHC-doors and rear steel panels on wooden frame, 2 doors), 4 seats		All-steel, 4 doors (DHC-doors and rear steel panels on wooden frame, 2 doors), 4 seats	
Weather protection, top mechanism	Enclosed-drive, manually operated steel sunroof (DHC manually operated top)		Enclosed-drive, manually operated steel sunroof (DHC manually operated top)	
Length, width, height (mm)	4750 x 1753 x 1588		4750 x 1753 x 1588	
Length, width, height (inches)	187 x 69 x 62 1/2		187 x 69 x 62 1/2	
Wheelbase, front, rear track (mm)	3048 x 1422/1460		3048 x 1422/1460	
Wheelbase, front, rear track (inches)	120 x 56/57 1/2		120 x 56 57 1/2	
Ground clearance, turning circle, curb weight	190mm, 12m, 1700kg		190mm, 12m, 1700kg	
Max speed, acceleration 0-60 mph	140kph, 18 sec		150kph, 15 sec	
Max power, standard, revs	102 SAE-HP/4600		120 SAE-HP/4250	
Max torque, revs	181 Nm/2500		247 Nm/2000	
Engine type, position, number and configuration of cylinders	Four-stroke gasoline, front longitudinally, 6 cylinders straight		Four-stroke gasoline, front longitudinally, 6 cylinders straight	
Bore x Stroke (mm), capacity (cc), compression ratio	73 x 106, 2663cc, 7.3 : 1		82 x 110, 3485cc, 6.75 : 1	
Designation of engine and cylinder head	Engine "Standard 2.5-Liter," head "Weslake"		Engine "Standard 3.5-Liter," head "Weslake"	
Engine block and cylinder head material, number of main bearings, type of liners	Block and head cast chrome-iron, 7 main bearings, n/a		Block and head cast chrome-iron, 7 main bearings, n/a	
Number of valves per cylinder, configuration, valve gearing, timing variants	2 overhead valves, pushrod/rocker, 1 side camshaft, sprocket, fixed		2 overhead valves, pushrod/rocker, 1 side camshaft, sprocket, fixed	
Air supply, type of inlet manifold, air tempering	Normally aspirated, one-stage inlet manifold, n/a		Normally aspirated, one-stage inlet manifold, n/a	
Type, position, make, and designation of mixture preparation	2 horizontal carb., SU H3		2 horizontal carb., SU H4	
Energy source, type, make, and designation of ignition system	Battery, breaker, Lucas		Battery, breaker, Lucas	
Make of alternator, voltage, earthing	DC dynamo, 12 V, positive		DC dynamo, 12 V, positive	
Engine coolant, drive, regulation of cooling	Liquid, pump, thermostat		Liquid, pump, thermostat	
Type of clutch, number of gears in manual box, synchronized gears	Single-plate dry clutch, 4, 2–4		Single-plate dry clutch, 4, 2–4	
Gear ratios in manual box	3.375, 1.98, 1.365, 1, unknown : 1		3.375, 1.98, 1.365, 1, unknown : 1	
Make, type, ratio of overdrive	n/a		n/a	
Type of clutch, number of gears, make and model of automatic box	n/a		n/a	
Gear ratios in automatic gearbox	n/a		n/a	
Driven axle, type of diff, traction control	Rear, hypoid bevel, n/a		Rear, hypoid bevel, n/a	
Axle ratios	4.55 : 1		4.3, later 4.27 : 1	
Type of chassis	Separate boxed-in chassis		Separate boxed-in chassis	
Suspension, springing front	Double-wishbone, torsion bars		Double-wishbone, torsion bars	
Suspension, springing rear	Live axle, half-elliptic leaf springs		Live axle, half-elliptic leaf springs	
Reduction of roll	Torsion bar front		Torsion bar front	
Type of shock absorbers	Telescopic, rear lever		Telescopic, rear lever	
Type and dimensions of wheels	Steel discs, painted, 5 J x 16		Steel discs, painted, 5 J x 16	
Type, dimensions, make of tires	Dunlop Super Comfort, super-balloon 6.70 x 16		Dunlop Super Comfort, super-balloon 6.70 x 16	
Type of braking front	Drums with two leading shoes		Drums with two leading shoes	
Type of braking rear	Outboard drums with two leading shoes		Outboard Drums with two leading shoes	
Braking mechanism, number of circuits, servo assistance, electronic aids	Hydraulics, 1 circuit, n/a		Hydraulics, 1 circuit, n/a	
Steering gear, make and model of power steering	Recirculating ball, n/a		Recirculating ball, n/a	

* 2 "Mark VI" with XK 120 engine

Mk V

Make, range	**Jaguar Mark VII**		**Jaguar Mark VIII and IX**	
Type	*Sedan**	*Sedan M*	*Mark VIII Sedan*	*Mark IX Sedan****
Public debut	17/10/1950	15/10/1954	11/10/1956	8/10/1958
End of production	9/1954	7/1957	12/1958	9/1961
Production figure	20,937	10,060	6427	10,012
First, last chassis number RHD	710001-722754	722755-729999**	760001-764644	770001-775984
First, last chassis number LHD	730001-738183	738184-740200	780001-781688	790001-794021
Body type	All-steel, 4 doors, 5 seats		All-steel, 4 doors, 5 seats	
Weather protection, top mechanism	Enclosed-drive, manually operated steel sunroof		Enclosed-drive, manually operated steel sunroof	
Length, width, height (mm)	4991 x 1854 x 1600		4991 x 1854 x 1600	
Length, width, height (inches)	196 1/2 x 73 x 63		1961/2 x 73 x 63	
Wheelbase, front, rear track (mm)	3048 x 1422/1460		3048 x 1422/1460	
Wheelbase, front, rear track (inches)	120 x 56 x 57 1/2		120 x 56 x 57 1/2	
Ground clearance, turning circle, curb weight	190mm, 12m, 1750kg		190mm, 12m, 1800kg	
Max speed, acceleration 0-60 mph	164kph, 14 sec (with C-head and VII M 170kph, 12 sec)		172kph, 12 sec (Mark IX 183kph, 11 sec)	
Max power, standard, revs	160 SAE-HP/5200 (with C-head 210 SAE-HP/5750,VII M 190 SAE-HP/5500)		210 SAE-HP/5500 (Mark IX 220 SAE-HP/5500)	
Max torque, revs	265 Nm/2500 (with C-head 294 Nm/2500, VII M 282 Nm/2500)		294 Nm/3000 (Mark IX 328 Nm/3000)	
Engine type, position, number and configuration of cylinders	Four-stroke gasoline, front longitudinally, 6 cylinders straight		Four-stroke gasoline, front longitudinally, 6 cylinders straight	
Bore x Stroke (mm), capacity (cc), compression ratio	83 x 106, 3442cc, 8 (optional 7, with C-head 9) : 1		83 x 106, 3442cc (Mark IX 87 x 106, 3781cc), 8 (optional 7 or 9) : 1	
Designation of engine and cylinder head	Engine "XK", head "A" (from 4/53 optional "C-Type")		Engine "XK," head "B" hellblaugrün (Mark IX blaumetallic) painted	
Engine block and cylinder head material, number of main bearings, type of liners	Block cast chrome-iron, head aluminum, 7 main bearings, n/a		Block cast chrome-iron, head aluminum, 7 main bearings, n/a (Mark IX: dry liners)	
Number of valves per cylinder, configuration, valve gearing, timing variants	2 overhead valves, bucket tappets, 2 overhead camshafts, 2 duplex-chains, fixed		2 overhead valves, bucket tappets, 2 overhead camshafts, 2 duplex-chains, fixed	
Air supply, type of inlet manifold, air tempering	Normally aspirated, one-stage inlet manifold, n/a		Normally aspirated, one-stage inlet manifold, n/a	
Type, position, make, and designation of mixture preparation	2 horizontal carb., SU H6		2 horizontal carb., SU HD6	
Energy source, type, make, and designation of ignition system	Battery, breaker, Lucas		Battery, breaker, Lucas	
Make of alternator, voltage, earthing	DC dynamo, 12 V, positive		DC dynamo, 12 V, positive	
Engine coolant, drive, regulation of cooling	Liquid, pump, thermostat		Liquid, pump, thermostat	
Type of clutch, number of gears in manual box, synchronized gears	Single-plate dry clutch, 4, 2–4		Single-plate dry clutch, 4, 2–4	
Gear ratios in manual box	3.375, 1.98, 1.365, 1, unknown (optional 2.98, 1.75, 1.21, 1, unknown) : 1		3.375, 1.98, 1.365, 1, unknown (optional 2.98, 1.75, 1.21, 1, unknown) : 1	
Make, type, ratio of overdrive	From 1/54 optional, Laycock-de Normanville, electrically, 0.78 : 1		Optional, Laycock-de Normanville, electrically, 0.78 : 1	
Type of clutch, number of gears, make and model of automatic box	From 3/53 optional hydraulic torque converter, 3, Borg-Warner DG		Optional hydraulic torque converter, 3, Borg-Warner DG	
Gear ratios in automatic gearbox	2.31, 1.44, 1, 2 : 1		2.31, 1.44, 1, 2 : 1	
Driven axle, type of diff, traction control	Rear, hypoid bevel, n/a		Rear, hypoid bevel, n/a	
Axle ratios	4.27 (with overdrive 4.55) : 1		4.27 (with overdrive 4.55) : 1	
Type of chassis	Separate boxed-in chassis		Separate boxed-in chassis	
Suspension, springing front	Double-wishbone, torsion bars		Double-wishbone, torsion bars	
Suspension, springing rear	Live axle, half-elliptic leaf springs		Live axle, half-elliptic leaf springs	
Reduction of roll	Torsion bar front		Torsion bar front	
Type of shock absorbers	Telescopic, rear lever (from 1953 telescopic)		Telescopic	
Type and dimensions of wheels	Steel discs, painted, 5 (from 1952 5.5) J x 16		Steel discs, painted, 5.5 J x 16	
Type, dimensions, make of tires	Dunlop Super Comfort, super-balloon 6.70 x 16		Dunlop Super Comfort, super-balloon 6.70 x 16	
Type of braking front	Drums with two trailing shoes		Drums with two trailing shoes (Mark IX massive discs)	
Type of braking rear	Outboard drums with one leading shoe		Outboard drums with one leading shoe (Mark IX massive outboard discs)	
Braking mechanism, number of circuits, servo assistance, electronic aids	Hydraulics, 1 circuit, vacuum servo assistance, n/a		Hydraulics, 1 circuit, vacuum servo assistance, n/a	
Steering gear, make and model of power steering	Recirculating ball, n/a		Recirculating ball, optional (Mark IX always) hydraulics servo Burman	

* Plus two prototype convertibles, which have been scrapped

** Further chassis numbers 750001-750898

*** 27 "MK VIII B" without servo-assisted steering, but with separation

Mk VII / VIII / IX

Make, range	**Jaguar XK 120**			**Jaguar XK 120 S.E. or M**		
Type	*OTS**	*FHC*	*DHC*	*OTS*	*FHC*	*DHC*
Public debut	22/10/1948	8/3/1951	4/1953	8/3/1951	8/3/1951	4/1953
End of production	8/1954	7/1954	8/1954	9/1954	9/1954 9/1954	
Production figure	240 aluminum +5120**	1867	1024	2253	811	743
First, last chassis number RHD	660001-661176***	669001-669195	667001-667295	S660733-S661176	S669001-S669195	S667001-S667295
First, last chassis number LHD	670001-676438***	679001-681485	677001-678472	S671205-S676438	S679001-S681485	S677001-S678472
Body type	Aluminum panels on wooden frame (from 4/50 as S.E.), 2 doors, 2 seats			All-steel, doors, hood and trunklid aluminum, 2 doors, 2 seats		
Weather protection, hood mechanism	Manually operated top (FHC enclosed-drive)			Manually operated top (FHC enclosed-drive)		
Length, width, height (mm)	4420 x 1574 x 1332 (FHC 4420 x 1574 x 1359)			4420 x 1574 x 1332 (FHC 4420 x 1574 x 1359)		
Length, width, height (inches)	174 x 62 x 52 (FHC 174 x 62 x 53 1/2)			174 x 62 x 52 (FHC 174 x 62 x 53 1/2)		
Wheelbase, front, rear track (mm)	2591 x 1295/1295			2591 x 1295/1295		
Wheelbase, front, rear track (inches)	102 x 51/51			102 x 51/51		
Ground clearance, turning circle, curb weight	140mm, 10m, 1300kg			140mm, 10m, 1300kg		
Max speed, acceleration 0-60 mph	192kph, 10 sec			200kph, 10 sec, (with C-head 202kph, 9 sec)		
Max power, standard, revs	160 SAE-HP/5000			180 SAE-HP/5300 (from 1954 190 SAE-HP/5500, with C-head 210 SAE-HP/5750)		
Max torque, revs	265 Nm/2500			284 Nm/2500 (272/2500, with C-head 294/2500)		
Engine type, position, number and configuration of cylinders	Four-stroke gasoline, front longitudinally, 6 cylinders straight			Four-stroke gasoline, front longitudinally, 6 cylinders straight		
Bore x Stroke (mm), capacity (cc), compression ratio	83 x 106, 3442cc, 8 (optional 7 or 9) : 1			83 x 106, 3442cc, 8 (optional 7 or, with C-head always 9) : 1		
Designation of engine and cylinder head	Engine "XK," head "A"			Engine "XK," head "A" (from 4/54 optional "C-Type")		
Engine block and cylinder head material, number of main bearings, type of liners	Block cast chrome-iron, head aluminum, 7 main bearings, n/a			Block cast chrome-iron, head aluminum, 7 main bearings, n/a		
Number of valves per cylinder, configuration, valve gearing, timing variants	2 overhead valves, bucket tappets, 2 overhead camshafts, 2 duplex chains, fixed			2 overhead valves, bucket tappets, 2 overhead camshafts, 2 duplex chains, fixed		
Air supply, type of inlet manifold, air tempering	Normally aspirated, one-stage inlet manifold, n/a			Normally aspirated, one-stage inlet manifold, n/a		
Type, position, make, and designation of mixture preparation	2 horizontal carb., SU H6 (occasionally H8)			2 horizontal carb., SU H6 (occasionally H8)		
Energy source, type, make, and designation of ignition system	Battery, breaker, Lucas			Battery, breaker, Lucas		
Make of alternator, voltage, earthing	DC dynamo, 12 V, positive			DC dynamo, 12 V, positive		
Engine coolant, drive, regulation of cooling	Liquid, pump, thermostat			Liquid, pump, thermostat		
Type of clutch, number of gears in manual box, synchronized gears	Single-plate dry clutch, 4, 2–4			Single-plate dry clutch, 4, 2–4		
Gear ratios in manual box	3.375, 1.98, 1.365, 1, unknown (optional 2.98, 1.75, 1.21, 1, unknown) : 1			3.375, 1.98, 1.365, 1, unknown (optional 2.98, 1.75, 1.21, 1, unknown) : 1		
Make, type, ratio of overdrive	n/a			n/a		
Type of clutch, number of gears, make and model of automatic box	n/a			n/a		
Gear ratios in automatic gearbox	n/a			n/a		
Driven axle, type of diff, traction control	Rear, hypoid bevel, n/a			Rear, hypoid bevel, n/a		
Axle ratios	3.64, from 3/53 3.54 : 1 (optional until 3/52 3.27, 3.92, 4.3 or 4.56, from 11/51 optional 2.93, 3.31, 3.77, 4.09 or 4.27 : 1			3.64, from 3/53 3.54 : 1 (optional until 3/52 3.27, 3.92, 4.3 or 4.56, from 11/51 optional 2.93, 3.31, 3.77, 4.09 or 4.27 : 1)		
Type of chassis	Separate boxed-in chassis			Separate boxed-in chassis		
Suspension, springing front	Double-wishbone, torsion bars			Double-wishbone, torsion bars		
Suspension, springing rear	Live axle, half-elliptic leaf springs			Live axle, half-elliptic leaf springs		
Reduction of roll	Torsion bar front			Torsion bar front		
Type of shock absorbers	Telescopic, rear lever (from 1953 telescopic)			Telescopic, rear lever (from 1953 telescopic)		
Type and dimensions of wheels	Steel discs, painted, (from'51 optional steel spokes) 5 (from '52 5.5) J x 16			Steel spokes, painted, 5 (from 1952 5.5) J x 16		
Type, dimensions, make of tires	Dunlop Super Comfort, super-balloon 6.00 x 16			Dunlop Super Comfort, super-balloon 6.00 x 16		
Type of braking front	Drums with two leading shoes			Drums with two leading shoes		
Type of braking rear	Outboard drums with two (from 1/50 one) leading shoes			Outboard drums with one leading shoe		
Braking mechanism, number of circuits, servo assistance, electronic aids	Hydraulics, 1 circuit, n/a			Hydraulics, 1 circuit, n/a		
Steering gear, make and model of power steering	Recirculating ball, n/a			Recirculating ball, n/a		

* 1948: 1 XK 100 chassis no. 470001, 4 cyl., 80.5x98=1995cc, 105 SAE at 5000/min, compression ratio 7:1, 3 main bearings, combined gear and axle ratios 13.79/8.1/5.59/4.09 : 1

** 6 supplied as chassis without bodies

*** All-steel from 660059 and 670185, 670172 also has all-steel body

XK 120

Make, range	Jaguar XK 140			Jaguar XK 140 S.E. or M		
Type	*OTS*	*FHC*	*DHC*	*OTS S.E.*	*FHC S.E.*	*DHC S.E.*
Public debut	15/10/1954	15/10/1954	15/10/1954	15/10/1954	15/10/1954	15/10/1954
End of production	1/1957	1/1957	1/1957	1/1957	1/1957	1/1957
Production figure	3356*	2809*	2791	2808		
First, last chassis number RHD	800001-800074	804001-804843	807001-807480	S800001-S800074**	S804001-S804843**	S807001-S807480**
First, last chassis number LHD	810001-813282	814001-815964	817001-819311	S810001-S813282**	S814001-S815964**	S817001-S819311**
Body type	All-steel (FHC and DHC doors, hood and trunklid aluminum -7/56), 2 doors, 2 (FHC 2 + 2) seats			All-steel (FHC and DHC doors, hood and trunklid aluminum -7/56), 2 doors, 2 (FHC 2 + 2) seats		
Weather protection, top mechanism	Manually operated top (FHC enclosed-drive)			Manually operated top (FHC enclosed-drive)		
Length, width, height (mm)	4470 x 1638 x 1358 (FHC 4470 x 1638 x 1397)			4470 x 1638 x 1358 (FHC 4470 x 1638 x 1397)		
Length, width, height (inches)	176 x 64 1/2 x 53 1/2 (FHC 176 x 64 1/2 x 55)			176 x 64 1/2 x 53 1/2 (FHC 176 x 64 1/2 x 55)		
Wheelbase, front, rear track (mm)	2591 x 1299/1299			2591 x 1299/1299		
Wheelbase, front, rear track (inches)	102 x 51/51			102 x 51/51		
Ground clearance, turning circle, curb weight	140mm, 10m, 1350kg			140mm, 10m, 1350kg		
Max speed, acceleration 0-60 mph	200kph, 10 sec			202kph, 9 sec		
Max power, standard, revs	190 SAE-HP/5500			210 SAE-HP/5750		
Max torque, revs	282 Nm/2500			285 Nm/2500		
Engine type, position, number and configuration of cylinders	Four-stroke gasoline, front longitudinally, 6 cylinders straight			Four-stroke gasoline, front longitudinally, 6 cylinders straight		
Bore x Stroke (mm), capacity (cc), compression ratio	83 x 106, 3442cc, 8 (optional 7 or 9) : 1			83 x 106, 3442cc, 8 (optional 7 or, with C-head always 9) : 1		
Designation of engine and cylinder head	Engine "XK," head "A"			Engine "XK," head "A" (optional "C-Type" rot painted)		
Engine block and cylinder head material, number of main bearings, type of liners	Block cast chrome-iron, head aluminum, 7 main bearings, n/a			Block cast chrome-iron, head aluminum, 7 main bearings, n/a		
Number of valves per cylinder, configuration, valve gearing, timing variants	2 overhead valves, bucket tappets, 2 overhead camshafts, 2 duplex chains, fixed			2 overhead valves, bucket tappets, 2 overhead camshafts, 2 duplex chains, fixed		
Air supply, type of inlet manifold, air tempering	Normally aspirated, one-stage inlet manifold, n/a			Normally aspirated, one-stage inlet manifold, n/a		
Type, position, make, and designation of mixture preparation	2 horizontal carb. SU H6 (occasionally H8)			2 horizontal carb. SU H6 (occasionally H8)		
Energy source, type, make, and designation of ignition system	Battery, breaker, Lucas			Battery, breaker, Lucas		
Make of alternator, voltage, earthing	DC dynamo, 12 V, positive			DC dynamo, 12 V, positive		
Engine coolant, drive, regulation of cooling	Liquid, pump, thermostat			Liquid, pump, thermostat		
Type of clutch, number of gears in manual box, synchronized gears	Single-plate dry clutch, 4, 2–4			Single-plate dry clutch, 4, 2–4		
Gear ratios in manual box	3.375, 1.98, 1.365, 1, unknown (optional 2.98, 1.75, 1.21, 1, unknown) : 1			3.375, 1.98, 1.365, 1, unknown (optional 2.98, 1.75, 1.21, 1, unknown) : 1		
Make, type, ratio of overdrive	Optional, Laycock-de Normanville, electrically, 0.78 : 1			Optional, Laycock-de Normanville, electrically, 0.78 : 1		
Type of clutch, number of gears, make and model of automatic box	FHC and DHC from 1956 optional hydraulic torque converter, 3, Borg-Warner DG			FHC and DHC from 1956 optional hydraulic torque converter , 3, Borg-Warner DG		
Gear ratios in automatic gearbox	2.31, 1.44, 1, 2 : 1			2.31, 1.44, 1, 2 : 1		
Driven axle, type of diff, traction control	Rear, hypoid bevel, n/a			Rear, hypoid bevel, n/a		
Axle ratios	3.54 (with overdrive 4.09; optional 4.27 or 3.31) : 1			3.54 (with overdrive 4.09; optional 4.27 or 3.31) : 1		
Type of chassis	Separate boxed-in chassis			Separate boxed-in chassis		
Suspension, springing front	Double-wishbone, torsion bars			Double-wishbone, torsion bars		
Suspension, springing rear	Live axle, half-elliptic leaf springs			Live axle, half-elliptic leaf springs		
Reduction of roll	Torsion bar front			Torsion bar front		
Type of shock absorbers	Telescopic			Telescopic		
Type and dimensions of wheels	Steel discs, painted (optional steel spokes), 5.5 J x 16			Steel spokes, painted, 5.5 J x 16		
Type, dimensions, make of tires	Dunlop Super Comfort, super-balloon 6.00 x 16			Dunlop Super Comfort, super-balloon 6.00 x 16		
Type of braking front	Drums with two leading shoes			Drums with two leading shoes		
Type of braking rear	Outboard drums with two leading shoes			Outboard drums with two leading shoes		
Braking mechanism, number of circuits, servo assistance, electronic aids	Hydraulics, 1 circuit, n/a			Hydraulics, 1 circuit, n/a		
Steering gear, make and model of power steering	Rack and pinion, n/a			Rack and pinion, n/a		

* Two OTS and eight FHC supplied as chassis without bodies

** S.E. without C-head have "A" instead of "S" prefix

XK 140

Make, range	**Jaguar XK 150 3.4**			**Jaguar XK 150 3.8**		
Type	*3.4 OTS and S.E. (S)*	*3.4 FHC and S.E. (S)*	*3.4 DHC and S.E. (S)*	*3.8 OTS (S)*	*3.8 FHC (S)*	*3.8 DHC (S)*
Public debut	3/1958	22/5/1957, (3/1958)	22/5/1957, (3/1958)	10/1958	10/1958	10/1958
End of production	11/1960 (10/1960)	5/1961 (10/1961)	3/1961 (10/1960)	10/1960	10/1961	10/1960
Production figure	1300* (S 888)	3457* (S 199)	1893 (S 104)	42 (S 36) 656 (S 150)	586 (S 89) First, last chassis number RHD	
	S820001-820093**	S824001-825369**	S827001-827663**	S820001-820093**	S824001-825369**	S827001-827663**
First, last chassis number LHD	S830001-832174**	S834001-836999**, ***	S837001-839010**	S830001-832174**	S834001-836999**, ***	S837001-839010**
Body type	All-steel (hood and trunklid aluminum), 2 doors 2 (FHC 2 + 2) seats			All-steel (hood and trunklid aluminum), 2 doors, 2 (FHC 2 + 2) seats		
Weather protection, top mechanism	Manually operated top (FHC enclosed-drive)			Manually operated top (FHC enclosed-drive)		
Length, width, height (mm)	4496 x 1638 x 1372 (FHC 4496 x 1638 x 1397)			4496 x 1638 x 1372 (FHC 4496 x 1638 x 1397)		
Length, width, height (inches)	177 x 64 1/2 x 54 (FHC 177 x 64 1/2 x 55)			177 x 64 1/2 x 54 (FHC 177 x 64 1/2 x 55)		
Wheelbase, front, rear track (mm)	2591 x 1311/1311			2591 x 1311/1311		
Wheelbase, front, rear track (inches)	102 x 51 1/2/51 1/2			102 x 51 1/2/51 1/2		
Ground clearance, turning circle, curb weight	140mm, 10m, 1400kg			140mm, 10m, 1400kg		
Max speed, acceleration 0-60 mph	200kph, 10 sec (S.E. 202kph, 9 sec, S 215kph, 8 sec)			202kph, 9 sec (S 215kph, 8 sec)		
Max power, standard, revs	190 SAE-HP/5500 (S.E. 210 SAE-HP/5750, S 250 SAE-HP/5500)			220 SAE-HP/5500 (S 265 SAE-HP/5500)		
Max torque, revs	282 Nm/2500 (S.E. 289 Nm/3000, S 314 Nm/4500)			314 Nm/3000 (3.8 S 348 Nm/4000)		
Engine type, position, number and configuration of cylinders	Four-stroke gasoline, front longitudinally, 6 cylinders straight			Four-stroke gasoline, front longitudinally, 6 cylinders straight		
Bore x Stroke (mm), capacity (cc), compression ratio	83 x 106, 3442cc, 8 (optional 7 or 9, S 8, optional 9) : 1			87 x 106, 3781cc, 8 (optional 7 or 9, S only 9) : 1		
Designation of engine and cylinder head	Engine "XK," head "B" light blue green painted (S orange)			Wie 3.4 (head "B" blue metallic painted, S "Straight Port" orange painted)		
Engine block and cylinder head material, number of main bearings, type of liners	Block cast chrome-iron, head aluminum, 7 main bearings, n/a			Block cast chrome-iron, head aluminum, 7 main bearings, dry liners		
Number of valves per cylinder, configuration, valve gearing, timing variants	2 overhead valves, bucket tappets, 2 overhead camshafts, 2 duplex chains, fixed			2 overhead valves, bucket tappets, 2 overhead camshafts, 2 duplex chains, fixed		
Air supply, type of inlet manifold, air tempering	Normally aspirated, one-stage inlet manifold, n/a			Normally aspirated, one-stage inlet manifold, n/a		
Type, position, make, and designation of mixture preparation	2 (S 3) horizontal carb. SU HD6 (S HD8)			2 (S 3) horizontal carb. SU HD6 (S HD8)		
Energy source, type, make, and designation of ignition system	Battery, breaker, Lucas			Battery, breaker, Lucas		
Make of alternator, voltage, earthing	DC dynamo, 12 V, positive			DC dynamo, 12 V, positive		
Engine coolant, drive, regulation of cooling	Liquid, pump, thermostat			Liquid, pump, thermostat		
Type of clutch, number of gears in manual box, synchronized gears	Single-plate dry clutch, 4, 2–4			Single-plate dry clutch, 4, 2–4		
Gear ratios in manual box	3.375, 1.98, 1.365, 1, unknown (optional 2.98, 1.75, 1.21, 1, unknown) : 1			3.375, 1.98, 1.365, 1, unknown (optional 2.98, 1.75, 1.21, 1, unknown) : 1		
Make, type, ratio of overdrive	Optional (S always), Laycock-de Normanville, electrically, 0.78 : 1			Optional (S always), Laycock-de Normanville, electrically, 0.78 : 1		
Type of clutch, number of gears, make and model of automatic box	Optional (except S) hydraulic torque converter, 3, Borg-Warner DG			Optional (except S) hydraulic torque converter, 3, Borg-Warner DG		
Gear ratios in automatic gearbox	2.31, 1.44, 1, 2 : 1			2.31, 1.44, 1, 2 : 1		
Driven axle, type of diff, traction control	Rear, hypoid bevel, n/a (S limited-slip)			Rear, hypoid bevel, n/a (S limited-slip)		
Axle ratios	3.54 (with overdrive 4.09, optional 3.31 or 4.27) : 1			3.54 (with overdrive 4.09, optional 3.31 or 4.27) : 1		
Type of chassis	Separate boxed-in chassis			Separate boxed-in chassis		
Suspension, springing front	Double-wishbone, torsion bars			Double-wishbone, torsion bars		
Suspension, springing rear	Live axle, half-elliptic leaf springs			Live axle, half-elliptic leaf springs		
Reduction of roll	Torsion bar front			Torsion bar front		
Type of shock absorbers	Telescopic			Telescopic		
Type and dimensions of wheels	Steel discs, painted, optional steel spokes, 5.5 J x 16			Steel discs, painted, optional steel spokes, 5.5 J x 16		
Type, dimensions, make of tires	Dunlop RS3 (from 1958 RS4), super-balloon 6.00 x 16			Dunlop RS3 (from 1958 RS4), super-balloon 6.00 x 16		
Type of braking front	Drums with two leading shoes, (optional, from 210 HP always massive discs)			Massive discs		
Type of braking rear	Outboard Drums with two leading shoes (a.W, from 210 HP stets massive outboard discs)			Massive outboard discs		
Braking mechanism, number of circuits, servo assistance, electronic aids	Hydraulics, 1 circuit, vacuum servo assistance, n/a			Hydraulics, 1 circuit, vacuum servo assistance, n/a		
Steering gear, make and model of power steering	Rack and pinion, n/a			Rack and pinion, n/a		

* Eight OTS and ten FHC supplied as chassis without bodies
** With 190 HP no "S," late S have "T" instead of "S" prefixes
*** Further chassis numbers 847000 to 847095

XK 150

Make, range	**Jaguar XK 120 C**		**Jaguar XK 120 C**	
Type	*1951**	*1952*	*1953*	*C/D-Prototype or XKC 054*
Public debut	26/6/1951	5/1952	5/1953	1953
End of production	8/1953	5/1952	5/1953	1953
Production figure	49	1	3	1 (scrapped)
First, last chassis number RHD	XKC 001-010 and 012-050	XKC 011	XKC 051-053	XKC 201
First, last chassis number LHD	n/a	n/a	n/a	n/a
Body type	Aluminum pop-riveted, 1 or 2 doors, 2 seats		Aluminum riveted, 1 door, 2 seats	
Weather protection, hood mechanism	n/a	n/a		
Length, width, height (mm)	3988 x 1638 x 1080 (1952 4242 x 1638 x 1080)		3988 x 1638 x 1080 (C/D 3912 x 1610 x 1080)	
Length, width, height (inches)	157 x 64 1/2 x 42 1/2 (1952 167 x 64 1/2 x 42 1/2)		157 x 64 1/2 x 42 1/2 (C/D 154 x 63 1/2 x 42 1/2)	
Wheelbase, front, rear track (mm)	2438 x 1295/1295		2438 x 1295/1295	
Wheelbase, front, rear track (inches)	96 x 51/51		96 x 51/51	
Ground clearance, turning circle, curb weight	140mm, 10m, 950 (1952 940) kg		140mm, 10m, 880kg	
Max speed, acceleration 0-60 mph	232kph, 8 sec (1952 245kph, 8 sec)		245kph, 8 sec (C/D 286kph, 8 sec)	
Max power, standard, revs	200 SAE-HP/5500 (1952 210 SAE-HP/5800)		220 SAE-HP/5200 (C/D 246 SAE-HP/6000)	
Max torque, revs	314 Nm/unknown (1952 unknown)		Unknown	
Engine type, position, number and configuration of cylinders	Four-stroke gasoline, front longitudinally, 6 cylinders straight		Four-stroke gasoline, front longitudinally, 6 cylinders straight	
Bore x Stroke (mm), capacity (cc), compression ratio	83 x 106, 3442cc, 8 (1952 9) : 1		83 x 106, 3442cc, 9 : 1	
Designation of engine and cylinder head	Engine "XK," head "C-Type"		Engine "XK," head "C-Type"	
Engine block and cylinder head material, number of main bearings, type of liners	Block cast chrome-iron, head aluminum, 7 main bearings, n/a		Block cast chrome-iron, head aluminum, 7 main bearings, n/a	
Number of valves per cylinder, configuration, valve gearing, timing variants	2 overhead valves, bucket tappets, 2 overhead camshafts, 2 duplex chains, fixed		2 overhead valves, bucket tappets, 2 overhead camshafts, 2 duplex chains, fixed	
Air supply, type of inlet manifold, air tempering	Normally aspirated, one-stage inlet manifold, n/a		Normally aspirated, one-stage inlet manifold, n/a	
Type, position, make, and designation of mixture preparation	2 horizontal carb., SU H8		3 horizontal twin carb., Weber 40 DCOE	
Energy source, type, make, and designation of ignition system	Battery, breaker, Lucas		Battery, breaker, Lucas	
Make of alternator, voltage, earthing	DC dynamo, 12 V, positive		DC dynamo, 12 V, positive	
Engine coolant, drive, regulation of cooling	Liquid, pump, thermostat		Liquid, pump, thermostat	
Type of clutch, number of gears in manual box, synchronized gears	Single-plate dry clutch, 4, 2–4		Three-plate dry clutch, 4, 2–4	
Gear ratios in manual box	2.98, 1.75, 1.21, 1, unknown : 1		2.98, 1.75, 1.21, 1, unknown : 1	
Make, type, ratio of overdrive	n/a		n/a	
Type of clutch, number of gears, make and model of automatic box	n/a		n/a	
Gear ratios in automatic gearbox	n/a		n/a	
Driven axle, type of diff, traction control	Rear, hypoid bevel, n/a		Rear, hypoid bevel, n/a	
Axle ratios	3.31 (optional 3.54, 1952 optional 4.27) : 1		3.31 (optional 3.54, or 4.27) : 1	
Type of chassis	Tubular chassis		Tubular chassis (C/D aluminum tubular front subframe welded to unitary aluminum body)	
Suspension, springing front	Double-wishbone, torsion bars		Double-wishbone, torsion bars	
Suspension, springing rear	Live axle, trailing arms, torsion bars		Live axle, trailing arms and Panhard rod, torsion bars	
Reduction of roll	Torsion bar front		Torsion bar front	
Type of shock absorbers	Lever		Lever	
Type and dimensions of wheels	Steel spokes, painted, 5.5 J x 16		Steel spokes, painted, 5.5 J x 16	
Type, dimensions, make of tires	Dunlop, balloon 6.50 x 16		Dunlop, balloon 6.50 x 16	
Type of braking front	Drums with two leading shoes (Dunlop, self-adjusting)		Massive discs	
Type of braking rear	Outboard drums with two leading shoes (Dunlop, self-adjusting)		Massive outboard discs	
Braking mechanism, number of circuits, servo assistance, electronic aids	Lockheed-Hydraulics, 1 circuit, n/a		Hydraulics, 1 circuit, Girling vacuum servo assistance, n/a	
Steering gear, make and model of power steering	Rack and pinion, n/a		Rack and pinion, n/a	

* Plus one "Brontosaurus" with enclosed wheels

XK 120 C C-Type

Make, range	**Jaguar D-Type**			**Jaguar E1A and E2A**	
Type	*1954 (1955)**	*1956*	*XK-SS*	*E1A*	*E2A***
Public debut	5/1954 (5/1955)	8/1956	21/1/1957	5/1957	25/6/1960
End of production	8/1955 (5/1955)	8/1956	2/1957	5/1957	6/1960
Production figure	6 (8)	6	(17)**	1 (scrapped)	1
First, last chassis number RHD	XKC401-406 (XKD501-575)	XKD 601-606	XKSS 701-716	Unknown	Unknown
First, last chassis number LHD	n/a	n/a	n/a	n/a	n/a
Body type	Aluminum, pop-riveted, 1 or 2 (1955 1, 1956 2) doors, 2 seats			Aluminum, pop-riveted, 2 doors, 2 seats	
Weather protection, hood mechanism	n/a (XK-SS manually operated top)			n/a	
Length, width, height (mm)	3920 (1955 3910, 1956 4110, XK-SS 3990) x 1661 x 1118			4320 x 1600 x 1100 (E2A 4320 x 1590 x 1350)	
Length, width, height (inches)	154 1/4 (1955 154, 1956 162, XK-SS 157) x 65 1/2 x 44			170 x 63 x 43 1/4 (E2A 170 x 62 1/2 x 53)	
Wheelbase, front, rear track (mm)	2286 x 1270/1270			2286 x 1270/1270 (E2A 2438 x 1220/1220)	
Wheelbase, front, rear track (inches)	90 x 50/50			90 x 50/50 (E2A 96 x 48/48)	
Ground clearance, turning circle, curb weight	140mm, 10m, 880 (XK-SS 920) kg			160mm, 12m, 850 (E2A 873) kg	
Max speed, acceleration 0-60 mph	250kph, 8 sec (1955 270kph, 8 sec, 1956 280kph, 7 sec, XK-SS 230kph, 7 sec)			200kph, 11 sec (E2A 265kph, 7 sec)	
Max power, standard, revs	250 (1955 275, 1956 285) SAE-HP/5750			120 SAE-HP/5750 (E2A 294 SAE-HP/6750)	
Max torque, revs	324 Nm/4000			193 Nm/2000 (E2A 308 Nm/6000)	
Engine type, position, number and configuration of cylinders	Four-stroke gasoline, front longitudinally, 6 cylinders straight			Four-stroke gasoline, front longitudinally, 6 cylinders straight	
Bore x Stroke (mm), capacity (cc), compression ratio	83 x 106, 3442cc, 9 : 1			83 x 76.5, 2483cc, 8 : 1 (E2A 85 x 88, 2997cc, 10 : 1)	
Designation of engine and cylinder head	Engine "XK," head-"Straight Port" (from 1955 "Wide Angle")			Engine "XK," head "B" (E2A head "Wide Angle")	
Engine block and cylinder head material, number of main bearings, type of liners	Block cast chrome-iron, head aluminum, 7 main bearings, n/a			Block cast chrome-iron, head aluminum, 7 main bearings, n/a (E2A dry liners)	
Number of valves per cylinder, configuration, valve gearing, timing variants	2 overhead valves, bucket tappets, 2 overhead camshafts, 2 duplex chains, fixed			2 overhead valves, bucket tappets, 2 overhead camshafts, 2 duplex chains, fixed	
Air supply, type of inlet manifold, air tempering	Normally aspirated, one-stage inlet manifold, n/a			Normally aspirated, one-stage inlet manifold, n/a	
Type, position, make, and designation of mixture preparation	3 horizontal twin carb., Weber 45 DCOE			2 horizontal carb., SU HD 8 (E2A mechanical injection to manifold Lucas)	
Energy source, type, make, and designation of ignition system	Battery, breaker, Lucas			Battery, breaker, Lucas	
Make of alternator, voltage, earthing	DC dynamo, 12 V, positive			DC dynamo, 12 V, positive	
Engine coolant, drive, regulation of cooling	Liquid, pump, thermostat			Liquid, pump, thermostat	
Type of clutch, number of gears in manual box, synchronized gears	Three-plate dry clutch, 4, fully			Three-plate dry clutch, 4, fully	
Gear ratios in manual box	2.98, 1.75, 1.21, 1, unknown : 1			2.98, 1.75, 1.21, 1, unknown : 1	
Make, type, ratio of overdrive	n/a			n/a	
Type of clutch, number of gears, make and model of automatic box	n/a			n/a	
Gear ratios in automatic gearbox	n/a			n/a	
Driven axle, type of diff, traction control	Rear, hypoid bevel, n/a			Rear, hypoid bevel, n/a	
Axle ratios	2.79 to 3.92 (1956 also 2.54,)			3.77 (E2A 3.31): 1	
Type of chassis	Magnesium (from 1955 steel) tubular front subframe welded to aluminum unitary body			Tubular front subframe bolted to aluminum unitary body (E1A as late D-Type)	
Suspension, springing front	Double-wishbone, torsion bars (E1A rear also)			Double-wishbone, torsion bars	
Suspension, springing rear	Live axle, trailing arms and Panhard rod, torsion bars			Transverse and trailing arms (E2A Wishbones and driveshafts, 2 coil springs each**)	
Reduction of roll	Torsion bar front			Torsion bar front, E2A also rear	
Type of shock absorbers	Telescopic			Telescopic	
Type and dimensions of wheels	Magnesium discs, painted, 5.5 J x 16			Magnesium discs, painted, 5.5 J x 16	
Type, dimensions, make of tires	Dunlop, balloon 6.00 x 16			Dunlop Stabilia, balloon 6.50 x 16	
Type of braking front	Massive discs			Massive discs	
Type of braking rear	Massive outboard discs			Massive inboard discs	
Braking mechanism, number of circuits, servo assistance, electronic aids	Hydraulics, 1 circuit, from 1955 vacuum servo assistance, n/a			Hydraulics, 1 circuit, n/a (E2A vacuum servo assistance), n/a	
Steering gear, make and model of power steering	Rack and pinion, n/a			Rack and pinion, n/a	

* XKC 405 (spare for Le Mans) possibly never completed, "Production" as 1955, but short nose and no W.A.-head, chassis nr. from XKD 509, 67 made until 1956, axle ratio 3.54 : 1

** XKD555 became XKSS701, 563 became 704, 564 became 707, 568 became 710, 569 became 713, 575 became 716, 572 became 719, 539 became 722, 562 became 725, 547 became 728, 542 became 754, 559 became 757, 557 became 760, 566 became 763, 567 became 766, 550 became 769, XKD 533 became a works-transformed XKSS but retained its chassis no.

*** Later increased to 3.8-liter capacity, Weber carburetor, 294 bhp

D-Type

Make, range	**Jaguar 2.4-Liter/3.4-Liter**		**Jaguar Mark II**		
Type	*2.4-Liter Sedan (S.E.)*	*3.4-Liter Sedan**	*Mark II 2.4*	*Mark II 3.4**	*Mark II 3.8**
Public debut	28/9/1955	26/2/1957	2/10/1959	2/10/1959	2/10/1959
End of production	28/8/1959	15/9/1959	4/7/1967	21/8/1967	22/9/1967
Production figure	19,891	17,404	25,173	28,663	30,140
First, last chassis number RHD	S900001-S916250	S970001-S978946	100001-121769**	150001-172095**	200001-209999**, ***
First, last chassis number LHD	S940001-S943742	S985001-S993460	125001-128405**	175001-181571**	210001-224758**
Body type	All-steel, 4 doors, 5 seats		All-steel, 4 doors, 5 seats		
Weather protection, hood mechanism	Enclosed-drive, optional manually operated folding sunroof		Enclosed-drive, optional manually operated folding sunroof		
Length, width, height (mm)	4591 x 1695 x 1461		4591 x 1695 x 1467		
Length, width, height (inches)	180 3/4 x 66 3/4 x 57 1/2		180 3/4 x 66 3/4 x 57 3/4		
Wheelbase, front, rear track (mm)	2727 x 1387/1273		2727 x 1397/1356		
Wheelbase, front, rear track (inches)	107 1/2 x 54 1/2/50		107 1/2 x 55/53 1/2		
Ground clearance, turning circle, curb weight	180mm, 11m, 1300 (3.4-Liter 1480) kg		180mm, 11m, 1450 (from 3.4 1500) kg		
Max speed, acceleration 0-60 mph	162kph, 14 sec (3.4-Liter 192kph, 10 sec)		155kph, 17 sec (3.4 192kph, 10 sec, 3.8 198kph, 9 sec)		
Max power, standard, revs	112 SAE-HP/5750 (3.4-Liter 210 SAE-HP/5500)		120 SAE-HP/5750 (3.4 210 SAE-HP/5500, 3.8 220 SAE-HP/5500)		
Max torque, revs	191Nm/2000 (3.4-Liter 294 Nm/3000)		196 Nm/2000 (3.4 294 Nm/3000, 3.8 328 Nm/3000)		
Engine type, position, number and configuration of cylinders	Four-stroke gasoline, front longitudinally, 6 cylinders straight		Four-stroke gasoline, front longitudinally, 6 cylinders straight		
Bore x Stroke (mm), capacity (cc), compression ratio	83 x 76.5, 2483cc (3.4-Liter 83 x 106, 3442cc), 8 (optional 7) : 1		As 2.4/3.4-Liter (optional from 1966 9 : 1, 3.8 87 x 106, 3781cc)		
Designation of engine and cylinder head	Engine "XK," head "B" (3.4-Liter head "B" painted light blue green)		Wie 2.4/3.4-Liter (3.8 head "B" painted blue metallic)		
Engine block and cylinder head material, number of main bearings, type of liners	Block cast chrome-iron, head aluminum, 7 main bearings, n/a		Block cast chrome-iron, head aluminum, 7 main bearings,n/a (3.8 dry liners)		
Number of valves per cylinder, configuration, valve gearing, timing variants	2 overhead valves, bucket tappets, 2 overhead camshafts, 2 duplex chains, fixed		2 overhead valves, bucket tappets, 2 overhead camshafts, 2 duplex chains, fixed		
Air supply, type of inlet manifold, air tempering	Normally aspirated, one-stage inlet manifold, n/a		Normally aspirated, one-stage inlet manifold, n/a		
Type, position, make, and designation of mixture preparation	2 downdraught carb., Solex B32PBI5S (3.4-Liter 2 horizontal carb., SU HD6)		2 downdraught carb., Solex B32PBI5S (from 3.4 2 horizontal carb., SU HD6)		
Energy source, type, make, and designation of ignition system	Battery, breaker, Lucas		Battery, breaker, Lucas		
Make of alternator, voltage, earthing	DC dynamo, 12 V, positive		DC dynamo (from 1965 alternator), 12 V, positive (from 1965 negative)		
Engine coolant, drive, regulation of cooling	Liquid, pump, thermostat		Liquid, pump, thermostat		
Type of clutch, number of gears in manual box, synchronized gears	Single-plate dry clutch, 4, 2–4		Single-plate dry clutch, 4, 2–4 (from 9/65 fully)		
Gear ratios in manual box	3.375, 1.98, 1.365, 1, unknown (optional 2.98, 1.75, 1.21, 1, unknown) : 1		Wie 2.4 (from 9/65 3.03, 1.97, 1.33, 1, 3.49, optional 2.68, 1.74, 1.27, 1, 3.38) : 1		
Make, type, ratio of overdrive	Optional Laycock-de Normanville, electrically, 0.78 : 1		Optional Laycock-de Normanville, electrically, 0.78 : 1		
Type of clutch, number of gears, make and model of automatic box	Ab 10/57 optional hydraulic torque converter, 3, Borg-Warner DG		Optional hydraulic torque converter, 3, Borg-Warner DG (from 1965 Borg-Warner 8)		
Gear ratios in automatic gearbox	2.31, 1.44, 1, 2 : 1		2.31, 1.44, 1, 2 : 1		
Driven axle, type of diff, traction control	Rear, hypoid bevel, n/a		Rear, hypoid bevel, n/a (3.8 limited-slip)		
Axle ratios	4.27 (with overdrive 4.55, 3.4-Liter 3.54, with overdrive 3.77) : 1		4.27 (2.4 with overdrive 4.55, 3.4 and 3.8 3.54, 3.4 and 3.8 with overdrive 3.77) : 1		
Type of chassis	Unitary with front subframe		Unitary with front subframe		
Suspension, springing front	Double-wishbone, coil springs		Double-wishbone, coil springs		
Suspension, springing rear	Live axle, cantilever leaf springs, Panhard rod		Live axle, cantilever leaf springs, Panhard rod		
Reduction of roll	Torsion bar front		Torsion bar front		
Type of shock absorbers	Telescopic		Telescopic		
Type and dimensions of wheels	Steel discs, painted 4.5 J x 15		Steel discs, painted 4.5 (from 9/60 5) J x 15		
Type, dimensions, make of tires	Dunlop Road Speed (from 2/57 RS 3, from 1958 RS 4) super-balloon 6.40 x 15		Dunlop RS 4 (from 1961 RS 5) super-balloon 6.40 x 15		
Type of braking front	Drums, (from 10/57 optional massive discs)		Massive discs		
Type of braking rear	Outboard drums (from 10/57 optional massive outboard discs)		Massive outboard discs		
Braking mechanism, number of circuits, servo assistance, electronic aids	Hydraulics, 1 circuit, vacuum servo assistance, n/a		Hydraulics, 1 circuit, vacuum servo assistance, n/a		
Steering gear, make and model of power steering	Recirculating ball, n/a		Recirculating ball, n/a (optional hydraulic servo Burman, from 1967 Adwest Varamatic)		

* S977046 1961 provided with Daimler 2.5-Liter engine; for Sweden Mark II 3.4 LWB; 1 or 2 Mark II 3.8 on works order transformed by Jones Brothers Ltd to Mark II "County" estate cars

** Prefix "P" denotes servo-assisted steering, "A" or "B" CKD for export

*** Further chassis numbers: 230000-235383

2.4/3.4

Make, range	**Daimler V-8**			**Jaguar 240 and 340**		
Type	*Daimler 2.5-Liter V-8*	*Daimler V-8 250*		*240*	*340*	*340 3.8***
Public debut	10/1962	26/9/1967		26/9/1967	26/9/1967	26/9/1967
End of production	8/6/1967	9/7/1969		11/3/1969	29/8/1968	5/1968
Production figure	12,999	4885		4446	2788	12
First, last chassis number RHD	1A 1001-13377*	1K 1001-1K 5780*	1J 1001-1J 4716*	1J 50001-1J 52265*	1J 50001-1J 52265*	
First, last chassis number LHD	1A 20001-20622*	1K 30001-1K 30105*	1J 30001-1J 30730*	1J 80001-1J 80535*	1J 80001-1J 80535*	
Body type	All-steel, 4 doors, 5 seats			All-steel, 4 doors, 5 seats		
Weather protection, hood mechanism	Enclosed-drive, optional manually operated folding sunroof			Enclosed-drive, optional manually operated folding sunroof		
Length, width, height (mm)	4591 x 1695 x 1467			4591 x 1695 x 1467		
Length, width, height (inches)	180 3/4 x 66 3/4 x 57 3/4			180 3/4 x 66 3/4 x 57 3/4		
Wheelbase, front, rear track (mm)	2727 x 1397/1356			2727 x 1397/1356		
Wheelbase, front, rear track (inches)	107 1/2 x 55/53 1/2			107 1/2 x 55/53 1/2		
Ground clearance, turning circle, curb weight	180mm, 11m, 1450kg			180mm, 11m, 1450 (from 340 1500) kg		
Max speed, acceleration 0-60 mph	176kph, 12 sec			170kph, 13 sec (340 192kph, 10 sec, 340 3.8 198kph, 9 sec)		
Max power, standard, revs	140 SAE-HP/5800			133 SAE-HP/5000 (340 210 SAE-HP/5500, 340 3.8 220 SAE-HP/5500)		
Max torque, revs	210 Nm3600			200 Nm/3700 (340 294 Nm/3000, 340 3.8 328 Nm/3000)		
Engine type, position, number and configuration of cylinders	Four-stroke gasoline, front longitudinally, 8 cylinders, 90 degree-V			Four-stroke gasoline, front longitudinally, 6 cylinders straight		
Bore x Stroke (mm), capacity (cc), compression ratio	76.2 x 69.85, 2548cc, 8.2 : 1			As Mark II (340 3.8 optional only 9 : 1)		
Designation of engine and cylinder head	Engine "Daimler V-8," head "Turner"			Engine "XK," head "Straight Port" (from 340 head "B")		
Engine block and cylinder head material, number of main bearings, type of liners	Block cast chrome-iron, head aluminum, 5 main bearings, dry liners			Block cast chrome-iron, head aluminum., 7 main bearings, n/a (3.8 dry liners)		
Number of valves per cylinder, configuration, valve gearing, timing variants	2 overhead valves, pushrod/rocker, 1 central camshaft, sprocket, fixed			2 overhead valves, bucket tappets, 2 overhead camshafts, 2 duplex chains, fixed		
Air supply, type of inlet manifold, air tempering	Normally aspirated, one-stage inlet manifold, n/a			Normally aspirated, one-stage inlet manifold, n/a		
Type, position, make, and designation of mixture preparation	2 horizontal carb., SU HD6			2 horizontal carb., SU HD6		
Energy source, type, make, and designation of ignition system	Battery, breaker, Lucas			Battery, breaker, Lucas		
Make of alternator, voltage, earthing	DC dynamo, (from 1965 alternator), 12 V, positive (from 1965 negative)			Alternator, 12 V, negative		
Engine coolant, drive, regulation of cooling	Liquid, pump, thermostat			Liquid, pump, thermostat		
Type of clutch, number of gears in manual box, synchronized gears	Single-plate dry clutch, 4, fully			Single-plate dry clutch, 4, fully		
Gear ratios in manual box	3.03, 1.97, 1.33, 1, 3.49 (optional 2.68, 1.74, 1.27, 1, 3.38) : 1			3.03, 1.97, 1.33, 1, 3.49 (optional and 240 always 2.68, 1.74, 1.27, 1, 3.38) : 1		
Make, type, ratio of overdrive	Stets, Laycock-de Normanville, electrically, 0.78 : 1			Optional, Laycock-de Normanville, electrically, 0.78 : 1		
Type of clutch, number of gears, make and model of automatic box	Optional (until 3/67 always) hydraulic torque converter , 3, Borg-Warner 35			Optional hydraulic torque converter, 3, Borg-Warner 8 (240 35)		
Gear ratios in automatic gearbox	2.4, 1.45, 1, 2: 1			2.31, 1.44, 1, 2 (240 2.4, 1.45, 1, 2) : 1		
Driven axle, type of diff, traction control	Rear, hypoid bevel, n/a			Rear, hypoid bevel, n/a (3.8 limited-slip)		
Axle ratios	4.55 (from 1/64 4.27, with overdrive 4.55) : 1			4.27 (240 with overdrive 4.55, from 340 3.54, with overdrive 3.77) : 1		
Type of chassis	Unitary with front subframe			Unitary with front subframe		
Suspension, springing front	Double-wishbone, coil springs			Double-wishbone, coil springs		
Suspension, springing rear	Live axle, cantilever leaf springs, Panhard rod			Live axle, cantilever leaf springs, Panhard rod		
Reduction of roll	Torsion bar front			Torsion bar front		
Type of shock absorbers	Telescopic			Telescopic		
Type and dimensions of wheels	Steel discs, painted, 5 J x 15			Steel discs, painted, 5 J x 15		
Type, dimensions, make of tires	Dunlop RS5, super-balloon 6.40 x 15			Dunlop RS5, super-balloon 6.40 x 15		
Type of braking front	Massive discs			Massive discs		
Type of braking rear	Massive outboard discs			Massive outboard discs		
Braking mechanism, number of circuits, servo assistance, electronic aids	Hydraulics, 1 circuit, vacuum servo assistance, n/a			Hydraulics, 1 circuit, vacuum servo assistance, n/a		
Steering gear, make and model of power steering	Recirculating ball, n/a (optional hydraulic servo Burman, from 1967 like the 240)			Recirculating ball, n/a (optional hydraulic servo Adwest Varamatic)		

* Prefix "P" denotes servo-assisted steering, "A" or "B" CKD for export

** 340 3.8 have engine number prefixes "SE" or "EE"

Mark II

Make, range	**Jaguar 3.4 and 3.8 S**		**420 and Daimler Sovereign**	
Type	*3.4 S*	*3.8 S*	*420*	*Daimler Sovereign*
Public debut	30/9/1963	30/9/1963	13/10/1966	13/10/1966
End of production	8/1968	6/1968	9/1968	9/1969
Production figure	9928	15,065	10,236	5824
First, last chassis number RHD	1B 1001-9665*	1B 50001-59717*	1F 1001-8595*	1A 30001-35476*
First, last chassis number LHD	1B 25001-26371*	1B 75001-80418*	1F 25001-27629*	1A 70001-70355*
Body type	All-steel, 4 doors, 5 seats		All-steel, 4 doors, 5 seats	
Weather protection, hood mechanism	Enclosed-drive, optional manually operated folding sunroof		Enclosed-drive, optional manually operated folding sunroof	
Length, width, height (mm)	4750 x 1683 x 1416		4763 x 1702 x 1429	
Length, width, height (inches)	187 x 66 1/4 x 55 3/4		187 1/2 x 67 x 56 1/4	
Wheelbase, front, rear track (mm)	2730 x 1403/1375		2730 x 1403/1375	
Wheelbase, front, rear track (inches)	107 1/2 x 55 1/4/54		107 1/2 x 55 1/4/54	
Ground clearance, turning circle, curb weight	180mm, 12m, 1650kg		180mm, 12m, 1650kg	
Max speed, acceleration 0-60 mph	186kph, 14 sec (3.8 S 194kph, 11 sec)		196kph, 10 sec	
Max power, standard, revs	210 (3.8 S 220) SAE-HP/5500		245 SAE-HP/5500	
Max torque, revs	294 (3.8 S 328) Nm/3000		382 Nm/3750	
Engine type, position, number and configuration of cylinders	Four-stroke gasoline, front longitudinally, 6 cylinders straight		Four-stroke gasoline, front longitudinally, 6 cylinders straight	
Bore x Stroke (mm), capacity (cc), compression ratio	83 x 106, 3442cc (3.8 87 x 106, 3781cc), 8 (optional 7 or 9) : 1		92.07 x 106, 4235cc, 8 (optional 7 or 9) : 1	
Designation of engine and cylinder head	Engine "XK," head "B" hellblaugrün (3.8 metallicblau) painted		Engine "XK," head "Straight Port"	
Engine block and cylinder head material, number of main bearings, type of liners	Block cast chrome-iron, head aluminum, 7 main bearings, n/a (3.8 dry liners)		Block cast chrome-iron, head aluminum, 7 main bearings, dry liners	
Number of valves per cylinder, configuration, valve gearing, timing variants	2 overhead valves, bucket tappets, 2 overhead camshafts, 2 duplex chains, fixed		2 overhead valves, bucket tappets, 2 overhead camshafts, 2 duplex chains, fixed	
Air supply, type of inlet manifold, air tempering	Normally aspirated, one-stage inlet manifold, n/a		Normally aspirated, one-stage inlet manifold, n/a	
Type, position, make, and designation of mixture preparation	2 horizontal carb., SU HD6		2 horizontal carb., SU HD6	
Energy source, type, make, and designation of ignition system	Battery, breaker, Lucas	Battery, breaker, Lucas		
Make of alternator, voltage, earthing	DC dynamo (from 1965 alternator), 12 V, positive (from 1965 negative)		Alternator, 12 V, negative	
Engine coolant, drive, regulation of cooling	Liquid, pump, thermostat		Liquid, pump, thermostat	
Type of clutch, number of gears in manual box, synchronized gears	Single-plate dry clutch, 4, 2–4 (from 1965 fully)		Single-plate dry clutch, 4, fully	
Gear ratios in manual box	3.375, 1.98, 1.365, (optional 2.98, 1.75, 1.21), 1, unknown, (from 9/65 wie 420) : 1		3.03, 1.97, 1.33, 1, 3.49, optional 2.68, 1.74, 1.27, 1, 3.38 : 1	
Make, type, ratio of overdrive	Optional, Laycock-de Normanville, electrically, 0.78 : 1		Optional, Laycock-de Normanville, electrically, 0.78 : 1	
Type of clutch, number of gears, make and model of automatic box	Optional hydraulic torque converter 3, Borg-Warner DG (from 1965 Borg-Warner 8)		Optional hydraulic torque converter 3, Borg-Warner 8	
Gear ratios in automatic gearbox	2.31, 1.44, 1, 2 : 1		2.31, 1.44, 1, 2 : 1	
Driven axle, type of diff, traction control	Rear, hypoid bevel, n/a (3.8 limited-slip)		Rear, hypoid bevel, limited-slip	
Axle ratios	3.54 (with overdrive 3.77) : 1		3.54 (with overdrive 3.77) : 1	
Type of chassis	Unitary with front and rear subframes		Unitary with front and rear subframes	
Suspension, springing front	Double-wishbone, coil springs		Double-wishbone, coil springs	
Suspension, springing rear	Transverse and trailing arms, driveshafts, 2 coil springs each		Transverse and trailing arms, driveshafts, 2 coil springs each	
Reduction of roll	Torsion bar front		Torsion bar front	
Type of shock absorbers	Telescopic		Telescopic	
Type and dimensions of wheels	Steel discs, painted, 5.5 x 15		Steel discs, painted, 5.5 x 15	
Type, dimensions, make of tires	Dunlop RS5, super-balloon 6.40 x 15		Dunlop RS5, super-balloon 6.40 x 15	
Type of braking front	Massive discs		Massive discs	
Type of braking rear	Massive inboard discs		Massive inboard discs	
Braking mechanism, number of circuits, servo assistance, electronic aids	Hydraulics, 2 circuits, vacuum servo assistance, n/a		Hydraulics, 2 circuits, vacuum servo assistance, n/a	
Steering gear, make and model of power steering	Recirculating ball, n/a (optional hydraulic servo Burman, from 1967 Adwest Varamatic)		Recirculating ball, n/a (optional hydraulic servo Burman, from 1967 Adwest Varamatic)	

* Prefix "P" denotes servo-assisted steering, "A" or "B" CKD for export

S-Type

Make, range	**Daimler Majestic etc.**			**Daimler SP 250**
Type	*Majestic*	*Majestic Major*	*DR 450*	*Roadster**
Public debut	7/1958	2/10/1959	2/10/1959	2/10/1959
End of production	1962	2/1968	2/1968	9/1964
Production figure	940	1184	865	2645
First, last chassis number RHD	98300-99774	136701-137891	136001-139176	100000-104456
First, last chassis number LHD	98750-99794	n/a	n/a	100010-101585
Body type	All-steel, 4 doors, 5 (DR 450 7) seats			Polyester, 2 doors, 2 seats
Weather protection, hood mechanism	Enclosed-drive			Manually operated top
Length, width, height (mm)	4980 x 1850 x 1590 (Major 5130 x 1850 x 1590, DR 450 5640 x 1850 x 1610)			4080 x 1520 x 1280
Length, width, height (inches)	196 x 73 x 62 1/2 (Major 202 x 73 x 62 1/2, DR 450 222 x 62 1/2 x 63 1/2)			160 1/2 x 60 x 50 1/2
Wheelbase, front, rear track (mm)	2896 (DR 450 3505) x 1478/1478			2337 x 1270/1270
Wheelbase, front, rear track (inches)	114 (DR 450 138) x 58/58			92 x 50/50
Ground clearance, turning circle, curb weight	170mm, 12 (DR 450 14) m, 1800 (DR 2000) kg			150mm, 10m, 1000kg
Max speed, acceleration 0-60 mph	168 (Major and DR 450 190) kph, 14 (Major 12) sec			192kph, 10 sec
Max power, standard, revs	147 SAE-HP/4400 (Major and DR 450 220 SAE-HP/5500)			140 SAE-HP/5800
Max torque, revs	Unknown (Major and DR 450 384 Nm/3200)			210 Nm/3600
Engine type, position, number and configuration of cylinders	Four-stroke gasoline, front longitudinally, 6 cylinders straight (Major and DR 450 8, 90-degree-V)			Four-stroke gasoline, front longitudinally, 8 cylinders, 90-degree-V
Bore x Stroke (mm), capacity (cc), compression ratio	86.36 x 107.95, 3794cc, 7.5 : 1 (Major and DR 450 95.25 x 80, 4561cc, 8 : 1)			76.2 x 69.85, 2548cc, 8.2 : 1
Designation of engine and cylinder head	Engine "Daimler 3.8-Liter," (Major and DR 450 Engine "Daimler V-8", head "Turner")			Engine "Daimler V8", head "Turner"
Engine block and cylinder head material, number of main bearings, type of liners	Block cast chrome-iron, head aluminum, 7 (Major and DR 450 5) main bearings, dry liners			Block cast chrome-iron, head aluminum, 5 main bearings, dry liners
Number of valves per cylinder, configuration, valve gearing, timing variants	As SP 250 (Majestic 1 side camshaft)			2 overhead valves, pushrod/rocker, 1 central camshaft, sprocket, fixed
Air supply, type of inlet manifold, air tempering	Normally aspirated, one-stage inlet manifold, n/a			Normally aspirated, one-stage inlet manifold, n/a
Type, position, make, and designation of mixture preparation	2 horizontal carb., SU HD6 (Major and DR 450 SU HD8)			2 horizontal carb., SU HD6
Energy source, type, make, and designation of ignition system	Battery, breaker, Lucas			Battery, breaker, Lucas
Make of alternator, voltage, earthing	DC dynamo (from 1965 alternator), 12 V, positive (from 1965 negative)			DC dynamo, 12 V, positive
Engine coolant, drive, regulation of cooling	Liquid, pump, thermostat			Liquid, pump, thermostat
Type of clutch, number of gears in manual box, synchronized gears	n/a			Single-plate dry clutch, 4, 2–4
Gear ratios in manual box	n/a			Unknown
Make, type, ratio of overdrive	n/a			Optional, Laycock-de Normanville, electrically, 0.78 : 1
Type of clutch, number of gears, make and model of automatic box	Hydraulic torque converter, 3, Borg-Warner DG (from 1965 8)			Optional hydraulic torque converter, 3, Borg-Warner 35
Gear ratios in automatic gearbox	2.31, 1.44, 1, 2 : 1			2.4, 1.45, 1, 2: 1
Driven axle, type of diff, traction control	Rear, hypoid bevel, n/a (from 1964 limited-slip)		Rear, hypoid bevel, n/a	
Axle ratios	3.92 (from 1960 3.77) : 1			3.58 : 1
Type of chassis	boxed-in chassis			boxed-in chassis
Suspension, springing front	Double-wishbone, coil springs			Double-wishbone, coil springs
Suspension, springing rear	Live axle, half-elliptic leaf springs			Live axle, half-elliptic leaf springs
Reduction of roll	Torsion bar front			Torsion bar front
Type of shock absorbers	Telescopic			Telescopic
Type and dimensions of wheels	Steel discs, painted, unknown			Steel discs, painted, unknown
Type, dimensions, make of tires	Dunlop, unknown			Dunlop Road Speed, 5.50 x 14
Type of braking front	Massive discs			Massive discs
Type of braking rear	Massive outboard discs			Massive outboard discs
Braking mechanism, number of circuits, servo assistance, electronic aids	Hydraulics, 1 circuit, vacuum servo assistance, n/a			Hydraulics, 1 circuit, vacuum servo assistance, n/a
Steering gear, make and model of power steering	Recirculating ball, n/a (from Major optional and from 1964 always hydraulic servo Burman)			Recirculating ball, n/a

* From 4/61 reinforcing structures introduced by and by, "B Specification"

Daimler

Make, range	**Jaguar E-Type**			**Jaguar E-Type Lightweight**
Type	*3.8 OTS*	*Semi-Lightweight*	*3.8 FHC*	*Lightweight*
Public debut	15/3/1961	9/7/1962	15/3/1961	3/1963
End of production	8/1964	9/7.1962	8/1964	1963
Production figure	7818 incl. Semi-LW	1	7678	11, plus 1 later modified car
First, last chassis number RHD	850001-850943	EC 1001	860001-861799	S850659-S850669
First, last chassis number LHD	875001-881886	n/a	885001-890879	n/a
Body type	All-steel, 2 doors, 2 seats			Steel and aluminum, 2 doors, 2 seats
Weather protection, top mechanism	Manually operated top* (FHC enclosed-drive, optional manually operated folding sunroof)			Steel hardtop
Length, width, height (mm)	4458 x 1657 x 1194 (FHC 4458 x 1657 x 1219)			4400 x 1657 x 1219
Length, width, height (inches)	175 1/2 x 65 1/4 x 47 (FHC 175 1/2 x 65 1/4 x 48)			173 x 65 1/4 x 48
Wheelbase, front, rear track (mm)	2438 x 1295/1295			2438 x 1295/1295
Wheelbase, front, rear track (inches)	96 x 51/51			96 x 51/51
Ground clearance, turning circle, curb weight	130mm, 12m, 1250kg			130mm, 12m, 1150kg
Max speed, acceleration 0-60 mph	240kph, 8 sec (Semi-Lightweight 270kph, 6 sec) 288kph, 5 sec			
Max power, standard, revs	265 SAE-HP/5500 (Semi-Lightweight 291 SAE-HP/7000)			293 SAE-HP/6750
Max torque, revs	378 Nm/4000 (Semi-Lightweight 285 Nm/6000)			308 Nm/6000
Engine type, position, number and configuration of cylinders	Four-stroke gasoline, front longitudinally, 6 cylinders straight			Four-stroke gasoline, front longitudinally, 6 cylinders straight
Bore x Stroke (mm), capacity (cc), compression ratio	87 x 106, 3781cc, 9 (optional 8) : 1			85 x 88, 2997cc, 9 : 1
Designation of engine and cylinder head	Engine "XK," head "Straight Port" golden, originally orange painted			Engine "XK," head "Straight Port"
Engine block and cylinder head material, number of main bearings, type of liners	Block cast chrome-iron, head aluminum, 7 main bearings, dry liners			Block and head aluminum, 7 main bearings, dry liners
Number of valves per cylinder, configuration, valve gearing, timing variants	2 overhead valves, bucket tappets, 2 overhead camshafts, 2 duplex chains, fixed			2 overhead valves, bucket tappets, 2 overhead camshafts, 2 duplex chains, fixed
Air supply, type of inlet manifold, air tempering	Normally aspirated, one-stage inlet manifold, n/a			Normally aspirated, one-stage inlet manifold, n/a
Type, position, make, and designation of mixture preparation	3 horizontal carb. SU HD 8 (Semi-Lightweight wie Lightweight)			Mechanical injection to manifold Lucas, optional 3 horizontal-twin carb Weber 45 DCOE
Energy source, type, make, and designation of ignition system	Battery, breaker, Lucas	Battery, breaker, Lucas		
Make of alternator, voltage, earthing	DC dynamo, 12 V, positive			DC dynamo, 12 V, positive
Engine coolant, drive, regulation of cooling	Liquid, pump, thermostat			Liquid, pump, thermostat
Type of clutch, number of gears in manual box, synchronized gears	Single-plate dry clutch, 4, 2–4			Three-plate dry clutch, 4 (optional 5), 2–4 (optional fully)
Gear ratios in manual box	2.98, 1.75, 1.21, 1, unknown : 1			2.98, 1.75, 1.21, 1, unknown : 1
Make, type, ratio of overdrive	n/a			n/a
Type of clutch, number of gears, make and model of automatic box	n/a			n/a
Gear ratios in automatic gearbox	n/a			n/a
Driven axle, type of diff, traction control	Rear, hypoid bevel, limited-slip			Rear, hypoid bevel, limited-slip
Axle ratios	3.31 (optional 3.07 to 4.09) : 1			Unknown
Type of chassis	Unitary with front tubular subframe and rear subframe			Unitary with front tubular subframe and rear subframe
Suspension, springing front	Double-wishbone, torsion bars			Double-wishbone, torsion bars
Suspension, springing rear	Transverse and trailing arms, driveshafts, 2 coil springs each			Transverse and trailing arms, driveshafts, 2 coil springs each
Reduction of roll	Torsion bar front			Torsion bar front
Type of shock absorbers	Telescopic			Telescopic
Type and dimensions of wheels	Steel spokes, painted or chromed, 5 J x 15			Magnesium discs, painted, 5 J x 16
Type, dimensions, make of tires	Dunlop, super-balloon 6.40 x 15			Dunlop, super-balloon 6.40 x 15
Type of braking front	Massive discs			Massive discs
Type of braking rear	Massive inboard discs			Massive inboard discs
Braking mechanism, number of circuits, servo assistance, electronic aids	Hydraulics, 2 circuits, vacuum servo assistance, n/a			Hydraulics, 2 circuits, vacuum servo assistance, n/a
Steering gear, make and model of power steering	Rack and pinion, n/a			Rack and pinion, n/a

E-Type

Make, range	**Jaguar E-Type 4.2**			**Jaguar E-Type Series 2**		
Type	*OTS*	*FHC*	*2 + 2*	*Series 2 OTS*	*Series 2 FHC*	*Series 2 2 + 2*
Public debut	9/10/1964	9/10/1964	3/1966	18/10/1968	18/10/1968	18/10/1968
End of production	8/1968	8/1968	8/1968	12/1970	12/1970	9/1970
Production figure	9550	7772	5600	8629	4857	5326
First, last chassis number RHD	1E 1001-2183	1E 20001-21958	1E 50001-51379	1R 1001-1776*	1R 20001-21071*	1R 35001-36040*
First, last chassis number LHD	1E 10001-18367	1E 30001-35814	1E 75001-79221	1R 7001-14853*	1R 25001-28786*	1R 40001-44286*
Body type	All-steel, 2 doors, 2 ("2 + 2" 2 + 2) seats			All-steel, 2 doors, 2 ("2 + 2" 2 + 2) seats		
Weather protection, top mechanism	Manually operated top (FHC and 2 + 2 as Series 2)			As 4.2 (FHC and 2 + 2 enclosed-drive, optional manually operated folding sunroof)		
Length, width, height (mm)	4458 x 1657 x 1194 (FHC 4458 x 1657 x 1219, 2 + 2 4686 x 1657 x 1295)			4458 x 1657 x 1194 (FHC 4458 x 1657 x 1219, 2 + 2 4686 x 1657 x 1295)		
Length, width, height (inches)	175 1/2 x 65 1/4 x 47 (FHC 175 1/2 x 65 1/4 x 48, 2 + 2 184 1/2 x 65 1/4 x 51)			175 1/2 x 65 1/4 x 47 (FHC 175 1/2 x 65 1/4 x 48, 2 + 2 184 1/2 x 65 1/4 x 51		
Wheelbase, front, rear track (mm)	2438 (2 + 2 2667) x 1295/1295			2438 (2 + 2 2667) x 1295/1295		
Wheelbase, front, rear track (inches)	96 (2 + 2 105) x 51/51			96 (2 + 2 105) x 51/51		
Ground clearance, turning circle, curb weight	130mm, 12m, 1300 (2 + 2 1400) kg			130mm, 12m, 1300 (2 + 2 1400) kg		
Max speed, acceleration 0-60 mph	235kph, 8 sec (2 + 2 220kph, 9 sec)			235kph, 8 sec (2 + 2 220kph, 9 sec)		
Max power, standard, revs	265 SAE-HP/5400			265 SAE-HP/5400		
Max torque, revs	382 Nm/4000			382 Nm/4000		
Engine type, position, number and configuration of cylinders	Four-stroke gasoline, front longitudinally, 6 cylinders straight			Four-stroke gasoline, front longitudinally, 6 cylinders straight		
Bore x Stroke (mm), capacity (cc), compression ratio	92.07 x 106, 4235cc, 9 (optional 8) : 1			92.07 x 106, 4235cc, 9 (optional 8) : 1		
Designation of engine and cylinder head	Engine "XK", head "Straight Port" golden painted			Engine "XK", head "Straight Port"		
Engine block and cylinder head material, number of main bearings, type of liners	Block cast chrome-iron, head aluminum, 7 main bearings, dry liners			Block cast chrome-iron, head aluminum, 7 main bearings, dry liners		
Number of valves per cylinder, configuration, valve gearing, timing variants	2 overhead valves, bucket tappets, 2 overhead camshafts, 2 duplex chains, fixed			2 overhead valves, bucket tappets, 2 overhead camshafts, 2 duplex chains, fixed		
Air supply, type of inlet manifold, air tempering	Normally aspirated, one-stage inlet manifold, n/a (US from 1967 pre-heating)			Normally aspirated, one-stage inlet manifold, n/a (US pre-heating)		
Type, position, make, and designation of mixture preparation	3 horizontal carb., SU HD 8 (US from 1967 US 2 Zenith/Stromberg 175 CDSE)			3 horizontal carb., SU HD 8 (US 2 Zenith/Stromberg 175 CDSE)		
Energy source, type, make, and designation of ignition system	Battery, breaker, Lucas			Battery, breaker, Lucas		
Make of alternator, voltage, earthing	Alternator, 12 V, negative Alternator, 12 V, negative					
Engine coolant, drive, regulation of cooling	Liquid, pump, thermostat			Liquid, pump, thermostat		
Type of clutch, number of gears in manual box, synchronized gears	Single-plate dry clutch, 4, fully			Single-plate dry clutch, 4, fully		
Gear ratios in manual box	2.68, 1.74, 1.27, 1, 3.38 : 1			2.68, 1.74, 1.27, 1, 3.38 : 1		
Make, type, ratio of overdrive	n/a			n/a		
Type of clutch, number of gears, make and model of automatic box	n/a (2 + 2 optional hydraulic torque converter, 3, Borg-Warner 8)			n/a (2 + 2 optional hydraulic torque converter, 3, Borg-Warner 8)		
Gear ratios in automatic gearbox	2.31, 1.44, 1, 2 : 1			2.31, 1.44, 1, 2 : 1		
Driven axle, type of diff, traction control	Rear, hypoid bevel, limited-slip			Rear, hypoid bevel, limited-slip		
Axle ratios	3.07 or 3.31 : 1			3.07 or 3.31 : 1		
Type of chassis	Unitary with front tubular subframe and rear subframe			Unitary with front tubular subframe and rear subframe		
Suspension, springing front	Double-wishbone, torsion bars			Double-wishbone, torsion bars		
Suspension, springing rear	Transverse and trailing arms, driveshafts, 2 coil springs each			Transverse and trailing arms, driveshafts, 2 coil springs each		
Reduction of roll	Torsion bar front			Torsion bar front		
Type of shock absorbers	Telescopic			Telescopic		
Type and dimensions of wheels	Steel spokes, painted or chromed, 5 x 15			Steel spokes, painted or chromed, 5 x 15		
Type, dimensions, make of tires	Dunlop SP Super, low section 185 x 15			Dunlop SP Super, low section 185 x 15		
Type of braking front	Massive discs			Massive discs		
Type of braking rear	Massive inboard discs			Massive inboard discs		
Braking mechanism, number of circuits, servo assistance, electronic aids	Hydraulics, 2 circuits, vacuum servo assistance, n/a			Hydraulics, 2 circuits, vacuum servo assistance, n/a		
Steering gear, make and model of power steering	Rack and pinion, n/a (from 1967 optional Adwest Varamatic)			Rack and pinion, n/a (from 1967 optional Adwest Varamatic)		

*From 1.9.70 for US chassis number prefix "2R", Prefix "P" denotes servo-assisted steering

Make, range	**Jaguar E-Type Series 3**			**Jaguar XJ 13**
Type	*Series 3 OTS*	*Series 3 2 + 2**	*SCCA racing car*	*Racing prototype*
Public debut	29/3/1971	29/3/1971	1974	3/1966
End of production	9/1974	10/1973	1974	3/1966
Production figure	7992	7299	2	1
First, last chassis number RHD	1S 1001-2872	1S 50001-52116	n/a	Unknown
First, last chassis number LHD	1S 20001-26120**	1S 70001-75183**		See Series 3 OTS n/a
Body type	All-steel, 2 doors, 2 ("2 + 2" 2 + 2) seats			aluminum and steel, 2 doors, 2 seats
Weather protection, top mechanism	Manually operated top, (FHC and 2 + 2 as Series 2, SCCA n/a)			n/a
Length, width, height (mm)	4674 x 1683 x 1245 (2 + 2 4674 x 1683 x 1295, SCCA 4684 x 1678 x 1226)			4810 x 1850 x 980
Length, width, height (inches)	184 x 66 1/4 x 49 (2 + 2 184 x 66 1/4 x 51, SCCA 184 1/2 x 66 x 48 1/4)			189 1/2 x 73 x 38 1/2
Wheelbase, front, rear track (mm)	2667 x 1378/1353			2430 x 1422/1422
Wheelbase, front, rear track (inches)	105 x 54 1/4/53 1/4			95 1/2 x 56/56
Ground clearance, turning circle, curb weight	130mm, 12m, 1500 (SCCA 1200) kg			100mm, 15m, 1000kg
Max speed, acceleration 0-60 mph	230kph, 7 sec (SCCA 280kph, 5 sec)			286kph, 4 sec
Max power, standard, revs	315 SAE-HP/5850 (SCCA 460 SAE-HP/7000)			502 SAE-HP/7000
Max torque, revs	420 Nm/3600 (SCCA unknown)			517 Nm/6300
Engine type, position, number and configuration of cylinders	Four-stroke gasoline, front longitudinally, 12 cylinders, 60-degree-V			Four-stroke gasoline, central longitudinally, 12 cylinders, 60-degree-V
Bore x Stroke (mm), capacity (cc), compression ratio	90 x 70, 5343cc, 9 (SCCA unknown) : 1			87 x 70, 4991cc, 10.4 : 1
Designation of engine and cylinder head	Engine "Jaguar V-12," head "Heron"			Engine "Jaguar V-12," head "Heron"
Engine block and cylinder head material, number of main bearings, type of liners	Block and head aluminum, 7 main bearings, wet liners			Block and head aluminum, 7 main bearings, wet liners
Number of valves per cylinder, configuration, valve gearing, timing variants	2 overhead valves, bucket tappets, 1 overhead camshaft, duplex chain, fixed			2 overhead valves, bucket tappets, 1 overhead camshaft, duplex chain, fixed
Air supply, type of inlet manifold, air tempering	Normally aspirated, one-stage inlet manifold, n/a (US pre-heating)			Normally aspirated, one-stage inlet manifold, n/a
Type, position, make, and designation of mixture preparation	4 horizontal carb., Zenith/Stromberg 175 CDSE (for US CD2SE)			6 horizontal carb., SU HD8
Energy source, type, make, and designation of ignition system	Battery, solid-state, Lucas OPUS (SCCA unknown)			Battery, breaker, Lucas
Make of alternator, voltage, earthing	Alternator, 12 V, negative			Alternator, 12 V, negative
Engine coolant, drive, regulation of cooling	Liquid, pump, thermostat			Liquid, pump, thermostat
Type of clutch, number of gears in manual box, synchronized gears	Single-plate dry clutch, 4 (SCCA 5), fully			Racing clutch, 5, fully
Gear ratios in manual box	2.68, 1.74, 1.27, 1, 3.38 (SCCA unknown) : 1			Unknown
Make, type, ratio of overdrive	n/a			n/a
Type of clutch, number of gears, make and model of automatic box	Optional hydraulic torque converter, 3, Borg-Warner 12 (SCCA n/a)			n/a
Gear ratios in automatic gearbox	2.4, 1.45, 1, 2 : 1			n/a
Driven axle, type of diff, traction control	Rear, hypoid bevel, limited-slip			Rear, hypoid bevel, n/a
Axle ratios	3.31 (with automatic 3.07, SCCA unknown) : 1			4.2 : 1
Type of chassis	Unitary with front tubular subframe and rear subframe			Unitary
Suspension, springing front	Double-wishbone, torsion bars			Double-wishbone, coil springs
Suspension, springing rear	Transverse and trailing arms, driveshafts, 2 coil springs each			Transverse and trailing arms, driveshafts, 2 coil springs each
Reduction of roll	Torsion bar front			Torsion bar front
Type of shock absorbers	Telescopic			Telescopic
Type and dimensions of wheels	Steel discs, chromed, 6 x 15 (SCCA aluminum discs, polished, unknown)			Aluminum discs with holes, unknown
Type, dimensions, make of tires	Dunlop SP, E 70 VR 15 (SCCA Goodyear, unknown)			Dunlop, unknown
Type of braking front	Ventilated discs			Massive discs
Type of braking rear	Massive inboard discs			Massive inboard discs
Braking mechanism, number of circuits, servo assistance, electronic aids	Hydraulics, 2 circuits, vacuum servo assistance, n/a			Hydraulics, 1 circuit, vacuum servo assistance, n/a
Steering gear, make and model of power steering	Rack and pinion, hydraulic servo Adwest Varamatic			Rack and pinion, n/a

*5 prototypes with Series 2 engines (chassis nos. EX 100 to EX 104 and 1S 50106)

**Prefix "UC" (1972), "UD" (73) "UE" (74) denotes US destination

E-Type

Make, range	Jaguar MK X and 420 G			Daimler DS 420	
Type	*3.8 Sedan*	*4.2 Sedan**	*420 G**	*Limousine*	*Landaulette*
Public debut	11/10/1961	9/ 10/1964	13/10/1966	11/6/1968	7/1973
End of production	8/1964	12/1966	6/1970	11/1992	1974
Production figure	12,961	5672	5542	4937	2
First, last chassis number RHD	300001-309129	1D 50001-53720	G1D 53721-58149	1M 1001-3616 VIN 010001-010209, 200001-201631, 400001-400425	
First, last chassis number LHD	350001-353848	1D 75001-76960	G1D 76961-78086	1M 20001-20151, VIN 010001-010209, 200001-201631, 400001-400425	
Body type	All-steel, 4 doors, 5 seats			All-steel, 4 doors, 7 seats	
Weather protection, top mechanism	Enclosed-drive, optional manually operated folding sunroof			Enclosed-drive (Landaulette rear manually operated top)	
Length, width, height (mm)	5131 x 1930 x 1391			5740 x 1969 x 1619	
Length, width, height (inches)	202 x 76 x 54 3/4			226 x 77 1/2 x 63 3/4	
Wheelbase, front, rear track (mm)	3048 x 1473/1473			3581 x 1473/1473	
Wheelbase, front, rear track (inches)	120 x 58/58			141 x 58/58	
Ground clearance, turning circle, curb weight	140mm, 12m, 1900kg			140mm, 14m, 2150kg	
Max speed, acceleration 0-60 mph	192kph, 11 sec (4.2 and 420 G 194kph, 10 sec)			176kph, 13 sec	
Max power, standard, revs	265 SAE-HP/5500			245 SAE-HP/4750, from 1973 164 DIN-HP/4250, from 1985 178 DIN-HP/4750	
Max torque, revs	353 Nm/4000 (4.2 and 420 G 382 Nm/4000)			380 Nm/3750, from 1973 309 Nm/3000, from 1985 297 Nm/2500)	
Engine type, position, number and configuration of cylinders	Four-stroke gasoline, front longitudinally, 6 cylinders straight			Four-stroke gasoline, front longitudinally, 6 cylinders straight	
Bore x Stroke (mm), capacity (cc), compression ratio	87 x 106, 3781 (4.2 and 420 G 92.07 x 106, 4235) cc, 8 (optional 7 or 9) : 1			92.07 x 106, 4235cc, 8 (optional 7 or 9) : 1	
Designation of engine and cylinder head	Engine "XK," head "Straight Port" golden painted (420 G unpainted)			Engine "XK," head "Straight Port"	
Engine block and cylinder head material, number of main bearings, type of liners	Block cast chrome-iron, head aluminum, 7 main bearings, dry liners			Block cast chrome-iron, head aluminum, 7 main bearings, dry liners	
Number of valves per cylinder, configuration, valve gearing, timing variants	2 overhead valves, bucket tappets, 2 overhead camshafts, 2 duplex chains, fixed			2 overhead valves, bucket tappets, 2 overhead camshafts, 2 duplex chains, fixed	
Air supply, type of inlet manifold, air tempering	Normally aspirated, one-stage inlet manifold, n/a			Normally aspirated, one-stage inlet manifold, n/a	
Type, position, make, and designation of mixture preparation	3 horizontal carb., SU HD8			2 horizontal carb., SU HD8 (from '85 electronic injection to manifold L-Jetronic)	
Energy source, type, make, and designation of ignition system	Battery, breaker, Lucas	Battery, breaker, Lucas			
Make of alternator, voltage, earthing	DC dynamo (from 4.2 alternator), 12 V, positive (from 4.2 negative)			Alternator, 12 V, negative	
Engine coolant, drive, regulation of cooling	Liquid, pump, thermostat			Liquid, pump, thermostat	
Type of clutch, number of gears in manual box, synchronized gears	Single-plate dry clutch, 4, 2–4 (4.2 and 420 G fully)			n/a	
Gear ratios in manual box	3.37, 1.98, 1.365, 1, 3.37 (from 4.2 3.04, 1.973, 1.328, 1, 3.49) : 1			n/a	
Make, type, ratio of overdrive	Optional Laycock-de Normanville, electrically, 0.78 : 1			n/a	
Type of clutch, number of gears, make and model of automatic box	Optional hydraulic torque converter, 3, Borg-Warner 8			Hydraulic torque converter, 3, Borg-Warner 8 (from 7/70 12, from 11/73 65)	
Gear ratios in automatic gearbox	2.31, 1.44, 1, 2 : 1			2.31, 1.44, 1, 2 (from 7/70 2.4, 1.45, 1, 2) : 1	
Driven axle, type of diff, traction control	Rear, hypoid bevel, n/a			Rear, hypoid bevel, n/a	
Axle ratios	3.54 (with overdrive 3.77) : 1			3.54 : 1	
Type of chassis	Unitary, front and rear subframes			Unitary, front and rear subframes	
Suspension, springing front	Double-wishbone, coil springs			Double-wishbone, coil springs	
Suspension, springing rear	Transverse and trailing arms, driveshafts, 2 coil springs each			Transverse and trailing arms, driveshafts, 2 coil springs each	
Reduction of roll	Torsion bar front			Torsion bar front	
Type of shock absorbers	Telescopic			Telescopic	
Type and dimensions of wheels	Steel discs, painted 5.5 J x 14			Steel discs, painted, 5.5 J x 15	
Type, dimensions, make of tires	Dunlop RS low section 7.50 x 14, 4.2 u. 420 G Dunlop SP 205 x 14			Dunlop, 205 x 15	
Type of braking front	Massive discs			Massive discs	
Type of braking rear	Massive inboard discs			Massive inboard discs	
Braking mechanism, number of circuits, servo assistance, electronic aids	Hydraulics, 2 circuits, vacuum servo assistance, n/a			Hydraulics, 2 circuits, vacuum servo assistance, n/a	
Steering gear, make and model of power steering	Recirculating ball, hydraulic servo Burman (4.2 and 420 G Adwest Varamatic)			Rack and pinion, hydraulic servo Adwest Varamatic	

* 18 Mark X 4.2 and 24 420 G 24 with separation

DS 420

Make, range	**Jaguar XJ 6 Series 1 2.8 and Daimler Sovereign**			**Jaguar XJ 6 Series 1 4.2 and Daimler Sovereign**		
Type	*XJ 6 2.8-Liter*	*XJ 6 2.8-Liter de Luxe*	*Daimler Sovereign 2.8*	*XJ 6 4.2-Liter* (XJ 6 L)*	*Daimler Sovereign 4.2*	*Daimler Sovereign LWB*
Public debut	26/9/1968	26/9/1968	9/10/1969	26/9/1968 (10/1972)	9/10/1969	10/1972
End of production	1971	9/73	1972	9/1973	9/1973	9/1973
Production figure		19,426	3234	58,972 (584)	11,620	395
First, last chassis number RHD	1G 1001-14301		1T 1001-4069	1L 1001-34467**	1U 1001-11894	2D 1001-1394
First, last chassis number LHD	1G 50001-56125		1T 50001-50165	1L 50001-75505**, ***	1U 50001-50726	2D 50001
Body type	All-steel, 4 doors, 5 seats			All-steel, 4 doors, 5 seats		
Weather protection, top mechanism	Enclosed-drive, optional manually operated folding sunroof			Enclosed-drive, optional manually operated folding sunroof		
Length, width, height (mm)	4813 x 1759 x 1372			4813 (L and LWB 4913) x 1759 x 1372		
Length, width, height (inches)	189 1/2 x 69 1/4 x 54			189 1/2 (L and LWB 193 1/4) x 69 1/4 x 54		
Wheelbase, front, rear track (mm)	2762 x 1473/1486			2762 (L and LWB 2864) x 1473/1486		
Wheelbase, front, rear track (inches)	108 3/4 x 58/58 1/2			108 3/4 (L and LWB 112 3/4) x 58/58 1/2		
Ground clearance, turning circle, curb weight	150mm, 12m, 1650kg			150mm, 12m, 1700 (L and LWB 1750) kg		
Max speed, acceleration 0-60 mph	184kph, 12 sec			196kph, 9 sec		
Max power, standard, revs	149 DIN-HP/6000, from 1971 142 DIN-HP/5500			186 DIN-HP/5500 (with low compression 181, from 1972 175 DIN-HP/4750)		
Max torque, revs	240 Nm/3750 (from 1971 203 Nm/4250)			370 Nm/3750 (with low compression 310, from 1972 307 Nm/3000)		
Engine type, position, number and configuration of cylinders	Four-stroke gasoline, front longitudinally, 6 cylinders straight			Four-stroke gasoline, front longitudinally, 6 cylinders straight		
Bore x Stroke (mm), capacity (cc), compression ratio	83 x 86, 2792cc, 9 (optional 8) : 1			92.07 x 106, 4235cc, 9 (optional 8) : 1		
Designation of engine and cylinder head	Engine "XK," head "Straight Port"			Engine "XK," head "Straight Port"		
Engine block and cylinder head material, number of main bearings, type of liners	Block cast chrome-iron, head aluminum, 7 main bearings, n/a			Block cast chrome-iron, head aluminum, 7 main bearings, dry liners		
Number of valves per cylinder, configuration, valve gearing, timing variants	2 overhead valves, bucket tappets, 2 overhead camshafts, 2 duplex chains, fixed			2 overhead valves, bucket tappets, 2 overhead camshafts, 2 duplex chains, fixed		
Air supply, type of inlet manifold, air tempering	Normally aspirated, one-stage inlet manifold, n/a (US pre-heating)			Normally aspirated, one-stage inlet manifold, n/a (US pre-heating)		
Type, position, make, and designation of mixture preparation	2 horizontal carb., SU HD8			2 horizontal carb., SU HD8		
Energy source, type, make, and designation of ignition system	Battery, breaker, Lucas			Battery, breaker, Lucas		
Make of alternator, voltage, earthing	Alternator, 12 V, negative			Alternator, 12 V, negative		
Engine coolant, drive, regulation of cooling	Liquid, pump, thermostat			Liquid, pump, thermostat		
Type of clutch, number of gears in manual box, synchronized gears	Single-plate dry clutch, 4, fully			Single-plate dry clutch, 4, fully		
Gear ratios in manual box	2.93, 1.905, 1.39, 1, 3.378 : 1			2.93, 1.905, 1.39, 1, 3.378 : 1		
Make, type, ratio of overdrive	Optional (Sovereign always), Laycock-de Normanville, electrically, 0.78 : 1			Optional (Sovereign always), Laycock-de Normanville, electrically, 0.78 : 1		
Type of clutch, number of gears, make and model of automatic box	Optional hydraulic torque converter, 3, Borg-Warner 35			Optional hydraulic torque converter, 3, Borg-Warner 8 (from 7/70 Borg-Warner 12)		
Gear ratios in automatic gearbox	2.4, 1.45, 1, 2 : 1			2.31, 1.44, 1, 2 (from 7/70 2.4, 1.45, 1, 2) : 1		
Driven axle, type of diff, traction control	Rear, hypoid bevel, n/a			Rear, hypoid bevel, n/a		
Axle ratios	4.27 (with overdrive 4.55, with automatic from 1/69 4.09) : 1			3.31 (with overdrive 3.77) : 1		
Type of chassis	Unitary, front and rear subframes			Unitary, front and rear subframes		
Suspension, springing front	Double-wishbone, coil springs			Double-wishbone, coil springs		
Suspension, springing rear	Transverse and trailing arms, driveshafts, 2 coil springs each			Transverse and trailing arms, driveshafts, 2 coil springs each		
Reduction of roll	Torsion bar front			Torsion bar front		
Type of shock absorbers	Telescopic			Telescopic		
Type and dimensions of wheels	Steel discs, painted (optional chromed), 6 J x 15			Steel discs, painted (optional chromed), 6 J x 15		
Type, dimensions, make of tires	Dunlop SP, E 70 VR 15			Dunlop SP, E 70 VR 15		
Type of braking front	Massive discs			Massive discs		
Type of braking rear	Massive inboard discs			Massive inboard discs		
Braking mechanism, number of circuits, servo assistance, electronic aids	Hydraulics, 2 circuits, vacuum servo assistance, n/a			Hydraulics, 2 circuits, vacuum servo assistance, n/a		
Steering gear, make and model of power steering	Rack and pinion, optional (from de Luxe always) hydraulic servo Adwest Varamatic			Rack and pinion, hydraulic servo Adwest Varamatic		

* Incl. one coupe prototype of 1969
** XJ 6L 2E 1001-1583 and (LHD) 2E 50001
*** Prefix "UC" (1972) or "UD" (1973) denotes US destination

XJ

Make, range	**Jaguar XJ 12 Series 1 and Daimler Double-Six**		**Jaguar XJ 12 L Series 1 and Daimler Double-Six Vanden Plas**	
Type	*XJ 12 Sedan*	*Daimler Double-Six*	*XJ 12 L*	*Daimler Double-Six Vanden Plas*
Public debut	27/7/1972	27/7/1972	10/1972	26/9/1972
End of production	8/1973	8/1973	8/1973	8/1973
Production figure	2482	535	753	342
First, last chassis number RHD	1P 1001-1720	2A 1001-1524	2C 1001-1750	2B 1001-1337
First, last chassis number LHD	1P50001-51762*	2A 50001-50011	2C 50001-50003	2B 50001-50005
Body type	All-steel, 4 doors, 5 seats		All-steel, 4 doors, 5 seats	
Weather protection, top mechanism	Enclosed-drive, optional manually operated folding sunroof		Enclosed-drive, optional manually operated folding sunroof	
Length, width, height (mm)	4813 x 1759 x 1372		4913 x 1759 x 1372	
Length, width, height (inches)	189 1/2 x 69 1/4 x 54		193 1/2 x 69 1/4 x 54	
Wheelbase, front, rear track (mm)	2762 x 1473/1486		2864 x 1473/1486	
Wheelbase, front, rear track (inches)	108 3/4 x 58/58 1/2		112 3/4 x 58/58 1/2	
Ground clearance, turning circle, curb weight	150mm, 12m, 1800kg		150mm, 12m, 1850kg	
Max speed, acceleration 0-60 mph	224kph, 8 sec		224kph, 8 sec	
Max power, standard, revs	269 DIN-HP/6000 (US 241 NET-HP/5750)		269 DIN-HP/6000	
Max torque, revs	407 Nm/3500 (US 385 Nm/3500)		407 Nm/3500	
Engine type, position, number and configuration of cylinders	Four-stroke gasoline, front longitudinally, 12 cylinders, 60-degree-V		Four-stroke gasoline, front longitudinally, 12 cylinders, 60-degree-V	
Bore x Stroke (mm), capacity (cc), compression ratio	90 x 70, 5343cc, 9 : 1		90 x 70, 5343cc, 9 : 1	
Designation of engine and cylinder head	Engine "Jaguar V-12", head "Heron"		Engine "Jaguar V-12", head "Heron"	
Engine block and cylinder head material, number of main bearings, type of liners	Block and head aluminum, 7 main bearings, wet liners		Block and head aluminum, 7 main bearings, wet liners	
Number of valves per cylinder, configuration, valve gearing, timing variants	2 overhead valves, bucket tappets, 1 ohc per bank, duplex chain, fixed		2 overhead valves, bucket tappets, 1 ohc per bank, duplex chain, fixed	
Air supply, type of inlet manifold, air tempering	Normally aspirated, one-stage inlet manifold, n/a (US pre-heating)		Normally aspirated, one-stage inlet manifold, n/a	
Type, position, make, and designation of mixture preparation	4 horizontal carb., Zenith/Stromberg 175 CDSE (US CD2SE)		4 horizontal carb., Zenith/Stromberg 175 CDSE	
Energy source, type, make, and designation of ignition system	Battery, solid-state, Lucas OPUS		Battery, solid-state, Lucas OPUS	
Make of alternator, voltage, earthing	Alternator, 12 V, negative		Alternator, 12 V, negative	
Engine coolant, drive, regulation of cooling	Liquid, pump, thermostat		Liquid, pump, thermostat	
Type of clutch, number of gears in manual box, synchronized gears	n/a		n/a	
Gear ratios in manual box	n/a		n/a	
Make, type, ratio of overdrive	n/a		n/a	
Type of clutch, number of gears, make and model of automatic box	Hydraulic torque converter, 3, Borg-Warner 12		Hydraulic torque converter, 3, Borg-Warner 12	
Gear ratios in automatic gearbox	2.4, 1.45, 1, 2 : 1		2.4, 1.45, 1, 2 : 1	
Driven axle, type of diff, traction control	Rear, hypoid bevel, limited-slip		Rear, hypoid bevel, limited-slip	
Axle ratios	3.31 : 1		3.31 : 1	
Type of chassis	Unitary, front and rear subframes		Unitary, front and rear subframes	
Suspension, springing front	Double-wishbone, coil springs		Double-wishbone, coil springs	
Suspension, springing rear	Transverse and trailing arms, driveshafts, 2 coil springs each		Transverse and trailing arms, driveshafts, 2 coil springs each	
Reduction of roll	Torsion bar front		Torsion bar front	
Type of shock absorbers	Telescopic		Telescopic	
Type and dimensions of wheels	Steel discs, painted (optional chromed), 6 J x 15		Steel discs, painted (optional, Vanden Plas always chromed), 6 J x 15	
Type, dimensions, make of tires	Dunlop SP, E 70 VR 15		Dunlop SP, E 70 VR 15	
Type of braking front	Ventilated discs		Ventilated discs	
Type of braking rear	Massive inboard discs		Massive inboard discs	
Braking mechanism, number of circuits, servo assistance, electronic aids	Hydraulics, 2 circuits, front/rear balance valve, vacuum servo assistance, n/a		Hydraulics, 2 circuits, front/rear balance valve, vacuum servo assistance, n/a	
Steering gear, make and model of power steering	Rack and pinion, hydraulic servo Adwest Varamatic		Rack and pinion, hydraulic servo Adwest Varamatic	

*Prefixes "UC" (1972) or "UD" (1973) denote US destination

XJ

Make, range	**Jaguar XJ 6 Series 2 and Daimler Sovereign**			**Jaguar XJ 6 C and Daimler Sovereign Two-Door**	
Type	*XJ 6 2.8*	*XJ 4.2*	*Daimler Sovereign 4.2*	*XJ 4.2 C**	*Daimler Sovereign Two-Door*
Public debut	13/9/1973	13/9/1973	13/9/1973	13/9/1973	13/9/1973
End of production	2/7/1974	11/11/1974	8/11/1974	8/11/1977	8/11/1977
Production figure	170	12,368	2428	6505	1698
First, last chassis number RHD	n/a	2N 1001-8463	2M 1001–3313	2J 1001-3606	2H 1001–2586
First, last chassis number LHD	2U 50001-50170	2N 50001-54907	2M 50001-50115	2J 50001-53899**	2H 50001–50112
Body type	All-steel, 4 doors, 5 seats			All-steel, 2 doors, 5 seats	
Weather protection, top mechanism	Enclosed-drive, optional manually operated folding sunroof			Enclosed-drive, optional manually operated folding sunroof	
Length, width, height (mm)	4845 x 1770 x 1375			4845 x 1770 x 1375	
Length, width, height (inches)	190 3/4 x 69 3/4 x 54			190 3/4 x 69 3/4 x 54	
Wheelbase, front, rear track (mm)	2762 x 1473/1486			2762 x 1473/1486	
Wheelbase, front, rear track (inches)	108 3/4 x 58/58 1/2			108 3/4 x 58/58 1/2	
Ground clearance, turning circle, curb weight	150mm, 12m, 1700kg			150mm, 12m, 1700kg	
Max speed, acceleration 0-60 mph	190kph, 10 sec (2.8 184kph, 12 sec)			190kph, 10 sec	
Max power, standard, revs	137 DIN-HP/5500 (4.2 172 o. 182 (from 1975 170 bzw. 180 DIN-HP/4500)			As XJ 4.2 (US from 1977 164 DIN-HP/4750)	
Max torque, revs	192 Nm/4250 (4.2 305 or 313/3000)			305 or 313 Nm/3000 (US from 1977 306 Nm/2500)	
Engine type, position, number and configuration of cylinders	Four-stroke gasoline, front longitudinally, 6 cylinders straight			Four-stroke gasoline, front longitudinally, 6 cylinders straight	
Bore x Stroke (mm), capacity (cc), compression ratio	83 x 86, 2792cc, 8 : 1 (4.2 92.07 x 106, 4235cc, 8, optional 9 : 1)			92.07 x 106, 4235cc, 8, optional 9, US from 1977 always 7.5 : 1	
Designation of engine and cylinder head	Engine "XK," head "Straight Port"			Engine "XK," head "Straight Port"	
Engine block and cylinder head material, number of main bearings, type of liners	Block cast chrome-iron, head aluminum, 7 main bearings, n/a (4.2 dry liners)			Block cast chrome-iron, head aluminum, 7 main bearings, dry liners	
Number of valves per cylinder, configuration, valve gearing, timing variants	2 overhead valves, bucket tappets, 2 overhead camshafts, 2 duplex chains, fixed			2 overhead valves, bucket tappets, 2 overhead camshafts, 2 duplex chains, fixed	
Air supply, type of inlet manifold, air tempering	Normally aspirated, one-stage inlet manifold, pre-heating			Normally aspirated, one-stage inlet manifold, pre-heating	
Type, position, make, and designation of mixture preparation	2 horizontal carb., SU HS8			2 horizontal carb., SU HS8 (from 1977 HIF7)	
Energy source, type, make, and designation of ignition system	Battery, breaker, Lucas			Battery, breaker, Lucas	
Make of alternator, voltage, earthing	Alternator, 12 V, negative			Alternator, 12 V, negative	
Engine coolant, drive, regulation of cooling	Liquid, pump, thermostat			Liquid, pump, thermostat	
Type of clutch, number of gears in manual box, synchronized gears	Single-plate dry clutch, 4, fully			Single-plate dry clutch, 4, fully	
Gear ratios in manual box	2.93, 1.905, 1.39, 1, 3.378 : 1			2.93, 1.905, 1.39, 1, 3.378 (from 4/75 3.03, 1.905, 1.39, 1, 3.428) : 1	
Make, type, ratio of overdrive	Optional (Sovereign always), Laycock-de Normanville, electrically, 0.78 : 1			Always (XJ 4.2 C until 1974 optional), Laycock-de Normanville, electrically, 0.78 : 1	
Type of clutch, number of gears, make and model of automatic box	Optional hydraulic torque converter, 3, Borg-Warner 12 (from 12/73 65)			Optional hydraulic torque converter, 3, Borg-Warner 12 (from 12/73 65)	
Gear ratios in automatic gearbox	2.4, 1.45, 1, 2 : 1			2.4, 1.45, 1, 2.09 (from 4/75 2) : 1	
Driven axle, type of diff, traction control	Rear, hypoid bevel, n/a (optional limited-slip)			Rear, hypoid bevel, n/a (optional limited-slip)	
Axle ratios	4.27, with overdrive 4.55 (4.2 3.31, with overdrive 3.77) : 1			3.31, with overdrive 3.77 : 1	
Type of chassis	Unitary, front and rear subframes			Unitary, front and rear subframes	
Suspension, springing front	Double-wishbone, coil springs			Double-wishbone, coil springs	
Suspension, springing rear	Transverse and trailing arms, driveshafts, 2 coil springs each			Transverse and trailing arms, driveshafts, 2 coil springs each	
Reduction of roll	Torsion bar front			Torsion bar front	
Type of shock absorbers	Telescopic			Telescopic	
Type and dimensions of wheels	Steel discs, painted (optional chromed), 6 J x 15			Steel discs, painted (optional chromed), 6 J x 15	
Type, dimensions, make of tires	Dunlop SP, E 70 VR 15			Dunlop SP, E 70 VR 15 (from 1975 Pirelli P5, 205 VR 15)	
Type of braking front	Massive discs			Massive discs	
Type of braking rear	Massive inboard discs			Massive inboard discs	
Braking mechanism, number of circuits, servo assistance, electronic aids	Hydraulics, 2 circuits, front/rear balance valve, vacuum servo assistance, n/a			Hydraulics, 2 circuits, front/rear balance valve, vacuum servo assistance, n/a	
Steering gear, make and model of power steering	Rack and pinion, hydraulic servo Adwest Varamatic			Rack and pinion, hydraulic servo Adwest Varamatic	

** Prefixes "UF" (1975), "UG" (1976), "UH" (1977), or "UJ" (1978) denote US destination

* Some early examples for works use with 3.4 engines

Make, range	**Jaguar XJ 3.4 Series 2 and Daimler Sovereign**		**Jaguar XJ 6 L Series 2 and Daimler**		
Type	*XJ 3.4*	*Daimler Sovereign 3.4*	*XJ 4.2 L*	*Daimler Sovereign LWB*	*Daimler 4.2 Vanden Plas*
Public debut	4/1975	4/1975	13/9/1973	13/9/1973	30/4/1975
End of production	3/1979	3/1979	2/1979	2/1979	2/1979
Production figure	6880	2349	57,804	14,531	883
First, last chassis number RHD	3A 1001-6004*	3B 1001-3345	2T 1001-27236*	2S 1001-12816*	3C 1001-1818*
First, last chassis number LHD	3A 50001-51486	3B 50001-50004	2T 50001-74676*, **	2S 1001-50704*	3C 50001-50012*
Body type	All-steel, 4 doors, 5 seats		All-steel, 4 doors, 5 seats		
Weather protection, top mechanism	Enclosed-drive, optional manually operated folding sunroof		Enclosed-drive, optional manually operated folding sunroof		
Length, width, height (mm)	4945 x 1770 x 1375		4945 x 1770 x 1375		
Length, width, height (inches)	194 3/4 x 69 3/4 x 54		194 3/4 x 69 3/4 x 54		
Wheelbase, front, rear track (mm)	2864 x 1473/1486		2864 x 1473/1486		
Wheelbase, front, rear track (inches)	112 3/4 x 58/58 1/2		112 3/4 x 58/58 1/2		
Ground clearance, turning circle, curb weight	150mm, 12m, 1750kg		150mm, 12m, 1750 (Vanden Plas 1800) kg		
Max speed, acceleration 0-60 mph	185kph, 11 sec		190kph, 10 sec		
Max power, standard, revs	161 DIN-HP/5500 or 163 DIN-HP/5000		172 or 182 (from 1975 170 or 180 DIN /4500***)		
Max torque, revs	255 Nm/3500		305 or 313 Nm/3000 (US from 1977 306 Nm/2500, from 5/78 297 Nm/2500)		
Engine type, position, number and configuration of cylinders	Four-stroke gasoline, front longitudinally, 6 cylinders straight		Four-stroke gasoline, front longitudinally, 6 cylinders straight		
Bore x Stroke (mm), capacity (cc), compression ratio	83 x 106, 3442cc, 8.8 : 1		92.07 x 106, 4235cc, 7.8 (optional 9, US from 1977 always 7.5, from 5/78 7.8) : 1		
Designation of engine and cylinder head	Engine "XK," head "Straight Port"		Engine "XK," head "Straight Port"		
Engine block and cylinder head material, number of main bearings, type of liners	Block cast chrome-iron, head aluminum, 7 main bearings, n/a		Block cast chrome-iron, head aluminum, 7 main bearings, dry liners		
Number of valves per cylinder, configuration, valve gearing, timing variants	2 overhead valves, bucket tappets, 2 overhead camshafts, 2 duplex chains, fixed		2 overhead valves, bucket tappets, 2 overhead camshafts, 2 duplex chains, fixed		
Air supply, type of inlet manifold, air tempering	Normally aspirated, one-stage inlet manifold, pre-heating		Normally aspirated, one-stage inlet manifold, pre-heating (US from 5/78 n/a)		
Type, position, make, and designation of mixture preparation	2 horizontal carb., SU HS8 (from 1977 HIF7)		As XJ 3.4 (US from 5/78 electronic injection to manifold Bosch/Lucas L-Jetronic)		
Energy source, type, make, and designation of ignition system	Battery, breaker, Lucas		Battery, breaker, Lucas		
Make of alternator, voltage, earthing	Alternator, 12 V, negative		Alternator, 12 V, negative		
Engine coolant, drive, regulation of cooling	Liquid, pump, thermostat		Liquid, pump, thermostat		
Type of clutch, number of gears in manual box, synchronized gears	Single-plate dry clutch, 4, fully		Single-plate dry clutch, 4, fully		
Gear ratios in manual box	3.235, 1.905, 1.39, 1, 3.428 : 1		2.93, 1.905, 1.39, 1, 3.378 (from 4/75 3.03, 1.905, 1.39, 1, 3.428) : 1		
Make, type, ratio of overdrive	Always Laycock-de Normanville, electrically, 0.78 : 1		Always (4.2 L until 1974 optional) Laycock-de Normanville, electrically, 0.78 : 1		
Type of clutch, number of gears, make and model of automatic box	Optional hydraulic torque converter, 3, Borg-Warner 35 (from 12/73 65)		Optional (Vanden Plas always) as XJ 3.4, Borg-Warner 12 (from 12/73 Borg-Warner 65)		
Gear ratios in automatic gearbox	2.4, 1.45, 1, 2 : 1		2.4, 1.45, 1, 2 (from 4/75 2) : 1		
Driven axle, type of diff, traction control	Rear, hypoid bevel, n/a (optional limited-slip)		Rear, hypoid bevel, n/a (optional limited-slip)		
Axle ratios	3.54 : 1		3.31 (with overdrive 3.77) : 1		
Type of chassis	Unitary, front and rear subframes		Unitary, front and rear subframes		
Suspension, springing front	Double-wishbone, coil springs		Double-wishbone, coil springs		
Suspension, springing rear	Transverse and trailing arms, driveshafts, 2 coil springs each		Transverse and trailing arms, driveshafts, 2 coil springs each		
Reduction of roll	Torsion bar front		Torsion bar front		
Type of shock absorbers	Telescopic		Telescopic		
Type and dimensions of wheels	Steel discs, painted (optional chromed), 6 J x 15		Steel discs, painted (optional, Vanden Plas always chromed), 6 J x 15		
Type, dimensions, make of tires	Dunlop SP, E 70 (from 1975 Pirelli P5, 205) VR 15		Dunlop SP, E 70 (from 1975 Pirelli P5, 205) VR 15		
Type of braking front	Massive discs		Massive discs		
Type of braking rear	Massive inboard discs		Massive inboard discs		
Braking mechanism, number of circuits, servo assistance, electronic aids	Hydraulics, 2 circuits, front/rear balance valve, vacuum servo assistance, n/a		Hydraulics, 2 circuits, front/rear balance valve, vacuum servo assistance, n/a		
Steering gear, make and model of power steering	Rack and pinion, hydraulic servo Adwest Varamatic		Rack and pinion, hydraulic servo Adwest Varamatic		

*From 5/78 VIN 100001 to 111.727, without "UJ" prefix

**Prefix "UF" (1975), "UG" (1976), "UH" (1977), or "UJ" (1978) denote US destination

*** US from 1977 164, from 5/78 178 NET-HP/4750

Make, range	**Jaguar XJ 12 Series 2 and Daimler Double-Six**			**Jaguar XJ 12 C and Daimler Double-Six Two-Door**		
Type	*XJ 5.3 L*	*Daimler Double-Six*	*Double-Six Vanden Plas*	*XJ 5.3 C*****	*Daimler Double-Six Two-Door*	*XJ 12 C Broadspeed*
Public debut	13/9/1973	13/9/1973	13/9/1973	13/9/1973	13/9/1973	1976
End of production	2/1979	2/1979	2/1979	8/11/1977	8/11/1977	1976
Production figure	16,010	2608	1726	1873	399	See XJ 5.3 C
First, last chassis number RHD	2R 1001-5157*	2K 1001-2925*	2P 1001-2220*	2G 1001-1604	2F 1001-1372	See XJ 5.3 C
First, last chassis number LHD	2R 50001-60069*, **	2K 50001-50227*	2P 50001-50355*	2G 50001-51269**	2F 50001-50027	n/a
Body type	All-steel, 4 doors, 5 seats			All-steel (Broadspeed fiberglass), 2 doors, 5 seats		
Weather protection, top mechanism	Enclosed-drive, optional manually operated folding sunroof			Enclosed-drive (optional manually operated folding sunroof, not for Broadspeed)		
Length, width, height (mm)	4945 x 1770 x 1375			4845 x 1770 x 1375 (Broadspeed 4750 x 1900 x 1280)		
Length, width, height (inches)	194 3/4 x 69 3/4 x 54			190 3/4 x 69 3/4 x 54		
Wheelbase, front, rear track (mm)	2864 x 1473/1486			2762 x 1473/1486		
Wheelbase, front, rear track (inches)	112 3/4 x 58/58 1/2			108 3/4 x 58/58 1/2		
Ground clearance, turning circle, curb weight	150mm, 12m, 1850 (Vanden Plas 1900) kg			150 (Broadspeed 80)mm, 12m, 1800 (Broadspeed 1450) kg		
Max speed, acceleration 0-60 mph	224kph, 8 sec			224kph, 8 sec (Broadspeed 273kph, 6 sec)		
Max power, standard, revs	253 DIN-HP/6000 (from 5/75: 287 DIN-HP/5750***)			As 5.3 L (Broadspeed 560 SAE-HP/8000)		
Max torque, revs	407 Nm/3500 (from 5/75 399 Nm/3500, some markets and US 365 Nm/4500)			As 5.3 L (Broadspeed unknown)		
Engine type, position, number and configuration of cylinders	Four-stroke gasoline, front longitudinally, 12 cylinders, 60-degree-V			Four-stroke gasoline, front longitudinally, 12 cylinders, 60-degree-V		
Bore x Stroke (mm), capacity (cc), compression ratio	90 x 70, 5343cc, 9 (US from 5/75 7.8) : 1			As XJ 5.3 L (Broadspeed 90.6 x 70, 5416cc, unknown)		
Designation of engine and cylinder head	Engine "Jaguar V 12," head "Heron"			Engine "Jaguar V 12," head "Heron"		
Engine block and cylinder head material, number of main bearings, type of liners	Block and head aluminum, 7 main bearings, wet liners			Block and head aluminum, 7 main bearings, wet liners		
Number of valves per cylinder, configuration, valve gearing, timing variants	2 overhead valves, bucket tappets, 1 ohc per bank, duplex chain, fixed			2 overhead valves, bucket tappets, 1 ohc per bank, duplex chain, fixed		
Air supply, type of inlet manifold, air tempering	Normally aspirated, one-stage inlet manifold, n/a (US until 5/75 pre-heating)			Normally aspirated, one-stage inlet manifold, n/a (US until 5/75 pre-heating)		
Type, position, make, and designation of mixture preparation	4 horizontal carb., Zenith/Stromberg 175 CDSE (from 5/75 as 5.3 C)			As 5.3 L (from 5/75 electronic injection to manifold Bosch/Lucas D-Jetronic***)		
Energy source, type, make, and designation of ignition system	Battery, solid-state, Lucas OPUS			Battery, solid-state, Lucas OPUS		
Make of alternator, voltage, earthing	Alternator, 12 V, negative			Alternator, 12 V, negative		
Engine coolant, drive, regulation of cooling	Liquid, pump, thermostat			Liquid, pump, thermostat		
Type of clutch, number of gears in manual box, synchronized gears	n/a			n/a (Broadspeed AP racing clutch, 4, fully)		
Gear ratios in manual box	n/a			Unknown		
Make, type, ratio of overdrive	n/a			n/a		
Type of clutch, number of gears, make and model of automatic box	Hydraulic torque converter, 3, Borg-Warner 12 (from 4/77 GM 400)			Hydraulic torque converter, 3, Borg-Warner 12 (Broadspeed n/a)		
Gear ratios in automatic gearbox	2.4, 1.45, 1, 2 (from 4/77 2.48, 1.48.1, 2.08) : 1			2.4, 1.45, 1, 2 (from 4/77 2.48, 1.48, 1, 2.08) : 1		
Driven axle, type of diff, traction control	Rear, hypoid bevel, limited-slip			Rear, hypoid bevel, limited-slip		
Axle ratios	3.07 : 1			3.07 : 1		
Type of chassis	Unitary, front and rear subframes			Unitary, front and rear subframes		
Suspension, springing front	Double-wishbone, coil springs			Double-wishbone, coil springs		
Suspension, springing rear	Transverse and trailing arms, driveshafts, 2 coil springs each			Transverse and trailing arms, driveshafts, 2 coil springs each		
Reduction of roll	Torsion bar front			Torsion bar front		
Type of shock absorbers	Telescopic			Telescopic		
Type and dimensions of wheels	Steel discs, painted (optional, Vanden Plas always chromed), 6 J x 15			As 5.3 L (Broadspeed Aluminum discs, unknown)		
Type, dimensions, make of tires	Dunlop SP, E 70 (from 1975 Pirelli P5, 205) VR 15			As 5.3 L (Broadspeed Dunlop, unknown)		
Type of braking front	Ventilated discs			Ventilated discs		
Type of braking rear	Massive inboard discs	Massive inboard discs				
Braking mechanism, number of circuits, servo assistance, electronic aids	Hydraulics, 2 circuits, front/rear balance valve, vacuum servo assistance, n/a			Hydraulics, 2 circuits, front/rear balance valve, vacuum servo assistance, n/a		
Steering gear, make and model of power steering	Rack and pinion, hydraulic servo Adwest Varamatic			Rack and pinion, hydraulic servo Adwest Varamatic		

* From 5/78 chassis numbers VIN 100001 to 111.727, without "UJ" prefix
** Prefixes "UE" (1974), "UF" (1975), "UG" (1976), "UH" (1977), or "UJ" (1978) denote US destination
*** From 5/75 some markets 275 DIN-HP/5400, US 244 NET-HP/5250, Broadspeed mechanical Lucas injection to manifold
**** 1975: 1 Coupe in Vanden Plas guise, 1850kg, chassis no. 2G 50002

Make, range	**Jaguar XJ 6 Series 3 and Daimler**			**Jaguar XJ 6 Series 3 and Daimler**		
Type	*Jaguar XJ 6 3.4*	*Jaguar XJ 6 4.2*	*Jaguar Sovereign 4.2*	*Daimler Sovereign 4.2*	*Jaguar Vanden Plas 4.2*	*Daimler 4.2 Vanden Plas*
Public debut	28/3/1979	28/3/1979	9/1982	28/3/1979	11/1980	28/3/1979
End of production	6/1986	5/1987	6/1986	9/1983	5/1987	6/1986
Production figure	5767	97,565	18,655	9049	18,837	1879
First, last chassis number RHD	VIN 300001-399999 and 410001-477824			VIN 300001-399999 and 410001-477824		
First, last chassis number LHD	VIN 300001-399999 and 410001-477824			VIN 300001-399999 and 410001-477824		
Body type	All-steel, 4 doors, 5 seats			All-steel, 4 doors, 5 seats		
Weather protection, top mechanism	Enclosed-drive, optional electrically operated steel sunroof			Enclosed-drive, optional electrically operated steel sunroof		
Length, width, height (mm)	4958 x 1771 x 1372			4958 x 1771 x 1372		
Length, width, height (inches)	195 1/4 x 69 3/4 x 54			195 1/4 x 69 3/4 x 54		
Wheelbase, front, rear track (mm)	2864 x 1473/1486			2864 x 1473/1486		
Wheelbase, front, rear track (inches)	112 3/4 x 58/58 1/2			112 3/4 x 58/58 1/2		
Ground clearance, turning circle, curb weight	150mm, 12m, 1800kg			150mm, 12m, 1800 (Vanden Plas 1850) kg		
Max speed, acceleration 0-60 mph	185kph, 11 sec (4.2 205kph, 9 sec)			205kph, 9 sec		
Max power, standard, revs	161 DIN-HP/5000 (4.2 205 DIN-HP/5000, US 178 NET-HP/4750, CH as Vanden Plas)			As 4.2 (CH 1982 179 DIN-HP/4500, 1983 181/5000, from 1984 178/5000)		
Max torque, revs	255 Nm/3500 (4.2 310 Nm/1500, US 297 Nm/2500, CH from 1982 300 Nm/3500)			310 Nm/1500 (US 297 Nm/2500, CH from 1982 300 Nm/3500)		
Engine type, position, number and configuration of cylinders	Four-stroke gasoline, front longitudinally, 6 cylinders straight			Four-stroke gasoline, front longitudinally, 6 cylinders straight		
Bore x Stroke (mm), capacity (cc), compression ratio	83 x 106, 3442cc, 8.8 (4.2 wie Daimler and Vanden Plas)			92.07 x 106, 4235cc, 8.7 (US 7.8, CH from 1983 8.1) :1		
Designation of engine and cylinder head	Engine "XK," head "Straight Port"			Engine "XK," head "Straight Port"		
Engine block and cylinder head material, number of main bearings, type of liners	Block cast chrome-iron, head aluminum, 7 main bearings, n/a (4.2 dry liners)			Block cast chrome-iron, head aluminum, 7 main bearings, dry liners		
Number of valves per cylinder, configuration, valve gearing, timing variants	2 overhead valves, bucket tappets, 2 overhead camshafts, 2 duplex chains, fixed			2 overhead valves, bucket tappets, 2 overhead camshafts, 2 duplex chains, fixed		
Air supply, type of inlet manifold, air tempering	Normally aspirated, one-stage inlet manifold, n/a			Normally aspirated, one-stage inlet manifold, n/a		
Type, position, make, and designation of mixture preparation	2 horizontal carb., SU (4.2 as Vanden Plas)			Electronic injection to manifold Bosch/Lucas L-Jetronic		
Energy source, type, make, and designation of ignition system	Battery, breaker (4.2 solid-state), Lucas			Battery, solid-state, Lucas		
Make of alternator, voltage, earthing	Alternator, 12 V, negative			Alternator, 12 V, negative		
Engine coolant, drive, regulation of cooling	Liquid, pump, thermostat			Liquid, pump, thermostat		
Type of clutch, number of gears in manual box, synchronized gears	n/a (from 1982 single-plate dry clutch, 5, fully)		n/a (from 1982 single-plate dry clutch, 5, fully)			
Gear ratios in manual box	3.32, 2.09, 1.4, 1, 0.79, 3.428 : 1			3.32, 2.09, 1.4, 1, 0.79, 3.428 : 1		
Make, type, ratio of overdrive	n/a			n/a		
Type of clutch, number of gears, make and model of automatic box	Optional hydraulic torque converter, 3, Borg-Warner 65 (from 6/79 66)			Optional (Vanden Plas always) hydraulic torque converter, 3, Borg-Warner 65 (from 6/79 66)		
Gear ratios in automatic gearbox	2.4, 1.45, 1, 2 : 1			2.4, 1.45, 1, 2 : 1		
Driven axle, type of diff, traction control	Rear, hypoid bevel, n/a (optional limited-slip)			Rear, hypoid bevel, n/a (optional limited-slip)		
Axle ratios	3.54 (4.2 3.31, 4.2 with automatic 3.07) : 1			3.31 (with automatic 3.07) : 1		
Type of chassis	Unitary, front and rear subframes			Unitary, front and rear subframes		
Suspension, springing front	Double-wishbone, coil springs			Double-wishbone, coil springs		
Suspension, springing rear	Transverse and trailing arms, driveshafts, 2 coil springs each			Transverse and trailing arms, driveshafts, 2 coil springs each		
Reduction of roll	Torsion bar front			Torsion bar front		
Type of shock absorbers	Telescopic			Telescopic		
Type and dimensions of wheels	Steel discs, painted (Sovereign aluminum discs), 6 J x 15			Aluminum discs, 6 J x 15		
Type, dimensions, make of tires	Pirelli P5, 205 VR 15			Pirelli P5, 205 VR 15		
Type of braking front	Massive discs			Massive discs		
Type of braking rear	Massive inboard discs			Massive inboard discs		
Braking mechanism, number of circuits, servo assistance, electronic aids	Hydraulics, 2 circuits, front/rear balance valve, vacuum servo assistance, n/a			Hydraulics, 2 circuits, front/rear balance valve, vacuum servo assistance, n/a		
Steering gear, make and model of power steering	Rack and pinion, hydraulic servo Adwest Varamatic			Rack and pinion, hydraulic servo Adwest Varamatic		

Make, range	**Jaguar XJ 12 Series 3 and Daimler Double-Six**			**Jaguar XJ 12 Series 3 and Daimler Double-Six**	
Type	*Jaguar XJ 12**	*Daimler Double-Six*	*D. Double-Six Vanden Plas***	*Jaguar Sovereign*	*Jaguar Vanden Plas*
Public debut	28/3/1979	28/3/1979	28/3/1979	9/1982	9/1982
End of production	8/1983	8/1983	11/1992	11/1992	1992
Production figure	2861	2581	9757	7753	2952
First, last chassis number RHD	VIN 300001-399999 and 410001-487641			VIN unknown-399999 and 410001-487641	
First, last chassis number LHD	VIN 300001-399999 and 410001-487641			VIN unknown-399999 and 410001-487641	
Body type	All-steel, 4 doors, 5 seats			All-steel, 4 doors, 5 seats	
Weather protection, top mechanism	Enclosed-drive, optional (standard for Vanden Plas) electrically operated steel sunroof			Enclosed-drive, optional (standard for Vanden Plas) electrically operated steel sunroof	
Length, width, height (mm)	4958 x 1771 x 1372			4958 x 1771 x 1372	
Length, width, height (inches)	195 1/4 x 69 3/4 x 54			195 1/4 x 69 3/4 x 54	
Wheelbase, front, rear track (mm)	2864 x 1473/1486			2864 x 1473/1486	
Wheelbase, front, rear track (inches)	112 3/4 x 58/58 1/2			112 3/4 x 58/58 1/2	
Ground clearance, turning circle, curb weight	150mm, 12m, 1900 (Vanden Plas 1950) kg			150mm, 12m, 1900 (Vanden Plas 1950) kg	
Max speed, acceleration 0-60 mph	230kph, 8 sec			230kph, 8 sec	
Max power, standard, revs	287 DIN-HP/5750*** (from 7/80 290 or 299 DIN-HP/5400, from 6/81 as Sovereign)			295 DIN-HP/5500 (catalyst 266 NET-HP/5000, from 1990 268 DIN-HP/5000)****	
Max torque, revs	399 Nm/3500*** (from 7/80 436 Nm/3900 or 434 Nm/4000, from 6/81 as Sovereign)			432 Nm/3300, catalyst 393 Nm/3000, from 1990 384 Nm/3000)****	
Engine type, position, number and configuration of cylinders	Four-stroke gasoline, front longitudinally, 12 cylinders, 60-degree-V			Four-stroke gasoline, front longitudinally, 12 cylinders, 60-degree-V	
Bore x Stroke (mm), capacity (cc), compression ratio	90 x 70, 5343cc, 9 (US 7.8, from 7/80 10, from 6/81 12.5 (with catalyst 11.5) : 1			90 x 70, 5343cc, 12.5 (with catalyst 11.5) : 1	
Designation of engine and cylinder head	Engine "Jaguar V-12," head "Heron" (from 6/81 "Fireball")			Engine "Jaguar V-12," head "Fireball"	
Engine block and cylinder head material, number of main bearings, type of liners	Block and head aluminum, 7 main bearings, wet liners			Block and head aluminum, 7 main bearings, wet liners	
Number of valves per cylinder, configuration, valve gearing, timing variants	2 overhead valves, bucket tappets, 1 ohc per bank, duplex chain, fixed			2 overhead valves, bucket tappets, 1 ohc per bank, duplex chain, fixed	
Air supply, type of inlet manifold, air tempering	Normally aspirated, one-stage inlet manifold, n/a			Normally aspirated, one-stage inlet manifold, n/a	
Type, position, make, and designation of mixture preparation	Electronic injection to manifold Bosch/Lucas D- (from 6/81 L-) Jetronic			Electronic injection to manifold Bosch/Lucas L-Jetronic	
Energy source, type, make, and designation of ignition system	Battery, solid-state, Lucas OPUS			Battery, solid-state, Lucas OPUS	
Make of alternator, voltage, earthing	Alternator, 12 V, negative			Alternator, 12 V, negative	
Engine coolant, drive, regulation of cooling	Liquid, pump, thermostat			Liquid, pump, thermostat	
Type of clutch, number of gears in manual box, synchronized gears	n/a			n/a	
Gear ratios in manual box	n/a			n/a	
Make, type, ratio of overdrive	n/a			n/a	
Type of clutch, number of gears, make and model of automatic box	Hydraulic torque converter, 3, GM 400			Hydraulic torque converter, 3, GM 400	
Gear ratios in automatic gearbox	2.48, 1.48.1, 2.08 : 1			2.48, 1.48.1, 2.08 : 1	
Driven axle, type of diff, traction control	Rear, hypoid bevel, limited-slip			Rear, hypoid bevel, limited-slip	
Axle ratios	3.07 (from 6/81 2.88) : 1			2.88 : 1	
Type of chassis	Unitary, front and rear subframes			Unitary, front and rear subframes	
Suspension, springing front	Double-wishbone, coil springs			Double-wishbone, coil springs	
Suspension, springing rear	Transverse and trailing arms, driveshafts, 2 coil springs each			Transverse and trailing arms, driveshafts, 2 coil springs each	
Reduction of roll	Torsion bar front			Torsion bar front	
Type of shock absorbers	Telescopic			Telescopic	
Type and dimensions of wheels	Steel discs, painted (from 6/81 Daimler aluminum discs), 6 J x 15			Aluminum discs, 6 J x 15	
Type, dimensions, make of tires	Pirelli P5, 205 VR 15 (from 6/81 215/70 VR 15)			Pirelli P5, 215/70 VR 15	
Type of braking front	Ventilated discs			Ventilated discs	
Type of braking rear	Massive inboard discs			Massive inboard discs	
Braking mechanism, number of circuits, servo assistance, electronic aids	Hydraulics, 2 circuits, front/rear balance valve, vacuum servo assistance, antilock from 1989			Hydraulics, 2 circuits, front/rear balance valve, vacuum servo assistance, antilock from 1989	
Steering gear, make and model of power steering	Rack and pinion, hydraulic servo Adwest Varamatic			Rack and pinion, hydraulic servo Adwest Varamatic	

* US deliveries ended 1979 after less than 40 examples

** 9/83 re-named Daimler Double-Six

*** US 247 NET-HP/5250, some markets 275 DIN-HP/5400, both 365 Nm/4500

**** CH '83-86 269, then 264 DIN-HP/5250, some markets from '91 225/5000; 1983-86 394 Nm/3000, then 377 Nm/2750, some markets from 1991389 Nm/3000

Make, range	**Early Jaguar XJ-S**			**Jaguar XJ-S "Digital P"**
Type	*Coupe '75*	*SCCA 1976*	*(1981)*	*Coupe '80*
Public debut	10/9/1975	1976	(1981)	7/1980
End of production	6/1980	1976	(1981)	6/1981
Production figure	14,927	2	(2)	See Coupe '75
First, last chassis number RHD	2W 1001-5000* and VIN 100001-104145			VIN 104146-105047
First, last chassis number LHD	2W 50001-55915* and VIN 100001-104145			VIN 104146-105047
Body type	All-steel (SCCA with fiberglass, 1981 with aluminum), 2 doors, 2+2 seats			All-steel, 2 doors, 2 + 2 seats
Weather protection, top mechanism	Enclosed-drive			Enclosed-drive
Length, width, height (mm)	4864 x 1793 x 1262 (SCCA 4700 x 1900 x 1180)			4864 x 1793 x 1262
Length, width, height (inches)	191 1/2 x 70 1/2 x 49 3/4 (SCCA 185 x 75 x 47)			191 1/2 x 70 1/2 x 49 3/4
Wheelbase, front, rear track (mm)	2593 x 1473/1486 (SCCA 2593 x 1549/1524, 1981 2593 x 1575/1524)			2593 x 1473/1486
Wheelbase, front, rear track (inches)	102 x 58/58 1/2			102 x 58/58 1/2
Ground clearance, turning circle, curb weight	140mm (SCCA 80mm), 11m, 1750 (SCCA 1450, 1981 1150) kg			140mm, 11m, 1750kg
Max speed, acceleration 0-60 mph	235kph, 7 sec (SCCA 300kph, 5 sec)			235kph, 7 sec
Max power, standard, revs	287 DIN-HP/5750 (US 247 DIN-HP/5250**)			299 DIN-HP/5400 (some markets 290 DIN-HP/5500, US 262 NET-HP/5000)
Max torque, revs	399Nm/3500 (US 365 Nm/4500, SCCA unknown)			436 Nm/3900 (some markets 434 Nm/4000, US 392 Nm/4000)
Engine type, position, number and configuration of cylinders	Four-stroke gasoline, front longitudinally, 12 cylinders, 60-degree-V			Four-stroke gasoline, front longitudinally, 12 cylinders, 60-degree-V
Bore x Stroke (mm), capacity (cc), compression ratio	90 x 70, 5343cc, 9 (US 7.8, SCCA 10) : 1			90 x 70, 5343cc, 10 (US 9) : 1
Designation of engine and cylinder head	Engine "Jaguar V-12," head "Heron"			Engine "Jaguar V-12," head "Heron"
Engine block and cylinder head material, number of main bearings, type of liners	Block and head aluminum, 7 main bearings, wet liners			Block and head aluminum, 7 main bearings, wet liners
Number of valves per cylinder, configuration, valve gearing, timing variants	2 overhead valves, bucket tappets, 1 ohc per bank, duplex chain, fixed			2 overhead valves, bucket tappets, 1 ohc per bank, duplex chain, fixed
Air supply, type of inlet manifold, air tempering	Normally aspirated, one-stage inlet manifold, n/a			Normally aspirated, one-stage inlet manifold, n/a
Type, position, make, and designation of mixture preparation	Electronic injection to manifold Bosch/Lucas D-Jetronic (SCCA 6 twin carb., Weber)			Electronic injection to manifold Bosch/Lucas D-Jetronic digital
Energy source, type, make, and designation of ignition system	Battery, solid-state, Lucas OPUS (SCCA unknown)			Battery, solid-state, Lucas OPUS
Make of alternator, voltage, earthing	Alternator, 12 V, negative			Alternator, 12 V, negative
Engine coolant, drive, regulation of cooling	Liquid, pump, thermostat			Liquid, pump, thermostat
Type of clutch, number of gears in manual box, synchronized gears	Single-plate dry clutch, 4, fully (SCCA racing clutch, 5, fully)			n/a
Gear ratios in manual box	3.235, 1.905, 1.39, 1, 3.428 (SCCA unknown) : 1			n/a
Make, type, ratio of overdrive	n/a			n/a
Type of clutch, number of gears, make and model of automatic box	Optional (from 1979 always, SCCA n/a) hydraulic torque converter, 3, GM 400 (until 4/77 Borg-Warner 12)			Hydraulic torque converter, 3, GM 400
Gear ratios in automatic gearbox	2.4, 1.45, 1, 2 (from 4/77 2.48, 1.48.1, 2.08) : 1			2.48, 1.48.1, 2.08 : 1
Driven axle, type of diff, traction control	Rear, hypoid bevel, limited-slip			Rear, hypoid bevel, limited-slip
Axle ratios	3.07 (SCCA unknown) : 1			3.07 : 1
Type of chassis	Unitary, front and rear subframes (SCCA tubular chassis)			Unitary, front and rear subframes
Suspension, springing front	Double-wishbone, coil springs			Double-wishbone, coil springs
Suspension, springing rear	Transverse and trailing arms, driveshafts, 2 coil springs each			Transverse and trailing arms, driveshafts, 2 coil springs each
Reduction of roll	Torsion bars front and rear			Torsion bars front and rear
Type of shock absorbers	Telescopic			Telescopic
Type and dimensions of wheels	Aluminum discs, 6 (SCCA 10) J x 15			Aluminum discs, 6 J x 15
Type, dimensions, make of tires	Pirelli P5, 205 VR 15 (SCCA Goodyear, unknown)			Pirelli P5, 205 VR 15
Type of braking front	Ventilated discs			Ventilated discs
Type of braking rear	Massive inboard discs			Massive inboard discs
Braking mechanism, number of circuits, servo assistance, electronic aids	Hydraulics, 2 circuits, front/rear balance valve, vacuum servo assistance, n/a			Hydraulics, 2 circuits, front/rear balance valve, vacuum servo assistance, n/a
Steering gear, make and model of power steering	Rack and pinion, hydraulic servo Adwest Varamatic			Rack and pinion, hydraulic servo Adwest Varamatic

* Prefix "UG" ('76'), "UH" ('77) or "UJ" ('78) denote US destination
** SCCA 525 SAE-HP/7500, 1981 570 SAE-HP/8000

Make, range	**Jaguar XJ-S 3.6**	**Jaguar XJ-SC 3.6**
Type	*XJ-S 3.6*	*XJ-SC 3.6*
Public debut	12/10/1983	12/10/1983
End of production	4/1991	10/1986
Production figure	8867	1150
First, last chassis number RHD	VIN 112586-179736	VIN 112588-148594
First, last chassis number LHD	VIN 112586-179736	VIN 112588-148594
Body type	All-steel, 2 doors, 2 + 2 seats	All-steel, 2 doors, 2 seats
Weather protection, top mechanism	Enclosed-drive	Targa roof, rear manually operated top
Length, width, height (mm)	4765 x 1793 x 1262	4765 x 1793 x 1262
Length, width, height (inches)	187 3/4 x 70 1/2 x 49 3/4	187 3/4 x 70 1/2 x 49 3/4
Wheelbase, front, rear track (mm)	2593 x 1473/1486	2593 x 1473/1486
Wheelbase, front, rear track (inches)	102 x 58/58 1/2	102 x 58/58 1/2
Ground clearance, turning circle, curb weight	140mm, 11m, 1650kg	140mm, 11m, 1650kg
Max speed, acceleration 0-60 mph	220kph, 7 sec	220kph, 7 sec
Max power, standard, revs	As SC (from 1987 224 DIN-HP/5100, from 1988 optional 198 or 202 DIN-HP/5250)	228 DIN-HP/5300 (some markets 220 DIN-HP/5250)
Max torque, revs	As SC (from 1987 337 Nm/4000, from 1988 optional 302 Nm/4000)	325 Nm/4000 (some markets 325 Nm/4000)
Engine type, position, number and configuration of cylinders	Four-stroke gasoline, front longitudinally, 6 cylinders straight	Four-stroke gasoline, front longitudinally, 6 cylinders straight
Bore x Stroke (mm), capacity (cc), compression ratio	91 x 92, 3590cc, 9.6 : 1	91 x 92, 3590cc, 9.6 : 1
Designation of engine and cylinder head	Engine and head "AJ 6"	Engine and head "AJ 6"
Engine block and cylinder head material, number of main bearings, type of liners	Block and head aluminum, 7 main bearings, dry liners	Block and head aluminum, 7 main bearings, dry liners
Number of valves per cylinder, configuration, valve gearing, timing variants	4 overhead valves, bucket tappets, 2 overhead camshafts, 2 duplex chains, fixed	4 overhead valves, bucket tappets, 2 overhead camshafts, 2 duplex chains, fixed
Air supply, type of inlet manifold, air tempering	Normally aspirated, one-stage inlet manifold, n/a	Normally aspirated, one-stage inlet manifold, n/a
Type, position, make, and designation of mixture preparation	Electronic injection to manifold Bosch/Lucas D-Jetronic	Electronic injection to manifold Bosch/Lucas D-Jetronic
Energy source, type, make, and designation of ignition system	Battery, solid-state, Lucas 9CU	Battery, solid-state, Lucas 9CU
Make of alternator, voltage, earthing	Alternator, 12 V, negative	Alternator, 12 V, negative
Engine coolant, drive, regulation of cooling	Liquid, pump, thermostat	Liquid, pump, thermostat
Type of clutch, number of gears in manual box, synchronized gears	Single-plate dry clutch, 5, fully	Single-plate dry clutch, 5, fully
Gear ratios in manual box	3.57, 2.96, 1.39, 1, 0.76, 3.46 : 1	3.57, 2.96, 1.39, 1, 0.76, 3.46 : 1
Make, type, ratio of overdrive	n/a	n/a
Type of clutch, number of gears, make and model of automatic box	From 1987 optional hydraulic torque converter, 4, ZF 4 HP 22	n/a
Gear ratios in automatic gearbox	2.48, 1.48.1, 0.73, 2.09 : 1	n/a
Driven axle, type of diff, traction control	Rear, hypoid bevel, limited-slip	Rear, hypoid bevel, limited-slip
Axle ratios	3.54 : 1	3.54 : 1
Type of chassis	Unitary, front and rear subframes	Unitary, front and rear subframes
Suspension, springing front	Double-wishbone, coil springs	Double-wishbone, coil springs
Suspension, springing rear	Transverse and trailing arms, driveshafts, 2 coil springs each	Transverse and trailing arms, driveshafts, 2 coil springs each
Reduction of roll	Torsion bars front and rear	Torsion bars front and rear
Type of shock absorbers	Telescopic	Telescopic
Type and dimensions of wheels	Aluminum discs, 7.5 J x 15	Aluminum discs, 7.5 J x 15
Type, dimensions, make of tires	Pirelli P5, 215/70 VR 15 (from 9/87 Pirelli P 600 235/60 VR 15)	Pirelli P5, 215/70 VR 15
Type of braking front	Ventilated discs	Ventilated discs
Type of braking rear	Massive inboard discs	Massive inboard discs
Braking mechanism, number of circuits, servo assistance, electronic aids	Hydraulics, 2 circuits, front/rear balance pipe, vacuum servo assistance, antilock from 1989	Hydraulics, 2 circuits, front/rear balance valve, vacuum servo assistance, antilock from 1989
Steering gear, make and model of power steering	Rack and pinion, hydraulic servo Adwest Varamatic	Rack and pinion, hydraulic servo Adwest Varamatic

Make, range	**Jaguar XJ-S H.E.**		**Jaguar XJ-SC H.E.**	
Type	*XJ-S H.E.**	*XJR-S*	*XJ-SC H.E.***	*Convertible*
Public debut	6/1981	22/8/1988	7/1985	2/1988
End of production	11/1990	8/1989	12/1987	11/1990
Production figure	43,950	293	3863	12,371
First, last chassis number RHD	VIN 105048-179736	VIN unknown-unknown	VIN 125021-148594	VIN 147269-179736
First, last chassis number LHD	VIN 105048-179736	VIN unknown-unknown	VIN 125021-148594	VIN 147269-179736
Body type	All-steel, 2 doors, 2 + 2 seats		All-steel, 2 doors, 2 seats	
Weather protection, top mechanism	Enclosed-drive		Targa roof, rear manually (convertible electrically) operated top	
Length, width, height (mm)	4765 x 1793 x 1262		4765 x 1793 x 1262	
Length, width, height (inches)	187 3/4 x 70 1/2 x 49 3/4		187 3/4 x 70 1/2 x 49 3/4	
Wheelbase, front, rear track (mm)	2593 x 1473/1486		2593 x 1473/1486	
Wheelbase, front, rear track (inches)	102 x 58/58 1/2		102 x 58/58 1/2	
Ground clearance, turning circle, curb weight	140mm, 11m, 1750kg		140mm, 11m, 1750 (convertible 1850) kg	
Max speed, acceleration 0-60 mph	240kph, 7 sec		240kph, 7 sec	
Max power, standard, revs	295 DIN-HP/5500 (from 12/89 some markets 290 DIN-HP/5150, catalyst as SC)***		As XJ-S H.E. (catalyst 269 DIN-HP/5250, from 12/89 264 DIN-HP/5150)	
Max torque, revs	432 Nm/3300 (from 12/89 some markets 420 Nm/2800, catalyst as SC)***		As XJ-S H.E. (catalyst 394 Nm/3000, from 12/89 420 Nm/2800)	
Engine type, position, number and configuration of cylinders	Four-stroke gasoline, front longitudinally, 12 cylinders, 60-degree-V		Four-stroke gasoline, front longitudinally, 12 cylinders, 60-degree-V	
Bore x Stroke (mm), capacity (cc), compression ratio	90 x 70, 5343cc, 12.5 (US and catalyst 11.5) : 1		90 x 70, 5343cc, 12.5 (US and catalyst 11.5) : 1	
Designation of engine and cylinder head	Engine "Jaguar V-12," head "Fireball"		Engine "Jaguar V-12," head "Fireball"	
Engine block and cylinder head material, number of main bearings, type of liners	Block and head aluminum, 7 main bearings, wet liners		Block and head aluminum, 7 main bearings, wet liners	
Number of valves per cylinder, configuration, valve gearing, timing variants	2 overhead valves, bucket tappets, 1 ohc per bank, duplex chain, fixed		2 overhead valves, bucket tappets, 1 ohc per bank, duplex chain, fixed	
Air supply, type of inlet manifold, air tempering	Normally aspirated, one-stage inlet manifold, n/a		Normally aspirated, one-stage inlet manifold, n/a	
Type, position, make, and designation of mixture preparation	Electronic injection to manifold Bosch/Lucas L-Jetronic		Electronic injection to manifold Bosch/Lucas L-Jetronic	
Energy source, type, make, and designation of ignition system	Battery, solid-state, Lucas OPUS		Battery, solid-state, Lucas OPUS	
Make of alternator, voltage, earthing	Alternator, 12 V, negative		Alternator, 12 V, negative	
Engine coolant, drive, regulation of cooling	Liquid, pump, thermostat		Liquid, pump, thermostat	
Type of clutch, number of gears in manual box, synchronized gears	n/a		n/a	
Gear ratios in manual box	n/a		n/a	
Make, type, ratio of overdrive	n/a		n/a	
Type of clutch, number of gears, make and model of automatic box	Hydraulic torque converter, 3, GM 400		Hydraulic torque converter, 3, GM 400	
Gear ratios in automatic gearbox	2.48, 1.48, 1, 2.08 : 1		2.48, 1.48, 1, 2.08 : 1	
Driven axle, type of diff, traction control	Rear, hypoid bevel, limited-slip		Rear, hypoid bevel, limited-slip	
Axle ratios	2.88 : 1		2.88 : 1	
Type of chassis	Unitary, front and rear subframes		Unitary, front and rear subframes	
Suspension, springing front	Double-wishbone, coil springs		Double-wishbone, coil springs	
Suspension, springing rear	Transverse and trailing arms, driveshafts, 2 coil springs each		Transverse and trailing arms, driveshafts, 2 coil springs each	
Reduction of roll	Torsion bars front and rear		Torsion bars front and rear	
Type of shock absorbers	Telescopic		Telescopic	
Type and dimensions of wheels	Aluminum discs, 6.5 J x 15		Aluminum discs, 6.5 J x 15	
Type, dimensions, make of tires	Pirelli P5, 215/70 VR 15		Pirelli P5, 215/70 VR 15	
Type of braking front	Ventilated discs		Ventilated discs	
Type of braking rear	Massive inboard discs		Massive inboard discs	
Braking mechanism, number of circuits, servo assistance, electronic aids	Hydraulics, 2 circuits, front/rear balance valve, vacuum servo assistance, antilock from 1989		Hydraulics, 2 circuits, front/rear balance valve, vacuum servo assistance, antilock from 1989	
Steering gear, make and model of power steering	Rack and pinion, hydraulic servo Adwest Varamatic		Rack and pinion, hydraulic servo Adwest Varamatic	

* 1 prototype with 2760mm wheelbase

*** US –1989: 266 NET-HP/5000 and 393 Nm/3000, then as SC with catalyst

** 1 prototype as Coupe Daimler Double-Six S with fixed roof

Make, range	**Jaguar XJ-S TWR**	**XJR-S 6.0**
Type	*Sports Touring Car*	*XJR-S 6.0*
Public debut	1982	19/10/1989
End of production	1984	4/1991
Production figure	Unknown	448
First, last chassis number RHD	Unknown VIN	179737-unknown
First, last chassis number LHD	n/a	VIN 179737-unknown
Body type	All-steel, 2 doors, 2 + 2 seats	All-steel, 2 doors, 2 + 2 seats
Weather protection, top mechanism	Enclosed-drive	Enclosed-drive
Length, width, height (mm)	4786 x 1790 x 1210	4765 x 1793 x 1262
Length, width, height (inches)	188 1/2 x 70 1/2 x 47 3/4	187 3/4 x 70 1/2 x 49 3/4
Wheelbase, front, rear track (mm)	2593 x 1473/1486	2593 x 1473/1486
Wheelbase, front, rear track (inches)	102 x 58/58 1/2	102 x 58/58 1/2
Ground clearance, turning circle, curb weight	140mm, 11m, 1750kg	140mm, 11m, 1750kg
Max speed, acceleration 0-60 mph	300kph, 5 sec	248kph, 7 sec
Max power, standard, revs	460 DIN-HP/5750	309 or 323 DIN-HP/5250
Max torque, revs	520 Nm/unknown	468 Nm/3000 or 491 Nm/3750
Engine type, position, number and configuration of cylinders	Four-stroke gasoline, front longitudinally, 12 cylinders, 60-degree-V	Four-stroke gasoline, front longitudinally, 12 cylinders, 60-degree-V
Bore x Stroke (mm), capacity (cc), compression ratio	90 x 70, 5343cc, 9 : 1	90 x 78.5, 5993cc, 11.2 : 1
Designation of engine and cylinder head	Engine "Jaguar V-12," head "TWR"	Engine "Jaguar V-12," head "TWR"
Engine block and cylinder head material, number of main bearings, type of liners	Block and head aluminum, 7 main bearings, wet liners	Block and head aluminum, 7 main bearings, wet liners
Number of valves per cylinder, configuration, valve gearing, timing variants	2 overhead valves, bucket tappets, 1 ohc per bank, duplex chain, fixed	2 overhead valves, bucket tappets, 1 ohc per bank, duplex chain, fixed
Air supply, type of inlet manifold, air tempering	Normally aspirated, one-stage inlet manifold, n/a	Normally aspirated, one-stage inlet manifold, n/a
Type, position, make, and designation of mixture preparation	Electronic injection to manifold Bosch-Lucas D-Jetronic	Electronic injection to manifold Lucas L-Jetronic
Energy source, type, make, and designation of ignition system	Battery, solid-state, unknown	Battery, solid-state, Lucas/Zytec
Make of alternator, voltage, earthing	Alternator, 12 V, negative	Alternator, 12 V, negative
Engine coolant, drive, regulation of cooling	Liquid, pump, thermostat	Liquid, pump, thermostat
Type of clutch, number of gears in manual box, synchronized gears	Single-plate dry clutch, 4 or 5, fully	n/a
Gear ratios in manual box	Unknown	n/a
Make, type, ratio of overdrive	n/a	n/a
Type of clutch, number of gears, make and model of automatic box	n/a	Hydraulic torque converter, 3, GM 400
Gear ratios in automatic gearbox	n/a	2.48, 1.48, 1, 2.08 : 1
Driven axle, type of diff, traction control	Rear, hypoid bevel, limited-slip	Rear, hypoid bevel, limited-slip
Axle ratios	Unknown	2.88 : 1
Type of chassis	Unitary, front and rear subframes	Unitary, front and rear subframes
Suspension, springing front	Double-wishbone, coil springs	Double-wishbone, coil springs
Suspension, springing rear	Transverse and trailing arms, driveshafts, 2 coil springs each	Transverse and trailing arms, driveshafts, 2 coil springs each
Reduction of roll	Torsion bars front and rear	Torsion bars front and rear
Type of shock absorbers	Telescopic	Telescopic
Type and dimensions of wheels	Aluminum discs, 6.5 J x 15	Aluminum discs, 6.5 J x 15
Type, dimensions, make of tires	Dunlop, unknown	Pirelli P5, 215/70 VR 15 (from 10/90 Dunlop D40, 225/60, rear 245/55 VR 15)
Type of braking front	Ventilated discs	Ventilated discs
Type of braking rear	Massive inboard discs	Massive inboard discs
Braking mechanism, number of circuits, servo assistance, electronic aids	Hydraulics, 2 circuits, front/rear balance valve, vacuum servo assistance, n/a	Hydraulics, 2 circuits, front/rear balance valve, vacuum servo assistance, antilock
Steering gear, make and model of power steering	Rack and pinion, n/a	Rack and pinion, hydraulic servo Adwest Varamatic

Make, range	**Early facelift Jaguar XJS 4.0**		**Early facelift Jaguar XJS V12**		
Type	*XJS 4.0 Coupe*	*XJS 4.0 Convertible*	*XJS V 12 Coupe (Conv.)*	*XJR-S 6.0*	*XJR-S Convertible*
Public debut	1/5/1991	19/5/1992	1/5/1991	11/9/1991	5/2/1993
End of production	4/1993	4/1993	4/1993	8/1993	1993
Production figure	1660	3803*	4399 (2875)	339	50
First, last chassis number RHD	VIN 179737-188104	VIN 184574-188104	VIN 179737-188104	VIN unknown	VIN unknown
First, last chassis number LHD	VIN 179737-188104	VIN 184574-188104	VIN 179737-188104	VIN unknown	VIN unknown
Body type	All-steel, 2 doors, 2 + 2 (convertible 2, from 1992 optional 2 + 2) seats		All-steel, 2 doors, 2 + 2 (convertible 2, from 1992 optional 2 + 2) seats		
Weather protection, top mechanism	Enclosed-drive (convertible electrically operated top)		Enclosed-drive (convertible electrically operated top)		
Length, width, height (mm)	4765 x 1793 x 1262		4765 x 1793 x 1262		
Length, width, height (inches)	187 3/4 x 70 1/2 x 49 3/4		187 3/4 x 70 1/2 x 49 3/4		
Wheelbase, front, rear track (mm)	2591 x 1473/1486		2591 x 1473/1486		
Wheelbase, front, rear track (inches)	102 x 58/58 1/2		102 x 58/58 1/2		
Ground clearance, turning circle, curb weight	140mm, 11m, 1650 (convertible 1800) kg		140mm, 11m, 1750 (convertible 1900) kg		
Max speed, acceleration 0-60 mph	230kph, 8 sec		240kph, 7 sec (RS 250kph, 6 sec)		
Max power, standard, revs	222 or 226 (optional until 1992 238) DIN-HP/4750		282 or 284 DIN-HP/5550 (optional until 1992 290 DIN-HP/4800)**		
Max torque, revs	371 Nm/3950, 377 Nm/3650 (optional until 1992 387 Nm/3750)		408 or 415 Nm/2800 (optional until 1992 420 Nm/3150)*		
Engine type, position, number and configuration of cylinders	Four-stroke gasoline, front longitudinally, 6 cylinders straight		Four-stroke gasoline, front longitudinally, 12 cylinders, 60-degree-V		
Bore x Stroke (mm), capacity (cc), compression ratio	91 x 102, 3980cc, 9.5 : 1		90 x 70, 5343cc, 11.5 : 1 (RS 90 x 78.5, 5993cc, 11, optional 11.2 : 1)		
Designation of engine and cylinder head	Engine and head "AJ 6"		Engine "Jaguar V-12," head "Fireball" (RS "TWR")		
Engine block and cylinder head material, number of main bearings, type of liners	Block and head aluminum, 7 main bearings, wet liners		Block and head aluminum, 7 main bearings, wet liners		
Number of valves per cylinder, configuration, valve gearing, timing variants	4 overhead valves, bucket tappets, 2 overhead camshafts, 2 duplex chains, fixed		2 overhead valves, bucket tappets, 1 ohc per bank, duplex chain, fixed		
Air supply, type of inlet manifold, air tempering	Normally aspirated, one-stage inlet manifold, n/a		Normally aspirated, one-stage inlet manifold, n/a		
Type, position, make, and designation of mixture preparation	Electronic injection to manifold, Lucas		Electronic injection to manifold, Lucas		
Energy source, type, make, and designation of ignition system	Battery, solid-state, Lucas 15 CU		Battery, solid-state, Lucas OPUS (RS Lucas/Zytec)		
Make of alternator, voltage, earthing	Alternator, 12 V, negative		Alternator, 12 V, negative		
Engine coolant, drive, regulation of cooling	Liquid, pump, thermostat		Liquid, pump, thermostat		
Type of clutch, number of gears in manual box, synchronized gears	Single-plate dry clutch, 5, fully		n/a		
Gear ratios in manual box	3.57, 2.96, 1.39, 1, 0.76, 3.46 : 1		n/a		
Make, type, ratio of overdrive	n/a		n/a		
Type of clutch, number of gears, make and model of automatic box	Optional hydraulic torque converter, 4, ZF 4 HP 24		Hydraulic torque converter, 3, GM 400		
Gear ratios in automatic gearbox	2.48, 1.48.1, 0.73, 2.09 : 1		2.48, 1.48.1, 2.08 : 1		
Driven axle, type of diff, traction control	Rear, hypoid bevel, limited-slip		Rear, hypoid bevel, limited-slip		
Axle ratios	3.58 : 1		2.88 : 1		
Type of chassis	Unitary, front and rear subframes		Unitary, front and rear subframes		
Suspension, springing front	Double-wishbone, coil springs		Double-wishbone, coil springs		
Suspension, springing rear	Transverse and trailing arms, driveshafts, 2 coil springs each		Transverse and trailing arms, driveshafts, 2 coil springs each		
Reduction of roll	Torsion bars front and rear		Torsion bars front and rear		
Type of shock absorbers	Telescopic		Telescopic		
Type and dimensions of wheels	Aluminum discs, 6.5 J x 16		Aluminum discs, 6.5 J x 16 (RS 7.5 J x 16)		
Type, dimensions, make of tires	Pirelli P 4000 E, 225/60 ZR 16 (4.0 Coupe 225/55 ZR 16)		As 4.0 (RS Goodyear Eagle, 225/60, rear 245/55 ZR 16)		
Type of braking front	Ventilated discs		Ventilated discs		
Type of braking rear	Massive inboard discs		Massive inboard discs		
Braking mechanism, number of circuits, servo assistance, electronic aids	Hydraulics, 2 circuits, front/rear balance valve, vacuum servo assistance, antilock		Hydraulics, 2 circuits, front/rear balance valve, vacuum servo assistance, antilock		
Steering gear, make and model of power steering	Rack and pinion, hydraulic servo Adwest Varamatic		Rack and pinion, hydraulic servo Adwest Varamatic		

* Incl. 1852 two-seater

** XJ-RS 324, optional 330 or 337 DIN-HP/5250 and 484, optional 491 Nm/3750

Make, range	Late Jaguar XJS 4.0		Late Jaguar XJS V12	
Type	*XJS 4.0 Coupe*	*XJS 4.0 Convertible*	*XJS V 12 Coupe*	*XJS V 12 Convertible*
Public debut	5/1993	5/1993	5/1993	5/1993
End of production	4/1996	4/1996	7/1995	7/1995
Production figure	4007	10,061	774	1787 (incl. 81 two-seater)
First, last chassis number RHD	VIN 188105-226645		VIN 188105-226645	
First, last chassis number LHD	VIN 188105-226645		VIN 188105-226645	
Body type	All-steel, 2 doors, 2 + 2 seats (convertible 2 doors, 2 or 2 + 2 seats)		All-steel, 2 doors, 2 + 2 seats, (convertible 2 doors, 2 or 2 + 2 seats)	
Weather protection, top mechanism	Enclosed-drive (convertible electrically operated top)		Enclosed-drive (convertible electrically operated top)	
Length, width, height (mm)	4820 x 1793 x 1255		4820 x 1793 x 1255	
Length, width, height (inches)	189 3/4 x 70 1/2 x 49 3/4		189 3/4 x 70 1/2 x 49 3/4	
Wheelbase, front, rear track (mm)	2591 x 1490/1505		2591 x 1490/1505	
Wheelbase, front, rear track (inches)	102 x 58 3/4/59 1/4		102 x 58 3/4/59 1/4	
Ground clearance, turning circle, curb weight	140mm, 11m, 1650 (Convertible 1800) kg		140mm, 11m, 1750 (Convertible 1900) kg	
Max speed, acceleration 0-60 mph	230kph, 8 sec		250kph, 6 sec	
Max power, standard, revs	222 or 226 DIN-HP/4750 (from 7/94 249 DIN or 241 ECE-HP/4750)		308 DIN or 302 ECE-HP/5350 (US 305 NET-HP/5500)	
Max torque, revs	371 Nm/3950 or 377 Nm/3650 (from 7/94 392 or 375 Nm/4000)		481 Nm/2850 (US 471 Nm/2850)	
Engine type, position, number and configuration of cylinders	Four-stroke gasoline, front longitudinally, 6 cylinders straight		Four-stroke gasoline, front longitudinally, 12 cylinders, 60-degree-V	
Bore x Stroke (mm), capacity (cc), compression ratio	91 x 102, 3980cc, 9.5 (from 7/94 10) : 1		90 x 78.5, 5993cc, 11.5 : 1	
Designation of engine and cylinder head	Engine and head "AJ 6," (from 7/94 "AJ 16")		Engine "Jaguar V-12," head "Fireball"	
Engine block and cylinder head material, number of main bearings, type of liners	Block and head aluminum, 7 main bearings, dry liners		Block and head aluminum, 7 main bearings, wet liners	
Number of valves per cylinder, configuration, valve gearing, timing variants	4 overhead valves, bucket tappets, 2 overhead camshafts, 2 duplex chains, fixed		2 overhead valves, bucket tappets, 1 ohc per bank, duplex chain, fixed	
Air supply, type of inlet manifold, air tempering	Normally aspirated, one-stage inlet manifold, n/a		Normally aspirated, one-stage inlet manifold, n/a	
Type, position, make, and designation of mixture preparation	Electronic injection to manifold, Lucas		Electronic injection to manifold, Lucas	
Energy source, type, make, and designation of ignition system	Battery, solid-state, Lucas 15 CU (from 7/94 separate coils, SAGEM-Lucas)		Battery, solid-state, Lucas OPUS	
Make of alternator, voltage, earthing	Alternator, 12 V, negative		Alternator, 12 V, negative	
Engine coolant, drive, regulation of cooling	Liquid, pump, thermostat		Liquid, pump, thermostat	
Type of clutch, number of gears in manual box, synchronized gears	Single-plate dry clutch, 5, fully		n/a	
Gear ratios in manual box	3.57, 2.96, 1.39, 1, 0.76, 3.46 : 1		n/a	
Make, type, ratio of overdrive	n/a		n/a	
Type of clutch, number of gears, make and model of automatic box	Optional hydraulic torque converter, 4, ZF 4 HP 24		Hydraulic torque converter, 4, GM 4L80E	
Gear ratios in automatic gearbox	2.48, 1.48.1, 0.73, 2.09 : 1		2.48, 1.48, 1, 0.75, 2.08 : 1	
Driven axle, type of diff, traction control	Rear, hypoid bevel, limited-slip		Rear, hypoid bevel, limited-slip	
Axle ratios	3.58 : 1		2.88 : 1	
Type of chassis	Unitary, front and rear subframes		Unitary, front and rear subframes	
Suspension, springing front	Double-wishbone, coil springs		Double-wishbone, coil springs	
Suspension, springing rear	Transverse and trailing arms, driveshafts, 2 coil springs each		Transverse and trailing arms, driveshafts, 2 coil springs each	
Reduction of roll	Torsion bars front and rear		Torsion bars front and rear	
Type of shock absorbers	Telescopic		Telescopic	
Type and dimensions of wheels	Aluminum discs, 6.5 J x 16 (Coupe 7 J x 16)		Aluminum discs, 7.5 J x 16	
Type, dimensions, make of tires	Pirelli P 4000 E, 225/60 ZR 16 (Coupe 225/55 ZR 16)		Pirelli P 4000 E, 225/60 ZR 16	
Type of braking front	Ventilated discs		Ventilated discs	
Type of braking rear	Massive outboard discs		Massive outboard discs	
Braking mechanism, number of circuits, servo assistance, electronic aids	Hydraulics, 2 circuits, front/rear balance valve, vacuum servo assistance, antilock		Hydraulics, 2 circuits, front/rear balance valve, vacuum servo assistance, antilock	
Steering gear, make and model of power steering	Rack and pinion, hydraulic servo Adwest Varamatic		Rack and pinion, hydraulic servo Adwest Varamatic	

Make, range	Aston Martin DB 7		Aston Martin DB 7 Vantage	
Type	*Coupe*	*Volante*	*Coupe*	*Volante*
Public debut	1/5/1993	2/1996	8/3/1999	8/3/1999
End of production	2000	2000	12/2003	12/2003
Production figure	3300		7000	
First, last chassis number RHD	VIN 0001-unknown		VIN unknown-unknown	
First, last chassis number LHD	VIN 0001-unknown		VIN unknown-unknown	
Body type	All-steel, 2 doors, 2 + 2 seats		All-steel, 2 doors, 2 + 2 seats	
Weather protection, top mechanism	Enclosed-drive (Volante electrically operated top)		Enclosed-drive (Volante electrically operated top)	
Length, width, height (mm)	4645 x 1830 x 1240 (Volante 1260)		4666 x 1830 x 1240 (Volante 1260)	
Length, width, height (inches)	182 3/4 x 72 x 48 3/4 (Volante 49 1/2)		183 x 72 x 48 3/4 (Volante 49 1/2)	
Wheelbase, front, rear track (mm)	2591 x 1525/1530		2591 x 1525/1530	
Wheelbase, front, rear track (inches)	102 x 60/60 1/4		102 x 60/60 1/4	
Ground clearance, turning circle, curb weight	140mm, 11m, 1700 (Volante 1800) kg		140mm, 11m, 1800 (Volante 1850) kg	
Max speed, acceleration 0-60 mph	266kph, 6 sec		298 (Volante 266) kph, 5 sec	
Max power, standard, revs	340 DIN-HP/5750 (automatic 317 DIN-HP/5500)		420 ECE-HP/6000	
Max torque, revs	490 Nm/3000 (automatic 457 Nm/3000)		540 Nm/5000	
Engine type, position, number and configuration of cylinders	Four-stroke gasoline, front longitudinally, 6 cylinders straight		Four-stroke gasoline, front longitudinally, 12 cylinders, 60-degree-V	
Bore x Stroke (mm), capacity (cc), compression ratio	91 x 83, 3239cc, 8.3 : 1		89 x 79.5, 5933cc, 10.3 : 1	
Designation of engine and cylinder head	Engine and head "AJ 16"		Engine "Cosworth V-12"	
Engine block and cylinder head material, number of main bearings, type of liners	Block and head aluminum, 7 main bearings, dry liners		Block and head aluminum, 7 main bearings, cast-in liners	
Number of valves per cylinder, configuration, valve gearing, timing variants	4 overhead valves, bucket tappets, 2 overhead camshafts, 2 duplex chains, fixed		4 overhead valves, bucket tappets, 2 overhead camshafts, duplex chain, fixed	
Air supply, type of inlet manifold, air tempering	Roots supercharger, one-stage inlet manifold, intercooler		Normally aspirated, one-stage inlet manifold, n/a	
Type, position, make, and designation of mixture preparation	Electronic injection to manifold, Lucas-Bosch		Electronic injection to manifold, Lucas-Bosch	
Energy source, type, make, and designation of ignition system	Battery, solid-state, Lucas 15 CU		Battery, separate coils, Nippondenso	
Make of alternator, voltage, earthing	Alternator, 12 V, negative		Alternator, 12 V, negative	
Engine coolant, drive, regulation of cooling	Liquid, pump, thermostat		Liquid, pump, thermostat	
Type of clutch, number of gears in manual box, synchronized gears	Single-plate dry clutch, 5, fully		Single-plate dry clutch, 6, fully	
Gear ratios in manual box	3.55, 2.04, 1.39, 1, 0.755, 3.55 : 1		2.66, 1.78, 1.3, 1, 0.8, 0.63 (optional 0.5), 2.9 : 1	
Make, type, ratio of overdrive	n/a		n/a	
Type of clutch, number of gears, make and model of automatic box	Optional hydraulic torque converter, 4, GM 4L80E		Optional hydraulic torque converter, 5, Mercedes-Benz W5A580	
Gear ratios in automatic gearbox	2.48, 1.48, 1, 0.73, 2.09 : 1		3.55, 2.24, 1.55, 1, 0.79, 3.68 : 1	
Driven axle, type of diff, traction control	Rear, hypoid bevel, limited-slip		Rear, spiral bevel, electronic traction control	
Axle ratios	3.54 : 1		3.77 (with automatic 3.06) : 1	
Type of chassis	Unitary, front and rear subframes		Unitary, front and rear subframes	
Suspension, springing front	Double-wishbone, coil springs		Double-wishbone, coil springs	
Suspension, springing rear	Transverse and trailing arms, driveshafts, 2 coil springs each		Transverse and trailing arms, driveshafts, 2 coil springs each	
Reduction of roll	Torsion bars front and rear		Torsion bars front and rear	
Type of shock absorbers	Telescopic		Telescopic	
Type and dimensions of wheels	Aluminum discs, 8 J x 18		Aluminum discs, 8 (rear 9) J x 18	
Type, dimensions, make of tires	Bridgestone, 245/40 ZR 18		Bridgestone, 245/40 (rear 265/35) ZR 18	
Type of braking front	Ventilated discs		Ventilated discs	
Type of braking rear	Ventilated outboard discs		Ventilated outboard discs	
Braking mechanism, number of circuits, servo assistance, electronic aids	Hydraulics, 2 circuits, front/rear balance valve, vacuum servo assistance, antilock		Hydraulics, 2 circuits, front/rear balance valve, vacuum servo assistance, antilock	
Steering gear, make and model of power steering	Rack and pinion, hydraulic servo Adwest Varamatic		Rack and pinion, hydraulic servo Adwest Varamatic	

DB 7

Make, range	**Aston Martin DB 7 GT**	**Aston Martin DB 7 Zagato etc.**	
Type	*GT Coupe*	*DB 7 Zagato*	*AR 1 (American Roadster)*
Public debut	10/2002	8/2002	2/2003
End of production	2003	2003	2003
Production figure	Unknown	99	99
First, last chassis number RHD	VIN unknown	VIN unknown	
First, last chassis number LHD	VIN unknown	VIN unknownn	
Body type	All-steel, 2 doors, 2 + 2 seats	Steel and aluminum, 2 doors, 2 seats	
Weather protection, top mechanism	Enclosed-drive	Enclosed-drive (AR 1 electrically operated top)	
Length, width, height (mm)	4645 x 1830 x 1240	4480 (AR 1 4692) x 1869 x 1245	
Length, width, height (inches)	183 x 72 x 48 3/4	176 1/2 (AR 1 184 3/4) x 13 1/2 x 49	
Wheelbase, front, rear track (mm)	2591 x 1525/1530	2591 x 1535/1540	
Wheelbase, front, rear track (inches)	102 x 60/60 1/4	102 x 60/60 1/4	
Ground clearance, turning circle, curb weight	120mm, 12m, 1780kg	120mm, 12m, 1740 (AR 1 1700) kg	
Max speed, acceleration 0-60 mph	298 (Automatik: 265) kph, 5 sec	298kph, 5 sec	
Max power, standard, revs	435 ECE-HP/6000	440 ECE-HP/6000	
Max torque, revs	556/5000	556/5000	
Engine type, position, number and configuration of cylinders	Four-stroke gasoline, front longitudinally, 12 cylinders, 60-degree-V	Four-stroke gasoline, front longitudinally, 12 cylinders, 60-degree-V	
Bore x Stroke (mm), capacity (cc), compression ratio	89 x 79.5, 5933cc, 10.3 : 1	89 x 79.5, 5933cc, 10.3 : 1	
Designation of engine and cylinder head	Engine and head "Cosworth V-12"	Engine and head "Cosworth V-12"	
Engine block and cylinder head material, number of main bearings, type of liners	Block and head aluminum, 7 main bearings, cast-in liners	Block and head aluminum, 7 main bearings, cast-in liners	
Number of valves per cylinder, configuration, valve gearing, timing variants	4 overhead valves, bucket tappets, 2 ohc per bank, duplex chain, fixed	4 overhead valves, bucket tappets, 2 ohc per bank, duplex chain, fixed	
Air supply, type of inlet manifold, air tempering	Normally aspirated, one-stage inlet manifold, n/a	Normally aspirated, one-stage inlet manifold, n/a	
Type, position, make, and designation of mixture preparation	Electronic injection to manifold, Lucas-Bosch	Electronic injection to manifold, Lucas-Bosch	
Energy source, type, make, and designation of ignition system	Battery, separate coils, Nippondenso	Battery, separate coils, Nippondenso	
Make of alternator, voltage, earthing	Alternator, 12 V, negative	Alternator, 12 V, negative	
Engine coolant, drive, regulation of cooling	Liquid, pump, thermostat	Liquid, pump, thermostat	
Type of clutch, number of gears in manual box, synchronized gears	Single-plate dry clutch, 5, fully	Two-plate dry clutch, 6, fully	
Gear ratios in manual box	2.66, 1.78, 1.3, 1, 0.8, 0.63 (optional 0.5), 2.9 : 1	2.66, 1.78, 1.3, 1, 0.8, 0.63, 2.9 : 1	
Make, type, ratio of overdrive	n/a	n/a	
Type of clutch, number of gears, make and model of automatic box	Optional hydraulic torque converter, 5, Mercedes-Benz W5A580	n/a	
Gear ratios in automatic gearbox	3.55, 2.24, 1.55, 1, 0.79, 3.68 : 1	n/a	
Driven axle, type of diff, traction control	Rear, spiral bevel, electronic traction control	Rear, spiral bevel, electronic traction control	
Axle ratios	3.77 or 3.73 (with automatic 3.06) : 1	4.09 : 1	
Type of chassis	Unitary, front and rear subframes	Unitary, front and rear subframes	
Suspension, springing front	Double-wishbone, coil springs	Double-wishbone, coil springs	
Suspension, springing rear	Transverse and trailing arms, driveshafts, 2 coil springs each	Transverse and trailing arms, driveshafts, 2 coil springs each	
Reduction of roll	Torsion bars front and rear	Torsion bars front and rear	
Type of shock absorbers	Telescopic	Telescopic	
Type and dimensions of wheels	Aluminum discs, 8 (rear 9) J x 18	Aluminum discs, painted, 8 (rear 9) J x 18 (AR1 8, rear 9 J x 19)	
Type, dimensions, make of tires	Bridgestone, 245/40 (rear 265/35) R 18	Bridgestone, 245/40 (rear 265/35) R 18 (AR1 245/35 R 19, rear 265/30 R 19)	
Type of braking front	Ventilated discs	Ventilated discs	
Type of braking rear	Ventilated outboard discs	Ventilated outboard discs	
Braking mechanism, number of circuits, servo assistance, electronic aids	Hydraulics, 2 circuits, front/rear balance valve, vacuum servo assistance, antilock	Hydraulics, 2 circuits, front/rear balance valve, vacuum servo assistance, antilock	
Steering gear, make and model of power steering	Rack and pinion, hydraulic servo Adwest Varamatic	Rack and pinion, hydraulic servo Adwest Varamatic	

DB 7

Make, range	**Group 44 Jaguar XJR-5**	**Group 44 Jaguar XJR-7 and 8**	
Type	*XJR-5*	*XJR-7*	*XJR-8*
Public debut	3/1982	12/1985	1987
End of production	1984	1986	1987
Production figure	4	2	1
First, last chassis number RHD	Unknown	Unknown	
First, last chassis number LHD	n/a	n/a	
Body type	Fiberglass, 2 doors, 2 seats	Fiberglass, 2 doors, 2 seats	
Weather protection, top mechanism	Enclosed-drive	Enclosed-drive	
Length, width, height (mm)	4750 x 1980 x 1040	4750 x 1980 x 1040	
Length, width, height (inches)	187 x 78 x 41	187 x 78 x 41	
Wheelbase, front, rear track (mm)	2765 x 1680/1570	2765 x 1680/1570	
Wheelbase, front, rear track (inches)	109 x 66/62	109 x 66/62	
Ground clearance, turning circle, curb weight	100mm, 15m, 900kg	100mm, 15m, 900kg	
Max speed, acceleration 0-60 mph	300kph, 4 sec	300kph, 4 sec	
Max power, standard, revs	600 (650) NET-HP/8000	650 NET-HP/8000*	
Max torque, revs	690 Nm/unknown	Unknown	
Engine type, position, number and configuration of cylinders	Four-stroke gasoline, central longitudinally, 12 cylinders, 60-degree-V	Four-stroke gasoline, central longitudinally, 12 cylinders, 60-degree-V	
Bore x Stroke (mm), capacity (cc), compression ratio	90 x 78.5, 5993cc, unknown	90 x 78.5, 5993cc*, unknown	
Designation of engine and cylinder head	Engine "Jaguar V-12," head "Heron"	Engine "Jaguar V-12," head "Heron"	
Engine block and cylinder head material, number of main bearings, type of liners	Block and head aluminum, 7 main bearings, wet liners	Block and head aluminum, 7 main bearings, wet liners	
Number of valves per cylinder, configuration, valve gearing, timing variants	2 overhead valves, bucket tappets, 1 ohc per bank, duplex chain, fixed	2 overhead valves, bucket tappets, 1 ohc per bank, duplex chain, fixed	
Air supply, type of inlet manifold, air tempering	Normally aspirated, one-stage inlet manifold, n/a	Normally aspirated, one-stage inlet manifold, n/a	
Type, position, make, and designation of mixture preparation	6 twin carb., Weber	Electronic injection to manifold Lucas-MICOS	
Energy source, type, make, and designation of ignition system	Battery, solid-state, unknown	Battery, solid-state, unknown	
Make of alternator, voltage, earthing	Alternator, 12 V, negative	Alternator, 12 V, negative	
Engine coolant, drive, regulation of cooling	Liquid, pump, thermostat	Liquid, pump, thermostat	
Type of clutch, number of gears in manual box, synchronized gears	Three-plate dry clutch, 5, fully	Three-plate dry clutch, 5, fully	
Gear ratios in manual box	Unknown	Unknown	
Make, type, ratio of overdrive	n/a	n/a	
Type of clutch, number of gears, make and model of automatic box	n/a	n/a	
Gear ratios in automatic gearbox	n/a	n/a	
Driven axle, type of diff, traction control	Rear, hypoid bevel, limited-slip	Rear, hypoid bevel, limited-slip	
Axle ratios	Unknown	Unknown	
Type of chassis	Tubular chassis (aluminum and steel)	Tubular chassis (aluminum and steel)	
Suspension, springing front	Double-wishbone, coil springs	Double-wishbone, coil springs	
Suspension, springing rear	Double-wishbone, coil springs	Double-wishbone, coil springs	
Reduction of roll	Torsion bars front and rear	Torsion bars front and rear	
Type of shock absorbers	Telescopic	Telescopic	
Type and dimensions of wheels	Aluminum discs, unknown	Aluminum discs, unknown	
Type, dimensions, make of tires	Goodyear, 23.5 x 11.5 – 16 (rear 27 x 14 – 16)	Goodyear, 23.5 x 11.5 – 16 (rear 27 x 14 – 16)	
Type of braking front	Ventilated discs	Ventilated discs	
Type of braking rear	Ventilated outboard discs	Ventilated outboard discs	
Braking mechanism, number of circuits, servo assistance, electronic aids	Hydraulics, 2 circuits, vacuum servo assistance, n/a	Hydraulics, 2 circuits, vacuum servo assistance, n/a	
Steering gear, make and model of power steering	Rack and pinion, hydraulic servo	Rack and pinion, hydraulic servo	

* From 1986 690 NET-HP, 6500cc

Group 44

Make, range	**Jaguar XJ 6 2.9 (XJ 40)**		**Jaguar XJ 6 3.6 and Daimler 3.6 (XJ 40)**		
Type	*XJ 6 2.9*	*2.9 Sovereign*	*XJ 6 3.6 (XJ-R)*	*3.6 Sovereign*	*Vanden Plas (Daimler 3.6)*
Public debut	9/1986	9/1986	9/1986 (18/10/1988)	9/1986	5/1987 (9/1986)
End of production	8/1990	8/1990	9/1989	9/1989	9/1989 (9/1989)
Production figure	11,191	2957	9349	56,291	7319 (10,314)
First, last chassis number RHD	VIN 500515-unknown		VIN 500515-unknown		
First, last chassis number LHD	VIN 500515-unknown		VIN 500515-unknown		
Body type	All-steel, 4 doors, 5 seats		All-steel, 4 doors, 5 seats		
Weather protection, top mechanism	Enclosed-drive, optional electrically operated steel sunroof		Enclosed-drive, optional electrically operated steel sunroof		
Length, width, height (mm)	4988 x 1780 x 1380		4988 x 1780 x 1380		
Length, width, height (inches)	196 1/2 x 70 x 54 1/4		196 1/2 x 70 x 54 1/4		
Wheelbase, front, rear track (mm)	2870 x 1501/1499		2870 x 1501/1499		
Wheelbase, front, rear track (inches)	113 x 59/59		113 x 59/59		
Ground clearance, turning circle, curb weight	150mm, 12m, 1700kg		150mm, 12m, 1770kg		
Max speed, acceleration 0-60 mph	187kph, 10 sec		215kph, 8 sec		
Max power, standard, revs	165 DIN-HP/5600 (from 1989 catalyst 150 DIN-HP/5000)		224 DIN-HP/5000 (some markets 212/5000 or from 1987 202 DIN-HP/5250)*		
Max torque, revs	239 Nm/4000 (from 1989 catalyst 225 Nm/4300)		337 Nm/4000 (some markets 324 Nm/4000 or from 1987 302 Nm/4000)		
Engine type, position, number and configuration of cylinders	Four-stroke gasoline, front longitudinally, 6 cylinders straight		Four-stroke gasoline, front longitudinally, 6 cylinders straight		
Bore x Stroke (mm), capacity (cc), compression ratio	91 x 74.8, 2919cc, 12.6 : 1		91 x 92, 3590cc, 9.6 (Kat 8.2) : 1		
Designation of engine and cylinder head	Engine "AJ 6," head "Fireball"		Engine and head "AJ 6"		
Engine block and cylinder head material, number of main bearings, type of liners	Block and head aluminum, 7 main bearings, dry liners		Block and head aluminum, 7 main bearings, dry liners		
Number of valves per cylinder, configuration, valve gearing, timing variants	2 overhead valves, bucket tappets, 1 overhead camshaft, duplex chain, fixed		4 overhead valves, bucket tappets, 2 overhead camshafts, 2 duplex chains, fixed		
Air supply, type of inlet manifold, air tempering	Normally aspirated, one-stage inlet manifold, n/a		Normally aspirated, one-stage inlet manifold, n/a		
Type, position, make, and designation of mixture preparation	Electronic injection to manifold, Bosch/Lucas L-Jetronic		Electronic injection to manifold, Bosch/Lucas		
Energy source, type, make, and designation of ignition system	Battery, solid-state, Lucas 9CU		Battery, solid-state, Lucas 9CU		
Make of alternator, voltage, earthing	Alternator, 12 V, negative		Alternator, 12 V, negative		
Engine coolant, drive, regulation of cooling	Liquid, pump, thermostat		Liquid, pump, thermostat		
Type of clutch, number of gears in manual box, synchronized gears	Single-plate dry clutch, 5, fully		Single-plate dry clutch, 5, fully		
Gear ratios in manual box	3.57, 2.96, 1.39, 1, 0.76, 3.46 : 1		3.57, 2.96, 1.39, 1, 0.76, 3.46 : 1		
Make, type, ratio of overdrive	n/a		n/a		
Type of clutch, number of gears, make and model of automatic box	Optional hydraulic torque converter, 4, ZF 4 HP 22		Optional hydraulic torque converter, 4, ZF 4 HP 22		
Gear ratios in automatic gearbox	2.73, 1.56, 1, 0.73, 2.09 : 1		2.48, 1.48.1, 0.73, 2.09 : 1		
Driven axle, type of diff, traction control	Rear, hypoid bevel, limited-slip		Rear, hypoid bevel, limited-slip		
Axle ratios	3.77 (with automatic 4.09) : 1		3.54 : 1		
Type of chassis	Unitary, front and rear subframes		Unitary, front and rear subframes		
Suspension, springing front	Double-wishbone, coil springs		Double-wishbone, coil springs		
Suspension, springing rear	Forked transverse arms and driveshafts, coil springs		Forked transverse arms and driveshafts, coil springs		
Reduction of roll	Torsion bar front		Torsion bar front		
Type of shock absorbers	Telescopic		Telescopic		
Type and dimensions of wheels	Steel (optional, Sovereign always aluminum) discs, 390 x 180		Steel (optional, from XJR always aluminum) discs, 390 x 180 (US 6.5 J x 15)		
Type, dimensions, make of tires	Michelin TD 220/65 VR 390		Michelin TD 220/65 VR 390 (US Pirelli P5, 215/70 VR 15)		
Type of braking front	Ventilated discs		Ventilated discs		
Type of braking rear	Massive outboard discs		Massive outboard discs		
Braking mechanism, number of circuits, servo assistance, electronic aids	Hydraulics, 2 circuits, balance valve front/rear, hydraulic servo assistance, antilock		Hydraulics, 2 circuits, balance valve front/rear, hydraulic servo assistance, antilock		
Steering gear, make and model of power steering	Rack and pinion, hydraulic servo Adwest Varamatic		Rack and pinion, hydraulic servo Adwest Varamatic		

* Catalyst 184 DIN-HP/4750 and 300 Nm/3750

Make, range	Jaguar XJ 6 3.2 (XJ 40)			Jaguar XJ 6 3.2 Majestic (XJ 40)	
Type	*XJ 6 3.2*	*3.2 S*	*3.2 Sovereign*	*3.2 Gold Majestic*	*3.2 Sovereign Majestic*
Public debut	18/9/1990	9/1993	18/9/1990	20/10/1992	20/10/1992
End of production	1994	1994	1994	1994	1994
Production figure	13,053	3117	4986	3	4
First, last chassis number RHD	VIN unknown-708757			VIN unknown-708757	
First, last chassis number LHD	VIN unknown-708757			VIN unknown-708757	
Body type	All-steel, 4 doors, 5 seats			All-steel, 4 doors, 5 seats	
Weather protection, top mechanism	Enclosed-drive, optional electrically operated steel sunroof			Enclosed-drive, optional electrically operated steel sunroof	
Length, width, height (mm)	4988 x 1780 x 1380			5120 x 1780 x 1430	
Length, width, height (inches)	196 1/2 x 70 x 54 1/4			201 1/2 x 70 x 54 1/4	
Wheelbase, front, rear track (mm)	2870 x 1501/1499			2997 x 1501/1499	
Wheelbase, front, rear track (inches)	113 x 59/59			118 x 59/59	
Ground clearance, turning circle, curb weight	150mm, 12m, 1770kg			150mm, 12m, 1850kg	
Max speed, acceleration 0-60 mph	210kph, 8 sec			210kph, 8 sec	
Max power, standard, revs	200 DIN-HP/5250 (from 1991 some markets 197 DIN-HP/5300)			200 DIN-HP/5250 (some markets 197 DIN-HP/5300)	
Max torque, revs	298 Nm/4000			298 Nm/4000	
Engine type, position, number and configuration of cylinders	Four-stroke gasoline, front longitudinally, 6 cylinders straight			Four-stroke gasoline, front longitudinally, 6 cylinders straight	
Bore x Stroke (mm), capacity (cc), compression ratio	91 x 83, 3239cc, 9.75 : 1			91 x 83, 3239cc, 9.75 : 1	
Designation of engine and cylinder head	Engine and head "AJ 6"			Engine and head "AJ 6"	
Engine block and cylinder head material, number of main bearings, type of liners	Block and head aluminum, 7 main bearings, dry liners			Block and head aluminum, 7 main bearings, dry liners	
Number of valves per cylinder, configuration, valve gearing, timing variants	4 overhead valves, bucket tappets, 2 overhead camshafts, 2 duplex chains, fixed			4 overhead valves, bucket tappets, 2 overhead camshafts, 2 duplex chains, fixed	
Air supply, type of inlet manifold, air tempering	Normally aspirated, one-stage inlet manifold, n/a			Normally aspirated, one-stage inlet manifold, n/a	
Type, position, make, and designation of mixture preparation	Electronic injection to manifold, Lucas			Electronic injection to manifold, Lucas	
Energy source, type, make, and designation of ignition system	Battery, solid-state, Lucas 15 CU			Battery, solid-state, Lucas 15 CU	
Make of alternator, voltage, earthing	Alternator, 12 V, negative			Alternator, 12 V, negative	
Engine coolant, drive, regulation of cooling	Liquid, pump, thermostat			Liquid, pump, thermostat	
Type of clutch, number of gears in manual box, synchronized gears	Single-plate dry clutch, 5, fully			Single-plate dry clutch, 5, fully	
Gear ratios in manual box	3.57, 2.96, 1.39, 1, 0.76, 3.46 : 1			3.57, 2.96, 1.39, 1, 0.76, 3.46 : 1	
Make, type, ratio of overdrive	n/a			n/a	
Type of clutch, number of gears, make and model of automatic box	Optional hydraulic torque converter, 4, ZF 4 HP 24			Optional hydraulic torque converter, 4, ZF 4 HP 24	
Gear ratios in automatic gearbox	2.48, 1.48, 1, 0.75, 2.08 : 1			2.48, 1.48, 1, 0.75, 2.08 : 1	
Driven axle, type of diff, traction control	Rear, hypoid bevel, limited-slip			Rear, hypoid bevel, limited-slip	
Axle ratios	3.77 (with automatic 4.09) : 1			3.77 (with automatic 4.09) : 1	
Type of chassis	Unitary, front and rear subframes			Unitary, front and rear subframes	
Suspension, springing front	Double-wishbone, coil springs			Double-wishbone, coil springs	
Suspension, springing rear	Forked transverse arms and driveshafts, coil springs			Forked transverse arms and driveshafts, coil springs	
Reduction of roll	Torsion bar front			Torsion bar front	
Type of shock absorbers	Telescopic			Telescopic	
Type and dimensions of wheels	Steel (optional, from 3.2 S always aluminum) discs, 390 x 180 (from '93 7 J x 16)			Aluminum discs, 390 x 180 (from '93 7 J x 16)	
Type, dimensions, make of tires	Michelin TD 220/65 VR 390 (from 1993 Dunlop SP 2000 225/55 ZR 16)			Michelin TD 220/65 VR 390 (from 1993 Dunlop SP 2000 225/55 ZR 16)	
Type of braking front	Ventilated discs			Ventilated discs	
Type of braking rear	Massive outboard discs			Massive outboard discs	
Braking mechanism, number of circuits, servo assistance, electronic aids	Hydraulics, 2 circuits, front/rear balance valve, hydraulic servo assistance, antilock			Hydraulics, 2 circuits, front/rear balance valve, hydraulic servo assistance, antilock	
Steering gear, make and model of power steering	Rack and pinion, hydraulic servo Adwest Varamatic			Rack and pinion, hydraulic servo Adwest Varamatic	

Make, range	**Jaguar XJ 6 4.0 (XJ 40)**			**Jaguar Vanden Plas and Daimler 4.0 (XJ 40)**		
Type	*XJ 6 4.0 (XJ-R*)*	*4.0 S*	*Sovereign***	*Vanden Plas*	*Daimler 4.0*	*Jaguar (Daimler) Majestic*
Public debut	13/9/1989 (19/10/1989)	9/1993	13/9/1989	9/1989	13/9/1989	20/10/1992
End of production	1994	1994	1994	1994	1994	1994
Production figure	13,576	500	56,450	6864	8876	72 (Daimler 42)
First, last chassis number RHD	VIN unknown-708757			VIN unknown-708757		
First, last chassis number LHD	VIN unknown-708757			VIN unknown-708757		
Body type	All-steel, 4 doors, 5 seats			All-steel, 4 doors, 5 seats		
Weather protection, top mechanism	Enclosed-drive, optional electrically operated steel sunroof			Enclosed-drive, optional electrically operated steel sunroof		
Length, width, height (mm)	4988 x 1780 x 1380			4988 x 1780 x 1380 (Majestic 5120 x 1780 x 1430)		
Length, width, height (inches)	196 1/2 x 70 x 54 1/4			196 1/2 x 70 x 54 1/4 (Majestic 201 1/2 x 70 x 54 1/4)		
Wheelbase, front, rear track (mm)	2870 x 1501/1499			2870 (Majestic 2997) x 1501/1499		
Wheelbase, front, rear track (inches)	113 x 59/59			113 (Majestic 118) x 59/59		
Ground clearance, turning circle, curb weight	150mm, 12m, 1800kg			150mm, 12m, 1800 (Majestic 1950) kg		
Max speed, acceleration 0-60 mph	225kph, 8 sec (XJ-R 235kph, 7 sec)			225kph, 8 sec		
Max power, standard, revs	226 DIN-HP/4750 (some markets as Daimler, XJ-R 252 DIN-HP/5250)			As XJ 6 (some markets 222 DIN-HP/5250 or until 1992 238 DIN-HP/4750)		
Max torque, revs	377 Nm/3650 (XJ-R 377 Nm/4000)			377 Nm/3650		
Engine type, position, number and configuration of cylinders	Four-stroke gasoline, front longitudinally, 6 cylinders straight			Four-stroke gasoline, front longitudinally, 6 cylinders straight		
Bore x Stroke (mm), capacity (cc), compression ratio	91 x 102, 3980cc, 9.5 : 1			91 x 102, 3980cc, 9.5 : 1		
Designation of engine and cylinder head	Engine and head "AJ 6"			Engine and head "AJ 6"		
Engine block and cylinder head material, number of main bearings, type of liners	Block and head aluminum, 7 main bearings, dry liners			Block and head aluminum, 7 main bearings, dry liners		
Number of valves per cylinder, configuration, valve gearing, timing variants	4 overhead valves, bucket tappets, 2 overhead camshafts, 2 duplex chains, fixed			4 overhead valves, bucket tappets, 2 overhead camshafts, 2 duplex chains, fixed		
Air supply, type of inlet manifold, air tempering	Normally aspirated, one-stage inlet manifold, n/a			Normally aspirated, one-stage inlet manifold, n/a		
Type, position, make, and designation of mixture preparation	Electronic injection to manifold, Lucas			Electronic injection to manifold, Lucas		
Energy source, type, make, and designation of ignition system	Battery, solid-state, Lucas 15 CU			Battery, solid-state, Lucas 15 CU		
Make of alternator, voltage, earthing	Alternator, 12 V, negative			Alternator, 12 V, negative		
Engine coolant, drive, regulation of cooling	Liquid, pump, thermostat			Liquid, pump, thermostat		
Type of clutch, number of gears in manual box, synchronized gears	Single-plate dry clutch, 5, fully			Single-plate dry clutch, 5, fully		
Gear ratios in manual box	3.57, 2.96, 1.39, 1, 0.76, 3.46 : 1			3.57, 2.96, 1.39, 1, 0.76, 3.46 : 1		
Make, type, ratio of overdrive	n/a			n/a		
Type of clutch, number of gears, make and model of automatic box	Optional hydraulic torque converter, 4, ZF 4 HP 24			Optional hydraulic torque converter, 4, ZF 4 HP 24		
Gear ratios in automatic gearbox	2.48, 1.48, 1, 0.75, 2.08 : 1			2.48, 1.48, 1, 0.75, 2.08 : 1		
Driven axle, type of diff, traction control	Rear, hypoid bevel, limited-slip			Rear, hypoid bevel, limited-slip		
Axle ratios	3.58 : 1			3.58 : 1		
Type of chassis	Unitary, front and rear subframes			Unitary, front and rear subframes		
Suspension, springing front	Double-wishbone, coil springs			Double-wishbone, coil springs		
Suspension, springing rear	Forked transverse arms and driveshafts, coil springs			Forked transverse arms and driveshafts, coil springs		
Reduction of roll	Torsion bar front			Torsion bar front		
Type of shock absorbers	Telescopic			Telescopic		
Type and dimensions of wheels	Steel (optional, from XJR and S always aluminum) discs, wie VdP (XJ-R 6.5 J x 16)			Aluminum discs, 390 x 180 (US 6.5 J x 15, all from 1993 7 J x 16)		
Type, dimensions, make of tires	Michelin TD 220/65 VR 390 (US etc. as VdP, XJ-R Pirelli 225/55 ZR 16)			As XJ 6 (US Pirelli P5 215/70 VR 15, all from 1993 P4000 225/65 ZR 16)		
Type of braking front	Ventilated discs			Ventilated discs		
Type of braking rear	Massive outboard discs			Massive outboard discs		
Braking mechanism, number of circuits, servo assistance, electronic aids	Hydraulics, 2 circuits, front/rear balance valve, hydraulic servo assistance, antilock			Hydraulics, 2 circuits, balance valve front/rear, hydraulic servo assistance, antilock		
Steering gear, make and model of power steering	Rack and pinion, hydraulic servo Adwest Varamatic			Rack and pinion, hydraulic servo Adwest Varamatic		

* XJ-R re-styled 7/90

** One prototype four-door estate car

XJ

Make, range	**Jaguar XJ 12 and Daimler Double-Six (XJ 81)**		**Jaguar XJ 12 and Daimler Double-Six Majestic (XJ 81)**	
Type	*XJ 12**	*Daimler Double-Six*	*XJ 12 Majestic*	*Daimler Double-Six Majestic*
Public debut	3/2/1993	2/3/1993	2/3/1993	2/3/1993
End of production	1994	1994	1994	1994
Production figure	2764	985	20	30
First, last chassis number RHD	VIN unknown-708757		VIN unknown-708757	
First, last chassis number LHD	VIN unknown-708757		VIN unknown-708757	
Body type	All-steel, 4 doors, 5 seats		All-steel, 4 doors, 5 seats	
Weather protection, top mechanism	Enclosed-drive, optional electrically operated steel sunroof		Enclosed-drive, optional electrically operated steel sunroof	
Length, width, height (mm)	4988 x 1780 x 1380		5120 x 1780 x 1430	
Length, width, height (inches)	196 1/2 x 70 x 54 1/4		201 1/2 x 70 x 54 1/4	
Wheelbase, front, rear track (mm)	2870 x 1501/1499		2997 x 1501/1499	
Wheelbase, front, rear track (inches)	113 x 59/59		118 x 59/59	
Ground clearance, turning circle, curb weight	150mm, 12m, 1800kg		150mm, 12m, 1950kg	
Max speed, acceleration 0-60 mph	248kph, 7 sec		248kph, 7 sec	
Max power, standard, revs	318 DIN or 311 ECE-HP/5400 (US 315 NET or 305 ECE-HP/5350)		318 DIN or 311 ECE-HP/5400 (US 315 NET or 305 ECE-HP/5350)	
Max torque, revs	463 or 453 Nm/3750 (US 455 Nm/3750)		463 or 453 Nm/3750 (US 455 Nm/3750)	
Engine type, position, number and configuration of cylinders	Four-stroke gasoline, front longitudinally, 12 cylinders, 60-degree-V		Four-stroke gasoline, front longitudinally, 12 cylinders, 60-degree-V	
Bore x Stroke (mm), capacity (cc), compression ratio	90 x 78.5, 5993cc, 11 : 1		90 x 78.5, 5993cc, 11 : 1	
Designation of engine and cylinder head	Engine "Jaguar V-12," head "Fireball"		Engine "Jaguar V-12," head "Fireball"	
Engine block and cylinder head material, number of main bearings, type of liners	Block and head aluminum, 7 main bearings, wet liners		Block and head aluminum, 7 main bearings, wet liners	
Number of valves per cylinder, configuration, valve gearing, timing variants	2 overhead valves, bucket tappets, 1 ohc per bank, duplex chain, fixed		2 overhead valves, bucket tappets, 1 ohc per bank, duplex chain, fixed	
Air supply, type of inlet manifold, air tempering	Normally aspirated, one-stage inlet manifold, n/a		Normally aspirated, one-stage inlet manifold, n/a	
Type, position, make, and designation of mixture preparation	Electronic injection to manifold, Lucas		Electronic injection to manifold, Lucas	
Energy source, type, make, and designation of ignition system	Battery, solid-state, Lucas OPUS		Battery, solid-state, Lucas OPUS	
Make of alternator, voltage, earthing	Alternator, 12 V, negative		Alternator, 12 V, negative	
Engine coolant, drive, regulation of cooling	Liquid, pump, thermostat		Liquid, pump, thermostat	
Type of clutch, number of gears in manual box, synchronized gears	n/a		n/a	
Gear ratios in manual box	n/a		n/a	
Make, type, ratio of overdrive	n/a		n/a	
Type of clutch, number of gears, make and model of automatic box	Hydraulic torque converter, 4, GM 4L80E		Hydraulic torque converter, 4, GM 4L80E	
Gear ratios in automatic gearbox	2.48, 1.48, 1, 0.75, 2.08 : 1		2.48, 1.48, 1, 0.75, 2.08 : 1	
Driven axle, type of diff, traction control	Rear, hypoid bevel, limited-slip		Rear, hypoid bevel, limited-slip	
Axle ratios	2.88 : 1		2.88 : 1	
Type of chassis	Unitary, front and rear subframes		Unitary, front and rear subframes	
Suspension, springing front	Double-wishbone, coil springs		Double-wishbone, coil springs	
Suspension, springing rear	Forked transverse arms and driveshafts, coil springs		Forked transverse arms and driveshafts, coil springs	
Reduction of roll	Torsion bar front		Torsion bar front	
Type of shock absorbers	Telescopic		Telescopic	
Type and dimensions of wheels	Aluminum discs, 390 x 180 (US 6.5J x 15, all from 1993 7J x 16)		Aluminum discs, 390 x 180 (US 6.5J x 15, all from 1993 7J x 16)	
Type, dimensions, make of tires	Michelin TD 220/65 VR 390 (US Pirelli P5, 215/70 VR 15, from 93 as Majestic)		As XJ 12 (from 1993 Dunlop SP 2000 225/55 ZR 16), Daimler Pirelli P4000 225/65 ZR 15	
Type of braking front	Ventilated discs		Ventilated discs	
Type of braking rear	Massive outboard discs		Massive outboard discs	
Braking mechanism, number of circuits, servo assistance, electronic aids	Hydraulics, 2 circuits, front/rear balance valve, hydraulic servo assistance, antilock		Hydraulics, 2 circuits balance valve front/rear, hydraulic servo assistance, antilock	
Steering gear, make and model of power steering	Rack and pinion, hydraulic servo Adwest Varamatic		Rack and pinion, hydraulic servo Adwest Varamatic	

* One prototype two-door Coupe of 1994, shortened by 457mm, chassis no. SAJJHAES3AR000069

Make, range	**Jaguar XJ 6 3.2 (X 300)**			**Jaguar XJ 6 3.2 LWB (X 300)**	
Type	*XJ 6 (Business)*	*Sport (Executive)*	*Sovereign*	*XJ 6 LWB*	*Sovereign LWB*
Public debut	28/9/1994	28/9/1994	28/9/1994	28/6/1995	28/6/1995
End of production	7/1997	7/1997	7/1997	7/1997	7/1997
Production figure	92,225 (incl. 4.0 and 6.0)			92,225 (incl. 4.0 and 6.0)	
First, last chassis number RHD	VIN 720000-812255			VIN 720000-812255	
First, last chassis number LHD	VIN 720000-812255			VIN 720000-812255	
Body type	All-steel, 4 doors, 5 seats			All-steel, 4 doors, 5 seats	
Weather protection, top mechanism	Enclosed-drive, optional electrically operated steel sunroof			Enclosed-drive, optional electrically operated steel sunroof	
Length, width, height (mm)	5025 x 1780 x 1380			5150 x 1780 x 1380	
Length, width, height (inches)	198 x 70 x 54 1/4			203 x 70 x 54 1/4	
Wheelbase, front, rear track (mm)	2870 x 1501/1499			2997 x 1501/1499	
Wheelbase, front, rear track (inches)	113 x 59/59			118 x 59/59	
Ground clearance, turning circle, curb weight	150mm, 12m, 1800kg			150mm, 12m, 1850kg	
Max speed, acceleration 0-60 mph	220kph, 8 sec			220kph, 8 sec	
Max power, standard, revs	211 DIN-HP/5100			211 DIN-HP/5100	
Max torque, revs	301 Nm/4500			301 Nm/4500	
Engine type, position, number and configuration of cylinders	Four-stroke gasoline, front longitudinally, 6 cylinders straight			Four-stroke gasoline, front longitudinally, 6 cylinders straight	
Bore x Stroke (mm), capacity (cc), compression ratio	91 x 83, 3239cc, 10 : 1			91 x 83, 3239cc, 10 : 1	
Designation of engine and cylinder head	Engine and head "AJ 16"			Engine and head "AJ 16"	
Engine block and cylinder head material, number of main bearings, type of liners	Block and head aluminum, 7 main bearings, dry liners			Block and head aluminum, 7 main bearings, dry liners	
Number of valves per cylinder, configuration, valve gearing, timing variants	4 overhead valves, bucket tappets, 2 overhead camshafts, 2 duplex chains, fixed			4 overhead valves, bucket tappets, 2 overhead camshafts, 2 duplex chains, fixed	
Air supply, type of inlet manifold, air tempering	Normally aspirated, one-stage inlet manifold, n/a			Normally aspirated, one-stage inlet manifold, n/a	
Type, position, make, and designation of mixture preparation	Electronic injection to manifold, Lucas			Electronic injection to manifold, Lucas	
Energy source, type, make, and designation of ignition system	Battery, separate coils, SAGEM-Lucas			Battery, separate coils, SAGEM-Lucas	
Make of alternator, voltage, earthing	Alternator, 12 V, negative			Alternator, 12 V, negative	
Engine coolant, drive, regulation of cooling	Liquid, pump, thermostat			Liquid, pump, thermostat	
Type of clutch, number of gears in manual box, synchronized gears	Single-plate dry clutch, 5, fully			Single-plate dry clutch, 5, fully	
Gear ratios in manual box	3.57, 2.96, 1.39, 1, 0.76, 3.46 : 1			3.57, 2.96, 1.39, 1, 0.76, 3.46 : 1	
Make, type, ratio of overdrive	n/a			n/a	
Type of clutch, number of gears, make and model of automatic box	Optional hydraulic torque converter, 4, ZF 4 HP 24			Optional hydraulic torque converter, 4, ZF 4 HP 24	
Gear ratios in automatic gearbox	2.48, 1.48, 1, 0.75, 2.08 : 1			2.48, 1.48, 1, 0.75, 2.08 : 1	
Driven axle, type of diff, traction control	Rear, hypoid bevel, limited-slip			Rear, hypoid bevel, limited-slip	
Axle ratios	3.77 (with automatic 4.09) : 1			3.77 (with automatic 4.09) : 1	
Type of chassis	Unitary, front and rear subframes			Unitary, front and rear subframes	
Suspension, springing front	Double-wishbone, coil springs			Double-wishbone, coil springs	
Suspension, springing rear	Forked transverse arms and driveshafts, coil springs			Forked transverse arms and driveshafts, coil springs	
Reduction of roll	Torsion bar front, optional rear also			Torsion bar front, optional rear also	
Type of shock absorbers	Telescopic			Telescopic	
Type and dimensions of wheels	Steel (from Business aluminum) discs, 7 J x 16 (Sport 8 J x 16)			Aluminum discs, 7 J x 16	
Type, dimensions, make of tires	Pirelli P 4000 E, 225/60 ZR 16 (Sport 225/55 ZR 16)			Pirelli P 4000 E, 225/60 ZR 16	
Type of braking front	Ventilated discs			Ventilated discs	
Type of braking rear	Massive outboard discs			Massive outboard discs	
Braking mechanism, number of circuits, servo assistance, electronic aids	Hydraulics, 2 circuits, front/rear balance valve, hydraulic servo assistance, antilock, optional traction control			Hydraulics, 2 circuits, front/rear balance valve, hydraulic servo assistance, antilock, optional traction control	
Steering gear, make and model of power steering	Rack and pinion, hydraulic servo ZF Servotronic			Rack and pinion, hydraulic servo ZF Servotronic	

XJ

Make, range	**Jaguar XJ 6 4.0 and Daimler Six (X 300)**			**Jaguar XJ 6 4.0 and Daimler Six LWB (X 300)**		
Type	*XJ 6 (XJR)*	*Sport (Executive)*	*Sovereign (Daimler Six*)*	*XJ 6 LWB*	*Daimler Six LWB***	*Sovereign LWB*
Public debut	8/1995 (28/9/1994)	28/9/1994	28/9/1994	28/6/1995	28/6/1995	8/1995
End of production	7/1997	7/1997	7/1997	7/1997	7/1997	7/1997
Production figure	92,225 (incl. 3.2 and 6.0)			92,225 (incl. 3.2 and 6.0)		
First, last chassis number RHD	VIN 720000-812255			VIN 720000-812255		
First, last chassis number LHD	VIN 720000-812255			VIN 720000-812255		
Body type	All-steel, 4 doors, 5 seats			All-steel, 4 doors, 5 seats		
Weather protection, top mechanism	Enclosed-drive, optional electrically operated steel sunroof			Enclosed-drive, optional electrically operated steel sunroof		
Length, width, height (mm)	5025 x 1780 x 1380			5150 x 1780 x 1380		
Length, width, height (inches)	198 x 70 x 54 1/4			203 x 70 x 54 1/4		
Wheelbase, front, rear track (mm)	2870 x 1501/1499			2997 x 1501/1499		
Wheelbase, front, rear track (inches)	113 x 59/59			118 x 59/59		
Ground clearance, turning circle, curb weight	150mm, 12m, 1800kg			150mm, 12m, 1850kg		
Max speed, acceleration 0-60 mph	230kph, 7 sec (XJR 250kph, 6 sec)			230kph, 7 sec		
Max power, standard, revs	249 DIN-HP/4800 (XJR 326 DIN-HP/5000)			249 DIN-HP/4800		
Max torque, revs	392 Nm/4000 (XJR 512 Nm/3050)			392 Nm/4000		
Engine type, position, number and configuration of cylinders	Four-stroke gasoline, front longitudinally, 6 cylinders straight			Four-stroke gasoline, front longitudinally, 6 cylinders straight		
Bore x Stroke (mm), capacity (cc), compression ratio	91 x 102, 3980cc, 10 (XJR 8.5) : 1			91 x 102, 3980cc, 10 : 1		
Designation of engine and cylinder head	Engine and head "AJ 16"			Engine and head "AJ 16"		
Engine block and cylinder head material, number of main bearings, type of liners	Block and head aluminum, 7 main bearings, dry liners			Block and head aluminum, 7 main bearings, dry liners		
Number of valves per cylinder, configuration, valve gearing, timing variants	4 overhead valves, bucket tappets, 2 overhead camshafts, 2 duplex chains, fixed			4 overhead valves, bucket tappets, 2 overhead camshafts, 2 duplex chains, fixed		
Air supply, type of inlet manifold, air tempering	Normally aspirated, one-stage inlet manifold, n/a (XJR Roots supercharger, intercooler)			Normally aspirated, one-stage inlet manifold, n/a		
Type, position, make, and designation of mixture preparation	Electronic injection to manifold, Lucas			Electronic injection to manifold, Lucas		
Energy source, type, make, and designation of ignition system	Battery, separate coils, SAGEM-Lucas			Battery, separate coils, SAGEM-Lucas		
Make of alternator, voltage, earthing	Alternator, 12 V, negative			Alternator, 12 V, negative		
Engine coolant, drive, regulation of cooling	Liquid, pump, thermostat			Liquid, pump, thermostat		
Type of clutch, number of gears in manual box, synchronized gears	Single-plate dry clutch, 5, fully			Single-plate dry clutch, 5, fully		
Gear ratios in manual box	3.57, 2.96, 1.39, 1, 0.76, 3.46 : 1			3.57, 2.96, 1.39, 1, 0.76, 3.46 : 1		
Make, type, ratio of overdrive	n/a			n/a		
Type of clutch, number of gears, make and model of automatic box	Optional hydraulic torque converter, 4, ZF 4 HP 24 (XJR GM 4L80E)			Optional hydraulic torque converter, 4, ZF 4 HP 24		
Gear ratios in automatic gearbox	2.48, 1.48, 1, 0.75, 2.08 : 1			2.48, 1.48, 1, 0.75, 2.08 : 1		
Driven axle, type of diff, traction control	Rear, hypoid bevel, limited-slip			Rear, hypoid bevel, limited-slip		
Axle ratios	3.58 (XJR with manual gearchange 3.27) : 1			3.58 : 1		
Type of chassis	Unitary, front and rear subframes			Unitary, front and rear subframes		
Suspension, springing front	Double-wishbone, coil springs			Double-wishbone, coil springs		
Suspension, springing rear	Forked transverse arms and driveshafts, coil springs			Forked transverse arms and driveshafts, coil springs		
Reduction of roll	Torsion bar front, optional (XJR always) rear also			Torsion bar front, optional rear also		
Type of shock absorbers	Telescopic			Telescopic		
Type and dimensions of wheels	Aluminum discs, 7 J x 16 (Sport 8 J x 16, XJR 8 J x 17)			Aluminum discs, 7 J x 16		
Type, dimensions, make of tires	Pirelli P 4000 E, 225/60 ZR 16 (Sport 225/55 ZR 16, XJR Pirelli P Zero 225/45 ZR 17)			Pirelli P 4000 E, 225/60 ZR 16		
Type of braking front	Ventilated discs			Ventilated discs		
Type of braking rear	Massive outboard discs			Massive outboard discs		
Braking mechanism, number of circuits, servo assistance, electronic aids	Hydraulics, 2 circuits, front/rear balance valve, hydraulic servo assistance, antilock, optional (Sovereign, Daimler, XJR always) traction control			Hydraulics, 2 circuits, front/rear balance valve, hydraulic servo assistance, antilock, optional (Sovereign and Daimler always) traction control		
Steering gear, make and model of power steering	Rack and pinion, hydraulic servo ZF Servotronic			Rack and pinion, hydraulic servo ZF Servotronic		

* 1 shorter prototype convertible Corsica, mechanically completed only 2007 (VIN SAJDSVOJDHTDMG001)

** 1996 100 examples of limited-edition Century

XJ

Make, range	**Jaguar XJ 12 6.0 and Daimler Double-Six (X 300)**			**Jaguar XJ 12 6.0 and Daimler Double-Six LWB (X 300)**		
Type	*XJ 12*	*Vanden Plas*	*Daimler Double-Six*	*XJ 12 LWB*	*Vanden Plas LWB*	*Daimler Double-Six LWB**
Public debut	28/9/1994	10/1994	28/9/1994	28/6/1995	8/1995	28/6/1995
End of production	10/1996	1995	10/1996	10/1996	5/1997	5/1997
Production figure	92,225 (incl. 3.2 and 4.0)			92,225 (incl. 3.2 and 4.0)		
First, last chassis number RHD	VIN 720000-unknown			VIN unknown-812255		
First, last chassis number LHD	VIN 720000-unknown			VIN unknown-812255		
Body type	All-steel, 4 doors, 5 seats			All-steel, 4 doors, 5 seats		
Weather protection, top mechanism	Enclosed-drive, optional electrically operated steel sunroof			Enclosed-drive, optional electrically operated steel sunroof		
Length, width, height (mm)	5025 x 1780 x 1380			5150 x 1780 x 1380		
Length, width, height (inches)	198 x 70 x 54 1/4			203 x 70 x 54 1/4		
Wheelbase, front, rear track (mm)	2870 x 1501/1499			2997 x 1501/1499		
Wheelbase, front, rear track (inches)	113 x 59/59			118 x 59/59		
Ground clearance, turning circle, curb weight	150mm, 12m, 1900kg			150mm, 12m, 1950kg		
Max speed, acceleration 0-60 mph	250kph, 7 sec			250kph, 7 sec		
Max power, standard, revs	318 DIN or 311 ECE-HP/5400 (US 315 NET or 305 ECE-HP/5350)			318 DIN or 311 ECE-HP/5400 (US 315 NET or 305 ECE-HP/5350)		
Max torque, revs	463 or 453 Nm/3750 (US 455 Nm/3750)			463 or 453 Nm/3750 (US 455 Nm/3750)		
Engine type, position, number and configuration of cylinders	Four-stroke gasoline, front longitudinally, 12 cylinders, 60-degree-V			Four-stroke gasoline, front longitudinally, 12 cylinders, 60-degree-V		
Bore x Stroke (mm), capacity (cc), compression ratio	90 x 78.5, 5993cc, 11 : 1			90 x 78.5, 5993cc, 11 : 1		
Designation of engine and cylinder head	Engine "Jaguar V-12," head "Fireball"			Engine "Jaguar V-12," head "Fireball"		
Engine block and cylinder head material, number of main bearings, type of liners	Block and head aluminum, 7 main bearings, wet liners			Block and head aluminum, 7 main bearings, wet liners		
Number of valves per cylinder, configuration, valve gearing, timing variants	2 overhead valves, bucket tappets, 1 ohc per bank, duplex chain, fixed			2 overhead valves, bucket tappets, 1 ohc per bank, duplex chain, fixed		
Air supply, type of inlet manifold, air tempering	Normally aspirated, one-stage inlet manifold, n/a			Normally aspirated, one-stage inlet manifold, n/a		
Type, position, make, and designation of mixture preparation	Electronic injection to manifold, Lucas			Electronic injection to manifold, Lucas		
Energy source, type, make, and designation of ignition system	Battery, solid-state, Lucas OPUS			Battery, solid-state, Lucas OPUS		
Make of alternator, voltage, earthing	Alternator, 12 V, negative			Alternator, 12 V, negative		
Engine coolant, drive, regulation of cooling	Liquid, pump, thermostat			Liquid, pump, thermostat		
Type of clutch, number of gears in manual box, synchronized gears	n/a			n/a		
Gear ratios in manual box	n/a			n/a		
Make, type, ratio of overdrive	n/a			n/a		
Type of clutch, number of gears, make and model of automatic box	Hydraulic torque converter, 4, GM 4L80E			Hydraulic torque converter, 4, GM 4L80E		
Gear ratios in automatic gearbox	2.48, 1.48, 1, 0.75, 2.08 : 1			2.48, 1.48, 1, 0.75, 2.08 : 1		
Driven axle, type of diff, traction control	Rear, hypoid bevel, limited-slip			Rear, hypoid bevel, limited-slip		
Axle ratios	3.58 : 1			3.58 : 1		
Type of chassis	Unitary, front and rear subframes			Unitary, front and rear subframes		
Suspension, springing front	Double-wishbone, coil springs			Double-wishbone, coil springs		
Suspension, springing rear	Forked transverse arms and driveshafts, coil springs			Forked transverse arms and driveshafts, coil springs		
Reduction of roll	Torsion bar front, optional rear also			Torsion bar front, optional rear also		
Type of shock absorbers	Telescopic			Telescopic		
Type and dimensions of wheels	Aluminum discs, 8 (Vanden Plas and Daimler 7) J x 16			Aluminum discs, 8 (Vanden Plas and Daimler 7) J x 16		
Type, dimensions, make of tires	Pirelli P 6000 225/55 ZR 16 (Vanden Plas and Daimler P 4000 E, 225/60 ZR 16)			Pirelli P 6000 225/55 ZR 16 (Vanden Plas and Daimler P 4000 E, 225/60 ZR 16)		
Type of braking front	Ventilated discs			Ventilated discs		
Type of braking rear	Massive outboard discs			Massive outboard discs		
Braking mechanism, number of circuits, servo assistance, electronic aids	Hydraulics, 2 circuits, balance valve front/rear, hydraulic servo assistance, antilock, traction control			Hydraulics, 2 circuits, balance valve front/rear, hydraulic servo assistance, antilock, traction control		
Steering gear, make and model of power steering	Rack and pinion, hydraulic servo ZF Servotronic			Rack and pinion, hydraulic servo ZF Servotronic		

* 1 prototype extended by 200mm; 1996 100 examples of limited-edition Century

Make, range	**Jaguar XJ 8 3.2 (X 308)**			**Jaguar XJ 8 3.2 LWB (X 308)**
Type	*XJ 8 3.2*	*3.2 Sport*	*3.2 Executive (S.E.)*	*3.2 Executive (S.E.) LWB*
Public debut	9/9/1997	9/9/1997	9/9/1997 (8/2001)	10/1998 (8/2001)
End of production	6/2001	6/2001	18/7/02	18/7/02
Production figure	126,260 (incl. 4.0 and supercharged cars)			126,260 (incl. 4.0 and supercharged cars)
First, last chassis number RHD	VIN 812256-878714 and F00001-59525			VIN 812256-878714 and F00001-59525
First, last chassis number LHD	VIN 812256-878714 and F00001-59525			VIN 812256-878714 and F00001-59525
Body type	All-steel, 4 doors, 5 seats			All-steel, 4 doors, 5 seats
Weather protection, top mechanism	Enclosed-drive, optional electrically operated steel sunroof			Enclosed-drive, optional electrically operated steel sunroof
Length, width, height (mm)	5023 x 1799 x 1314			5148 x 1799 x 1333
Length, width, height (inches)	197 3/4 x 70 3/4 x 51 3/4			202 3/4 x 70 3/4 x 52 1/2
Wheelbase, front, rear track (mm)	2870 x 1500/1498			2997 x 1500/1498
Wheelbase, front, rear track (inches)	113 x 59/59			118 x 59/59
Ground clearance, turning circle, curb weight	150mm, 12m, 1710kg			150mm, 12m, 1770kg
Max speed, acceleration 0-60 mph	225kph, 8 sec			225kph, 8 sec
Max power, standard, revs	237 ECE-HP/6350			237 ECE-HP/6350
Max torque, revs	310 Nm/4350			310 Nm/4350
Engine type, position, number and configuration of cylinders	Four-stroke gasoline, front longitudinally, 8 cylinders, 90-degree-V			Four-stroke gasoline, front longitudinally, 8 cylinders, 90-degree-V
Bore x Stroke (mm), capacity (cc), compression ratio	86 x 70, 3248cc, 10.5 : 1			86 x 70, 3248cc, 10.5 : 1
Designation of engine and cylinder head	Engine and head "AJ 26"			Engine and head "AJ 26"
Engine block and cylinder head material, number of main bearings, type of liners	Block and head aluminum, 5 main bearings, Nikasil (from 2000 cast-in liners)			Block and head aluminum, 5 main bearings, Nikasil (from 2000 cast-in liners)
Number of valves per cylinder, configuration, valve gearing, timing variants	4 overhead valves, bucket tappets, 2 ohc per bank, chain, fixed			4 overhead valves, bucket tappets, 2 ohc per bank, chain, fixed
Air supply, type of inlet manifold, air tempering	Normally aspirated, 2-stage inlet manifold, n/a			Normally aspirated, 2-stage inlet manifold, n/a
Type, position, make, and designation of mixture preparation	Electronic injection to manifold, Lucas			Electronic injection to manifold, Lucas
Energy source, type, make, and designation of ignition system	Battery, separate coils, Nippondenso			Battery, separate coils, Nippondenso
Make of alternator, voltage, earthing	Alternator, 12 V, negative			Alternator, 12 V, negative
Engine coolant, drive, regulation of cooling	Liquid, pump, thermostat			Liquid, pump, thermostat
Type of clutch, number of gears in manual box, synchronized gears	n/a			n/a
Gear ratios in manual box	n/a			n/a
Make, type, ratio of overdrive	n/a			n/a
Type of clutch, number of gears, make and model of automatic box	Hydraulic torque converter, 5, ZF 5 HP 24			Hydraulic torque converter, 5, ZF 5 HP 24
Gear ratios in automatic gearbox	3.57, 2.2, 1.51, 1, 0.8, 4.1 : 1			3.57, 2.2, 1.51, 1, 0.8, 4.1 : 1
Driven axle, type of diff, traction control	Rear, hypoid bevel, n/a			Rear, hypoid bevel, n/a
Axle ratios	3.27 : 1			3.27 : 1
Type of chassis	Unitary, front and rear subframes			Unitary, front and rear subframes
Suspension, springing front	Double-wishbone, coil springs			Double-wishbone, coil springs
Suspension, springing rear	Forked transverse arms and driveshafts, coil springs			Forked transverse arms and driveshafts, coil springs
Reduction of roll	Torsion bar front, optional rear also			Torsion bar front, optional rear also
Type of shock absorbers	Telescopic, optional CATS			Telescopic, optional CATS
Type and dimensions of wheels	Steel (from Sport and Executive aluminum) discs, 7 x 16			Aluminum discs, 7 x 16
Type, dimensions, make of tires	225/60 ZR 16			225/60 ZR 16
Type of braking front	Ventilated discs			Ventilated discs
Type of braking rear	Ventilated outboard discs			Ventilated outboard discs
Braking mechanism, number of circuits, servo assistance, electronic aids	Hydraulics, 2 circuits, electronic front/rear balance, hydraulic servo assistance, antilock, ASC+T			Hydraulics, 2 circuits, electronic front/rear balance, hydraulic servo assistance, antilock, ASC+T
Steering gear, make and model of power steering	Rack and pinion, hydraulic servo ZF Servotronic (from 9/98 Servotronic II)			Rack and pinion, hydraulic servo ZF Servotronic (from 9/98 Servotronic II)

Make, range	**Jaguar XJ 8 4.0 and Daimler V8 (X 308)**			**Jaguar XJ 8 4.0 and Daimler V8 LWB (X 308)**		
Type	*XJ 8 4.0**	*4.0 Executive*	*4.0 Sovereign*	*Sovereign LWB (XJ 8L)*	*Vanden Plas LWB***	*Daimler V8 LWB***
Public debut	9/9/1997	9/9/1997	9/9/1997	9/9/1997	9/9/1997	9/9/1997
End of production	18/7/2002	18/7/2002	18/7/2002	18/7/2002	18/7/2002	18/7/2002
Production figure	126,260 (incl. 3.2 and supercharged cars)			126,260 (incl. 3.2 and supercharged cars)		
First, last chassis number RHD	VIN 812256-878714 and F00001-59525			VIN 812256-878714 and F00001-59525		
First, last chassis number LHD	VIN 812256-878714 and F00001-59525			VIN 812256-878714 and F00001-59525		
Body type	All-steel, 4 doors, 5 seats			All-steel, 4 doors, 5 seats		
Weather protection, top mechanism	Enclosed-drive, optional electrically operated steel sunroof			Enclosed-drive, optional electrically operated steel sunroof		
Length, width, height (mm)	5023 x 1799 x 1314			5148 x 1799 x 1333		
Length, width, height (inches)	197 3/4 x 70 3/4 x 51 3/4			202 3/4 x 70 3/4 x 52 1/2		
Wheelbase, front, rear track (mm)	2870 x 1500/1498			2997 x 1500/1498		
Wheelbase, front, rear track (inches)	113 x 59/59			118 x 59/59		
Ground clearance, turning circle, curb weight	150mm, 12m, 1710kg			150mm, 12m, 1770kg		
Max speed, acceleration 0-60 mph	240kph, 7 sec			240kph, 7 sec		
Max power, standard, revs	284 ECE-HP/6100			284 ECE-HP/6100		
Max torque, revs	375 Nm/4250			375 Nm/4250		
Engine type, position, number and configuration of cylinders	Four-stroke gasoline, front longitudinally, 8 cylinders, 90-degree-V			Four-stroke gasoline, front longitudinally, 8 cylinders, 90-degree-V		
Bore x Stroke (mm), capacity (cc), compression ratio	86 x 86, 3996cc, 10.75 : 1			86 x 86, 3996cc, 10.75 : 1		
Designation of engine and cylinder head	Engine and head "AJ 26"			Engine and head "AJ 26"		
Engine block and cylinder head material, number of main bearings, type of liners	Block and head aluminum, 5 main bearings, Nikasil (from 2000 cast-in liners)			Block and head aluminum, 5 main bearings, Nikasil (from 2000 cast-in liners)		
Number of valves per cylinder, configuration, valve gearing, timing variants	4 overhead valves, bucket tappets, 2 ohc per bank, otherwise as LWB			As XJ 8 4.0, chain, 2-stage variable timing (from 10/98 continously variable)		
Air supply, type of inlet manifold, air tempering	Normally aspirated, 2-stage inlet manifold, n/a			Normally aspirated, 2-stage inlet manifold, n/a		
Type, position, make, and designation of mixture preparation	Electronic injection to manifold, Lucas			Electronic injection to manifold, Lucas		
Energy source, type, make and designation of ignition system	Battery, separate coils, Nippondenso			Battery, separate coils, Nippondenso		
Make of alternator, voltage, earthing	Alternator, 12 V, negative			Alternator, 12 V, negative		
Engine coolant, drive, regulation of cooling	Liquid, pump, thermostat			Liquid, pump, thermostat		
Type of clutch, number of gears in manual box, synchronized gears	n/a			n/a		
Gear ratios in manual box	n/a			n/a		
Make, type, ratio of overdrive	n/a			n/a		
Type of clutch, number of gears, make and model of automatic box	Hydraulic torque converter, 5, ZF 5 HP 24			Hydraulic torque converter, 5, ZF 5 HP 24		
Gear ratios in automatic gearbox	3.57, 2.2, 1.51, 1, 0.8, 4.1 : 1			3.57, 2.2, 1.51, 1, 0.8, 4.1 : 1		
Driven axle, type of diff, traction control	Rear, hypoid bevel, n/a			Rear, hypoid bevel, n/a		
Axle ratios	3.06 : 1			3.06 : 1		
Type of chassis	Unitary, front and rear subframes			Unitary, front and rear subframes		
Suspension, springing front	Double-wishbone, coil springs			Double-wishbone, coil springs		
Suspension, springing rear	Forked transverse arms and driveshafts, coil springs			Forked transverse arms and driveshafts, coil springs		
Reduction of roll	Torsion bar front, optional rear also			Torsion bar front, optional rear also		
Type of shock absorbers	Telescopic, optional CATS			Telescopic, optional CATS		
Type and dimensions of wheels	Aluminum discs, 7 x 16			Aluminum discs, 7 x 16		
Type, dimensions, make of tires	225/60 ZR 16			225/60 ZR 16		
Type of braking front	Ventilated discs			Ventilated discs		
Type of braking rear	Ventilated outboard discs			Ventilated outboard discs		
Braking mechanism, number of circuits, servo assistance, electronic aids	Hydraulics, 2 circuits, electronic front/rear balance, hydraulic servo assistance, antilock, ASC+T			Hydraulics, 2 circuits, electronic front/rear balance, hydraulic servo assistance, antilock, ASC+T		
Steering gear, make and model of power steering	Rack and pinion, hydraulic servo ZF Servotronic (from 9/98 Servotronic II)			Rack and pinion, hydraulic servo ZF Servotronic (from 9/98 Servotronic II)		

* Optional with lwb

** Optional with swb

Make, range	**Jaguar XJR (X 308)**	**Jaguar Vanden Plas and Daimler V8 super (X 308)**	
Type	*XJR**	*Vanden Plas Supercharged***	*Daimler V8 super***
Public debut	9/9/1997	9/9/1997	9/9/1997
End of production	18/7/2002	18/7/2002	18/7/2002
Production figure	126,260 (incl. 3.2 and unsupercharged 4.0)	126,260 (incl. 3.2 and unsupercharged 4.0)	
First, last chassis number RHD	VIN 812256-878714 and F00001-59525	VIN 812256-878714 and F00001-59525	
First, last chassis number LHD	VIN 812256-878714 and F00001-59525	VIN 812256-878714 and F00001-59525	
Body type	All-steel, 4 doors, 5 seats	All-steel, 4 doors, 5 seats	
Weather protection, top mechanism	Enclosed-drive, optional electrically operated steel sunroof	Enclosed-drive, optional electrically operated steel sunroof	
Length, width, height (mm)	5023 x 1799 x 1314	5148 x 1799 x 1333	
Length, width, height (inches)	197 3/4 x 70 3/4 x 51 3/4	202 3/4 x 70 3/4 x 52 1/2	
Wheelbase, front, rear track (mm)	2870 x 1500/1498	2997 x 1500/1498	
Wheelbase, front, rear track (inches)	113 x 59/59	118 x 59/59	
Ground clearance, turning circle, curb weight	150mm, 12m, 1775kg	150mm, 12m, 1850kg	
Max speed, acceleration 0-60 mph	250kph, 6 sec	250kph, 6 sec	
Max power, standard, revs	363 ECE-HP/6150	363 ECE-HP/6150	
Max torque, revs	505 Nm/3600	505 Nm/3600	
Engine type, position, number and configuration of cylinders	Four-stroke gasoline, front longitudinally, 8 cylinders, 90-degree-V	Four-stroke gasoline, front longitudinally, 8 cylinders, 90-degree-V	
Bore x Stroke (mm), capacity (cc), compression ratio	86 x 86, 3996cc, 8.9 : 1	86 x 86, 3996cc, 8.9 : 1	
Designation of engine and cylinder head	Engine and head "AJ 26"	Engine and head "AJ 26"	
Engine block and cylinder head material, number of main bearings, type of liners	Block and head aluminum, 5 main bearings, Nikasil (from 2000 cast-in liners)	Block and head aluminum, 5 main bearings, Nikasil (from 2000 cast-in liners)	
Number of valves per cylinder, configuration, valve gearing, timing variants	4 overhead valves, bucket tappets, 2 ohc per bank, chain, fixed	4 overhead valves, bucket tappets, 2 ohc per bank, chain, fixed	
Air supply, type of inlet manifold, air tempering	Roots supercharger, one-stage inlet manifold, intercooler	Roots supercharger, one-stage inlet manifold, intercooler	
Type, position, make, and designation of mixture preparation	Electronic injection to manifold, Lucas	Electronic injection to manifold, Lucas	
Energy source, type, make, and designation of ignition system	Battery, separate coils, Nippondenso	Battery, separate coils, Nippondenso	
Make of alternator, voltage, earthing	Alternator, 12 V, negative	Alternator, 12 V, negative	
Engine coolant, drive, regulation of cooling	Liquid, pump, thermostat	Liquid, pump, thermostat	
Type of clutch, number of gears in manual box, synchronized gears	n/a	n/a	
Gear ratios in manual box	n/a	n/a	
Make, type, ratio of overdrive	n/a	n/a	
Type of clutch, number of gears, make and model of automatic box	Hydraulic torque converter, 5, Mercedes-Benz W5A580	Hydraulic torque converter, 5, Mercedes-Benz W5A580	
Gear ratios in automatic gearbox	3.59, 2.19, 1.41, 1, 0.83, 3.16 : 1	3.59, 2.19, 1.41, 1, 0.83, 3.16 : 1	
Driven axle, type of diff, traction control	Rear, hypoid bevel, n/a	Rear, hypoid bevel, n/a	
Axle ratios	3.06 : 1	3.06 : 1	
Type of chassis	Unitary, front and rear subframes	Unitary, front and rear subframes	
Suspension, springing front	Double-wishbone, coil springs	Double-wishbone, coil springs	
Suspension, springing rear	Forked transverse arms and driveshafts, coil springs	Forked transverse arms and driveshafts, coil springs	
Reduction of roll	Torsion bars front and rear	Torsion bar front, optional rear also	
Type of shock absorbers	Telescopic, CATS	Telescopic, optional CATS	
Type and dimensions of wheels	Aluminum discs, 8 x 18	Aluminum discs, 7.5 J x 17	
Type, dimensions, make of tires	255/40 ZR 18	235/50 ZR 17	
Type of braking front	Ventilated discs	Ventilated discs	
Type of braking rear	Ventilated outboard discs	Ventilated outboard discs	
Braking mechanism, number of circuits, servo assistance, electronic aids	Hydraulics, 2 circuits, electronic front/rear balance, hydraulic servo assistance, antilock, ASC+T	Hydraulics, 2 circuits, electronic front/rear balance, hydraulic servo assistance, antilock, ASC+T	
Steering gear, make and model of power steering	Rack and pinion, hydraulic servo ZF Servotronic (from 9/98 Servotronic II)	Rack and pinion, hydraulic servo ZF Servotronic (from 9/98 Servotronic II)	
	* 2001 100 examples of limited-edition "XJR 100"	** Optional with swb	

XJ

Make, range	**TWR Jaguar XJR-6 bis 9**			**TWR Jaguar XJR-12**
Type	*XJR-6*	*XJR-8*	*XJR-9*	*XJR-12***
Public debut	02/07/1985	06/02/1987	20/08/1987	28/02/1990
End of production	6/1986	5/1987	6/1988	12/1992
Production figure	6*	3	6**	4
		(plus 2 former XJR-6)	(plus 3 former XJR-8**)	(+ 3 former XJR-9 and 1 former XJR-6)
First, last chassis number RHD	185, 285, 385, 186-386	187-387	188-688	190, 290, 990, 1090
First, last chassis number LHD	n/a	n/a	n/a	n/a
Body type	Fiberglass and Kevlar, 2 doors, 2 seats			Fiberglass and Kevlar, 2 doors, 2 seats
Weather protection, top mechanism	Enclosed-drive			Enclosed-drive
Length, width, height (mm)	4800 (XJR-8 and XJR-9 for Le Mans 5000) x 2000 x 1100			4800 x 2000 x 1100
Length, width, height (inches)	189 (XJR-8 und XJR-9 for Le Mans 5000) x 79 x 43			189 x 79 x 43
Wheelbase, front, rear track (mm)	2780 x 1500/1500			2780 x 1500/1500
Wheelbase, front, rear track (inches)	109 1/2 x 59/59			109 1/2 x 59 x 59
Ground clearance, turning circle, curb weight	100mm, 15m, 890 (from XJR-8 850, XJR-9 for IMSA 900) kg			100mm, 15m, 850kg
Max speed, acceleration 0-60 mph	300kph, 3 sec			300kph, 3 sec
Max power, standard, revs	650 (XJR-8 720, XJR-9 WSPC 750) DIN-HP/8000 750 DIN-HP/8000			
Max torque, revs	700 Nm/6000 (XJR-8 780 Nm/6000, XJR-9 800 Nm/6000)			800 Nm/6000
Engine type, position, number and configuration of cylinders	Four-stroke gasoline, central longitudinally, 12 cylinders, 60-degree-V			Four-stroke gasoline, central longitudinally, 12 cylinders, 60-degree-V
Bore x Stroke (mm), capacity (cc), compression ratio	92 x 78, 6222*** (from XJR-8 94 x 84, 6995***) cc, 11 : 1			94 x 84, 6995cc, 11 : 1
Designation of engine and cylinder head	Engine "Jaguar V-12," head "TWR"			Engine "Jaguar V-12," head "TWR"
Engine block and cylinder head material, number of main bearings, type of liners	Block and head aluminum, 7 main bearings, wet liners			Block and head aluminum, 7 main bearings, wet liners
Number of valves per cylinder, configuration, valve gearing, timing variants	2 overhead valves, bucket tappets, 1 ohc per bank, duplex chain, fixed			2 overhead valves, bucket tappets, 1 ohc per bank, duplex chain, fixed
Air supply, type of inlet manifold, air tempering	Normally aspirated, one-stage inlet manifold, n/a			Normally aspirated, one-stage inlet manifold, n/a
Type, position, make, and designation of mixture preparation	Electronic injection to manifold Lucas-MICOS			Electronic injection to manifold Lucas-MICOS
Energy source, type, make, and designation of ignition system	Battery, solid-state, unknown			Battery, solid-state, unknown
Make of alternator, voltage, earthing	Alternator, 12 V, negative			Alternator, 12 V, negative
Engine coolant, drive, regulation of cooling	Liquid, pump, thermostat			Liquid, pump, thermostat
Type of clutch, number of gears in manual box, synchronized gears	Three-plate dry clutch, 5, fully			Three-plate dry clutch, 5, fully
Gear ratios in manual box	Unknown			Unknown
Make, type, ratio of overdrive	n/a			n/a
Type of clutch, number of gears, make and model of automatic box	n/a			n/a
Gear ratios in automatic gearbox	n/a			n/a
Driven axle, type of diff, traction control	Rear, hypoid bevel, limited-slip			Rear, hypoid bevel, limited-slip
Axle ratios	Unknown			Unknown
Type of chassis	Unitary			Unitary
Suspension, springing front	Double-wishbone, coil springs (horizontal)			Double-wishbone, coil springs
Suspension, springing rear	Double-wishbone and trailing arm, coil springs			Double-wishbone and trailing arm, coil springs
Reduction of roll	Torsion bars front and rear			Torsion bars front and rear
Type of shock absorbers	Telescopic (front horizontal)			Telescopic
Type and dimensions of wheels	Magnesium discs, 17 (rear 19, XJR-9 for IMSA 17")			Magnesium discs, 17"
Type, dimensions, make of tires	Dunlop, unknown			Goodyear, unknown
Type of braking front	Ventilated discs			Ventilated discs
Type of braking rear	Ventilated outboard discs			Ventilated outboard discs
Braking mechanism, number of circuits, servo assistance, electronic aids	Hydraulics, 2 circuits, hydraulic servo assistance, n/a			Hydraulics, 2 circuits, hydraulic servo assistance, n/a
Steering gear, make and model of power steering	Rack and pinion, hydraulic servo			Rack and pinion, hydraulic servo

* Incl. 3 with 6.5-liter engine

** For IMSA 900kg with 6.0-liter engine, 650 HP and 700 Nm

*** Incl. each 3 with 6.0-liter engine, 650 HP, 700 Nm; 7.0 with 4 valves 798 HP and 830 Nm

Make, range	**Jaguar XJ 220**			**Jaguar Sport XJR-15**		
Type	*Prototype*	*Series*	*C*	*Coupe*	*Racing car*	*7.0*
Public debut	10/1988	18/10/1991	1993	15/11/1990	11/05/1991	1991
End of production	10/1988	12/1993	1993	1991	5/1991	1991
Production figure	1	280	4	27	18	5
First, last chassis number RHD	VIN, unknown	VIN 220617-220900	VIN 220617-220900	Unknown	Unknown	Unknown
First, last chassis number LHD	n/a	VIN 220617-220900	n/a	n/a	n/a	n/a
Body type	Aluminum, bonded (C Kevlar and fiberglass), 2 doors, 2 seats			Fiberglass, 2 doors, 2 seats		
Weather protection, top mechanism	Enclosed-drive (Prototype and Production glass roof)			Enclosed-drive		
Length, width, height (mm)	5140 x 1980 x 1150 (Production 4860 x 1980 x 1150, C 4930 x 2020 x 1140)			4780 x 1900 x 1070		
Length, width, height (inches)	202 1/2 x 78 x 45 1/4 (Production 191 1/2 x 79 1/2 x 45 1/4, C 194 x 79 1/2 x 45			188 x 75 x 42		
Wheelbase, front, rear track (mm)	2845 (Production and C 2642) x 1651/1651			2780 x 1500/1500		
Wheelbase, front, rear track (inches)	112 (Production and C 101)			109 1/2 x 59/59		
Ground clearance, turning circle, curb weight	140mm, 16m, 1550 (Production 1350, C 1200) kg			140mm, 15m, 1050kg		
Max speed, acceleration 0-60 mph	345kph, 4 sec			297kph, 3 sec		
Max power, standard, revs	580 DIN-HP/7000 (Production 542 DIN-HP/7200, C 700 DIN-HP/6500)			450 DIN-HP/6250 (racing car and 7.0 above 450 DIN-HP)		
Max torque, revs	550 Nm/5100 (Production 642 Nm/4500, C unknown)			570 Nm/4500 (racing car unknown, 7.0 unknown)		
Engine type, position, number and configuration of cylinders	As XJR-15 (Production and C 6 cylinders, 60-degree-V, 4)			Four-stroke gasoline, central longitudinally, 12 cylinders, 60-degree-V		
Bore x Stroke (mm), capacity (cc), compression ratio	92 x 78, 6222cc, 10 : 1 (Production and C 94 x 84, 3498, 8.3 : 1)			90 x 78.5, 5993cc (7.0 94 x 84, 6995cc), 11 : 1		
Designation of engine and cylinder head	Engine "Jaguar V-12," head "TWR" (Production u. C Engine u. head "Cosworth")			Engine "Jaguar V-12," head "TWR"		
Engine block and cylinder head material, number of main bearings, type of liners	As XJR-15 (Production and C 4 main bearings, dry liners)			Block and head aluminum, 7 main bearings, wet liners		
Number of valves per cylinder, configuration, valve gearing, timing variants	4 overhead valves, otherwise as XJR-15 (Production u. C 2 ohc per bank, toothed belt)			2 overhead valves, bucket tappets, 1 ohc per bank, duplex chain, fixed		
Air supply, type of inlet manifold, air tempering	Normally aspirated, one-stage inlet manifold, n/a (Production u. C Garrett turbocharger, intercooler)			Normally aspirated, one-stage inlet manifold, n/a		
Type, position, make, and designation of mixture preparation	Electronic injection to manifold, Lucas			Electronic injection to manifold, Lucas		
Energy source, type, make, and designation of ignition system	Battery, solid-state, Lucas			Battery, solid-state, Lucas/Zytec		
Make of alternator, voltage, earthing	Alternator, 12 V, negative			Alternator, 12 V, negative		
Engine coolant, drive, regulation of cooling	Liquid, pump, thermostat			Liquid, pump, thermostat		
Type of clutch, number of gears in manual box, synchronized gears	Two-plate dry clutch, 5 , fully			Three-plate dry clutch, 5 (optional 6, standard on racing car and 7.0), fully		
Gear ratios in manual box	3, 1.95, 1.46, 1.13, 0.91, 2.58 (from 12/91 3.1, 1.95, 1.42, 1.09, 0.85, 2.58) : 1			Unknown		
Make, type, ratio of overdrive	n/a			n/a		
Type of clutch, number of gears, make and model of automatic box	n/a			n/a		
Gear ratios in automatic gearbox	n/a			n/a		
Driven axle, type of diff, traction control	As XJR-15 (Prototype all-wheel, hypoid bevels, central viscous)			Rear, hypoid bevel, limited-slip		
Axle ratios	2.88 (Prototype front 2.76) : 1			Unknown : 1		
Type of chassis	Tubular chassis			Tubular chassis		
Suspension, springing front	Double-wishbone, coil springs			Double-wishbone, coil springs (horizontal)		
Suspension, springing rear	Double-wishbone and trailiong arm, coil springs			Double-wishbone and trailing arm, coil springs		
Reduction of roll	Torsion bars front and rear			Torsion bars front and rear		
Type of shock absorbers	Telescopic			Telescopic, electronically adjustable		
Type and dimensions of wheels	Aluminum discs, 9J x 17 (rear 14J x 18, C 9 or 13J x 19)			Magnesium discs, 9.5 (rear 13) J x 17		
Type, dimensions, make of tires	Bridgestone Expedia 245/40 ZR 17, rear 345/35 ZR 18*			Bridgestone Expedia, 245/40 ZR 17, rear 345/40 ZR 17		
Type of braking front	Ventilated discs			Ventilated discs		
Type of braking rear	Ventilated outboard discs			Ventilated outboard discs		
Braking mechanism, number of circuits, servo assistance, electronic aids	Hydraulics, 2 circuit, front/rear balance, hydraulic servo assistance, antilock			Hydraulics, 2 circuits, front/rear balance, hydraulic servo assistance, antilock		
Steering gear, make and model of power steering	Rack and pinion, hydraulic servo			Rack and pinion, hydraulic servo		

* Prototype Pirelli P Zero 295/40 ZR 17, C unknown

XJ 220

Make, range	**TWR Jaguar XJR Six-cylinder**		**TWR Jaguar XJR Eight-cylinder**
Type	*XJR-10 (16)*	*XJR-11 (17)*	*XJR-14*
Public debut	31/03/1989 (28/04/1991)	08/02/1989 (1/1992)	20/03/1991
End of production	1990 (4/1991)	4/1990 (1/1992)	7/1991
Production figure	4 or 5 (2)	3 (plus 1 former XJR-16), 1	3
First, last chassis number RHD	389-589, 390 (?), 690 (191, 291)	189, 289, 490 (291)	591-791
First, last chassis number LHD	n/a	n/a	n/a
Body type	Fiberglass and Kevlar, 2 doors, 2 seats		Fiberglass and Kevlar, 2 doors, 2 seats
Weather protection, top mechanism	Enclosed-drive		Enclosed-drive
Length, width, height (mm)	Unknown		Unknown
Length, width, height (inches)	Unknown		Unknown
Wheelbase, front, rear track (mm)	Unknown		Unknown
Wheelbase, front, rear track (inches)	Unknown		Unknown
Ground clearance, turning circle, curb weight	80mm, 15m, 953 (XJR-11 unknown) kg		80mm, 15m, 750kg
Max speed, acceleration 0-60 mph	above 300kph, 3 sec		above 300kph, 3 sec
Max power, standard, revs	650 NET-HP/unknown (XJR-11 750 DIN-HP/unknown)		700 DIN-HP/unknown
Max torque, revs	Unknown		Unknown
Engine type, position, number and configuration of cylinders	Four-stroke gasoline, central longitudinally, 6 cylinders, 90-degree-V		Four-stroke gasoline, central longitudinally, 8 cylinders, 90-degree-V
Bore x Stroke (mm), capacity (cc), compression ratio	unknown, 3000 (XJR-11 and XJR-17 3500) cc, unknown		unknown, 3500cc, unknown
Designation of engine and cylinder head	Engine and head "Cosworth V6"		Engine and head "Cosworth V8"
Engine block and cylinder head material, number of main bearings, type of liners	Block and head aluminum, 4 main bearings, dry liners		Block and head aluminum, 5 main bearings, dry liners
Number of valves per cylinder, configuration, valve gearing, timing variants	4 overhead valves, bucket tappets, 2 ohc per bank, toothed belt, fixed		4 overhead valves, bucket tappets, 1 ohc per bank, duplex chain, fixed
Air supply, type of inlet manifold, air tempering	2 Garrett turbocharger, one-stage inlet manifold, intercooler (XJR-17 as XJR-14)		Normally aspirated, one-stage inlet manifold, n/a
Type, position, make, and designation of mixture preparation	Electronic injection to manifold, Bosch		Electronic injection to manifold, Bosch
Energy source, type, make, and designation of ignition system	Battery, solid-state, Bosch (XJR-16 and 17 Bosch Motronic 1.8)		Battery, solid-state, Bosch Motronic 1.8
Make of alternator, voltage, earthing	Alternator, 12 V, negative		Alternator, 12 V, negative
Engine coolant, drive, regulation of cooling	Liquid, pump, thermostat		Liquid, pump, thermostat
Type of clutch, number of gears in manual box, synchronized gears	Three-plate dry clutch, 5, fully		Three-plate dry clutch, 6, fully
Gear ratios in manual box	Unknown		Unknown
Make, type, ratio of overdrive	n/a		n/a
Type of clutch, number of gears, make and model of automatic box	n/a		n/a
Gear ratios in automatic gearbox	n/a		n/a
Driven axle, type of diff, traction control	Rear, hypoid bevel, limited-slip		Rear, hypoid bevel, limited-slip
Axle ratios	Unknown		Unknown
Type of chassis	Unitary		Unitary
Suspension, springing front	Double-wishbone, coil springs (horizontal)		Double-wishbone, coil springs (horizontal)
Suspension, springing rear	Double-wishbone and trailing arm, coil springs		Double-wishbone and trailing arm, coil springs
Reduction of roll	Torsion bars front and rear		Torsion bars front and rear
Type of shock absorbers	Telescopic (front horizontal)		Telescopic (front horizontal)
Type and dimensions of wheels	Magnesium discs, 17″ (rear 18″)		Magnesium discs, unknown, 17″ (rear 18″)
Type, dimensions, make of tires	Goodyear, unknown		Goodyear, unknown
Type of braking front	Ventilated discs		Carbon discs
Type of braking rear	Ventilated outboard discs		Outboard Carbon discs
Braking mechanism, number of circuits, servo assistance, electronic aids	Hydraulics, 2 circuits, hydraulic servo assistance, n/a		Hydraulics, 2 circuits, hydraulic servo assistance, n/a
Steering gear, make and model of power steering	Rack and pinion, hydraulic servo		Rack and pinion, hydraulic servo

TWR

Make, range	**Jaguar XK 8 4.0 (X 100)**		**Jaguar XKR 4.0 (X 100)**		
Type	*XK 8 Coupe*	*XK 8 Convertible*	*XKR Coupe*, **	*XKR Convertible***	*XK 180*
Public debut	3/10/1996	3/10/1996	3/3/1998	3/3/1998	28/9/1998
End of production	6/2002	6/2002	6/2002	6/2002	1999
Production figure	Unknown	Unknown	Unknown	Unknown	2
First, last chassis number RHD	VIN 001001-042775 and A00001-unknown		VIN 001001-042775 and A00001-unknown (XK 180 unknown)		
First, last chassis number LHD	VIN 001001-042775 and A00001-unknown		VIN 001001-042775 and A00001-unknown (XK 180 unknown)		
Body type	All-steel, 2 doors, 2 + 2 seats		All-steel, 2 doors, 2 + 2 seats (XK 180 aluminum, 2 doors, 2 seats)		
Weather protection, top mechanism	Enclosed-drive (convertible electrically operated top)		Enclosed-drive (XK 180 n/a)		
Length, width, height (mm)	4760 x 1829 x 1296 (convertible 1306)		4760 x 1829 x 1296 (convertible 1306, XK 180 4415 x 1828 x 1100)		
Length, width, height (inches)	187 1/2 x 72 x 51 (convertible 51 1/2)		187 1/2 x 72 x 51 (convertible 51 1/2, XK 180 174 x 72 x 43)		
Wheelbase, front, rear track (mm)	2588 x 1504/1498		2588 x 1504/1498 (XK 180 2476 x 1504/1498)		
Wheelbase, front, rear track (inches)	102 x 59 1/4/59		102 x 59 1/4/59 (XK 180 97 1/2 x 59 1/4/59)		
Ground clearance, turning circle, curb weight	140mm, 11m, 1600 (convertible 1700) kg		140mm, 11m, 1640 (convertible 1750, XK 180 1600) kg		
Max speed, acceleration 0-60 mph	250kph, 7 sec		250kph, 6 sec (XK 180 275kph, 5 sec)		
Max power, standard, revs	284 ECE-HP/6100		363 ECE-HP/6150 (XK 180 450 DIN-HP/6250)		
Max torque, revs	393 Nm/4250		505 Nm/3600 (XK 180 500 Nm/4500)		
Engine type, position, number and configuration of cylinders	Four-stroke gasoline, front longitudinally, 8 cylinders, 90-degree-V		Four-stroke gasoline, front longitudinally, 8 cylinders, 90-degree-V		
Bore x Stroke (mm), capacity (cc), compression ratio	86 x 86, 3996cc, 10.75 : 1		86 x 86, 3996cc, 9 : 1		
Designation of engine and cylinder head	Engine and head "AJ 26"		Engine and head "AJ 26"		
Engine block and cylinder head material, number of main bearings, type of liners	Block and head aluminum, 5 main bearings, Nikasil (from 2000 cast-in liners)		Block and head aluminum, 5 main bearings, Nikasil (from 2000 cast-in liners)		
Number of valves per cylinder, configuration, valve gearing, timing variants	As XKR, chain, 2-stage variable timing (from 10/98 continously variable)		4 overhead valves, bucket tappets, 2 ohc per bank, chain, fixed		
Air supply, type of inlet manifold, air tempering	Normally aspirated, 2-stage inlet manifold, n/a		Roots supercharger, one-stage inlet manifold, intercooler		
Type, position, make, and designation of mixture preparation	Electronic injection to manifold, Lucas		Electronic injection to manifold, Lucas		
Energy source, type, make, and designation of ignition system	Battery, separate coils, Nippondenso		Battery, separate coils, Nippondenso		
Make of alternator, voltage, earthing	Alternator, 12 V, negative		Alternator, 12 V, negative		
Engine coolant, drive, regulation of cooling	Liquid, pump, thermostat		Liquid, pump, thermostat		
Type of clutch, number of gears in manual box, synchronized gears	n/a		n/a		
Gear ratios in manual box	n/a		n/a		
Make, type, ratio of overdrive	n/a		n/a		
Type of clutch, number of gears, make and model of automatic box	Hydraulic torque converter, 5, ZF 5 HP 24		Hydraulic torque converter, 5, Mercedes-Benz W5A580		
Gear ratios in automatic gearbox	3.57, 2.2, 1.51, 1, 0.8, 4.1 : 1		3.59, 2.19, 1.41, 1, 0.83, 3.16 : 1		
Driven axle, type of diff, traction control	Rear, hypoid bevel, n/a		Rear, hypoid bevel, n/a		
Axle ratios	3.06 : 1		3.06 : 1		
Type of chassis	Unitary, front and rear subframes		Unitary, front and rear subframes		
Suspension, springing front	Double-wishbone, coil springs		Double-wishbone, coil springs		
Suspension, springing rear	Forked transverse arms and driveshafts, coil springs		Forked transverse arms and driveshafts, coil springs		
Reduction of roll	Torsion bars front and rear		Torsion bars front and rear		
Type of shock absorbers	Telescopic, optional CATS		Telescopic, CATS		
Type and dimensions of wheels	Aluminum discs, 8 J x 17		Aluminum discs, 8 (rear 9 J x 18, XK 180 9, rear 10 J x 20)		
Type, dimensions, make of tires	245/50 ZR 17		Pirelli Direzionale 245/45 (rear Asimmetrico 255/45 ZR 18***)		
Type of braking front	Ventilated discs		Ventilated discs		
Type of braking rear	Ventilated outboard discs		Ventilated outboard discs		
Braking mechanism, number of circuits, servo assistance, electronic aids	Hydraulics, 2 circuits, electronic front/rear balance, hydraulic servo assistance, antilock, ASC+T		Hydraulics, 2 circuits, electronic front/rear balance, hydraulic servo assistance, antilock, ASC+T		
Steering gear, make and model of power steering	Rack and pinion, hydraulic servo ZF Servotronic (from 9/98, Servotronic II)		Rack and pinion, hydraulic servo ZF Servotronic II		

* 2000: 200 examples of limited-edition "Silverstone"; 8/01 1 XKR-R, 460 HP

** 2001: Each 100 examples of limited edition "XKR 100" coupe and convertible

*** XK 180, 255/35 ZR 20, rear 285/30 ZR 20

Make, range	**Jaguar XK 8 4.2 (X 100)**		**Jaguar XKR 4.2 (X 100)**	
Type	*Coupe*	*Convertible*	*XKR Coupe*	*XKR Convertible*
Public debut	1/8/2002	1/8/2002	1/8/2002	1/8.2002
End of production	6/2005	6/2005	6/2005	6/2005
Production figure	Unknown	Unknown	Unknown	Unknown
First, last chassis number RHD	VIN unknown		VIN unknown	
First, last chassis number LHD	VIN unknown		VIN unknown	
Body type	All-steel, 2 doors, 2 + 2 seats		All-steel, 2 doors, 2 + 2 seats	
Weather protection, top mechanism	Enclosed-drive (convertible electrically operated top)		Enclosed-drive (convertible electrically operated top)	
Length, width, height (mm)	4760 (from 4/2004 4776) x 1829 x 1296 (convertible 1306)		4760 (from 4/2004 4776) x 1829 x 1296 (convertible 1306)	
Length, width, height (inches)	187 1/2 (from 4/2004 188) x 72 x 51 (convertible 51 1/2)		187 1/2 (from 4/2004 188) x 72 x 51 (convertible 51 1/2)	
Wheelbase, front, rear track (mm)	2588 x 1504/1498		2588 x 1504/1498	
Wheelbase, front, rear track (inches)	102 x 59 1/4/59		102 x 59 1/4/59	
Ground clearance, turning circle, curb weight	140mm, 11m, 1700 (convertible 1800) kg		140mm, 11m, 1700 (convertible 1800) kg	
Max speed, acceleration 0-60 mph	250kph, 6 sec		250kph, 5 sec	
Max power, standard, revs	298 ECE-HP/6000		395 ECE-HP/6100	
Max torque, revs	411 Nm/1050		541 Nm/3500	
Engine type, position, number and configuration of cylinders	Four-stroke gasoline, front longitudinally, 8 cylinders, 90-degree-V		Four-stroke gasoline, front longitudinally, 8 cylinders, 90-degree-V	
Bore x Stroke (mm), capacity (cc), compression ratio	86 x 90.3, 4196cc, 11 : 1		86 x 90.3, 4196cc, 9.1 : 1	
Designation of engine and cylinder head	Engine and head "AJ 34"		Engine and head "AJ 34"	
Engine block and cylinder head material, number of main bearings, type of liners	Block and head aluminum, 5 main bearings, cast-in liners		Block and head aluminum, 5 main bearings, cast-in liners	
Number of valves per cylinder, configuration, valve gearing, timing variants	As XKR, chain, continously variable timing		4 overhead valves, bucket tappets, 2 ohc per bank, chain, fixed	
Air supply, type of inlet manifold, air tempering	Normally aspirated, 2-stage inlet manifold, n/a		Roots supercharger, one-stage inlet manifold, intercooler	
Type, position, make, and designation of mixture preparation	Electronic injection to manifold, Lucas		Electronic injection to manifold, Lucas	
Energy source, type, make, and designation of ignition system	Battery, separate coils, Nippondenso		Battery, separate coils, Nippondenso	
Make of alternator, voltage, earthing	Alternator, 12 V, negative		Alternator, 12 V, negative	
Engine coolant, drive, regulation of cooling	Liquid, pump, thermostat		Liquid, pump, thermostat	
Type of clutch, number of gears in manual box, synchronized gears	n/a		n/a	
Gear ratios in manual box	n/a		n/a	
Make, type, ratio of overdrive	n/a		n/a	
Type of clutch, number of gears, make and model of automatic box	Hydraulic torque converter, 6, ZF 6 HP 26		Hydraulic torque converter, 6, ZF 6 HP 26	
Gear ratios in automatic gearbox	4.17, 2.34, 1.52, 1.14, 0.87, 0.69, 3.4 : 1		4.17, 2.34, 1.52, 1.14, 0.87, 0.69, 3.4 : 1	
Driven axle, type of diff, traction control	Rear, hypoid bevel, n/a		Rear, hypoid bevel, n/a	
Axle ratios	3.06 : 1		3.06 : 1	
Type of chassis	Unitary, front and rear subframes		Unitary, front and rear subframes	
Suspension, springing front	Double-wishbone, coil springs		Double-wishbone, coil springs	
Suspension, springing rear	Forked transverse arms and driveshafts, coil springs		Forked transverse arms and driveshafts, coil springs	
Reduction of roll	Torsion bars front and rear		Torsion bars front and rear	
Type of shock absorbers	Telescopic, optional CATS		Telescopic, CATS	
Type and dimensions of wheels	Aluminum discs, 8 J x 17		Aluminum discs, 8, rear 9 J x 18	
Type, dimensions, make of tires	245/50 ZR 17		Pirelli Direzionale 245/45 (rear Asimmetrico 255/45 ZR 18)	
Type of braking front	Ventilated discs		Ventilated discs	
Type of braking rear	Ventilated outboard discs		Ventilated outboard discs	
Braking mechanism, number of circuits, servo assistance, electronic aids	Hydraulics, 2 circuits, electronic front/rear balance, hydraulic servo assistance, antilock, DSC		Hydraulics, 2 circuits, electronic front/rear balance, hydraulic servo assistance, antilock, DSC	
Steering gear, make and model of power steering	Rack and pinion, hydraulic servo ZF Servotronic II		Rack and pinion, hydraulic servo ZF Servotronic II	

Make, range	Jaguar S-Type V-6 (X 200)			Jaguar S-Type V-8 (X 200)	
Type	*V-6*	*V-6 Sport*	*V-6 Executive (S.E.)*	*V-8 Sport*	*V-8*
Public debut	3/1999	5/12/2000	3/1999	5/12/2000	3/1999
End of production	9/2001	9/2001	9/2001	9/2001	9/2001
Production figure	Unknown	Unknown	Unknown	Unknown	Unknown
First, last chassis number RHD	VIN L00001-unknown			VIN L00001-unknown	
First, last chassis number LHD	VIN L00001-unknown			VIN L00001-unknown	
Body type	All-steel, 4 doors, 5 seats			All-steel, 4 doors, 5 seats	
Weather protection, top mechanism	Enclosed-drive, optional electrically operated glass sunroof			Enclosed-drive, optional electrically operated glass sunroof	
Length, width, height (mm)	4861 x 1819 x 1444			4861 x 1819 x 1444	
Length, width, height (inches)	191 1/2 x 71 1/2 x 57			191 1/2 x 71 1/2 x 57	
Wheelbase, front, rear track (mm)	2909 x 1537/1544			2909 x 1537/1544	
Wheelbase, front, rear track (inches)	114 1/2 x 60 1/2/60 3/4			114 1/2 x 60 1/2/60 3/4	
Ground clearance, turning circle, curb weight	140mm, 11m, 1650kg			140mm, 11m, 1700kg	
Max speed, acceleration 0-60 mph	230kph, 8 sec			240kph, 7 sec	
Max power, standard, revs	238 ECE-HP/6800			276 ECE-HP/6100	
Max torque, revs	293 Nm/4500			378 Nm/4300	
Engine type, position, number and configuration of cylinders	Four-stroke gasoline, front longitudinally, 6 cylinders, 60 degree-V			Four-stroke gasoline, front longitudinally, 8 cylinders, 90-degree-V	
Bore x Stroke (mm), capacity (cc), compression ratio	89 x 79.5, 2967cc, 10.5 : 1			86 x 86, 3996cc, 10.75 : 1	
Designation of engine and cylinder head	Engine and head "AJ V-6"			Engine and head "AJ 26"	
Engine block and cylinder head material, number of main bearings, type of liners	Block and head aluminum, 4 main bearings, cast-in liners			Block and head aluminum, 5 main bearings, cast-in liners	
Number of valves per cylinder, configuration, valve gearing, timing variants	4 overhead valves, bucket tappets, 2 ohc per bank, otherwise as S-Type V-8			As S-Type V-6, chain, continously variable timing	
Air supply, type of inlet manifold, air tempering	Normally aspirated, 3-stage inlet manifold, n/a			Normally aspirated, 2-stage inlet manifold, n/a	
Type, position, make, and designation of mixture preparation	Electronic injection to manifold, Nippondenso			Electronic injection to manifold, Nippondenso	
Energy source, type, make, and designation of ignition system	Battery, separate coils, Nippondenso			Battery, separate coils, Nippondenso	
Make of alternator, voltage, earthing	Alternator, 12 V, negative			Alternator, 12 V, negative	
Engine coolant, drive, regulation of cooling	Liquid, pump, thermostat			Liquid, pump, thermostat	
Type of clutch, number of gears in manual box, synchronized gears	Single-plate dry clutch, 5, fully			n/a	
Gear ratios in manual box	4.23, 2.52, 1.67, 1.22, 1, 4.14 : 1			n/a	
Make, type, ratio of overdrive	n/a			n/a	
Type of clutch, number of gears, make and model of automatic box	Optional hydraulic torque converter, 5, Ford 5R55N			Hydraulic torque converter, 5, ZF 5 HP 24	
Gear ratios in automatic gearbox	3.25, 2.44, 1.55, 1, 0.75, 3.07 : 1			3.57, 2.2, 1.51, 1, 0.8, 4.1 : 1	
Driven axle, type of diff, traction control	Rear, hypoid bevel, n/a			Rear, hypoid bevel, n/a	
Axle ratios	3.07 : 1			3.31 : 1	
Type of chassis	Unitary, front and rear subframes			Unitary, front and rear subframes	
Suspension, springing front	Double-wishbone, coil springs			Double-wishbone, coil springs	
Suspension, springing rear	Double-wishbone, coil springs			Double-wishbone, coil springs	
Reduction of roll	Torsion bars front and rear			Torsion bars front and rear	
Type of shock absorbers	Telescopic, optional CATS			Telescopic, optional CATS	
Type and dimensions of wheels	Aluminum discs, 7 J x 16 (Sport 7.5 J x 18)			Aluminum discs, 7.5 J x 16, (Sport 7.5 J x 18)	
Type, dimensions, make of tires	Pirelli P 6000 225/55 ZR 16 (Sport Pirelli P Zero 245/40 ZR 18)			Pirelli P 6000 225/55 ZR 16 (Sport Pirelli P Zero 245/40 ZR 18)	
Type of braking front	Ventilated discs			Ventilated discs	
Type of braking rear	Ventilated outboard discs			Ventilated outboard discs	
Braking mechanism, number of circuits, servo assistance, electronic aids	Hydraulics, 2 circuits, electronic front/rear balance, hydraulic servo assistance, antilock, from 7/00 DSC			Hydraulics, 2 circuits, electronic front/rear balance, hydraulic servo assistance, antilock, from 7/00 DSC	
Steering gear, make and model of power steering	Rack and pinion, hydraulic servo ZF Servotronic (from 9/98 Servotronic II)			Rack and pinion, hydraulic servo ZF Servotronic (from 9/98 Servotronic II)	

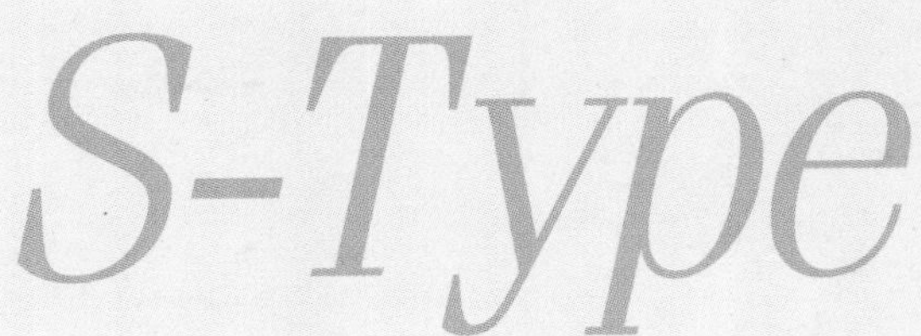

Make, range	**Jaguar S-Type 2.5 and 3.0 (X 202)**			**Jaguar S-Type 4.2 (X 202)**		
Type	*2.5 (2.5 Sport)*	*2.5 Executive (S.E.)*	*3.0 Sport (3.0 Executive or S.E.)*	*4.2 Sport*	*4.2 Executive (S.E.)*	*S-Type R*
Public debut	4/1/2002	4/1/2002	4/1/2002	4/1/2002	4/1/2002	4/1/2002
End of production	12/2003	12/2003	12/2003	12/2003	12/2003	12/2003
Production figure	Unknown	Unknown	Unknown	Unknown	Unknown	Unknown
First, last chassis number RHD	VIN unknown-unknown			VIN unknown-unknown		
First, last chassis number LHD	VIN unknown-unknown			VIN unknown-unknown		
Body type	All-steel, 4 doors, 5 seats			All-steel, 4 doors, 5 seats		
Weather protection, top mechanism	Enclosed-drive, optional electrically operated glass sunroof			Enclosed-drive, optional electrically operated glass sunroof		
Length, width, height (mm)	4877 x 1818 x 1423			4877 x 1818 x 1423		
Length, width, height (inches)	192 x 71 1/2 x 56			192 x 71 1/2 x 56		
Wheelbase, front, rear track (mm)	2909 x 1534/1542			2909 x 1534/1542		
Wheelbase, front, rear track (inches)	114 1/2 x 60 1/2/60 3/4			114 1/2 x 60 1/2/60 3/4		
Ground clearance, turning circle, curb weight	140mm, 11m, 1735kg			140mm, 11m, 1800kg		
Max speed, acceleration 0-60 mph	225kph, 10 sec (3.0 230kph, 8 sec)			250kph, 7 sec (R 250kph, 6 sec)		
Max power, standard, revs	200 ECE-HP/6800 (3.0 238 ECE-HP/6800)			298 ECE-HP/6000 (R 395 ECE-HP/6100)		
Max torque, revs	245 Nm/4000 (3.0 293 Nm/4500)			411 Nm/4100 (R 541 Nm/3500)		
Engine type, position, number and configuration of cylinders	Four-stroke gasoline, front longitudinally, 6 cylinders, 60 degree-V			Four-stroke gasoline, front longitudinally, 8 cylinders, 90-degree-V		
Bore x Stroke (mm), capacity (cc), compression ratio	81.65 x 79.5, 2497cc (3.0 89 x 79.5, 2967cc), 10.5 : 1			86 x 90.3, 4196cc, 11 (R 9.1) : 1		
Designation of engine and cylinder head	Engine and head "AJ V-6"			Engine and head "AJ 26"		
Engine block and cylinder head material, number of main bearings, type of liners	Block and head aluminum, 4 main bearings, cast-in liners			Block and head aluminum, 5 main bearings, cast-in liners		
Number of valves per cylinder, configuration, valve gearing, timing variants	4 overhead valves, bucket tappets, 2 ohc per bank, otherwise as 4.2			As 2.5, chain, continously variable timing (S-Type R chain, fixed)		
Air supply, type of inlet manifold, air tempering	Normally aspirated, 3-stage inlet manifold, n/a			Normally aspirated, 2-stage inlet manifold, n/a (R Roots supercharger, one-stage, intercooler)		
Type, position, make, and designation of mixture preparation	Electronic injection to manifold, Nippondenso			Electronic injection to manifold, Nippondenso		
Energy source, type, make, and designation of ignition system	Battery, separate coils, Nippondenso			Battery, separate coils, Nippondenso		
Make of alternator, voltage, earthing	Alternator, 12 V, negative			Alternator, 12 V, negative		
Engine coolant, drive, regulation of cooling	Liquid, pump, thermostat			Liquid, pump, thermostat		
Type of clutch, number of gears in manual box, synchronized gears	Single-plate dry clutch, 5, fully			n/a		
Gear ratios in manual box	4.23, 2.52, 1.67, 1.22, 1, 4.14 : 1			n/a		
Make, type, ratio of overdrive	n/a			n/a		
Type of clutch, number of gears, make and model of automatic box	Optional hydraulic torque converter, 6, ZF 6 HP 26			Hydraulic torque converter , 6, ZF 6 HP 26		
Gear ratios in automatic gearbox	4.17, 2.34, 1.52, 1.14, 0.87, 0.69, 3.4 : 1			4.17, 2.34, 1.52, 1.14, 0.87, 0.69, 3.4 : 1		
Driven axle, type of diff, traction control	Rear, hypoid bevel, n/a			Rear, hypoid bevel, n/a		
Axle ratios	3.07 (with automatic: 3.31) : 1			2.87 : 1		
Type of chassis	Unitary, front and rear subframes			Unitary, front and rear subframes		
Suspension, springing front	Double-wishbone, coil springs			Double-wishbone, coil springs		
Suspension, springing rear	Double-wishbone, coil springs			Double-wishbone, coil springs		
Reduction of roll	Torsion bars front and rear			Torsion bars front and rear		
Type of shock absorbers	Telescopic, optional CATS			Telescopic, optional (R always) CATS		
Type and dimensions of wheels	Aluminum discs, 6.5 J (Executive 7.5 J x 16, Sport 7.5 J x 17)			Aluminum discs, 7.5 J x 17 (R 8 J x 18)		
Type, dimensions, make of tires	Pirelli P 6000 205/60 ZR 16 (Executive 225/55 ZR 16, Sport as 4.2)			Pirelli P Zero 235/50 ZR 17 (R 245/40 ZR 18)		
Type of braking front	Ventilated discs			Ventilated discs		
Type of braking rear	Ventilated outboard discs			Ventilated outboard discs		
Braking mechanism, number of circuits, servo assistance, electronic aids	Hydraulics, 2 circuits, electronic front/rear balance, hydraulic servo assistance, antilock, DSC			Hydraulics, 2 circuits, electronic front/rear balance, hydraulic servo assistance, antilock, DSC		
Steering gear, make and model of power steering	Rack and pinion, hydraulic servo ZF Servotronic II			Rack and pinion, hydraulic servo ZF Servotronic II		

S-Type

Make, range	**Jaguar S-Type 2.5 and 3.0 (X 204)**			**Jaguar S-Type 4.2 (X 204)**		
Type	*2.5 or 2.5 S (2.5 Sport)*	*2.5 Executive (S.E.)*	*3.0 Sport (3.0 Executive or S.E.)*	*4.2 Sport*	*4.2 Executive (S.E.)*	*S-Type R*
Public debut	3/2004	3/2004	3/2004	3/2004	3/2004	3/2004
End of production	6/2007	6/2007	6/2007	6/2007	6/2007	6/2007
Production figure	Unknown	Unknown	Unknown	Unknown	Unknown	Unknown
First, last chassis number RHD	VIN unknown			VIN unknown		
First, last chassis number LHD	VIN unknown			VIN unknown		
Body type	All-steel, 4 doors, 5 seats			All-steel, 4 doors, 5 seats		
Weather protection, top mechanism	Enclosed-drive, optional electrically operated glass sunroof			Enclosed-drive, optional electrically operated glass sunroof		
Length, width, height (mm)	4905 x 1819 x 1448			4905 x 1819 x 1448		
Length, width, height (inches)	193 x 71 1/2 x 57			193 x 71 1/2 x 57		
Wheelbase, front, rear track (mm)	2909 x 1534/1542			2909 x, 1534/1542		
Wheelbase, front, rear track (inches)	114 1/2 x 60 1/2/60 3/4			114 1/2 x 60 1/2/60 3/4		
Ground clearance, turning circle, curb weight	140mm, 11m, 1735kg			140mm, 11m, 1800kg		
Max speed, acceleration 0-60 mph	225kph, 9 sec (3.0 230kph, 8 sec)			250kph, 7 sec (R 250kph, 6 sec)		
Max power, standard, revs	200 ECE-HP/6800 (3.0 238 ECE-HP/6800)			298 ECE-HP/6000 (R 395 ECE-HP/6100)		
Max torque, revs	245 Nm/4000 (3.0 293 Nm/4500)			411 Nm/4100 (R 541 Nm/3500)		
Engine type, position, number and configuration of cylinders	Four-stroke gasoline, front longitudinally, 6 cylinders, 60 degree-V			Four-stroke gasoline, front longitudinally, 8 cylinders, 90-degree-V		
Bore x Stroke (mm), capacity (cc), compression ratio	81.65 x 79.5, 2497cc (3.0 89 x 79.5, 2967cc), 10.5 : 1			86 x 90.3, 4196cc, 11 (R 9.1) : 1		
Designation of engine and cylinder head	Engine and head "AJ V-6"			Engine and head "AJ 26"		
Engine block and cylinder head material, number of main bearings, type of liners	Block and head aluminum, 4 main bearings, cast-in liners			Block and head aluminum, 5 main bearings, cast-in liners		
Number of valves per cylinder, configuration, valve gearing, timing variants	4 overhead valves, bucket tappets, 2 ohc per bank, otherwise as 4.2			As 2.5, chain, continously variable timing (S-Type R chain, fixed)		
Air supply, type of inlet manifold, air tempering	Normally aspirated, 3-stage inlet manifold, n/a			Normally aspirated, 2-stage inlet manifold, n/a (S-Type R Roots supercharger, one-stage, intercooler)		
Type, position, make, and designation of mixture preparation	Electronic injection to manifold, Nippondenso			Electronic injection to manifold, Nippondenso		
Energy source, type, make, and designation of ignition system	Battery, separate coils, Nippondenso			Battery, separate coils, Nippondenso		
Make of alternator, voltage, earthing	Alternator, 12 V, negative			Alternator, 12 V, negative		
Engine coolant, drive, regulation of cooling	Liquid, pump, thermostat			Liquid, pump, thermostat		
Type of clutch, number of gears in manual box, synchronized gears	Single-plate dry clutch, 5, fully			n/a		
Gear ratios in manual box	4.23, 2.52, 1.67, 1.22, 1, 4.14 : 1			n/a		
Make, type, ratio of overdrive	n/a			n/a		
Type of clutch, number of gears, make and model of automatic box	Optional hydraulic torque converter, 6, ZF 6 HP 26			Hydraulic torque converter , 6, ZF 6 HP 26		
Gear ratios in automatic gearbox	4.17, 2.34, 1.52, 1.14, 0.87, 0.69, 3.4 : 1			4.17, 2.34, 1.52, 1.14, 0.87, 0.69, 3.4 : 1		
Driven axle, type of diff, traction control	Rear, hypoid bevel, n/a			Rear, hypoid bevel, n/a		
Axle ratios	3.07 (with automatic: 3.31) : 1			2.87 : 1		
Type of chassis	Unitary, front and rear subframes			Unitary, front and rear subframes		
Suspension, springing front	Double-wishbone, coil springs			Double-wishbone, coil springs		
Suspension, springing rear	Double-wishbone, coil springs			Double-wishbone, coil springs		
Reduction of roll	Torsion bars front and rear			Torsion bars front and rear		
Type of shock absorbers	Telescopic, optional CATS			Telescopic, optional (R always) CATS		
Type and dimensions of wheels	Aluminum discs, 6.5 J (Executive 7.5 J x 16, Sport 7.5 J x 17)			Aluminum discs, 7.5 J x 17 (R 8 J x 18)		
Type, dimensions, make of tires	Pirelli P 6000 205/60 ZR 16 (Executive 225/55 ZR 16, Sport as 4.2)			Pirelli P Zero 235/50 ZR 17 (R 245/40 ZR 18)		
Type of braking front	Ventilated discs			Ventilated discs		
Type of braking rear	Ventilated outboard discs			Ventilated outboard discs		
Braking mechanism, number of circuits, servo assistance, electronic aids	Hydraulics, 2 circuits, electronic front/rear balance, hydraulic servo assistance, antilock, DSC, brake assistant			Hydraulics, 2 circuits, electronic front/rear balance, hydraulic servo assistance, antilock, DSC, brake assistant		
Steering gear, make and model of power steering	Rack and pinion, hydraulic servo ZF Servotronic II			Rack and pinion, hydraulic servo ZF Servotronic II		

Make, range	**Jaguar S-Type 2.7 d (X 204)**		
Type	*2.7 d or 2.7 d S*	*2.7 d Sport*	*2.7 d Executive (S.E.)*
Public debut	15/5/2004 (2005)	15/5/2004	15/5/2004
End of production	6/2007	6/2007	6/2007
Production figure	Unknown	Unknown	Unknown
First, last chassis number RHD	VIN unknown		
First, last chassis number LHD	VIN unknown-unknown		
Body type	All-steel, 4 doors, 5 seats		
Weather protection, top mechanism	Enclosed-drive, optional electrically operated glass sunroof		
Length, width, height (mm)	4905 x 1819 x 1448		
Length, width, height (inches)	193 x 71 1/2 x 57		
Wheelbase, front, rear track (mm)	2909 x 1534/1542		
Wheelbase, front, rear track (inches)	114 1/2 x 60 1/2/60 3/4	Unknown	
Ground clearance, turning circle, curb weight	140mm, 11m, 1750kg	50mm, 15m, unknown	
Max speed, acceleration 0-60 mph	Above 300kph, 2 sec		
Max power, standard, revs	207 ECE-HP/4000n		
Max torque, revs	435 Nm/1900		
Engine type, position, number and configuration of cylinders	Four-stroke diesel, front longitudinally, 6 cylinders, 60 degree-V		
Bore x Stroke (mm), capacity (cc), compression ratio	81 x 86, 2720cc, 17.3 : 1		
Designation of engine and cylinder head	Engine and head "Diesel"		
Engine block and cylinder head material, number of main bearings, type of liners	Block and head aluminum, 4 main bearings, cast-in liners		
Number of valves per cylinder, configuration, valve gearing, timing variants	4 overhead valves, rocker, 2 ohc per bank, toothed belt, fixed		
Air supply, type of inlet manifold, air tempering	2 turbochargers, one-stage inlet manifold, intercooler		
Type, position, make, and designation of mixture preparation	Electronic common-rail direct injection, n/a	Electronic injection to manifold, unknown	
Energy source, type, make, and designation of ignition system	Battery, glow plugs, n/a	Battery, unknown	
Make of alternator, voltage, earthing	Alternator, 12 V, negative	Unknown	
Engine coolant, drive, regulation of cooling	Liquid, pump, thermostat		
Type of clutch, number of gears in manual box, synchronized gears	Single-plate dry clutch, 6, fully		
Gear ratios in manual box	Unknown : 1		
Make, type, ratio of overdrive	n/a		
Type of clutch, number of gears, make and model of automatic box	Optional hydraulic torque converter, 6, ZF 6 HP 26		
Gear ratios in automatic gearbox	4.17, 2.34, 1.52, 1.14, 0.87, 0.69, 3.4 : 1		
Driven axle, type of diff, traction control	Rear, hypoid bevel, n/a	Rear, unknown	
Axle ratios	2.69 (with automatic: 3.07) : 1		
Type of chassis	Unitary, front and rear subframes		
Suspension, springing front	Double-wishbone, coil springs		
Suspension, springing rear	Double-wishbone, coil springs		
Reduction of roll	Torsion bars front and rear		
Type of shock absorbers	Telescopic, optional CATS		
Type and dimensions of wheels	Aluminum discs, 6.5 J (Executive 7.5 J x 16, Sport 7.5 J x 17)		
Type, dimensions, make of tires	Pirelli P 6000 205/60 ZR 16 (Executive 225/55 ZR 16, Sport as 4.2)		
Type of braking front	Ventilated discs		
Type of braking rear	Ventilated outboard discs		
Braking mechanism, number of circuits, servo assistance, electronic aids	Hydraulics, 2 circuits, electronic front/rear balance, hydraulic servo assistance, antilock, DSC, brake assistant		
Steering gear, make and model of power steering	Rack and pinion, hydraulic servo ZF Servotronic II		

Make, range	**Jaguar Formula 1 racing cars**		
Type	*R1 (R2)*	*R3 (R4)*	*R5*
Public debut	1/2000 (1/2001)	1/2002 (1/2003)	1/2004
End of production	2000 (2001)	2002 (2003)	2004
Price on introduction, currency (€for Germany)	n/a	n/a	n/a
Production figure	6 (6)	6 (6)	6
First, last chassis number RHD	R1 01-06 (R2 01-06)	R3 01-06 (R4 01-06)	R5 01-06
First, last chassis number LHD	n/a	n/a	n/a
Body type	Fiberglass and Kevlar, no doors, 1 seat		
Weather protection, top mechanism	n/a		
Length, width, height (mm)	Unknown		
Length, width, height (inches)	Unknown		
Wheelbase, front, rear track (mm)	Unknown		
Wheelbase, front, rear track (inches)	Unknown		
Ground clearance, turning circle, curb weight	Unknown		
Max speed, acceleration 0-60 mph	Above 300kph, 2 sec		
Max power, standard, revs	820 SAE-HP/18.000 (from R-2 17.300), from R4 unknown		
Max torque, revs	Unknown		
Engine type, position, number and configuration of cylinders	Four-stroke gasoline, central longitudinally, 10 cylinders, 72-degree-V (from R4 90 degree-V)		
Bore x Stroke (mm), capacity (cc), compression ratio	unknown, 3000cc, unknown		
Designation of engine and cylinder head	Engine and head "Cosworth C-R 2" (R2 "C-R3", R3 "C-R 4", R4 "C-R5", R5 "C-R6")		
Engine block and cylinder head material, number of main bearings, type of liners	Block and head aluminum, 6, cast-in liners		
Number of valves per cylinder, configuration, valve gearing, timing variants	4 overhead valves, bucket tappets, 2 ohc per bank, toothed belt, fixed		
Air supply, type of inlet manifold, air tempering	Normally aspirated, one-stage inlet manifold, n/a		
Type, position, make, and designation of mixture preparation	Electronic injection to manifold, unknown		
Energy source, type, make, and designation of ignition system	Battery, unknown		
Make of alternator, voltage, earthing	Unknown		
Engine coolant, drive, regulation of cooling	Liquid, pump, thermostat		
Type of clutch, number of gears in manual box, synchronized gears	Three-plate dry clutch, 7, 7		
Gear ratios in manual box	Unknown		
Make, type, ratio of overdrive	n/a		
Type of clutch, number of gears, make and model of automatic box	n/a		
Gear ratios in automatic gearbox	n/a		
Driven axle, type of diff, traction control	Rear, unknown, unknown		
Axle ratios	Unknown		
Type of chassis	Unitary		
Suspension, springing front	Double-wishbone, Drehstab		
Suspension, springing rear	2 transverse arms, trailing arm, coil springs		
Reduction of roll	Telescopic, electronically adjustable		
Type and dimensions of wheels	Aluminum discs, unknown		
Type, dimensions, make of tires	Bridgestone (R-2 Michelin), 12.5 (from R4 12.7) x 13 (rear 13.4 x 13")		
Type of braking front	Carbon discs with six calipers		
Type of braking rear	Carbon discs with six calipers		
Braking mechanism, number of circuits, servo assistance, electronic aids	Hydraulic, 1 circuit, unknown		
Steering gear, make and model of power steering	Unknown		

Formula 1

Make, range	**Jaguar prototype**	**Jaguar prototypes**	
Type	*F-Type*	*R-Coupe*	*R-D6*
Public debut	11/1/2001	11/9/2001	9/9/2003
End of production	11/1/2001	11/9/2001	9/9/2003
Production figure	1	1	1
First, last chassis number RHD	VIN unknown	n/a	
First, last chassis number LHD	n/a	VIN unknown	
Body type	aluminum, 2 doors, 2 seats	aluminum, 2 doors, 4 seats (R-D 6 aluminum, 4 doors, 4 seats)	
Weather protection, top mechanism	n/a	Enclosed-drive	
Length, width, height (mm)	4115 x 1732 x 1090	4925 x 1890 x 1347 (R-D 6 4330 x 2150 x 1390)	
Length, width, height (inches)	162 x 68 x 43	194 x 74 1/2 x 53 (R-D 6 170 1/2 x 84 1/2 x 54 3/4)	
Wheelbase, front, rear track (mm)	2400 x 1537/1544	2909 x 1540/1540 (R-D 6 (2840 x unknown/unknown)	
Wheelbase, front, rear track (inches)	94 1/2 x 60 1/2/60 3/4	114 1/2 x 60 1/260 1/2	
Ground clearance, turning circle, curb weight	140mm, 11m, 1400kg	140mm, 12m, 1700kg (R-D 6 1600kg)	
Max speed, acceleration 0-60 mph	250kph, 6 sec	n/a (R-D 6 250kph, 6 sec)	
Max power, standard, revs	238 ECE-HP/6800	n/a (R-D 6 207 ECE-HP/4000)	
Max torque, revs	293 Nm/4500	n/a (R-D 6 435 Nm/1900)	
Engine type, position, number and configuration of cylinders	Four-stroke gasoline, front longitudinally, 6 cylinders, 60-degree-V	n/a (R-D 6 Four-stroke diesel, front longitudinally, 6 cylinders, 60-degree-V)	
Bore x Stroke (mm), capacity (cc), compression ratio	89 x 79.5, 2967cc, 10.5 : 1	n/a (R-D 6 81 x 86, 2720cc, 17.3 : 1)	
Designation of engine and cylinder head	Engine and head "AJ V-6"	n/a (R-D 6 Engine and head "Diesel")	
Engine block and cylinder head material, number of main bearings, type of liners	Block and head aluminum, 4 main bearings, cast-in liners	n/a (R-D 6 Block cast chrome-iron, 4 main bearings, cast-in liners)	
Number of valves per cylinder, configuration, valve gearing, timing variants	4 overhead valves, bucket tappets, 2 ohc per bank, chain, continuously variable timing	n/a (R-D 6 as F-Type, toothed belt, fixed)	
Air supply, type of inlet manifold, air tempering	Normally aspirated, 3-stage inlet manifold, n/a	n/a (R-D 6 2 turbochargers, one-stage inlet manifold, intercooler)	
Type, position, make, and designation of mixture preparation	Electronic injection to manifold, Nippondenso	n/a (R-D 6 Elektron. common rail direct injection, unknown)	
Energy source, type, make, and designation of ignition system	Battery, separate coils, Nippondenso	n/a (R-D 6 Battery, glow plugs, n/a)	
Make of alternator, voltage, earthing	Alternator, 12 V, negative	n/a (R-D 6 alternator, 12 V, negative)	
Engine coolant, drive, regulation of cooling	Liquid, pump, thermostat	n/a (R-D 6 Liquid, pump, thermostat)	
Type of clutch, number of gears in manual box, synchronized gears	Single-plate dry clutch, 5, fully	n/a (R-D 6 Single-plate dry clutch, 6, fully)	
Gear ratios in manual box	Unknown	n/a (R-D 6 unknown)	
Make, type, ratio of overdrive	n/a	n/a	
Type of clutch, number of gears, make and model of automatic box	n/a	n/a	
Gear ratios in automatic gearbox	n/a	n/a	
Driven axle, type of diff, traction control	Rear, hypoid bevel, electronic traction control	n/a (R-D 6 Rear, hypoid bevel, electronic traction control)	
Axle ratios	Unknown	n/a (R-D 6 Unknown)	
Type of chassis	Unitary	Unitary	
Suspension, springing front	Double-wishbone, coil springs	Unknown	
Suspension, springing rear	Double-wishbone, coil springs	Unknown	
Reduction of roll	Torsion bars front and rear	Unknown	
Type of shock absorbers	Telescopic	Unknown	
Type and dimensions of wheels	Aluminum discs, unknown	Aluminum discs, unknown (R-D 6 21")	
Type, dimensions, make of tires	Unknown	Unknown (R-D 6 255/30 R 21, rear 275/30 R 21)	
Type of braking front	Ventilated discs	n/a (R-D 6 ventilated discs)	
Type of braking rear	Ventilated outboard discs	n/a (R-D 6 ventilated outboard discs)	
Braking mechanism, number of circuits, servo assistance, electronic aids	Hydraulics, 2 circuits, electronic front/rear balance, hydraulic servo assistance, antilock, n/a	n/a (R-D 6 unknown)	
Steering gear, make and model of power steering	Rack and pinion, hydraulic servo ZF Servotronic II	n/a (R-D 6 unknown)	

F-Type

Make, range	**Jaguar X-Type 2.0 (X 400)**			**Jaguar X-Type 2.0 Estate (X 400)**		
Type	*2.0*	*Sport*	*Executive or S.E.*	*2.0*	*Sport*	*Executive or S.E.*
Public debut	10/12/2001	10/12/2001	10/12/2001	4/3/2004	4/3/2004	4/3/2004
End of production	5/2005	5/2005	5/2005	5/2005	5/2005	5/2005
Production figure	Unknown	Unknown	Unknown	Unknown	Unknown	Unknown
First, last chassis number RHD	VIN unknown			VIN unknown		
First, last chassis number LHD	VIN unknown			VIN unknown		
Body type	All-steel, 4 doors, 5 seats			All-steel, 4 doors, 5 seats		
Weather protection, top mechanism	Enclosed-drive, optional electrically operated glass sunroof			Enclosed-drive, optional electrically operated glass sunroof		
Length, width, height (mm)	4672 x 1789 x 1392			4716 x 1789 x 1483		
Length, width, height (inches)	184 x 70 1/2 x 54 3/4			185 1/2 x 70 1/2 x 58 1/2		
Wheelbase, front, rear track (mm)	2710 x 1522/1537			2710 x 1522/1537		
Wheelbase, front, rear track (inches)	106 1/2 x 60/60 1/2			106 1/2 x 60/60 1/2		
Ground clearance, turning circle, curb weight	140mm, 11m, 1600kg			140mm, 11m, 1600kg		
Max speed, acceleration 0-60 mph	210kph, 11 sec			210kph, 11 sec		
Max power, standard, revs	156 ECE-HP/6800			156 ECE-HP/6800		
Max torque, revs	196 Nm/4100			196 Nm/4100		
Engine type, position, number and configuration of cylinders	Four-stroke gasoline, front transverse, 6 cylinders, 60-degree-V			Four-stroke gasoline, front transverse, 6 cylinders, 60-degree-V		
Bore x Stroke (mm), capacity (cc), compression ratio	81.6 x 66.8, 2099cc, 10.75 : 1			81.6 x 66.8, 2099cc, 10.75 : 1		
Designation of engine and cylinder head	Engine and head "AJ V-6"			Engine and head "AJ V-6"		
Engine block and cylinder head material, number of main bearings, type of liners	Block and head aluminum, 4 main bearings, cast-in liners			Block and head aluminum, 4 main bearings, cast-in liners		
Number of valves per cylinder, configuration, valve gearing, timing variants	4 overhead valves, bucket tappets, 2 ohc per bank, chain, continously variable timing			4 overhead valves, bucket tappets, 2 ohc per bank, chain, continously variable timing		
Air supply, type of inlet manifold, air tempering	Normally aspirated, 3-stage inlet manifold, n/a			Normally aspirated, 3-stage inlet manifold, n/a		
Type, position, make, and designation of mixture preparation	Electronic injection to manifold, Nippondenso			Electronic injection to manifold, Nippondenso		
Energy source, type, make, and designation of ignition system	Battery, separate coils, Nippondenso			Battery, separate coils, Nippondenso		
Make of alternator, voltage, earthing	Alternator, 12 V, negative			Alternator, 12 V, negative		
Engine coolant, drive, regulation of cooling	Liquid, pump, thermostat			Liquid, pump, thermostat		
Type of clutch, number of gears in manual box, synchronized gears	Single-plate dry clutch, 5, fully			Single-plate dry clutch, 5, fully		
Gear ratios in manual box	3.42, 2.14, 1.45, 1.03, 0.77, 3.47 : 1			3.42, 2.14, 1.45, 1.03, 0.77, 3.47 : 1		
Make, type, ratio of overdrive	n/a			n/a		
Type of clutch, number of gears, make and model of automatic box	Optional hydraulic torque converter, 5, JATCO FPD			Optional hydraulic torque converter, 5, JATCO FPD		
Gear ratios in automatic gearbox	3.8, 2.13, 1.37, 0.94, 0.69, 2.97 : 1			3.8, 2.13, 1.37, 0.94, 0.69, 2.97 : 1		
Driven axle, type of diff, traction control	Front, hypoid bevel, n/a			Front, hypoid bevel, n/a		
Axle ratios	4.15 : 1			4.15 : 1		
Type of chassis	Unitary, rear subframe			Unitary, rear subframe		
Suspension, springing front	McPherson, coil springs			McPherson, coil springs		
Suspension, springing rear	2 transverse and 1 trailing arms, coil springs			2 transverse and 1 trailing arms, coil springs		
Reduction of roll	Torsion bars front and rear			Torsion bars front and rear		
Type of shock absorbers	Telescopic, optional CATS			Telescopic, optional CATS		
Type and dimensions of wheels	Aluminum discs, 6.5 J x 16 (Sport 7 J x 17)			Aluminum discs, 6.5 J x 16 (Sport 7 J x 17)		
Type, dimensions, make of tires	205/55 R 16 (Sport 225/45 R 17)			205/55 R 16 (Sport 225/45 R 17)		
Type of braking front	Ventilated discs			Ventilated discs		
Type of braking rear	Ventilated outboard discs			Ventilated outboard discs		
Braking mechanism, number of circuits, servo assistance, electronic aids	Hydraulics, 2 circuits, electronic front/rear balance, hydraulic servo assistance, antilock, optional (from 3/02 always) DSC			Hydraulics, 2 circuits, electronic front/rear balance, hydraulic servo assistance, antilock, optional (from 3/02 always) DSC		
Steering gear, make and model of power steering	Rack and pinion, hydraulic servo ZF Servotronic II			Rack and pinion, hydraulic servo ZF Servotronic II		

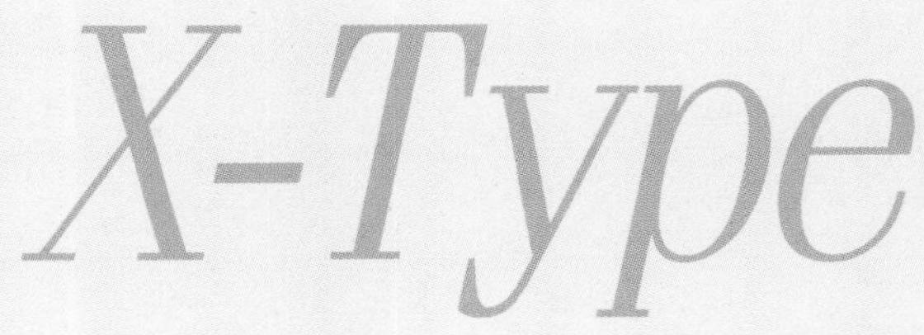

Make, range	**Jaguar X-Type 2.0 d (X 400)**			**Jaguar X-Type 2.0 d Estate (X 400)**		
Type	*2.0 d (S)*	*Sport (Sport Premium)*	*Executive or S.E. (Sovereign)*	*2.0 d (S)*	*Sport (Sport Premium)*	*Executive or S.E.(Sovereign)*
Public debut	12/6/2003 (9/2005)	12/6/2003 (9/2005)	12/6/2003 (9/2005)	4/3/2004 (9/2005)	4/3/2004 (9/2005)	4/3/2004 (9/2005)
End of production	7/2007 (...)	7/2007 (...)	...	7/2007 (...)	7/2005 (...)	...
Production figure	Unknown (...)	Unknown (...)	...	Unknown (...)	Unknown (...)	...
First, last chassis number RHD	VIN unknown			VIN unknown		
First, last chassis number LHD	VIN unknown			VIN unknown		
Body type	All-steel, 4 doors, 5 seats			All-steel, 4 doors, 5 seats		
Weather protection, top mechanism	Enclosed-drive, optional electrically operated glass sunroof			Enclosed-drive, optional electrically operated glass sunroof		
Length, width, height (mm)	4672 x 1789 x 1392			4716 x 1789 x 1483		
Length, width, height (inches)	184 x 70 1/2 x 54 3/4			185 1/2 x 70 1/2 x 58 1/2		
Wheelbase, front, rear track (mm)	2710 x 1522/1537			2710 x 1522/1537		
Wheelbase, front, rear track (inches)	106 1/2 x 60/60 1/2			106 1/2 x 60/60 1/2		
Ground clearance, turning circle, curb weight	140mm, 11m, 1600kg			140mm, 11m, 1600kg		
Max speed, acceleration 0-60 mph	201kph, 10 sec			198kph, 10 sec		
Max power, standard, revs	130 ECE-HP/3800			130 ECE-HP/3800		
Max torque, revs	330 Nm/1800			330 Nm/1800		
Engine type, position, number and configuration of cylinders	Four-stroke diesel, front transverse, 4 cylinders straight			Four-stroke diesel, front transverse, 4 cylinders straight		
Bore x Stroke (mm), capacity (cc), compression ratio	86 x 86, 1998cc, 18.2 : 1			86 x 86, 1998cc, 18.2 : 1		
Designation of engine and cylinder head	Engine and head "Ford TDCi"			Engine and head "Ford TDCi"		
Engine block and cylinder head material, number of main bearings, type of liners	Block cast chrome-iron, head aluminum, 5 main bearings, cast-in liners			Block cast-chrome-iron, head aluminum, 5 main bearings, cast-in liners		
Number of valves per cylinder, configuration, valve gearing, timing variants	4 overhead valves, rocker, 2 overhead camshafts, chain, fixed			4 overhead valves, rocker, 2 overhead camshafts, chain, fixed		
Air supply, type of inlet manifold, air tempering	Turbocharger, one-stage inlet manifold, intercooler			Turbocharger, one-stage inlet manifold, intercooler		
Type, position, make, and designation of mixture preparation	Electronic common-rail direct injection, unknown			Electronic common-rail direct injection, unknown		
Energy source, type, make, and designation of ignition system	Battery, glow plugs, n/a			Battery, glow plugs, n/a		
Make of alternator, voltage, earthing	Alternator, 12 V, negative			Alternator, 12 V, negative		
Engine coolant, drive, regulation of cooling	Liquid, pump, thermostat			Liquid, pump, thermostat		
Type of clutch, number of gears in manual box, synchronized gears	Single-plate dry clutch, 5, fully			Single-plate dry clutch, 5, fully		
Gear ratios in manual box	3.42, 2.14, 1.45, 1.03, 0.77, 3.47 : 1			3.42, 2.14, 1.45, 1.03, 0.77, 3.47 : 1		
Make, type, ratio of overdrive	n/a			n/a		
Type of clutch, number of gears, make and model of automatic box	n/a			n/a		
Gear ratios in automatic gearbox	n/a			n/a		
Driven axle, type of diff, traction control	Front, hypoid bevel, n/a			Front, hypoid bevel, n/a		
Axle ratios	4.15 : 1			4.15 : 1		
Type of chassis	Unitary, rear subframe			Unitary, rear subframe		
Suspension, springing front	McPherson, coil springs			McPherson, coil springs		
Suspension, springing rear	2 transverse and 1 trailing arms, coil springs			2 transverse and 1 trailing arms, coil springs		
Reduction of roll	Torsion bars front and rear			Torsion bars front and rear		
Type of shock absorbers	Telescopic, optional CATS			Telescopic, optional CATS		
Type and dimensions of wheels	Aluminum discs, 6.5 J x 16 (Sport and Sport Premium 7 J x 17)			Aluminum discs, 6.5 J x 16 (Sport and Sport Premium 7 J x 17)		
Type, dimensions, make of tires	205/55 R 16 (Sport and Sport Premium 225/45 R 17)			205/55 R 16 (Sport and Sport Premium 225/45 R 17)		
Type of braking front	Ventilated discs			Ventilated discs		
Type of braking rear	Ventilated outboard discs			Ventilated outboard discs		
Braking mechanism, number of circuits, servo assistance, electronic aids	Hydraulics, 2 circuits, electronic front/rear balance, hydraulic servo assistance, antilock, DSC			Hydraulics, 2 circuits, electronic front/rear balance, hydraulic servo assistance, antilock, DSC		
Steering gear, make and model of power steering	Rack and pinion, hydraulic servo ZF Servotronic II			Rack and pinion, hydraulic servo ZF Servotronic II		

Make, range	**Jaguar X-Type 2.2 d (X 400)**			**Jaguar X-Type 2.2 d Estate (X 400)**		
Type	*2.2 d (S)*	*Sport (Sport Premium)*	*Executive or S.E. (Sovereign)*	*2.2 d (S)*	*Sport Executive or S.E. (Sovereign) (Sport Premium)*	
Public debut	9/2005	9/2005	9/2005	9/2005	9/2005	9/2005
End of production	7/2007 (...)	7/2007 (...)	...	7/2007 (...)	7/2007 (...)	...
Production figure	Unknown (...)	Unknown (...)	...	Unknown (...)	Unknown (...)	...
First, last chassis number RHD	VIN unknown			VIN unknown		
First, last chassis number LHD	VIN unknown			VIN unknown		
Body type	All-steel, 4 doors, 5 seats			All-steel, 4 doors, 5 seats		
Weather protection, top mechanism	Enclosed-drive, optional electrically operated glass sunroof			Enclosed-drive, optional electrically operated glass sunroof		
Length, width, height (mm)	4672 x 1789 x 1392			4716 x 1789 x 1483		
Length, width, height (inches)	184 x 70 1/2 x 54 3/4			185 1/2 x 70 1/2 x 58 1/2		
Wheelbase, front, rear track (mm)	2710 x 1522/1537			2710 x 1522/1537		
Wheelbase, front, rear track (inches)	106 1/2 x 60/60 1/2			106 1/2 x 60/60 1/2		
Ground clearance, turning circle, curb weight	140mm, 11m, 1600kg			140mm, 11m, 1600kg		
Max speed, acceleration 0-60 mph	216kph, 9 sec			211kph, 9 sec		
Max power, standard, revs	145 ECE-HP/3500			145 ECE-HP/3500		
Max torque, revs	360 Nm/1800			360 Nm/1800		
Engine type, position, number and configuration of cylinders	Four-stroke diesel, front transverse, 4 cylinders straight			Four-stroke diesel, front transverse, 4 cylinders straight		
Bore x Stroke (mm), capacity (cc), compression ratio	86 x 94.6, 2198cc, 17.5 : 1			86 x 94.6, 2198cc, 17.5 : 1		
Designation of engine and cylinder head	Engine and head "Ford TDCi"			Engine and head "Ford TDCi"		
Engine block and cylinder head material, number of main bearings, type of liners	Block cast chrome-iron, head aluminum, 5 main bearings, cast-in liners			Block cast chrome-iron, head aluminum, 5 main bearings, cast-in liners		
Number of valves per cylinder, configuration, valve gearing, timing variants	4 overhead valves, rocker, 2 overhead camshafts, chain, fixed			4 overhead valves, rocker, 2 overhead camshafts, chain, fixed		
Air supply, type of inlet manifold, air tempering	Turbocharger, one-stage inlet manifold, intercooler			Turbocharger, one-stage inlet manifold, intercooler		
Type, position, make, and designation of mixture preparation	Electronic common-rail direct injection, unknown			Electronic common-rail direct injection, unknown		
Energy source, type, make, and designation of ignition system	Battery, glow plugs, n/a			Battery, glow plugs, n/a		
Make of alternator, voltage, earthing	Alternator, 12 V, negative			Alternator, 12 V, negative		
Engine coolant, drive, regulation of cooling	Liquid, pump, thermostat			Liquid, pump, thermostat		
Type of clutch, number of gears in manual box, synchronized gears	Single-plate dry clutch, 6, fully			Single-plate dry clutch, 6, fully		
Gear ratios in manual box	Unknown			Unknown		
Make, type, ratio of overdrive	n/a			n/a		
Type of clutch, number of gears, make and model of automatic box	n/a			n/a		
Gear ratios in automatic gearbox	n/a			n/a		
Driven axle, type of diff, traction control	Front, hypoid bevel, n/a			Front, hypoid bevel, n/a		
Axle ratios	4.15 : 1			4.15 : 1		
Type of chassis	Unitary, rear subframe			Unitary, rear subframe		
Suspension, springing front	McPherson, coil springs			McPherson, coil springs		
Suspension, springing rear	2 transverse and 1 trailing arms, coil springs			2 transverse and 1 trailing arms, coil springs		
Reduction of roll	Torsion bars front and rear			Torsion bars front and rear		
Type of shock absorbers	Telescopic, optional CATS			Telescopic, optional CATS		
Type and dimensions of wheels	Aluminum discs, 6.5 J x 16 (Sport and Sport Premium 7 J x 17)			Aluminum discs, 6.5 J x 16 (Sport and Sport Premium 7 J x 17)		
Type, dimensions, make of tires	205/55 R 16 (Sport and Sport Premium 225/45 R 17)			205/55 R 16 (Sport and Sport Premium 225/45 R 17)		
Type of braking front	Ventilated discs			Ventilated discs		
Type of braking rear	Ventilated outboard discs			Ventilated outboard discs		
Braking mechanism, number of circuits, servo assistance, electronic aids	Hydraulics, 2 circuits, electronic front/rear balance, hydraulic servo assistance, antilock, DSC			Hydraulics, 2 circuits, electronic front/rear balance, hydraulic servo assistance, antilock, DSC		
Steering gear, make and model of power steering	Rack and pinion, hydraulic servo ZF Servotronic II			Rack and pinion, hydraulic servo ZF Servotronic II		

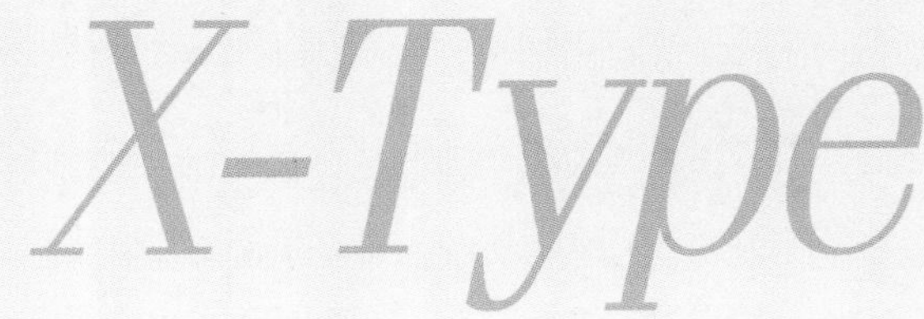

Make, range	**Jaguar X-Type 2.5 (X 400)**			**Jaguar X-Type 2.5 Estate (X 400)**		
Type	*2.5 (S)*	*Sport (Sport Premium)*	*Executive or S.E. (Sovereign)*	*2.5 (S)*	*Sport (Sport Premium)*	*Executive or S.E. (Sovereign)*
Public debut	23/5/2001 (9/2005)	23/5/2001 (9/2005)	23/5/2001 (9/2005)	4/3/2004 (9/2005)	4/3/2004 (9/2005)	4/3/2004 (9/2005)
End of production	7/2007 (...)	7/2007 (...)	...	7/2007 (...)	7/2007 (...)	...
Production figure	Unknown (...)	Unknown (...)	...	Unknown (...)	Unknown (...)	...
First, last chassis number RHD	VIN unknown			VIN unknown		
First, last chassis number LHD	VIN unknown			VIN unknown		
Body type	All-steel, 4 doors, 5 seats			All-steel, 4 doors, 5 seats		
Weather protection, top mechanism	Enclosed-drive, optional electrically operated glass sunroof			Enclosed-drive, optional electrically operated glass sunroof		
Length, width, height (mm)	4672 x 1789 x 1392			4716 x 1789 x 1483		
Length, width, height (inches)	184 x 70 1/2 x 54 3/4			185 1/2 x 70 1/2 x 58 1/2		
Wheelbase, front, rear track (mm)	2710 x 1522/1537			2710 x 1522/1537		
Wheelbase, front, rear track (inches)	106 1/2 x 60/60 1/2			106 1/2 x 60/60 1/2		
Ground clearance, turning circle, curb weight	140mm, 11m, 1600kg			140mm, 11m, 1600kg		
Max speed, acceleration 0-60 mph	225kph, 9 sec			220kph, 9 sec		
Max power, standard, revs	196 ECE-HP/6800			196 ECE-HP/6800		
Max torque, revs	241 Nm/3000			241 Nm/3000		
Engine type, position, number and configuration of cylinders	Four-stroke gasoline, front transverse, 6 cylinders, 60-degree-V			Four-stroke gasoline, front transverse, 6 cylinders, 60-degree-V		
Bore x Stroke (mm), capacity (cc), compression ratio	81.6 x 79.5, 2495cc, 10.3 : 1			81.6 x 79.5, 2495cc, 10.3 : 1		
Designation of engine and cylinder head	Engine and head "AJ V-6"			Engine and head "AJ V-6"		
Engine block and cylinder head material, number of main bearings, type of liners	Block and head aluminum, 4 main bearings, cast-in liners			Block and head aluminum, 4 main bearings, cast-in liners		
Number of valves per cylinder, configuration, valve gearing, timing variants	4 overhead valves, bucket tappets, 2 ohc per bank, chain, continously variable timing			4 overhead valves, bucket tappets, 2 ohc per bank, chain, continously variable timing		
Air supply, type of inlet manifold, air tempering	Normally aspirated, 3-stage inlet manifold, n/a			Normally aspirated, 3-stage inlet manifold, n/a		
Type, position, make, and designation of mixture preparation	Electronic injection to manifold, Nippondenso			Electronic injection to manifold, Nippondenso		
Energy source, type, make, and designation of ignition system	Battery, separate coils, Nippondenso			Battery, separate coils, Nippondenso		
Make of alternator, voltage, earthing	Alternator, 12 V, negative			Alternator, 12 V, negative		
Engine coolant, drive, regulation of cooling	Liquid, pump, thermostat			Liquid, pump, thermostat		
Type of clutch, number of gears in manual box, synchronized gears	Single-plate dry clutch, 5, fully			Single-plate dry clutch, 5, fully		
Gear ratios in manual box	3.42, 2.14, 1.45, 1.03, 0.77, 3.47 : 1			3.42, 2.14, 1.45, 1.03, 0.77, 3.47 : 1		
Make, type, ratio of overdrive	n/a			n/a		
Type of clutch, number of gears, make and model of automatic box	Optional hydraulic torque converter, 5, JATCO FPD			Optional hydraulic torque converter, 5, JATCO FPD		
Gear ratios in automatic gearbox	3.8, 2.13, 1.37, 0.94, 0.69, 2.97 : 1			3.8, 2.13, 1.37, 0.94, 0.69, 2.97 : 1		
Driven axle, type of diff, traction control	All-wheel, hypoid bevels, central viscous, n/a			All-wheel, hypoid bevels, central viscous, n/a		
Axle ratios	3.8 (with automatic 3.9) : 1			3.8 (with automatic 3.9) : 1		
Type of chassis	Unitary, rear subframe			Unitary, rear subframe		
Suspension, springing front	McPherson, coil springs			McPherson, coil springs		
Suspension, springing rear	2 transverse and 1 trailing arms, coil springs			2 transverse and 1 trailing arms, coil springs		
Reduction of roll	Torsion bars front and rear			Torsion bars front and rear		
Type of shock absorbers	Telescopic, optional CATS			Telescopic, optional CATS		
Type and dimensions of wheels	Aluminum discs, painted, 6.5 J x 16 (Sport and Sport Premium 7 J x 17)			Aluminum discs, painted, 6.5 J x 16 (Sport and Sport Premium 7 J x 17)		
Type, dimensions, make of tires	205/55 R 16 (Sport and Sport Premium 225/45 R 17)			205/55 R 16 (Sport and Sport Premium 225/45 R 17)		
Type of braking front	Ventilated discs			Ventilated discs		
Type of braking rear	Ventilated outboard discs			Ventilated outboard discs		
Braking mechanism, number of circuits, servo assistance, electronic aids	Hydraulics, 2 circuits, electronic front/rear balance, hydraulic servo assistance, antilock, optional (from 3/02 always) DSC			Hydraulics, 2 circuits, electronic front/rear balance, hydraulic servo assistance, antilock, DSC		
Steering gear, make and model of power steering	Rack and pinion, hydraulic servo ZF Servotronic II			Rack and pinion, hydraulic servo ZF Servotronic II		

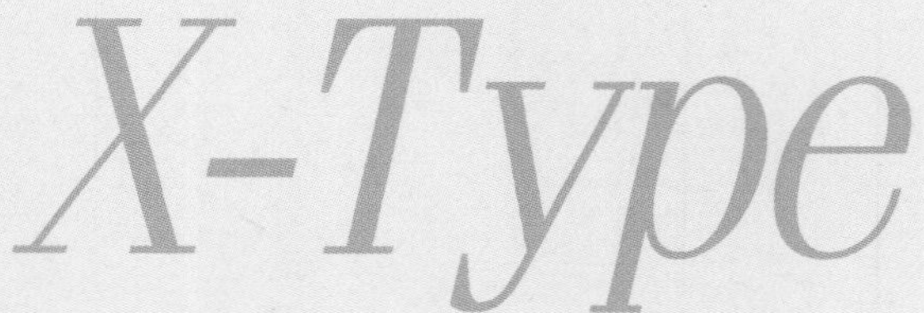

Make, range	**Jaguar X-Type 3.0 (X 400)**			**Jaguar X-Type 3.0 Estate (X 400)**		
Type	*3.0*	*Sport (Sport Premium)*	*Executive or S.E. (Sovereign)*	*3.0*	*Sport (Sport Premium)*	*Executive or S.E. (Sovereign)*
Public debut	1/2004	23/5/2001 (9/2005)	23/5/2001 (9/2005)	4/3/2004	4/3/2004 (9/2005)	4/3/2004 (9/2005)
End of production	7/2007	7/2007	7/2007	7/2007	7/2007	7/2007 (...)
Production figure	Unknown	Unknown	Unknown	Unknown	Unknown	Unknown (...)
First, last chassis number RHD	VIN unknown			VIN unknown		
First, last chassis number LHD	VIN unknown			VIN unknown		
Body type	All-steel, 4 doors, 5 seats			All-steel, 4 doors, 5 seats		
Weather protection, top mechanism	Enclosed-drive, optional electrically operated glass sunroof			Enclosed-drive, optional electrically operated glass sunroof		
Length, width, height (mm)	4672 x 1789 x 1392			4716 x 1789 x 1483		
Length, width, height (inches)	184 x 70 1/2 x 54 3/4			185 1/2 x 70 1/2 x 58 1/2		
Wheelbase, front, rear track (mm)	2710 x 1522/1537			2710 x 1522/1537		
Wheelbase, front, rear track (inches)	106 1/2 x 60/60 1/2			106 1/2 x 60/60 1/2		
Ground clearance, turning circle, curb weight	140mm, 11m, 1600kg			140mm, 11m, 1600kg		
Max speed, acceleration 0-60 mph	235kph, 8 sec			230kph, 8 sec		
Max power, standard, revs	231 ECE-HP/6800			231 ECE-HP/6800		
Max torque, revs	279 Nm/3000			279 Nm/3000		
Engine type, position, number and configuration of cylinders	Four-stroke gasoline, front transverse, 6 cylinders, 60-degree-V			Four-stroke gasoline, front transverse, 6 cylinders, 60-degree-V		
Bore x Stroke (mm), capacity (cc), compression ratio	89 x 79.5, 2967cc, 10.5 : 1			89 x 79.5, 2967cc, 10.5 : 1		
Designation of engine and cylinder head	Engine and head "AJ V-6"			Engine and head "AJ V-6"		
Engine block and cylinder head material, number of main bearings, type of liners	Block and head aluminum, 4 main bearings, cast-in liners			Block and head aluminum, 4 main bearings, cast-in liners		
Number of valves per cylinder, configuration, valve gearing, timing variants	4 overhead valves, bucket tappets, 2 ohc per bank, chain, continously variable timing			4 overhead valves, bucket tappets, 2 ohc per bank, chain, continously variable timing		
Air supply, type of inlet manifold, air tempering	Normally aspirated, 3-stage inlet manifold, n/a			Normally aspirated, 3-stage inlet manifold, n/a		
Type, position, make, and designation of mixture preparation	Electronic injection to manifold, Nippondenso			Electronic injection to manifold, Nippondenso		
Energy source, type, make, and designation of ignition system	Battery, separate coils, Nippondenso			Battery, separate coils, Nippondenso		
Make of alternator, voltage, earthing	Alternator, 12 V, negative			Alternator, 12 V, negative		
Engine coolant, drive, regulation of cooling	Liquid, pump, thermostat			Liquid, pump, thermostat		
Type of clutch, number of gears in manual box, synchronized gears	Single-plate dry clutch, 5, fully			Single-plate dry clutch, 5, fully		
Gear ratios in manual box	3.42, 2.14, 1.45, 1.03, 0.77, 3.47 : 1			3.42, 2.14, 1.45, 1.03, 0.77, 3.47 : 1		
Make, type, ratio of overdrive	n/a			n/a		
Type of clutch, number of gears, make and model of automatic box	Optional hydraulic torque converter, 5, JATCO FPD			Optional hydraulic torque converter, 5, JATCO FPD		
Gear ratios in automatic gearbox	3.8, 2.13, 1.37, 0.94, 0.69, 2.97 : 1			3.8, 2.13, 1.37, 0.94, 0.69, 2.97 : 1		
Driven axle, type of diff, traction control	All-wheel, hypoid bevels, central viscous, n/a			All-wheel, hypoid bevels, central viscous, n/a		
Axle ratios	3.8 (with automatic 3.9) : 1			3.8 (with automatic 3.9) : 1		
Type of chassis	Unitary, rear subframe			Unitary, rear subframe		
Suspension, springing front	McPherson, coil springs			McPherson, coil springs		
Suspension, springing rear	2 transverse and 1 trailing arms, coil springs			2 transverse and 1 trailing arms, coil springs		
Reduction of roll	Torsion bars front and rear			Torsion bars front and rear		
Type of shock absorbers	Telescopic, optional CATS			Telescopic, optional CATS		
Type and dimensions of wheels	Aluminum discs, 6.5 J x 16 (Sport and Sport Premium 7 J x 17)			Aluminum discs, 6.5 J x 16 (Sport and Sport Premium 7 J x 17)		
Type, dimensions, make of tires	205/55 R 16 (Sport and Sport Premium 225/45 R 17)			205/55 R 16 (Sport and Sport Premium 225/45 R 17)		
Type of braking front	Ventilated discs			Ventilated discs		
Type of braking rear	Ventilated outboard discs			Ventilated outboard discs		
Braking mechanism, number of circuits, servo assistance, electronic aids	Hydraulics, 2 circuits, electronic front/rear balance, hydraulic servo assistance, antilock, optional (from 3/02 always) DSC			Hydraulics, 2 circuits, electronic front/rear balance, hydraulic servo assistance, antilock, DSC		
Steering gear, make and model of power steering	Rack and pinion, hydraulic servo ZF Servotronic II			Rack and pinion, hydraulic servo ZF Servotronic II		

Make, range	**Jaguar XJ 6 3.0 (X 350)**			**Jaguar XJ 8 3.5 (X 350)**	
Type	*3.0*	*3.0 Sport*	*3.0 Executive (S.E.)*	*3.5 Executive (S.E.)*	*3.5 LWB*
Public debut	4/2003	4/2003	4/2003	4/2003	7/4/2004
First, last chassis number RHD	VIN unknown			VIN unknown	
First, last chassis number LHD	VIN unknown			VIN unknown	
Body type	Aluminum, bonded and riveted, 4 doors, 5 seats			Aluminum, bonded and riveted, 4 doors, 5 seats	
Weather protection, top mechanism	Enclosed-drive, optional electrically operated glass sunroof			Enclosed-drive, optional electrically operated glass sunroof	
Length, width, height (mm)	5080 x 1868 x 1448			5080 x 1868 x 1448 (LWB 5215 x 1868 x 1455)	
Length, width, height (inches)	200 x 73 1/2 x 57			200 x 73 1/2 x 57 (LWB 205 1/4 x 73 1/3 x 57 1/4)	
Wheelbase, front, rear track (mm)	3034 x 1556/1546			3034 (LWB 3159) x 1556/1546	
Wheelbase, front, rear track (inches)	119 1/2 x 61 1/4/61			119 1/2 (LWB 124 1/2 x 61 1/4/61	
Ground clearance, turning circle, curb weight	150mm, 11m, 1620kg			150mm, 11m, 1650kg	
Max speed, acceleration 0-60 mph	235kph, 8 sec			240kph, 7 sec	
Max power, standard, revs	238 ECE-HP/6800			258 ECE-HP/6250	
Max torque, revs	279 Nm/3000			335 Nm/4200	
Engine type, position, number and configuration of cylinders	Four-stroke gasoline, front longitudinally, 6 cylinders, 60-degree-V			Four-stroke gasoline, front longitudinally, 8 cylinders, 90-degree-V	
Bore x Stroke (mm), capacity (cc), compression ratio	89 x 79.5, 2967cc, 10.5 : 1			86 x 76.5, 3555cc, 11 : 1	
Designation of engine and cylinder head	Engine and head "AJ V-6"			Engine and head "AJ 34"	
Engine block and cylinder head material, number of main bearings, type of liners	Block and head aluminum, 4 main bearings, cast-in liners			Block and head aluminum, 5 main bearings, cast-in liners	
Number of valves per cylinder, configuration, valve gearing, timing variants	4 overhead valves, bucket tappets, 2 ohc per bank, chain, continously variable timing			4 overhead valves, bucket tappets, 2 ohc per bank, chain, fixed	
Air supply, type of inlet manifold, air tempering	Normally aspirated, 3-stage inlet manifold, n/a			Normally aspirated, 2-stage inlet manifold, n/a	
Type, position, make, and designation of mixture preparation	Electronic injection to manifold, Nippondenso			Electronic injection to manifold, Nippondenso	
Energy source, type, make, and designation of ignition system	Battery, separate coils, Nippondenso			Battery, separate coils, Nippondenso	
Make of alternator, voltage, earthing	Alternator, 12 V, negative			Alternator, 12 V, negative	
Engine coolant, drive, regulation of cooling	Liquid, pump, thermostat			Liquid, pump, thermostat	
Type of clutch, number of gears in manual box, synchronized gears	n/a			n/a	
Gear ratios in manual box	n/a			n/a	
Make, type, ratio of overdrive	n/a			n/a	
Type of clutch, number of gears, make and model of automatic box	Hydraulic torque converter, 6, ZF 6 HP 26			Hydraulic torque converter, 6, ZF 6 HP 26	
Gear ratios in automatic gearbox	4.17, 2.34, 1.52, 1.14, 0.87, 0.69, 3.4 : 1			4.17, 2.34, 1.52, 1.14, 0.87, 0.69, 3.4 : 1	
Driven axle, type of diff, traction control	Rear, hypoid bevel, n/a			Rear, hypoid bevel, n/a	
Axle ratios	3.31 : 1			3.07 : 1	
Type of chassis	Unitary, rear subframe			Unitary, rear subframe	
Suspension, springing front	Double-wishbone, air springing*			Double-wishbone, air springing	
Suspension, springing rear	Double-wishbone, air springing*			Double-wishbone, air springing	
Reduction of roll	Torsion bars front and rear			Torsion bars front and rear	
Type of shock absorbers	n/a, optional CATS			n/a, optional CATS	
Type and dimensions of wheels	Aluminum discs, 7.5 J x 17			Aluminum discs, 7.5 J x 17 (LWB 8 J x 18)	
Type, dimensions, make of tires	235/55 R 17			235/55 R 17 (LWB 235/50 R 18)	
Type of braking front	Ventilated discs			Ventilated discs	
Type of braking rear	Ventilated outboard discs			Ventilated outboard discs	
Braking mechanism, number of circuits, servo assistance, electronic aids	Hydraulics, 2 circuits, electronic front/rear balance, hydraulic servo assistance, antilock, DSC			Hydraulics, 2 circuits, electronic front/rear balance, hydraulic servo assistance, antilock, DSC	
Steering gear, make and model of power steering	Rack and pinion, hydraulic servo ZF Servotronic II			Rack and pinion, hydraulic servo ZF Servotronic II	

* 3.0 base model with coil springs/telescopic dampers front and rear

X 350

Make, range	**Jaguar XJ 6 2.7 d (X 350)**			**Jaguar XJ 6 2.7 d LWB (X 350)**		
Type	*2.7 d Classic (Executive)*	*2.7 d Sport (Sport Premium)*	*2.7 d Sovereign*	*2.7 d Executive*	*2.7 d Sport Premium*	*2.7 d Sovereign*
Public debut	9/2005	9/2005	9/2005	20/7/2006	20/7/2006	20/7/2006
End of production	...	...	9/2006	...		
First, last chassis number RHD	VIN unknown			VIN unknown		
First, last chassis number LHD	VIN unknown			VIN unknown		
Body type	Aluminum, bonded and riveted, 4 doors, 5 seats			Aluminum, bonded and riveted, 4 doors, 5 seats		
Weather protection, top mechanism	Enclosed-drive, optional electrically operated glass sunroof			Enclosed-drive, optional electrically operated glass sunroof		
Length, width, height (mm)	5080 x 1868 x 1448			5215 x 1868 x 1455		
Length, width, height (inches)	200 x 73 1/2 x 57			205 1/4 x 73 1/2 x 57 1/4		
Wheelbase, front, rear track (mm)	3034 x 1556/1546			3159 x 1556/1546		
Wheelbase, front, rear track (inches)	119 1/2 x 61 1/4/61			124 1/2 x 61 1/4/61		
Ground clearance, turning circle, curb weight	150mm, 11m, 1650kg			150mm, 11m, 1650kg		
Max speed, acceleration 0-60 mph	230kph, 9 sec			230kph, 9 sec		
Max power, standard, revs	207 ECE-HP/4000			207 ECE-HP/4000		
Max torque, revs	435 Nm/1900			435 Nm/1900		
Engine type, position, number and configuration of cylinders	Four-stroke diesel, front longitudinally, 6 cylinders, 60 degree-V			Four-stroke diesel, front longitudinally, 6 cylinders, 60 degree-V		
Bore x Stroke (mm), capacity (cc), compression ratio	81 x 86, 2720cc, 17.3 : 1			81 x 86, 2720cc, 17.3 : 1		
Designation of engine and cylinder head	Engine and head "Diesel"			Engine and head "Diesel"		
Engine block and cylinder head material, number of main bearings, type of liners	Block and head aluminum, 4 main bearings, cast-in liners			Block and head aluminum 4 main bearings, cast-in liners		
Number of valves per cylinder, configuration, valve gearing, timing variants	4 overhead valves, rocker, 2 ohc per bank, toothed belt, fixed			4 overhead valves, rocker, 2 ohc per bank, toothed belt, fixed		
Air supply, type of inlet manifold, air tempering	2 turbochargers, one-stage inlet manifold, intercooler			2 turbochargers, one-stage inlet manifold, intercooler		
Type, position, make, and designation of mixture preparation	Electronic Common-Rail direct injection, n/a			Electronic Common-Rail direct injection, n/a		
Energy source, type, make, and designation of ignition system	Battery, glow plugs, n/a			Battery, glow plugs, n/a		
Make of alternator, voltage, earthing	Alternator, 12 V, negative			Alternator, 12 V, negative		
Engine coolant, drive, regulation of cooling	Liquid, pump, thermostat			Liquid, pump, thermostat		
Type of clutch, number of gears in manual box, synchronized gears	n/a			n/a		
Gear ratios in manual box	n/a			n/a		
Make, type, ratio of overdrive	n/a			n/a		
Type of clutch, number of gears, make and model of automatic box	Hydraulic torque converter, 6, ZF 6 HP 26			Hydraulic torque converter, 6, ZF 6 HP 26		
Gear ratios in automatic gearbox	4.17, 2.34, 1.52, 1.14, 0.87, 0.69, 3.4 : 1			4.17, 2.34, 1.52, 1.14, 0.87, 0.69, 3.4 : 1		
Driven axle, type of diff, traction control	Rear, hypoid bevel, n/a			Rear, hypoid bevel, n/a		
Axle ratios	3.07 : 1			3.07 : 1		
Type of chassis	Unitary, rear subframe			Unitary, rear subframe		
Suspension, springing front	Double-wishbone, air springing			Double-wishbone, air springing		
Suspension, springing rear	Double-wishbone, air springing			Double-wishbone, air springing		
Reduction of roll	Torsion bars front and rear			Torsion bars front and rear		
Type of shock absorbers	n/a, optional CATS			n/a, optional CATS		
Type and dimensions of wheels	Aluminum discs, 7.5 J x 17			Aluminum discs, 8 J x 18		
Type, dimensions, make of tires	235/55 R 17			235/50 R 18)		
Type of braking front	Ventilated discs			Ventilated discs		
Type of braking rear	Ventilated outboard discs			Ventilated outboard discs		
Braking mechanism, number of circuits, servo assistance, electronic aids	Hydraulics, 2 circuits, electronic front/rear balance, hydraulic servo assistance, antilock, DSC			Hydraulics, 2 circuits, electronic front/rear balance, hydraulic servo assistance, antilock, DSC		
Steering gear, make and model of power steering	Rack and pinion, hydraulic servo ZF Servotronic II			Rack and pinion, hydraulic servo ZF Servotronic II		

X 350

Make, range	**Jaguar XJ 8 4.2 (X 350)**			**Jaguar XJR and Super V8 (X 350)**		
Type	*4.2 Sport*	*4.2 Executive (S.E.)*	*Sovereign*	*XJR*	*Super V-8*	*Vanden Plas*
Public debut	4/2003	4/2003	9/9/2004	4/2003	4/2003	9/2003
End of production	...	...	...	...	...	7/2004
First, last chassis number RHD	VIN unknown			VIN unknown		
First, last chassis number LHD	VIN unknown			VIN unknown		
Body type	Aluminum, bonded and riveted, 4 doors, 5 seats			Aluminum, bonded and riveted, 4 doors, 5 seats		
Weather protection, top mechanism	Enclosed-drive, optional electrically operated glass sunroof			Enclosed-drive, optional electrically operated glass sunroof		
Length, width, height (mm)	5080 x 1868 x 1448			5080 x 1868 x 1448		
Length, width, height (inches)	200 x 73 1/2 x 57			200 x 73 1/2 x 57		
Wheelbase, front, rear track (mm)	3034 x 1556/1546			3034 x 1556/1546		
Wheelbase, front, rear track (inches)	119 1/2 x 61 1/4/61			119 1/2 x 61 1/4/61		
Ground clearance, turning circle, curb weight	150mm, 11m, 1700kg			150mm, 11m, 1700kg		
Max speed, acceleration 0-60 mph	250kph, 6 sec			250kph, 5 sec		
Max power, standard, revs	298 ECE-HP/6000			395 ECE-HP/6100		
Max torque, revs	411 Nm/3500			541 Nm/3500		
Engine type, position, number and configuration of cylinders	Four-stroke gasoline, front longitudinally, 8 cylinders, 90-degree-V			Four-stroke gasoline, front longitudinally, 8 cylinders, 90-degree-V		
Bore x Stroke (mm), capacity (cc), compression ratio	86 x 90.3, 4196cc, 11 : 1			86 x 90.3, 4196cc, 9.1 : 1		
Designation of engine and cylinder head	Engine and head "AJ 34"			Engine and head "AJ 34"		
Engine block and cylinder head material, number of main bearings, type of liners	Block and head aluminum, 5 main bearings, cast-in liners			Block and head aluminum, 5 main bearings, cast-in liners		
Number of valves per cylinder, configuration, valve gearing, timing variants	4 overhead valves, bucket tappets, 2 ohc per bank, chain, continously variable timing			4 overhead valves, bucket tappets, 2 ohc per bank, chain, fixed		
Air supply, type of inlet manifold, air tempering	Normally aspirated, 2-stage inlet manifold, n/a			Roots supercharger, one-stage inlet manifold, intercooler		
Type, position, make, and designation of mixture preparation	Electronic injection to manifold, Nippondenso			Electronic injection to manifold, Nippondenso		
Energy source, type, make, and designation of ignition system	Battery, separate coils, Nippondenso			Battery, separate coils, Nippondenso		
Make of alternator, voltage, earthing	Alternator, 12 V, negative			Alternator, 12 V, negative		
Engine coolant, drive, regulation of cooling	Liquid, pump, thermostat			Liquid, pump, thermostat		
Type of clutch, number of gears in manual box, synchronized gears	n/a			n/a		
Gear ratios in manual box	n/a			n/a		
Make, type, ratio of overdrive	n/a			n/a		
Type of clutch, number of gears, make and model of automatic box	Hydraulic torque converter, 6, ZF 6 HP 26			Hydraulic torque converter, 6, ZF 6 HP 26		
Gear ratios in automatic gearbox	4.17, 2.34, 1.52, 1.14, 0.87, 0.69, 3.4 : 1			4.17, 2.34, 1.52, 1.14, 0.87, 0.69, 3.4 : 1		
Driven axle, type of diff, traction control	Rear, hypoid bevel, n/a			Rear, hypoid bevel, n/a		
Axle ratios	2.87 : 1			2.87 : 1		
Type of chassis	Unitary, front and rear subframes			Unitary, front and rear subframes		
Suspension, springing front	Double-wishbone, air springing			Double-wishbone, air springing		
Suspension, springing rear	Double-wishbone, air springing			Double-wishbone, air springing		
Reduction of roll	Torsion bars front and rear			Torsion bars front and rear		
Type of shock absorbers	n/a, optional CATS			n/a, CATS		
Type and dimensions of wheels	Aluminum discs, 8 J x 17			Aluminum discs, 8.5 J x 18		
Type, dimensions, make of tires	235/55 R 17			235/50 R 18		
Type of braking front	Ventilated discs			Ventilated discs		
Type of braking rear	Ventilated outboard discs			Ventilated outboard discs		
Braking mechanism, number of circuits, servo assistance, electronic aids	Hydraulics, 2 circuits, electronic front/rear balance, hydraulic servo assistance, antilock, DSC			Hydraulics, 2 circuits, electronic front/rear balance, hydraulic servo assistance, antilock, DSC		
Steering gear, make and model of power steering	Rack and pinion, hydraulic servo ZF Servotronic II			Rack and pinion, hydraulic servo ZF Servotronic II		

X 350

Make, range	**Jaguar XJ 8 4.2 LWB (X 350)**		**Jaguar super V8 and Daimler Super Eight**		
Type	*4.2 S.E.*	*Sovereign*	*Super V-8*	*Jaguar Vanden Plas (Portfolio)*	*Daimler Super-Eight*
Public debut	9/9/2004	9/9/2004	9/9/2004	9/9/2004 (9/2005)	9/2005
End of production	...	...	...	... (2006)	...
Production figure	...	...	...	... (150)	...
First, last chassis number RHD	VIN unknown		VIN unknown		
First, last chassis number LHD	VIN unknown		VIN unknown		
Body type	Aluminum, bonded and riveted, 4 doors, 5 seats		Aluminum, bonded and riveted, 4 doors, 5 seats		
Weather protection, top mechanism	Enclosed-drive, optional electrically operated glass sunroof		Enclosed-drive, optional electrically operated glass sunroof		
Length, width, height (mm)	5215 x 1868 x 1455		5215 x 1868 x 1455		
Length, width, height (inches)	205 1/4 x 73 1/2 x 57 1/4		205 1/4 x 73 1/2 x 57 1/4		
Wheelbase, front, rear track (mm)	3159 x 1556/1546		3159 x 1556/1546		
Wheelbase, front, rear track (inches)	124 1/2 x 61 1/4/61		124 1/2 x 61 1/4/61		
Ground clearance, turning circle, curb weight	150mm, 11m, 1700kg		150mm, 11m, 1700kg		
Max speed, acceleration 0-60 mph	250kph, 6 sec		250kph, 5 sec		
Max power, standard, revs	298 ECE-HP/6000		395 ECE-HP/6100		
Max torque, revs	411 Nm/3500		541 Nm/3500		
Engine type, position, number and configuration of cylinders	Four-stroke gasoline, front longitudinally, 8 cylinders, 90-degree-V		Four-stroke gasoline, front longitudinally, 8 cylinders, 90-degree-V		
Bore x Stroke (mm), capacity (cc), compression ratio	86 x 90.3, 4196cc, 11 : 1		86 x 90.3, 4196cc, 9.1 : 1		
Designation of engine and cylinder head	Engine and head "AJ 34"		Engine and head "AJ 34"		
Engine block and cylinder head material, number of main bearings, type of liners	Block and head aluminum, 5 main bearings, cast-in liners		Block and head aluminum, 5 main bearings, cast-in liners		
Number of valves per cylinder, configuration, valve gearing, timing variants	4 overhead valves, bucket tappets, 2 ohc per bank, chain, continously variable timing		4 overhead valves, bucket tappets, 2 ohc per bank, chain, fixed		
Air supply, type of inlet manifold, air tempering	Normally aspirated, 2-stage inlet manifold, n/a		Roots supercharger, one-stage inlet manifold, intercooler		
Type, position, make, and designation of mixture preparation	Electronic injection to manifold, Nippondenso		Electronic injection to manifold, Nippondenso		
Energy source, type, make, and designation of ignition system	Battery, separate coils, Nippondenso		Battery, separate coils, Nippondenso		
Make of alternator, voltage, earthing	Alternator, 12 V, negative		Alternator, 12 V, negative		
Engine coolant, drive, regulation of cooling	Liquid, pump, thermostat		Liquid, pump, thermostat		
Type of clutch, number of gears in manual box, synchronized gears	n/a		n/a		
Gear ratios in manual box	n/a		n/a		
Make, type, ratio of overdrive	n/a		n/a		
Type of clutch, number of gears, make and model of automatic box	Hydraulic torque converter, 6, ZF 6 HP 26		Hydraulic torque converter, 6, ZF 6 HP 26		
Gear ratios in automatic gearbox	4.17, 2.34, 1.52, 1.14, 0.87, 0.69, 3.4 : 1		4.17, 2.34, 1.52, 1.14, 0.87, 0.69, 3.4 : 1		
Driven axle, type of diff, traction control	Rear, hypoid bevel, n/a		Rear, hypoid bevel, n/a		
Axle ratios	2.87 : 1		2.87 : 1		
Type of chassis	Unitary, front and rear subframes		Unitary, front and rear subframes		
Suspension, springing front	Double-wishbone, air springing		Double-wishbone, air springing		
Suspension, springing rear	Double-wishbone, air springing		Double-wishbone, air springing		
Reduction of roll	Torsion bars front and rear		Torsion bars front and rear		
Type of shock absorbers	n/a, optional CATS		n/a, CATS		
Type and dimensions of wheels	Aluminum discs, 8 J x 18		Aluminum discs, 8.5 J x 18		
Type, dimensions, make of tires	235/50 R 18		235/50 R 18		
Type of braking front	Ventilated discs		Ventilated discs		
Type of braking rear	Ventilated outboard discs		Ventilated outboard discs		
Braking mechanism, number of circuits, servo assistance, electronic aids	Hydraulics, 2 circuits, electronic front/rear balance, hydraulic servo assistance, antilock, DSC		Hydraulics, 2 circuits, electronic front/rear balance, hydraulic servo assistance, antilock, DSC		
Steering gear, make and model of power steering	Rack and pinion, hydraulic servo ZF Servotronic II		Rack and pinion, hydraulic servo ZF Servotronic II		

X 350

Make, range	**Jaguar XK 4.2 (X 150)**	**Jaguar XXR (X 150)**
Type	*Advanced Lightweight Coupe*	*Coupe** *Convertible* *Coupe* *Convertible*
Public debut	10/1/2005	9/13/2005 9/13/2005 7/20/2006 7/20/2006
End of production	1/2005	... ...
Production figure	...	...
First, last chassis number RHD	VIN unknown-unknown	VIN unknown-unknown
First, last chassis number LHD	VIN unknown-unknown	VIN unknown-unknown
Body type	Aluminum bonded and riveted, 2 doors, 2+2 seats	Aluminum bonded and riveted, 2 doors, 2+2 seats
Weather protection, top mechanism	Enclosed-drive (convertible electircally operated top)	Enclosed-drive (convertible electrically operated top)
Length, width, height (mm)	4791 x 2030 x 1322 (convertible 1329)	4791 x 2030 x 1322 (convertible 1329)
Length, width, height (inches)	188 1/2 x 80 x 52 (convertible 52 1/4)	188 1/2 x 80 x 52 (convertible 52 1/4)
Wheelbase, front, rear track (mm)	2752 x 1545/1565	2752 x 1545/1565
Wheelbase, front, rear track (inches)	108 1/2 x 61/61 1/2	108 1/2 x 61/61 1/2
Ground clearance, turning circle, curb weight	140mm, 11m, 1595kg (convertible 1635kg)	140mm, 11m, 1665kg (convertible 1715kg)
Max speed, acceleration 0-60 mph	250kph, 6 sec	250kph (restricted), 5 sec
Max power, standard, revs	298 ECE-HP/6000	416 ECE-HP/6250
Max torque, revs	411 Nm//3500	560 Nm/3500
Engine type, position, number and configuration of cylinders	Four-stroke gasoline, front longitudinally, 8 cylinders, 90-degree-V	Four-stroke gasoline, front longitudinally, 8 cylinders, 90-degree-V
Bore x Stroke (mm), capacity (cc), compression ratio	86 x 90.3, 4196cc, 11 : 1	86 x 90.3, 4196cc, 9.1 : 1
Designation of engine and cylinder head	Engine and head "AJ 34"	Engine and head "AJ 34"
Engine block and cylinder head material, number of main bearings, type of liners	Block and head aluminum, 5 main bearings, cast-in liners	Block and head aluminum, 5 main bearings, cast-in liners
Number of valves per cylinder, configuration, valve gearing, timing variants	4 overhead valves, bucket tappets, 2 ohc per bank, chain, continously variable timing	4 overhead valves, bucket tappets, 2 ohc per bank, chain, continously variable timing
Air supply, type of inlet manifold, air tempering	Normally aspirated, 2-stage inlet manifold, n/a	Roots supercharger, 2-stage inlet manifold, intercooler
Type, position, make, and designation of mixture preparation	Electronic injection to manifold, Nippondenso	Electronic injection to manifold, Nippondenso
Energy source, type, make, and designation of ignition system	Battery, separate coils, Nippondenso	Battery, separate coils, Nippondenso
Make of alternator, voltage, earthing	Alternator, 12 V, negative	Alternator, 12 V, negative
Engine coolant, drive, regulation of cooling	Liquid, pump, thermostat	Liquid, pump, thermostat
Type of clutch, number of gears in manual box, synchronized gears	n/a	n/a
Gear ratios in manual box	n/a	n/a
Make, type, ratio of overdrive	n/a	n/a
Type of clutch, number of gears, make and model of automatic box	Hydraulic torque converter, 6, ZF 6 HP 26	Hydraulic torque converter, 6, ZF 6 HP 26
Gear ratios in automatic gearbox	4.17, 2.34, 1.52, 1.14, 0.87, 0.69, 3.4 : 1	4.17, 2.34, 1.52, 1.14, 0.87, 0.69, 3.4 : 1
Driven axle, type of diff, traction control	Rear, hypoid bevel, n/a	Rear, hypoid bevel, n/a
Axle ratios	2.87 : 1	2.87 : 1
Type of chassis	Unitary, front and rear subframes	Unitary, front and rear subframes
Suspension, springing front	Double-wishbone, coil springs	Double-wishbone, coil springs
Suspension, springing rear	Double-wishbone, coil springs	Double-wishbone, coil springs
Reduction of roll	Torsion bars front and rear	Torsion bars front and rear
Type of shock absorbers	Telescopic, CATS	Telescopic, CATS
Type and dimensions of wheels	Aluminum discs, 8 J x 18 (ALC 8.5 J x 21)	Aluminum discs, 8.5 J x 19
Type, dimensions, make of tires	245/45 R 18, rear 275/40 R 18 (ALC 285/30 R 21)	245/40 R 19, rear 275/35 R 19
Type of braking front	Ventilated discs	Ventilated discs
Type of braking rear	Ventilated outboard discs	Ventilated outboard discs
Braking mechanism, number of circuits, servo assistance, electronic aids	Hydraulics, 2 circuits, electronic front/rear balance, hydraulic servo assistance, antilock, DSC	Hydraulics, 2 circuits, electronic front/rear balance, hydraulic servo assistance, antilock, DSC
Steering gear, make and model of power steering	Rack and pinion, hydraulic servo ZF Servotronic II	Rack and pinion, hydraulic servo ZF Servotronic II

* 150 examples of limited edition 3.5 Coupe with 3.5-liter engine of X 350, debut 6/2007, Price 77,900 €

X 150

Make, range	**Jaguar XF 2.7 d (X 250)**	
Type	*Luxury Premium*	*Luxury*
Public debut	09/13/2007	09/13/2007
End of production	…	…
Production figure Unknown Unknown		
First, last chassis number RHD	VIN unknown-unknown	
First, last chassis number LHD	VIN unknown-unknown	
Body type	All-steel, 4 doors, 5 seats	
Weather protection, top mechanism	Enclosed-drive, optional electrically operated glass sunroof	
Length, width, height (mm)	4961 x 1877 x 1460	
Length, width, height (inches)	195 1/4 x 74 x 57 1/2	
Wheelbase, front, rear track (mm)	2909 x 1559/1542	
Wheelbase, front, rear track (inches)	114 1/2 x 61 1/2/63	
Ground clearance, turning circle, curb weight	140mm, 11m, 1750kg	
Max speed, acceleration 0-60 mph	230kph, 9 sec	
Max power, standard, revs	207 ECE-HP/4000	
Max torque, revs	435 Nm/1900	
Engine type, position, number and configuration of cylinders	Four-stroke diesel, front longitudinally, 6 cylinders, 60 degree-V	
Bore x Stroke (mm), capacity (cc), compression ratio	81 x 86, 2720cc, 17.3 : 1	
Designation of engine and cylinder head	Engine and head “Diesel”	
Engine block and cylinder head material, number of main bearings, type of liners	Block and head aluminum, 4 main bearings, cast-in liners	
Number of valves per cylinder, configuration, valve gearing, timing variants	4 overhead valves, rocker, 2 ohc per bank, toothed belt, fixed	
Air supply, type of inlet manifold, air tempering	2 turbochargers, one-stage inlet manifold, intercooler	
Type, position, make, and designation of mixture preparation	Electronic common-rail direct injection, n/a	
Energy source, type, make, and designation of ignition system	Battery, glow plugs, n/a	
Make of alternator, voltage, earthing	Alternator, 12 V, negative	
Engine coolant, drive, regulation of cooling	Liquid, pump, thermostat	
Type of clutch, number of gears in manual box, synchronized gears	n/a	
Gear ratios in manual box	n/a	
Make, type, ratio of overdrive	n/a	
Type of clutch, number of gears, make and model of automatic box	Hydraulic torque converter, 6, ZF 6 HP 26	
Gear ratios in automatic gearbox	4.17, 2.30, 1.52, 1.14, 0.87, 0.69, 3.4 : 1	
Driven axle, type of diff, traction control	Rear, hypoid bevel, n/a	
Axle ratios	3.07 : 1	
Type of chassis	Unitary, front and rear subframes	
Suspension, springing front	Double-wishbone, coil springs	
Suspension, springing rear	Double-wishbone, coil springs	
Reduction of roll	Torsion bars front and rear	
Type of shock absorbers	Telescopic, optional CATS	
Type and dimensions of wheels	Aluminum discs, 7.5 J x 17 (Premium 8.5 J x 18)	
Type, dimensions, make of tires		
Type of braking front	Ventilated discs	
Type of braking rear	Ventilated outboard discs	
Braking mechanism, number of circuits, servo assistance, electronic aids	Hydraulics, 2 circuits, electronic front/rear balance, hydraulic servo assistance, antilock, DSC, brake assistant	
Steering gear, make and model of power steering	Rack and pinion, hydraulic servo ZF Servotronic II	

X 250

Make, range	**Jaguar XF V-6 (X 250)**		**Jaguar XF V-8 (X 250)**	
Type	*Luxury*	*Premium Luxury*	*Premium Luxury*	*S V-8*
Public debut	*09/13/2007*	*09/13/2007*	*09/13/2007*	*09/13/2007*
First, last chassis number RHD	VIN unknown		VIN unknown	
First, last chassis number LHD	VIN unknown		VIN unknown	
Body type	All-steel, 4 doors, 5 seats		All-steel, 4 doors, 5 seats	
Weather protection, top mechanism	Enclosed-drive, optional electrically operated glass sunroof		Enclosed-drive, optional electrically operated glass sunroof	
Length, width, height (mm)	4961 x 1877 x 1460		4961 x 1877 x 1460	
Length, width, height (inches)	195 1/4 x 74 x 57 1/2		195 1/4 x 74 x 57 1/2	
Wheelbase, front, rear track (mm)	2909 x 1559/1542		2909 x 1559/1542 (S V-8: 1571)	
Wheelbase, front, rear track (inches)	114 1/2 x 61 1/2/63		114 1/2 x 61 1/2/63 (S V-8: 62)	
Ground clearance, turning circle, curb weight	140mm, 11m, 1735kg		140mm, 11m, 1800kg	
Max speed, acceleration 0-60 mph	230kph, 8 sec		250kph, 7 sec (S V-8 250kph, 6 sec)	
Max power, standard, revs	238 ECE-HP/6800		298 ECE-HP/6000 (S V-8 416 ECE-HP/6250)	
Max torque, revs	245 Nm/4000 (3.0 293 Nm/4500)		411 Nm/4100 (S V-8 560 Nm/3500)	
Engine type, position, number and configuration of cylinders	Four-stroke gasoline, front longitudinally, 6 cylinders, 60 degree-V		Four-stroke gasoline, front longitudinally, 8 cylinders, 90-degree-V	
Bore x Stroke (mm), capacity (cc), compression ratio	81.65 x 79.5, 2497cc (3.0 89 x 79.5, 2967cc), 10.5 : 1		86 x 90.3, 4196cc, 11 (SV-8 9.1) : 1	
Designation of engine and cylinder head	Engine and head “AJ V-6”		Engine and head “AJ 26”	
Engine block and cylinder head material, number of main bearings, type of liners	Block and head aluminum, 4 main bearings, cast-in liners		Block and head aluminum, 5 main bearings, cast-in liners	
Number of valves per cylinder, configuration, valve gearing, timing variants	4 overhead valves, bucket tappets, 2 ohc per bank, chain, continously variable timing		4 overhead valves, bucket tappets, 2 ohc per bank, chain, continously variable timing	
Air supply, type of inlet manifold, air tempering	Normally aspirated, 3-stage inlet manifold, n/a		Normally aspirated, 2-stage inlet manifold, n/a (S-V-8 Roots supercharger, one-stage, intercooler)	
Type, position, make, and designation of mixture preparation	Electronic injection to manifold, Nippondenso		Electronic injection to manifold, Nippondenso	
Energy source, type, make, and designation of ignition system	Battery, separate coils, Nippondenso		Battery, separate coils, Nippondenso	
Make of alternator, voltage, earthing	Alternator, 12 V, negative		Alternator, 12 V, negative	
Engine coolant, drive, regulation of cooling	Liquid, pump, thermostat		Liquid, pump, thermostat	
Type of clutch, number of gears in manual box, synchronized gears	n/a		n/a	
Gear ratios in manual box	n/a		n/a	
Make, type, ratio of overdrive	n/a		n/a	
Type of clutch, number of gears, make and model of automatic box	Hydraulic torque converter, 6, ZF 6 HP 26		Hydraulic torque converter , 6, ZF 6 HP 26	
Gear ratios in automatic gearbox	4.17, 2.30, 1.52, 1.14, 0.87, 0.69, 3.4 : 1		4.17, 2.30, 1.52, 1.14, 0.87, 0.69, 3.4 : 1	
Driven axle, type of diff, traction control	Rear, hypoid bevel, n/a		Rear, hypoid bevel, n/a	
Axle ratios	3.31 : 1		3.31 (SV-8 3.07) : 1	
Type of chassis	Unitary, front and rear subframes		Unitary, front and rear subframes	
Suspension, springing front	Double-wishbone, coil springs		Double-wishbone, coil springs	
Suspension, springing rear	Double-wishbone, coil springs		Double-wishbone, coil springs	
Reduction of roll	Torsion bars front and rear		Torsion bars front and rear	
Type of shock absorbers	Telescopic, CATS		Telescopic, CATS	
Type and dimensions of wheels	Aluminum discs, 7.5 J x 17 (Premium 8.5 J x 18)		Aluminum discs, 7.5 J x 17 (Premium 8.5 J x 18, S V-8 8.5 J x 20))	
Type, dimensions, make of tires				
Type of braking front	Ventilated discs		Ventilated discs	
Type of braking rear	Ventilated outboard discs		Ventilated outboard discs	
Braking mechanism, number of circuits, servo assistance, electronic aids	Hydraulics, 2 circuits, electronic front/rear balance, hydraulic servo assistance, antilock, DSC, brake assistant		Hydraulics, 2 circuits, electronic front/rear balance, hydraulic servo assistance, antilock, DSC, brake assistant	
Steering gear, make and model of power steering	Rack and pinion, hydraulic servo ZF Servotronic II		Rack and pinion, hydraulic servo ZF Servotronic II	

X 250

Jaguar Development Codes

XJ Project numbers explained

XJ 1:	V-12 racing engine
XDM 2:	Daimler 2.5-liter V-8
XJ 3:	Jaguar 3.4 S and 3.8 S
XDM 3:	Daimler DR 450, later DS 420
XJ 4 and XDM 4:	XJ 6 Series I
XJ 5:	Mark X 4.2 or GT sports car (see XJ 27)
XJ 6:	V-12 and V-8 engines for XJ 4
XJ 7:	Mark II 2.4-liter with SU carburetors
XJ 8:	E-Type 2 + 2 (late 1964), abandoned project
XJ 10:	Mark X V-12, abandoned project
XJ 12:	E-Type 4.2 with synchromesh gearbox, later used for XJ 4 with V-12 engine
XJ 13:	Miscellaneous (e.g., lightweight XJ-C, antilock braking system, adaptation of GM Automatic, compression ratio 7.5:1 for 4.2 engine and 7.8:1 for V-12 engine) and mid-engined racing prototype
XJ 15:	Compact overdrive unit for Mark II
XJ 16 and XDM 16:	420 and first Daimler Sovereign
XJ 17:	E-Type with more inclined A posts (abandoned project) or compact 3-liter 4-seater
XJ 18:	3-liter XK engine (for XJ 6)
XJ 21:	E-Type-successor for 1968 (OTS and 2 + 2), abandoned project
XJ 22:	E-Type Series II
XJ 23:	E-Type Series III for 1969, abandoned project
XJ 25:	E-Type Series III 2 + 2
XJ 26:	E-Type Series III OTS
XJ 27:	XJ-S coupe V-12
XJ 28:	XJ-S cabriolet V-12
XJ 29:	XJ 6 L Series I and Vanden Plas
XJ 30:	XJ 12 L Series I
XJ 31:	XJ 6 LWB Series II
XJ 32:	XJ 12 LWB Series II
XJ 33:	XJ 6 SWB, abandoned project
XJ 34:	XJ 12 SWB Series 2, abandoned project
XJ 35:	XJ 6 C (as produced)
XJ 36:	XJ 12 C (as produced)
XJ 37:	XJ 6 C (perhaps with 3.4-liter engine)
XJ 38:	XJ 12 C Series 1
XJ 39:	XJ Series III body with special equipment
XJ and XDM 40:	XJ 12 L Series I with diesel engine, later XJ 6 for 1987
XJ 41:	Successor to XJ-S coupe, abandoned in favor of X 100
XJ 42:	XJ 6 C 3.4 Series II, later successor to XJ-S convertible, abandoned project
XJ 43:	Daimler Vanden Plas 4.2 Series II or XJ 40 LWB
XJ 44:	XJ 30 with VM six-cylinder Diesel engine
XJ and XDM 45:	Limousine based on XJ Series III, abandoned project
XJ 47:	Super sports car (see also XJ 99)
XJ 48:	Convertible version of XJ 47
XJ and XDM 50:	XJ 12 Series III
XJ 51:	XJ 6 3.4 Series III
XJ 52:	XJ 6 4.2 Series III
XJ 53:	Daimler Vanden Plas 4.2 Series III
XJ 54:	Daimler Double-Six Vanden Plas Series III
XJ 57:	XJ-S 3.6
XJ 58:	XJ-SC 3.6
XJ 59:	XJ Series III with BMW six-cylinder Diesel engine, abandoned 29/9/1982
XJ 60:	XJ Series III with XJ 40 engine and rear suspension (for testing only)
XDM 62:	Daimler limousine for Middle East markets, abandoned project
XJ 63:	GETRAG gearbox for XJ 57
XJ 64:	Sports car, abandoned project
XDM 65:	Daimler limousine for North America, abandoned project
XJ 66:	Dana differential
XJ 67:	New differential seals for existing models
XJ 68:	Tracteck "Truetral" limited slip differential
XJ 69:	XJ 40 with all-wheel drive
XJ 71:	XJ-S on XJ 41 platform (for testing only)
XJ 77:	XJ-S V-12 convertible for 1988
XJ 78:	XJ-S six-cylinder convertible, abandoned project
XJ 79:	XJ-S with all-wheel drive, abandoned February, 1989
XJ 80:	Compact sedan for 1987, abandoned project
XJ and XDM 81:	XJ 40 with V-12 engine
XJ 82:	XJ 81 LWB, abandoned project
XJ 83:	XJ 40 LWB
XJ 84:	XJ 81 LWB with 6.4-liter engine
XJ 85:	XJ 84 coupe, abandoned project
XJ 86:	XJ 40 coupe or XJS supercharged, both abandoned project
XJ 87:	XJS V-12 coupe for 1991
XJ 88:	XJS 4.0 coupe for 1991
XJ 89:	XJ-SC facelift, abandoned project
XJ 90:	XJ 40 revamp, abandoned in favor of X 300
XJ 91:	XJ 81 facelift, abandoned project
XJ and XDM 92:	XJ 40 facelift with AJ 26 V-8 engine and LWB (119˝), abandoned project
XJ 93:	XJ 84 facelift with AJ 26 V-12 engine and LWB (119˝), abandoned project
XJ 94:	Close-coupled XJ 90 (113 in wheelbase)
XJ 95:	XJ 84 convertible, abandoned project
XJ 96:	XJ 40 convertible, abandoned project
XJ 97:	XJS V-12 convertible for 1991
XJ 98:	XJS 4.0 convertible for 1992
XJ 99:	Super sports car, abandoned project
XJ 100:	XJ 40 facelift, became X 300
XJ 101:	XJ 81 facelift
XJ 102:	XJ 84 facelift
XJ 103:	XJ 40 LWB facelift
XJ 104:	XJ 83 facelift
XJ 105:	XJ 84 facelift
XJ 220:	Sports prototype, abandoned project
XJ 230:	Sports GT supercar, for testing only
XJR 6:	XJR (XJ 40)

When Ford took over Jaguar, XJ 90, XJ 91, XJ 92, and XJ 93 were combined to X 90 but soon abandoned in favor of X 300 with less radical changes. New projects under Ford regime had the following designations:

X 100:	XK 8
XJ 102:	XK 8 coupe
XJ 103:	XK 8 coupe with V-12 engine, abandoned project
XJ 112:	XK 8 convertible
XJ 113:	XK 8 convertible with V-12 engine, abandoned project
X 150:	XK for 2006
X 200:	S-Type
XJ 201:	S-Type V-6
XJ 202:	S-Type V-8
X 202:	S-Type facelift for 2002
X 202 R:	S-Type R
X 250:	XF for 2008
X 300:	XJ 40 successor
X 308:	X 300 and X 330 with V-8 engines
X 330:	X 300 LWB
X 350:	XJ with aluminum body for 2003
X 390:	Successor to X 350 for 2011
X 400:	X-Type
X 400 R:	X-Type facelift for 2004
X 450:	X-Type successor for 2009
X 600:	F-Type for 2007, abandoned project
X 700:	Daimler limousine, abandoned project

Sales and Export Figures

Year	Supplies Total	Sales UK	Export Total	Export US	Export Australia	Export South Africa*	Export Malaysia*	Export Argentina	Export India	Export Portugal	Export Spain	Export Holland	Export Switzerland
1931	0	0	0	0	0	0	0	0	0	0	0	0	0
1932	776	736	40	0	5	0	0	0	4	4	0	1	5
1933	1,525	1,394	131	0	15	0	0	0	17	17	9	26	6
1934	1,793	1,567	226	0	29	0	0	23	16	8	43	43	2
1935	1,720	1,506	214	8	51	0	0	19	5	4	31	25	15
1936	2,469	2,292	177	29	9	15	4	7	6	5	9	22	24
1937	3,554	3,320	234	9	23	17	12	6	4	9	0	9	66
1938	2,209	2,035	174	1	9	16	10	6	12	5	0	7	45
1939	5,454	5,228	226	0	19	19	24	2	27	0	0	1	50
1940	823	746	77	0	9	5	18	4	12	2	0	0	11
1941	0		0	0	0	0	0	0	0	0	0	0	0
1942	0		0	0	0	0	0	0	0	0	0	0	0
1943	0		0	0	0	0	0	0	0	0	0	0	0
1944	0		0	0	0	0	0	0	0	0	0	0	0

*All exports via Tozer, Kemsley & Milbourn included in Australia

Year	Sales Total	Sales UK	Export Total	Export US	Export Canada	Export Japan	Export Europe	Export France	Export Italy	Export Germany	Registered Germany	Export Austria	Export Switzerland
1945	0	0	0	0	0	0	0	0	0	0	0	0	0
1946	1,132	827	305	0	0			2	0	0			53
1947	4,342	3,432	910	9	0			21	0	0			196
1948	4,186	2,082	2,104	245**	0			26	0	0			191
1949	3,313	2,122	1,191	135**	12			15	0	2		5	70
1950	6,647	2,721	3,926	729**	225			76	0	22		17	156
1951	5,805	1,532	4,273	1,553**	182			70	4	83		8	95
1952	8,979	1,001	7,978	3,243**	96			278	16	288		6	222
1953	10,114	2,471	7,643	5,218	313			175	19	93		14	62
1954	10,131	4,796	5,335	2,834	217			235	24	107		5	54
1955	9,900	4,462	5,438	3,239	183			167	9	118		8	41
1956	12,152	5,305	6,847	3,871	351			230	29	138		15	197
1957	12,952	6,338	6,614	3,592	348			267	50	93		17	180
1958	17,552	8,375	9,177	4,607	512			314	77	119	420	32	274
1959	20,876	10,400	10,476	5,596	814			303	99	144		20	299
1960	19,341	9,664	9,677	4,934	524			389	121	201	266	34	322
1961	24,018	13,844	10,174	3,422	612			755	348	323		88	707
1962	22,030	10,895	11,135	5,716	444			645	456	349		68	589
1963	24,989*	12,754	12,235*	4,113*	212*			997	721	556*		84	932*
1964	24,348	14,142	10,206	4,037	227			735	314	351		69	316
1965	24,601	15,041	9,560	3,669	241			617	245	302		88	534
1966	25,936	13,838	12,098	5,418	351			675	389	369		80	491

* Including Daimler from then on **New car registrations in U.S. 1948–1952: 238, 158, 912, 1702, and 3349; 1959 5843 and 1967 5839

Year	Sales Total	Sales UK	Export Total	Export US	Export Canada	Export Japan	Export Europe	Export France	Export Italy	Export Germany	Registered Germany	Export Austria	Export Switzerland
1967	22,650	10,624	12,026	6,715	323			508	469	257		88	399
1968***	24,315	14,515	9,800	4,430	382			426	127	336		202	363
1969	24,636	11,105	13,531	6,833	418			493	502	379		229	633
1970	30,423	12,001	18,422	7,384	433			906	1,323	425		345	842
1971	32,589	14,183	18,406	5,500	217			996	1,317	982		255	1,453
1972	22,988	12,043	10,945	4,734	297			551	143	253	3,023	327	124
1973	29,875	12,932	16,943	7,650	475			512	507	408	3,225	206	656
1974	26,632	14,475	12,157	5,299	528		2,391			376	3,102	119	394
1975	24,469	12,258	12,211	6,799	430		2,164			772	2,966	148	335
1976***	25,042	10,401	14,641	7,382	500		3,579			1,557	2,944	282	389
1977	21,953	9,387	12,566	4,349	402		4,309			1,367	2,965	260	452
1978	24,980	12,812	12,168	4,754	329		4,650			1,547	2,950	110	417
1979	17,160	8,035	9,125	3,748	325		3,313			1,158	2,908	100	272
1980	15,011	5,290	9,091	3,021	311		3,541			1,112	2,708	106	394
1981	15,562	5,688	9,874	4,695	331		2,983			974	2,393	60	340
1982	21,619	6,440	15,179	10,349	304		2,508			744	2,063	66	400
1983	29,175	7,069	22,106	15,815	530		3,175			1,234	4,702	99	353
1984	33,417	7,544	25,873	18,044	1,002		3,995			1,938	7,466	102	430
1985	37,745	8,049	29,696	20,528	1,315		4,838			2,350	12,024	133	426
1986	40,971	7,579	33,392	24,464	2,032		4,332			1,793	15,018	117	418
1987	46,643	11,102	35,541	22,919	2,660		6,550			2,175	17,624	158	655
1988	49,494	14,504	34,990	20,727	2,154		7,876			2,291	21,428	151	797
1989	47,400	14,243	33,157	18,967	1,606	1,856			8,199	2,391	25,114	168	768
1990	42,754	10,664	32,090	18,728	1,005	2,502			8,094	2,353	28,536	175	777
1991	25,661	5,809	19,852	9,376	740	2,438			6,304	2,148	31,676	194	464
1992	22,478	5,607	16,835	8,681	581	1,501			5,021	1,930	35,118	131	326
1993	27,338	6,215	21,123	12,734	630	1,510			4,866	2,020	38,712	147	362
1994	30,020	6,685	23,335	15,195	713	1,445			4,641	1,449	41,710	167	402
1995	39,727	8,798	30,929	18,085	945	2,311			7,215	2,667	44,836	279	527
1996	39,001	8,422	30,579	17,878	1,051	2,335			6,917	2,512	48,390	221	635
1997	43,775	9,524	34,251	19,514	1,020	2,366			8,665	3,180	52,468	256	703
1998	50,220	11,695	38,565	22,503	1,293	2,049			10,522	4,136		315	
1999													
2000			43,738										
2001													
2002													
2003													
2004	118,918	32,598					24,337						

*** Overlong business year (14 or 15 months), ending until 1968 by July 31, 1969–1975 by September 30, since 1976 by December 31

VEHICLE IDENTIFICATION NUMBERS & COLOR CODES

Vehicle Identification Numbers

Vehicle Identification Numbers as introduced by Jaguar in spring 1978 followed an international standard of 14, or from April 1981, 17 letters. Since April 1981 the first four letters denoted the manufacturer:

- D Daimler (1978 until April 1981)
- J Jaguar (1978 until April 1981)
- SADD Daimler (XJ April 1981 to 1987)
- SAJA Jaguar (S-Type, from 2000 all models incl. Daimler)
- SAJD Daimler (XJ and DS 420 from 1987 to 2000)
- SAJJ Jaguar (April 1981 until 2000, except S-Type)

The fifth letter denoted the model range:

- A XJ 6 Series 2 or 3
- B XJ 12 Series 2 or 3
- C Sovereign Series 2 or 3
- D Double-Six and Vanden Plas Series 2 and 3
- E XJ 220
- F XJ 40 base model
- G XK 8
- H XJ 40 and X 300 Sovereign, XJ 12
- J X 300 base model and Executive
- K XJ 81, X 300/308 Daimler Six, Double-Six and Vanden Plas/Daimler V-8
- M XJ 40 Majestic
- N XJS
- P XJ 40 and X 300, XJR and XJ Sport variants
- S XJR-S
- T XJ-S Special Edition
- W DS 420

The sixth letter denoted the interior equipment:

- A Base models
- G Vanden Plas for Japan
- J Normal Japan models
- K Japan models with airbag
- L Canada models
- M Mexico models with airbag
- N Canada models Vanden Plas and XK 8
- R Vanden Plas Series 3
- S XK 8 with airbag for Mexico
- V US models with normal safety belts
- W & X US models with airbag
- Y US models with automatic safety belts

Letter seven denoted the body style:

- C Two-door cabriolet
- D Two-door convertible
- E Two-door coupe
- F Two-door four-seater convertible
- L Four-door sedan
- M Five-seater LWB sedan
- N Four-seater LWB sedan
- T Limousine
- W Chassis without body

Letter eight denoted the engine:

- A XJ—3.4-liter
- B AJ 6—3.6-liter
- C AJ 6—3.6-liter
- D AJ 6—3.6-liter
- D AJ 6—4.0-liter
- D V-8—4.0-liter
- E AJ 6—3.6-liter
- E AJ 6—4.0-liter
- E V-8—4.0-liter with better ventilation
- F AJ 6—4.0-liter supercharged
- F AJ 6—2.9-liter
- F V-8—4.0-liter supercharged
- G AJ 6—2.9-liter
- G AJ 6—3.2-liter
- G V-8—3.2-liter
- H XK—4.2-liter
- H AJ 6—3.6-liter
- H AJ 6—2.9-liter
- K XK—4.2-liter
- K V 12—5.3-liter
- L AJ 6—4.0-liter supercharged with improved ventilation
- L AJ 6—2.9-liter
- L XK—4.2-liter
- N XK—4.2-liter
- P XK—4.2-liter
- R XK—4.2-liter
- S XK—4.2-liter
- S V-12—6.0-liter
- T XK—4.2-liter
- V V-12—5.3-liter
- W V-12—5.3-liter
- X V-12—5.3-liter
- X V-6—3.5-liter for XJ 220
- Y V-12—5.3-liter
- Z V-12—5.3-liter

Since 1981, letters five to eight follow a different system for North American cars (e.g., AV13 for Series 3 XJ 6 and BN18 for XJ 12 Series 3).

Letter nine denoted transmission and position of steering wheel:

- 3 RHD automatic
- 4 LHD automatic
- 7 RHD manual
- 8 LHD manual

Letter ten denoted the model variant:

- A XJ 40, XJ-S, DS 420, XJ 220, and XK 8
- B XJ Series 2, XJ-S H.E., and X 300
- C XJ Series 3, XJ-S and SC 3.6, X 308
- D XJ-S convertible
- E XJS from 1991

In some countries this letter denoted the year of manufacture, starting with 1981 (B).

Letter eleven denoted emission control. Due to the sheer number of varieties it was not possible to find a system that could be described within this framework.

The last six digits denoted the individual vehicle.

Upon introduction of S-Type, and XJ/XK models with cast-in liners instead of Nikasil (2000), the system was changed as follows:

Letter four now denoted destination (country) and driver and passenger restraint systems, letter five transmission and steering.

Letters six and seven now indicated the model:

- 01 S-Type
- 03 S-Type R
- 41 XK and XKR coupe (X 100)
- 42 XK and XKR convertible (X100)
- 43 XK and XKR coupe (X 150)
- 44 XK and XKR convertible (X150)
- 51 X-Type
- 71 XJ (X 350)
- 73 XJR (X 350)
- 74 Vanden Plas (X 350)
- 79 XJ 8L (X 350)
- 82 Super V-8 (X 350)

Letter eight now indicated emission control and letter nine was a check digit.

Letter ten denoted the model year, starting with 1 for 2001, while information varies about the meaning of letter eleven.

Letter twelve denotes the model range:

- A XK (X100)
- B XK (X 150)
- D, E X-Type
- F XJ (X 308)
- G, H XJ (X 350)
- L,M,N S-Type

The last five digits denoted the individual vehicle.

Aston Martin used a different system for DB 7, starting with "SCFA" for the manufacturer. Letter five denotes V-6 ("A") and V-12 engines ("B"). Letter six denotes body style (1 and 2 for coupe, 3 and 4 for Volante) and position of steering wheel (smaller digit for RHD, higher one for LHD). The next two letters indicate the engine, (11 for European-spec six-cylinders, 12 for U.S.-spec six-cylinders, 23 for V-12). Letter nine denotes model year, starting with "S" for 1994 and "1" for 2001. Letters ten to twelve denote place of manufacture (Bloxham) and model variant: Six-cylinder coupe ("K10"), six-cylinder Volante ("K20"), Vantage coupe ("K30") and Vantage Volante ("K40"). The remaining four digits are individual to each vehicle and start with 0001.

Paint Codes

Body

Code Nitro cellulose	Paint designation	from model year 1930	to model year 1952
	Beige	1933	1935
	Buff	1931	1934
284015	Belco Brown		
D 3111	Bronze Metallic	1949	1952
D 3120	Red	1950	1952
	Carnation Red	1931	1935
D1670, 2572, 2925 and 3107	Maroon	1936	1948
	Crimson Lake	1930	1935
	Violet	1930	1932
	Primrose	1931	1934
D2032 or 2672	Honeysuckle	1937	1948
D1828	Light Apple Green	1930	1935
D2397	Suede Green	1935	1952
D 3108	Pastel Green Metallic	1949	1952
7440	Mountain Ash Green	1937	1949
	Deep Leaf Green	1930	1932
D1319 and 2720	Olive Green	1934	1949
284114	Belco Light Blue		
D 3107	Pastel Blue Metallic	1949	1952
D1306	Nile Blue	1931	1935
	Twilight Blue	1951	1952
D1327 or 3138	Dark Blue	1933	1949
	Dove Gray	1949	1951
D1184	Birch Gray	1930	1933
D 3104	Birch Gray	1933	1952
	Silver (Pearl Essence)	1933	1940
D 3124	Silver Metallic	1949	1952
	Lavender Gray	1933	1952
D1283	Swallow Gray	1933	1934
	Battleship Gray	1930	1932
	Battleship Gray	1937	1952
2298M	Gunmetal	1937	1952
D1267	Ivory	1930	1937
D1267	Ivory	1946	1952
	Cream	1930	1940
67S and 122	Black	1930	1952
	Ivory and Dark Blue	1930	1932
	Ivory and Black	1930	1932
	Ivory and Crimson	1930	1932
	Ivory and Violet	1930	1932
	Cream and Crimson	1930	1932
	Cream and Violet	1930	1932
	Cream and Green	1930	1932
	Birch Gray and Battleship Gray	1930	1932
	Gray and Green	1930	1932
	Apple Green and Deep Leaf Green	1930	1932
	Light Mole Brown and Deep Suede Brown	1930	1932
	Cherry Red and Maroon	1930	1932
	Sky Blue and Danish Blue	1930	1932

Synthetic		**1952**	**1979**
	Sand	1963	1964
J1066	Golden Sand	1962	1968
2050M	Rose Beige Metallic		
2680M	Driftwood Beige Metallic		
	Beige	1966	1968
	Ascot Fawn	1968	1972
ADR	Sable	1968	1976
ADS	Carriage Brown	1976	1979
J1055	Opalescent Bronze	1960	1964
BDB	Moroccan Bronze	1975	1979
Q 1089	Red	1952	1960
Q 1190 or ICI 1-21948	Carmine Red, from '58 Carmen Red	1954	1968
CDF	Signal Red	1968	1978
	Sebring Red	1978	1979
ICI 1-19277, J 1015, Q 1230 and Q 1230/1	Claret	1954	1962
	Light Maroon	1959	1960
	Light Maroon	1965	1968
CDM	Imperial Crimson	1960	1962
Q 1135 or Q 1135/1	Maroon	1954	1960
J 1011, Q 1229, Q 1229/1 or ICI 1-18475	Imperial Maroon	1956	1962
2662M, TDC	Opalescent Maroon	1961	1968
FDA	Green Sand	1972	1977
120	Yellow		
FDB	Pale Primrose	1963	1976
FDD	Yellow Gold	1976	1978
J 873, Q 1080 or Q 1080/1	Suede Green	1952	1956
19255 or Q 1231	Sherwood Green	1956	1967
	Meadow Green	1964	1965
J 877, Q 1081 or Q 1081/1	Pastel Green	1952	1956
Q 1191	Arbor Green	1954	1960
HDH	Fern Grey	1972	1977
	Willow Green	1966	1972
16712, J 860, ICI 1-16712 or Q 1076	British Racing Green	1952	1964
	British Racing Green	1966	1970
HDJ	British Racing Green	1970	1979
J 1051	Opalescent Dark Green	1960	1965
HDL	Dark Green		
HDM	Juniper Green	1975	1979
J 867	Pastel Blue	1952	1956
19224 or Q 1234	Mediterranean Blue	1952	1956
ebenso	Cotswold Blue	1956	1964
J 1050	Opalescent Dark Blue	1960	1964
Q 1132 or Q 1132/1	Pacific Blue	1952	1956
	Twilight Blue	1952	1953
27153 or Q 1233	Indigo Blue	1954	1962
JDG	Dark Blue	1964	1979
J 1082	Light Blue	1968	1972
JDH	Lavender blue	1972	1974
J 1054	Opalescent Silver Blue	1960	1968
2049M	Mountain Blue	1961	1968
JDJ	Squadron Blue	1974	1979
JDN	Azure Blue	1972	1974
KDA	Heather	1972	1974
J 861	Dove Gray	1952	1956
J 861	Dove Gray	1963	1964

ICI 1-18043, Q 1129, Q 1129/1 or /2	Pearl Gray	1952	1964
J 865 or Q 1079	Birch Gray	1952	1956
J 871, Q 1072 or Q 1072/1	Lavender Gray	1952	1956
19180, J 889, J 809 or Q 1235	Mist Gray	1956	1964
J 875, Q 1075 or Q 1075/1	Battleship Gray	1952	1956
19164 or Q 1236	Cornish Gray	1956	1960
J 932	Warwick Gray	1965	1972
	Light Gray	1952	1955
LDD	Light Gray		
J 1053	Opalescent Silver Gray	1961	1968
J 1084, MDC	Light Silver	1972	1974
MDD	Silver Gray Metallic	1974	1979
2125M or 2216M	Gray Metallic		
2298 M or J 1052	Opalescent Gunmetal Gray	1961	1964
	Ivory	1952	1953
J 863, J 863 C	Cream or Old English White	1952	1970
J 932, NDB	Cream or Old English White	1970	1977
NDF	Special Police White	1964	1973
J 869 or Q 1073, later PMA	Black	1952	1974
3801	Roman Purple		
TDD	Regency Red	1968	1978
TDD	Damson Red	1978	1979
UDA	Turquoise	1972	1974
	Claret over Imperial Maroon	1957	1961
	Black over Claret	1957	1961
	Black over Sherwood Green	1957	1961
	Black over Forest Green	1957	1961
	Black over Old English White	1959	1961
	Cornish over Mist Gray	1957	1961
	Indigo over Cotswold Blue	1957	1961
	Black over Golden Sand	1966	1968
	Black over Silver Gray	1966	1968
	Dark Blue over Silver Blue	1966	1968
	Dark Green over Willow Green	1966	1968
	Black over Ascot Fawn	1968	1970
	Black over Warwick Gray	1968	1970
	Dark Blue over Light Blue	1968	1970
	British Racing over Willow Green	1968	1970
Vanden Plas		**1972**	**1979**
ADA	Caramel Metallic	1972	1979
DDC	Mink Metallic	1976	1979
EDA	Coral Metallic	1972	1979
HDG	Sage Metallic	1972	1976
HDK	Mistletoe Metallic	1976	1979
JDF	Aegean Blue	1972	1976
JDK	Biascan Blue	1976	1979
KDB	Amethyst Metallic	1976	1979
MDB	Silver Sand	1972	1979
TDA	Morello Cherry	1972	1976
TDB und TDE	Aubergine	1972	1976
Limousine (1979)	Black, Carlton Grey		
	Dark Blue, Dark Green		
	Light Grey		
	Maroon		

Thermoplastic Acrylic		**1979**	**1986**
ACM	Brazilia	1979	1983
	Caramel Metallic	1979	1983
AEA	Portland Beige	1981	1983
AEB	Grosvenor Brown	1981	1985
AFK and AFM	Antelope Metallic	1983	1986
AFT	Curlew Brown Metallic	1986	
ANC	Cirrus, Purbeck	1983	1986
BDA	Chestnut Brown Metallic	1979	1983
CCE	Richelieu		
CDG	Damson Red	1979	1982
CDJ	Sebring Red	1979	1986
CDN	Garnet Red	1981	1982
CEA	Claret Metallic	1982	1986
CEE	Cranberry Red Metallic	1983	1986
CEL	Burgundy		
FCB	Turmeric		
FDE	Cotswold Yellow	1979	1980
GDA	Silver Sand Metallic	1979	1986
GDB	Coronet Gold Metallic	1981	1984
GDD	Regal Gold	1986	
GDJ	Filigree Gold		
HAF	Poseidon		
HDN	Racing Green Metallic	1979	1985
HEF	Evergreen Metallic	1981	1982
HEG	Sage Green Metallic	1983	1986
HEH and HEL	Dark Green	1979	1983
HEM	Opaline Green		
HEP	Gavin Green		
JCF	Atlantis	1979	1983
JDM	Cobalt Blue Metallic	1979	1986
JEA	Quartz Blue Metallic	1979	1980
JEB	Indigo Blue	1981	1983
JEC, later JEY	Sapphire Blue Metallic	1981	1985
JED	Kingfisher Metallic	1981	1982
JEE	Biascon Blue Metallic	1979	1983
JEJ	Mineral Blue Metallic	1981	1982
JER	Clarendon Blue	1983	1985
JEV	Windsor Blue	1985	1986
LDC	Carlton Grey	1984	1986
LDL and LDR	Regent Grey Metallic	1983	1986
LEC	Steel Blue Metallic	1985	1986
MCA and MDD	Silver Frost Metallic	1979	1981
MDE and MDM	Rhodium Silver	1980	1986
NCF	Pendelican		
NDC	Tudor White	1979	1986
NDE	Ivory		
NDG	Cumulus White	1986	
PDE	Black	1980	1986
PDF	Sable Black Metallic	1981	1983

Clear-over-base-paint		**1986**	**—**
AFV and AGA	Woodsmoke	1986	1987
AFV and AGA	Satin Beige	1986	1990
	Roman Bronze Micatallic	2000	2002
	Winter Gold Micatallic	2008	—
CEH	Grenadier Red	1986	1990
CEH and CFS	Carnival Micatallic	1995	2002
	Madeira Micatallic	1997	1999
CEJ	Amaranth Micatallic	1997	1999
CEK	Bordeaux Red Metallic	1986	1991
CEV	Crimson Metallic	1986	1988
CFF	Crimson Metallic	1988	1989
CFA	Regency Red Micatallic	1989	1994
CFC	Signal Red	1987	1996
CFG	Morocco Red Micatallic	1992	1996
CFH	Flamenco Red Micatallic	1991	1995
CFJ	Meteor Red	1991	1993
	Cabernet Red	1996	1997
	Phoenix Red	1998	2003
	Salsa Red	2003	2006
	Garnet	2005	—
	Chili Micatallic	2005	—
	Radiance Micatallic	2002	—
GDF	Sovereign Gold Metallic	1986	1987
HED	Brooklands Green	1990	1992
HEN and HER	Jaguar Racing Green	1986	1990
HET	Moorland Green	1987	1989
HES	Alpine Green Metallic	1986	1989
HEV	Jade Green Micatallic	1988	1997
	Alpine Green Metallic	1997	2000
	Seafrost Micatallic	1998	—
HFB	British Racing Green	1992	—
HFD	Catkin Micatallic	1992	1992
HFE	Kingfisher Blue Metallic	1991	1996
	Sherwood Green	1996	1999
HFL	Spruce Micatallic	1995	1998
	Aspen Green	2001	2002
	Emerald Green Micatallic	1999	2002
	Jaguar Racing Green Metallic	2002	2007
	Botanical Green	2008	—
	Emerald Fire Micatallic	2008	—
JEW, later JFJ	Solent Blue Metallic	1986	1994
JEX	Tungsten Grey Metallic	1986	1991
JFE	Arctic Blue Metallic	1986	1992
JEU	Westminster Blue	1986	1994
JFG	Westminster Blue	1999	2002
	Westminster Blue	2005	—
	Diamond Blue Metallic	1989	1994
JFN	Mistral Metallic	1998	2001
	Antigua Blue Micatallic	1996	1999
	Aquamarine Blue Metallic	1996	1998
JGE and JHE	Sapphire Blue Metallic	1993	2002
	Pacific Blue Metallic	2000	2007
	Adriatic Blue Metallic	2001	2003
	Zircon Blue Micatallic	2002	2006
	Midnight Micatallic	2003	—
	Indigo Micatallic	2007	—

	Blue Prism Micatallic	2008	—
LDP	Dorchester Grey Metallic	1986	1989
LED and LEK	Savoy Grey Metallic	1989	1991
LEH	Gunmetal Micatallic	1989	1993
LEP	Platinum Metallic	1991	1993
LEV	Steel Grey Micatallic	1993	1996
LFA	Titanium Micatallic	1993	2002
	Quartz Micatallic	2002	2007
	Slate Micatallic	2002	—
MDF	Talisman Silver Metallic	1986	1990
	Pearl Grey Micatallic	2008	—
	Lunar Grey Micatallic	2008	—
	Shadow Grey Micatallic	2008	—
MDJ	Silver Birch Metallic	1986	1989
MDK	Silver Frost Metallic	1990	1995
	Liquid Silver Micatallic	2008	—
	Meteorite Micatallic	1997	2000
	Platinum Silver	1999	—
MDP	Ice Blue Metallic	1993	1997
NDH, NDM and NEE	Spindrift	1995	1999
	White Onyx	1999	—
NDJ	Nimbus White	1986	1987
	Porcelain	2007	—
NDK and NDP	Glacier White	1987	1995
PDH	Black or Jet Black	1986	1993
PDP	Black Cherry Micatallic	1990	1993
PDT	Black	1993	1996
	Ebony	2002	—
	Midnight Black Micatallic	2002	—
PDV	Nautilus Micatallic	1995	1996
PED	Anthracite	1996	2002
SDD	Tuscany Bronze Metallic	1990	1991
SDE	Oyster Beige Metallic	1990	1993
SDL	Rose Bronze Micatallic	1993	
SDN	Topaz Metallic	1993	1996
SEC	Topaz Metallic	1996	—
UDA	Turquoise Metallic	1993	1996
	Ultraviolet Blue Micatallic	2002	—
XJ 220	Spa Silver	1991	1993
	Monza Red	1991	1993
	Silverstone Green	1991	1993
	Le Mans Blue	1991	1993
	Daytona Black	1991	1993
Insignia		**1992**	**1994**
NDT	White Pearl Micatallic	1992	1994
FDH	Primrose Pearl Micatallic	1992	1994
ANZ	Saturn Orange Micatallic	1992	1994
AGB	Sandstone Metallic	1992	1994
ANY	Mahogany Micatallic	1992	1994
HFF	Mineral Green Micatallic	1992	1994
HFM	Peppermint Metallic	1992	1994
JGH	Crystal Blue Metallic	1992	1994
JGP	Amethyst Blue Metallic	1992	1994
JGR	Lavender Metallic	1992	1994

Interior Trim

Leather		1929	2008
	Pigskin Grain Tan	1929	1950
VM 3234	Beige	1933	1974
ADB	Antelope	1971	1974
ADD	Cinnamon	1967	1980
	Amber	1982	1983
	Cashmere	1997	2002
ADE	Biscuit	1949	1988
ADL, VM 3880	(Dark) Tan	1949	1974
AEC	County Tan	1980	1983
AED	Burnt Umber	1982	1983
AEE	Doe Skin (from '91 optional Autolux)	1980	1994
AEM	Magnolia (from '91 optional Autolux)	1985	1993
	Cream	1960	1962
	Oatmeal	1993	2002
	Ivory	1997	—
	Champagne	2003	—
	Almond	1999	2002
VM 3104	Light Tan	1959	1974
	Heritage Tan	2000	2006
	Sand	2000	2006
AFR	Buck Skin	1983	1991
AFS	Parchment	1989	1997
	Crimson	1934	1935
AFW	Barley	1985	1994
ANS	Brown	1929	1956
	Maroon	1935	1948
CDA	Maroon	1957	1975
CDB	Russet Red	1971	1980
CDB	Grey	1949	1970
CEB	Mandarin Red	1980	1981
CEF, CES, CEX and CFP	Red	1929	1969
	Crimson Lake	1934	1935
CEM	Mulberry Red	1983	1991
CFK	Cherry Red	1991	1993
	Cranberry	2001	2005
DBB	Terracotta	1972	1974
DDA	Cerise	1972	1974
	Green	1929	1935
VM 3510	Suede Green	1935	1974
	Olive Green	1935	1948
HDB	Olive	1971	1977
HDD	Sage Green (piping)	1988	1994
	Moss Green	1970	1977
	Teal	1997	1999
	Catkin	1997	2001
HEZ	Stone	1991	1993
	Dark Blue or Blue	1929	1955
JDA	French Blue	1970	1974
JDB, VM 3199	Dark Blue	1956	1980
JDD, VM 3244	Light Blue	1934	1974
JDD	Pale Blue	1947	1960
JEF	Isis Blue	1979	1994
JEF	Regatta	1993	1996

LDA	Blue-Grey	1978	1980
	Grey	1948	1974
LDY	Savile Grey (from '91 optional Autolux)	1982	1994
	Nimbus Grey	1993	2000
	Dove Grey	2000	—
	Pewter	1998	2001
	Stone Gray	2001	—
	Silver and Black	1931	1950
LEG	Charcoal	1985	1994
LEG	Warm Charcoal	1994	—
PDA and PMA	Black	1929	1986
SDC	Coffee	1993	1997
SDP	Cream	1990	1997
	Biscuit/Tan	1949	1955
	Biscuit/Red	1949	1956
	Biscuit/Pigskin	1949	1954
	Light/Dark Blue	1949	1956
	Duotone Red	1955	1956
Leather Vanden Plas		**1972**	**1980**
ADF	Chamois	1972	1980
HDC	Deep Olive	1972	1980
ADG	Tuscan, later Tan	1972	1979
Leather Insignia		**1992**	**1990**
	Silk White	1992	1996
	Pale and Dark Mushroom	1992	1994
	Pale and Dark Stone	1992	1994
	Yellow Pearl	1992	1994
	Saddle Tan	1992	1994
	Aqua	1992	1994
	Powder Blue	1992	1994
	Thistle	1992	1994
Leather XJ 220		**1991**	**1993**
	Smoke Gray	1991	1993
	Sand Beige	1991	1993
Vinyl		**1967**	**1969**
AEJ	Oatmeal	1967	1969
AFA	County Tan	1967	1969
	Red	1967	1969
PDH	Blue Gray	1967	1969
	Dark Blue	1967	1969
LDV	Gray, later Savile Gray	1967	1969
PDL	Black	1967	1969
DS 420 (mostly velour cloth)		**1978**	**1992**
	Leather Gray		
	Leather Fawn		
	Fawn Cloth		
AFF	Beige		
AFH	Amber		
	Maroon		
	Green		
	Light Blue		

JFB	Fleet Blue		
	Dark Blue		
LDM	Graphite		1978
LDJ	Savile Gray	1978	
PDK	Black	1968	1992
	Blue/Gray	1979	
Polyester velours		**1975**	**1985**
ADJ and ADN	Sand	1975	1982
ADH	Fawn	1979	1982
BDC	Copper	1980	1982
	Amber	1982	1985
	Beige	1982	1985
CDC	Garnet	1977	1980
CDD	Red	1975	1977
CED	Loganberry	1982	1985
HDE	Jade	1975	1980
JDE or JDC	Navy	1975	1980
JEG	Marine	1980	1985
	Graphite	1983	1985
	Black	1983	1985
PDB	Ebony	1977	1982
Raschelle velours		**1983**	**1985**
ADK, ADM or AFB	Beige	1983	1985
AFC	Amber	1983	1985
	Parchment	1985	1985
JEM oder JET	Fleet Blue	1983	1985
LDG	Graphite	1983	1985
Tweed		**1986**	**1993**
AFX	Cotswold Tweed	1986	1993
AFY	Cheviot Tweed	1986	1993
LEE	Pennine Tweed	1986	1993
LEF	Chiltern Tweed	1986	1993
LES	Ocean Tweed	1988	1993
Solid color fabric		**1993**	**2008**
AFD	Magnolia	1993	1994
	Doe Skin	1993	1994
	Oatmeal	1994	2003
	Sand	2003	2005
	Champagne	2005	—
	Barley	1993	1994
	Coffee	1994	1996
	Mocha	2007	—
	Cashmere	1996	2002
	Almond	1998	2001
AFS	Parchment	1993	1994
	Isis	1993	1994
	Regatta Blue	1994	1996
LDZ	Charcoal, Warm Charcoal	1995	—
	Marbled black with leather Warm Charcoal	1994	1997
	Alcantara Warm Charcoal		
LET	Savile Gray	1993	1994
	Nimbus Gray	1994	2000

	Marbled gray with leather Oatmeal	1994	1997
	Pewter	1998	2001
	Dove	2001	—
Top Cloth		**1932**	**1998**
	Fawn	1953	1960
	French Gray	1932	1960
	Sand over Dark Sand	1937	1960
ANF	Brown	1985	1996
ANR	Beige	1988	1996
	Stone	1996	1998
	Light Beige	1998	—
	Dark Beige	1998	—
	Red	1957	1960
CFL	Dark Red	1993	1996
	Blue over Dark Blue	1954	1960
	Light Blue	1957	1960
JFF	Blue	1985	—
	Green	1996	—
	Gunmetal	1937	1960
	Black	1932	1967
	Black	1967	1974
PDM	Black	1983	—
Top Vinyl		**1928**	**1979**
	Beige	1931	1936
	Chocolate Brown	1929	1933
	Carnation Red	1931	1936
	Crimson Lake	1928	1936
	Olive Green	1929	1933
	Blue	1928	1936
	Birch Gray	1933	1936
	Lavender Gray	1933	1936
	Ivory	1931	1936
	Cream	1931	1936
	Black	1928	1936
	Black	1972	1979

Index

Index